Writing
Inquiry

Texas A&M Commerce

Shannon Carter, Donna Dunbar-Odom
Tabetha J. Adkins, Jessica Pauszek

FOUNTAINHEAD
PRESS

Our green initiatives include:

Electronic Products

We deliver products in non-paper form whenever possible. This includes pdf downloadables, flash drives, & CDs.

Electronic Samples

We use Xample, a new electronic sampling system. Instructor samples are sent via a personalized web page that links to pdf downloads.

FSC Certified Printers

All of our printers are certified by the Forest Service Council which promotes environmentally and socially responsible management of the world's forests. This program allows consumer groups, individual consumers, and businesses to work together hand-in-hand to promote responsible use of the world's forests as a renewable and sustainable resource.

Recycled Paper

Most of our products are printed on a minimum of 30% post-consumer waste recycled paper.

Support of Green Causes

When we do print, we donate a portion of our revenue to green causes. Listed below are a few of the organizations that have received donations from Fountainhead Press. We welcome your feedback and suggestions for contributions, as we are always searching for worthy initiatives.

Rainforest 2 Reef

Environmental Working Group

Contents

Chapter 3 Dominant and Vernacular Literacies   149

Chapter 4 (Re)defining Literacy in Our Lives   219

PREFACE

Writing Inquiry is for first-year writing courses that emphasize and bring together ideas, reflection, critical thinking, research, and academic writing. What makes this text unique is the way the reading and writing assignments build on each other and, more importantly, build on students' experiences as language users and learners.

At the center of *Writing Inquiry* is the field of literacy studies. What makes our book different from the Writing-about-Writing approach (see Downs and Wardle) is our students are looking to and working from their own experiences as language learners so they are taking their places alongside experts in the field.

What this means is that this text helps students develop an understanding of argument and research as dialectical processes rather than a series of formulaic steps. So *Writing Inquiry* emphasizes the role that active, critical reading plays in academic work. This book is also unique in that it stresses field research in order to enrich student researchers' sense of expertise and to help them see themselves as participants in an ongoing academic conversation rather than eavesdroppers.

How *Writing Inquiry* is Organized

This book is divided into 3 parts. Parts I and II serve as a textbook for writing classes that introduce students to expository writing and the importance of close reading in the production of academic arguments. Part III serves as a textbook for a research writing class for which students engage in field research and produce a final ethnographic project. (However, the book could easily be used for a one-semester writing course.)

The thrust of the entire book is literacy—how literacy is acquired, experienced, defined, policed, and grown. At the heart are students' experiences of everyday literacies in the contexts of their own lives.

Part II introduces students to the concept of literacy. Students are asked to write, read, consider, revise, then begin the process again, continually expanding their understanding and knowledge base and continually re-evaluating how their experiences are reflected or are not reflected in what they're reading for class and hearing in class.

Part III asks students to continue considering literacy practice with the goal of developing a project, conducting field research, and completing a final ethnographic written project. As part of this work, students will continue reading published essays to help them grapple with new ways of seeing what it means to be literate and will also seriously consider what it means to do ethical research.

All parts of the book position students to speak with some measure of authority from the first assignment. Every student has expertise on which to draw; every student is the "star" of his or her own literacy narrative, whether that student is a traditional student, a nontraditional student, an athlete, a commuter, a parent, and so on. The assignment sequences enable students to build on that expertise so that they can enter into a larger conversation—one that teachers and researchers carry on every day in every college across the country.

PART I

Getting Started

Learning Habits of Reflection

Donna Dunbar-Odom

A key component of any good writer's toolbox is the habit of reflection. Unfortunately, most writing classes don't address reflection in any real depth because there's just so little time in a term and so much intellectual ground to cover.

Many of us who teach writing attempt to have our students reflect on what they've written as well as why and how they've written it by requiring revision. My fellow writing teachers and I define revision as re-seeing and re-imagining the writing project in light of the first working drafts and the thinking that results from having written them. That is, revision should reflect greater understanding and awareness of the topic being developed in the process of writing multiple drafts and responding to peer and teacher comments. My students largely, however, tend to see revision in terms of addition and editing—in other words, they, by and large, want to "fix" any problems I've identified in my comments on those first drafts by adding a paragraph or a sentence or two and by correcting surface errors. I can't blame them. They're under enormous time constraints—so many work part- or full-time, some are athletes with rigorous practice and game schedules, and others have families to care for—all in addition to being students.

In a real sense, reflection is a luxury. But it's a luxury that can enable your growing facility as a writer and thinker. What follows is a variety of strategies you may check out to see if they can help you continue your efforts to produce the best possible work you can.

Taking Time

Time is the easiest reflective tool in some respects, but also the most difficult if you're a typical, time-crunched student.

The idea, of course, is to finish a draft then leave it alone, letting it get "cold." I am the first to admit that I hate revising my writing—but I'm also the first to admit that my writing always needs a lot of revision. If I try to revise too soon after I've produced a draft, I just can't see any ways to do anything differently and resist making any global changes that would result in major revamping of what's already there. Like many of my students, I want to make minimal changes and preserve as much as possible.

If, however, I ignore the draft for a couple of days or so, I am far more likely to re-see my writing in ways that can take it in interesting and fruitful directions—directions that take me beyond where I started. My goal is to look back at my writing with pride—"Wow, I wrote that!"—rather than with indifference or worse—"It's OK, I guess."

The kind of reading and writing you're being asked to do will, ideally, lead to dialectical thinking—or learning. The way that dialectical thinking was described to me years ago was a thesis encounters an antithesis, and the result is a synthesis of the two positions. In other words, when one big idea is met with another big idea, we are generally led to synthesize them—that is, rethink and re-see them both—so that they lead us to something new. This is another way of describing intellectual growth.

As I described early on in this book, I've tried to create reading and writing assignments that won't lead to knee-jerk, ironclad positions but will encourage considerations of topics from several perspectives and to positions that will shift and grow as you read, write, and learn more about those positions.

Keeping a Writer's Journal

Many good writers keep a writer's journal. By journal, I don't mean a diary accounting for our daily activities but a place where you can engage and experiment and explore with your writing topics and the reading you do as part of your writing assignments.

For instance, you may use a journal to write down chunks of text from your reading that you find evocative for whatever reason. For example, when I read Robert Johnson's essay "Teaching the Forbidden: Literature and the Religious Student" for the first time, I was irritated by his characterization of his students, but I was particularly infuriated by his use of "pardner" near the end of his essay. I grew up in the same region he's describing and now teach in that same region (after 20 years of teaching and studying and working in other parts of the country) and never have I heard anyone use the word "pardner" seriously. So I wrote out a pretty angry response to Mr. Johnson in an "idea" journal that I kept as part of the long process of preparing this book. That angry response eventually calmed down and evolved into a writing assignment and became the reason Johnson's article is the first reading in the "Faith and Religion on Campus" sequence.

You can also keep a free-writing journal to help you jump start writing projects. You might use some key words or a key sentence from the assignment to serve as your starting point. You can likely mine some good stuff from a series of linked free-writing responses for your writing assignment.

Your teacher may also give you questions or topics to focus your journal responses to lead to more informed class discussion or to a more formal writing assignment.

Talking with Others

My favorite means of reflection is to talk about my reading and writing with others. In a certain sense, this habit of reflection also requires the luxury of time since not all students are able to spend out-of-class time discussing ideas that arise from their reading and writing. But for those students who have the time and have fellow students or friends or significant others willing to try out and talk about the ideas they're wrestling with, this kind of reflection can be the most rewarding of their college careers.

I always recommend to my students that they form study groups. If you can work with others with whom you're comfortable but by whom you're intellectually challenged, you'll end up smarter than you began—I guarantee it!

A group can also help you consider how others will view your position and your writing. This is one way to anticipate your opposition, but, of course, it's also much more than this, too, in that you're also reflecting on what moves some readers and alienates or antagonizes others. Imagining and writing for an audience of real readers is probably the most difficult element of accomplished writing. Sharing our ideas and our writing with others can only help us produce writing that others will not only find convincing but that they might actually want to read.

Looking Backward

At the end of each term, I almost always ask my students to write a reflective essay or letter. The idea behind this project is to explicitly require reflection.

I ask them to return to all the reading and writing they did over the term and to consider how and where their writing and thinking changed. In other words, what can they see in their writing that reveals change taking place in their thinking about and approaches to the issues we've focused on for a whole term.

Rarely does it happen that students see no change. Generally, in fact, they're pretty excited to see the ways their writing has developed and deepened over the course of 16 weeks. And if they don't see change, I ask them to reflect on what sorts of factors might have prevented change, so they can also reflect on problems with the assignment sequence, which I need to be made aware of, or problems with their performance as students (say, for example, excessive absences), which they need to be aware of.

So looking back can help you also look forward. In a very real sense, I'm asking that you find ways to observe yourself as a reader, writer, and learner—and to make those methods of observation a habit.

Active Reading

Donna Dunbar-Odom

The majority of the writing you will produce in college will be done to demonstrate how well you have read and understood something. For exams and short papers, you'll have to show how well you've understood your textbooks and other class readings. For long papers or projects, you'll have to demonstrate how well you have comprehended and synthesized some of the written work of several experts or other authors in the field you're studying. Indeed, virtually all of the academic writing you will do will be in response to close, active reading of the work of others. To produce effective academic discourse, then, you must be able to understand what you read fully; and to do this, you must learn to read actively and critically.

Active may seem an odd adjective to associate with reading; after all, we usually think of reading as a passive activity, done lying on a couch or with our feet up on a hassock. Reading is not like watching television, however. A book does not spoon-feed meaning to its readers; rather, each reader must actively construct meaning from the words on each page. The more engaged and active a reader is in this task of constructing meaning from the text, the richer his or her construction of meaning will be. Try rethinking your perception of reading as a passive activity. This chapter is included here to give you some guidelines for active reading and to get you into the habit of reading actively and critically.

Getting Ready for Active Reading

Many students enter or return to college without having read extensively. Those who have read a lot generally have read for pleasure (science fiction novels, mysteries, thrillers) or for information (textbooks) or for a combination of the two (magazines, newspapers, Web sites). Novels carry readers along with a plot and characters, making us want to find out what happens next. Textbooks help readers along with the use of bold type, subheadings, chapter summaries, and review questions. You may not find the readings in this book to be quite so "user-friendly." Therefore, some suggestions and guidelines may help you prepare yourself to approach more demanding reading assignments.

To begin with, follow these practical steps to prepare for serious, active reading:

1. Make sure your work environment is comfortable and helps you concentrate. You need a quiet place free of television or stereo noise. If you're using music to drown out dorm or family noise, choose music that can become part of the background, and turn it up just enough to blur other people's noise but not so much that it detracts from your attention to your studies. Good lighting is important, so invest in a reading lamp if you don't already have one. Sit upright so as to stay alert and focused.

2. Read with the dictionary within easy reach, and use it. Avoid the temptation to skip over words you don't know—doing so will cut down on your comprehension. When you look up a word, write down its definition in your book so you can refresh your memory more easily.

Strategies for Critical Reading

Reading, whether for pleasure, for information, or for a college course, requires varying amounts of concentration, depending on the particular piece of writing you're engaged with. You'll find, for instance, that some of the readings in this text are easier than others. You might find some of the readings difficult to comprehend because of arcane vocabulary, complex organization, or challenging ideas and concepts. Some such difficulties can get worked out in class discussions, in journals, or after reading additional assignments later in the term that help you see something you missed the first time around. None of these difficulties can be overcome, however, without paying close attention to each reading the first time you encounter it. Following are a few strategies that will help you improve your comprehension each time you delve into a written work.

Contemplate the title

The title is your first point of entry into the text. Short though it may be, it contains key information. Take a minute, for example, to consider the title of Alexander W. Astin's essay "The Cause of Citizenship." It's not as simple as it first appears, since "cause" can be read two ways: both in terms of the process that produces citizens (as in "cause and effect") and in terms of the goal of promoting citizenship (as in "a worthy cause"). Paying close attention to this title, then, might give the reader the sense that Astin will be discussing both definitions of "cause" in his essay, giving him or her a head start in constructing meaning from the essay.

Some titles will appear at first to make no sense at all. The title of Sven Birkerts's piece "Mahvahhuhpuh," for example, looks like nonsense. But once you've read the essay (actually an excerpt from his book *The Gutenberg Elegies*—another title worth deciphering), you'll see what the title refers to, and keeping the title in mind as you read will help you gain additional insight into his argument. In other words, titles aren't just fillers; they're important to the meaning of the texts you'll be working with.

Read the introduction

If there is any kind of introductory text before the main part of the reading begins, pay close attention to the information it contains. It's there to provide context for the reading, to help you better understand it. "Head notes" and other introductory comments are included to acquaint you with the writer and perhaps something about his or her purpose for writing that particular piece. Sometimes there will be specific information there to help you see what the writer wants you to take from your reading. In this book, for example, each reading begins with a brief head note to provide you with general background information on the writer or the specific piece and a sense of what the writer's focus or argument will be. The head note to Lynne Cheney's "Students of Success," for example, explains very briefly what Cheney's purpose for writing the piece was and invites you to compare your experience of choosing a major with what she argues a "good" student should consider when choosing his or her major.

Skim the reading

Before you begin to read in earnest, skim the essay once through. Try to get a sense of where the writer is coming from and what point he or she is arguing (although this won't always be clear from a quick pass-through). Pay close attention to subheadings, terms printed in boldface type or italics, photos and captions, and use them to help you make predictions about the argument. What do the closing paragraphs indicate about the writer's argument? Knowing something about where the writer is going can help you read the beginning and the body of the essay more closely and with greater comprehension. You can practice this strategy on this book. Before you read the following chapters, take a few minutes to skim each one. Jot down what you think the key terms and arguments are. What is the most important information in each chapter? Spending just a short amount of time skimming the material you are about to read can make a real difference in your comprehension and retention of it.

Annotate the reading

Sit down to read with a pen or pencil and two highlighters of different colors. Designate one color to highlight sections of the reading you find important or significant, for whatever reason, and use the other color to mark passages you find confusing, obscure, or completely impenetrable. Then use the pen or pencil to write brief comments to yourself about what you've highlighted—that is, why you connected with a certain passage or why you found others to be completely off base. These steps may seem time-consuming to you at this point, but they'll save you considerable time when you move on to writing about the essay. You'll also be more likely to remember material that you've paid such close attention to.

Take part in the argument

As you read, highlighters and pencil in hand, think of yourself as entering into a dialogue with the writer about what he or she has written. To provide intelligent responses to the writer's work, you'll need to read it with two purposes in mind. First, you'll want to gain a strong sense of what the writer is trying to communicate and what he or she wants to accomplish by doing so. Thus, your first goal should be to identify the writer's central argument and the reasons for advancing it. Second, you'll want to pinpoint where and why you do or don't agree with the writer, where and how you think he or she made a particularly strong point or perhaps missed something. Once you understand the writer's argument, you can begin to compare it to your personal experience or to other reading you've done, and to make judgments about its validity and persuasiveness.

Assume authority and take responsibility

Readers often approach a difficult reading thinking that they either have to agree with it totally or disagree totally, but the more complex a reading, the more likely it is that both the writer's argument and your response to it will be much less clear-cut. Second, my personal experience makes it possible for me to begin to read "against the grain," maintaining a healthy skepticism about his argument. Likewise, you will draw on your own experience as you read for this and other college courses. I've chosen the culture of higher education as a unifying theme for the readings specifically to draw out this aspect of close reading, to get you into the habit of reflecting on your reading from your personal experience. This habit will help you approach your academic reading as an authority in your own right. You can be an authority and at the same time remain open to the ideas you encounter in

---

Figure 1.1

Discourse V　　　**Knowledge: Its Own End**

1

I have said that all branches of knowledge are connected together, because the subject-matter of knowledge is intimately united in itself, as being the acts and works of the Creator. Hence it is that the Sciences, into which our knowledge may be said to be cast, have multiplied gearings one on another, and an internal sympathy, and admit, or rather demand, comparison and adjustment. They complete, correct, balance one another. This consideration, if well-founded, must be taken into account, not only as regards the attainment of truth, which is their common end, but as regards the influence which they exercise upon those whose education consists in the study of them. I have said that already, that to give undue prominence to one is to be unjust to another; to neglect or supersede these is to divert those from their proper object. It is to unsettle the boundary lines between science and science, to disturb their action, to destroy the harmony which binds them together. Such a proceeding will have a corresponding effect when introduced into a place of education. There is no science but tells a different tale, when viewed as a portion of a whole, from what is likely to suggest when taken by itself, without the safeguard, as I may call it, of others.

Margin annotations:

Is he saying everything is connected because God made it?

What kind of Sciences is he talking about?

Sciences have to be brought together to provide the "big picture." Is this one of the purposes for colleges, then?

But isn't destruction a bad thing?

your reading, some of which may even persuade you to modify your own position on an issue.

The fact that you have this book in front of you indicates that you've considered the importance of higher education in your life, and the fact that you've survived orientation, registration, getting an e-mail account, buying books, and getting to this class long enough to reach this point indicates that you've already invested considerable energy in your pursuit of higher education. All of this places you in the perfect position to enter into a dialogue with every writer in this book. Furthermore, as you read more and more essays in each assignment sequence, you'll be able to bring in the authority of multiple writers, to help you continue to develop and complicate your position.

Why, you might ask, should you engage in conversation with the writers you read for this and other courses? First, you should do it because it is a way of working with ideas that characterizes educated persons, work that will serve you well in your professional life beyond your college years. Engaging in conversation with other writers allows you to present yourself as an authority, to take a position of responsibility on issues that concern you personally. The issues addressed by the readings in this book provide a good example. In my state, educators, legislators, and citizens are arguing over legislation that will affect general education requirements. Debates in other parts of the country concern affirmative action and its alternatives, whether or not to get rid of remedial courses in four-year colleges and universities, as well as many, many other issues. You, as both a student and a citizen, have a vested interest in these discussions, which will potentially affect where you can take classes, how many classes you can take, and how much you'll pay for them. If you don't enter these conversations, your voice won't be heard, and these decisions will be left entirely to others.

Second, engaging in conversation with the many materials you read will give you the ability to bring together, comprehend, and synthesize a variety of sources of information and ultimately make critical judgments about their validity and relevance. As we tread further into the twenty-first century, we will need to keep up with lightning-fast changes in technology, deal with threats to the global environment, and make wise decisions that will position us well in the global economy. As the world continues to shrink, it becomes more and more vital that we be able to hear, evaluate, and respond to others' concerns and desires. It has never been more necessary for our society to be able to draw from a diverse pool of educated, thoughtful citizens who are critically aware and capable of producing reasonable, clear discourse. A major goal of this book is to help you become a contributing member of such a pool.

Closing Thoughts on Active Reading

Finally, I challenge you to take responsibility for your own confusion. Some of these readings are difficult, it's true; but the ones that are hard challenge all readers, not just you alone. I tell my students each term, "It's hard because it's hard." In other words, reading scholarly or difficult texts isn't hard because you're not smart enough or tall enough or rich enough; they're hard because they're hard. Serious scholars don't read quickly; they read slowly, pen or pencil in hand, over and over again. What I've tried to do in this chapter is to help you learn to work with "difficult" texts and challenging ideas so that you no longer have to feel that any reading is "over your head" and so that you can approach any reading you have to do with the confidence that comes from knowing you can find your way into it and take something valuable away from it. With this chapter, you now have strategies at hand to help you approach any reading you need to do, for any class, as an active, critical participant.

Writing as a Process

Donna Dunbar-Odom

I've been teaching writing in one form or another and at one school or another for a long time now, and I can safely say that there is no one tried-and-true writing process, system, or method that will work for everyone. I've come to this realization by observing my own writing efforts as well as those of my colleagues and students. I've learned that my writing process differs markedly from the way some other people get words down on paper. For example, I'm a slow writer, for whom every page is generally produced with pain, but I'm usually able to keep what I write very focused. By contrast, a friend of mine can rapidly produce page after page, but what she writes is usually all over the place. We were in a study group together some time ago, and although we drafted by entirely different methods, we were a good team when it came time to revise, because she could help me expand and develop and I could help her cut. We each had our own individual process that we went through to produce a first draft, and we learned from observing each other's methods.

Exposure to other people's writing processes has made me a better, less constricted writer. I'm still slow, but I don't approach my writing projects with quite the same level of anxiety as before, because I have more strategies to rely on now. This chapter offers you some strategies for writing an essay or research paper that you may not have tried. Sample some of the methods that are less familiar to you to see if, perhaps, you can improve your own writing process.

Enhancing Your Repertoire of Writing Strategies

The writing assignments in this book may be unlike any you've tackled before, and you might need to refine your repertoire of writing strategies to respond to them. You may need to try different ways of planning and drafting—that is, you may need to experiment with your writing process, as I have done at times when faced with new writing challenges.

On the following pages you'll find an overview of a writing process you can use to complete the assignment sequences in this book. But remember, it's up to you to customize your own strategies for writing successfully. I'll offer suggestions, but you need to keep in mind the kind of learner, thinker, and writer you are so that you can come up with creative strategies specifically geared to your inclinations and needs. Talking about how to write is like trying to describe how to dance or how to serve a volleyball; there are certain moves everyone must make, but not everyone will execute those moves in the same way. Most people who become truly proficient at an activity develop their own unique style. You can likely identify your favorite basketball player or guitarist by the moves or sounds he or she makes. I'm hoping you'll be able to use this book to develop your own unique, proficient learning and writing style.

Developing a Writing Process that Works for You

Following is a step-by-step description of a thinking and writing process that you can use or adapt to suit your own requirements and preferences. Although the process is specifically geared to completing the assignment sequences in this book, the overall process is applicable to other writing projects as well. It is provided here as a model, a starting point that you can use to develop your own unique writing process.

Before you write anything

Maybe you keep a personal journal or diary. Perhaps you're a fine, productive poet. You might even be a songwriter. Personal or creative writing usually does not require you to respond to specific assignments or readings. Academic writing, on the other hand, almost always does, so you will benefit from some prior consideration of the assignment, the readings, your goals, and your potential audience. The following paragraphs describe some preliminary steps to take in completing any academic writing project, before you ever put pen to paper.

Assess the Assignment. The first step of the academic writing process is to assess the assignment, or "prompt." Always read your assignment through at least twice before you begin to write anything. Underline or highlight the textual clues that will give you a sense of how you're expected to approach the assignment. Words like argue, compare, contrast, summarize, persuade, and analyze clearly indicate how you are to approach the assignment.

For example, if an assignment asks for an analysis of another writer's arguments, then an essay that merely restates those arguments won't fulfill the requirements of the assignment. An analysis requires that you not only make observations but also draw conclusions from them. For instance, if your instructor were to ask you to analyze a television talk show, you would, of course, describe the set, the format, and who appeared and what happened in the episodes you watched. What you would then have would be a report. To move beyond a report to an analysis, you would have to draw conclusions from your observations, finding significance in the details and identifying the show's strengths and weaknesses. You might, for example, note that although the advertisements for the show seem to be aimed at attracting a young audience, its guests seem geared to a much older audience. Then you would go on to discuss your conclusions concerning why this is so and offer evidence to support those conclusions.

Ask for Help if You Need It. If at any time you're not clear about what the assignment requires, don't hesitate to ask your instructor to go over it with you. Even if you feel you have a pretty solid understanding of the assignment, ask yourself, "If I had to come up with a question about this assignment for my instructor, what would it be?" This step may seem like a waste of time, but I've found that many times what I think I've asked students to do and what my students think I've asked them to do aren't necessarily the same thing. When I have my students write questions about an assignment, even if they think they understand it completely, I often find that it helps us get a better sense of each other's goals and expectations for the assignment. Finally, make notes on the assignment as you hear other people's questions and your teacher's responses. You never know what might help you later when it's just you and the blank page or computer screen.

Read the Reading. With your answers to key focus or prereading journal questions in mind, highlight and annotate sections of the text that you think might be useful as supporting evidence or that you might want to argue against. (For a detailed discussion of active reading strategies, see Chapter 1. Also, as noted in Chapter 1, don't try to answer all of the prereading questions for the assignment sequences in this book. Instead, pursue those questions that, for whatever reason, draw your attention most forcefully.)

Define Your Purpose. Defining your reasons for writing and who you are writing for is related to the step of assessing your assignment, insofar as it will cause you to focus your assessment further. For example, suppose your assignment asks you to analyze Robert Johnson's argument in his essay "Teaching the Forbidden: Literature and the Religious Student." Right off the bat, you would know that your overall purpose will be to perform that analysis. But let's say that you are put off by the way Johnson represents his students in his essay; you would then want to communicate that concern as part of your analysis, and this would become part of your purpose in writing your essay. At this point you probably wouldn't know exactly how you would accomplish this, but it would be part of your purpose, nonetheless. Defining your purpose for writing is an important habit of reflection that will help you go beyond simply reacting to your assignments and instead shape unique, carefully considered responses to them.

Identify Your Audience. You also need to begin thinking about your audience at this stage. Certainly, you know that writing for your best friend is radically different from writing for a college course. Not only does your purpose for writing differ, but the expectations of your readers differ as well. Your friend will be a generous, interested, and sympathetic reader, disposed to be persuaded by whatever you have to say because of your friendship. Academic readers, who do not know you or care about you, are much more demanding. In general, academic audiences have a shared set of expectations—that you use solid logical argumentation and backing, that your prose is precise and well-structured, and that you rely as little as possible on emotional appeals. The assignment sequences in this book ask you to produce papers that conform to these conventions. However, even among academic readers, expectations may vary. Your biology or history or business professors will have different expectations from those of your English professors concerning what a successful writing project should include and how it should look. Even two English professors at the same college can differ in what they find valuable or what they wish you to emphasize in your writing. Thus, each writing situation requires that you shift "rhetorical gears" to a degree, and that you give some thought for whom you are writing. Don't let this keep you from getting started, however. If you're not sure how to write for a particular audience, you can always revise your paper later to suit that audience once you've figured out what its expectations are likely to be.

The next time you read the newspaper, take a longer-than-usual look at the letters to the editor and consider how well each writer has imagined and addressed his or her audience. What kind of person do you imagine each letter writer to be, and what kind of people do you think each was writing for? In other words, what is each writer's rhetorical stance? Did these writers imagine a particular audience and attempt to communicate their concerns to that audience, specifically? How persuasive were they, ultimately?

Each time you write, you want to accomplish something—get a good grade, secure a job interview, obtain more votes for the candidate you favor. If you want to be as successful as possible, then you should take the time to define exactly who you are trying to persuade and what you are trying to persuade them of—this will help you establish an effective rhetorical stance. Once you've done this, then you can consider how best to approach your project for the specific audience and purpose you've defined:

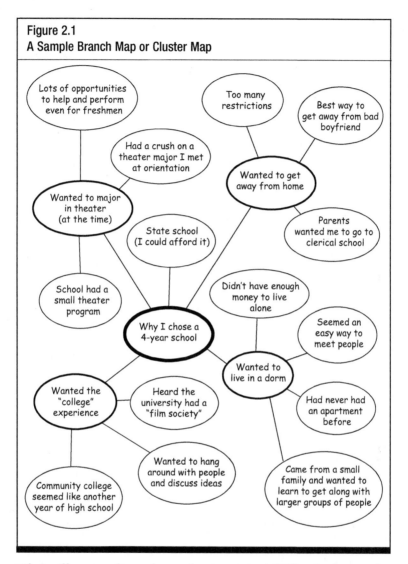

Figure 2.1
A Sample Branch Map or Cluster Map

- What will your audience know about your topic? What background information will you need to provide?
- Will your audience understand your approach to your topic, or do you need to explain it?
- Where is your audience likely to stand on the issue you're addressing? Will they agree with you or disagree?
- Will you have to convince them that your approach or position is worth caring about?

All of the assignments in this book ask you to keep your experience as a student (in whatever setting and at whatever point in your life you're experiencing it) at the center of your responses. If you're a student who has been out of school for several years, you'll have to decide how likely it is that your audience will know how your experience of student life differs from that of someone right out of high school. If you're a first-generation college student at a school where most of the students have college-educated parents, you'll need to decide if your background enables you to see some things your classmates can't. If it does, you'll need to explain something of your background to your audience so that you can teach them what you've observed. Your answers to the questions in the preceding bulleted list will affect what you include in your draft and how you shape it. They'll also help you decide how to persuade your audience to appreciate and understand where your responses come from.

The invention and planning stage

Now that you've analyzed your assignment, perhaps done some reading on your topic, defined your purpose for writing, and identified your audience, you're ready to start planning the content of your essay. You are still very much in the thinking stages of your writing process, and so you should strive to remain as unfettered as possible. At this stage you need to discover new possibilities and explore various different avenues. Later you'll pick and choose from the options you develop at this point, so don't limit your menu; let your mind roam free.

Revisit the Readings and the Prereading Questions. You will often find that at this stage of your writing process it is useful to reflect on any reading you've done on your topic, whatever your writing project may be. Since this book specifically asks you to read and respond to a number of essays for each assignment sequence, you'll definitely have done some reading on your topic by this point for the assignments in this book. In fact, you'll likely find that you've done some reading of outside sources by this stage no matter what your assignment is, and whether or not you've yet done any formal library research.

At this point you might want to revisit your answers to the prereading focus questions in the assignment sequences (or, for other assignments, any prereading questions you compiled yourself). If you took the trouble to highlight and annotate your reading the first time through, then you'll have a head start on this stage. If there were sections that angered you or struck you as especially true or compelling for any reason, copy them down (if they're not too long) and take notes about what made them work or not work for you.

If you found nothing worth pursuing in the readings, then you'll have your work cut out for you in terms of completing the assignment sequences. When students find a reading "boring," it's usually because there are obstacles to their understanding it. The writing may be above their reading level. Or perhaps they couldn't find a "quick" way into the text and were unsure how to proceed. It can also mean that they tried to read the material too quickly. You may encounter difficulties with some of the readings in this book, for a variety of reasons. If you do, stick with the readings. Believe that you'll find a way to make yourself interested in them. In this class, you're learning intellectual strategies and skills, not just information to be repeated for a test, and engaging with the readings in the assignment sequences is an important part of learning those skills.

Answer the Prewriting Questions. If you're unsure how or where to begin, try working with the prewriting questions following each essay in the assignment sequences (or, for other assignments, try compiling prewriting questions yourself). The prewriting questions should serve as prompts to help you move from the readings into the writing assignments that follow them. After you've answered some of the prewriting questions, choose two or three of the questions within the writing assignment itself that you feel are the most promising. Next, revisit the readings briefly, with those particular questions in mind. Mark the places that seem to connect, and make quick notes that convey some sense of what those connections are.

Brainstorm to Get Ideas. What you do next will largely depend on how you work as a writer. I generally brainstorm on the topic at this point, trying to write down as many ideas and observations as I can. I used to try to formulate a thesis sentence and outline at this point, but I (slowly) learned that doing this too soon kept me from developing ideas and associating those ideas with other ideas that would make my writing more interesting and complex. Also, on a number of occasions, I'd think of something I'd left out after I had completed the outline.

When you brainstorm, try to associate your topic with as many other ideas as you can. Leave nothing out. Some writers prefer to do this with nothing more than a pen and a pad of unlined paper. Others do it at the computer keyboard. Some people use huge numbers of sticky notes of different sizes and colors. Still others use lots of different colored pens. Whatever method you use, cover the page or screen with as many possible directions that your writing can take that you can think of.

Branch- or Cluster-map Your Ideas. This is a variation on brainstorming, with the added advantage of helping you organize your ideas sooner. At the center of a sheet of paper, write down a possible idea or argument you think you might want to work with (perhaps a key term from the assignment). Then draw lines branching out from that central point as additional, related ideas occur to you. (See Figure 2.1 for an example.) For example, if you were working with the first assignment in the "Idea of a University" sequence, you might write that phrase at the center of your page. Your branching lines might go to topics like "career preparation," "leave home," or "meet diverse people." From each of these you would then draw more lines, branching out to more specific kinds of information. For instance, branching out from "leave home" might be "time management," "handle own problems," or "budget money." From there you could keep going, jotting down examples and specifics that support or clarify each idea or point. Just keep going until you run out of "twigs" for your branches.

Make a Chart or Table. If your writing assignment seems too complicated for a cluster map, try making a chart or table of the different issues involved. For example, if the assignment asks you to compare your idea of a university to John Henry Newman's or Caroline Bird's ideas, draw three lines down your paper and list what you can about each viewpoint in the appropriate column. You can also have a fourth column for ideas that occur to you that don't seem to fit in the other three columns but may be helpful as you begin drafting your essay.

Freewrite. You can also try freewriting to get your ideas flowing. To do this, write for several minutes without stopping, and see what ideas emerge. Even if you get stuck, don't stop writing. If you have to, you can write "stuck, stuck, stuck" over and over again until the ideas start flowing; the point is to break through writer's block to find possibilities to develop in your draft. If you find this strategy useful, you can do a series of freewritings, taking the best parts of each as the jumping-off place for the next.

Think out Loud. If you're more comfortable talking through ideas rather than writing them down, experiment with a tape recorder or a very good friend who is willing to listen and take notes on what you say. Many of my students have found this an effective strategy. When you "replay" your comments, jot down or otherwise indicate which parts seem to you to be worth exploring further or about which you had the most to say or became the most animated and engaged.

Collaborate with Others. A variation on thinking out loud is to work with a study group composed of other people in your class. When you work with a group of peers committed to helping one another, this technique can be fun as well as effective. The purpose is to bounce ideas off one another and help one another develop ideas by asking questions and making suggestions. The important thing to remember is that each member of the group does his or her own work and writes his or her own essay. I only ask that my students who work together like this add a note in their essays acknowledging the collaboration. Check with your teacher to make sure this is an acceptable strategy.

Stay Flexible. Remember that nothing is cast in stone in the early stages. These are just a few strategies for getting your ideas out where you can see and work with them. Your job is to find some way to begin writing—one of the ways just discussed or one you invent for yourself or one you see a classmate using—so that when you begin to draft your essay, you have more than enough material to work with and you are in a position to make choices about what to include and what to leave out as you write.

Planning what you're going to write in your first rough draft should always be seen as provisional—that is, it can be changed and reworked and redirected. When I used to require outlines, I found that most of my students did them after they had written their essays. Most strong writers, however, have some form of plan from which to begin. Experiment with loose, quick outlines (you don't have to use Roman numerals) or notes to help you find and follow a direction for your draft. It may seem like extra work, but it will pay off in the long run.

Organizing and drafting your essay

The temptation always looms to write an exploratory draft before you decide how to organize your final paper. But thinking about possibilities for organization first, before you begin to write, can give you a sense of direction that will help you as you face that first blank page. Thus, many writers first decide how they will organize their paper, before they begin drafting.

The writing assignments in this book ask you to try out a variety of organizational methods. One assignment in the "Higher Learning/Cyber-Learning" sequence asks that you work through some of the ideas and terms in Paul Saffo's essay "Quality in an Age of Electronic Incunabula" and see how those ideas and terms fit or do not fit your experience of computers and learning. Whether or not you're a computer programmer or "hacker," as a college student you are in a position to speculate about the future of technology in both your college career and your economic career. As part of your essay, you will likely have stories and examples to tell from your own experience that will either mirror or contrast Saffo's stories and examples as you tell how computers have "transformed [your] intellectual life"; you'll need to narrate those events in detail, providing a chronological description of who said and did what. You'll also have to show clearly how your position compares with Saffo's position. And, of course, you'll need to present your point of view, your argument, in the most effective, persuasive way possible. This is a lot to juggle, and it will help to at least sketch out where in your essay you want to perform each of these tasks—narrating events, making comparisons, and presenting your arguments.

As I sat writing the first exploratory draft of this part of this book, I was surrounded by many pieces of paper—notes, brainstorming cluster maps, a very rough outline, suggestions from others, old handouts I'd given classes. I shifted these around as I worked, staring at them, making more notes on them, and pawing through them each of the many times that I got stuck. It was a messy sight. As you begin to write your first draft of an essay, I suggest you spread your notes, your plans, your prewriting questions, and your readings around you. For one thing, having all this writing around you makes your blank page or computer screen less intimidating. For another, you're less likely to leave things out. And finally, ideas can generate other ideas.

Observe Your Writing Rituals. Do you have writing rituals? What can you do to make your writing time as productive as possible? I try to work at the computer, but if my brain won't work fast enough, I find I'm more comfortable writing longhand. (Of course, I then have to find exactly the right pen.) Do you find that music helps you think, or do you need silence? Do you need a clear desk, or do you prefer to sprawl out on the floor? Is the library a place where you find it easier to get writing done, or is your kitchen table a better workplace? Are you an early-morning writer or a late-night writer? Spend some time thinking about what you might do to get yourself in the frame of mind for some serious writing. You might also ask other students what works for them. Experiment, and perhaps you'll find new rituals that can help you get to work more quickly and efficiently.

Find a Good Starting Point. Where to begin is another consideration. Do you feel you absolutely have to have a solid introduction before you can move on, or does the introduction seem to you to be something you should come back to once you've worked on the body of your essay? Beginning is difficult, so experiment to find ways to get yourself going. Do you find it difficult to make that first mark? Try freewriting again. Sometimes when you're stuck on a particular paragraph, try brainstorming material for just that one paragraph to see what the possibilities are and where you can go with it. Keep in mind that you can always change it. (In fact, I require that my students revise their essays extensively to help them get over thinking that the first draft they turn in has to be perfect.)

If you can, formulate at least a rough thesis or central claim to start out with. It can be a single sentence or several sentences. This will help you focus your essay and pin down what point of view you are going to express. A thesis statement is like a memorable, effective photograph: It gives the reader a sense of what's happening and what the story is behind it. A good photograph not only shows the subject, it also gives the viewer a sense of what the photographer wants him or her to think about that subject. Similarly, your job in your thesis is to provide that element of direction to your subject—that is, to convey what you personally find significant about your topic.

Maintain Your Momentum. Don't let yourself get blocked if a perfectly formulated thesis doesn't flow from your brain to the page. Instead, try to come up with a "working" thesis that can begin to give you a sense of how you might narrow and focus your particular take on your topic. Let it be as broad as you need it to be at this point, as long as it gives you some sense of direction to follow in the rest of your draft.

As you write the body of your essay, keep your plan and notes at hand, and find ways to get as much done as possible. Ask yourself questions and make notes with different-colored pens or sticky notes or in brackets and capital letters on your screen. If you get stuck, make a note and work on another section; then come back later to the place where you got stuck, when you're fresh or when an idea shakes loose as you work on that other section.

Here's a key tip: When you take a break, don't stop at a place where you're stuck; stop at a place where you have a good idea of what's coming next. If you stop because you're blocked, you'll likely dread picking up where you left off, and once you make yourself begin again, it will be even harder to gather writing steam. If you know what your next move is going to be, however, you'll face picking up where you left off with a lot less anxiety. Again, if you've begun with a rough outline, you'll have other sections you can work on when you run dry. Remember that it doesn't have to be perfect at this stage—it just has to get written!

Revision means more than fixing the commas

The revision stage of the writing process is where the real craft of writing comes in. Some students think revising is the same thing as editing or proofreading (that is, checking spelling, punctuation, and grammar), but these are two radically different stages in the writing process. Think of revising as re-envisioning your project and where you can take it. If you can do this, many more writing opportunities will open up for you.

It is especially helpful at this stage to be writing on a computer. After making a copy of your draft, try experimenting with major changes to your copy—and I really do mean major. What happens if you move your conclusion to the beginning? What other stories could you offer in your introduction to lead up to and clarify your thesis? Or, now that you've done all this thinking and writing to produce this draft, is there a more interesting or compelling argument you could make in your thesis? Are there big block quotes in the middle that need to be broken down and explained? What anecdotes, examples, or personal observations could you add to make your essay more engaging for your readers?

Even though it may not seem like it, your writing is the result of a series of choices: Will I argue from this point of view or that one? Will I include this example or that one? Does this phrase say exactly what I want it to, or can I say it differently? As I tell my students, no draft is ever "final"; there's always something else that could be developed or reimagined. Writing is an intellectual process, and as you write, new ideas develop. The revision stage is the perfect time for you to reflect on the ideas you've developed so far and to play with your writing and your ideas. The more time you can devote to your writing at this stage, the better your paper is likely to be.

When you have your paper or essay pretty much in the shape you want to stick with, try to let it get "cold." If you've been writing for four hours straight, you're probably not going to have much perspective about its quality if you try to evaluate it immediately. A day or two can help you "hear" it much more clearly. Almost no one completes an academic paper in time to let it sit for two days, but if you do, the payoff can be amazing. When you read your revised draft, make notes in the margins or on another sheet of paper so you'll know where to focus your attention after you finish reading the whole thing. Also, ask someone else to read and to note places he or she thinks are particularly strong and what sections need more work and why. The following is a kind of checklist you can use to help "road test" your essay.

1. Analyze the argument and organization:
   - What's the focus or thesis of your paper, and where can you find it?

- Does the way you have arranged or organized your essay—that is, what comes first, second, third, and so on—make sense?
- How much support have you provided for your thesis? Have you broken down your main argument for your reader and provided examples and supporting information to back up your arguments?
- Could your introduction be more effective or compelling?
- Does your conclusion bring your essay to a satisfying close without relying on stock closing phrases?
- Where could you add more, or what could you leave out?
- Is everything in your essay relevant to your thesis?

2. Analyze the rhetorical stance:
  - Who is your essay written for?
  - Will that audience need to know more background information about your topic before you introduce your thesis?
  - How would you describe your essay's tone? Have you addressed your audience as you would want to be addressed? (No one likes being talked down to or being told things we already know very well.)
  - How do you come across to your audience? Are you someone others will want to listen to?
  - Where and how have you attempted to engage your audience's interest?
  - Does your essay get bogged down anywhere? Does it move too quickly through any difficult issues or ideas?

3. Analyze the style:
  - What are your key terms? Are they clearly and adequately defined?
  - What section of your essay is the strongest? What makes it strong? Can you use that source of strength in other sections of your essay to strengthen them as well?
  - How many of your sentences begin with there or this or it? If you find more than a couple, rewrite those sentences.

Editing and proofreading your essay

Editing and proofreading, or reading your essay for correct grammar, punctuation, and spelling, is the very last thing you should do before sharing it with a serious reader. Read your essay aloud, as if you have an audience right there that you must keep interested. Don't mumble through it in a monotone. If any sentences or sections are confusing or make you stumble, make a mark in the margin to go over them again; if something makes you stumble, it will likely do the same to your reader.

Run a spell-checking program if you've used a word processing program on a computer. If you haven't written with a computer, read your essay backwards with a dictionary at hand. Look up the words you're not sure about. If you're still not sure after checking your dictionary, ask your teacher before you turn in your essay. Also be aware that spell checkers are not foolproof. A spell-check program won't catch incorrect homonyms (words that sound alike but have different spellings and meanings), for instance. The most common homonym errors involve they're, their, and there; to, too, and two; you're and your; and accept and except. Just remember that the ultimate responsibility for making sure your essay is as error free as possible is yours, not your computer's.

Over the course of this term, keep a list in your notebook of problems that occur in your writing. For example, if you've had trouble remembering the difference between *there*, *they're*, and *their*, include these in a chart in your notebook, and consult that chart as part of your final editing process. Finally, ask someone you trust to read your essay to catch anything you might have missed.

Closing Thoughts on Writing as a Process

The idea behind this chapter was not to overwhelm you with rules to follow and hoops to jump through but to let you know that people aren't born writers; they learn to be writers. Think about yourself as a writer—your pleasures, your anxieties, your strengths, your weaknesses. How can you use what you know about yourself and what you've read here to expand and develop the pleasures and strengths? There is no one "right" step-by-step formula, but there are strategies available to you if you're willing to experiment and invest the necessary time. As a teacher and a still-growing writer, I believe it's worth it.

Some Things We Know about the Teaching & Learning of Writing from 50 Years of Research

Mark Hall

1. There is no single "good" writing because writing practices, including rules and conventions, vary from one context to another. (Thus, "good" writing in English is not "good" writing in business, biology, nursing, computer science, or construction management.)

2. Literacy practices are *situated*. Students learn to write by *practicing* writing *in a particular context*, or situation, repeatedly over time. (First-Year Composition teaches students to write in First-Year Composition; writing in biology teaches students to write in biology.) There is no universally good writing, and "transfer" is considerably less common than we wish.)

3. *Process* comes before *product*. Writing *practices* are more important than individual papers. In a pedagogical setting, attention to and guidance in writing processes leads to improved products.

4. Students learn to write by *writing*, not by sitting on the sidelines and hearing a lecture on how to write.

5. Students do not learn the "basics" of grammar, punctuation, and mechanics *before* they can write in a particular context. Rather, they learn sentence-level rules and conventions by *practicing* meaningful writing—for a real *purpose* to a real *audience* in a real *form*—repeatedly over time.

6. Learning to write requires room to make mistakes. Novice writers in any field cannot be expected to produce writing "like a professional" or expert. Novices need to be taught and need to practice the rules and conventions of a particular field, but they are *learners*, not *professionals*. Developing

independent writers is more important than getting an error-free paper. "Error-free" is impossible for most novices, and thus, an unrealistic expectation.

7. Students learn to write by writing like professionals in their fields, by doing *real* writing in the *genres*—or forms—used by a particular community of experts. Disciplinary experts are essential to the learning process. (English teachers can't teach writing in nursing; experts in nursing know best the ways of seeing, ways of being, and ways of communicating in nursing.)

8. Informal writing is an effective way to learn course content. Teachers need not choose writing over content, or vice versa.

9. In a pedagogical setting, writing is *meaningful* when it is like the writing that people do outside of school: professional, personal, or public writing. Meaningful writing accomplishes some goal or objective important to the writer. When writing is meaningful, students find it engaging. When writing is engaging, students learn.

10. Marking errors on one paper does not lead to improvement on the next. Rather, students learn by revising one paper before going on to the next.

11. Correcting errors prompts no improvement. Editing & proofreading *for* a student teaches nothing. It merely makes a better paper.

12. Students improve as writers only when they revise repeatedly over time. Students must write *frequently* in order to develop.

13. Students improve proofreading & editing by having a small number of repeated errors pointed out at one time, then self-correcting and collaborating with peers.

14. Peer responses may help students improve writing, provided students are trained to respond effectively through repeated modeling.

15. Writing in any situation is concerned, first and foremost, not with sentence-level correction, but with *communicating meaning to a real audience*. Over-concern with error too early in the writing process actually *hinders* meaning-making and the development of ideas.

16. *Form* follows *function*. Writing is effectively assessed when higher order concerns such as *content* and *organization* are considered first and most important, and when lower order concerns, such as grammar, punctuation, and mechanics, are considered *later* and less important.

17. All errors are not created equal. Those that interfere with *clear meaning* are more important than, say, a misspelled word, or *affect* when the writer means *effect*. Effective feedback *prioritizes* revision suggestions from most important to least.

18. Marking every error discourages learning. *Minimal marking* (merely pointing out) is effective, while excessive marking is overwhelming, confusing.

19. Grammar, punctuation, and mechanics are not learned in isolation; rather, they are learned *in the context* of writing.

20. Effective writing assessment distinguishes among "mistakes" (the result of carelessness), "error" (the result of misunderstanding), and "stylistic" preferences (*viscous* instead of *thick*, for example).

21. Errors are social and local, not universal. Errors are what experts in a field agree are errors. Error in one situation may be a preferred convention in another. We mark what we expect to find.

22. If students don't know, then we must teach them. Telling students that they should have learned "X" in 4th grade or high school or First-Year Composition does not help them to develop.

23. Assigning writing, marking and grading it, then returning it is not *teaching* writing. Teaching requires explicit instruction, repeated modeling, frequent feedback during the writing process, multiple opportunities for writing in a variety of genres, both formal and informal, and practice over an extended period of time.

24. Mistakes may be evidence of learning; while learning new content or forms, writers may backslide, making mistakes on matters they previously handled successfully. Not all evidence of learning shows up in a single semester; rather writing development occurs slowly over extended time.

25. Non-native speakers of English may always write with an accent. Penalizing them for their status as multilingual writers is unjust

Plagiarism

Tabetha Adkins

What Is Plagiarism?

Plagiarism isn't simply the use of another source's words without giving credit to that source. In fact, this issue is far more complicated. For example:

1. If you write an entire paragraph based on information from a source and only cite that source at the end of the paragraph, this practice can be considered a form of plagiarism.

2. If you use an author's idea without crediting the author, this practice can be considered a form of plagiarism.

3. If you turn in an essay you've used in another course, you can be accused of plagiarism. Yes, you can plagiarize yourself!

4. If you buy a paper from an online "paper mill," this is definitely plagiarism.

5. If someone writes your paper for you, this is definitely plagiarism.

6. If you "lift" sentences, phrases, or paragraphs from a source (online, a book, a peer's paper, etc.) without giving credit to the source, that is definitely plagiarism.

Why It's a Big Deal

As a freshman student, you're entering a new culture. Anytime you enter a new culture (as you'll learn in ENG 1302), understanding the rules of that culture is very important. Here are some facts to help you understand why plagiarism is a "big deal" in academic cultures:

1. Academics have to write to keep their jobs. Professors have to publish in order to earn tenure and promotion. Graduate assistants have to write papers and eventually a thesis or dissertation in order to earn their degree. When students do not do their own writing or "steal" someone else's writing, many academics feel as though their livelihood is being robbed from them.

2. Since the invention of Google, plagiarism is easily detectable. Also, teachers of writing are experts in discourse, so they often have a sense for when students have plagiarized. These two facts lead teachers to feel as though students who plagiarize are trying to "outsmart" them, and their reaction is often one of anger.

3. To give you an idea of how seriously academics take plagiarism: the words "plagiarism" and "kidnapping" share the same Latin root.

4. Because the offense is viewed by academics with such seriousness, there can be severe consequences. Students can be expelled. Professors can be fired. Karl-Theodor Zu Guttenberg, the former defense minister of German, lost his job once he was accused of plagiarism despite the fact that he was a well-liked member of the German government.

The Department of Literature and Language's Official Plagiarism Policy

Instructors in the Department of Literature and Languages do not tolerate plagiarism and other forms of academic dishonesty. Instructors uphold and support the highest academic standards, and students are expected to do likewise. Penalties for students guilty of academic dishonesty include disciplinary probation, suspension, and expulsion. (Texas A&M University-Commerce Code of Student Conduct 5.b [1,2,3]).

Some Tips for Avoiding Plagiarism

1. Take good notes so you'll know which sources are making which claims.

2. If you find information in three or more sources, that information is probably considered "common knowledge" and does not need to be cited.

3. Start working on your assignments early to avoid temptation to turn in something you did not write in an act of desperation.

4. If you run out of time on an assignment and are tempted to turn in something you didn't write, talk to your instructors. Chances are that if you ask for an extension in advance, you'll get one.

5. Ask for help if you're confused. Your writing instructor and tutors in the Writing Center are here to help you. For great information about plagiarism and how to avoid it, visit this site on Purdue University's Online Writing Lab (OWL) page: http://owl.english.purdue.edu/owl/resource/589/01/.

The Writing Program's Policy on Turnitin.com and Other Plagiarism Detection Software

The writing program at Texas A&M University-Commerce does not use turnitin. com or other proprietary tools like it to detect plagiarism because these tools are ineffective and expensive. To read more about turnitin.com, see this story in the East Texan: http://www.theeasttexan.com/turnitin-raisesquestions-of-privacy-copyrights-1.2223313

PART II

Experiencing Literacy

If among the o
of its pervading
whic significan
idden from all
depts the preg

How to approach the assignments

Broadly speaking, the reading and writing assignments in this book are sequenced—that is, they build on each other, deepening and complicating the resulting conversations. The reading, writing, and research assignments are designed to build on one another. Generally, we will ask that you move gradually from your personal perceptions to a series of increasingly complex responses based on reading, writing, and, eventually other forms of research. Thus you'll be asked to progress in two directions—from the personal to the global, in terms of your audience, and from the general to the specific, in terms of your subject matter.

The assignments are structured to help you make connections among what you experience, what you read, and what you write. You'll start by writing about some of your own responses and experiences. Next you'll read an essay that complicates/enriches what you've written, and then you'll reconsider your original ideas in light of what that reading argues. After that, another essay will be brought into the mix. And, of course, you'll have class discussion to further complicate your thinking. And so on. (For us, complication is a good thing, by the way.)

The goal is for you to bring together ideas from a number of writers, combine them with your own thoughts and experiences, and ultimately develop a rich understanding of literacy practices.

CHAPTER 1

Narrating Literacies

We will begin our exploration of literacies in context by looking at the ways in which a variety of people (different ages, different backgrounds) have developed new literacies. According to Deborah Brandt, a professor of English at University of Wisconsin-Madison and author of the award-winning study *Literacy in American Lives* (2001), literacy development depends on literacy "sponsors." In the article that follows, Brandt "trace[s the] sponsors of literacy . . . as they appear in the accounts of ordinary Americans recalling how they learned to write and read" (167). She urges us to stop thinking of "literacy as an individual development" and instead begin to understand "literacy as an economic development, at least as the two have played out over the last ninety years or so" (166).

BEFORE YOU READ, spend some time with the interview protocol Brandt used to collect the literacy narratives that would eventually inform her book *Literacy in American Lives*. A literacy narrative explores a person's experiences with reading and writing over their lifetime. Use this interview protocol to interview a classmate about their literacy experiences. Your instructor may not require you to address every question. Instead, you may be encouraged to generate a literacy narrative based on just a handful of questions. You can use these at least two different ways:

1. Interview a classmate about their memories of reading and writing. Your instructor may ask you to draw from this information as a way to introduce your interviewee to the rest of the class.

2. Interview yourself, using the interview protocol as guide. Whether or not you interview a classmate, you should plan to use these questions to generate ideas for the first major writing assignment (see pg. 48).

   Before you begin, review the questions below and decide a plan of action. What are you most interested in learning about yourself and/or your classmate(s)? Hone in on that section of questions. If it is not as fruitful as you hoped, you can always move to a different line of questioning. The goal here is to stimulate memories of reading and writing—specific, detailed, and compelling.

Interview Protocol

From Deborah Brandt's *Literacy in American Lives* (New York: Cambridge UP, 2001, 208-210)

Demographic
Date of birth
Place of birth
Place of rearing
Gender/race
Type of household (childhood)
Type of household (current)
Great grandparents schooling and occupations, if known
Grandparents' schooling and occupations, if known
Parents'/guardians' schooling and occupations, in known
Names and locations of all schools attended
Other training
Degrees, dates of graduation, size of graduating class
Past/current/future occupations

Early Childhood Memories
Earliest memories of seeing other people writing/reading
Earliest memories of self writing/reading
Earliest memories of direct or indirect instruction
Memories of places writing/reading occurred
Occasions associated with writing/reading
People associated with writing/reading
Organizations associated with writing/reading
Materials available for writing/reading
Ways materials entered households
Kinds of materials used
Role of technologies

Writing and Reading in School
Earliest memories of reading/writing in school
Memories of kinds of writing/reading done in school
Memories of direct instruction
Memories of self-instruction

Memories of peer instruction
Memories of evaluation
Uses of assignments/other school writing and reading
Audiences of school-based writing
Knowledge drawn on to complete assignments
Resources drawn on to complete assignments
Kinds of materials available for school-based writing/reading
Kinds of materials used
Role of technologies

Writing and Reading with Peers
Memories of sharing writing and reading
Memories of writing and writing to/with friends
Memories of writing and reading in play
Memories of seeing friends reading and writing
Memories of reading friends' writing

Extracurricular Writing and Reading
Organizations or activities that may have involved writing or reading
Writing contests, pen pals, and so forth
Self-Initiated Writing or Reading
Purposes for writing and reading at different states
Genres
Audiences/uses
Teaching/learning involved

Writing on the Job
Same questions as above

Civic or Political Writing

Influential People
Memories of people who had a hand in one's learning to write or read

Influential Events
Significant events in the process of learning to write

Purposes for Writing and Reading Overall

Values
Relative importance of writing and reading
Motivations
Consequences

Current Uses of Reading and Writing
All reading and writing done in the six months prior to the interview

Senses of Literacy Learning
Interviewee's own sense of how he or she learned to read and write
Sense of how people in general learn to read and write

READING

Sponsors of Literacy

Deborah Brandt

BEFORE YOU READ

1. Who or what has encouraged you the most in your efforts to become a more effective reader or writer in a particular context? Do you have any memories of someone or something specific that may have discouraged your efforts to read and/or write more pleasurably or flexibly? What are those memories?

2. From your own observations or experience, what factors prevent people, especially adults, from increasing their literacy skills?

3. What experiences does the term "sponsor" bring up for you? What do you think about when you hear that word? How do you think someone may actually "sponsor" a particular facet of education?

AS YOU READ the following article, be sure to consider your responses to the above questions. You should also . . .

READ IT ONCE (quickly), just to see where it is going. We know from the title of the essay that Brandt is going to discuss what "sponsorship" may have to do with literacy and who may actually "sponsor" literacy. She's tracing this term as it functions in the lives of several specific people. Who are these people? How did they learn to read and write (and for what purposes)? As you do this first quick read-through, you should also consider this: Why does Brandt use the term "sponsor" in conjunction with the term "literacy"?

READ IT A SECOND TIME, much more carefully. This time, read with a pen in your hand so you can jot down notes, mark important passages (or other passages you'd like to talk about in class), and find yourself in this text by agreeing with portions of her arguments (if you do), dismissing other portions of her argument (if you can't agree), relating to some of the things she says with stories from your own life (if you can), and basically reading her argument against your own arguments in order to (1) understand her position as best you can so you can (2) expand on it and/or resist it—if need be—in order to advance your own arguments, ideas, and experiences.

Sponsors of Literacy

Deborah Brandt

In his sweeping history of adult learning in the United States, Joseph Kett describes the intellectual atmosphere available to young apprentices who worked in the small, decentralized print shops of antebellum American. Because printers also were the solicitors and editors of what they published, their workshops served as lively incubators for literacy and political discourse. By the mid-nineteenth century, however, this learning space was disrupted when the invention of the steam press reorganized the economy of the print industry. Steam presses were so expensive that they required capital outlays beyond the means of many printers. As a result, print jobs were outsourced, the processes of editing and printing were split, and, in tight competition, print apprentices became low-paid mechanics with no more access to the multi-skilled environment of the craftshop (Kett 67-70). While this shift in working conditions may be evidence of the deskilling of workers induced by the Industrial Revolution (Nicholas and Nicholas), it also offers a site for reflecting upon the dynamic sources of literacy and literacy learning. The reading and writing skills of print apprentices in this period were the achievements not simply of teachers and learners nor of the discourse practices of the printer community. Rather, these skills existed fragilely, contingently within an economic moment. The pre-steam press economy enabled some of the most basic aspects of the apprentices' literacy, especially their access to material production and the public meaning or worth of their skills. Paradoxically, even as the steam-powered penny press made print more accessible (by making publishing more profitable), it brought an end to a particular form of literacy sponsorship and a drop in literate potential.

The apprentices' experience invites rumination upon literacy learning and teaching today. Literacy looms as one of the great engines of profit and competitive advantage in the 20th century: a lubricant for consumer desire; a means for integrating corporate markets; a foundation for the deployment of weapons and other technology; a raw material in the mass production of information. As ordinary citizens have been compelled into these economies, their reading and writing skills have grown sharply more central to the everyday trade of information and goods as well as to the pursuit of education, employment, civil rights, status. At the same time, people's literate skills have grown vulnerable to unprecedented turbulence in their economic value, as conditions, forms, and standards of literacy achievement seem to shift with almost every new generation of learners. How are we to understand the vicissitudes of individual literacy development in relationship to the large-scale economic forces that set the routes and determine the wordly worth of that literacy?

The field of writing studies has had much to say about individual literacy development. Especially in the last quarter of the 20th century, we have theorized, researched, critiqued, debated, and sometimes even managed to enhance the literate potentials of ordinary citizens as they have tried to cope with life as they find it. Less easily and certainly less steadily have we been able to relate what we see, study, and do to these larger contexts of profit making and competition. This even as we recognize that the most pressing issues we deal with—tightening associations between literate skill and social viability, the breakneck pace of change in communications technology, persistent inequities in access and reward—all relate to structural conditions in literacy's bigger picture. When economic forces are addressed in our work, they appear primarily as generalities: contexts, determinants, motivators, barriers, touchstones. But rarely are they systematically related to the local conditions and embodied moments of literacy learning that occupy so many of us on a daily basis.[1]

This essay does not presume to overcome the analytical failure completely. But it does offer a conceptual approach that begins to connect literacy as an individual development to literacy as an economic development, at least as the two have played out over the last ninety years or so. The approach is through what I call sponsors of literacy. Sponsors, as I have come to think of them, are any agents, local or distant, concrete or abstract, who enable, support, teach, model, as well as recruit, regulate, suppress, or withhold literacy—and gain advantage by it in some way. Just as the ages of radio and television accustom us to having programs *brought* to us by various commercial sponsors, it is useful to think about who or what underwrites occasions of literacy learning and use. Although the interests of the sponsor and the sponsored do not have to converge (and, in fact, may conflict) sponsors nevertheless set the terms for access to literacy and wield powerful incentives for compliance and loyalty. Sponsors are a tangible remind that literacy learning throughout history has always required permission, sanction, assistance, coercion, or, at minimum, contact with existing trade routes. Sponsors are delivery systems for the economies of literacy, the means by which these forces present themselves to—and through—individual learners. They also represent the causes into which people's literacy usually gets recruited.[2] For the last five years I have been tracing sponsors of literacy across the 20th century as they appear in the accounts of ordinary Americans recalling how they learned to write and read. The investigation is grounded in more than 100 in-depth interviews that I collected from a diverse group of people born roughly between 1900 and 1980. In the interviews, people explored in great detail their memories of learning to read and write across their lifetimes, focusing especially on the people, institutions, materials, and motivations involved in the process. The more I worked with these accounts, the more I came to realize that they were filled with references to sponsors, both explicit and latent, who appeared in formative roles at the scenes of literacy learning. Patterns of sponsorship became an illuminating site through which to track the different cultural attitudes people developed towards writing vs. reading as well as the ideological congestion faced by late-century literacy learners as their sponsors proliferated and diversified (see my essays on "Remembering Reading" and "Accumulating Literacy"). In this essay I set out a case for why the concept of sponsorship is so richly suggestive for exploring economies of literacy and their effects. Then, through use of extended case examples, I demonstrate the practical application of this approach for interpreting current conditions of literacy teaching and learning, including persistent stratification of opportunity and escalating standards for literacy achievement. A final section addresses implications for the teaching of writing.

Sponsorship

Intuitively, *sponsors* seemed a fitting term for the figures who turned up most typically in people's memories of literacy learning: older relatives, teachers, priests, supervisors, military officers, editors, influential authors. Sponsors, as we ordinarily think of them, are powerful figures who bankroll events or smooth the way for initiates. Usually richer, more knowledgeable, and more entrenched than the sponsored, sponsors nevertheless enter a reciprocal relationship with those they underwrite. They lend their resources or credibility to the sponsored but also stand to gain benefits from their success, whether by direct repayment or, indirectly, by credit of association. *Sponsors* also proved an appealing term in my analysis because of all the commercial references that appeared in these 20th-century accounts—the magazines, peddled encyclopedias, essay contests, radio and television programs, toys fan clubs, writing tools, and so on, from which so much experience with literacy was derived. As the 20th century turned the abilities to read and write into widely exploitable resources, commercial sponsorship abounded.

In whatever form, sponsors deliver the ideological freight that must be borne for access to what they have. Of course, the sponsored can be oblivious to or innovative with this ideological burden. Like Little Leaguers who wear the logo of a local insurance agency on their uniforms, not out of a concern for enhancing the agency's image but as a means for getting to play ball, people throughout history have acquired literacy pragmatically under the banner of others' causes. In the days before free, public schooling in England, Protestant Sunday Schools warily offered basic reading instruction to working-class families as part of evangelical duty. To the horror of many in the church sponsorship, these families insistently, sometimes riotously demanded of their Sunday Schools more instruction, including in writing and math, because it provided means for upward mobility.[3] Through the sponsorship of Baptist and Methodist ministries, African Americans in slavery taught each other to understand the Bible in subversively liberatory ways. Under a conservative regime, they developed forms of critical literacy that sustained religious, educational, and political movements both before and after emancipation (Cornelius). Most of the time, however, literacy takes its shape from the interests of its sponsors. And, as we will see below, obligations toward one's sponsors run deep, affecting what, why, and how people write and read.

The concept of sponsors helps to explain, then, a range of human relationships and ideological pressures that turn up at the scenes of literacy learning—from benign sharing between adults and youths, to euphemized coercions in schools and workplaces, to the most notorious impositions and deprivations by church or state. It also is a concept useful for tracking literacy's material: the things that accompany writing and reading and the ways they are manufactured and distributed. Sponsorship as a sociological term is even more broadly suggestive for thinking about economies of literacy development. Studies of patronage in Europe and *compradrazgo* in the Americas shows how patron-client relationships in the past grew up around the need to manage scarce resources and promote political stability (Bourne; Lynch; Horstman and Kurtz). Pragmatic, instrumental, ambivalent, patron-client relationships integrated otherwise antagonistic social classes into relationships of mutual, albeit unequal dependencies. Loaning land, money, protection, and other favors allowed the politically powerful to extend their influence and justify their exploitation of clients. Clients traded their labor and deference for access to opportunities for themselves or their children and for leverage needed to improve their social standing. Especially under conquest in Latin America, *compradrazgo* reintegrated native societies badly fragmented by the diseases and other disruptions that followed foreign invasions. At the same time, this system was susceptible to its own stresses, especially when patrons became clients themselves of still more centralized or distant overlords, with all the shifts in loyalty and perspective that entailed (Horstman and Kurtz 13-14).

In raising this association with formal systems of patronage, I do not wish to overlook the very different economic, political, and educational systems within which U.S. literacy has developed. But where we find the sponsoring of literacy, it will be useful to look for its function within larger political and economic arenas. Literacy, like land, is a valued commodity in this economy, a key resource in gaining profit and edge. This value helps to explain, of course, the lengths people will go to secure literacy fro themselves or their children. But it also explains why the powerful work so persistently to conscript and ration the powers of literacy. The competition to harness literacy, to manage, measure, teach, and exploit it, has intensified throughout the century. It is vital to pay attention to this development because it largely sets the terms for individuals' encounters with literacy. This competition shapes the incentives and barriers (including uneven distributions of opportunity) that greet literacy learners in any particular time and place. It is this competition that has made access to the right kinds of literacy sponsors so crucial for political and economic well being. And it also has spurred the rapid, complex changes that now make the pursuit of literacy feel so turbulent and precarious for so many.

In the next three sections, I trace the dynamics of literacy sponsorship through the life experiences of several individuals, showing how their opportunities for literacy learning emerge out of the jockeying and skirmishing for economic and political advantage going on among sponsors of literacy. Along the way, the analysis addresses three key issues: (1) how, despite ostensible democracy in educational chances, stratification of opportunity continues to organize access and reward in literacy learning; (2) how sponsors contribute to what is called "the literacy crisis," that is, the perceived gap between rising standards for achievement and people's ability to meet them; and (3) how encounters with literacy sponsors, especially as they are configured at the end of the 20th century, can be sites for the innovative rerouting of resources into projects of self-development and social change.

Sponsorship and Access

A focus on sponsorship can force a more explicit and substantive link between literacy learning and systems of opportunity and access. A statistical correlation between high literacy achievement and high socioeconomic, majority-race status routinely shows up in results of national tests of reading and writing performance.[4]These findings capture yet, in their shorthand way, obscure the unequal conditions of literacy sponsorship that lie behind differential outcomes in academic performance. Throughout their lives, affluent people from high-caste racial groups have multiple and redundant contacts with powerful literacy sponsors as a routine part of their economic and political privileges. Poor people and those from low-caste racial groups have less consistent, less politically secured access to literacy sponsors—especially to the ones that can grease their way to academic and economic success. Differences in their performances are often attributed to family background (namely education and income of parents) or to particular norms and values operating within different ethnic groups or social classes. But in either case, much more is usually at work.

As a study in contrasts in sponsorship patterns and access to literacy, consider the parallel experiences of Raymond Branch and Dora Lopez, both of whom were born in 1969 and, as young children, moved with their parents to the same, mid-sized university town in the midwest.[5] Both were still residing in this town at the time of our interviews in 1995. Raymond Branch, a European American, had been born in southern California, the son of a professor father and a real estate executive mother. He recalled that his first grade classroom in 1975 was hooked up to a mainframe computer at Stanford University and that, as a youngster, he enjoyed fooling around with computer programming in the company of "real users" at his father's science lab. This process was not interrupted much when, in the late 1970s, his family moved to the Midwest. Raymond received his first personal computer as a Christmas present from his parents when he was twelve years old, and a modem the year after that. In the 1980s, computer hardware and software stores began popping up within a bicycle-ride's distance from where he lived. The stores were serving the university community and, increasingly, the high-tech industries that were becoming established in that vicinity. As an adolescent, Raymond spent his summers roaming these stores, sampling new computer games, making contact with founders of some of the first electronic bulletin boards in the nation, and continuing, through reading and other informal means, to develop his programming techniques. At the time of our interview he had graduated from the local university and was a successful freelance writer of software and software documentation, with clients in both the private sector and the university community.

Dora Lopez, a Mexican American, was born in the same year as Raymond Branch, 1969, in a Texas border town, where her grandparents, who worked as farm laborers, lived most of the year. When Dora was still a baby her family moved to the same Midwest university town as had the family of Raymond Branch. Her father pursued an accounting degree at a local technical college and found work as a shipping and receiving clerk at the university. Her mother, who also attended technical college briefly, worked part-time in a bookstore. In the early 1970s, when the Lopez family made its move to the Midwest, the Mexican-American population in the university town was barely one percent. Dora recalled that the family had to drive seventy miles to a big city to find not only suitable groceries but also Spanish-language newspapers and magazines that carried information of concern and interest to them. (Only when reception was good could they catch Spanish-language radio programs coming from Chicago, 150 miles away.) During her adolescence, Dora Lopez undertook to teach herself how to read and write in Spanish, something, she said, the neither her brother nor her U.S.-born cousins knew how to do. Sometimes, with the help of her mother's employee discount at the bookstore, she sought out novels by South American and Mexican writers, and she practiced her written Spanish by corresponding with relatives in Colombia. She was exposed to computers for the first time at the age of thirteen when she worked as a teacher's aide in a federally-funded summer school program for the children of migrant workers. The computers were being used to help the children to be brought up to grade level in their reading and writing skills. When Dora was admitted to the same university that Raymond Branch attended, her father bought her a used word processing machine that a student had advertised for sale in a bulletin board in the building where Mr. Lopez worked. At the time of our interview, Dora Lopez had transferred from the university to a technical college. She was working for a cleaning company, where she performed extra duties as a translator, communicating on her supervisor's behalf with the largely Latina cleaning staff. "I write in Spanish for him, what he needs to be translated, like job duties, what he expects them to do, and I write lists for him in English and Spanish," she explained.

In Raymond Branch's account of his early literacy learning we are able to see behind the scenes of his majority-race membership, male gender, and high-end socioeconomic family profile. There lies a thick and, to him, relatively accessible economy of institutional and commercial supports that cultivated and subsidized his acquisition of a powerful form of literacy. One might be tempted to say that Raymond Branch was born at the right time and lived in the right place—except that the experience of Dora Lopez troubles that thought. For Raymond Branch, a university town in the 1970s and 1980s provided an information-rich, resource-rich learning environment in which to pursue his literacy development, but for Dora Lopez, a female member of a culturally unsubsidized ethnic minority, the same town at the same time was information- and resource-poor. Interestingly, both young people were pursuing projects of self-initiated learning, Raymond Branch in computer programming and Dora Lopez in biliteracy. But she had to reach much further afield for the material and communicative systems needed to support her learning. Also, while Raymond Branch, as the son of an academic, was sponsored by some of the most powerful agents of the university (its laboratories, newest technologies, and most educated personnel), Dora Lopez was being sponsored by what her parents could pull from the peripheral service systems of the university (the mail room, the bookstore, the second-hand technology market). In these accounts we also can see how the development and eventual economic worth of Raymond Branch's literacy skills were underwritten by late-century transformations in communication technology that created a boomtown need for programmers and software writers. Dora Lopez's biliterate skills developed and paid off much further down the economic-reward ladder, in government-sponsored youth programs and commercial enterprises, that, in the 1990s, were absorbing surplus migrant workers into low-wage, urban service economy.[6] Tracking patterns of literacy sponsorship, then, gets beyond SES shorthand to expose more fully how unequal literacy chances relate to systems of unequal subsidy and reward for literacy. These are the systems that deliver large-scale economic, historical, and political conditions to the scenes of small-scale literacy use and development.

This analysis of sponsorship forces us to consider not merely how one social group's literacy practices may differ from another's, but how everybody's literacy practices are operating in differential degrees of sponsoring power, and different scales of monetary worth to the practices in use. In fact, the interviews I conducted are filled with examples of how economic and political forces, some of them originating in quite distant corporate and government policies, affect people's day-to-day ability to seek out and practice literacy. As a telephone company employee, Janelle Hampton enjoyed a brief period in the early 1980s as a fraud investigator, pursuing inquiries and writing up reports of her efforts. But when the breakup of the telephone utility reorganized its workforce, the fraud division was moved two states away and she was returned to less interesting work as a data processor. When, as a seven-year-old in the mid-1970s, Yi Vong made his way with his family from Laos to rural Wisconsin as part of the first resettlement group of Hmong refugees after the Vietnam War, his school district—which had no ESL programming—placed him in a school for the blind and dear, where he learned English on audio and visual language machines. When a meager retirement pension forced Peter Hardaway and his wife out of their house and into a trailer, the couple stopped receiving newspapers and magazines in order to avoid cluttering up the small space they had to share. An analysis of sponsorship systems of literacy would help educators everywhere to think through the effects that economic and political changes in their regions are having on various people's ability to write and read, their chances to sustain that ability, and their capacities to pass it along to others. Recession, relocation, immigration, technological change, government retreat all can—and do—condition the course by which literate potential develops.

Sponsorship and the Rise in Literacy Standards

As I have been attempting to argue, literacy as a resource becomes available to ordinary people largely through the mediations of more powerful sponsors. These sponsors are engaged in ceaseless processes of positioning and repositioning, seizing and relinquishing control over meanings and materials of literacy as part of their participation in economic and political competition. In the give and take of these struggles, forms of literacy and literacy learning take shape. This section examines more closely how forms of literacy are created out of competitions between institutions. It especially considers how this process relates to the rapid rise in literacy standards since World War II. Resnick and Resnick lay out the process by which the demand for literacy achievement has been escalating, from basic, largely rote competence to more complex analytical and interpretive skills. More and more people are now being expected to accomplish more and more things with reading and writing. As print and its spinoffs have entered virtually every sphere of life, people have grown increasingly dependent on their literacy skills for earning a living and exercising and protecting their civil rights. This section uses one extended case example to trace the role of institutional sponsorship in raising the literacy stakes. It also considers how one man used available forms of sponsorship to cope with this escalation in literacy demands.

The focus is on Dwayne Lowery, whose transition in the early 1970s from line worker in an automobile manufacturing plant to field representative for a major public employees union exemplified the major transition of the post-World War II economy—from a thing-making, thing-swapping society to an information-making, service-swapping society. In the process, Dwayne Lowery had to learn to read and write in ways that he had never done before. How his experiences with writing developed and how they were sponsored—and distressed—by institutional struggle will unfold in the following narrative.

A man of Eastern European ancestry, Dwayne Lowery was born in 1938 and raised in a semi-rural area in the upper midwest, the third of five children of a rubber workers father and a homemaker mother. Lowery recalled how, in his childhood home, his father's feisty union publications and left-leaning newspapers and radio shows helped to create a political climate in his household. "I was sixteen years old before I knew that goddamn Republicans was two words," he said. Despite this influence, Lowery said he shunned politics and newspaper reading as a young person, except to read the sports page. A diffident student, he graduated near the bottom of his class from a small high school in 1956 and, after a stint in the Army, went to work on the assembly line of a major automobile manufacturer. In the late 1960s, bored with the repetition of spraying primer paint on the right door checks of 57 cars an hour, Lowery traded in his night shift at the auto plant for a day job reading water meters in a municipal utility department. It was at that time, Lowery recalled, that he rediscovered newspapers, reading them in the early morning in his department's break room. He said:

> At the time I guess I got a little more interested in the state of things within the state. I started to get a little political at that time and got a little more information about local people. So I would buy [a metropolitan paper] and I would read that paper in the morning. It was a pretty conservative paper but I got some information.

At about the same time Lowery became active in a rapidly growing public employees union, and, in the early 1970s, he applied for and received a union-sponsored grant that allowed him to take off four months of work and travel to Washington, D.C. for training in union activity. Here is his extended account of that experience:

> When I got to school, then there was a lot of reading. I often felt bad. If I had read more [as a high school student] it wouldn't have been so tough. But they pumped a lot of stuff at us to read. We lived in a hotel and we had to some extent homework we had to do and reading we had to do and not make written reports but make some presentation on our part of it. What they were trying to teach us, I believe, was regulations, systems, laws. In case anything in court came up along the way, we would know that. We did a lot of work on organizing, you know, learning how to negotiate contracts, contractual language, how to write it. Gross National Product, how that affected the Consumer Price Index. It was pretty much a crash course. It was pretty much crammed in. And I'm not sure we were all that well prepared when we got done, but it was interesting.

After a hands-on experience organizing sanitation workers in the west, Lowery returned home and was offered a full-time job as a field staff representative for the union, handling worker grievances and contract negotiations for a large, active local near his state capital. His initial writing and rhetorical activities corresponded with the heady days of the early 1970s when the union was growing in strength and influence, reflecting in part the exponential expansion in information workers and service providers within all branches of government. With practice, Lowery said he became "good at talking," "good at presenting the union side," "good at slicing chunks off the employers case." Lowery observed that, in those years, the elected officials with whom he was negotiating often lacked the sophistication of their Washington-trained counterparts. "They were part-time people," he said. "And they didn't know how to calculate. We got things in contracts that didn't cost them much at the time but were going to cost them a ton down the road." In time, through, even small municipal and county governments responded to the public employees' growing power by hiring specialized attorneys to represent them in grievance and contract negotiations. "Pretty soon," Lowery observed, "ninety percent of the people I was dealing with across the table were attorneys."

This move brought dramatic changes in the writing practices of union reps, and, in Lowery's estimation, a simultaneous waning of the power of the workers and the power of his own literacy. "It used to be we got our way through muscle or through political connections," he said. "Now we had to get it through legalistic stuff. It was no longer just sit down and talk about it. Can we make a deal?" Instead, all activity became rendered in writing: the exhibit, the brief, the transcript, the letter, the appeal. Because briefs took longer to write, the wheels of justice took longer to turn. Delays in grievance hearings became routine, as lawyers and union reps alike asked hearing judges for extensions on their briefs. Things went, in Lowery's words, "from quick, competent justice to expensive and long term justice."

In the meantime, Lowery began spending up to 70 hours a week at work, sweating over the writing of briefs, which are typically fifteen to thirty-page documents laying out precedents, arguments, and evidence for a grievant's case. These documents were being forced by the new political economy in which Lowery's union was operating. He explained:

> When employers were represented by an attorney, you were going to have a written brief because the attorney needs to get paid. Well, what do you think if you were a union grievant and the attorney says, well, I'm going to write a brief and Dwayne Lowery says, well, I'm not going to. Does the worker somehow feel that their representation is less now?

To keep up with the new demands, Lowery occasionally traveled to major cities for two or three-day union-sponsored workshops on arbitration, new legislation, and communication skills. He also took short courses at a historic School for Workers at a nearby university. His writing instruction consisted mainly of reading the briefs of other field reps, especially those done by the college graduates who increasingly being assigned to his district from union headquarters. Lowery said he kept a file drawer filled with other people's briefs from which he would borrow formats and phrasings. At the time of our interview in 1995, Dwayne Lowery had just taken an early and somewhat bitter retirement from the union, replaced by a recent graduate forma master's degree program in Industrial Relations. As a retiree, he was engaged in local Democratic party politics and was getting informal lessons in word processing at home from his wife.

Over a 20-year period, Lowery's adult writing took its character from a particular juncture in labor relations, when even small units of government began wielding (and, as a consequence, began spreading) a "legalistic" form of literacy in order to restore political dominance over public workers. This struggle for dominance shaped the kinds of literacy skills required of Lowery, the kinds of genres he learned and used, and the kinds of literate identity he developed. Lowery's rank-and-file experience and his talent for representing that experience around a bargaining table became increasingly peripheral to his ability to prepare documents that could compete in kind with those written by formally-educated, professional adversaries. Face-to-face meetings became occasions mostly for a ritualistic exchange of texts, as arbitrators generally deferred decisions, reaching them in private, after solitary deliberation over complex sets of documents. What Dwayne Lowery was up against as a working adult in the second half of the 20th century was more than just living through a rising standard in literacy expectations or a generalized growth in professionalization, specialization, or documentary power—although certainly all of those things are, generically, true. Rather, these developments should be seen more specifically, as outcomes of ongoing transformations in the history of literacy as it has been wielded as part of economic and political conflict. These transformations become the arenas in which new standards of literacy develop. And for Dwayne Lowery—as well as many like him over the last 25 years—these are the arenas in which the worth of existing literate skills become degraded. A consummate debater and deal maker, Lowery saw his value to the union bureaucracy subside, as power shifted to younger, university-trained staffers whose literacy credentials better matched the specialized forms of escalating pressure coming form the other side.

In the broadest sense, the sponsorship of Dwayne Lowery's literacy experiences lies deep within the historical conditions of industrial relations in the 20th century and, more particularly, within the changing nature of work and labor struggle over the last several decades. Edward Stevens Jr. has observed the rise in this century of an "advanced contractarian society" (25) by which formal relationships of all kinds have come to rely on "a jungle of rules and regulations" (139). For labor, these conditions only intensified in the 1960s and 1970s when a flurry of federal and state civil rights legislation curtailed the previously unregulated hiring and firing power of management. These developments made the appeal to law as central as collective bargaining for extending employee rights (Heckscher 9). I mention this broader picture, first, because it relates to the forms of employer backlash that Lowery began experiencing by the early 1980s and, more important, because a history of unionism serves as a guide for a closer look at he sponsors of Lowery's literacy.

These resources begin with the influence of his father, whose membership in the United Rubber Workers during the ideologically potent 1930s and 1940s, grounded Lowery in class-conscious progressivism and its favorite literate form: the newspaper. On top of that, though, was a pragmatic philosophy of worker education that developed in the U.S. after the Depression as an anti-communist antidote to left-wing intellectual influences in unions. Lowery's parent union, in fact, had been a central force in refocusing worker education away from an earlier emphasis on broad crucial study and toward discrete techniques for organizing and bargaining. Workers began to be trained in the discrete bodies of knowledge, written formats, and idioms associated with those strategies. Characteristic of this legacy, Lowery's crash course at the Washington-based training center in the early 1970s emphasized technical information, problem solving, and union-building skills and methods. The transformation in worker education from critical, humanistic study to problem-solving skills was also lived out at the school for workers where Lowery took short courses in the 1980s. Once a place where factory workers came to write and read about economics, sociology, and labor history, the school is now part of a university extension service offering workshops—often requested by management—on such topics as work restructuring, new technology, health and safety regulations, and joint labor-management cooperation.[7] Finally, in this inventory of Dwayne Lowery's literacy sponsors, we must add the latest incarnations shaping union practices: the attorneys and college-educated co-workers who carried into Lowery's workplace forms of legal discourse and "essayist literacy."[8]

What should we notice about this pattern of sponsorship? First, we can see form yet another angle how the course of an ordinary person's literacy learning—its occasions, materials, applications, potentials—follows the transformations going on within sponsoring institutions as those institutions fight for economic and ideological position. As a result of wins, losses, or compromises, institutions undergo change, affecting the kinds of literacy they promulgate and the status that such literacy has in the larger society. So where, how, why, and what Lowery practiced as a writer—and what he didn't practice—took shape as part of the post-industrial jockeying going on over the last thirty years by labor, government, and industry. Yet there is more to be seen in this inventory of literacy sponsors. It exposes the deeply textured history that lies within the literacy practices of institutions and within any individual's literacy experiences. Accumulated layers of sponsoring influences—in families, workplaces, schools, memory—carry forms of literacy that have been shaped out of ideological and economic struggles of the past. This history, on the one hand, is a sustaining resource in the quest for literacy. It enables an older generation to pass its literacy resources onto another. Lowery's exposure to his father's newspaper-reading and supper-table political talk kindled his adult passion for news, debate, and for language that rendered relief and justice. This history also helps to create infrastructures of opportunity. Lowery found crucial supports for extending his adult literacy in the educational networks that unions established during the first half of the 20th century as they were consolidating into national powers. On the other hand, this layered history of sponsorship is also deeply conservative and can be maladaptive because it teaches forms of literacy that oftentimes are in the process of being overtaken by new political realities and by ascendant forms of literacy. The decision to focus worker education on practical strategies of recruiting and bargaining—devised in the thick of Cold War patriotism and galloping expansion in union memberships—became, by the Reagan years, a fertile ground for new forms of management aggression and cooptation.

It is actually this lag or gap in sponsoring forms that we call the rising standard of literacy. The pace of change and the place of literacy in economic competition have both intensified enormously in the last half of the 20th century. It is as if the history of literacy is in fast forward. Where once the same sponsoring arrangements could maintain value across a generation or more, forms of literacy and their sponsors can now rise and recede many times within a single life span. Dwayne Lowery experienced profound changes in forms of union-based literacy not only between his father's time and his but between the time he joined the union and the time he left it, twenty-odd years later. This phenomenon is what makes today's literacy feel so advanced and, at the same time, so destabilized.

Sponsorship and Appropriation in Literacy Learning

We have seen how literacy sponsors affect literacy learning in two powerful ways. They help to organize and administer stratified systems of opportunity and access, and they raise the literacy stakes in struggles for competitive advantage. Sponsors enable and hinder literacy activity, often forcing the formation of new literacy requirements while decertifying older ones. A somewhat different dynamic of literacy sponsorship is treated here. It pertains to the potential of the sponsored to divert sponsors' resources toward ulterior projects, often projects of self-interest or self-development. Earlier I mentioned how Sunday School parishioners in England and African Americans in slavery appropriated church-sponsored literacy for economic and psychic survival. "Misappropriation" is always possible at the scene of literary transmission, a reason for the tight ideological control that usually surrounds reading and writing instruction. The accounts that appear below are meant to shed light on the dynamics of appropriation, including the role of sponsoring agents in that process. They are also meant to suggest that diversionary tactics in literacy learning may be invited now by the sheer proliferation of literacy activity in contemporary life. The uses and networks of literacy crisscross through many domains, exposing people to multiple, often amalgamated sources of sponsoring powers, secular, religious, bureaucratic, commercial, technological. In other words, what is so destabilized about contemporary literacy today also makes it so available and potentially innovative, ripe for picking, one might say, for people suitably positioned. The rising level of schooling in the general population is also an inviting factor in this process. Almost everyone now has some sort of contact, for instance, with college educated people, whose movements through workplaces, justice systems, social service organizations, houses of worship, local government, extended families, or circles of friends spread dominant forms of literacy (whether wanted or not, helpful or not) into public and private spheres. Another condition favorable for appropriation is the deep hybridity of literacy practices extant in many settings. As we saw in Dwayne Lowery's case, workplaces, schools, families bring together multiple strands of the history of literacy in complex and influential forms. We need models of literacy that more astutely account for these kinds of multiple contacts, both in and out of school and across a lifetime. Such models could begin to grasp the significance of re-appropriation, which, for a number of reasons, is becoming a key requirement for literacy learning at the end of the 20th century.

The following discussion will consider two brief cases of literacy diversion. Both involve women working in subordinate positions as secretaries, in print-rich settings where better educated male supervisors were teaching them to read and write in certain ways to perform their clerical duties. However, as we will see shortly, strong loyalties outside the workplace prompted these two secretaries to lift these literate resources for use in other spheres. For one, Carol White, it was on behalf of her work as a Jehovah's Witness. For the other, Sarah Steele, it was on behalf of upward mobility for her lower middle-class family.

Before turning to their narratives, though, it will be wise to pay some attention to the economic moment in which they occur. Clerical work was the largest and fastest growing occupation for women in the 20th century. Like so much employment for women, it offered a mix of gender-defined constraints as well as avenues for economic independence and mobility. As a new information economy created an acute need for typists, stenographers, bookkeepers and other office workers, white, American-born women and, later, immigrant and minority women saw reason to pursue high school and business-college educations. Unlike male clerks of the 19th century, female secretaries in this century had little chance for advancement. However, office work represented a step up from the farm or the factory for women of the working class and served as a respectable occupation from which educated, middle-class women could await or avoid marriage (Anderson, Strom). In a study of clerical work through the first half of the 20th century, Christine Anderson estimated that secretaries might encounter up to 97 different genres in the course of doing dictation or transcription. They routinely had contact with an array of professionals, including lawyers, auditors, tax examiners, and other government overseers (52-53). By 1930, 30% of women office workers used machines other than typewriters (Anderson 76) and, in contemporary offices, clerical workers have often been the first employees to learn to operate CRTs and personal computers and to teach others how to use them. Overall, the daily duties of 20th-century secretaries could serve handily as an index to the rise of complex administrative and accounting procedures, standardization of information, expanding communication, and developments in technological systems.

With the background, consider the experiences of Carol White and Sarah Steele. An Oneida, Carol White was born into a poor, single-parent household in 1940. She graduated from high school in 1960 and, between five maternity leaves and a divorce, worked continuously in a series of clerical positions in both the private and public sectors. One of her first secretarial jobs was with an urban firm that produced and disseminated Catholic missionary films. The vice-president with whom she worked most closely also spent much of his time producing a magazine for a national civic organization that he headed. She discussed how typing letters and magazine articles and occasionally proofreading for this man taught her rhetorical strategies in which she was keenly interested. She described the scene of transfer this way:

> [My boss] didn't just write to write. He wrote in a way to make his letters appealing. I would have to write what he was writing in this magazine too. I was completely

enthralled. He would write about the people who were in this [organization] and the different works they were undertaking and people that died and people who were sick and about their personalities. And he wrote little anecdotes. Once in a while I made some suggestions too. He was a man who would listen to you.

The appealing and persuasive power of the anecdote became especially important to Carol White when she began doing door-to-door missionary work for the Jehovah's Witnesses, a pan-racial, millenialist religious faith. She now uses colorful anecdotes to prepare demonstrations that she performs with other women at weekly service meetings at their Kingdom Hall. These demonstrations, done in front of the congregation, take the form of skits designed to explore daily problems through Bible principles. Further, at the time of our interview, Carol White was working as a municipal revenue clerk and had recently enrolled in an on-the-job training seminar called Persuasive Communication, a two-day class offered free to public employees. Her motivation for taking the course stemmed from her desire to improve her evangelical work. She said she wanted to continue to develop speaking and writing skills that would be "appealing," "motivating," and "encouraging" to people she hoped to convert.

Sarah Steele, a woman of Welsh and German descent, was born in 1920 into a large, working-class family in a coal mining community in eastern Pennsylvania. In 1940, she graduated from a two-year commercial college. Married soon after, she worked as a secretary in a glass factory until becoming pregnant with the first of four children. In the 1960s, in part to help pay for her children's college educations, she returned to the labor force as a receptionist and bookkeeper in a law firm, where she stayed until her retirement in the late 1970s.

Sarah Steele described how, after joining the law firm, she began to model her household management on principles of budgeting that she was picking up from one of the attorneys with whom she worked most closely. "I learned cash flow from Mr. B____," she said. "I would get all the bills and put a tape in the adding machine and he and I would sit down together to be sure there was going to be money ahead." She said that she began to replicate that process at home with the household bills. "Before that," she observed, "I would just cook beans when I had to instead of meat." Sarah Steele also said she encountered the genre of the credit report during routine reading and typing on the job. She figured out what constituted a top rating, making sure her husband followed these steps in preparation for their financing a new car. She also remembered typing up documents connected to civil suits being brought against local businesses, teacher her, she said, which firms never to hire for home repairs. "It just changes the way you think," she observed about the reading and writing she did on her job. "You're not a pushover after you learn how a business operates."

The dynamics of sponsorship alive in these narratives expose important elements of literacy appropriation, at least as it is practiced at the end of the 20th century. In a pattern now familiar from the earlier sections, we see how opportunities for literacy learning—this time for diversions of resources—open up in the clash between long-standing, residual forms of sponsorship and the new: between the lingering presence of literacy's conservative history and its pressure for change. So, here, two women—one Native American and both working-class—filch contemporary literacy resources (public relations techniques and accounting practices) from more educated, higher-status men. The women are emboldened in these acts by ulterior identities beyond the workplace: Carol White with faith and Sarah Steele with family. These affiliations hark back to the first sponsoring arrangements through which American women were gradually allowed to acquire literacy and education. Duties associated with religious faith and child rearing helped literacy to become, in Gloria Main's words, "a permissible feminine activity" (579). Interestingly, these roles, deeply sanctioned within the history of women's literacy—and operating beneath the newer permissible feminine activity of clerical work—become grounds for covert, innovative appropriation even as they reinforce traditional female identities.

Just as multiple identities contribute to the ideologically hybrid character of these literacy formations, so do institutional and material conditions. Carol White's account speaks to such hybridity. The missionary film company with the civic club vice president is a residual site for two of literacy's oldest campaigns—Christian conversion and civic participation—enhanced here by 20th century advances in film and public relations techniques. This ideological reservoir proved a pleasing instructional site for Carol White, whose interests in literacy, throughout her life, have been primarily spiritual. So literacy appropriation draws upon, perhaps even depends upon, conservative forces in the history of literacy sponsorship that are always hovering at the scene of acts of learning. This history serves as both a sanctioning force and a reserve of ideological and material support.

At the same time, however, we see in these accounts how individual acts of appropriation can divert and subvert the course of literacy's history, how changes in individual literacy experiences relate to larger scale transformations. Carol White's redirection of personnel management techniques to the cause of the Jehovah's witnesses is an almost ironic transformation in this regard. Once a principle sponsor in the initial spread of mass literacy, evangelism is here rejuvenated through late-literate corporate sciences of secular persuasion, fund-raising, and bureaucratic management that Carol White finds circulating in her contemporary workplaces. By the same token, through Sarah Steele, accounting practices associated with corporations are, in a sense, tracked into the house, rationalizing and standardizing even domestic practices. (Even though Sarah Steele did not own an adding machine, she penciled her budge figures onto adding-machine tape that she kept for that purpose.) Sarah Steele's act of appropriation in some sense explains how dominant forms of literacy migrate and penetrate into private spheres, including private consciousness. At the same time, though, she accomplishes a subversive diversion of literate power. Her efforts to move her family up in the middle class involved not merely contributing a second income but also, from her desk as a bookkeeper, reading her way into an understanding of middle-class economic power.

Teaching and the Dynamics of Sponsorship

It hardly seems necessary to point out to the readers of *CCC* that we haul a lot of freight for the opportunity to teach writing. Neither rich nor powerful enough to sponsor literacy on our own terms, we serve instead as conflicted brokers between literacy's buyers and sellers. At our most worthy, perhaps, we show the sellers how to beware and try to make sure these exchanges will be a little fairer, maybe, potentially, a little more mutually rewarding. This essay has offered a few working case studies that link patterns of sponsorship to processes of stratification, competition, and reappropriation. How much these dynamics can be generalized to classrooms is an ongoing empirical question.

I am sure that sponsors play even more influential roles at the scenes of literacy learning and use than this essay has explored. I have focused on some of the most tangible aspects—material supply, explicit teaching, institutional aegis. But the ideological pressure of sponsors affects many private aspects of writing processes as well as public aspects of finished texts. Where one's sponsors are multiple or even at odds, they can make writing maddening. Where they are absent, they make writing unlikely. Many of the cultural formations we associate with writing development—community practices, disciplinary traditions, technological potentials—can be appreciated as made-do responses to the economics of literacy, past and present. The history of literacy is a catalogue of obligatory relations. That this catalogue is so deeply conservative and, at the same time, so ruthlessly demanding of change is what fills contemporary literacy learning and teaching with their most paradoxical choices and outcomes.[9]

In bringing attention to economies of literacy learning I am not advocating that we prepare students more efficiently for the job markets they must enter. What I have tried to suggest is that as we assist and study individuals in pursuit of literacy, we also recognize how literacy is in pursuit of them. When this process stirs ambivalence, on their part or on ours, we need to be understanding.

Acknowledgments: This research was sponsored by the NCTE Research Foundation and the Center on English Learning and Achievement. The Center is supported by the U.S. Department of Education's Office of Educational Research and Improvement, whose views do not necessarily coincide with the author's. A version of this essay was given as a lecture in the Department of English, University of Louisville, in April 1997/ Thanks to Anna Syvertsen and Julie Nelson for their help with archival research. Thanks too to colleagues who lent an ear along the way: Nelson Graff, Jonna Gjevre, Anne Gere, Kurt Spellmeyer, Tom Fox, and Bob Gundlach.

Notes

[1]Three of the keenest and most eloquent observers of economic impacts on writing teaching and learning have been Lester Faigley, Susan Miller, and Kurt Spellmeyer.

[2]My debt to the writings of Pierre Bourdieu will be evident throughout this essay. Here and throughout I invoke his expansive notion of "economy," which is not restricted to literal and ostensible systems of money making but to the many spheres where people labor, invest, and exploit energies—their own and others'—to maximize advantage. See Bordieu and Wacquant, especially 117-120 and Bourdieu, Chapter 7.

[3]Thomas Laqueur (124) provides a vivid account of a street demonstration in Bolton, England, in 1834 by a "pro-writing" faction of Sunday School students and their teachers. This faction demanded that writing instruction continue to be provided on Sundays, something that opponents of secular instruction on the Sabbath were trying to reverse.

[4]See, for instance, National Assessments of Educational Progress in reading and writing (Applebee et al,; and "Looking").

[5]All names used in this essay are pseudonyms.

[6]I am not suggesting that literacy that does not "pay off" in terms of prestige or monetary reward is less valuable. Dora Lopez's ability to read and write in Spanish was a source of great strength and pride, especially when she was able to teach it to her young child. The resource of Spanish literacy carried much of what Bourdieu calls cultural capital in her social and family circles. But I want to point out here how people who labor equally to acquire literacy do so under systems of unequal subsidy and unequal reward.

[7]For useful accounts of this period in union history, see Heckscher; Nelson.

[8]Marcia Farr associates "essayist literacy" with written genres esteemed in the academy and noted for their explicitness, exactness, reliance on reasons and evidence, and impersonal voice.

[9]Lawrence Cremin makes similar points about education in general in his essay "The Cacophony of Teaching." He suggests that complex economic and social changes since World War Two, including the popularization of schooling and the penetration of mass media, have created "a far great range

and diversity of language, competencies, values, personalities, and approaches to the world and to its educational opportunities" than at one time existed. The diversity most of interest to him (and me) resides not so much in the range of different ethnic groups there are in society but in the different cultural formulas by which people assemble their educational—or, I would say, literate—experience.

Works Cited

Anderson, Mary Christine. "Gender, Class, and Culture: Women Secretarial and Clerical Workers in the United States, 1925-1955." Diss. Ohio State U, 1986

Applebee, Arthur N., Judith A. Langer, and Ida V.S. Mullis. *The Writing Report Card: Writing Achievement in American Schools.* Princeton: ETS, 1986.

Bourdieu, Pierre. *The Logic of Practice.* Trans. Richard Nice. Cambridge: Polity, 1990.

Bourdieu, Pierre and Loic J.D. Wacquant. *An Invitation to Reflexive Sociology.* Chicago: Chicago UP, 1992.

Bourne, J.M. *Patronage and Society in Nineteenth-Century England.* London: Edward Arnold, 1986.

Brandt, Deborah. "Remembering Reading, Remembering Writing." *CCC* 45 (1994): 459-79.

Brandt, Deborah. "Accumulating Literacy: Writing and Learning to Write in the 20th Century." *College English* 57 (1995): 649-68.

Cornelius, Janet Duitsman. *'When I Can Ready My Title Clear': Literacy, Slavery, and Religion in the Antebellum South.* Columbia: U of South Carolina, 1991.

Cremin, Lawrence. "The Cacophony of Teaching." *Popular Education and Its Discontents.* New York: Harper, 1990.

Faigley, Lester. "Veterans' Stories on the Porch." *History, Reflection and Narrative: The Professionalization of Composition, 1963-1983.* Eds. Beth Boehm, Debra Journet, and Mary Rosner. Norwood: Ablex, in press.

Farr, Marcia. "Essayist Literacy and Other Verbal Performances." *Written Communication* 8 (1993): 4-38.

Heckscher, Charles C. *The New Unionism: Employee Involvement in the Changing Corporation.* New York: Basic, 1988.

Hortsman, Connie and Donald V. Kurtz. *Compradrazgo in Post-Conquest Middle America.* Milwaukee-UW Center for Latin America, 1978.

Kett, Joseph F. *The Pursuit of Knowledge Under Difficulties: From Self Improvement to Adult Education in America 1750-1990.* Stanford: Stanford UP, 1994.

Laqueur, Thomas. *Religion and Respectability: Sunday Schools and Working Class Culture 1780-1850.* New Haven: Yale UP, 1976.

Looking at How Well Our Students Read: The 1992 National Assessment of Educational Progress in Reading. Washington: US Dept. of Education, Office of Educational Research and Improvement, Educational Resources Information Center, 1992.

Lynch, Joseph H. *Godparents and Kinship in Early Medieval Europe.* Princeton: Princeton UP, 1986.

Main, Gloria L. "An Inquiry Into When and Why Women Learned to Write in Colonial New England." *Journal of Social History* 24 (1991): 579-89.

Miller, Susan. *Textual Carnivals: The Politics of Composition.* Carbondale: Southern Illinois UP, 1991.

Nelson, Daniel. *American Rubber Workers & Organized Labor, 1900-1941.* Princeton: Princeton UP, 1988.

Nicholas, Stephen J. and Jacqueline M. Nicholas. "Male Literacy, 'Deskilling,' and the Industrial Revolution." *Journal of Interdisciplinary History* 23 (1992): 1-18.

Resnick, Daniel P., and Lauren B. Resnick. "The Nature of Literacy: A Historical Explanation." *Harvard Educational Review* 47 (1977): 370-85.

Spellmeyer, Kurt. "After Theory: From Textuality to Attunement With the World." *College English* 58 (1996): 893-913.

Stevens, Jr., Edward. *Literacy, Law, and Social Order.* DeKalb: Northern Illinois UP, 1987.

Strom, Sharon Hartman. *Beyond the Typewriter: Gender, Class, and the Origins of Modern American Office Work, 1900-1930.* Urbana: U of Illinois P, 1992.

NOW THAT YOU'VE READ, what do you think? Don't forget to offer responses that both accept the arguments and evidence Brandt offers in this article and "resist" them. That is, share what you know and respect about her arguments before working to resist them or aspects of them (which is the next, very important step).

1. What is the function of a "sponsor of literacy," according to Brandt?

2. Brandt argues that you are not just in pursuit of literacy but that "literacy is in pursuit of [you]." What does she mean by this? How might a sponsor "permit" literacy? How might a sponsor "prohibit" literacy?

3. Is your experience more like Raymond Branch or Dora Lopez's? How?

4. Who are the key agents sponsoring your own literacy history? How do you know?

5. Who may be the agents "prohibiting" literacy? What advantages might they gain from this prohibition?

WRITING ASSIGNMENT

NARRATING LITERACY

You have read Deborah Brandt's essay about how our abilities to read and write are intimately tied with connections to people in our lives. You've also interviewed a classmate using Brandt's questions so you have some further information about literacy acquisition to work with.

In this assignment, please create a literacy narrative that reflects on your acquisition of literacy and the roles that others played in that process. This assignment can take multiple forms and can include various media (images, text, audio, video, digital links, etc). That is, as you're thinking about this assignment, think about the types of literacies that you would like to include to make your project unique.

Rather than writing in general and broad terms about learning to read and write, develop an emblematic moment(s) from that process and provide rich, specific detail so that it comes alive for your reader. Remember, these moments can occur at many different times throughout your life. Be sure to include a meaningful title.

What we would like to see in your project:

- Is your writing and work original? Is it interesting? Do you experiment with various forms (beyond an essay) and understandings of literacy development?
- Does your work demonstrate careful thought about literacy and language? Does it provide rich detail about your own experiences? Does your work show complex thinking about the topics that extend beyond repetition of definitions and summary?
- Does your work emerge from, or is it informed by, the content, conversations, and activities from class? That is, your assignment should clearly reflect your engagement with the content of the class and your colleagues. "Engagement" here does not have to mean agreement.

STUDENT EXAMPLE

LITERACY NARRATIVE

What follows is a literacy narrative not unlike the one you are being asked to write in the writing assignment ("Narrating Literacy"). This is, of course, longer than your own literacy narrative will be. However, like you, Megan is responding to Deborah Brandt's work. Like you, she used the interview questions from Brandt's study to generate ideas for this essay. She was also part of a class where the instructor invited students to introduce one another to the class based on information gleaned from the interview protocol. You'll notice her referencing this experience at the beginning of her essay. Her experiences with reading and writing, she argues, did not echo those of her classmates in this graduate-level English class—students working on MAs and PhDs in English.

Megan Opperman

ENG 680

Dr. Shannon Carter

February 28, 2017

Not That Kind of Reader

At the beginning of the semester, we were asked to introduce ourselves by giving a snippet from our literacy narratives which we would develop over the duration of the course. As English graduate students, everyone's answer fit a similar narrative: loved to read at a young age; were seen as different or odd for their obsession with books and learning; read books far above their reading level; straight As or at least As within reading/writing based courses. Some students even created their own library card system in their bedrooms and played school.

This is not my story.

This writing project offered me a moment to step away from the whirlwind of education opportunities that swept me seemingly from one level of literacy to another and consider how my narrative compares to those of others. I've thought more deeply about those "agents, local or distant, concrete or abstract, who enable, support, teach, and model, as well as recruit, regulate, suppress, or withhold, literacy – and gain advantage by it in some way" that Deborah Brandt calls sponsors of literacy (*American Lives* 19). Without these people, and sometimes circumstances, that found their way into my life, I realize long after the fact that they were the guiding force that kept me searching for a little bit more.

When I reflect upon my literacy history, I realize I began like many average students begin and had a complicated relationship with reading and books. I was not a voracious reader like so many literacy narratives express. Instead, my reading came in bursts which would always fizzle out. I showed no markers of a future graduate student or instructor of English; but I wasn't a problem student either. My grades hovered between Cs and As and my behavior was good. When I chose to go to college, it wasn't a shock to anyone; but I wasn't seen as destined for glory either. Statistically, I should have struggled more to get a higher education—my family didn't set aside funds toward either my sister's nor my education, my father died of cancer the summer following my senior year of high school, and no one in our early lives were college educated—yet somehow we both always knew college was a given in our lives.

Like Donna Dunbar-Odom in her personal reflections on class in *Defying the Odds*, I failed to realize I was from working class parents; I most associated myself with middle class—though a lower middle class than others. But as I look at my history, I realize that we were solidly working class. My father, who was forty-six when I was born, worked his entire life as an in-town truck driver, propane truck driver, fense builder, and other hourly and often manual jobs associated with working class men of his generation. My mother moved to Denver with her family at age 16; but when they arrived, her parents told her to grab a newspaper and answer an ad for a live in nanny before leaving her on the street to fend for herself. By the end of the day, she took a job with an upper class family. She eventually finished her GED and has lived the rest of her life bouncing from one hourly position to another, even taking a detour to nail tech school; though she only worked at a nail salon for about a year before moving to something else. It was always something else with the dream of something more, though more never happened. They, like their families before them, were not college educated and their parents never pushed them toward higher literacy.

But my parents encouraged me, and I have achieved something better, not only through my undergraduate, but also a masters and approximately half of my PhD despite such an unlikely path. The secret to my success is certainly not my own efforts; I know for a fact I went to college highly unprepared and that four years, while opening my mind, did not fully prepare me for higher literacy throughout the rest of my life. What got me here was not my hard work but rather luck. I was lucky to have encountered a series of well-placed sponsors of literacy. These sponsors, for me, came in many forms, often as teachers, and guided me into this path to deeper thinking, to asking questions of readings, as well as selecting more challenging texts.

When I ask her, my sister, like me, does not remember specific instances in which our parents sat us down and spoke to us about college; but they are solidly our biggest sponsors of literacy when it came to our position on education. There were no family college visits nor expectations that we would carry on some tradition of attending a particular school. Instead my mother claims that her and my father often pointed out schools stating "look at this school! You will love school. Elementary, high school, and then college, too." According to her, discussion of our future college attendance was handled so casually that neither of us remember it being discussed, but feel strongly its effects on our views of education. College was simply something everyone did, in our eyes, despite the fact that neither of our parents ever attended a college or university. For them, the reward for their sponsorship was not just our own successful futures, but theirs as they could at least say they helped their children do what they never could. However, the message wasn't that they expected us to go to college, that we should go to college because they never got to, or that college was the best option for future success. They simply spoke to us as if we had already made the decision to go to college and it was just the way things were. And then they were.

At school I received a similar message about higher education as I did at home, though teachers and staff were more overt in their sponsorship. In our small community of mostly white, agricultural and working class people, somehow college was a major emphasis. Perhaps my success was due to the small class sizes (I graduated with 32 in my class) and the partnership our school had with Morgan Community College to offer dual credit courses for free; but I also had more than enough support in filling out applications and visiting schools during school hours and with school provided transportation. My position was one of privilege which ultimately outweighed the class disadvantage I faced. While my parents sponsored my drive to go to college, me actually getting into college was the direct result of two teachers: Eve Pugh and Joey Venable. Mrs. Pugh, the guidance counselor, took time to sit down with each senior and plan with them their next step after high school. She knew at this time my father was dying of cancer and that I had no college money set aside, so she searched for a scholarship that fit my circumstances. Due to her nomination, I received the Governor's Opportunity Scholarship which paid for eight semesters of tuition, fees, books, supplies, housing, and food. Ms. Venable, my band and choir director my senior year, saw potential in me, somehow, to become a music major and she encouraged me to attend the same university she did. She sponsored my entrance into the world of music study, even signing me up for a music theory summer course nearby in order for me to catch up to students who would be entering the university with a background in music theory absent in small school music education. Additionally, she opened her home to me when my dad, who I lived with full time, went into hospice care, allowing me to have some stability in my last months of high school. While my parents taught me that I would be going to college, they had neither the knowledge, or tools to get me there. Fortunately for them, and me, the rural school I attended had an excellent guidance counselor along with teachers who identified the unique needs and potential in their students, something not as common as one would hope.

At the point in my story where I went off to college, I was not an avid reader; I read only the novels I was assigned in school and since we worked from anthologies in my high school, this meant very few. I also had no plans of studying English, thinking I would teach elementary music some day. One would assume that while my dad was dying of cancer, a true book nerd would retreat into the safety of novels for a sense of escape; but this was not the case. Reading was, however, a large part of my childhood and for a brief period of time, I did spend a large portion of my time being read to.

I'm told I learned to read at age three but I don't remember this firsthand. The memory has been implanted in my mind, secured there with photographs and worn copies of picture books containing these early words. I do remember for my birthday one year, subscribing to the Dr. Seuss Book Club and receiving a new book for my shelf every month. I remember the mailman leaving the books, one by one, in my mailbox and the place they sat on my shelf, but not reading the books themselves. There were also many library books in canvas bags that we shared together at bedtime. I remember fragments of plots and illustrations and that we ate shredded coconut directly from the bag when we read *The Gollywopper Egg.* But overall, I remember very little about the act of reading in general; I cannot recall learning to read, and instead have a strong sense of what these books, and many others to follow, meant.

From the time I was three until I was ten, my family lived down a dirt road in a community of farmers with neighbors whose houses we could see in a distance, but not well enough to see when someone came or left the front door. This small community was almost a town of it's own at one point named Leader after the road that connected many farm houses and is the first home I remember. My family didn't farm, but had followed their desires for an idyllic childhood for me and my sister to this unusual community, thirty miles away from Byers, CO where the population hovered around one thousand. Leader, even smaller and more spread out than Byers, was in stark contrast with the busyness of Denver where we had previously lived. In Leader people have owned their land for many years, often generations, cultivating crops and livestock with their family and occasionally hired hands. There were no businesses for miles and trips to the store were intentional because they require venturing into "town" thirty minutes away. We read Laura Ingles Wilder here and I didn't have to imagine the places she describes; I was living it say with the added technologies of the early nineties.

My parents' decision to move to a place where walking to a friend's house was impossible and homeschooling me, followed closely by their decision to divorce, caused a type of isolation which in a way sponsored the development of my imagination. My sister and I stayed in Leader with our mother and our father moved an hour away to live temporarily with his brother. Again, a moment in which an individual would usually fall into books caused me to search outside myself instead. I spent three years from first through third grades learning from Abecca home school books and exploring the property we lived on. School was difficult for me because every lesson contained in these books revolved around one theme, but I had to do them anyway with no variation or supplemental assignments to ease the monotony. Even now the infamous year of exclusively Maine lobster themed math, science, reading, and writing lessons comes up in conversation with my family. I dreaded school-time to the point to where looking back I remember the desk being larger and taller than I'm sure it was. I would lie on the floor, playing dead, refusing to climb into the chair and do my work. Where I thrived was creating. I spent entire days outdoors where I would invent elaborate games with a cast of characters consisting of toys, dolls, logs, and even kitchen chairs and other stolen objects with plots that spanned days. I would also drag out my mother's craft boxes, with permission and without, and create works of art that were both decorative and functional. If I needed a prop for my stuffed animals, a life jacket for my Barbies, or a tool to fix a broken car wheel, I would scavenge the house until I had something to build it with, once even sneaking a swatch of fabric from the back of the sofa. Our kitchen contained an impressive, oak microwave stand where our family created a junk drawer. My sister and I would pull chairs up to that junk drawer and spend hours creating our inventions by connecting odds and ends which we would then describe in great detail to anyone who would listen. I would then tell my sister impressive tales of pirates and ghosts, even a sad old painter I named Pink Pod who all lived in our backyard which caused her to avoid a particular tree as to not make him think she was out to steal his crab apples.

Smith and Wilhelm discuss the multiple literacies of boys who, as they grow, seek challenging, active, and social activities which often do not include reading.[1] While I cannot speak to the experience of boys, I can see how for me things which involved multiple literacies interested me far more than sitting and reading a book. I was hands on, and while I enjoyed the concept of books and reading, and enjoyed being read too, I struggled with activities that put me in traditional school settings and contained academic structures. To this day I prefer a good audiobook to reading in print as I doodle, drive, or clean my house. Homeschool may have remedied this had my mother seen my need for diversified learning; but she chose instead to follow rigid homeschool textbooks on the recommendation from other local homeschool moms who claimed it was the best possible method.

I remained homeschooled through third grade, but my parents decided it best for me to return to public school when I was in fourth grade and my sister was in Kindergarten. I was not good with sitting still and doing activities in workbooks, so the transition

---

1 Deborah Brandt also discusses multiple literacies within *Literacy in American Lives.*

into the classroom where I would be required to work in one desk without the freedom of multiple breaks required an adjustment. I was quiet and reserved, tricking people into believing I was introverted when really I thrived on the energy of others. It was at this time that my extroverted need for the company of others left me distracted when I should have been reading and soon Mrs. Theel requested I get my vision tested to improve my reading comprehension. I misunderstood her concern, thinking that my long held trouble with focusing on reading and working from workbooks was something that glasses could correct. I loved books and stories, but not sitting alone to read them. I loved learning and creating, but not repetitive and solo school work.

At the eye doctor, they had me look through various machines and read different lines out loud. At the end, the eye doctor asked me if I was having trouble in school and if it was hard to read the board or my books. I told him I had trouble with books which elicited a nod as if I had just confirmed the results from the machines. I continued to tell him that I always got to the end of the page and had completely forgotten everything I had read. He laughed and stated something to the effect of "don't we all" but still wrote me a prescription for glasses. When I got my new glasses, I truly thought they were the missing piece, the magic tool which would transform me from a distracted reader and learner into an A plus student. I loved learning, and I enjoyed school in general, so when I put on these glasses, my belief that they would help was a self fulfilling prophecy.

But the magic reading glasses didn't turn me into a lifelong voracious reader. After a summer of intense reading between the fourth and fifth grade during which I discovered *The Babysitters' Club* series, I went back to my old ways of reading what was assigned and passing my classes unremarkably. When I stepped onto the Adams State College[2] campus in 2004 I was eager yet wildly unprepared. What was possibly worse, was that I didn't even realize I was so unprepared; in short, I didn't know what I didn't know. I cited the Bible as a historical text with no secondary sources to back me up in a music history class; I practically had no skills in grammar beyond diagramming sentences which I was amazed to find wasn't a big deal in college; I had no understanding of how to tackle large papers or keep up with the demands of a hefty reading schedule; I had no grasp of the varied experiences of a suddenly diverse world around me. That I let my

---

2 Now Adams State University

narrow world view and inexperience be known to my professors and fellow classmates is embarrassing now, but I am forever grateful to each and every one of them who took the time to explain to me my shortcomings and gave me the tools in which to fill the gaps in my knowledge. I wonder now what I looked like to those professors, particularly those who accepted me into the university community and further sponsored my drive to keep going against the odds. I must have seemed lost and naive, but with some potential as they kept pushing me forward. I'm glad that I didn't know I was supposed to fail; that I was not really college material. Had I known that, I probably would have sought a different route. I may have even been happy with it; but I would like to think I would prefer my life of higher literacy I have been so fortunate enough to achieve.

Works Cited

Barton, David. Literacy: An Introduction to the Ecology of the Written Language, 2nd Edition. Blackwell Publishing, 2007.

Brandt, Deborah. Literacy as Involvement: The Acts of Writers, Readers, and Texts. Southern Illinois UP, 2011 (1990).

—-. Literacy in American Lives. Cambridge UP, 2001.

Dunbar-Odom, Donna. Defying the Odds. State University of New York Press, 2007.

Goldblatt, Eli. Writing Home: A Literacy Autobiography. Southern Illinois UP, 2012.

Goodman, Ken, Peter H. Fries, and Steven L. Strauss Reading: The Grand Illusion. Routledge,

Salvatori, Mariolina R. and Patricia A. Donahue. The Elements (and Pleasures) of Difficulty. Pearson, 2004.

Smith, Michael W. and Jeffrey D. Wilhelm. "Going with the Flow." PDF file.(Footnotes)

READING

Learning to Read

Malcolm X

BEFORE YOU READ

1. What do you expect to read based on this title?

2. What are your own early memories of learning to read?

3. What are some motivators to learn to read as an adult who, for whatever reasons, was unable to learn to read at the typical age?

Learning to Read

MALCOLM X

It was because of my letters that I happened to stumble upon starting to acquire some kind of a homemade education.

I became increasingly frustrated at not being able to express what I wanted to convey in letters that I wrote, especially those to Mr. Elijah Muhammad. In the street, I had been the most articulate hustler out there—I had commanded attention when I said something. But now, trying to write simple English, I not only wasn't articulate, I wasn't even functional. How would I sound writing in slang, the way I would *say* it, something such as, "Look, daddy, let me pull your coat about a cat, Elijah Muhammad-"

Many who today hear me somewhere in person, or on television, or those who read something I've said, will think I went to school far beyond the eighth grade. This impression is due entirely to my prison studies.

It had really begun back in the Charlestown Prison, when Bimbi first made me feel envy of his stock of knowledge. Bimbi had always taken charge of any conversations he was in, and I had tried to emulate him. But every book I picked up had few sentences which didn't contain anywhere from one to nearly all of the words that might as well have been in Chinese. When I just skipped those words, of course, I really ended up with little idea of what the book said. So I had come to the Norfolk Prison Colony still going through only book-reading motions. Pretty soon, I would have quit even these motions, unless I had received the motivation that I did.

I saw that the best thing I could do was get hold of a dictionary—to study, to learn some words. I was lucky enough to reason also that I should try to improve my penmanship. It was sad. I couldn't even write in a straight line. It was both ideas together that moved me to request a dictionary along with some tablets and pencils from the Norfolk Prison Colony school.

I spent two days just riffling uncertainly through the dictionary's pages. I'd never realized so many words existed! I didn't know *which* words I needed to learn. Finally, just to start some kind of action, I began copying.

In my slow, painstaking, ragged handwriting, I copied into my tablet everything printed on that first page, down to the punctuation marks.

I believe it took me a day. Then, aloud, I read back, to myself, everything I'd written on the tablet. Over and over, aloud, to myself, I read my own handwriting.

I woke up the next morning, thinking about those words—immensely proud to realize that not only had I written so much at one time, but I'd written words that I never knew were in the world. Moreover, with a little effort, I also could remember what many of these words meant. I reviewed the words whose meanings I didn't remember. Funny thing, from the dictionary first page right now, that "aardvark" springs to my mind. The dictionary had a picture of it, a long-tailed, long-eared, burrowing African mammal, which lives off termites caught by sticking out its tongue as an anteater does for ants.

I was so fascinated that I went on—I copied the dictionary's next page. And the same experience came when I studied that. With every succeeding page, I also learned of people and places and events from history. Actually the dictionary is like a miniature encyclopedia. Finally the dictionary's A section had filled a whole tablet—and I went on into the B's. That was the way I started copying what eventually became the entire dictionary. It went a lot faster after so much practice helped me to pick up handwriting speed. Between what I wrote in my tablet, and writing letters, during the rest of my time in prison I would guess I wrote a million words.

I suppose it was inevitable that as my word-base broadened, I could for the first time pick up a book and read and now begin to understand what the book was saying. Anyone who has read a great deal can imagine the new world that opened. Let me tell you something: from then until I left that prison, in every free moment I had, if I was not reading in the library, I was reading on my bunk. You couldn't have gotten me out of books with a wedge. Between Mr. Muhammad's teachings, my correspondence, my visitors,... and my reading of books, months passed without my even thinking about being imprisoned. In fact, up to then, I never had been so truly free in my life.

The Norfolk Prison Colony's library was in the school building. A variety of classes was taught there by instructors who came from such places as Harvard and Boston universities. The weekly debates between inmate teams were also held in the school building. You would be astonished to know how worked up convict debaters and audiences would get over subjects like "Should Babies Be Fed Milk?"

Available on the prison library's shelves were books on just about every general subject. Much of the big private collection that Parkhurst[1] had willed to the prison was still in crates and boxes in the back of the library—thousands of old books. Some of them looked ancient: covers faded, oldtime parchment-looking binding. Parkhurst... seemed to have been principally interested in history and religion. He had the money and the special interest to have a lot of books that you wouldn't have in a general circulation. Any college library would have been lucky to get that collection.

As you can imagine, especially in a prison where there was heavy emphasis on rehabilitation, an inmate was smiled upon if he demonstrated an unusually intense interest in books. There was a sizable number of well-read inmates, especially the popular debaters. Some were said by many to be practically walking encyclopedias. They were almost celebrities. No university would ask any student to devour literature as I did when this new world opened to me, of being able to read and *understand*.

I read more in my room than in the library itself. An inmate who was known to read a lot could check out more than the permitted maximum number of books. I preferred reading in the total isolation of my own room.

---

1 Charles H. Parkhurst (1842-1933); American clergyman, reformer, and president of the Society for the Prevention of Crime.

When I had progressed to really serious reading, every night at about ten P.M. I would be outraged with the "lights out." It always seemed to catch me right in the middle of something engrossing.

Fortunately, right outside my door was a corridor light that cast a glow into my room. The glow was enough to read by, once my eyes adjusted to it. So when "lights out" came, I would sit on the floor where I could continue reading in that glow.

At one-hour intervals at night guards paced past every room. Each time I heard the approaching footsteps, I jumped into bed and feigned sleep. And as soon as the guard passed, I got back out of bed onto the floor area of that light-glow, where I would read for another fifty-eight minutes until the guard approached again. That went on until three or four every morning. Three or four hours of sleep a night was enough for me. Often in the years in the streets I had slept less than that.

The teachings of Mr. Muhammad stressed how history had been "whitened"— when white men had written history books, the black man simply had been left out. Mr. Muhammad couldn't have said anything that would have struck me much harder. I had never forgotten how when my class, me and all of those whites, had studied seventh-grade United States history back in Mason, the history of the Negro had been covered in one paragraph, and the teacher had gotten a big laugh with his joke, "Negroes' feet are so big that when they walk, they leave a hole in the ground."

This is one reason why Mr. Muhammad's teachings spread so swiftly all over the United States, among *all* Negroes, whether or not they became followers of Mr. Muhammad. The teachings ring true-to every Negro. You can hardly show me a black adult in America—or a white one, for that matter—who knows from the history books anything like the truth about the black man's role. In my own case, once I heard of the "glorious history of the black man," I took special pains to hunt in the library for books that would inform me on details about black history.

I can remember accurately the very first set of books that really impressed me. I have since bought that set of books and I have it at home for my children to read as they grow up. It's called *Wonders of the World*. It's full of pictures of archeological finds, statues that depict, usually, non-European people.

I found books like Will Durant's *Story of Civilization*. I read H. G. Wells' *Outline of History*. *Souls of Black Folk* by W. E. B. Du Bois gave me a glimpse into the black people's history before they came to this country. Carter G. Woodson's *Negro History* opened my eyes about black empires before the black slave was brought to the United States, and the early Negro struggles for freedom.

J. A. Rogers' three volumes of *Sex and Race* told about race-mixing before Christ's time; and Aesop being a black man who told fables; about Egypt's Pharaohs; about the great Coptic Christian Empire[2]; about Ethiopia, the earth's oldest continuous black civilization, as China is the oldest continuous civilization.

Mr. Muhammad's teaching about how the white man had been created led me to *Findings in Genetics,* by Gregor Mendel. (The dictionary's G section was where I had learned what "genetics" meant.) I really studied this book by the Austrian monk. Reading it over and over, especially certain sections, helped me to understand that if you started with a black man, a white man could be produced; but starting with a white man, you never could produce a black man—because the white chromosome is recessive. And since no one disputes that there was but one Original Man, the conclusion is clear.

---

2 A native Egyptian Christian church that retains elements of its African origins.

During the last year or so, in *The New York Times,* Arnold Toynbeell used the word "bleached" in describing the white man. His words were: "White (i.e., bleached) human beings of North European origin…" Toynbee also referred to the European geographic area as only a peninsula of Asia. He said there was no such thing as Europe. And if you look at the globe, you will see for yourself that America is only an extension of Asia. (But at the same time Toynbee is among those who have helped to bleach history. He has written that Africa was the only continent that produced no history. He won't write that again. Every day now, the truth is coming to light.)

I never will forget how shocked I was when I began reading about slavery's total horror. It made such an impact upon me that it later became one of my favorite subjects when I became a minister of Mr. Muhammad's. The world's most monstrous crime, the sin and the blood on the white man's hands, are almost impossible to believe. Books like the one by Frederick Olmsted opened my eyes to the horrors suffered when the slave was landed in the United States. The European woman, Fanny Kemble, who had married a Southern white slaveowner, described how human beings were degraded. Of course I read *Uncle Tom's Cabin.* In fact, I believe that's the only novel I have ever read since I started serious reading.

Parkhurst's collection also contained some bound pamphlets of the Abolitionist Anti-Slavery Society of New England. I read descriptions of atrocities, saw those illustrations of black slave women tied up and flogged with whips; of black mothers watching their babies being dragged off, never to be seen by their mothers again; of dogs after slaves, and of the fugitive slave catchers, evil white men with whips and clubs and chains and guns. I read about the slave preacher Nat Turner, who put the fear of God into the white slave master. Nat Turner wasn't going around preaching pie-in-the-sky and "non-violent" freedom for the black man. There in Virginia one night in 1831, Nat and seven other slaves started out at his master's home and through the night they went from one plantation "big house" to the next, killing, until by the next morning 57 white people were dead and Nat had about 70 slaves following him. White people, terrified for their lives, fled from their homes, locked themselves up in public buildings, hid in the woods, and some even left the state. A small army of soldiers took two months to catch and hang Nat Turner. Somewhere I have read where Nat Turner's example is said to have inspired John Brown to invade Virginia and attack Harpers Ferry nearly thirty years later, with thirteen white men and five Negroes.

I read Herodotus, "the father of History," or, rather, I read about him. And I read the histories of various nations, which opened my eyes gradually, then wider and wider, to how the whole world's white men had indeed acted like devils, pillaging and raping and bleeding and draining the whole world's non-white people. I remember, for instance, books such as Will Durant's *The Story of Oriental Civilization,* and Mahatma Gandhi's accounts of the struggle to drive the British out of India.

Book after book showed me how the white man had brought upon the world's black, brown, red, and yellow peoples every variety of the suffering of exploitation. I saw how since the sixteenth century, the so-called "Christian trader" white man began to ply the seas in his lust for Asian and African empires, and plunder, and power. I read, I saw, how the white man never has gone among the non-white peoples bearing the Cross in the true manner and spirit of Christ's teachings—meek, humble, and Christlike.

I perceived, as I read, how the collective white man had been actually nothing but a piratical opportunist who used Faustian machinations[3] to make his own Christianity

---

3 Evil plots or schemes. Faust was a fictional character who sold his soul to the devil for knowledge and power.

his initial wedge in criminal conquests. First, always "religiously," he branded "heathen" and "pagan" labels upon ancient non-white cultures and civilizations. The stage thus set, he then turned upon his non-white victims his weapons of war.

I read how, entering India—half a *billion* deeply religious brown people—the British white man, by 1759, through promises, trickery, and manipulations, controlled much of India through Great Britain's East India Company. The parasitical British administration kept tentacling out to half of the sub-continent. In 1857, some of the desperate people of India finally mutinied—and, excepting the African slave trade, nowhere has history recorded any more unnecessary bestial and ruthless human carnage than the British suppression of the non-white Indian people.

Over 115 million African blacks—close to the 1930's population of the United States—were murdered or enslaved during the slave trade. And I read how when the slave market was glutted, the cannibalistic white powers of Europe next carved up, as their colonies, the richest areas of the black continent. And Europe's chancelleries for the next century played a chess game of naked exploitation and power from Cape Horn to Cairo.

Ten guards and the warden couldn't have torn me out of those books. Not even Elijah Muhammad could have been more eloquent than those books were in providing indisputable proof that the collective white man had acted like a devil in virtually every contact he had with the world's collective non-white man. I listen today to the radio, and watch television, and read the headlines about the collective white man's fear and tension concerning China. When the white man professes ignorance about why the Chinese hate him so, my mind can't help flashing back to what I read, there in prison, about how the blood forebears of this same white man raped China at a time when China was trusting and helpless. Those original white "Christian traders" sent into China millions of pounds of opium. By 1839, so many of the Chinese were addicts that China's desperate government destroyed twenty thousand chests of opium. The first Opium war[4] was promptly declared by the white man. Imagine! Declaring *war* upon someone who objects to being narcotized! The Chinese were severely beaten, with Chinese-invented gunpowder.

The Treaty of Nanking made China pay the British white man for the destroyed opium; forced open China's major ports to British trade; forced China to abandon Hong Kong; fixed China's import tariffs so low that cheap British articles soon flooded in, maiming China's industrial development.

After a second Opium War, the Tientsin Treaties legalized the ravaging opium trade, legalized a British-French-American control of China's customs. China tried delaying that Treaty's ratification; Peking was looted and burned.

"Kill the foreign white devils!" was the 1901 Chinese war cry in the Boxer Rebellion[5]. Losing again, this time the Chinese were driven from Peking's choicest areas. The vicious, arrogant white man put up the famous signs, "Chinese and dogs not allowed."

Red China after World War II closed its doors to the Western white world. Massive Chinese agricultural, scientific, and industrial efforts are described in a book that *Life* magazine recently published. Some observers inside Red China have reported that the world never has known such a hate-white campaign as is now going on in this non-white country where, present birth-rates continuing, in fifty more years

---

4 The "Opium War" of 1839-1842 was between Britain and China and ended when Hong Kong was handed over to Britain.
5 The Boxer Rebellion of 1898-1900. An uprising by members of a secret Chinese society who opposed foreign influence in Chinese affairs.

Chinese will be half the earth's population. And it seems that some Chinese chickens will soon come home to roost, with China's recent successful nuclear tests.

Let us face reality. We can see in the United Nations a new world order being shaped, along color lines—an alliance among the non-white nations. America's U.N. Ambassador Adlai Stevenson complained not long ago that in the United Nations "a skin game" was being played. He was right. He was facing reality. A "skin game" is being played. But Ambassador Stevenson sounded like Jesse James accusing the marshal of carrying a gun. Because who in the world's history ever has played a worse "skin game" than the white man?

Mr. Muhammad, to whom I was writing daily, had no idea of what a new world had opened up to me through my efforts to document his teachings in books.

When I discovered philosophy, I tried to touch all the landmarks of philosophical development. Gradually, I read most of the old philosophers, Occidental and Oriental. The Oriental philosophers were the ones I came to prefer; finally, my impression was that most Occidental philosophy had largely been borrowed from the Oriental thinkers. Socrates, for instance, traveled in Egypt. Some sources even say that Socrates was initiated into some of the Egyptian mysteries. Obviously Socrates got some of his wisdom among the East's wise men.

I have often reflected upon the new vistas that reading opened to me. I knew right there in prison that reading had changed forever the course of my life. As I see it today, the ability to read awoke inside me some long dormant craving to be mentally alive. I certainly wasn't seeking any degree, the way a college confers a status symbol upon its students. My homemade education gave me, with every additional book that I read, a little bit more sensitivity to the deafness, dumbness, and blindness that was afflicting the black race in America. Not long ago, an English writer telephoned me from London, asking questions. One was, "What's your alma mater?" I told him, "Books." You will never catch me with a free fifteen minutes in which I'm not studying something I feel might be able to help the black man.

Yesterday I spoke in London, and both ways on the plane across the Atlantic I was studying a document about how the United Nations proposes to insure the human rights of the oppressed minorities of the world. The American black man is the world's most shameful case of minority oppression. What makes the black man think of himself as only an internal United States issue is just a catch-phrase, two words, "civil rights." How is the black man going to get "civil rights" before first he wins his *human* rights? If the American black man will start thinking about his *human* rights, and then start thinking of himself as part of one of the world's great peoples, he will see he has a case for the United Nations.

I can't think of a better case! Four hundred years of black blood and sweat invested here in America, and the white man still has the black man begging for what every immigrant fresh off the ship can take for granted the minute he walks down the gangplank.

But I'm digressing. I told the Englishman that my alma mater was books, a good library. Every time I catch a plane, I have with me a book that I want to read—and that's a lot of books these days. If I weren't out here every day battling the white man, I could spend the rest of my life reading, just satisfying my curiosity—because you can hardly mention anything I'm not curious about. I don't think anybody ever got more out of going to prison than I did. In fact, prison enabled me to study far more intensively than I would have if my life had gone differently and I had attended some college. I imagine that one of the biggest troubles with colleges is there are too many distractions, too much panty-raiding, fraternities, and boola-boola and all of that. Where else but in a prison could I have attacked my ignorance by being able to study intensely sometimes as much as fifteen hours a day?

NOW THAT YOU'VE READ

1. What motivates Malcolm X to learn to read?

2. What is worth noting about the process Malcolm X followed in order to become educated?

3. What is he arguing about education?

4. What stories have you heard of individuals who worked hard to obtain an education? Family members? Fictional characters? Historical figures?

5. What might current students take from his story?

READING

Inventing the University

David Bartholomae

BEFORE YOU READ

1. What were some of your expectations about what college would be like? What has surprised you the most?

2. How do you prepare yourself to write for a college class?

3. What are the expectations you feel are being placed on you as someone writing for college classes?

Inventing the University[1]

David Bartholomae

> Education may well be, as of right, the instrument whereby every individual, in a society like our own, can gain access to any kind of discourse. But we well know that in its distribution, in what it permits and in what it prevents, it follows the well-trodden battle-lines of social conflict. Every educational system is a political means of maintaining or of modifying the appropriation of discourse, with the knowledge and the powers it carries with it.
>
> Foucault, "The Discourse on Language" (227)

Every time a student sits down to write for us, he has to invent the university for the occasion—invent the university, that is, or a branch of it, like History or Anthropology or Economics or English. He has to learn to speak our language, to speak as we do, to try on the peculiar ways of knowing, selecting, evaluating, reporting, concluding, and arguing that define the discourse of our community. Or perhaps I should say the various discourses of our community, since it is in the nature of a liberal arts education that a student, after the first year or two, must learn to try on a variety of voices and interpretive schemes—to write, for example, as a literary critic one day and an experimental psychologist the next, to work within fields where the rules governing the presentation of examples or the development of an argument are both distinct and, even to a professional, mysterious.

The students have to appropriate (or be appropriated by) a specialized discourse, and they have to do this as though they were easily and comfortably one with their audience, as though they were members of the academy, or historians or anthropologists or economists; they have to invent the university by assembling and mimicking its language, finding some compromise between idiosyncracy, a personal history, and the requirements of convention, the history of a discipline. They must learn to speak our language. Or they must dare to speak it, or to carry off the bluff, since speaking and writing will most certainly be required long before the skill is "learned." And this, understandably, causes problems.

Let me look quickly at an example. Here is an essay written by a college freshman, a basic writer:

> In the past time I thought that an incident was creative was when I had to make a clay model of the earth, but not of the classical or your everyday model of the earth which consists of the two cores, the mantle and the crust. I thought of these things in a dimension of which it would be unique, but easy to comprehend. Of course, your materials to work with were basic and limited at the same time, but thought help to put this limit into a right attitude or frame of mind to work with the clay.

> In the beginning of the clay model, I had to research and learn the different dimensions of the earth (in magnitude, quantity, state of matter, etc.) After this, I learned how to put this into the clay and come up with something different than any other person in my class at the time. In my opinion, color coordination and shape was the key to my creativity of the clay model of the earth.

> Creativity is the venture of the mind at work with the mechanics relay to the limbs from the cranium, which stores and triggers this action. It can be a burst of energy released at a precise time a thought is being transmitted. This can cause a frenzy of the human body, but it depends of the characteristics of the individual and how they can relay the message clearly enough through mechanics of the body to us as an observer. Then we must determine if it is creative or a learned process varied by the individuals thought process. Creativity is indeed a tool which has to exist, or our world will not succeed into the future and progress like it should.

I am continually impressed by the patience and good will of our students. This student was writing a placement essay during freshman orientation. (The problem set to him was, "Describe a time when you did something you felt to be creative. Then, on the basis of the incident you have described, go on to draw some general conclusions about 'creativity'.") He knew that university faculty would be reading and evaluating his essay, and so he wrote for them.

In some ways it is a remarkable performance. He is trying on the discourse even though he doesn't have the knowledge that makes the discourse more than a routine, a set of conventional rituals and gestures. And he does this, I think, even though he *knows* he doesn't have the knowledge that makes the discourse more than a routine. He defines himself as a researcher, working systematically, and not as a kid in a high school class: "I thought of these things in a dimension of … "; "had to research and learn the different dimensions of the earth (in magnitude, quantity, state of matter, etc.)." He moves quickly into a specialized language (his approximation of our jargon) and draws both a general, textbook-like conclusion ("Creativity is the venture of the mind at work ... ") and a resounding peroration ("Creativity is indeed a tool which has to exist, or our world will not succeed into the future and progress like it should.") The writer has even, with that "indeed" and with the qualifications and the parenthetical expressions of the opening paragraphs, picked up the rhythm of our prose. And through it all he speaks with an impressive air of authority.

There is an elaborate but, I will argue, a necessary and enabling fiction at work here as the student dramatizes his experience in a "setting"—the setting required by the discourse—where he can speak to us as a companion, a fellow researcher. As I read the essay, there is only one moment when the fiction is broken, when we are addressed differently. The student says, "Of course, your materials to work with were basic and limited at the same time, but thought help to put this limit into a right attitude or frame of mind to work with the clay." At this point, I think, we become students and he the teacher, giving us a lesson (as in, "You take your pencil in your right hand and put your paper in front of you."). This is, however, one of the most characteristic slips of basic writers. It is very hard for them to take on the role—the voice, the person—of an authority whose authority is rooted in scholarship, analysis, or research. They slip, then, into the more immediately available and realizable voice of authority, the voice of a teacher giving a lesson or the voice of a parent lecturing at the dinner table. They offer advice or homilies rather than "academic" conclusions. There is a similar break in the final paragraph, where the conclusion that pushes for a definition ("Creativity is the venture of the mind at work with the mechanics relay to the limbs from the cranium ... ") is replaced by a conclusion which speaks in the voice of an Elder ("Creativity is indeed a tool which has to exist, or our world will not succeed into the future and progress like it should.").

It is not uncommon, then, to find such breaks in the concluding sections of essays written by basic writers. Here is the concluding section of an essay written by a student about his work as a mechanic. He had been asked to generalize about "work" after reviewing an on-the-job experience or incident that "stuck in his mind" as somehow significant.

> How could two repairmen miss a leak? Lack of pride? No incentive? Lazy? I don't know.

At this point the writer is in a perfect position to speculate, to move from the problem to an analysis of the problem. Here is how the paragraph continues however (and notice the change in pronoun reference):

> From this point on, I take *my* time, do it right, and don't let customers get under your skin. If they have a complaint, tell them to call your boss and he'll be more than glad to handle it. Most important, worry about yourself, and keep a clear eye on everyone, for there's always someone trying to take advantage of you, anytime and anyplace.

We get neither a technical discussion nor an "academic" discussion but a Lesson on Life.[2] This is the language he uses to address the general question, "How could two repairmen miss a leak?" The other brand of conclusion, the more academic one, would have required him to speak of his experience in our terms; it would, that is, have required a special vocabulary, a special system of presentation, and an interpretive scheme (or a set of commonplaces) he could use to identify and talk about the mystery of human error. The writer certainly had access to the range of acceptable commonplaces for such an explanation: "lack of pride," "no incentive," "lazy." Each would dictate its own set of phrases, examples, and conclusions, and we, his teachers, would know how to write out each argument, just as we would know how to write out more specialized arguments of our own. A "commonplace," then, is a culturally or institutionally authorized concept or statement that carries with it its own necessary elaboration. We all use commonplaces to orient ourselves in the world; they provide a point of reference and a set of "prearticulated" explanations that are readily available to organize and interpret experience. The phrase "lack of pride" carries with it its own account for the repairman's error just as, at another point in time, a reference to "original sin" would provide an explanation, or just as, in a certain university classroom, a reference to "alienation" would enable a writer to continue and complete the discussion. While there is a way in which these terms are interchangeable, they are not all permissible. A student in a composition class would most likely be turned away from a discussion of original sin. Commonplaces are the "controlling ideas" of our composition textbooks, textbooks that not only insist upon a set form for expository writing but a set view of public life.[3]

When the student above says, "I don't know," he is not saying, then, that he has nothing to say. He is saying that he is not in a position to carry on this discussion. And so we are addressed as apprentices rather than as teachers or scholars. To speak to us as a person of status or privilege, the writer can either speak to us in our terms—in the privileged language of university discourse—or, in default (or in defiance), he can speak to us as though we were children, offering us the wisdom of experience.

I think it is possible to say that the language of the "Clay Model" paper has come *through* the writer and not from the writer. The writer has located himself (he has located the self that is represented by the *I* on the page) in a context that is, finally, beyond him, not his own and not available to his immediate procedures for inventing and arranging text. I would not, that is, call this essay an example of "writer-based" prose. I would not say that it is egocentric or that it represents the "interior monologue of a writer thinking and talking to himself" (Flower 63). It is, rather, the record of a writer who has lost himself in the discourse of his readers. There is a context beyond the reader that is not the world but a way of talking about the world, a way of talking that determines the use of examples, the possible conclusions, the acceptable commonplaces, and the key words of an essay on the construction of a clay model of the earth. This writer has entered the discourse without successfully approximating it.

Linda Flower has argued that the difficulty inexperienced writers have with writing can be understood as a difficulty in negotiating the transition between writer-based and reader-based prose. Expert writers, in other words, can better imagine how a reader will respond to a text and can transform or restructure what they have to say around a goal shared with a reader. Teaching students to revise for readers, then, will better prepare them to write initially with a reader in mind. The success of this pedagogy depends upon the degree to which a writer can imagine and conform to a reader's goals. The difficulty of this act of imagination, and the burden of such conformity, are so much at the heart of the problem that a teacher must pause and take stock before offering revision as a solution. Students like the student who wrote the "Clay Model" paper are not so much trapped in a private language as they are shut out from one of the privileged languages of public life, a language they are aware of but cannot control.

Our students, I've said, have to appropriate (or be appropriated by) a specialized discourse, and they have to do this as though they were easily or comfortably one with their audience. If you look at the situation this way, suddenly the problem of audience awareness becomes enormously complicated. One of the common assumptions of both composition research and composition teaching is that at some "stage" in the process of composing an essay a writer's ideas or his motives must be tailored to the needs and expectations of his audience. A writer has to "build bridges" between his point of view and his readers. He has to anticipate and acknowledge his readers' assumptions and biases. He must begin with "common points of departure" before introducing new or controversial arguments. There is a version of the pastoral at work here. It is assumed that a person of low status (like a shepherd) can speak to a person of power (like a courtier), but only (at least so far as the language is concerned) if he is not a shepherd at all, but actually a member of the court out in the fields in disguise.

Writers who can successfully manipulate an audience (or, to use a less pointed language, writers who can accommodate their motives to their readers' expectations) are writers who can both imagine and write from a position of privilege. They must, that is, see themselves within a privileged discourse, one that already includes and excludes groups of readers. They must be either equal to or more powerful than those they would address. The writing, then, must somehow transform the political and social relationships between basic writing students and their teachers.

If my students are going to write for me by knowing who I am—and if this means more than knowing my prejudices, psyching me out—it means knowing what I know; it means having the knowledge of a professor of English. They have, then, to know what I know and how I know what I know (the interpretive schemes that define the way I would work out the problems I set for them); they have to learn to write what I would write, or to offer up some approximation of that discourse. The problem of audience awareness, then, is a problem of power and finesse. It cannot be addressed, as it is in most classroom exercises, by giving students privilege and denying the situation of the classroom, by having students write to an outsider, someone excluded from their privileged circle: "Write about 'To His Coy Mistress,' not for your teacher, but for the students in your class": "Describe Pittsburgh to someone who has never been there"; "Explain to a high school senior how best to prepare for college"; "Describe baseball to a Martian."

Exercises such as these allow students to imagine the needs and goals of a reader and they bring those needs and goals forward as a dominant constraint in the construction of an essay. And they argue, implicitly, what is generally true about writing—that it is an act of aggression disguised as an act of charity. What they fail to address is the central problem of academic writing, where students must assume the right of speaking to someone who knows Pittsburgh or "To His Coy Mistress" better than they do, a reader for whom the general commonplaces and the readily available utterances about a subject are inadequate. It should be clear that when I say that I know Pittsburgh better than my basic writing students I am talking about a way of knowing that is also a way of writing. There may be much that they know that I don't know, but in the setting of the university classroom I have a way of talking about the town that is "better" (and for arbitrary reasons) than theirs.

I think that all writers, in order to write, must imagine for themselves the privilege of being "insiders"—that is, of being both inside an established and powerful discourse, and of being granted a special right to speak. And I think that right to speak is seldom conferred upon us—upon any of us, teachers or students—by virtue of the fact that we have invented or discovered an original idea. Leading students to believe that they are responsible for something new or original, unless they understand what those words mean with regard to writing, is a dangerous and counterproductive practice.

We do have the right to expect students to be active and engaged, but that is more a matter of being continually and stylistically working against the inevitable presence of conventional language; it is not a matter of inventing a language that is new.

When students are writing for a teacher, writing becomes more problematic than it is for the students who are describing baseball to a Martian. The students, in effect, have to assume privilege without having any. And since students assume privilege by locating themselves within the discourse of a particular community—within a set of specifically acceptable gestures and commonplaces—learning, at least as it is defined in the liberal arts curriculum, becomes more a matter of imitation or parody than a matter of invention and discovery.

What our beginning students need to learn is to extend themselves into the commonplaces, set phrases, rituals, gestures, habits of mind, tricks of persuasion, obligatory conclusions, and necessary connections that determine the "what might be said" and constitute knowledge within the various branches of our academic community. The course of instruction that would make this possible would be based on a sequence of illustrated assignments and would allow for successive approximations of academic or "disciplinary" discourse. Students will not take on our peculiar ways of reading, writing, speaking, and thinking all at once. Nor will the command of a subject like sociology, at least as that command is represented by the successful completion of a multiple choice exam, enable students to write sociology. Our colleges and universities, by and large, have failed to involve basic writing students in scholarly projects, projects that would allow them to act as though they were colleagues in an academic enterprise. Much of the written work students do is test-taking, report or summary, work that places them outside the working discourse of the academic community, where they are expected to admire and report on what we do, rather than inside that discourse, where they can do its work and participate in a common enterprise.[4] This is a failure of teachers and curriculum designers who, even if they speak of writing as a mode of learning, all too often represent writing as a "tool" to be used by an (hopefully) educated mind.

Pat Bizzell is one of the most important scholars writing now on basic writers and on the special requirements of academic discourse.[5] In a recent essay, "Cognition, Convention and Certainty: What We Need to Know About Writing," she argues that the problems of basic writers might be

> better understood in terms of their unfamiliarly with the academic discourse community, combined, perhaps, with such limited experience outside their native discourse communities that they are unaware that there is such a thing as a discourse community with conventions to be mastered. What is underdeveloped is their knowledge both of the ways experience is constituted and interpreted in the academic discourse community and of the fact that all discourse communities constitute and interpret experience. (230)

One response to the problems of basic writers, then, would be to determine just what the community's conventions are, so that those conventions can be written out, "demystified," and taught in our classrooms. Teachers, as a result, could be more precise and helpful when they ask students to "think," "argue," "describe," or "define." Another response would be to examine the essays written by basic writers— their approximations of academic discourse—to determine more clearly where the problems lie. If we look at their writing, and if we look at it in the context of other student writing, we can better see the points of discord when students try to write their way into the university.

The purpose of the remainder of this paper will be to examine some of the most striking and characteristic problems as they are presented in the expository essays of basic writers. I will be concerned, then, with university discourse in its most generalized form—that is, as represented by introductory courses—and not with the special conventions required by advanced work in the various disciplines. And I will be concerned with the difficult, and often violent, accommodations that occur when students locate themselves in a discourse that is not "naturally" or immediately theirs.

I have reviewed 500 essays written in response to the "creativity" question used during one of our placement exams. (The essay cited at the opening of this paper was one of that group.) Some of the essays were written by basic writers (or, more properly, those essays led readers to identify the writers as "basic writers"); some were written by students who "passed" (who were granted immediate access to the community of writers at the university). As I read these essays, I was looking to determine the stylistic resources that enabled writers to locate themselves within an "academic" discourse. My bias as a reader should be clear by now. I was not looking to see how the writer might represent the skills demanded by a neutral language (a language whose key features were paragraphs, topic sentences, transitions, and the like-features of a clear and orderly mind). I was looking to see what happened when a writer entered into a language to locate himself (a textual self) and his subject, and I was looking to see how, once entered, that language made or unmade a writer.

Here is one essay. Its writer was classified as a basic writer. Since the essay is relatively free of sentence level errors, that decision must have been rooted in some perceived failure of the discourse itself.

> I am very interested in music, and I try to be creative in my interpretation of music. While in high school, I was a member of a jazz ensemble. The members of the ensemble were given chances to improvise and be creative in various songs. I feel that this was a great experience for me, as well as the other members. I was proud to know that I could use my imagination and feelings to create music other than what was written.
>
> Creativity to me, means being free to express yourself in a way that is unique to you, not having to conform to certain rules and guidelines. Music is only one of the many areas in which people are given opportunities to show their creativity. Sculpting, carving, building, art, and acting are just a few more areas where people can show their creativity.
>
> Through my music I conveyed feelings and thoughts which were important to me. Music was my means of showing creativity. In whatever form creativity takes, whether it be music, art, or science, it is an important aspect of our lives because it enables us to be individuals.

Notice, in this essay, the key gesture, one that appears in all but a few of the essays I read. The student defines as his own that which is a commonplace. "Creativity, to me, means being free to express yourself in a way that is unique to you, not having to conform to certain rules and guidelines." This act of appropriation constitutes his authority; it constitutes his authority as a writer and not just as a musician (that is, as someone with a story to tell). There were many essays in the set that told only a story, where the writer's established presence was as a musician or a skier or someone who painted designs on a van, but not as a person removed from that experience interpreting it, treating it as a metaphor for something else (creativity). Unless those stories were long, detailed, and very well told (unless the writer was doing more than saying, "I am a skier or a musician or a van-painter"), those writers were all given low ratings.

Notice also that the writer of the jazz paper locates himself and his experience in relation to the commonplace (creativity is unique expression; it is not having to conform to rules or guidelines) regardless of whether it is true or not. Anyone who improvises "knows" that improvisation follows rules and guidelines. It is the power of the commonplace (its truth as a recognizable and, the writer believes, as a final statement) that justifies the example and completes the essay. The example, in other words, has value because it stands within the field of the commonplace. It is not the occasion for what one might call an "objective" analysis or a "close" reading. It could also be said that the essay stops with the articulation of the commonplace. The following sections speak only to the power of that statement. The reference to "sculpting, carving, building, art, and acting" attest to the universality of the commonplace (and it attests to the writer's nervousness with the status he has appropriated for himself—he is saying, "Now, I'm not the only one here who's done something unique."). The commonplace stands by itself. For this writer, it does not need to be elaborated. By virtue of having written it, he has completed the essay and established the contract by which we may be spoken to as equals: "In whatever form creativity takes, whether it be music, art, or science, it is an important aspect of *our* lives because it enables *us* to be individuals." (For me to break that contract, to argue that *my* life is not represented in that essay, is one way for me to begin as a teacher with that student in that essay.)

I said that the writer of the jazz paper offered up a commonplace regardless of whether it was "true" or not, and this, I said, was an example of the power of a commonplace to determine the meaning of an example. A commonplace determines a system of interpretation that can be used to "place" an example within a standard system of belief. You can see a similar process at work in this essay.

During the football season, the team was supposed to wear the same type of cleats and the same type socks, I figured that I would change this a little by wearing my white shoes instead of black and to cover up the team socks with a pair of my own white ones. I thought that this looked better than what we were wearing, and I told a few of the other people on the team to change too. They agreed that it did look better and they changed there combination to go along with mine. After the game people came up to us and said that it looked very good the way we wore our socks, and they wanted to know why we changed from the rest of the team.

I feel that creativity comes from when a person lets his imagination come up with ideas and he is not afraid to express them. Once you create something to do it will be original and unique because it came about from your own imagination and if any one else tries to copy it, it won't be the same because you thought of it first from your own ideas.

This is not an elegant paper, but it seems seamless, tidy. If the paper on the clay model of the earth showed an ill-fit between the writer and his project, here the discourse seems natural, smooth. You could reproduce this paper and hand it out to a class, and it would take a lot of prompting before the students sensed something fishy and one of the more aggressive ones might say, "Sure he came up with the idea of wearing white shoes and white socks. Him and Billy White-shoes Johnson. Come on. He copied the very thing he said was his own idea, 'original and unique'."

The "I" of this text, the "I" who "figured," "thought," and "felt" is located in a conventional rhetoric of the self that turns imagination into origination (I made it), that argues an ethic of production (I made it and it is mine), and that argues a tight scheme of intention (I made it because I decided to make it). The rhetoric seems invisible because it is so common. This "I" (the maker) is also located in a version of history that dominates classroom accounts of history. It is an example of the "Great Man" theory, where history is rolling along—the English novel is dominated by a central, intrusive narrative presence; America is in the throes of a great depression; during football season the team was supposed to wear the same kind of cleats and socks—until a figure appears, one who can shape history—Henry James, FDR, the writer of the football paper—and everything is changed. In the argument of the football paper, "I figured," "I thought," "I told," "They agreed," and, as a consequence, "I feel that creativity *comes from when* a person lets his imagination come up with ideas and he is not afraid to express them." The story of appropriation becomes a narrative of courage and conquest. The writer was able to write that story when he was able to imagine himself in that discourse. Getting him out of it will be difficult matter indeed.

There are ways, I think, that a writer can shape history in the very act of writing it. Some students are able to enter into a discourse, but, by stylistic maneuvers, to take possession of it at the same time. They don't originate a discourse, but they locate themselves within it aggressively, self-consciously.

Here is one particularly successful essay. Notice the specialized vocabulary, but also the way in which the text continually refers to its own language and to the language of others.

Throughout my life, I have been interested and intrigued by music. My mother has often told me of the times, before I went to school, when I would "conduct" the orchestra on her records. I continued to listen to music and eventually started to play the guitar and the clarinet. Finally, at about the age of twelve, I started to sit down and to try to write songs. Even though my instrumental skills were far from my own high standards, I would spend much of my spare time during the day with a guitar around my neck, trying to produce a piece of music.

Each of these sessions, as I remember them, had a rather set format. I would sit in my bedroom, strumming different combinations of the five or six chords I could play, until I heard a series which sounded particularly good to me. After this, I set the music to a suitable rhythm, (usually dependent on my mood at the time), and ran through the tune until I could play it fairly easily. Only after this section was complete did I go on to writing lyrics, which generally followed along the lines of the current popular songs on the radio.

At the time of the writing, I felt that my songs were, in themselves, an original creation of my own; that is, I, alone, made them. However, I now see that, in this sense of the word, I was not creative. The songs themselves seem to be an oversimplified form of the music I listened to at the time.

In a more fitting sense, however, I *was* being creative. Since I did not purposely copy my favorite songs, I was, effectively, originating my songs from my own "process of creativity." To achieve my goal, I needed what a composer would call "inspiration" for my piece. In this case the inspiration was the current hit on the radio. Perhaps with my present point of view, I feel that I used too much "inspiration" in my songs, but, at that time, I did not.

Creativity, therefore, is a process which, in my case, involved a certain series of "small creations" if you like. As well, it is something, the appreciation of which varies with one's point of view, that point of view being set by the person's experience, tastes, and his own personal view of creativity. The less experienced tend to allow for less originality, while the more experienced demand real originality to classify something a "creation." Either way, a term as abstract as this is perfectly correct, and open to interpretation.

This writer is consistently and dramatically conscious of herself forming something to say out of what has been said *and* out of what she has been saying in the act of writing this paper. "Creativity" begins, in this paper, as "original creation." What she thought was "creativity," however, she now calls "imitation" and, as she says, "in this sense of the word" she was not "creative." In another sense, however, she says that she *was* creative since she didn't purposefully copy the songs but used them as "inspiration."

The writing in this piece (that is, the work of the writer within the essay) goes on in spite of, or against, the language that keeps pressing to give another name to her experience as a song writer and to bring the discussion to closure. (Think of the quick closure of the football shoes paper in comparison.) Its style is difficult, highly qualified. It relies on quotation marks and parody to set off the language and attitudes that belong to the discourse (or the discourses) it would reject, that it would not take as its own proper location.[6]

In the papers I've examined in this essay, the writers have shown a varied awareness of the codes—or the competing codes—that operate within a discourse. To speak with authority student writers have not only to speak in another's voice but through another's "code"; and they not only have to do this, they have to speak in the voice and through the codes of those of us with power and wisdom; and they not only have to do this, they have to do it before they know what they are doing, before they have a project to participate in and before, at least in terms of our disciplines, they have anything to say. Our students may be able to enter into a conventional discourse and speak, not as themselves, but through the voice of the community. The university, however, is the place where "common" wisdom is only of negative value; it is something to work against. The movement toward a more specialized discourse begins (or perhaps, best begins) when a student can both define a position of privilege, a position that sets him against a "common" discourse, and when he can work self-consciously, critically, against not only the "common" code but his own.

The stages of development that I've suggested are not necessarily marked by corresponding levels in the type or frequency of error, at least not by the type or frequency of sentence level errors. I am arguing, then, that a basic writer is not necessarily a writer who makes a lot of mistakes. In fact, one of the problems with curricula designed to aid basic writers is that they too often begin with the assumption that the key distinguishing feature of a basic writer is the presence of sentence level error. Students are placed in courses because their placement essays show a high frequency of such errors and those courses are designed with the goal of making those errors go away. This approach to the problems of the basic writer ignores the degree to which error is not a constant feature but a marker in the development of a writer. Students who can write reasonably correct narratives may fall to pieces when faced with more unfamiliar assignments. More importantly, however, such courses fail to serve the rest of the curriculum. On every campus there is a significant number of college freshman who require a course to introduce them to the kinds of writing that are required for a university education. Some of these students can write correct sentences and some cannot, but as a group they lack the facility other freshmen possess when they are faced with an academic writing task.

The "White Shoes" essay, for example, shows fewer sentence level errors than the "Clay Model" paper. This may well be due to the fact, however, that the writer of that paper stayed well within the safety of familiar territory. He kept himself out of trouble by doing what he could easily do. The tortuous syntax of the more advanced papers on my list is a syntax that represents a writer's struggle with a difficult and unfamiliar language, and it is a syntax that can quickly lead an inexperienced writer into trouble. The syntax and punctuation of the "Composing Songs" essay, for example, shows the effort that is required when a writer works against the pressure of conventional discourse. If the prose is inelegant (although I'll confess I admire those dense sentences), it is still correct. This writer has a command of the linguistic and stylistic resources (the highly embedded sentences, the use of parentheses and quotation marks) required to complete the act of writing. It is easy to imagine the possible pitfalls for a writer working without this facility.

There was no camera trained on the "Clay Model" writer while he was writing, and I have no protocol of what was going through his mind, but it is possible to speculate that the syntactic difficulties of sentences like the following are the result of an attempt to use an unusual vocabulary and to extend his sentences beyond the boundaries that would be "normal" in his speech or writing:

> In past time I thought that an incident was creative was when I had to make a clay model of the earth, but not of the classical or your everyday model of the earth which consists of the two cores, the mantle and the crust. I thought of these things in a dimension of which it would be unique, but easy to comprehend.

There is reason to believe, that is, that the problem is with this kind of sentence, in this context. If the problem of the last sentence is a problem of holding together these units—"I thought," "dimension," "unique," and "easy to comprehend"—then the linguistic problem is not a simple matter of sentence construction.

I am arguing, then, that such sentences fall apart not because the writer lacks the necessary syntax to glue the pieces together but because he lacks the full statement within which these key words are already operating. While writing, and in the thrust of his need to complete the sentence, he has the key words but not the utterance. (And to recover the utterance, I suspect, he will need to do more than revise the sentence.) The invisible conventions, the prepared phrases remain too distant for the statement to be completed. The writer must get inside of a discourse he can only partially imagine. The act of constructing a sentence, then, becomes something like an act of transcription, where the voice on the tape unexpectedly fades away and becomes inaudible.

Mina Shaughnessy speaks of the advanced writer as a writer with a more facile but still incomplete possession of this prior discourse. In the case of the advanced writer, the evidence of a problem is the presence of dissonant, redundant, or imprecise language, as in a sentence such as this: "No education can be *total*, it must be *continuous*." Such a student Shaughnessy says, could be said to hear the "melody of formal English" while still unable to make precise or exact distinctions. And, she says, the pre-packaging feature of language, the possibility of taking over phrases and whole sentences without much thought about them, threatens the writer now as before. The writer, as we have said, inherits the language out of which he must fabricate his own messages. He is therefore in a constant tangle with the language, obliged to recognize its public, communal nature and yet driven to invent out of this language his own statements (19).

For the unskilled writer, the problem is different in degree and not in kind. The inexperienced writer is left with a more fragmentary record of the comings and goings of academic discourse. Or, as I said above, he often has the key words without the complete statements within which they are already operating.

It may very well be that some students will need to learn to crudely mimic the "distinctive register" of academic discourse before they are prepared to actually and legitimately do the work of the discourse, and before they are sophisticated enough with the refinements of tone and gesture to do it with grace or elegance. To say this, however, is to say that our students must be our students. Their initial progress will be marked by their abilities to take on the role of privilege, by their abilities to establish authority. From this point of view, the student who wrote about constructing the clay model of the earth is better prepared for his education than the student who wrote about playing football in white shoes, even though the "White Shoes" paper was relatively error-free and the "Clay Model" paper was not. It will be hard to pry the writer of the "White Shoes" paper loose from the tidy, pat discourse that allows him to dispose of the question of creativity in such a quick and efficient manner. He will have to be convinced that it is better to write sentences he might not so easily control, and he will have to be convinced that it is better to write muddier and more confusing prose (in order that it may sound like ours), and this will be harder than convincing the "Clay Model" writer to continue what he has begun.[7]

Notes

[1]This article represents an abridged version of a chapter in *When A Writer Can't Write: Studies in Writer's Block and Other Composing Problems*. Ed. Mike Rose. New York: The Guilford Press, 1985.

[2]David Olson has made a similar observation about school-related problems of language learning in younger children. Here is his conclusion: "Hence, depending upon whether children assumed language was primarily suitable for making assertions and conjectures or primarily for making direct or indirect commands, they will either find school texts easy or difficult" (107).

[3]For Aristotle there were both general and specific commonplaces. A speaker, says Aristotle, has a "stock of arguments to which he may turn for a particular need."

> If he knows the *topic* (regions, places, lines of argument)—and a skilled speaker will know them—he will know where to find what he wants for a special case. The general topics, or *common*places, are regions containing arguments that are common to all branches of knowledge. ... But there are also special topics (regions, places, *loci*) in which one looks for arguments appertaining to particular branches of knowledge, special sciences, such as ethics or politics. (154–155)

And, he says, "The topics or places, then, may be indifferently thought of as in the science that is concerned, or in the mind of the speaker." But the question of location is "indifferent" *only* if the mind of the speaker is in line with set opinion, general assumption. For the speaker (or writer) who is not situated so comfortably in the privileged public realm, this is indeed not an indifferent matter at all. If he does not have the commonplace at hand, he will not, in Aristotle's terms, know where to go at all.

[4]See especially Bartholomae and Rose for articles on curriculum designed to move students into university discourse. The movement to extend writing "across the cirriculum" is evidence of a general concern for locating students within the work of the university: see especially Bizzell and Maimon et al. For longer works directed specifically at basic writing, see Ponsot and Dean, and Shaughnessy. For a book describing a course for more advanced students, see Coles.

[5]See especially Bizzell, and Bizzell and Herzberg. My debt to Bizzell's work should be evident everywhere in this essay.

[6] In support of my argument that this is the kind of writing that does the work of the academy, let me offer the following excerpt from a recent essay by Wayne Booth ("The Company We Keep: Self-Making in Imaginative Art, Old and New"):

> I can remember making up songs of my own, no doubt borrowed from favorites like "Hello, Central, Give Me Heaven," "You Can't Holler Down My Rain Barrel," and one about the ancient story of a sweet little "babe in the woods" who lay down and died, with her brother.
>
> I asked my mother, in a burst of creative egotism, why nobody ever learned to sing *my* songs, since after all I was more than willing to learn *theirs*. I can't remember her answer, and I can barely remember snatches of two of "my" songs. But I can remember dozens of theirs, and when I sing them, even now, I sometimes feel again the emotions, and see the images, that they aroused then. Thus who I am now—the very shape of my soul—was to a surprising degree molded by the works of "art" that came my way.
>
> I set "art" in quotation marks, because much that I experienced in those early books and songs would not be classed as art according to most definitions. But for the purposes of appraising the effects of "art" on " life" or "culture," and especially for the purposes of thinking about the effects of the "media," we surely must include every kind of artificial experience that we provide for one another
>
> In this sense of the word, all of us are from the earliest years fed a steady diet of art ... (58–59).

While there are similarities in the paraphrasable content of Booth's arguments and my student's, what I am interested in is each writer's method. Both appropriate terms from a common discourse about (*art* and *inspiration*) in order to push against an established way of talking (about tradition and the individual). This effort of opposition clears a space for each writer's argument and enables the writers to establish their own "sense" of the key words in the discourse.

[7]Preparation of this manuscript was supported by the Learning Research and Development Center of the University of Pittsburgh, which is supported in part by the National Institute of Education. I am grateful also to Mike Rose, who pushed and pulled at this paper at a time when it needed it.

Works Cited

Aristotle. *The Rhetoric of Aristotle*. Trans. L. Cooper. Englewood Cliffs, NJ: Prentice, 1932.

Bartholomae, David. "Teaching Basic Writing: An Alternative to Basic Skills." *Journal of Basic Writing* 2(1979): 85-109.

———. "Writing Assignments: Where Writing Begins." *Forum*. Ed. P. Stock. Montclair, NJ: Boynton/ Cook, 1983. 300-312.

Bartholomae, David and Anthony Petrosky. *Facts, Artifacts and Counterfacts: A Basic Reading and Writing Course for the College Curriculum*. Montclair, NJ: Boynton/ Cook, forthcoming.

Bizzell, Patricia. "The Ethos of Academic Discourse." *College Composition and Communication* 29(1978): 351-55.

———. "Cognition, Convention and Certainty: What We Need to Know About." *Pre/Text* 3(1982): 213-244.

———. "College Composition: Initiation Into the Academic Discourse Communities." *Curriculum Inquiry* 12(1982): 191-207.

Bizzell, Patricia and Bruce Herzberg. " 'Inherent' Ideology, 'Universal' History, 'Empirical' Evidence, and 'Context-Free' Writing: Some Problems with E.D. Hirsch 's *The Philosophy of Composition*." *Modern Language Notes* 95(1980): 1181-1202.

Booth, Wayne. "The Company We Keep: Self-Making in Imaginative Art, Old and New." *The Pushcart Prize, VIII: Best of the Small Presses.* Ed. Bill Henderson. Wainscott, NY: Pushcart, 1983. 57-95.

Coles, William E., Jr. *The Plural I.* New York: Holt, 1978.

Flower, Linda S. "Revising Writer-Based Prose." *Journal of Basic Writing* 3(1981): 62-74.

Foucault, Michel. *The Archaeology of Knowledge.* Trans. A.M. Sheridan Smith. New York: Harper, 1972.

Maimon, Elaine P., G.L. Belcher, G.W. Hearn, B.F. Nodine, and F.X. O'Connor. *Writing in the Arts and Sciences.* Cambridge, MA: Winthrop, 1981.

Olson, David R. "Writing: The Divorce of the Author From the Text." *Exploring Speaking-Writing Relationships: Connections and Contrasts.* Eds. B. Kroll and R. Vann. Urbana, IL: NCTE, 1981.

Ponsot, Marie and Rosemary Deen. *Beat Not the Poor Desk.* Montclair, NJ: Boynton/ Cook, 1982.

Rose, Mike. "Remedial Writing Courses: A Critique and a Proposal." *College English* 45(1983): 109-128.

———. *When A Writer Can't Write: Studies in Writer's Block and Other Composing Problems.* New York: Guilford, 1985.

Shaughnessy, Mina. *Errors and Expectations.* New York: Oxford UP, 1977.

NOW THAT YOU'VE READ

1. Now that you've read the essay, what do you take the title to mean?

2. In what ways is it possible to "invent" the university?

3. How does Bartholomae get us to read the student papers he includes as examples?

4. What are some of the differences between "advanced" and "beginning" writers? Where do you see yourself? Why?

5. What is Bartholomae arguing in this essay?

READING

The Joy of Reading and Writing: Superman and Me

Sherman Alexie

BEFORE YOU READ

1. What do you expect from the title?

2. Did you read and love comics as a kid? Which ones? Do you still read them?

3. How would you describe yourself as a reader? Avid? Lukewarm?

4. What can parents do to help their kids enjoy reading? Is it beneficial to encourage a kid to read?

Superman and Me

Sherman Alexie

I learned to read with a Superman comic book. Simple enough, I suppose. I cannot recall which particular Superman comic book I read, nor can I remember which villain he fought in that issue. I cannot remember the plot, nor the means by which I obtained the comic book. What I can remember is this: I was 3 years old, a Spokane Indian boy living with his family on the Spokane Indian Reservation in eastern Washington state. We were poor by most standards, but one of my parents usually managed to find some minimum-wage job or another, which made us middle-class by reservation standards. I had a brother and three sisters. We lived on a combination of irregular paychecks, hope, fear and government surplus food.

My father, who is one of the few Indians who went to Catholic school on purpose, was an avid reader of westerns, spy thrillers, murder mysteries, gangster epics, basketball player biographies and anything else he could find. He bought his books by the pound at Dutch's Pawn Shop, Goodwill, Salvation Army and Value Village. When he had extra money, he bought new novels at supermarkets, convenience stores and hospital gift shops. Our house was filled with books. They were stacked in crazy piles in the bathroom, bedrooms and living room. In a fit of unemployment-inspired creative energy, my father built a set of bookshelves and soon filled them with a random assortment of books about the Kennedy assassination, Watergate, the Vietnam War and the entire 23-book series of the Apache westerns. My father loved books, and since I loved my father with an aching devotion, I decided to love books as well.

I can remember picking up my father's books before I could read. The words themselves were mostly foreign, but I still remember the exact moment when I first understood, with a sudden clarity, the purpose of a paragraph. I didn't have the vocabulary to say "paragraph," but I realized that a paragraph was a fence that held words. The words inside a paragraph worked together for a common purpose. They had some specific reason for being inside the same fence. This knowledge delighted me. I began to think of everything in terms of paragraphs. Our reservation was a small paragraph within the United States. My family's house was a paragraph, distinct from the other paragraphs of the LeBrets to the north, the Fords to our south and the Tribal School to the west. Inside our house, each family member existed as a separate paragraph but still had genetics and common experiences to link us. Now, using this logic, I can see my changed family as an essay of seven paragraphs: mother, father, older brother, the deceased sister, my younger twin sisters and our adopted little brother.

At the same time I was seeing the world in paragraphs, I also picked up that Superman comic book. Each panel, complete with picture, dialogue and narrative was a three-dimensional paragraph. In one panel, Superman breaks through a door. His suit is red, blue and yellow. The brown door shatters into many pieces. I look at the narrative above the picture. I cannot read the words, but I assume it tells me that "Superman is breaking down the door." Aloud, I pretend to read the words and say, "Superman is breaking down the door." Words, dialogue, also float out of Superman's mouth. Because he is breaking down the door, I assume he says, "I am breaking down the door." Once again, I pretend to read the words and say aloud, "I am breaking down the door" In this way, I learned to read.

This might be an interesting story all by itself. A little Indian boy teaches himself to read at an early age and advances quickly. He reads "Grapes of Wrath" in kindergarten when other children are struggling through "Dick and Jane." If he'd been anything but an Indian boy living on the reservation, he might have been called a prodigy. But he is an Indian boy living on the reservation and is simply an oddity. He grows into a man who often speaks of his childhood in the third-person, as if it will somehow dull the pain and make him sound more modest about his talents.

A smart Indian is a dangerous person, widely feared and ridiculed by Indians and non-Indians alike. I fought with my classmates on a daily basis. They wanted me to stay quiet when the non-Indian teacher asked for answers, for volunteers, for help. We were Indian children who were expected to be stupid. Most lived up to those expectations inside the classroom but subverted them on the outside. They struggled with basic reading in school but could remember how to sing a few dozen powwow songs. They were monosyllabic in front of their non-Indian teachers but could tell complicated stories and jokes at the dinner table. They submissively ducked their heads when confronted by a non-Indian adult but would slug it out with the Indian bully who was 10 years older. As Indian children, we were expected to fail in the non-Indian world. Those who failed were ceremonially accepted by other Indians and appropriately pitied by non-Indians.

I refused to fail. I was smart. I was arrogant. I was lucky. I read books late into the night, until I could barely keep my eyes open. I read books at recess, then during lunch, and in the few minutes left after I had finished my classroom assignments. I read books in the car when my family traveled to powwows or basketball games. In shopping malls, I ran to the bookstores and read bits and pieces of as many books as I could. I read the books my father brought home from the pawnshops and secondhand. I read the books I borrowed from the library. I read the backs of cereal boxes. I read the newspaper. I read the bulletins posted on the walls of the school, the clinic, the tribal offices, the post office. I read junk mail. I read auto-repair manuals. I read magazines. I read anything that had words and paragraphs. I read with equal parts joy and desperation. I loved those books, but I also knew that love had only one purpose. I was trying to save my life.

Despite all the books I read, I am still surprised I became a writer. I was going to be a pediatrician. These days, I write novels, short stories, and poems. I visit schools and teach creative writing to Indian kids. In all my years in the reservation school system, I was never taught how to write poetry, short stories or novels. I was certainly never taught that Indians wrote poetry, short stories and novels. Writing was something beyond Indians. I cannot recall a single time that a guest teacher visited the reservation. There must have been visiting teachers. Who were they? Where are they now? Do they exist? I visit the schools as often as possible. The Indian kids crowd the classroom. Many are writing their own poems, short stories and novels. They have read my books. They have read many other books. They look at me with bright eyes and arrogant wonder. They are trying to save their lives. Then there are the sullen and already defeated Indian kids who sit in the back rows and ignore me with theatrical precision. The pages of their notebooks are empty. They carry neither pencil nor pen. They stare out the window. They refuse and resist. "Books," I say to them. "Books," I say. I throw my weight against their locked doors. The door holds. I am smart. I am arrogant. I am lucky. I am trying to save our lives.

1. What is Alexie arguing in this short essay?

2. How does his Native American ethnicity figure into the narrative? Why is it important?

3. How does reading become something bigger than just one person and a book?

WRITING ASSIGNMENT
REVISION

Using the feedback you received from your teacher and peers on your first writing assignment, select the strongest part of your argument then complicate it with your reading of the second round of texts. Please note that we are looking for a re-vision—that is, a re-seeing of your project in light of new information and feedback. We are not interested in rewrites that contain sentences stuck into the first draft to "fix" the issues raised in your instructor's comments or to correct surface errors. This will be largely a new project. Of course, you can borrow from and make use of meaty sections or ideas of your first draft. But it's important to remember that editing is not the same thing as revision.

Your revision should be at least one page longer, or a suitable equivalent for digital projects that are not written essays. In addition, provide a brief explanation for how your revision differs from the original. This can take the form of a reflective piece, annotations throughout your project (such as inserting "Comments" into the margins to describe changes), audio reflections, etc.

CHAPTER 2

Expanding Notions of Literacy Practices

In this chapter, we continue our exploration of literacies as experienced by ordinary people in our everyday lives. We'll begin by considering the tensions writers have experienced when trying to compose for academic contexts, especially when the writing assignment requires the student author to draw from personal experiences. In "My Uncle's Guns," we encounter a student struggling to frame her lived experiences in the ways she anticipates her instructor will expect. The student believes her instructor will neither understand nor appreciate a truthful, honest essay about a significant experience in her life. As you will learn, she may very well be right. "Living Inside the Bible (Belt)" expands notions of literacy practices by considering the intellectual role to be played by faith-based texts in spaces in which they are often approached with trepidation (college classrooms, for example).

Many of the readings that you've done so far come from scholars in Composition and Rhetoric, or from popular writers (such as Malcolm X, Sherman Alexie, bell hooks). However, as we know, writing occurs beyond traditional educational spaces by writers from all different backgrounds. We will look at examples of writing from community members and students themselves. *Pro(se)letariets* is an example of this, as it is a publication by a community press called New City Community Press. Even more, *Pro(se)letariets* features writing from working-class people in both the United States and England. Some writers in this book, such as Oakley and Smart, discuss how their access to education or publishing opportunities differs based on socioeconomic identity, and yet, ultimately, they have been published in a book that you are reading as part of your college education. *Pro(se)letariets* emerged from a university-community partnership between Syracuse University's Writing Program and the *Federation of Worker Writers and Community Publishers* (FWWCP), a working-class writing network that began in London in 1976 and later spread transnationally. As you read these pieces, think about how literacy functions in various spaces (homes, schools, workplaces) and across geographic borders.

READING

My Uncle's Guns

Ann E. Green

In the essay that follows, Ann E. Green asks readers to look at the process of writing a "personal narrative" for a first-year composition class—like the one in which you are currently enrolled—from the perspective of the writer. Interspersed among the kind of safe and largely commonplace details so often associated with first-year composition are digressions into the real, complex, and fascinating lifewords and thoughts of the writer. These "Metacognitive Moments" are the things the writer decides not to include in the essay she's writing for class because she believes the events and choices that make up her life beyond school are not welcome in the academy—certainly not in this particular classroom where she feels certain she'll be judged as a "redneck" if she shares them.

BEFORE YOU READ

1. Have you ever been asked to write a personal essay about your life? Did you hesitate to include details you felt the teacher might judge as inappropriate or that you felt the teacher might not appreciate?

   a. Think about the process of writing that essay. What was going through your head?

   b. Green asks you to understand all non-blocked text as the prose the writer is generating for her teacher to read. You should understand all the blocked, italicized text as metacognitive moments—things the writer thinks about including but decides against. The first "metacognitive moment," for example, begins "I'm not sure how these essays are supposed to start. You said in class that a narrative should tell a story. How much of the story do I have to tell?" These are the things she remembers but worries are too "redneck" to include. Do any of these struggles seem familiar to you?

My Uncle's Guns

Ann E. Green

My uncle, who is not really my uncle but my father's best friend since grade school, bought an antique gun from the First World War. We saw it when we went over to my uncle's house to visit. Dad and T.J. were talking, having conversations with long pauses, while I watched out the living room window.

> I'm not sure how these essays are supposed to start. You said in class that a narrative should tell a story. How much of the story do I have to tell? Should I put in a reflection now? Should I tell you about smoking? Growing up, I watched men have conversations with each other filled with these long moments of silence where they smoked. One of them would light another cigarette or refill his pipe or, on a special occasion, smoke

a cigar. If they didn't smoke, they chewed, either wintergreen Skoal or a pipe stem or a long piece of hay. Dad smoked a pipe with Old Hickory Tobacco until he quit farming. T.J., according to Dad, used to have every vice imaginable and then some, but he had quit smoking both cigarettes and cigars, almost entirely stopped chewing tobacco, and even cut back on his drinking since his heart attack. Every time I watch Dad talk, I remember how he smoked. Should this be part of the story?

While I was looking out the window, two deer appeared from the woods and strolled out into the yard. Although T.J. and Dad hunted together every year, T.J. fed wild animals, birds and rabbits, deer and even stray dogs in his back yard. The two deer went to pick at the food that had fallen from the bird feeders. One was a good-size doe, the other a late-born fawn with spots on its rump yet. When I walked up to the window to get a closer look, the deer spooked and leaped over the stone wall separating the lawn from the woods. Dad said, "Damn it, T.J., where's your camera?"

"Don't own one. If I shoot something, it ain't going to be for a god damn picture, anyway." He paused and slowly stood up from his recliner. "Come here, I'll show you what I'll shoot it with come December."

Dad and I went into T.J.'s spare bedroom to his gun cabinet, and he pulled out the WWI gun, a rifle whose stock had been cut off and refinished, evidently as a deer hunting gun. T.J. said, "It's my gun from the First World War." And then he laughed long and hard at his own joke. His laugh, as usual, drowned out any other sound and ended with a couple of snorts after which he laughed again. T.J. hadn't seen any combat after he enlisted. His ROTC scholarship paid for Penn State, but instead of sending him to Korea where the fighting was, the Army sent him to West Germany as a stretcher carrier in a medical unit. For the Army, it hadn't been bad, T.J. said. They spent most of their time moving the mobile medical unit along the East German border, to practice in case of a communist attack.

My father took the gun from T.J.'s hands. "Nice job cutting it back. Craig .340."

The gun didn't look any different to me than the dozens of other guns I'd seen and handled. I didn't hunt, or at least I didn't shoot, but I occasionally had gone out for turkey with Dad in the spring. We'd never even seen one, but it was beautiful in the woods at dawn.

At twelve, my first date was a picnic on roast woodchuck in a field near home; the gun that shot the chuck was a bolt-action 30.30. Everyone in my class took the Hunter Safety course in sixth grade, before it was legal for us to hunt at twelve. All of my boyfriends and a good many of my girlfriends owned guns for shooting or hunting purposes, and school was canceled for the first day of buck season in December. In the fall, I was late home from dates because any boy I was with would use the drive home as a good opportunity to spotlight deer, to see how many there were before hunting season.

Are these the kinds of details that you mean when we talk in class about significant details? How am I supposed to know which details are important to you?

I feel like I have to tell you all the details about deer hunting so you won't think we're simple or backward or country, getting all excited about looking at somebody's gun. Even though you assign us those Tim O'Brien stories with lists, you really don't think we'll write like that do you? And you would tell us we were too repetitive if we did. You're not from around here, and I can see you don't like us sometimes when we go outside on break from class and smoke and talk too loud about how we hate our jobs.

You look at us and think that we don't know anything. You think that teaching us how to write can't help us cause we're not going to change our lives by reading some essays. But we all want to do well in this class. Can't you just tell us what you want us to write about?

As dad looked the Craig .340 over, peering down the barrel, checking to see if it was loaded, he said, "Let's try the son-of-a-bitch out in November at the fireman's shoot-in and pig roast." We left then, in our pickup, complete with spotlight and gun rack in the cab. Dad had to get home to go to work as a janitor at 7 A.M., while I had to make it in early to run the drive-by window at the bank. We saw twelve deer in a field on the way home, and nothing was unusual.

In fact, the night that it happened I had gone to the fair with Dad and his new woman, Louise. It was about time Dad found somebody else, and I was glad it was Louise, who was younger than Dad but older than me by quite a bit. I'd seen what other kinds of women men found after their first wives.

I'll cut Louise out of this paper later, because I know that you'll think she's extra, just one more person who's not really in the rising action of this story, but right now it's important to me that she stay in here. Most of the time I'm too busy trying to figure out how I'll pay for my next class and my car insurance to sit around and think about how I feel about somebody who's important in my life, but not a pain in my ass in some way. Louise has just been a fixture, a nice addition to Dad's life that makes him leave me alone more.

I rode down to the fair that night with Dad and Louise, knowing that I'd most certainly see somebody I knew and come home with whoever was there. T.J.'s volunteer fire company had beer at its fair, so it was a big event. It was high school reunion week, but nobody had called me to go as a date. I guess after this long, everybody brought their wives. What I didn't expect at the fair was that Mike would show up, looking better than the last I'd seen him, appearing between the clam and the beer tents while Dad brought Louise and me beers. He wasn't wearing anything Army. Evidently he no longer needed to show his pride in the uniform by wearing it to public events. He came over and asked Dad how he was and what he was doing since he wasn't farming. Mike nodded to Louise, but he was looking me up and down, checking to see if I had a wedding band, if weight had settled on my legs or on my ass, trying to see if the rumor about me taking college classes could be true. Dad said, "Mike, are you staying with your folks? Could you run Maria home on your way?"

I was mad that Dad was passing me off on Mike, even if I did plan on staying later. I could find my own way home and always had.

"I'll take her home. No problem," Mike said, grinning at me. "Does she have to be home at any particular time these days?"

We all laughed, because even when there were particular times, I had often missed them. Mike and I had another good long look at each other. No beer belly. No visible scars. Lines around his eyes. Teeth still straight and white. The Army has good dental.

The good dental is an important detail, and you probably don't know that. If you're on welfare, you get dental, same if you're in the Army, but if you work loading potato chips on tractor trailers you don't get dental, the bank gets some dental (because otherwise who'd deposit their paycheck with a teller-girl minus a front tooth?) but if you're self-employed or working in a stone quarry, you don't get dental. First thing that goes on people round here, makes them look older than they are, are teeth.

That's why kids in Head Start are fluoridated almost to death. Mary, from our class, her kid is in Head Start, and she says they make those kids brush their teeth twice in the three hours they're there. It's like that Head Start teacher believes Mary's teeth are bad because she doesn't brush them, not because her Mom raised her on potato chips and soda. If those kids don't look poor, if they have good teeth, a decent set, they just might make it.

"How's the babies doing?"

"Fine. Growing like weeds. They're still in Texas. This is a short trip, just me seeing Mom and Dad and going to the reunion. Karen's pregnant again, and she don't travel too good."

I remembered the one time I'd seen Karen, she was a dishwater blond with circles under her eyes and a crooked, white smile. Mike had met her at basic training in Oklahoma. Mike just came back from that last ten day brutal basic training hike in the desert and proposed. They were married before he was shipped to Germany, and they were in Germany when Mike got shipped to Saudi. She had stayed in Germany, praying that what was at first a conflict wouldn't last too long, and then praying that the war wouldn't kill him before their first child was born.

We decided to go get a drink at our favorite bar, the Tea Kettle, because it had been a good place to skip an afternoon of school when we were growing up. It seemed like a perfect place to fill Mike in on the local gossip.

Mike was driving a familiar car, his Dad's ancient, rust and white colored Ford Fairlane, the passenger seat littered with the usual collection of empty cigarette packages, a partially filled bottle of oil left over from a previous oil change, and an oil filter wrench. Mike threw the junk into the back seat on top of a light-weight fluorescent orange hunting vest with the license pinned in the back and an ancient red hunting cap. I smiled because the clutter in the back seat was so familiar. The extra flannel shirts and jumper cables didn't seem to have moved in the years since I'd ridden with him.

You said something in class about Tim O'Brien and parataxis. Is that a list or something? Does this description of Mike's back seat count? Should I describe the flannel shirts? Do you even know what an oil filter wrench looks like?

At the Tea Kettle, we started drinking shots and went through our high school classmates, listing births, deaths, marriages, divorces, and affairs. We'd each graduated with about seventy people, most we'd known all our lives, and we had talked about almost everybody when I started asking him about his time in the Gulf.

"It was lots of sand and way too hot," he said. "But in that way it was like Oklahoma and basic all over again. MREs and sweat. No black widow spiders, though. Did I tell you about that?"

"No. Don't we have black widow spiders around here? The males have the red hour glass on their backs?"

"No, the females. They bite their mates after they have sex and kill them."

"But, what about the Gulf? Your Mom told Dad that you were in the actual fighting and some of the digging the bodies out of the bunkers after stuff was over."

"It wasn't that big a deal. The hardest thing was losing the barracks to the Scud. I knew those people to speak to....They were Pennsylvanians, reserve, not career military. Stupid loss, shouldn't have been there.

"But anyway, I was on maneuvers in the Oklahoma desert," Mike continued. "Last ten day stretch of basic. The Army has convinced you, you can't brush your teeth unless somebody else says it's O.K. and shows you how, and we're supposed to be out surviving in combat conditions. I'm in my tent putting on socks..."

"Putting on socks?"

"Yeah. We had to mark ten miles back and my feet are blistered, so I'm putting on a pair of these stupid army issue socks. I'm pulling the left sock on and I feel this sharp pain, and I look down and there's a god damn black widow spider stuck to my leg. And we'd been told there are no black widow spiders in the Oklahoma desert, no dangerous spiders at all."

"Wait a second. No bad spiders. How in the hell did it end up on you then?"

"Christ, I don't know. But this drill sergeant has been giving me shit since the beginning, saying that it don't matter if my father was in Asia, that I'm such a smart ass that I'm not going to make it through basic. And since I think I'm so god damn intelligent, I should try for an ROTC scholarship in the Air Force, and just look at war on a computer screen, like Space Invaders. He's been busting on me for weeks, and now he's not going to let me finish basic. Or he's not going to believe me, and by the time he does I could be dead."

"Why are they such sons-of-bitches?"

"Right now you can only be career Army if they keep moving you up the chain of command. Career Army means retirement at thirty-eight and a new life. This weekend warrior shit means dying whenever somebody who's been away for a while forgets the rules and has an accident and you're in the line of fire or in the tank that he mistakes for the enemy."

I don't know if this is the kind of dialogue that you say "reveals character." We said "fuck" a lot more than I'm writing down now, but you probably don't want that in a paper. It's probably one of those things that a professional author can use, but that we can't yet. Like we have to get good at knowing how to use big words first, before we can write like we talk. See, for me the spider symbolizes what Mike's life has been like, something always biting him on the ass at a crucial moment and screwing things up, but I don't know if you'll get the spider comparison. It doesn't seem "realistic," but it's what he said really happened, so it must be true.

Is this the language of "the oppressed" that you've been talking about in class? Like that guy who taught those peasants, those peasants probably said "fuck" in Spanish a lot, too, but that probably wasn't included in their essays, right?

"So, anyway, you're still in the Army," I said, motioning the bartender to give me another chaser. "So what did you do about the spider?"

"Well, the Army gives you this stuff that freezes on contact. Why not just a bottle of bug spray, I don't know. So I'm hopping up and down and grabbing the can from my kit, dumping stuff all over, and the spider's trying to beat a hasty retreat and I'm hopping after it, knocking the tent down, till I finally freeze the sucker. I'm trying to figure out..."

The door to the Tea Kettle slams, and Candy Dimock, now married to a Brown, bursts in, talking before she's in the door.

"There's bodies in the road. Please come help. They're dead. We think they're dead, but we're not sure. Bodies..."

"What bodies, Candy?" I ask, but people are already standing up and pushing forward. "What road, where?"

"Up the hill," she says. I had seen her from a distance at the fair grounds earlier with her husband. They must have been driving home and seen something. "Danny went to call the state cops, the ambulance."

"Run over?" I ask. Candy says, "Blood in the road. I don't know..."

Mike grabs Candy by the arm. "Come show us where you saw them," he says. "We'll see if we can help. Maria, you know CPR, right?" He pulls Candy toward the Ford and throws open the back seat door for her. Reaches around and pulls a thirty-thirty out from underneath the hunting clothes. "Get in," he says, and pushes Candy inside, handing me the rifle. "There are shells in the glove box." Other people are getting into their cars, some still holding their beers. Some are unpacking knives and deer rifles from beneath their back seats. They are waiting to follow us. I fasten my seat belt and open the glove compartment while Mike gets in the car. When I open the glove box, Mike's grandpa's service issue revolver tumbles out with boxes of shells, pink registration information, and their Family Farm insurance card. Mike backs up fast, while I start slipping long yellow-colored bullets into the chamber of the thirty-thirty, load it and put the safety on. Candy says, "Maria, do you remember two-man CPR in case we need it? I can't remember how many breaths per second..."

"How far," Mike asks, voice calm. He doesn't wait for an answer before he says, "Load the Colt, too."

I am already filling the Colt from the other box of bullets. The only gun I have shot on a regular basis. Friday nights shooting bottles filled with water and watching them explode. Saturday nights shooting mailboxes at midnight driving too fast, throwing beer bottles at the mailboxes if it wasn't your turn with the gun.

"Here," Candy says, but at first we see nothing. Then we spot the white in the ditch, the unmoving white in the ditch.

I remember (from first aid class):
-gun shot wounds are to be treated as puncture wounds;
-knife wounds also puncture (don't remove the knife);
-cover and try and prevent bleeding with direct pressure.

Mike gets out of the car with the thirty-thirty, metal glinting, catching the light from a car pulling up behind us. Others pull up behind us, also get out. Slowly. Moments drag on and on. I hold the forty-five. The bodies are end to end in a ditch by the road side. Blood has run from the man's chest and onto the road and pools on the asphalt. In the headlights, it's not clear whether the woman's sweatshirt is gray or white. She lies on her side, and I can see that she was shot from the front because the exit wound on her back is big enough for me to put one of my hands in.

"Two," Mike says, his hand gently lifting the man's dark hair from his neck as he feels for the carotid pulse.

My fingers probe the woman's neck for the artery, any sign of life. Their clothes are red and maroon, fresh and bright, partly dried blood. Her eyes are wide open, but she is dead. It is silent as we gather around the bodies, not moving them. Sticking the guns back in the vehicles, finishing the beers, lighting cigarettes, waiting for the cops. No one recognizes the two dead.

We found out later it was a lover's triangle involving newcomers. The guy who did the killing went to the fair with his ex-girlfriend. She wanted to be friends and invited him to come with her to meet her new boyfriend. The old boyfriend was in the back seat of the car, pulled a gun, shot through the seat and killed the boyfriend.

She stopped the car, turned around, and said, "What the hell is going on?" and was shot in the chest. He panicked, threw the bodies in the ditch and drove off. Threw the revolver and its clip out at different places on his way out of town, but was caught before he hit the interstate because a cop stopped him and noticed the blood and rips on the passenger seat. The cops found the clip the first day, on the five mile strip of two lane that was most likely, but they couldn't find the gun. T.J.'s fire company cleaned up from the fair and then helped hunt for the gun. T.J. found the weapon three days later, ten yards from the road, in the rain. He knocked over some strands of purple and white vetch with a branch when the stick hit the gun. It was his sixtieth birthday, and after he found the gun, all the state cops shook his hand. His picture, holding his walking stick and grinning, was in the local paper.

That night, after we'd talked to the cops, Mike drove me home and finished telling me about the Gulf.

"Since I'm in for twenty years and already served almost half, they stuck me in a tank with more firepower than you'd ever imagine, guarding some West Point son-of-a-bitch commander who'd never even sweated in a desert. He was trained in jungle warfare, a kind of leftover. It was just miles and miles of tunnels, sand, and oil. And we were going to suffocate in their bunkers anyway."

As I sit here trying to write this story, I try and remember what was said about a good narrative, what a good narrative consists of, but I don't have a conclusion in this story, just more fragments: Dad and T.J. hunted deer and came back empty-handed; Mike's mother sent over a venison roast from one of their deer; we ate the venison roast today at noon, with potatoes. And I don't have any questions for peer reviewers, because now that I'm in these night classes with these eighteen-year-olds, they don't understand my life anyway. At least in the continuing ed classes we had a variety of experiences, like shitty jobs or boyfriends, and shared ideas about good writing, like no comma splices and clear words. These girls can't even tell the difference between a Honda and a Ford, a double barrel shot gun and a pellet gun, or eve, a buck and a doe. Some of them aren't even sure what their major is, while I'm trying to get enough algebra in my head to pass chemistry, qualify for the nursing program.

The assignment sheet said that this narrative should contain reflections, reveal something about ourselves and how we were changed by an event. But how should I be changed by finding a couple of bodies on a strip of two lane a couple of miles from home? Should I have a moral about how guns are dangerous and bad and nobody should have them anymore? Should I lie and tell you that I'll never be around guns anymore, that I'll be a good girl now and stay away from violent people and places?

How can I explain to you or to the other people in class that I finally decided that the noise I'm hearing outside the window as I write this isn't firecrackers, but gunfire. And that the phone just rang, and I talked to my neighbor who apologized for shooting his gun off, although it's ten on a Sunday night. I told him no big deal and he said, "I'm sorry for what I done, but I needed to do that, or I'd have to go somewhere and hit somebody." I don't tell him that Dad's not here, and that I'm trying to finish writing an essay.

And that he scared me.

And that while I've been listening to the shooting, I've propped the twelve-gauge at the front door and the thirty-thirty at the back.

NOW THAT YOU'VE READ

1. What stands out in your mind after reading Green's essay?

   a. Think about her key arguments by recasting them from the perspective of Malcolm X, for example, or Dora Lopez from Deborah Brandt's study. Do you think the experience would be the same for them?

   b. When they enroll in their first college classes, can you see them experiencing struggles similar to those illustrated in Green's study? Why or why not?

   c. How might those struggles manifest themselves?

   d. What about you? Do these experiences seem familiar to you? If so, how?

READING

"Preface" (from *Fashioning Lives: Black Queers and the Politics of Literacy*)

Eric Darnell Pritchard

Before You Read

1. What do you make of the quotation from Malea Powell at the very beginning of Pritchard's essay? What do you expect to follow?

2. What is your strongest memory (positive or negative or in between) of learning to read?

3. How would you describe the diversity of your elementary school? Did everyone look like you, or were you in a minority of some sort? How did the level of diversity affect what and how you learned?

Prologue from *Fashioning Lives*

Eric Darnell Pritchard

> This is a story. When I say "story," I don't mean for you to think "easy." Stories are anything but easy. When I say story, I mean an event in which I try to hold some of the complex shimmering strands of a constellative, epistemological space long enough to share them with you. When I say "story," I mean "theory..."
>
> —Malea Powell, "Stories Take Place: A Performance in One Act," 2012 CCCC Chair's Address

This *too* is a story—for this study flows from life stories by Black lesbian, gay, bisexual, transgender, and queer people to theorize the myriad ways individuals have learned and employed literacy in their quests to build a life on their own terms and, more specifically, toward the goals of self- and communal love, healing, care, and other modes of survival. As I investigate the voices, faces, and places that inform this book,

I am drawn over and over again to scenes of literacy within my life story that are crucial to narrativizing my life experience as a Black, queer, feminist, cisgender man who is a learner, teacher, scholar, artist, activist, and advocate; scenes that, when read alongside my later analysis, dovetail back to the themes of identity formation and affirmation, literacy concealment, ancestorship, and others explored in the chapters that follow.

I

My story. It was 1986. I was seven years old. My mother worked at the post office, and, having three children to take care of on her own, she worked as many evening hours as she could possibly get her supervisor to approve to generate more income. This meant that I hardly had any time to see my mother at all in the afternoon and evenings—she was never home when I returned from school. Occasionally, my big brother Avery would serve as our caretaker, but usually it was my mother's sister, Aunt Lorry, who helped us with homework and cooked dinner so that my mother had less to do when she came home. In essence, my mother and Aunt Lorry raised my two brothers, three female children of their brother, and me in one household; my family, like me, was always Black and queer. My mother, being the only source of income besides public assistance, didn't have much time for extracurricular activities with me or my siblings. However, I'll never forget that she always took the time to read to and with me. One book in particular featured the characters Bert and Ernie from the television program *Sesame Street*. I remember first that I loved the illustrations in the book and also the very animated way my mother would read the characters' lines. I mimicked the way she characterized their voices, and when she asked me to read aloud, I repeated back the story just as she had read it to me.

While I was able to recall the story word for word and scene-by-scene, my mother, teachers, and other relatives did not know that I could not actually read the book. I had made it to second grade without anyone ever finding out that I could not read. My recitation of the Bert and Ernie book was not a demonstration of my reading skills. My ability to recall the words was built around my supreme memorization skills (skills I still possess). By looking at the actual illustrations and listening to my mother's voice, I had memorized the book completely from cover to cover and could recite it on command. One day my mother received a phone call while we were reading the book. She continued her telephone conversation as I went on reciting the book from memory; however, while on the phone she never turned any of the pages. She noticed that the words I was reciting and pretending to follow with my index finger were not the words that appeared on the actual page. A look of worry and confusion came across her face. As she realized what was happening, that I was only reciting from memory, her eyes began to well with tears.

The very next day my mother went to meet with my teacher, Ms. Drew. When she attempted to engage Ms. Drew in a discussion about solutions to improving my reading abilities, my teacher became increasingly defensive throughout the conversation. At one point she suggested that my mother allow for my father to take on more hours at work so that she could focus on helping me read. My mother responded by telling her that there was no father and that she worked every minute she could to provide for my siblings and me. Ms. Drew's response was simply, "Well, Ms. Pritchard, these are difficult choices, in difficult times."

Though a sacrifice for her as a single parent, my mother made sure that my reading and writing improved quickly, and that it was not just skill related, but culturally centered and purposeful. One of the difficult decisions she made was to ask that I be placed back into a first-grade class the following school year so that I had a chance to learn all the things I hadn't the previous year. She also wanted me to be in the company of students at my skill level and not just passed along to the next grade. Though as a teen I had some self-esteem issues about having been "left back" and being a year behind students in my age cohort, I cannot dispute that my mother made the best decision she could have with the options she had available to assist me in catching up on the lost learning time.

My mother began to read to me not just from Bert and Ernie books but also from a pamphlet about African American history called *Black Facts*, a popular publication among many Black people. I couldn't understand all the words, or even the historical significance, but I remembered feeling special and having moments of clarity. I think those were also moments of clarity for my mother. She would often raise her eyebrows when we'd get to certain facts, saying she didn't know about that either, and smile. I learned things like Madame C. J. Walker was one of the first American women to become a self-made multimillionaire; that Booker T. Washington founded Tuskegee University, a Black college in Alabama; that George Washington Carver created about 145 different products from the peanut; and Rosa Parks was the "mother of the civil rights movement," made famous by her refusal to give in to prejudice aboard a segregated bus in Montgomery, Alabama. As my mother read to me, reading became much more of a routine, and I found it easier to do. Somehow learning about all those people taught me a little bit more about myself, but it also confused me when I looked around for those images elsewhere. I was even more confused about why those things didn't come up in my school lessons, and I found that, as one of a small group of students being bused from Corona, Queens, to a predominately White school in Rego Park, consideration for the experiences of the Black and Latinx students newly arriving to the school did not appear to concern my teachers. Even at home I would look through my grandfather's newspapers and books and wonder why there weren't any of the pictures or names in them that I had learned from *Black Facts*.

II

Another story. January 1988, 1 was in third grade. My family had recently moved to another side of Corona's major thoroughfare, Northern Boulevard, which meant that I, my brother Travis, and my cousins all went to a new school closer to home. No more Rego Park. My class was learning about Martin Luther King Jr. and preparing for Black History month. My teacher, Ms. Lowell, began to talk about Dr. King's "I Had a Dream" speech, stating that Dr. King saw all types of people—regardless of how they looked, talked, or behaved—living together in harmony. She asked us, "Where do you see Dr. King's dream?" Everyone's hand went up, and she called on us one at a time. Some students saw King's dream at their churches, in their neighborhoods, even in their families. I thought about where Dr. King's dream was for me and wanted to say it was at the school, but 1 knew that it wasn't true just by looking at how few people in the room looked like me, So, I thought about my neighborhood, my church, and realized that they didn't look a lot like the speech either. My neighborhood was pretty much all Black and brown people and, for the first time, that seemed odd. Not only did everyone look like me, but everyone lived like me too. My family struggled financially and we often had very little money to do anything extracurricular. We also lived in a neighborhood of broken-down houses and unclean streets with seemingly little hope of receiving any city resources toward improvement. No, Corona did not look like Dr. King's speech at all. There was not a diversity of people and it did not sound like much of a dream, at least in comparison to the experiences my classmates described back at Rego Park, or even at my new school. But I also loved home, and I felt more comfortable there than in school despite the fact that school had comparably better material conditions and literacy resources for me. In this moment I was, as Paulo Freire might say, reading the word *and* the world.

III

A different story. 1992. Ms. Kelly's "Rites of Passage" class was among the most popular among students at Wright Elementary School, an African culture immersion school located next door to a public housing project, and was required of all sixth-grade students. Being able to attend Ms. Kelly's class was in itself the end result of a rite of passage: the journey that brought you to the final year at Wright. I had attended Wright since 1989 when my family moved from Corona to South Jamaica. The purpose of "Rites of Passage" was to introduce students to Black culture through film, literature, history, lectures, and workshops. The course was named after traditional African cultural rites of passage, which mandate that every young male and female in a village must go through a period of learning and testing of culture, manhood, and womanhood before they can be considered an adult. The class met once per week. Males and females were separated as a part of Ms. Kelly's pedagogy and the rites of passage she followed, meeting with her at different times during the week. This philosophy was very African and Black culture-centered and traditional in terms of gender and sex, as men and women were seen as having different roles in the community. Rites of passage reinforced binary gender focusing on what males and females needed to know and learn separately. The distinctions drawn through binary gender were especially discussed in terms of labor, family, and leadership roles within a community. This understanding of gender shaped my own notions at the time of what it meant to be a Black man and Black boy. Though the course was helpful in terms of my early development of race consciousness, the ideas here would later be a source of struggle for me as I discovered the limitations and boundaries these lessons placed on what constituted manhood, women's roles, gender diversity, and, ultimately, sexuality. I didn't yet know exactly what it meant to be "queer" or how to express a gender that is nonconforming, but I did feel displaced by the expectations and definitions of what it meant to be a Black man or Black boy—I just couldn't articulate it. Despite this, Ms. Kelly's class remains one of the most successful educational experiences I ever had. I also credit this pedagogy with helping me to develop not only a sense of pride in myself and in community but also in empowerment and excellence. The paradox of this truth—that this literacy environment was one that was both liberating and constraining—is one that would continue to emerge at other points in my life and runs parallel to many of the experiences that sixty Black lesbian, gay, bisexual, transgender, and queer (LGBTQ) people I interviewed for the purposes of this book shared with me about their own literacy learning and identity formation and affirmation.

The words "Seek knowledge from the cradle to the grave" appear over the entry to Ms. Kelly's classroom and in the main hall as one entered Wright, just above the entrance to the auditorium. It peppered all of Ms. Kelly's lectures and classroom discussions. Ms. Kelly taught us about responsibility, revolution, honesty, and compassion—lessons coming through the history of Black people throughout the diaspora. We watched films such as *Roots*, *The Autobiography of Ms. Jane Pittman*, *The Color Purple*, and *Ethnic Notions*. Marlon Riggs, who directed *Ethnic Notions*, would later be reintroduced to me in a way, this time as a Black gay male ancestor. I was first introduced to his work only to know about and discuss issues of racial and ethnic stereotyping of Black folks, not the complex discussions around a more diverse sense of Black identity or the critical racialized gender and sexuality commentary for which he was also well known in his films *Black Is/Black Ain't* and *Tongues Untied*, which I would not learn of until graduate school. *Ethnic Notions* was a documentary about the stereotypes of African Americans in books, films, cartoons, and popular culture. I learned the names of these stereotypical figures: mammies, jezebels, sapphires, uncle toms, Black brutes, savages, and coons. This was an important lesson in my continued process of decoding, becoming visually literate. *Ethnic Notions* heightened my senses to issues of mainstream misrepresentations of Black people. I recall being very angry at this point in my life because I knew of many television shows and books that still represented Black people this way. I brought it up in class one day, and Ms. Kelly told me to write about it in the journal we were required to keep.

IV

I was fourteen years old when I first learned that there were African American lesbian, gay, bisexual, and transgender writers and literature. I did not discover this in school. By then I had dropped out of eighth grade at my new junior high just a fifteen-minute walk from Wright Elementary and made my local branch of the New York Public Library my classroom. On numerous occasions a librarian questioned if I was old enough to be at the library during school hours. Ms. Sinclair, the head librarian, would always come to my defense. "Leave him be," she'd say. "There's a lot worse things besides reading a child could be doing in these streets if they were skipping school." Once, after Ms. Sinclair intervened on my behalf, she said, "Eric, why don't you go to school? Does your mama know about this?" Standing there, mouth agape, I had so much I wanted to say but couldn't utter a single word. "You could be out there doing worse, though I am a little concerned about you reading them funny people's books and magazines all day," she said, referring to the gay and lesbian literature and magazines I read. She told me, "You're gonna have to finish school someday. So whatever you are running from, you better stop letting it rule you."

What was I running away from? School had ceased to be a place where learning was possible. Though I did not yet identify as gay, I had long since known and been treated differently than my peers whose parents made comments about how "sweet . . . funny acting . . . Kitty Pritchard's middle son was." Comments from parents gave way to being teased and beaten up at school multiple times. I stopped going to school to save myself the pain of fighting my way through a curriculum that held no meaning for me and to spare myself the beatings I would get throughout the day. Put simply, I was both bored and battered.

The library became my sanctuary and classroom for two consecutive years, and I would only go to school when the truant officers would threaten to take me and my brother away from my mother or there was a citywide test (which I would always ace because I didn't want to get left back again). At the library I remember reading all types of Black queer and Black feminist literary culture: the poems and poetry of Alice Walker, Audre Lorde, and Asha Bandele; the novels of James Baldwin; and national news stories about lesbian, gay, bisexual, and gender nonconforming people. I spent the most time with street literature like the novels of Donald Goines, a favorite of my mother—replete with tales of the illicit economies of drug dealers, pimps, sex workers, and other gender and sexual deviants—as well as the contemporary black gay fiction by authors James Earl Hardy and E. Lynn Harris. In Hardy's and Harris's work I saw for the first time Black same-gender loving and Black gay men depicted as happy, passionate about life, successful, in love with one another, desiring one another, and some openly doing so. These writers and their works were at the center of the pedagogy of empowerment and self-making I created for myself. My self-made curriculum, while focused on novels, poetry, and plays, also included activities such as research, writing, memorization, and reading the world to locate evidence in real life of what I saw in those books. I would learn the names of musical artists like Sylvester and Luther Vandross and others so popular among Black gay men and try to locate their music so I had better context for the moments when they were mentioned in what I read. I kept many journals with notes from my readings and research, I would go home and type my own stories in response to what I read that day, and I began to write poetry, short stories, and plays of my own. I would remember passages of the books and share them with friends. And in time the whispers about queer people in my neighborhood being sweet, sissies, dykes, bulldaggers, or fruity were almost completely silenced by the increased volume of a more affirming view of the lives of those same individuals, who I suddenly saw as more fully human than what had been modeled in the reductive descriptions of them because of assumptions about their sexuality, gender, and other aspects of their sense of self.

Through my self-created pedagogy and for the first time in my life I saw Black LGBTQ people depicted as brilliant thinkers, resilient people, lifelong warriors; I learned that they loved and were loved by others, that they laughed and danced and sang and painted and prayed and dreamed just like everyone else. I saw, especially in reading Hardy, that these Black LGBTQ people were not mutually exclusive of Black communities, but would be part of those communities, gay and lesbian communities, and making art completely comprised of the aesthetics of Black queer life. I created a place in which I could finally be "all of who I am in the same place.'" I began to gather the critical intellectual tools and personal affirmation to do as Ms. Sinclair had commanded me: to wrestle from my greatest fears the power it had stolen and the life I was being denied. Literacy was, and remains, key to that journey.

V

In 2002, at twenty-three years old, I was in my first semester of graduate school. I was sitting in the University of Wisconsin-Madison's "College Library" with a stack of books, searching for some substantial history that linked the Black civil rights and LGBT rights movements, but I couldn't find any connection. The one piece of information that did pop out to me dealt with the pivotal role that transgender women of color—namely Sylvia Rivera and Marcia P. Johnson, self-described Latina and Black "street queens"—played in the Stonewall Movement that kicked off the fight for LGBTQ liberation; however, that LGBTQ history was not articulated as part of anything I learned about histories focused on the contributions of Black or other people of color. These same stories only garnered what seemed like cursory mentions as part of LGBT history as well. I read pages of essays, speeches, and book reviews, looking for the answer to how I could work toward liberation and not have to fracture myself being forced to either be Black *or* gay, but not both. But it seemed like such a difficult task at the time. In doing that research I learned about Bayard Dustin, and this turned my attention from looking for information in the big narratives of the historiography that existed to the stories of individual people. This practice introduced me to a range of other people in Rustin's generation and the generation that followed who were freedom fighters working at the intersections of the Black Freedom and LGBT rights movements; people who identified with both at some point, and at other moments critiqued those movements individually and collectively, exploring the splitting of Black and LGBTQ identity and politics as a productive tension in the making of self, community, political identity, and other key matters. One of those people was Essex Hemphill.

I remember reading the book *Brother to Brother: New Writings by Black Gay Men*, an anthology edited by Hemphill. He completed it on behalf of Joseph Beam, a Black gay male writer and activist who had died of complications from AIDS before the volume was complete. Knowing that Hemphill finished the work of his brother-friend, and now ancestor was somehow more meaningful for me than the existence of a critical mass of Black queer history and literature itself because it directly informed the sense of purpose unfolding before me. Later Hemphill wrote about continuing Beam's work in the poem "When My Brother Fell," which he dedicated to him. Hemphill said, "When my brother fell, I picked up his weapons." I imagined those weapons Hemphill picked up as being the paper and pen he used to complete Beam's work, to act on the call he heard and chose to answer; Beam had initially taken on his work under the compulsion of the call he'd received as well.

Something resonated with me about this alliance, this continuum of Black queer family, working together for not just the causes of their race or sexuality or gender justice but also for social justice writ large. Just as I began to bring things together, expanding my antiracist work to a broader vision on gendered and sexual justice, this effort and my own personal identities as a Black queer man were affirmed by reading June Jordan, a Black bisexual writer, activist, and teacher. In the essay "A New Politics of Sexuality," Jordan wrote that "freedom is indivisible, or it is nothing at all." This was the essay that made intersectionality more tangible for me, and it also made my identity as an emerging Black gay feminist cisgender man much clearer. I read this essay in a graduate course taught by Stanlie James called "Black Feminisms," and I felt as if the dam had broken and out flowed fresh, replenishing waters, clear of the drudge that silenced me and kept myself from myself. As the Nina Simone song goes, I knew how it felt to be free.

A recurring space in my own literacy story, and in the literacy stories of many people, is the public library. Such was the subject of a series of paintings by famed artist Jacob Lawrence who used the public library as a central theme within several of his pieces, including his work 1967's *Dream Series No. 5: The Library*, which appears on the cover of this book. In his illustrious career, Lawrence sought to represent the fullest expressions of African American self-definition through paintings depicting the everydayness of Black life, from workplaces and churches to grocery shopping and children playing. Lawrence's quiet yet powerful images show the ways Black folks experience and express their humanity, the same humanity that is denied by the violence of systems of oppression and structural domination.

Outside of a handful of exceptions, including my own previously published work, narratives of Black LGBTQ literacy practices remain absent in literacy, composition, and rhetoric (LCR) generally as well as in work that centers on African American, Feminist, and LGBTQ literacies, composition, and rhetoric. For African American literacy, composition and rhetorical studies, this problematic is reflected in scholarship and pedagogical tools that fail to examine the diversity and complexity of Blackness and its intersectionalities. My work queers that theoretical and historical monolith. Likewise, queer theories of literacies do little to explore the uses of critical theories of racialized sexualities, despite the always already present characteristic of race in queer life and culture, and indeed the queerness of race itself and the necessity of engaging it for any adequate critique of power, privilege, and sexual, gender and LGBTQ identity that is always necessary to make possible progressive and radical interventions.

This book aims to live up to the promise of Lawrence's portraits in documenting, rendering, and engaging with the scenes of Black literacy in everyday life and to assume and represent a diversity of Black and queer lives as peopling those scenes of literacy. Lawrence's literacy portraits offer the raw material for imagining and engaging the possibilities of a more complex, multidimensional way of conceiving of a diversity of Black life stories within questions around Black literacy and literacy institutions.

Lawrence's portraits of libraries were often inspired by or were direct renderings of the 135th Street Branch of the New York Public Library, also part of the site of what is now the historic Schomburg Center for Research in Black Culture. The 135th Street library held a special significance for Lawrence because it served as his classroom after he dropped out of high school to take on a job and financially support his family as a teen. Of equal inspiration to Lawrence's library paintings are the patrons of the library in Harlem, who are a primary feature in his work. The representation of the patrons in his literacy portraits contain a range of Black figures, signaling attention to literacy stories of Black people and literate practices in its diverse forms.

For instance, looking at *Dream Series No, 5: The Library*, in which many of the figures present are gender neutral, my eyes are drawn to Lawrence's depiction of a person reading a book and another looking on over the reader's shoulder. The reader is frowning, eyes directed down toward the text, pupils turned up and to the side. This depiction of the eyes communicates some anxiety or frustration or perhaps serves as an indication that the person is more concerned with looking at something else rather than focusing on the book in hand. Across the table from the reader sit two other library patrons. They appear to be shrinking into a diminutive position, attempting to be unseen.

This is further demonstrated by the book they are reading, which appears to be much larger than the two patrons. They lean in toward one another; one wears an expression of laughter. The two appear to be talking about something humorous, but perhaps they are feigning discretion in doing so.

The spatial context for the painting—its seemingly quotidian setting and the rendering of library patrons—gives one set of interpretations of what is happening in Lawrence's work. The individual reading beneath the gaze of the imposing figure could be a child, one not particularly happy about having to spend time reading indoors when they could rather be at a playground. The person standing above may be a parent, determined that the child will be educated and well-read despite the child's wish to be left alone to play. The two people across from them are laughing, perhaps at the frustration of the child or possibly at the difficulty the child is having. Their physical effort to not be seen laughing could be motivated by the requirement that the library remain a quiet space, lest they draw the ire of the stereotypical all-seeing librarian. While my reading reveals details in how the painting visualizes literacy in the everyday, I am more interested in the queerness of these details and how attention to those details invites us into a reconsideration of African American and LGBTQ literacy activities that highlight the relationship between literacy and normativity, which is a primary concern of this book.

Consider, for instance, the ways in which the imposing figure standing over the reader is symbolic of a more frequent practice of literacies being surveilled, individuals being forced to read and conform to something with regard to literacy. In the painting, what is being enforced is being made to read; in everyday life, this might also expand to uses of literacy to regulate one into a practice, behavior, way of being or identifying, or other action that is oppressive, constraining, or just simply antithetical to what one might do without that imposing figure or force. This is the hallmark of literacy and normativity explored in this book: incidents where literacy operates with the power of regulation, imposition, surveillance, and other forces that do damage or inflict harm on individuals. Continuing this reading of the painting, the two patrons sitting across from the reader and the imposing figure offer a glimpse of literacy practices engaged on one's own terms. As they have no imposing figure standing over them, they possess something like freedom as they are not being monitored or expected to acquiesce to any particular practice in relationship to their reading. Compared to the person sitting across from them, literacy for them is protection; they have the support of the book obstructing their ability to be seen by the imposing figure standing across from them, and thus it functions as an article of distraction (or, to employ a term used in chapter 1, for the ends of *literacy concealment*) that allows them to have literacy their way and escape the regulatory presence of the imposing figure behind the reader just across the table from them.

I am also reminded of the life stories of many of my research participants when I view Lawrence's painting. Their stories form the basis of the theoretical interventions offered in this book, as they recall feelings of surveillance, unsafety, and regulation in relationship to literacy, sometimes because the act of reading was seen as being abnormal due to their race, class, sexuality, or gender identities; in other cases, they feared that the LGBTQ subjects of their books might reveal them as queer and subject them to violence and ostracization; and in more cases, literacy was used to wound them.

Examining Lawrence's painting, I think also of the queerness of the scene not only because of the gender neutrality of subjects in the painting but also given the very Blackness of the literacy scene itself. As cogently demonstrated by multiple literacy and language studies scholars, literacy is almost never assumed to be the property of African Americans, especially within historical and contemporary educational systems in the United States. Lawrence's painting positions this scene of Black literacy in general as queer by transgressing the normative view of literacy in relation to whiteness by centering Black literate subjects in a library, a standardized literacy institution if there ever was one. Finally, and perhaps most strikingly, I am drawn to the ways in which Lawrence's painting, in the abstract, does not provide a clear visual of the faces. Through this choice I see an invitation or opportunity to imagine most elements of the literacy story depicted in the painting, including those who may or may not have passed through the doors. And as I undertake a project whose central question asks where the Black queers are in African American and queer LCR, considering a scene that is historically situated in Harlem—one of the epicenters of Black queer life and culture in the United States—I read those abstract faces as possible Black LGBTQ patrons passing through the doors of Lawrence's library. I would even take the train to Harlem and visit the now Schomburg and the neighboring 136th Street library branch named for poet Countee Cullen myself as a teen, though it happened decades later than the scene in Lawrence's painting.

My desire then is to provide a framework through which literacy, composition, and rhetoric may see Black queerness generally and the theory I develop from the life stories of my research participants in Particular. Intersectionality demands nothing less than to imagine a world outside of our own as a point of entry into a more just, empathetic, complex and connected relationship to one another and also as a richer way of understanding ourselves, particularly with regard to our positional ties in the realities of power and difference. *Fashioning Lives: Black Queers and the Politics of Literacy* responds to this invitation in its aims to engage the truth of Black queerness that always was, is, and will be in histories, theories, and pedagogies of Black and LGBTQ literacies—whether we choose to see them or not is another matter. I also respond to this invitation as a literacy researcher who recognizes the ways in which Black queer studies, with its continued commitment to a deep analysis of Black queer cultural production, needs considered attention to theories in literacy, composition, and rhetorical studies to engage more productively with that project.

My request to you, the reader, is to be open to the ways in which everyday life and its stories, particularly those in this book, present a universe of possibles—a world of concepts, subjects, and interventions that are left marginal to the normative intellectual enterprise of a discipline—that may fuel new considerations of where the Black queer may be and go in LCR studies; where LCR may be within Black Queer Studies; what the universe of possibles, with all its seemingly ineffable questions, interventions, and challenges, may mean for your own stories and ways of being and doing in theory, history, and pedagogy, every day.

NOW THAT YOU'VE READ

1. What distinctions does Pritchard make between home and school? What is significant about those distinctions?

2. How does Martin Luther King's "I Have a Dream" speech figure into Pritchard's essay? How does it fit into his move to take ownership of his own education?

3. How does school change for Pritchard as he grows older? What prompts him to "school" himself?

4. What are some of Pritchard's arguments in "Fashioning Lives"?

READING

Living Inside the Bible (Belt)

Shannon Carter

BEFORE YOU READ

1. What do you understand the term "Bible Belt" to mean?

2. How and where might a university education and deeply held religious beliefs have the potential to be in conflict with each other?

3. Have you ever felt your beliefs were challenged in a classroom? Describe the situation.

4. What do you understand tolerance in the classroom to mean? How far should tolerance extend?

Living Inside the Bible (Belt)

Shannon Carter

Teaching writing in the Bible Belt for the past five years has taught me a number of things. Most significantly, perhaps—as much as I hate to admit—it has taught me the limits of my own tolerance for difference. In fact, the evangelical Christianity with which a number of my students most identify functions—rhetorically, ideologically, practically—in ways that appear completely and irreconcilably at odds with my pedagogical and scholarly goals. The social and cultural theories with which I most identify celebrate difference both empathically and explicitly, yet much of the traditional conservatism through which evangelical Christianity[1] resonates seems to embrace familiarity above all else, representing difference not as a benefit to embrace and learn from but as a threat to overcome (see Kintz). A key objective of my writing courses may be critical consciousness: awareness of one's subject position and the partial and socially situated nature of one's understanding of the world. However, the goal of "witnessing talk" or "testimonial" appears to be quite the opposite: to "convert" the listener to the speaker's ways of knowing and living, a conversion completely dependent upon the acceptance that the speaker's own subject position is far from "partial" or "socially situated" but rather universal, right, and—above all—"True."

Critics like Amy Goodburn, Priscilla Perkins, and Lizabeth Rand, however, have identified several rather ironic parallels between the critical position with which I most identify and the Christian position my Bible-believing students may use as, in Rand's words, "the primary sense of selfhood [. . .] they] draw upon in making meaning of their lives and the world around them" (350). In comparing the agenda of critical education with that of a Christian witnessing for Christ, for example, Rand suggests that both "act as witnesses hoping to convert others to the faith" (360). According to the former, "evil" results from a lack of critical consciousness, a blind faith in individualism and the myth of meritocracy that ignores the function of community and material conditions in determining our life paths; according to the latter, "evil" results from "a drive to make ourselves the centre of our world," ignoring the function of God's plan in determining our life path (Taylor, qtd. in Rand 360). Among the many similarities Goodburn points out is that both "desire to convert the 'other,' to persuade those whom they define as either 'unsaved' or 'uncritical'" (348). As my neighbor put it once after returning from a trip to India with the Church of Christ, the ultimate goal of his missionary work there was "to save [them] from themselves." So, too, it seems my goal as an educator[2] has often been to "save" my openly religious students "from themselves."

Despite the surprising number of similarities between these communities of practice, however, the fact remains that many evangelical students find the academy to be openly hostile to their faith-based ways of knowing, being, and expressing themselves. Likewise, much evangelical discourse seems openly hostile to already marginalized groups (homosexuals, women, those of non-Christian faiths, for example). For Luke, the Christian student who was the subject of Goodburn's study cited earlier, "valuing difference in perspectives leads to tolerating those whose lifestyles he finds irreconcilable with his religious beliefs. To tolerate difference undermines his faith that an individual must be saved in order to be accepted" (346). As Luke himself put it in a taped interview, "I don't need the university telling me that I should tolerate everybody [. . .] because not everybody's tolerable!" (qtd. in Goodburn 346).

It is a gap that liberal academics and evangelical Christians may find impossible to traverse—intolerable, in fact. Chris Anderson tells us that that "as academics, it's time that we were more aware that our position is not beyond point of view" (20). More recently, Priscilla Perkins asserts that "teachers write off evangelical students much too quickly." She suggests that instead we teach evangelical students to "put [their] reading[s] of the Bible into dialogue with sometimes competing, sometimes complementary sources of secular, academic knowledge" via "an explicitly hermeneutical approach" (586). Contributors to the recent collection *Negotiating Religious Faith in the Composition Classroom* address the disconnect between the academy and religious faith by encouraging students to "learn to use tension between faith [. . .] and academic inquiry as a way of learning more and learning better" (Vander Lei 8). Goodburn suggests we might best negotiate the gap by making use of what she sees as "the common thread between the discourses," which is "the language of social critique" (334); Rand contends that "we should invite students to explain why [. . .] [evangelical] discourse has had such significance in their lives" (364).

I argue that inasmuch as these believers "live in a world always already biblically written" (Kintz) and large segments of the academy are likely to remain hostile to faith-based ways of knowing, we would do better to help students speak to and across difference by employing what I have called elsewhere a pedagogy of rhetorical dexterity,[3] an approach that trains writers to effectively read, understand, manipulate, and negotiate the cultural and linguistic codes of a new community of practice (Lave and Wenger) based on a relatively accurate assessment of another, more familiar one. That familiar community of practice may be one associated with "play" (like fantasy football or quilting), or "work" (like plumbing or computer programming), or even, as I will explore here, one's faith (perhaps evangelical Christianity). While I agree that it is important for such students, as Rand suggests, to "examine the reasons evangelical discourse has had such significance in their lives," I believe rhetorical dexterity may be of more immediately practical value to students as it explicitly asks them to think of literacy in terms more conducive to maintaining both their faith-based and their academic literacies without being required to substitute one for the other. Rand suggests that our questions for students "might include: How does the struggle to overcome sin affect your life and the decisions you make about yourself or others?" and, perhaps, "How are you limited in your understanding of Truth?" (353). Though I can certainly see how responding to such questions might generate in our religious students the critical consciousness we desire, I can also see how some students (like Luke) might feel compelled to generate responses more defensive than reflective. Moreover, as so many of my students have said, true faith is a "feeling" that cannot be explained, so articulating the reasoning behind one's faith in terms the secular world can understand may seem impossible. As Chris Anderson puts it, faith is "a leap that cannot be justified to anyone who hasn't made that leap," making "religious experience [. . .] like a difficult language" (22, 26).

In the rest of this essay, I attempt to articulate the ways in which rhetorical dexterity might enable our students to use literacies they already possess (like deep knowledge of the Bible and its applications in day-to-day life) to negotiate those the academy expects them to exhibit. I begin with "James," a basic writer for whom, at least within his first semester of college, the Bible represented his primary sense of "selfhood." In that much of the current argument rests on the tensions between a community of practice that "lives inside the Bible" and one that is often perceived to be openly hostile to it, I continue with the stories of two graduate students in our program who—though they were able to maintain deep ties with both their religious communities and their academic ones—experienced some rather painful lessons early on about the irreconcilability of Christianity and the academy. The following section takes a much closer look at conservative and evangelical literacies as articulated in public discourse within and beyond the academy. Given the complex political, rhetorical, and intellectual maneuvers that conservatives and evangelicals have made to defend the conservative, evangelical student against those perceived to be threatening, we would do well to understand the conflicting epistemologies that fuel this perceived—and, in fact, often quite real—threat. Academics, particularly those of us in the humanities and social sciences, appear to many conservative and evangelical leaders as promoting agendas of "secular humanism" and "cultural relativism," agendas they view as antithetical to their own position. Building on the tensions and the conservative rhetoric that exposes these, I then return to James, who—despite our class's attention to "literacy" and my regular attempts to validate his Christian literacies—still found this biblical worldview slipping away from him. I end by discussing what I think may have contributed to this loss and how a pedagogy of rhetorical dexterity might have helped James "learn to use tensions between faith [. . .] and academic inquiry as a way of learning more and learning better" (Vander Lei 8).

Communicating Across Difference

When I asked students in a basic writing class two years ago to describe an object that best represented literacy for them, James started with what seemed most obvious to him: the Bible.

> Before I was [just] *a child that went to church*. I believed the Bible was something you read if you weren't sure that you were going to heaven [. . .] so I never read it. But one day I started to mature from a *child that went to church* to a *churchly child*. I started to understand the older Christians and the purpose of being a Christian and the role that the Bible played in a Christian's life. All because one day [. . .] I felt it was my job to be the clown. [. . .] When my mother [. . .] saw me acting like a fool she came slapped me in the back of the head in front of all my friends and maid [sic] me go to the front of the church to sit with the senior saints. [. . .] I couldn't even fall asleep because the old ladies wouldn't let me because they would either pinch to wake me or be making to [sic] much noise praising the Lord so I had to listen to the message. [. . .] I mean don't get me wrong I always heard the Message but I actually *listened* that time. [. . .] That's how the front pue [sic] saved my life. (emphasis mine)

That semester, James taught me the difference between "a child that goes to church" and "a churchly child"—an emotional shift as profound for him as it is valuable to the other "churchly" members of his "House." He was, however, surprised to hear that anyone could be so confused about what that difference might be, and it was only after several meetings with him that he began to understand the disconnect I experienced in reading his essays because of my own illiteracies in that community of practice. As James explained it to me when we met in my office to discuss revisions of the previous essay:

It's like this. A *child who just goes to church* is an illiterate Christian because he can't *feel* it. He may feel something somewhere else, like in school with his friends or at work, but that feeling ain't the Lord because he's not in his House. A *churchly child*, though, he [is] literate because he can feel it. Like I felt it.

From him, I learned that "living inside the Bible" the right way is a "feeling" that can "save" a person's life, but it is also a perspective that can be understood and truly appreciated only by others who have likewise experienced the "Message" in this way, a feeling that only other literate Christians can experience or understand and one that is central to who the person is—in the classroom, in the church, at home— everywhere, in fact. It is a feeling intimately connected with "the Lord's House" and one the person can "stay close to" only by reading the Bible—a book that, as many have found, is largely unwelcome in the academy.

In our rural East Texas university, graduate students are often no less likely to rely on a "spiritual identity as the primary source of selfhood." However, as English graduate students "Alex" and "Mona" explain, early in their college careers the disconnect between the same Bible-based reasoning with which they most identify and the hostile ways in which that Bible-based reasoning was received forced them to keep their Bible-believing identities "in check." These painful experiences taught them the impossibility of revealing their lives lived "inside the Bible" in terms legible to readers unconvinced of the Bible's "infallibility" (or even of its relevance to contexts extending beyond the churches that reproduce its value). This process is never easy, I am told, and many such students believe themselves to be playing an artificial role in academic contexts. Moreover, as Alex and Mona taught me, an awareness of the negative ways in which the Bible is viewed in the academy is often hard-won.

Alex, a PhD student in English who "for the past fifteen years" has been "continuously enrolled in school" (completing high school a year early and her BA in just two years) has experienced this dissonance rather sharply and consistently, despite (or perhaps because of) her ambition and intelligence: "I grew up in a Southern Baptist family [. . .]. When I was four, my bass-playing father changed his life from one of rock and roll at smoky night clubs to Black Gospel on Sunday mornings." From that point on, as Alex describes it, her "religious family functioned as either a well-oiled machine or a cult [. . .] I'm not sure which one."

The disconnect Alex experienced between the tacit expectations of the Baptist church and more secular ones was vast, but it was also a dissonance necessitated by her faith. As she explains,

> Because Christians are to go into the world of the unsaved, my cousins and I were sent to public schools[, . . .] an unsaved place where we were always to set a good example for our teachers and peers. School provided us an opportunity for witnessing and possible conversions; we were told to carry a Bible with us to school daily so that when the time came, we would use it to help others become saved.

But though her Bible was very much a part of her family, her church, and in fact her sense of self, she learned rather quickly that within many communities of practice in the academy, its use is strictly forbidden.

> Once I turned in a paper in which I used Biblical passages as an argument. I failed. After meeting with the teacher, I got the feeling that the reason I failed came directly from my choice to quote the Bible. I did nothing but remove the quotes and my paper received an "A." Even in a personal opinion paper, I was not allowed to use evidence that appealed to me. I am outraged by this incident to this day.

Despite the insensitivity of her professor's actions, however, Alex persevered, becoming a very successful undergraduate English major and, now, a top graduate student. Much of her ability to, in her words, "mesh my faith-based religious views with my fact-based academic view of the world" can be attributed to her hyperawareness of context. This is an ability, as Deborah Brandt puts it, to "amalgamate new reading and writing practices in response to rapid social change" ("Accumulating" 651).

An evangelical Christian herself, graduate student "Mona" articulates a similar point of dissonance between her faith and her schooling: "I was in a class several years ago when the instructor-led discussion drifted to the origin of mankind." There, she witnessed a fierce but rather empty debate between the professor and two students, the former dismissing creationism as "myth," the latter dismissing evolution in many of the same ways—neither, according to Mona, speaking with any real understanding of the opposition's argument but obviously relying on, as she explains, "what they'd been told by others." Still, believing the professor to be "a man of critical thinking and open-mindedness," she "approached him after class."

> Instead of listening and discussing, however, he dismissed me and my arguments by telling me that the Bible is to be viewed like ancient Greek mythology [. . .]. I said no more, but realized that my academic professor and my Evangelical student peers had much more in common than they realized.

Despite the many—sometimes ironic and largely unconscious—similarities between these two communities of practice, however, the dissonance remains. And, like Mona, Alex is well aware that the battle between these rather different communities of practice is not her own and, in fact, that they are largely irreconcilable. Alex says, "I understand that academics look at facts and evidence. However, religion is mostly about *feeling*. If God wanted to, He could easily give us evidence that He exists. If He did, though, believing in Him and trusting Him wouldn't be the same" (emphasis in original).

More than twenty years ago, feminists and other social theorists began treating feeling, emotion, and intuition as valid epistemological sites, taking seriously aspects of experience that a post-Cartesian worldview has regularly dismissed. Still, even scholarship in areas like these routinely ignores the function of faith, likely assuming it to be "anti-intellectual," "closed-minded," or even counterproductive. Faith does not seem knowledge, but rather its complete opposite.

Living Inside the Bible

In evangelical Christianity, the Bible serves as the primary source from which the power of familiarity resonates. As Linda Kintz explains, in this community of practice all "legitimate participants [. . .] live [. . .] inside a world of textual quotations and references to biblical passages, interpretations, and reinterpretations among a community of believers who know all the same stories and all the same passages [. . .] Liv[ing] inside the Book [. . .] gives believers a world always already biblically written" (33). Given that so many of my students "live inside the Book," it should not be surprising that some rely on the Bible and its teachings to make their arguments. However, the function of the college composition classroom seems to be, at the very least, to enable them to speak to readers who do not, likewise, "live inside the Book": readers like me, for instance. The goal of witnessing talk may be to "save" the listener so he or she will, likewise, "live inside the Book";[4] however, this is not an appropriate aim for academic rhetoric, whose goal is often pluralism. Inasmuch as, for our most religious students, this "biblically written" world is the one with which they most identify, it seems productive for us to ask that they think of what it takes to be considered literate within that world. To articulate this position would not require writers to accept the secular world as ultimately more valuable than the religious one (or even vice versa) but rather to help those not "Christian-literate" understand what it takes to be considered a literate member of the biblically written world. To articulate this position would require writers to think of literacy in much more situated, "people-oriented,"[5] and active terms than most commonsense, school-based versions of literacy allow.

Understanding literacy as social rather than alphabetic, situated rather than universal, and multiple rather than singular requires writers to consider themselves to be simultaneously literate and illiterate in a number of different contexts. I am, for example, literate in writing center studies and associated contexts but largely illiterate in matters relating to chemistry or video games like *Grand Theft Auto*. My devout Mormon student is, of course, a deeply "literate" Mormon, but may know very little about the Baptist communities of practice in which some of her classmates are quite likely *highly* literate. In other words, as the findings of the New Literacy Studies have proven, literacy is not a set of stable, portable, rule-based skills that enable the user to encode and decode all texts "correctly," regardless of the type of text, the conditions under which the text is encoded/decoded, the purpose of the text, the people surrounding the text, the place in which the text is situated, or the experiences of the readers/writers who put the text to use. Of course, developing in our students the flexibility and critical consciousness necessary to negotiate the texts they will encounter throughout college and in their lifeworlds beyond requires that they begin to think of literacy in a different way. In this process of development, we treat literacy not as an abstract set of rigid standards but rather as a blend of mutable social forces deeply situated in time and place.

Literate practices, at least as I am seeing them here, are those sanctioned and endorsed by others recognized as literate members of a particular *community* of practice. As in any community, the literate practices of evangelical traditions in Christianity are those sanctioned and endorsed by other literate members. Those of us who are not literate members of this particular community of practice are less likely to be able to tell the difference between someone who truly does "live inside the Bible" (Kintz)—what James calls "a churchly child"—and someone who is going through the motions (a "child that goes to church").

Literacy thus becomes both a set of socially sanctioned, community-based "skills" and *content* that is validated, produced, and reproduced within that same community of practice. Relevant content thus becomes shared knowledge among members of a given community of practice, and these members extend, reshape, validate, invalidate, reproduce, and archive the content most appropriate for them and their key objectives. From this perspective, developing new literacies depends not on a literacy learner's ability to obtain autonomous skills, nor on any generic content-knowledge, but rather on rhetorical dexterity. The latter, as I noted earlier, calls upon students to effectively read, understand, manipulate, and negotiate the cultural and linguistic codes of a new community of practice based on a relatively accurate assessment of a more familiar one.

Rhetorical dexterity relies on two overlapping theoretical traditions: the New Literacy Studies and activity theory. "NLS approaches," according to Brian V. Street, "focus on the everyday meanings and uses of literacy in specific cultural contexts and link directly to how we understand the work of literacy in educational contexts" (417). In other words, NLS is primarily concerned with the way literacy manifests itself in various out-of-school contexts and, through these findings, with exposing the artificiality and irrelevance of formal literacy education as it exists in most in-school contexts. NLS then redefines literacy education itself as a matter of reading and negotiating various contextualized forces that are deeply embedded in identity formation, political affiliations, material and social conditions, and ideological frameworks. This theoretical framework necessarily flattens hierarchies among literacies; instead of one literacy's being inherently more significant or valuable than another, their respective worth is determined by appropriateness to context.

In this sense, the anti-Bible hostility Alex and Mona experienced may be better understood as a dispute over appropriateness, rather than as a question of whether they suffer from "false consciousness" or, as I'm (unfortunately and often) quick to see it, outright "ignorance." The key issue becomes the ways in which the Bible functions in the communities of practice that reproduce themselves through the familiarity that resonates from that very same book, as well as how these activities (and the value-sets that perpetuate them) might conflict with activities and content reproduced within university communities of practice.

In any given community of practice—be it factory work or fishing, Xerox repair or midwifery, evangelism or the field of composition studies—some activities will be understood as appropriate and others as largely inappropriate, and most of these activities cannot be understood apart from the activity *system* in which they are carried out. Such systems are social and cultural rather than individual and objective. They are made up of groups who sanction and endorse particular ways of doing things and particular results, identifying some results and processes as innovative and valuable and condemning others as ineffective, inappropriate, or even unacceptable.

Thus Mona's Bible becomes at once an irrelevant "book of myths" in her college classroom and the "baseline source [. . .] [for all] reasoning" (Ault 210) among members of her church. There is, of course, nothing terribly insightful about this revelation. However, further exploration of the specific ways the Bible functions in Bible-believing communities of practice might help us understand better the complications our Bible-believing students often face when they begin to appropriate university discourses and value-sets.

Evangelism as a Community of Practice

Like any community of practice, evangelism is organic and dynamic. Therefore, no single representation can capture how it is practiced by all faith traditions in all contexts. Even the most influential leaders of this movement are unable to reach a consensus about what it means to be an evangelical Christian. As *New York Times* reporter Michael Luo explains, "like any dominating force, evangelism is not monolithic." As someone completely unaffiliated with any evangelical faith tradition and only marginally involved in Catholicism, I can at best offer a description of this community of practice as I understand it from an extensive survey of public and academic discourse on evangelism written by evangelists, as well as from informal interviews with students and colleagues who identify themselves as evangelical.[6]

There does appear to be a set of largely universal tenets of evangelism. According to Mark Noll, "evangelical denominations" are those that "stress the need for a supernatural new birth, profess a faith in the Bible as a revelation from God, encourage spreading the gospel through missions and personal evangelism, and emphasize the saving character of Jesus's death and resurrection" (9). Cal Thomas, a syndicated columnist and self-identified spokesperson for American evangelicals, offers a similar definition: "An evangelical Christian is one who believes that Jesus Christ is the Son of God and who has repented of sin and accepted Jesus as his or her savior. The evangelical believes he has the privilege and obligation to share the 'good news' that Jesus came to save sinners with others so they might go to heaven rather than hell."

"Spreading the gospel" is a commitment to what many Christians call the "Great Commission." Within this community of practice, it is widely understood that the Great Commission can be found in the Gospel of Matthew[7] in what is considered to be the "last recorded personal instruction given by Jesus to His disciples" ("The Great Commission"); those "living inside the Book" and calling themselves evangelicals understand the duty of all Christians to be to "make disciples of all the nations" (Matt. 28.18–20). Some evangelists argue that the Bible itself is the product of successful evangelism, with the twelve apostles chosen by Jesus functioning as Christianity's very first evangelists. As Robert Emerson Coleman asserts in the second edition of his popular instructional text The Master Plan of Evangelism, "the initial objective of Jesus's plan was to enlist men who could bear witness to his life and carry on his work after he returned to the Father" (27).

So what, then, does this "Great Commission" have to do with the disconnect James, Alex, and Mona experienced as they attempted to integrate the Bible into academic contexts? Because we are concerned with practices that replicate the community, as well as with the community as a whole, it is useful to examine evangelical Christianity as both a community and an activity system. According to this theoretical framework, the "acts" of relying on the Bible for wisdom and guidance (as James has) and using the Bible as evidence for a personal opinion paper (as Alex has) may be understood as unacceptable when evaluated by the communities of practice associated with the academy, but as completely acceptable and even mandatory when evaluated by those associated with their faith. The disconnect is profound when experienced by those for whom the Bible represents their "primary sense of selfhood" and merely obvious when judged by those for whom the Bible represents at best naivety and at worst "closed-mindedness" or even bigotry. The disconnect between these two communities of practice is not something to be glossed over as a "given" and irreconcilable, however, as I am attempting to prove here.

When attempting to make sense of an activity system within an unfamiliar community of practice, I have found it useful to identify the community's "input," "tools," and "output." Every activity system includes these three categories. Furthermore, they as well as the artifacts created are mediated by a series of "rules" established by the members of that community, reproduced through related activities and training, and likewise shaped by rules governing economic, political, cultural, and social behaviors in other social spaces of which these members are most assuredly a part. As I understand the "Great Commission" of evangelism, then, the input would be a nonbeliever, the output would be a converted believer,[8] and the tools would include, among other things, the Bible as the primary text communicating the teachings of Jesus Christ. In attempting to make sense of a chaotic world, James turned back to his Bible; thus, for him, the Bible is also the tool a Christian might use to "stay on the Lord's path" or "keep close to Jesus." Via the same analytical framework, then, the input here becomes the secular world and its challenges, the output a renewed worldview in keeping with biblical teachings. This also seems the way in which Alex made use of her Bible to support her personal opinion. Alex's professor dismissed her "tool" as irrelevant; Mona's professor went so far as to declare it heretical to the academic communities of practice he claimed to represent.

Alex and Mona attempted to use the Bible as a tool to support their own personal positions (where they are coming from), not as a tool to change the reader/writer in terms more in keeping with their Bible-believing identities (input—unsaved academic; output—saved Christian). For Alex, the Bible seemed an appropriate enough tool to integrate into her "personal opinion paper" because her personal opinion was shaped by the traditions perpetuated in Bible-based discourses. Mona attempted to make use of academic inquiry as tool to better understand—in community—the disconnects she'd just witnessed regarding the debate between her professor and two students (input—disconnect; output—understanding). The professor refused to entertain the debate on scholarly terms because, one must assume, he saw the debate itself (between creationism and evolution) as already settled and, therefore, not a product worth reproducing.

Among those for whom "Truth" is static, constant, and universal, speaking to and across our differences becomes a very different activity than what professors with critical consciousness as their goal might advocate. Among those for whom Bible-based discourses make up their primary sense of selfhood, the only reason to "communicate across difference" may be to change the minds of those who, for whatever reason, just aren't getting it or who have untrustworthy liberal and/or humanist agendas. As conservative talk show host Rush Limbaugh explains in "How to Deal with a Liberal Teacher," "*Evidence refutes liberalism*" (emphasis mine).

A rather common activity reproduced in evangelical communities of practice is organized training for future or current college students that works from similar assumptions about the role of evidence in debunking the liberal position. Each summer, for example, Summit Ministries in Colorado Springs[9] trains recent high school graduates to "refute" the liberalism they are likely to encounter in college, guided by a mission to "equip them to defend the biblical worldview" ("Mission"). This summer training Thomas Barnett calls "Faith Camp."[10] As one "camper" puts it, "I want to put on the *full armor of God* before I go into battle" (qtd. in Barnett, emphasis mine).

Though much less organized and formal, rhetorical "battle" strategies like these appear to be no less common among liberal academics working against conservative ideology and evangelical "dogma." "Evidence," we may insist, "refutes conservatism." Evidence may even refute faith, as Richard Hofstadter argued more than forty years ago in his regularly cited book *Anti-Intellectualism in American Life*. "Learning and cultivation," he asserts, "appear to be handicaps in the propagation of faith" (48–49). Thirty years later, *Washington Post* reporter Michael Weisskopf outraged members of the evangelical community by calling them "largely poor, uneducated and easy to command."[11]

On the face of it, conservatism and evangelism appear to be completely at odds with academic goals like open-mindedness and a high tolerance for ambiguity (see Jost et al.). Yet while I accept a more liberal worldview as ultimately more conducive to values like pluralism and equality, it is important to examine the ways in which a more conservative, faith-based worldview may, in fact, coexist with the end-stages of cognitive development as articulated via William Perry's model: relativism and commitment. To do so, we must examine the ways in which the evangelical community of practice makes sense of what many members of that community call the "Christian Mind" (see especially Nanez; Guinness; Lewis; Noll; Marsden; Budziszewski; Blamires).

Evangelism and the "Christian Mind"

Though matters of faith seem diametrically opposed to matters of the intellect, a growing number of evangelical academics and public intellectuals provide models for conflating this apparently artificial binary. Paul Anderson's collection *Professors Who Believe: The Spiritual Journeys of Christian Faculty* includes essays from "members of the faculty at major secular research universities" who have "found meaning and purpose and value, the essence of life, in their Christian faith" ("Introduction"). Likewise, in *Two Different Worlds* Charles E. Garrison argues that the Christian worldview can coexist with a more "academic" one as "biblical statements are not at odds with the view of knowledge expounded by cultural relativists." In fact, according to Garrison, "[t]he bible corresponds more to cultural relativism than absolutism in its presentation of knowing" (154).

By far the most compelling argument for the overlapping epistemological frameworks of Christianity and academic ways of knowing is, in my opinion, William G. Pollard's *Physicist and Christian: A Dialogue between Communities* (1961). In it, this physicist and priest[12] builds on the rather progressive assertion that "all knowledge is really imparted through community, and cannot be had in isolation or alienation from the community within which a particular segment of knowledge is known" (viii). The idea that knowledge is "imparted through community" differs, of course, from a more social and critical view that knowledge is, in fact, *created* within that community. For Pollard, a universal "Truth" does, in fact, exist outside of community but is only accessible *through* community; in other words, knowledge does not exist entirely within the minds of individuals but rather is imparted and sustained within a community of knowledge seekers. While accepting that his articulation of community is largely irreconcilable with a more critical worldview,[13] however, I argue that Pollard's arguments are useful to teachers shaped by more social theories as we may find in them a common ground between these conflicting worldviews. Pollard's perspective is, in fact, a view supported by even the most literal readings of the Bible (see Newbigin). As he insists, the Bible itself "is an integral part of the actual historic process by which a whole people came to know God in community" (Pollard 161). According to Pollard, "God spoke to Israel through the covenant relationship, and Israel, in turn, has spoken to us through the Bible" (162). Given that much of Pollard's treatment of knowledge as "community-based" is very much in keeping with more social and cultural theories that claim that knowledge, language, and learning are socially situated, I devote the next several pages to his key arguments and what they might offer us in teaching students like James who derive their "primary sense of selfhood" from the Bible.

Physics as a Community of Practice. The term "physics," Pollard argues, often brings to mind (or at least did in 1961) "a subject with a certain content dealing with matter and energy, space and time, force and motion" as well as "the instruments and apparatus which make up physics and are an integral part of it, such things as calorimeters, spectroscopes, galvanometers, Geiger counters, and cyclotrons." However, as he explains, physics must be understood as no less a subject matter than as "the product and the achievement of a human communal enterprise." Likewise, Christianity is "the product and the achievement of a human communal enterprise."

In both physics and Christianity, "the community is in an important sense prior to the subject matter content" (4).

Building on Harold K. Schilling's treatment of "science as community" (1958) and using terms surprisingly similar to those that would be used by scholars like James Paul Gee, Brian V. Street, and other New Literacy Studies scholars more than twenty-five years later, Pollard describes the processes of becoming both a priest and a physicist as "processes of incorporation into a community" (3) and, from these descriptions, two interesting points of contact emerge: (1) Faith is no less an integral part of physics than it is of Christianity, and (2) in physics, as in religion, one may be considered "orthodox" and thus embraced by the community or a "heretic" and subsequently banished from that community.

Faith. According to Pollard, faith is an essential part of the physics community. All participants must have faith in the discipline itself, the current scholarship and infrastructure that supports it, the history of the discipline, and "the scientific method" that sustains it. As he explains,

> The faith which is essential to the fruitful pursuit of scientific inquiry endows those who share it with the power to uncover and make manifest an underlying order and regularity beneath the surface turbulence of events by which these events are seen to be subject to the rule of universal laws. (16)

In similar ways, I must rely on my "faith" as both a teacher and a scholar in carrying out activities associated with my membership in the academy and relevant communities of practice. That is, I have faith in the principal tenets and values of activity theory and New Literacy Studies. Relying on these tenets and values in organizing a socially just classroom enables me to take risks and develop innovative course designs that others may find—at first glance—largely unworkable. When I lose faith in those theoretical frameworks to which I am most drawn—as I am beginning to with critical literacy—I find myself struggling in ways I find quite unsettling, but I have faith in the communities of writing studies and literacy studies (among others) and, therefore, I am able to learn from such experiences—perhaps locating a more appropriate theoretical framework, perhaps finding evidence that returns my faith to the original critical framework after I have temporarily lost my way.

Religious faith, according to Pollard, manifests itself in ways quite similar to this more "academic" version of faith. As he explains,

> [T]he faith which is essential to a fruitful pursuit of the Christian life endows those who share it with the power to know and respond to the hand of God operative behind the same surface turbulence of events by which these events are seen to be subject to the rule of providence and judgment. (17)

As James was transformed from "a child that went to Church" to a "churchly child," we may assume he gained the "faith" he needed not only to *understand* the "message" that day at the front of his church but also to *apply* it to his daily life. To put it to use. "A child that went to church," on the other hand, is not someone who is fully integrated into the community. He's someone who is, as James puts it, "just going through the motions." As I moved through graduate school into the field, I, too, was transformed from someone who could make use of the information in the field (though at times, perhaps, just "going through the motions") to someone who could apply it and, I hope, begin even to add to it. We both gained some level of faith in our target communities of practice and the value sets and expertise they represent.

Orthodoxy. In every community of practice, some activities and utterances will be understood by members as "acceptable" ("orthodox") and others as absolutely unacceptable ("unorthodox" or even "heretical"). This is no less true in faith-based communities than it is in academic ones. Consider the following definition of evangelism, this one offered by Mona:

> A myriad of beliefs and, subsequently, subgroups abound within the vaguely defined borders of Evangelical Christianity, however the expected beliefs are those espoused by the largest protestant denomination in America. These views are touted by Christian programs, held as mainstays by the political activist Christian groups, and echoed by grassroots Christians in the workplace. It is these views to which you must hold or at least not contradict if you are to be considered a "literate" member of the mainstream Evangelical movement.

We can, I hope, see many similarities between this articulation of "Evangelical Christian literacy" and the various disciplines in the academic community. For example, if I'm to be accepted as a "literate member" of the communities of practice that make up composition studies, I must "hold or at least not contradict" the views dominating current composition scholarship (unless I have a darn convincing reason for doing otherwise, which can be risky). Within the "vaguely defined borders" of composition studies, the subgroups to which I "belong" (writing center studies, basic writing studies) have their own standards, by which they identify members; in writing center studies, for example, such standards are usually based on, among other things, a core belief in the importance of one-on-one teaching. Anything counter to such writing center "orthodoxy" may be considered "heretical"—not, in Lorraine Code's words, "heard, understood, taken seriously" (xi), or at least not very easily.

According to Pollard, "[e]very community must have [orthodoxy and heresy] in order to be a community" (21). Sometimes the unorthodox, even the heretical, are completely aware of the "crucial loyalties, values, beliefs, and standards" maintained and reproduced in a particular community of practice. Yet they choose to violate them anyway. More often, however, the heretical behavior is not chosen but accidental. Alex included biblical evidence in her personal opinion paper and was punished for it. She removed the biblical materials and turned it in again and was rewarded for it. In many academic environments, she learned, the Bible is considered a heretical text. Orthodox behavior is determined by the communities of practice that validate, model, reproduce, and sustain it.

But how are we to give students like James some control over this environment, so that they don't commit heretical acts within this community of practice that considers the Bible heretical yet aren't required to give up that Bible entirely as their "primary sense of selfhood"? To this question, I now return.

Rhetorical Dexterity

During the semester in which James was enrolled, the basic writing curriculum asked students to think of literacy in terms more social than alphabetic.[14] It did not, however, ask students to examine the very specific ways in which literacy manifests itself in different communities of practice. By reading and responding to things like J. Elspeth Stuckey's *The Violence of Literacy* and Deborah Brandt's "Sponsors of Literacy," I asked students that semester to consider the ways in which literacy is often unfair; sanctioned and endorsed by those more powerful than us; and even at times "violent." I did not, however, ask them to articulate the shape and function of literacy in a community of practice with which they were familiar (e.g., James's Christian literacy), nor did I ask them to compare and contrast this literacy with a less familiar one (like those sanctioned and endorsed by various facets of the academy). In other words, I did not employ a pedagogy of rhetorical dexterity. If I had, perhaps James would have developed a better understanding of how he might make use of the tensions between his religious faith and the ways of knowing, being, and communicating perpetuated in much of the academic discourse he's expected to value and imitate.

A pedagogy of rhetorical dexterity would have encouraged James to investigate the "rhetorical spaces" of the communities of practice that shape his biblical worldview. According to Code, "rhetorical spaces" are "fictive but not fanciful locations whose (tacit, rarely spoken) territorial imperatives structure [. . .] and limit the kinds of utterances that can be voiced within them with a reasonable expectation of uptake and 'choral support'; an expectation of being heard, understood, taken seriously" (ix). A pedagogy of rhetorical dexterity would have guided James in articulating the "(tacit, rarely spoken) territorial imperatives" that separate those who "feel" it (a "churchly child"/the Christian-literate) from those who do not, likely by asking him questions like these: What does it meant to be a "churchly child" and how did you come to understand the valued status of the "churchly child" within the context under investigation? What are the "territorial imperatives" within this community of practice? That is, what are the "rules" that govern what one should or should not say, think, or feel in this context, as well as how one must behave, dress, and carry oneself in order to be considered a "churchly child" rather than merely "a child that goes to church"? How is membership in this context expressed? What strategies must one use to be "heard, understood, taken seriously" within this community of practice? In other words, what strategies or ways of being mark some children as "churchly" and others as children who just "go to church"? What can we learn from the fact that your faith tradition—according to you—calls members of the church "God's children"? What kinds of things did you have to do before you could consider yourself Christian-literate? What should the long-term goals of literate members be, as determined by what this community of practice finds valuable and possible? How does an incoming member know when he or she has reached these goals? What might you have to learn, recognize, and embody in the academy before you may be able to feel literate as a writer and reader in various school-based contexts, too?

By treating academic literacies as a dynamic sign system and academic discourse as an experience in overlapping communities of practice, I might have taught James to develop the flexibility and awareness he needed to negotiate the increasingly complex literacy contexts he might encounter throughout his college career, without sacrificing that "primary sense of selfhood" he derived from his Bible. Instead, I merely (though unknowingly) perpetuated the singular, "autonomous" model of literacy (Street) that I thought we had been resisting all along.

Keeping Close to Home

James was a student in our basic writing program more than two years ago. The following term, I began developing a curricular model based on a then-quite-vaguely defined pedagogy of rhetorical dexterity—first as the graduate-level course in which Mona and Alex were enrolled,[15] then as the curricular model for our basic writing program (and now as the theoretical framework for our new textbook *Literacies in Context* [Carter], designed for the second semester of first-year composition). It was not until the current term, however, that I was able to begin to make more direct use of rhetorical dexterity in the ways I wished I had been able to with James.

By the time Keneshia entered our basic writing program (August 2006), I had begun to develop a much better understanding of why so many of our basic writing students—despite our best efforts and an extensive focus on literacy as a social practice (the course theme)—continued to define literacy in terms much more in keeping with the autonomous model we were attempting to resist. It is this autonomous model— literacy as universal, portable skill-set and/or content—that led to the difficulties Alex, Mona, and James experienced in their attempts to integrate the Bible into academic communities. It was the autonomous model that may have led James to begin relying on his Bible less and less often.

The Pentecostal church in which Keneshia grew up is a close-knit one that functions as her "home" church in every sense of the word. Pastor Osborne is, according to Keneshia, "like my grandmother because she's always been there. [I] feel like I can really talk to her, [especially since] my real grandmother died." In fact, Pastor Osborne and her family were key fixtures in the Temple of God long before Keneshia was even born. Keneshia's mother grew up with the pastor's three daughters, the youngest of whom is Keneshia's godmother and all of whom (now with their own children) remain members of the church. For Keneshia, her church isn't just "like a family"; it is her family—literally and practically. They pray together, worship together, and play together; they spend their holidays together and eat many a meal together. "Every *body* in the church," Keneshia explains (quoting her Pastor) "is the body of the church. [. . .] We have unity at our church. [We are] 'loose knit individual believers that are equipped, ready, and trained to yield to God (L.I.B.E.R.T.Y.).' We even have a banner that says that!"

According to Keneshia, her choice to describe her church (as a familiar "community of practice"[16]) in her second formal essay written for our class stemmed from "the way you described how you felt when you went to that church last summer." About two weeks before the fall semester began, I had visited an evangelical church within the same part of Dallas where Keneshia's home church is located (a high-crime and poorer area of the city). This one (True Love Baptist Church) was the home church of one of the inmates involved with a prison literacy program I'm researching, and while I knew a little bit about the way this church might function (mainly from my reading of Beverly Moss's work), my functional illiteracies in this community of practice were apparent from the minute I walked through the door. I was at once illiterate and completely in awe. It was a beautiful service—quite different from anything I'd ever experienced before or since. Overwhelming and powerful. Still, I felt uncomfortable throughout much of it as I was utterly aware of my lack of belonging (despite the warmth with which I was welcomed by church members). I didn't know what I was doing. My clothing was too neutral (the colors worn by the members of this church were vibrant and alive), my knowledge of the Gospel lyrics sung was absolutely nonexistent (the songs were, almost without fail, sung without any reference to the hymnals tucked into the back of each church pew), and the seemingly spontaneous fainting, random screams, and crying exhibited by a few members of both the choir and the congregation (what I would later learn was called "being filled with the Spirit") confused me. As I've already noted, most of my experiences in church-based communities of practice have been Catholic. For me, services have been scripted (whereas True Love Baptist appears to be largely spontaneous though guided by the church bulletin read to congregants at the beginning of the service). For me, parishioners sit quietly and very still unless called upon by the priest, as scripted in the Missalette, to kneel or stand (whereas True Love Baptist members wave their hands about, close their eyes, cry out with "Thank you, Jesus" and "Tell it, Preacher! Amen!" and even at times move into the aisle, becoming even more animated as they become "filled with the Holy Spirit").

In that second writing assignment (entitled "What Makes Christianity Significant?"), Keneshia introduces her readers to her own very familiar, church-based community of practice by showing those of us unfamiliar with it what we would see were we to enter her church. In order to do this, she takes on the persona of an outsider entering the "Temple of God" for the first time:

> When we finally arrived at church I walked into the building looking around noticing all these amazing colorful hats that the lady's had on. Some were big, small, round, and even tall. I thought it was one of the amazing things I had seen in my life, then I looked at my grandmother as she begin to put her hands in the air so did I[.] [While] doing that, I looked up into the air as if I felt their were angels looking down up on me. As I looked out I seen people everywhere throwing there hair all over the place, running as well, and some were even yelling out Lord I thank you.

Perhaps even more interesting and important, however, were the moves Keneshia makes or fails to make to help her uninformed readers begin to understand "the rules and commandments of being in church." As she explains, "We all need beliefs [. . .] because they make some of us the people we have grown to be today." In this early draft of her second writing assignment, Keneshia offers an extensive quotation (labeled "Exodus 20: 1–17") as evidence ("[f]or instances") in support of her beliefs.

The problem here, of course, is one of conflicting communities of practice. Keneshia offers this extensive quotation, yet she fails to unpack it for readers who do not, like her and her church family, "live inside the Bible." For me, the familiarity that resonates from Exodus 20 as quoted in her paper ("I am the Lord your God [. . .]. Ye shall have no other gods before me. [. . .] [F]or I, the Lord your God, am a jealous God [. . .]. [. . .] Remember the Sabbath Day, to keep it holy. [. . .] [T]he Seventh Day [. . .] you shall not work [. . .]") are stories of intolerance and the Blue Laws I witnessed when I first arrived in Texas back in the late 1970s. For this reader, the long quotation Keneshia includes means something very different from what it means to her and other members of this faith tradition.

My feedback on this early draft included the following:

> Ambitious and so very interesting, Keneshia! I'm particularly intrigued by the ways in which you set your grandmother up as your guide into this community of practice. Powerful moment as we step into church with you and notice all those "amazing, colorful hats." Then you move into the "Rules and Commandments" for Christianity in general and a long quote from the Bible, which, while I'm sure quite relevant, takes us out of the game of articulating the ways in which literacy in this particular community of practice might play itself out. In revision, I'd like [. . .] [for you to] show us how these "rules" as outlined in Exodus might play themselves out in your church. For instance, what value sets and literacies might a literate churchgoer display by wearing a big, round, "colorful hat"? "put[ting] her hands in the air"? "throwing their hair all over the place"? "running"? "yelling out"? In other words, reread this scene for us so we can learn how literate behavior manifests itself in this community of practice (and why).

This was certainly difficult for Keneshia, and I expected it would be because it forced upon her levels of critical consciousness only available to us after "reading our world" in the ways Paulo Freire tells us we must. I see in Keneshia's notes on this draft in preparation for her revision the word "change" written above "Exodus 20: 1–17," which may have been a suggestion to herself to either "change" (revise) the way she deals with the quotation and/or "change" the scripture used to describe the church behavior she illustrates. Ultimately, she chose to change the scripture itself, first to something from the Book of Matthew (as indicated by her bracketing of the long quotation from Exodus followed by the word "Matt."). In her next and subsequent drafts of this essay (completed near midterm and again near the end of the term), Keneshia decided to go with Psalms 100.1–4: "Make a joyful noise unto the Lord [. . .]. Serve the Lord with gladness: come before his presence with singing [. . .]." As she explains, "[A]ll of these things we portray as Christians in my church. When entering the house of the Lord in my church, we do actually what it is said 'making a joyful noise unto the Lord,' just thanking him for waking us up to see another day. After we enter in, we have morning worship serving the Lord with gladness letting [Him] know that we give Him the entire honor and praise. Then we stand up and tell how the Lord has blessed us in our life."

Here we can begin to understand how the shape and function of the church might be informed by, among other things, this passage from the Book that makes up the core guidance in this community of practice. We see that the "joyful noise"—as instructed—begins with "morning worship" and that the key activity reproduced in that "morning worship" is "praise," "honor," and "gladness." However, it is still unclear to outsiders how this giving of "praise," "honor", and "gladness" might function—in other words, what does this literate behavior actually *look* like? From my single experience in a church that appears to function in ways somewhat similar to Keneshia's church (though True Love is Baptist and Keneshia's church is Pentecostal), I can begin to imagine that the behavior takes the form of high energy, laughter, loud music, and what members of the church call "praise dancing." These are exactly the same things Keneshia began to describe in her later draft, drawing parallels between the "freestyling" she did to prepare for her writing assignments (freewriting in her journal and her notes) and the "freestyling" she did to develop the "praise dances" she performed at her church. As she explains, these "praise dances" had to "come from the heart"; she had to "feel" the dance rather than think too much about it, for otherwise it wouldn't be "honest" (what's "honest" "honors Jesus"). Likewise, she had to "feel" what she wanted to say in her essays and in her journals rather than "think too much about it"; otherwise she'd be saying what she thought other people wanted to read rather than what she wanted to say. As Keneshia explains, "I like to keep it real."

Through all these drafts and face-to-face exchanges regarding her own faith-based community of practice and the academic ones she is attempting to enter, Keneshia developed ways to communicate across very different communities of practice (church-based and academic ones), attempting to make sense of her own Christian literacies in terms legible and accessible to those much less literate in Christianity as it manifests itself in evangelical churches like her own. But she also developed the "Christian mind" that evangelical scholars like Mark Noll, Rick Nanez, and J. Budziszewski (among others) tell us is the "good Christian's" responsibility. Perhaps by developing a deeper awareness of the various ways in which the Bible itself informs Christian literacy and the terms by which these faith-based activities are validated and reproduced, Keneshia is now in a better position to support her own faith- and Bible-based ways of knowing in communities of practice that may remain hostile to them. Perhaps these principles and the "Christian mind" she developed from them helped her better understand and begin to make use of an ideological model of literacy—treating secular and Bible-based literacies as situated, contextualized, place-based, people-oriented events. The ubiquitous autonomous model, on the other hand, would treat literacy as singular and, perhaps at some point, make her Bible-based ways of knowing seem as irrelevant to her as they appear to many of us representing university-based communities of practice (something we absolutely want to avoid). In any case, developing a deeper understanding of the way literacy lives in a particular context—among the people who reproduce themselves through a particular set of literate practices (time-based, situation-based, agent-based)—might enable Keneshia to develop the flexibility she'll need to negotiate the multiple, rapidly changing literacies she's likely to encounter beyond the overlapping communities of practice that made up her basic writing experience.

Notes

[1] Of course an evangelical Christian is not necessarily a political conservative. Liberal, very progressive movements are actually surprisingly common among the communities of practice identified as "evangelical." For me, the most intriguing of these progressive evangelical movements is *Sojourners/ Call to Renewal*, a Christian ministry with a stated mission "to articulate the biblical call to social justice, inspiring hope and building a movement to transform individuals, communities, the church, and the world" ("Mission").

[2] It may also be significant that I am a fallen-away Catholic suffering from a somewhat unhealthy relationship with my own religious past and, perhaps, my deeply religious extended family (while I was growing up, my nuclear family was not very religious).

[3] Please see the description of this pedagogy of rhetorical dexterity in my forthcoming book *The Way Literacy Lives: Rhetorical Dexterity and the "Basic" Writer* and article "Redefining Literacy as a Social Practice."

[4] As Maryann Whitaker, a devout Christian and current graduate student in our program, explained to me after reviewing a previous version of this article, only God can "convert" the listener, "not the evangelical."

[5] Jacqueline Jones Royster calls discourse a "people-centered enterprise." As she reminds us, "all language use [. . .] is an invention of a particular social milieu, not a natural phenomenon" (21). In other words, "discourses operate at the hands and the will of a *people*, rather than instruments or forces of nature" (25, emphasis in original).

[6] I am grateful for the many individuals who have been willing to share their insider perspectives from within the community of practice that is evangelical Christianity, especially Maryann Whitaker, a master's student at A&M–Commerce, Chandra Lewis-Qualls, an instructor at Abilene Christian University, and Keneshia Coleman, a basic writing student at A&M–Commerce.

[7] "Go ye therefore, and make disciples of all the nations, baptizing them into the name of the Father and of the Son and of the Holy Spirit: teaching them to observe all things whatsoever I commanded you: and lo, I am with you always, even unto the end of the world" (Matt. 28.19–20).

[8] Maryann Whitaker argues that it is not the evangelical who "converts" the "nonbeliever." Thus, rather than a "converted believer," "the output would be the communicated Word." In that "communication" of "the Word," however, as other evangelicals have suggested, God converts the believer. According to this line of argument, that very conversion is what confirms that "the Word" has been successfully communicated. The disconnect here brings to the surface the nuanced ways Bible-believing communities understand the rhetorical effects of "testimonial" in enacting "the Great Commission."

⁹Colorado Springs is quickly becoming a "headquarters" of sorts for conservative evangelical organizations, including James Dobson's Focus on the Family, among others.

¹⁰Leif Utne describes a similar movement in left-wing circles whereby "[i]n their fight to catch up with the right, progressives are sending their young to boot camp."

¹¹A flurry of calls and letters protesting this characterization forced the *Post* to issue a correction, noting simply, "There is no factual basis for that statement."

¹²Though it may seem counterintuitive to use a Catholic priest's words to represent ways our evangelical students might locate points of contact between their faith and the tacit expectations of the academy, I do so here for at least two reasons. The first is that the dissonance Pollard experiences between the academy and his faith seems quite comparable to the ways in which a number of evangelicals are describing this disconnect. The second is that, according to Mark Noll, Catholic leaders are beginning to join forces with evangelical leaders—a partnership he applauds.

¹³It is also important to note that Pollard views the community of Christians as "unique" and chosen by God; thus communities of practice that conflict with this Christian worldview are to be tolerated but understood as wrong and ultimately in need of saving.

¹⁴I describe this curriculum and the assignments as I've designed them in Chapter 3 of the forthcoming book *The Way Literacy Lives: Rhetorical Dexterity and the "Basic" Writer.*

¹⁵In the graduate-level course, we read several ethnographic studies designed to expand this concept of rhetorical dexterity beyond basic writers and their teachers to include society at large.

¹⁶Their second writing assignment was a "formal essay about the 'rules' and expectations governing 'literate' practices in a community of practice beyond those directly associated with school" (see http://faculty.tamu-commerce.edu/scarter/teaching.htm for additional information about this sequence, including copies of the writing assignments).

WORKS CITED

Anderson, Chris. "The Description of an Embarrassment: When Students Write about Religion." *Balancing Acts: Essays on the Teaching of Writing in Honor of William F. Irmscher.* Carbondale: Southern Illinois UP, 1991. 19–28.

Anderson, Paul M. "Introduction: This We Proclaim." *Professors Who Believe: The Spiritual Journeys of Christian Faculty.* Ed. Anderson. Downers Grove, IL: InterVarsity, 1998. 11–14.

Ault, James M. *Spirit and Flesh: Life in a Fundamentalist Baptist Church.* New York: Knopf, 2004.

Barnett, Thomas. "Faith Camp." *Chronicle of Higher Education* 23 Sept. 2005: A44–A46.

Blamires, Harry. *The Christian Mind: How Should a Christian Think?* Vancouver, BC: Regent, 2005.

Brandt, Deborah. "Accumulating Literacy: Writing and Learning to Write in the Twentieth Century." *College English* 57 (1995): 649–68.

———. "Sponsors of Literacy." *CCC* 49 (1998): 165–85.

Budziszewski, J. "Overcoming the Scandal of the Christian Mind." Rev. of *How Now Shall We Live?* by Charles Colson and Nancy Pearcey. *First Things* 100 (Feb. 2000): 52–56. 25 Apr. 2006 http://www.arn.org/docs/pearcey/np_ftbudziszewski0200.htm.

Carter, Shannon. "Redefining Literacy as a Social Practice." *Journal of Basic Writing,* #25 (Fall 2006): 94–125.

———. *The Way Literacy Lives: Rhetorical Dexterity and the "Basic" Writer.* Albany: SUNY P, March 2008

———, ed. *Literacies in Context.* Southlake, TX: Fountainhead, 2007.

Code, Lorraine. *Rhetorical Spaces: Essays on Gendered Locations.* New York: Routledge, 1995.

Coleman, Robert Emerson. *The Master Plan of Evangelism.* 2nd ed. Old Tappan, NJ: Revell, 1994. "Correction." *Washington Post.* 2 February 1993: D3.

Freire, Paulo. *Pedagogy of the Oppressed.* Trans. Myra Bergman Ramos. New York: Seabury, 1973.

Garrison, Charles E. *Two Different Worlds: Christian Absolutes and the Relativism of Social Science.* Newark: U of Delaware P, 1988.

Gee, James Paul. *What Video Games Have to Teach Us about Learning and Literacy.* New York: Palgrave, 2004.

Goodburn, Amy. "It's a Question of Faith: Discourses of Fundamentalism and Critical Pedagogy in the Writing Classroom." *JAC* (1998): 333–53.

"The Great Commission." *All about God Ministries, Inc.* 2 May 2006 http://www.allaboutjesuschrist.org/the-great-commission.htm.

Guinness, Os. *Fit Bodies, Fat Minds: Why Evangelicals Don't Think and What to Do about It.* Grand Rapids, MI: Baker, 1994.

Hofstadter, Richard. *Anti-Intellectualism in American Life.* New York: Vintage, 1962.

Jost, John T., Jack Glaser, Arie W. Kruglanski, and Frank J. Sulloway. "Political Conservatism as Motivated Social Cognition." *Psychological Bulletin* 129 (2003): 339–75. 11 Apr. 2006 http://www.wam.umd.edu/~hannahk/bulletin.pdf.

Kintz, Linda. *Between Jesus and the Market: The Emotions That Matter in Right-Wing America.* Durham, NC: Duke UP, 1997.

Lave, Jean, and Etienne Wenger. *Situated Learning: Legitimate Peripheral Participation.* New York: Cambridge UP, 1991.

Lewis, C. S. *Mere Christianity.* New York: Macmillan, 1952.

Limbaugh, Rush. "How to Deal with a Liberal Teacher." *Rush-Online.com.* 21 Feb. 2007 <http://www.rushonline.com/topics/r18htm>.

Luo, Michael. "Big Tent Religion: Evangelicals Debate the Meaning of 'Evangelical.'" *New York Times* Week in Review 16 Apr. 2006: 5.

Marsden, George. "The Sword of the Lord: How 'Otherwordly' Fundamentalism Became a Political Power." *Books and Culture: A Christian Review* Mar./Apr. 2006. 30 Apr. 2006 http://www.christianitytoday.com/bc/2006/002/3.10.html.

"Mission." *Sojourners/Call to Renewal.* 27 Feb. 2007 <http://www.sojo.net/index.cfm?action=about_us.mission>.

"Mission Statement." *Summit Ministries.* 25 Apr. 2006 http://www.summit.org/about/mission/.

Moss, Beverly. "Creating a Community: Literacy Events in African-American Churches." *Literacy across Communities.* Ed. Moss. Cresskill NJ: Hampton, 1994. 147–68.

Nanez, Rick M. *Full Gospel, Fractured Minds? A Call to Use God's Gift of the Intellect.* Grand Rapids, MI: Zondervan, 2006.

Newbigin, Lesslie. *Truth to Tell: The Gospel as Public Truth.* Grand Rapids, MI: Eerdmans, 1991.

Noll, Mark. *The Scandal of the Evangelical Mind.* Grand Rapids, MI: Eerdmans, 1995.

Perkins, Priscilla. "'A Radical Conversion of the Mind': Fundamentalism, Hermeneutics, and the Metanoic Classroom." *College English* 63 (2001): 585–611.

Perry, William. *Forms of Intellectual and Ethical Development in the College Years: A Scheme.* New York: Harcourt, 1968.

Pollard, William G. *Physicist and Christian: A Dialogue between the Communities.* Greenwich, CT: Seabury, 1961.

Rand, Lizabeth A. "Enacting Faith: Evangelical Discourse and the Discipline of Composition Studies." *CCC* 52 (2001): 349–67.

Royster, Jacqueline Jones. "Academic Discourses or Small Boats on a Big Sea." *AltDis: Alternative Discourses in the Academy.* Ed. Christopher Schroeder, Helen Fox, and Patricia Bizzell. Portsmouth, NH: Boynton, 2002. 23-30.

Schilling, Harold K. "A Human Enterprise." *Science* June 1958: 1324–27.

Sojourners: Christians for Justice and Peace. 3 May 2006 http://www.sojo.net.

Street, Brian V. "Recent Applications of New Literacy Studies in Educational Contexts." *Research in the Teaching of English* 39 (2005): 417–23.

Stuckey, J. Elspeth. *The Violence of Literacy.* Portsmouth, NH: Boynton, 1990.

Taylor, Charles. *Sources of the Self: The Making of the Modern Identity.* Cambridge, MA: Harvard UP, 1989.

Thomas, Cal. "God, Satan, and the Media." 5 Mar. 2003. 26 Apr. 2006 http://www.townhall.com/columnists/CalThomas/2003/03/05/god,_satan,_and_the_media.

Utne, Leif. "Training the Left to Win." *Utne Magazine* July/Aug. 2006. 19 Dec. 2006 http://www.utne.com/issues/2006_136/promo/12171-1.html.

Vander Lei, Elizabeth. "Coming to Terms with Religious Faith in the Composition Classroom: Introductory Comments." *Negotiating Religious Faith in the Composition Classroom.* Ed. Vander Lei and Bonnie Lenore Kyburz. Portsmouth, NH: Boynton, 2005. 1–10.

Weisskopf, Michael. "Energized by Pulpit or Passion, the Public Is Calling: 'Gospel Grapevine' Displays Strength in Controversy over Military Gay Ban." *Washington Post* 1 Feb. 1993: A1.

NOW THAT YOU'VE READ

1. Where do you see Carter working to respectfully express her concerns while expressing her students' positions?

2. What are some of the challenges to balancing tolerance with strongly held beliefs for the teacher? For the students?

3. What does "rhetorical dexterity" mean? How do you see it demonstrated in the essay?

4. How does Carter make use of her students' experiences and writings? Which are most effective? Why?

5. What conclusions does Carter draw? What conclusions do you draw?

6. What might you add about how to ensure respectful communication in the classroom?

WRITING ASSIGNMENT
EXPANDING LITERACY

In the reading we've done so far, we've been examining the ways language uses and literacy practices mark us as members of our communities and how some of those practices are less valued than others.

For this project (which can be a 3-4 page essay or a suitable equivalent*), please make use of your reading to reflect on how literacy practices we employ at home, at school, at work, and with friends shift according to the setting and context. In what situations are you most aware of how you're using language? In what situations are you most likely to try out new ways of using language? How do Green, Carter, and Pritchard help you deepen your analysis?

*NOTE: As you think of your literacy practices, you might choose to develop a project in a non-essay genre that represents these literacy practices and settings. We encourage this type of project that pushes the boundaries of how literacy is represented and used in your own lives. For example, how might you include Twitter posts? Social media examples? Writing in different languages? Visual artifacts? Comics? Innovate!

Please quote from some of the reading you've done, and please provide a meaningful title.

What We'll Be Looking For:

- Is your project engaging? Does it represent a nuanced and specific (rather than vague and abstract) understanding of literacy?
- Does your project show a variety of literacy practices across settings and contexts?
- Does your project present a simplistic view of literacy or does it grapple with possibilities, contradictions, and the nuances within these contexts?
- Does your project push the boundaries of academic writing to include multiple types of literacy practices?
- Do you engage with the readings, conversations, and activities from class in meaningful ways?

READING

So Black, I'm Blue

Vershawn Ashanti Young

BEFORE YOU READ answer the following questions:

1. What do you think the title might mean?

2. In this piece, Young talks about the "burden of racial performance" and how we *perform* identity (207). How would you describe your interactions with your family? Can you describe how you perform this identity? Does it differ from how you perform identity with other groups?

So Black, I'm Blue

Vershawn Ashanti Young

"White people don't know how to tell the difference between one black man and another," writes comedian Chris Rock in his book *Rock This!* "If they could, we'd all get along" (1997, 11). So Rock declares, "I love black people, but I hate niggers." For he believes that if whites could distinguish good blacks from bad ones, everything would be okay. We'd finally be able to determine which blacks to eliminate because, as Rock says, "the niggers have got to go" (17). Apparently, some whites agree. In Nella Larsen's *Passing,* John Bellew presents an earlier version of Rock's quip when he teases his wife, Clare. "She was as... white as a lily," he says. "But I declare she's gettin' darker and darker. I tell her if she don't look out, she'll wake up one these days and find she's turned into a nigger" (1997, 39). Both jokesters get laughs but are duped by the paradox they spin. Bellew learns that his wife really is a nigger. And Rock must answer, What am I?

Rock thus reproduces for himself what I call the burden of racial performance, the demand to prove what type of black person you are. It's a burden all blacks bear, and it is the core of the problem of black racial authenticity. It is the modern variant, I argue, of racial passing, making Bellew's racial distinction archetypal of Rock's performative differentiation.[1] Further, this burden not only supports racial discord between whites and blacks but provokes blacks to abhor other blacks, causing Rock to exclaim, "it's like our own personal civil war." This conflict, however, is not only interpersonal, as it is presented in Rock's example: "Every time black people want to have a good time . . . some ignorant ass niggers [are present,] fucking it up . . . Can't go to the movies first week it opens. Why? Because niggers are shooting at the screen" (1997, 17). It's also intrapersonal as I describe in a crack of my own, in a poem I've titled "shiny."

> as dark as i am and tryin' to pass
> somebody needs to kick my black ass
> for using proper english all the time
> when the rest o' my family's spittin' rhyme
> dressin' all prepy, talkin' all white,
> somebody tell me this ain't right

my skin so black folks think maybe it's blue;
who am i foolin', Two Eyes? Cain't be you
I wash and scrub and cosmetically bleach
but this doggone pigment just won't leach
so tryin' to be white ain't working at all,
since the only attention I get is in the mall
when heads turn to see the nigga with the silver dollar tongue
wondering, who dat talking deep from the diaphragm and lung?

as dark as i am and tryin' to pass
somebody really needs to kick my black ass
for walking like a white man with my rear end tight
but when someone calls me stuffy I'm ready to fight
do I bring it on myself with highfalutin' ways
livin' like whitey did in the brady bunch days?

i been walkin' so long down the other culture's path
that i'm gone need me a little nigga momma wrath
to kick my butt and do it good
the way a nigga momma should
for me paradin' 'round as white
when my skin is shiny as night
as black as I am and tryin' to pass
somebody pleeease kick my black ass

Thus my interest in this essay is not only in analyzing a literary problem but in helping to solve a social—even a personal—one.

"Sugaaarrr!" My sister Cookie screamed the half of my nickname that I can't shake. It was my turn to dance a jig, sing a tune, something to entertain the mostly women and kids who gathered in the living room of my apartment. My brothers, male cousins, and brothers-in-law were in the kitchen. I was there, too, trying to bond with them, participating in the men-talk they found so enjoyable and that I decided I no longer would avoid. "Sugar Bear!" She wasted no time calling again, this time using my full nickname—the version I like better since "Sugar" alone signifies so much of the effeminacy I hate. Cookie was the only person, family or friend, who was always careful to call me either by my full nick-name or just "Bear," rarely only "Sugar"— because "Bear" didn't so easily instigate the taunts that calling me "Sugar" did. "He got sugar in his tank," they used to say as a matter of fact, grownups and kids alike. "He a little sweet, ain't he?" they'd ask my family, mostly my brothers, as if I couldn't hear or answer back, as if I'd tell them I wasn't, which they presumed was a lie.

"Hold your panties," I told Cookie, trying to sound cool, or at least to get a laugh from one of the guys. But they seemed not to notice. So I just unfolded the paper that I had in my back pocket, waving it as I walked to the living room to indicate that I was doing a reading for my performance, not the modern dance routine that I used to do as my sister Y'shanda sang a Phyllis Hyman or Anita Baker tune in the background after we'd argue about who should be in front—the singer or the dancer. I gave that up at eleven after our last duet at a family reunion or some occasion like that. I had practiced until my routine was perfect, complete with a high kick, twirl, and a frozen pose in the fifth position at the end, with only my fingers moving, wiggling back and forth to affect leaves blowing in the wind. When Tyrone, a proud homosexual, the cousin of somebody's girlfriend, saw my routine, he took it as his cue to out dance me and everyone else at the party with even higher kicks, backbends, and Alvin Ailey leaps. My family egged on a challenge, even though they knew I couldn't outdance Tyrone. Afterward, Tyrone tried to talk to me, pointing out this and that technique, giving me advice about dancing, since he was professionally trained. But I ignored him, because during the competition when the disco tempo thumped, Tyrone launched into his jazz dance version of *Swan Lake*. And in between the crowd's "You go, boys," their "Hit its" and "Show 'em what cha gots," I heard "Look at that fag" and "Ain't that just like a sissy?" And since I couldn't tell which one of us they were talking about, I pretended to be tired and panted on the sidelines so it wouldn't be me. Tyrone kept right on going, and I admired him, even though I decided right then and there that I wouldn't be caught dead dancing like that again. I didn't want my family to see me as a Tyrone type of person.

After that I limited my performances to lip-synch routines—until that too lost its appeal when I first went to a bar and there was a drag queen entertainer lip-synching for a living. I found out that a whole culture and lifestyle revolved around the performance genre and that it was mostly gay. So I never went there again and felt like I was progressing well and fast toward losing the faggot identity that seemed to follow me like a shadow or stick like gum at the bottom of my shoe. Just when I'd turn the corner or scrape it off and walk a few steps, there it was again. And I wasn't about to go conjuring it up—not in the living room of my own apartment, even if there really was no way to avoid it.

I'm reading a poem this year, I announced, clearing my throat—loudly—so if there were any objections I could pretend not to hear them. And I promptly began: "As dark I am and trying to pass."

They roared.

"Somebody needs to kick my black ass."

They howled.

My family, enjoying themselves, participated call-and-response style in the performance. They didn't care so much about the poem's scanty aesthetics, knowing that anyone of them could write one better. My cousin, an amateur rapper and singer, was one of the few men to watch me perform. He was the yearly neighborhood talent show winner; he performed his own material only because his "shit was better than what those jive-ass popular punks did for the white man," as he used to say. Afterwards he told me that my poem was off-key. He said it lacked rhythm, that the flow was rough and the language forced and that he'd show me how to fix it, though he never did, because he was home for only a short time, during a respite in between trial dates for a murder he said he didn't commit but refused to say who had—a gangbanger's code of ethics or something like that. But what he mostly liked, he told me, and what also seemed to delight the rest of the family was the man's repeated plea. Every time I got to the refrain, "Somebody needs to . . ." they'd chime in, as if on cue, "kick your black ass." They obviously saw themselves as the poem's community and I, to them, was the failing-to-pass-for-white, dark-skinned black man, who needed them to help him get his act together, so he could just be black.

I was inspired to write the poem one night as Marilyn, my sometimes too-white friend, and I talked on the phone. It was a year after I was let go from the nearly all-white school district where she was still teaching. Every weekend she'd call to tell me how much she hated teaching there, though I couldn't figure out why at first, since I used to see her as whiter than I could ever be because she never slipped into the blackness I know. I used to see her whiteness as authentic and mine as made-up, since I had to mold myself so that I could proficiently sound and act white; but she just grew up that way, in Tacoma, Washington, an area heavily populated by white people. Marilyn told me that she and her sister were often the only two blacks at the schools they attended. I met her sister, a fledgling novelist, in and out of college writing programs, younger and worse than Marilyn. Too white, some of my family members would say if they'd met her—Tiger Woods, Tyra Banks white.

Marilyn's sister didn't talk much about black issues or racial politics. She deemed them pointless and outdated and said so once when she was visiting and we all went to dinner. Marilyn and I started joking with each other about who talks the whitest. Her sister playfully rolled her eyes and said, "You guys, people are people." Marilyn and I laughed away our self-consciousness, feeling a little hypocritical, since we are usually the ones to preach her sister's words to others. But when we say it, we mean in the long run, not in the meantime. We know that in this America, even as we've progressed in racial politics, that some black people, some who can racially pass for white, still feel it necessary to do so. And some people—like the white wife of Anatole Broyard—still find it necessary to out them. In 1990 Broyard was a seventy-year-old, retired "erudite book reviewer for the *New York Times*," whose wife could no longer live a lie or at least she wasn't going to let her husband die with one. So days before he died, she told their college-aged children that their father had black racial heritage (Thadious Davis 1997, xxv). I wonder: if Broyard had been one-eighth Native American, a quarter French, or maybe even one third Moroccan, would his wife have been compelled to reveal that part of his secret—to disrupt at death the racial identity he'd chosen?

The literary critic Thadious Davis cites Broyard's experience in her introduction to Larsen's *Passing* as one example of "several recent public revelations of racial passing [that] have revived interest in and speculation about its motives and consequences" (1997, xxiii). The literary critic Mae Henderson suggests novels about racial passing "educate" readers "ethnographically about black life." She emphasizes that this "renewed interest" stems from "a more general preoccupation with notions of hybridity, biraciality, and social constructionism as they structure contemporary conceptions of personal and social identity" (2002, xx-xxi). In other words, we contemporary readers look to passing novels to help us understand the forces that shape our racial identities—both those ascribed to us and those we avow. Henderson is interested in such questions as, What does it mean to be mixed raced? And how does one with both black and white racial heritages reconcile these identities?

For me, though, these novels address a more fundamental question: Why must blacks still pass? Thadious Davis admits that the answer "is less easy to decipher in the wake of the civil rights movement . . . which led to changes in the legal system" (1997, xxiii). And while Henderson recognizes how central the phenomenon of passing is to ongoing discussions of black racial identity, like Davis, she cannot account for its endurance. But the anthropologist Signithia Fordham does.

Fordham argues that passing not only persists, but is required—not just of blacks with light skin and "good hair" but even of those with nappy hair, wide noses, and skin so black you think maybe it's blue. That is, if they want to achieve success in America's mainstream and elevate their class status.[2] This, of course, includes Marilyn and me. We both are striving to become financially secure, trying to achieve a solidly middle-class status by working in the most mainstream of America's institutions—school—as English teachers, no less. And we both have to do this with our dark skin and kinky hair. But these physical traits don't matter, and it's good for Marilyn and me that they don't, since we could never literally look white. For us, then, "becoming white is not *the* issue" (Fordham 1996, 23). "Acting white" or "looking white on paper—behaving in ways and displaying the skills, abilities, and credentials that were traditionally associated with White Americans"—is what matters because acting white, Fordham stresses, "became the way to pass" after legal discrimination (44).

Fordham's account explains why Marilyn's sister believes that people are just people. As Fordham acknowledges, "acting white is . . . unavoidable," an "inescapable outcome of American citizenship" and "American schooling" (1996, 23). Marilyn's sister may believe that Marilyn and I don't really talk white, that we talk and act American, behaving in ways common to educated people. Her attitude is the result of what linguist Rosina Lippi-Green points out as "a general unwillingness to accept the speakers of [Black English] and the social choices they have made as viable and functional. Instead we relegate their experiences and capabilities to spheres which are secondary and out of the public eye" (1997, 201). Marilyn's sister refuses to acknowledge the language and cultural differences between blacks and whites, as well as people's negative perceptions about black culture. I believe that, like so many others who hold these views, she wants to excise Black English speakers from the public eye. But even if she doesn't wish to make them invisible, she likely thinks that they experience the problems they do because of their resistance to Americanization. But she's ignoring what Fordham calls the "subtle limitations" of assimilation. In other words, even though Marilyn and I have taken so much advantage of the American dream that we act white in our sleep, we face obstacles that whites don't. And we recognize these limitations in the lives of our black students, particularly when they insist upon using Black English. That's why we haven't completely chosen to pass as Marilyn's sister has—although we understand that she does it because the psycho-emotional pain of negotiating two cultural/racial worlds is far too great for many. For this same reason, we understand why there are those, like some of our students, who refuse to pass.

Reflecting on the decision he made to pass for white, the Ex-Colored Man in James Weldon Johnson's *The Autobiography of an Ex-Colored Man* (1912) expresses regret, saying: "I feel that I have been a coward, a deserter, and I am possessed by a strange longing for my mother's people" (1995, 99). And, although he says, "My love for my children makes me glad that I am what I am" (100), "an ordinarily successful white man" (99), his gladness cannot replace his anxiety. "I cannot repress the thought," he laments as the novel closes, "that, after all, I have chosen the lesser part, that I have sold my birthright for a mess of pottage" (100). This suggests a simple resolution: If you're unhappy passing for white, just be black. But it's not that easy. In my poem, what my family consider to be my white ways have always been or have become just as much a part of me as my black ways. In order for me to be like my family, to return, as it were, to my community, I must not only stop acting white, I must learn how to be black. Because it's impossible for me to recuperate or acquire the necessary blackness, I'm subject to my family's incessant expressions of dissatisfaction.

Similarly, when the Ex-Colored Man announces that he wants "to go back to the very heart of the South, and live among the people," his white patron asks: "What kind of Negro would you make now?" The patron's question is prompted by his perception that the Ex-Colored Man is "by blood, by appearance, by education, and by tastes a white man" (67). It's not the Ex-Colored Man's white skin alone that makes him insufficiently black. What makes the patron exclaim that "this idea you have of making a Negro out of yourself is nothing more than a sentiment" (67) is his conviction that the Ex-Colored Man's behavior, the performance of his racial identity, is sufficiently white.

In *The Mis-Education of the Negro* (1933), Carter G. Woodson sustains the patron's view of whiteness as not only a racial classification but a behavioral one—one that makes it possible for a black man to act white. "When a Negro has finished his education in our schools," Woodson writes, "then, he has been equipped to begin the life of an Americanized or Europeanized white man" (1990, 5). Woodson believes that because of education some blacks inhabit an improper relation to less educated blacks and can therefore be of no assistance to them in their struggle for equality. An educated black person, without the proper consciousness, is no more to under privileged blacks than your average white man. It's precisely because the Ex-Colored Man's white behaviors are by no means limited to his accent or gait but extend to areas that he cannot manipulate, like education, that his efforts to be black seem futile.

The problem that the Ex-Colored Man and I both face is that we fail to measure up, in ways beyond our control, to what's considered by both whites and blacks to be authentic blackness. Because he has white skin, however, the Ex-Colored Man can escape blackness by completely passing for white—what his patron advises him to do. Passing today, however, no longer mandates that you look white. It requires instead that you be black but act white, erasing the requirement of racial concealment and stressing racial performance.

My poem, then, recasts the significance that Jim Crow placed on skin color with an emphasis on performance. It replaces the light-skinned black who passes by hiding his blackness with a dark-skinned black who passes by performing his whiteness. The danger in both cases is the danger of discovery, although what's discovered isn't exactly the same. In the classic Jim Crow passing saga, such as the *Autobiography*, what's discovered when you're pretending to be white is that you're really black. In my post-Jim Crow passing saga everybody already knows I'm black. My fear is that they'll discover that I'm *really* black—ghetto black, what Chris Rock calls a "nigger." And, of course, in both stories the threat of failure is accompanied by what may be worse—the threat of success. For if I can keep my ghetto blackness from being detected, a move that will keep me estranged from the black community, I risk the same lingering psychoemotional torment that the Ex-Colored Man must bemoan for life.

As another consequence of success the male passer's masculinity and sexuality are inevitably called into question. In his analysis of *Autobiography* Phillip Brian Harper claims the literary passing subject has what he calls a "feminine function," which magnifies the femininity of even male passing characters. This femininity is signified, according to Harper, by the Ex-Colored Man's white racial features. Since passing today involves not looking white but acting white, this femininity is pronounced not by looking white but by the passer's language and behaviors that are racialized as white.

As a boy, especially at that family party, I knew that if I wanted to become fully a part of my black community, to be accepted as black, I also had to comply with the gender behaviors appropriate for my race and sex. Although my poem doesn't explicitly address concepts of masculinity and sexuality that are chained to blackness, I didn't want to put myself at risk of being called a fag. So I read the poem that night in a hip-hop style, trying to connect myself to the more thuggish rap music genre wherein even women refer to each other as man. Thus the post-Jim Crow problem of passing is the drama that my poem presents—the project I know firsthand.

I was hoping that my family would see themselves in my poem—see the folly in the performances blacks are called to give in order to prove our blackness to one another and our whiteness to whites and sometimes our whiteness to blacks and our blackness to whites and how tangled up this gets—and how confusing and frustrating it is. So much so, that we'd go insane if we didn't prevent it, if we didn't choose to live as either a Resisting Black, embracing the performance of blackness while resisting whiteness, like some in my family do, or as a Passing Black, striving towards whiteness and repudiating blackness, as I sometimes do.

"Shuck 'em both," some say, "I'll just be me," trying to find some way to escape race, to keep from identifying themselves as this or that type of black. But they soon find that they have to turn somewhere, perform for some group, before they belong to none, like Leanita McClain, who grew up in a Chicago ghetto, in the Ida B. Wells housing projects. At only thirty-two years old, right at the height of a highly successful journalism career, she "took an overdose of a powerful antidepression medicine and went to sleep" (Page 1996, 49).

"I am burdened," she wrote, "with trying to prove to whites that blacks are a people." She was also burdened by her "brothers and sisters," blacks she knew in the hood, "many of [whom] have abandoned me," she said "because they think that I have abandoned them" (Page 1996, 48). She was called to perform her blackness to keep from becoming estranged, feeling alienated, from the community she felt she belonged to.

Ironically, performing her blackness for whites also made her the success that she was: "I assuage white guilt," she wrote, and "I prove to whites that Blacks are a people." Before she became the first black editorial board member of the *Chicago Tribune*, her blackness had landed her a place at Northwestern University's Medill School of Journalism. Medill wanted to train blacks to meet the media demand, not for light skinned blacks who were racially passing for white, who couldn't or didn't say they were black, but for blacks who were black, who said it and showed it.

They didn't want blacks who were too black, though; talking that black talk and acting black—not that kind of black. McClain's "liberal white acquaintances" didn't see her as that type of black anyway. "They pat me on the head," she said "hinting that I am freak," thinking she was nothing like those in the projects she came from. Because of that she asked the world: "When they attempt to sever me from my own, how can I live with myself?" (Page 1996, 48). McClain got entangled in this racial double bind, called to give one performance to whites and another to blacks. And, inevitably, she gave out, writing: "I will never live long enough to see my people free anyway" (49).

Because McClain was at least three decades removed from separate but unequal and more than one hundred years beyond emancipation from decimation, Chicago journalist Clarence Page, who writes about his ex-wife's suicide in his essay "Survivors' Guilt," believes she already had the freedom she wanted. "Looking back, I see with greater clarity the freedom Leanita had at her disposal, whether she was willing to realize it or not. She did not have to march for it, fight for it, or crusade for it. All she had to do was . . . accept it" (1996, 69).

Page swears that McClain and other middle-class blacks "refuse to see" the freedom that came after Jim Crow, when "anti-discrimination laws made class differences more important arbiters of opportunity than racial differences" (58). He warns that too "many of us compensate by identifying excessively with our less fortunate brethren left behind in the ghetto" (59). Page regards this identification as unnecessary, harmful even, since lower-class blacks post-Jim Crow are separated from middle-class blacks not by race (we're all still black) but by class (some of us are just not poor). Page's confidence in the progress of anti-discrimination stems from his comparison of the legal status of blacks before Jim Crow to black class mobility after Jim Crow. But class isn't the only, nor even the primary factor that Page uses to separate blacks.

"Showing your color," Page says, was the term parents used to foster "the success stories of [his] generation." It "was just another way to say," like Chris Rock, "don't behave like those Negroes, those loud, lazy, godless, shiftless, doo-rag wearing, good-for-nothings who hang out on the corner and get themselves into trouble" (59). Page fingers contemporary gangster rappers, "Ice T., Ice Cube and Snoop Doggy Dog," who glorify the black ghetto in their lyrics and style of dress as examples of the types of Negroes he was told not to be like and cautions black people against imitating today. It doesn't matter to Page that Ice T., Ice Cube, and Snoop Doggy Dog make more money than he does and clearly enjoy greater celebrity. The problem is that they show their color. By advocating that these gangsta rappers hide their color, Page is not saying that they should hide their race, something their dark skin prohibits. He is suggesting that they act white.

Just as the *Autobiography* depicts the Jim Crow project of passing as personified by the nameless protagonist, it predicts the post-Jim-Crow project too—embodied by another nameless character: the upper-middle-class black doctor whom the Ex-Colored Man befriends aboard a ship as they travel from Europe to the United States. The doctor invites the Ex-Colored Man to spend a few weeks with him in the Boston area. While sightseeing, the doctor points out a group of lower-class blacks that he describes in terms curiously similar to Page's depiction of those who show their color, as "those lazy, loafing, good-for-nothing darkies." The doctor says, "They're not worth digging graves for; yet they are the ones who create impressions of the race." He exclaims to the Ex-Colored Man: "We are the race, and the race ought to be judged by us, not by them" (J. Johnson 1995, 73). Because the doctor's skin is too dark to pass in the way the Ex-Colored Man can, he worries not about whether he should reveal or conceal the fact that he is black, but about what blackness is taken to be—how it is defined and by which blacks. The doctor thus transforms the class difference between middle- and lower-class blacks into a racial difference—which ones are truly black?

I argue, then, that the doctor prefigures Page's contempt for lower-class blacks and represents the central problem of black authenticity. Like Johnson's doctor, Page thinks it's the middle class that embodies the race. Like Snoopy Doggy Dog, Ice T., and Ice Cube, my family thinks that being middle class—or, rather, acting middle class—is a way of betraying the race. McClain, pulled in both directions, wanted to reconcile the problem within the race. But neither lower-class blacks (her brothers and sisters in the ghetto), middle-class blacks (Page), nor whites (her colleagues) would allow her to do that. They wanted her to choose—and to prove it through her performance. This is why McClain believed that she would never live to see her people free—because blacks cannot achieve freedom from the burdens of racial performance, unless race ceases to exist as a category of distinction or you die. Knowing the former would not come in her lifetime, McClain hastened the latter.

McClain's racial dilemma and her heroic end uncannily parallels Clare Kendry's in Larsen's *Passing*. In the concluding episode of the novel Clare's white husband forces his way into an all-black party she is attending and demands to know if she is "a damned dirty nigger" (1997, 111). Clare frees herself from her husband's demand, and by extension the unspoken demand of the black guests, to claim either her whiteness or her blackness over the other by going through a window. Thadious Davis writes that "were it not for the view of Clare's body" on the ground outside, Clare's "disappearance out the window" could be read "not as death but as escape into a new life" (1997, xxx). However, I read Clare not as escaping into a new life, but as choosing, like McClain, to escape the racial limitations of the old one—one where she's forced to choose. As Mae Henderson writes of Clare, "her continued existence would menace both Bellew's [white] and Irene's [black] world, so [since Clare can't be both, she] must cease to exist" (2002, lxxiii). Larsen's ultimate accomplishment in the novel, Henderson says, "lies in the narrative performance of her refutation of essentialism" (lxxiv). But in jumping to her death, in refusing to choose either blackness or whiteness, Clare isn't just refusing essentialism. Neither is she embracing a performative account of race. *She's refusing to perform.* From this perspective, it's clear why Thadious Davis and Henderson can't explain why passing continues— because what's wrong with Henderson's antiessentialism is that it produces the demand for racial performance. Essentialism begets essentialism, even if we call it antiessentialism.

Like McClain and Clare, I want to be free from the burdens of racial performance, free from having to choose a passing identity or a resisting one, free from having to be this kind of black here, that kind there. I'm tired of being the family fag who tries to prove he's a man, of being the white boy, the academic scapegoat, the one who's book smart but not street smart, who's always running up behind white folks like a whipped puppy, sorry eyes, wet nose, and all, wagging for affection, hoping they'll accept me for who I am, asking them to forgive me when my blackness offends them.

I'm tired of seeing little black kids, too smart for their own good, who got it right, but their right is made their wrong, when they call school white and hate it. There's nothing left if their names are not Iverson, Shaq, or Jay-Z. The future is grave for them, because many of them end up in one, in jail, or on the streets, on drugs, and still poor, and they think it's okay, the way it should be: a cashier at the local burger joint at forty; on welfare at seventeen with one, maybe two, kids and pregnant again; a gas station attendant; a security guard at the local Chinese-owned clothing store, stealing a jersey here, a pair of sneakers there to make herself feel better. "Jobs somebody has to do," people say to make it seem like race is not the issue and point to white people who are in the same boat. But why does it have to be mostly black people?

Racial discrimination is now illegal, but performance discrimination that is based on that once-lawful, now fallacious, biologically mistaken, racist, though still race-concept-informing rule that rendered anyone black who had one or more drops of black blood, is not. Because of this concept we're called to perform our racial identities and should resist rather than conform.

But when Cookie came up at the end of my reading and kicked me smack dab in the rear end, and when my family's applause and cheers grew louder, entertained more by her performance than my poem, I knew they didn't get it. If they had, I wouldn't have been the only one getting kicked that night.

Works Cited

Davis, Thadious. Introduction. *Passing*. By Nella Larsen. New York: Penguin, 1997.

Fordham, Signithia. *Blacked Out: Dilemmas of Race, Identity, and Success at Capital High*. Chicago: U of Chicago P: 1996.

Henderson, Mae. Critical Foreword. *Passing.* By Nella Larsen. New York: Random House, 2002.

Johnson, James Weldon. *The Autobiography of an Ex-Colored Man. 1912*; 1927 Rpt. New York: Dover, 1995.

Larsen, Nella. *Passing.* 1929. Ed. Thadious Davis. New York: Penguin, 1997.

Page, Clarence. *Showing My Color: Impolite Essays on Race and Identity.* New York: HarperCollins, 1996.

Rock, Chris. *Rock This!* New York: Hyperion, 1997.

Notes

¹The distinction that Rock makes between blacks and niggers sounds like Bellew's distinction but it's not exactly the same. The difference for Bellew is a matter of race—"You can get as dark as you please" (40) he tells Clare because no matter how dark her skin may become, she is, he thinks, white. (The analogy is of a white person with a tan. No matter how dark she may get, it won't change her race.) That's what it means for Clare not to be a nigger. For Chris Rock, however, the alternative to being a nigger is not being white—it's being black. And blackness for Rock has nothing to do with skin color and neither, of course, does his distinction between blacks and niggers. Rather, Rock's difference is based on behavior, on how one performs her blackness.

²This, of course, is excepting the mainstream success that blacks achieve in entertainment industries and sports where blackness is celebrated—even lionized and imitated. For an account of why blacks have trouble succeeding in mainstream corporations and educational institutions but not in music and sports, see Chapter 9, "The Real Trouble with Black English" in Rosina Lippi-Green's *English with an Accent: Language, Ideology and Discrimination in the United States.* New York: Routledge, 1997. See also Cornel West's "Black Sexuality: A Taboo Subject" (in *Traps: African American Men on Gender and Sexuality.* Bloomington: Indiana UP, 2001. 301-07) where he points out the irony of the popularity and success of black male athletes and entertainers at a time when black men are increasingly being killed and incarcerated.

NOW THAT YOU'VE READ

1. What parts of this piece stand out to you and why? What makes them meaningful? Can you describe the writing style/tone/language?

2. Young describes what it means to "pass" or be forced into pushing aside part of yourself in order to look/act/feel a different way around certain groups. Have you ever experienced this before?

3. At the end, Young concludes about his family, "If they had [gotten it], I wouldn't have been the only one getting kicked that night" (216). What does he mean by this? Can you tease out his argument and perhaps the intention for this piece based on what he says here?

READING

From Outside, In

Barbara Mellix

BEFORE YOU READ answer the following questions:

1. How important to you is the way you talk (your dialect, accent, home language, slang, usage, etc.)?

2. Have you ever been asked or felt pressure to change the way you talk? Describe the situation.

3. Can an "outsider" always become an "insider" What does it take?

4. What are some of the reasons to learn to use "proper" English? Can you think of any reasons not to?

From Outside, In

Barbara Mellix

Two years ago, when I started writing this paper, trying to bring order out of chaos, my ten-year-old daughter was suffering from an acute attack of boredom. She drifted in and out of the room complaining that she had nothing to do, no one to "be with" because none of her friends were at home. Patiently I explained that I was working on something special and needed peace and quiet, and I suggested that she paint, read, or work with her computer. None of these interested her, Finally, she pulled up a chair to my desk and watched me, now and then heaving long, loud sighs. After two or three minutes (nine or ten sighs), I lost my patience. "Looka here, Allie," I said, "you too old for this kinda carryin' on. I done told you this is important. You wronger than dirt to be in here haggin' me like this and you know it. Now git on outta here and leave me off before I put my foot all the way down."

I was at home, alone with my family, and my daughter understood that this way of speaking was appropriate in that context. She knew, as a matter of fact, that it was almost inevitable; when I get angry at home, I speak some of my finest, most cherished black English. Had I been speaking to my daughter in this manner in certain other environments, she would have been shocked and probably worried that I had taken leave of my sense of propriety.

Like my children, I grew up speaking what I considered two distinctly different languages—black English and standard English (or as l thought of them then, the ordinary everyday speech of "country" coloreds and "proper" English)—and in the process of acquiring these languages, I developed an understanding of when, where, and how to use them. But unlike my children, I grew up in a world that was primarily black. My friends, neighbors, minister, teachers—almost everybody I associated with every day were black. And we spoke to one another in our own special language: *That sho is a pretty dress you got on. If she don' soon leave me off I'm gon tell her head a mess. I was so mad I could' a pissed a blue nail. He all the time trying to low-rate somebody. Ain't that just about the nastiest thing you ever set ears on?*

Then there were the "others," the "proper" blacks, transplanted relatives and one-time friends who came home from the city for weddings, funerals, and vacations. And the whites. To these we spoke standard English. "Ain't?" my mother would yell at me when I used the term in the presence of "others." "You know better than that." And l would hang my head in shame and say the "proper" word.

I remember one summer sitting in my grandmother's house in Greeleyville, South Carolina, when it was full of the chatter of city relatives who were home on vacation. My parents sat quietly, only now and then volunteering a comment or answering a question. My mother's face took on a strained expression when she spoke. I could see that she was being careful to say just the right words in just the right way. Her voice sounded thick, muffled. And when she finished speaking, she would lapse into silence, her proper smile on her face. My father was more articulate, more aggressive.

He spoke quickly, his words sharp and clear. But he held his proud head higher, a signal that he, too, was uncomfortable. My sisters and brothers and I stared at our aunts, uncles, and cousins, speaking only when prompted. Even then, we hesitated, formed our sentences in our minds, then spoke softly, shyly.

My parents looked small and anxious during those occasions, and I waited impatiently for our leave-taking when we would mock our relatives the moment we were out of their hearing. "Reeely," we would say to one another, flexing our wrists and rolling our eyes, "how dooo you stan this heat? Chile, it just tooo hy*ooo*-mid for words." Our relatives had made us feel "country," and this was our way of regaining pride in ourselves while getting a little revenge in the bargain. The words bubbled in our throats and rolled across our tongues, a balming.

As a child I felt this same doubleness in uptown Greeleyville where the whites lived. "Ain't that a pretty dress you're wearing!" Toby, the town policeman, said to me one day when I was fifteen. "Thank you very much," I replied, my voice barely audible in my own ears. The words felt wrong in my mouth, rigid, foreign. It was not that I had never spoken that phrase before—it was common in black English, too—but I was extremely conscious that this was an occasion for proper English. I had taken out my English and put it on as I did my church clothes, and I felt as if I were wearing my Sunday best in the middle of the week. It did not matter that Toby had not spoken grammatically correct English. He was white and could speak as he wished. I had something to prove. Toby did not.

Speaking standard English to whites was our way of demonstrating that we knew their language and could use it. Speaking it to standard-English-speaking blacks was our way of showing them that we, as well as they, could "put on airs." But when we spoke standard English, we acknowledged (to ourselves and to others—but primarily to ourselves) that our customary way of speaking was inferior. We felt foolish, embarrassed, somehow diminished because we were ashamed to be our real selves. We were reserved, shy in the presence of those who owned and/or spoke *the* language.

My parents never set aside time to drill us in standard English. Their forms of instruction were less formal. When my father was feeling particularly expansive, he would regale us with tales of his exploits in the outside world. In almost flawless English, complete with dialogue and flavored with gestures and embellishment, he told us about his attempt to get a haircut at a white barbershop; his refusal to acknowledge one of the town merchants until the man addressed him as "Mister"; the time he refused to step off the sidewalk uptown to let some whites pass; his airplane trip to New York City (to visit a sick relative) during which the stewardesses and porters—recognizing that he was a "gentleman"—addressed him as "Sir." I did not realize then—nor, I think, did my father—that he was teaching us, among other things, standard English and the relationship between language and power.

My mother's approach was different. Often, when one of us said, "I'm gon wash off my feet," she would say, "And what will you walk on if you wash them off!" Everyone would laugh at the victim of my mother's "proper" mood. But it was different when one of us children was in a proper mood. "You think you are so superior," I said to my oldest sister one day when we were arguing and she was winning. "Superior!" my sister mocked. "You mean I am acting 'bigidy'?" My sisters and brothers sniggered, then joined in teasing me. Finally, my mother said, "Leave your sister alone. There's nothing wrong with using proper English." There was a half-smile on her face. I had gotten "uppity," had "put on airs" for no good reason. I was at home, alone with the family, and I hadn't been prompted by one of my mother's proper moods. But there was also a proud light in my mother's eyes; her children were learning English very well.

Not until years later, as a college student, did I begin to understand our ambivalence toward English, our scorn of it, our need to master it, to own and be owned by it—an ambivalence that extended to the public-school classroom. In our school, where there were no whites, my teachers taught standard English but used black English to do it. When my grammar-school teachers wanted us to write, for example, they usually said something like, "I want y'all to write five sentences that make a statement. Anybody git done before the rest can color." It was probably almost those exact words that led me to write these sentences in 1953 when I was in the second grade:

> The white clouds are pretty.
> There are only 15 people in our room. We will go to gym.
> We have a new poster.
> We may go out doors.

Second grade came after "Little First" and "Big First," so by then I knew the implied rules that accompanied all writing assignments. Writing was an occasion for proper English. I was not to write in the way we spoke to one another: The white clouds pretty; There ain't but 15 people in our room; We going to gym; We got a new poster; We can go out in the yard. Rather I was to use the language of "other": clouds *are*, there *are*, we *will*, we *have*, we *may*.

My sentences were short, rigid, perfunctory, like the letters my mother wrote to relatives:

> *Dear Papa,*
>
> *How are you? How is Mattie? Fine I hope. We are fine. We will come to see you Sunday. Cousin Ned will give us a ride.*
>
> > *Love,*
> > *Daughter*

The language was not ours. It was something from outside us, something we used for special occasions.

But my coloring on the other side of that second-grade paper is different. I drew three hearts and a sun. The sun has a smiling face that radiates and envelops everything it touches. And although the sun and its world are enclosed in a circle, the colors I used—red, blue, green, purple, orange, yellow, black—indicate that I was less restricted with drawing and coloring than I was with writing standard English. My valentines were not just red. My sun was not just a yellow ball in the sky.

By the time I reached the twelfth grade, speaking and writing standard English had taken on new importance. Each year, about half of the newly graduated seniors of our school moved to large cities—particularly in the North—to live with relatives and find work. Our English teacher constantly corrected our grammar: "Not 'ain't,' but 'isn't.'" We seldom wrote papers, and even those few were usually plot summaries of short stories. When our teacher returned the papers, she usually lectured on the importance of using standard English: "I *am;* you *are;* he, she, or it *is,*" she would say, writing on the chalkboard as she spoke. "How you gon git a job talking about 'I is,' or 'I isn't' or 'I ain't'?"

In Pittsburgh, where I moved after graduation, I watched my aunt and uncle— who had always spoken standard English when in Greeleyville—switch from black English to standard English to a mixture of the two, according to where they were or who they were with. At home and with certain close relatives, friends, and neighbors, they spoke black English. With those less close, they spoke a mixture. In public and with strangers, they generally spoke standard English.

In time, I learned to speak standard English with ease and to switch smoothly from black to standard or a mixture, and back again. But no matter where I was, no matter what the situation or occasion, I continued to write as I had in school:

Dear Mommie,

How are you? How is everybody else? Fine I hope. I am fine. So are Aunt and Uncle. Tell everyone I said hello. I will write again soon.

> *Love,*
> *Barbara*

At work, at a health insurance company, I learned to write letters to customers. I studied form letters and letters written by co-workers, memorizing the phrases and the ways in which they were used. I dictated:

Thank you for your letter of January 5. We have made the changes in your coverage you requested. Your new premium will be $150 every three months. We are pleased to have been of service to you.

In a sense, I was proud of the letters I wrote for the company: they were proof of my ability to survive in the city, the outside world an indication of my growing mastery of English. But they also indicate that writing was still mechanical for me, something that didn't require much thought.

Reading also became a more significant part of my life during those early years in Pittsburgh. I had always liked reading, but now I devoted more and more of my spare time to it. I read romances, popular novels. Looking back, I realize that the books I liked best were simple, unambiguous: good versus bad and right versus wrong with right rewarded and wrong punished, mysteries unraveled and all set right in the end. It was how I remembered life in Greeleyville.

Of course I was romanticizing. Life in Greeleyville had not been so very uncomplicated. Back there I had been—first as a child, then as a young woman with limited experience in the outside world—living in a relatively closed-in society. But there were implicit and explicit principles that guided our way of life and shaped our relationships with one another and the people outside—principles that a newcomer would find elusive and baffling. In Pittsburgh, I had matured, become more experienced: I had worked at three different jobs, associated with a wider range of people, married, had children. This new environment with different prescripts for living required that I speak standard English much of the time, and slowly, imperceptibly, I had ceased seeing a sharp distinction between myself and "others." Reading romances and mysteries, characterized by dichotomy, was a way of shying away from change, from the person I was becoming.

But that other part of me—that part which took great pride in my ability to hold a job writing business letters—was increasingly drawn to the new developments in my life and the attending possibilities, opportunities for even greater change. If I could write letters for a nationally known business, could I not also do something better, more challenging, more important? Could I not, perhaps, go to college and become a school teacher? For years, afraid and a little embarrassed, I did no more than imagine this different me, this possible me. But sixteen years after coming north, when my younger daughter entered kindergarten, I found myself unable—or unwilling—to resist the lure of possibility. I enrolled in my first college course: Basic Writing, at the University of Pittsburgh.

For the first time in my life, I was required to write extensively about myself. Using the most formal English at my command, I wrote these sentences near the beginning of the term:

> One of my duties as a homemaker is simply picking up after others. A day seldom passes that I don't search for a mislaid toy, book, or gym shoe, etc. I change the Ty-D-Bol, fight "ring around the collar," and keep our laundry smelling "April fresh." Occasionally, I settle arguments between my children and suggest things to do when they're bored. Taking telephone messages for my oldest daughter is my newest (and sometimes most aggravating) chore. Hanging the toilet paper roll is my most insignificant.

My concern was to use "appropriate" language, to sound as if I belonged in a college classroom. But I felt separate from the language—as if it did not and could not belong to me. I couldn't think, and feel genuinely in that language, couldn't make it express what I thought and felt about being a housewife. A part of me resented, among other things, being judged by such things as the appearance of my family's laundry and toilet bowl, but in that language, I could only imagine and write about a conventional housewife.

For the most part, the remainder of the term was a period of adjustment, a time of trying to find my bearing as a student in college composition class, to learn to shut out my black English whenever I composed, and to prevent it from creeping into my formulations; a time for trying to grasp the language of the classroom and reproduce it in my prose; for trying to talk about myself in that language, reach others through it. Each experience of writing was like standing naked and revealing my imperfection, my "otherness." And each new assignment was another chance to make myself over in language, reshape myself, make myself "better" in my rapidly changing image of a student in a college composition class.

But writing became increasingly unmanageable as the term progressed, and by the end of the semester, my sentences sounded like this:

> My excitement was soon dampened, however, by what seemed like a small voice in the back of my head saying that I should be careful with my long awaited opportunity. I felt frustrated and this seemed to make it difficult to concentrate.

There is a poverty of language in these sentences. By this point, I knew that the clichéd language of my Housewife essay was unacceptable, and I generally recognized trite expressions. At the same time, I hadn't yet mastered the language of the classroom, hadn't yet come to see it as belonging to me. Most notable is the lifelessness of the prose, the apparent absence of a person behind the words. I wanted those sentences—and the rest of the essay—to convey the anguish of yearning to, at once, become something more and yet remain the same. I had the sensation of being split in two, part of me going into a future the other part didn't believe possible. As that person, the student writer at that moment, I was essentially mute. I could not—in the process of composing—use the language of the old me, yet I couldn't imagine myself in the language of "others."

I found this particularly discouraging because at mid-semester I had been writing in a much different way. Note the language of this introduction to an essay I had written then, near the middle of the term:

Pain is a constant companion to the people in "Footwork." Their jobs are physically damaging. Employers are insensitive to their feelings and in many cases add to their problems. The general public wounds them further by treating them with disgrace because of what they do for a living. Although the workers are as diverse as they are similar, there is a definite link between them. They suffer a great deal of abuse.

The voice here is stronger, more confident, appropriating terms like "physically damaging," "wounds them further," "insensitive," "diverse"—terms I couldn't have imagined using when writing about my own experience—and shaping them into sentences like "Although the workers are as diverse as they are similar, there is a definite link between them." And there is the sense of a personality behind the prose, someone who sympathizes with the workers. "The general public wounds them further by treating them with disgrace because of what they do for a living."

What caused these differences? I was, I believed, explaining other people's thoughts and feelings, and I was free to move about in the language of "others" so long as I was speaking of others. I was unaware that I was transforming into my best classroom language my own thoughts and feelings about people whose experiences and ways of speaking were in many ways similar to mine.

The following year, unable to turn back or to let go of what had become something of an obsession with language (and hoping to catch and hold the sense of control that had eluded me in Basic Writing), I enrolled in a research writing course. I spent most of the term learning how to prepare for and write a research paper. I chose sex education as my subject and spent hours in libraries, searching for information, reading, taking notes. Then (not without messiness and often-demoralizing frustration) I organized my information into categories, wrote a thesis statement, and composed my paper—a series of paraphrases and quotations spaced between carefully constructed transitions. The process and results felt artificial, but as I would later come to realize I was passing through a necessary stage. My sentences sounded like this:

This reserve becomes understandable with examination of who the abusers are. In an overwhelming number of cases they are people the victims know and trust. Family members, relatives, neighbors and close family friends commit seventy-five percent of all reported sex crimes against children, and parents, parent substitutes and relatives are the offenders in thirty to eighty percent of all reported cases. While assault by strangers does occur, it is less common, and is usually a single episode. But abuse by family members, relatives and acquaintances may continue for an extended period of time. In cases of incest, for example, children are abused repeatedly for an average of eight years. In such cases, "the use of physical force is rarely necessary because of the child's trusting, dependent relationship with the offender. The child's cooperation is often facilitated by the adult's position of dominance, an offer of material goods, a threat of physical violence, or a misrepresentation of moral standards."

The completed paper gave me a sense of profound satisfaction, and I read it often after my professor returned it. I know now that what I was pleased with was the language I used and the professional voice it helped me maintain. "Use better words," my teacher had snapped at me one day after reading the notes I'd begun accumulating from my research, and slowly I began taking on the language of my sources. In my next set of notes, I used the word "vacillating"; my professor applauded. And by the time I composed the final draft, I felt at ease with terms like "overwhelming number of critics," "single episode," and "reserve," and I shaped them into sentences similar to those of my "expert" sources.

If I were writing the paper today, I would of course do some things differently. Rather than open with an anecdote—as my teacher suggested—I would begin simply with a quotation that caught my interest as I was researching my paper (and which I scribbled without its source, in the margin of my notebook): "Truth does not do so much good in the world as the semblance of truth does evil." The quotation felt right because it captured what was for me the central idea of my paper—and expressed it in a way I would like to have said it. The anecdote, a hypothetical situation I invented to conform to the information in the paper, felt forced and insincere because it represented—to a great degree—my teacher's understanding of the essay, her idea of what in it was most significant. Improving upon my previous experiences with writing, I was beginning to think and feel in the language I used, to find my own voice in it, to sense that how one speaks influences how one means. But I was not yet secure enough, comfortable enough with the language to trust my intuition.

Now that I know that to seek knowledge, freedom, and autonomy means always to be in the concentrated process of becoming—always to be venturing into new territory, feeling one's way at first, then getting one's balance, negotiating, accommodating, discovering one's self in ways that previously defined "others"—I sometimes get tired. And I ask myself why I keep on participating in this highbrow form of violence, this slamming against perplexity. But there is no real futility in the question, no hint of that part of the old me who stood outside standard English, hugging to herself a disabling mistrust of language she thought could not represent a person with her history and experience. Rather, the question represents a person who feels the consequence of her education, the weight of her possibilities as a teacher and writer and human being, a voice in society. And I would not change that person, would not give back the good burden that accompanies my growing expertise, my increasing power to shape myself in language and share that self with "others."

"To speak," says Frantz Fanon, "means to be in a position to use a certain syntax, to grasp the morphology of this or that language, but it means above all to assume a culture, to support the weight of a civilization." To write means to do the same, but in a more profound sense. However, Fanon also says that to achieve mastery means to "get" in a position of power, to "grasp," to "assume." This, I have learned both as a student and subsequently as a teacher, can involve tremendous emotional and psychological conflict for those attempting to master academic discourse. Although as a beginning student writer I had a fairly good grasp of ordinary spoken English and was proficient at what Labov calls "code-switching" (and what John Baugh in *Black Street Speech* terms "style shifting"), when I came face to face with the demands of academic writing, I grew increasingly self-conscious, constantly aware of my status as a black and a speaker of one of the many black English vernaculars—a traditional outsider. For the first time, I experienced my sense of doubleness as something menacing, a built-in enemy. Whenever I turned inward for salvation, the balm so available during my childhood, I found instead this new fragmentation which spoke to me in many voices. It was the voice of my desire to prosper, but at the same time it spoke of what I had relinquished and could not regain: a safe way of being, a state of powerlessness which exempted me from responsibility for who I was and might be. And it accused me of betrayal, of turning away from blackness. To recover balance, I had to take on the language of the academy, the language of "others." And to do that, I had to learn to imagine myself a part of the culture of that language, and therefore someone free to manage that language, to take liberties with it. Writing and rewriting, practicing, experimenting, I came to comprehend more fully the generative power of language. I discovered—with the help of some especially sensitive teachers—that through writing one can continually bring new selves into being, each with new responsibilities and difficulties, but also with new possibilities. Remarkable power, indeed. I write and continually give birth to myself.

NOW THAT YOU'VE READ

1. What do you learn from Barbara Mellix's opening anecdote?

2. What is "code-switching"? Why is it useful—and even necessary?

3. What is Mellix saying when she describes her relatives as making her family "feel country"? Have you ever had a similar experience?

4. Mellix writes, ". . . I ask myself why I keep on participating in this highbrow form of violence, this slamming against perplexity." What does she mean here? How is she using the word *violence*? What does it mean to "slam against perplexity"?

READING

Confronting Class in the Classroom

bell hooks

BEFORE YOU READ answer the following questions:

1. Predict, on the basis of the title, how the word *class* will be used in this essay.

2. Why might class be an important factor in U.S. classrooms? Do you think it has a similar impact in classrooms in any other countries? Explain your answer.

3. Have you ever seen or heard of someone disrupting a class? What happened?

4. Describe a time when you felt that you didn't "fit in" with a particular group. How did you feel? Why?

Confronting Class in the Classroom

bell hooks

Class is rarely talked about in the United States; nowhere is there a more intense silence about the reality of class differences than in educational settings. Significantly, class differences are particularly ignored in classrooms. From grade school on, we are all encouraged to cross the threshold of the classroom believing we are entering a democratic space—a free zone where the desire to study and learn makes us all equal. And even if we enter accepting the reality of class differences, most of us still believe knowledge will be meted out in fair and equal proportions. In those rare cases where it is acknowledged that students and professors do not share the same class backgrounds, the underlying assumption is still that we are all equally committed to getting ahead, to moving up the ladder of success to the top. And even though many of us will not make it to the top, the unspoken understanding is that we will land somewhere in the middle, between top and bottom.

Coming from a nonmaterially privileged background, from the working poor, I entered college acutely aware of class. When I received notice of my acceptance at Stanford University, the first question that was raised in my household was how I would pay for it. My parents understood that I had been awarded scholarships, and allowed to take out loans, but they wanted to know where the money would come from for transportation, clothes, books. Given these concerns, I went to Stanford thinking that class was mainly about materiality. It only took me a short while to understand that class was more than just a question of money, that it shaped values, attitudes, social relations, and the biases that informed the way knowledge would be given and received. These same realizations about class in the academy are expressed again and again by academics from working-class backgrounds in the collection of essays *Strangers in Paradise* edited by Jake Ryan and Charles Sackrey.

During my college years, it was tacitly assumed that we all agreed that class should not be talked about, that there would be no critique of the bourgeois class biases shaping and informing pedagogical process (as well as social etiquette) in the classroom. Although no one ever directly stated the rules that would govern our conduct, it was taught by example and reinforced by a system of rewards. As silence and obedience to authority were most rewarded, students learned that this was the appropriate demeanor in the classroom. Loudness, anger, emotional outbursts, and even something as seemingly innocent as unrestrained laughter were deemed unacceptable, vulgar disruptions of classroom social order. These traits were also associated with being a member of the lower classes. If one was not from a privileged class group, adopting a demeanor similar to that of the group could help one to advance. It is still necessary for students to assimilate bourgeois values in order to be deemed acceptable.

Bourgeois values in the classroom create a barrier, blocking the possibility of confrontation and conflict, warding off dissent. Students are often silenced by means of their acceptance of class values that teach them to maintain order at all costs. When the obsession with maintaining order is coupled with the fear of "losing face," of not being thought well of by one's professor and peers, all possibility of constructive dialogue is undermined. Even though students enter the "democratic" classroom believing they have the right to "free speech," most students are not comfortable exercising this right to "free speech." Most students are not comfortable exercising this right—especially if it means they must give voice to thoughts, ideas, feelings that go against the grain, that are unpopular. This censoring process is only one way bourgeois values overdetermine social behavior in the classroom and undermine the democratic exchange of ideas. Writing about his experience in the section of *Strangers in Paradise* entitled "Outsiders," Karl Anderson confessed:

> Power and hierarchy, and not teaching and learning, dominated the graduate school I found myself in. "Knowledge" was one-upmanship, and no one disguised the fact.... The one thing I learned absolutely was the inseparability of free speech and free thought. I, as well as some of my peers, were refused the opportunity to speak and sometimes to ask questions deemed "irrelevant" when the instructors didn't wish to discuss or respond to them.

Students who enter the academy unwilling to accept without question the assumptions and values held by privileged classes tend to be silenced, deemed troublemakers.

Conservative discussions of censorship in contemporary university settings often suggest that the absence of constructive dialogue, enforced silencing, takes place as a by-product of progressive efforts to question canonical knowledge, critique relations of domination, or subvert bourgeois class biases. There is little or no discussion of the way in which the attitudes and values of those from materially privileged classes are imposed upon everyone via biased pedagogical strategies. Reflected in choice of subject matter and the manner in which ideas are shared, these biases need never be overtly stated. In his essay, Karl Anderson states that silencing is "the most oppressive aspect of middle-class life." He maintains:

> It thrives upon people keeping their mouths shut, unless they are actually endorsing whatever powers exist. The free marketplace of "ideas" that is so beloved of liberals is as much a fantasy as a free marketplace in oil or automobiles; a more harmful fantasy, because it breeds even more hypocrisy and cynicism. Just as teachers can control what is said in their classrooms, most also have ultra-sensitive antennae as to what will be rewarded or punished that is said outside them. And these antennae control them.

Silencing enforced by bourgeois values is sanctioned in the classroom by everyone.

Even those professors who embrace the tenets of critical pedagogy (many of whom are white and male) still conduct their classrooms in a manner that only reinforces bourgeois models of decorum. At the same time, the subject matter taught in such classes might reflect professorial awareness of intellectual perspectives that critique domination, that emphasize an understanding of the politics of difference, of race, class, gender, even though classroom dynamics remain conventional, business as usual. When contemporary feminist movement made its initial presence felt in the academy there was both an ongoing critique of conventional classroom dynamic and an attempt to create alternative pedagogical strategies. However, as feminist scholars endeavored to make Women's Studies a discipline administrators and peers would respect, there was a shift in perspective.

Significantly, feminist classrooms were the first spaces in the university where I encountered any attempt to acknowledge class difference. The focus was usually on the way class differences are structured in the larger society, not on our class position. Yet the focus on gender privilege in patriarchal society often meant that there was a recognition of the ways women were economically disenfranchised and therefore more likely to be poor or working class. Often, the feminist classroom was the only place where students (mostly female) from materially disadvantaged circumstances would speak from the class positionality, acknowledging both the impact of class on our social status as well as critiquing the class biases of feminist thought.

When I first entered university settings I felt estranged from this new environment. Like most of my peers and professors, I initially believed those feelings were there because of difference in racial and cultural background. However, as time passed it was more evident that this estrangement was in part a reflection of class difference. At Stanford, I was often asked by peers and professors if I was there on a scholarship. Underlying this question was the implication that receiving financial aid "diminished" one in some way. It was not just this experience that intensified my awareness of class difference, it was the constant evocation of materially privileged class experience (usually that of the middle class) as a universal norm that not only set those of us form working-class backgrounds apart but effectively excluded those who were not privileged from discussions, from social activities. To avoid feelings of estrangement, students from working-class backgrounds could assimilate into the mainstream, change speech patterns, points of reference, drop any habit that might reveal them to be from a nonmaterially privileged background.

Of course, I entered college hoping that a university degree would enhance my class mobility. Yet I thought of this solely in economic terms. Early on I did not realize that class was much more than one's economic standing, that it determined values, stand-point, and interests. It was assumed that any student coming from a poor or working-class background would willingly surrender all values and habits of being associated with this background. Those of us from diverse ethnic/racial backgrounds learned that no aspect of our vernacular culture could be voiced in elite settings. This was especially the case with vernacular language of a first language that was not English. To insist on speaking in any manner that did not conform to privileged class ideals and mannerisms placed one always in the position of interloper.

Demands that individuals from class backgrounds deemed undesirable surrender all vestiges of their past create psychic turmoil. We were encouraged, as many students are today, to betray our class origins. Rewarded if we chose to assimilate, estranged if we chose to maintain those aspects of who we were, some were all too often seen as outsiders. Some of us rebelled by clinging to exaggerated manners and behavior clearly marked as outside the accepted bourgeois norm. During my student years, and now as a professor, I see many students from "undesirable" class backgrounds become unable to complete their studies because the contradictions between the behavior necessary to "make it" in the academy and those that allowed them to be comfortable at home, with their families and friends, are just too great.

Often, African Americans are among those students I teach from poor and working-class backgrounds who are most vocal about issues of class. They express frustration, anger, and sadness about the tensions and stress the experience trying to conform to acceptable white, middle-class behaviors in university settings while retaining the ability to "deal" at home. Sharing strategies for coping for my own experience, I encourage students to reject the notion that they must choose between experiences. They must believe they can inhabit comfortably two different worlds, but they must make each space one of comfort. They must creatively invent ways to cross borders. They must believe in their capacity to alter the bourgeois settings they enter. All too often, students from nonmaterially privileged backgrounds assume a position of passivity—they behave as victims, as though they can only be acted upon against their will. Ultimately, they end up feeling they can only reject or accept the norms imposed upon them. This either/or often sets them up for disappointment and failure.

Those of us in the academy from working-class backgrounds are empowered when we recognize our own agency, our capacity to be active participants in the pedagogical process. This process is not simple or easy: it takes courage to embrace a vision of wholeness of being that does not reinforce the capitalist version that suggests that one must always give something up to gain another. In the introduction to the section of their book titled "Class Mobility and Internalized conflict," Ryan and Sackrey remind readers that "the academic work process is essentially antagonistic to the working class, and academics for the most part live in a different world of culture, different ways that make it, too, antagonistic to working class life." Yet those of us form working-class backgrounds cannot allow class antagonism to prevent us from gaining knowledge, degrees and enjoying the aspects of higher education that are fulfilling. Class antagonism can be constructively used, not made to reinforce the notion that students and professors from working-class backgrounds are "outsiders" and "interlopers," but to subvert and challenge the existing structure.

When I entered my first Women's Studies classes Stanford, white professors talked about "women" when they were making the experience of materially privileged white women a norm. It was both a matter of personal and intellectual integrity for me to challenge this biased assumption. By challenging, I refused to be complicit in the erasure of black and/or working-class women of all ethnicities. Personally, that meant I was not able to just sit in class, grooving on the good feminist vibes—that was a loss. The gain was that I was honoring the experience of poor and working-class women in my own family, in that very community that had encouraged and supported me in my efforts to be better educated. Even though my intervention was not wholeheartedly welcomed, it created a context for critical thinking, for dialectical exchange.

Any attempt on the part of individual students to critique the bourgeois biases that shape pedagogical process, particularly as they relate to epistemological perspectives (the points from which information is shared) will, in most cases, no doubt, be viewed as negative and disruptive. Given the presumed radical or liberal nature of early feminist classrooms, it was shocking to me to find those settings were also often closed to different ways of thinking. While it was acceptable to critique patriarchy in that context, it was not acceptable to confront issues of class, especially in ways that were not simply about the evocation of guilt. In general, despite their participation in different disciplines and the diversity of class backgrounds, African American scholars and other nonwhite professors have been no more willing to confront issues of class. Even when it became more acceptable to give at least lip service to the recognition of race, gender, and class, most professors and students just did not feel they were able to address class in anything more than a simplistic way. Certainly, the primary area where there was the possibility of meaningful critique and change was in relation to biased scholarship, work that used the experiences and thoughts of materially privileged people as normative.

In recent years, growing awareness of class differences in progressive academic circles has meant that students and professors committed to critical and feminist pedagogy have the opportunity to make spaces in the academy where class can receive attention. Yet there can be no intervention that challenges the status quo if we are not willing to interrogate the way our presentation of self as well as our pedagogical process is often shaped by middle-class norms. My awareness of class has been continually reinforced by my efforts to remain close to loved ones who remain in materially underprivileged class positions. This has helped me to employ pedagogical strategies that create ruptures in the established order, that promote modes of learning which challenger bourgeois hegemony.

One such strategy has been the emphasis on creating in classrooms learning communities where everyone's voice can be heard, their presence recognized and valued. In the section of *Strangers in Paradise* entitled "Balancing Class Locations," Jane Ellen Wilson shares the way an emphasis on personal voice strengthened her.

> Only by coming to terms with my own past, my own background, and seeing that in the context of the world at large, have I begun to find my true voice and to understand that, since it is my own voice, that no precut niche exists for it; that part of the work to be done is making a lace, with others, where my and our voices, can stand clear of the background noise and voice our concerns as part of a larger song.

When those of us in the academy who are working class or from working-class backgrounds share our perspectives, we subvert the tendency to focus only on the thoughts, attitudes, and experiences of those who are materially privileged. Feminist and critical pedagogy are two alternative paradigms for teaching which have really emphasized the issue of coming to voice. That focus emerged as central, precisely because it was so evident that race, sex, and class privilege empower some students more than others, granting "authority" to some voices more than others.

A distinction must be made between a shallow emphasis on coming to voice, which wrongly suggests there can be some democratization of voice wherein everyone's words will be given equal time and be seen as equally valuable (often the model applied in feminist classrooms), and the more complex recognition of the uniqueness of each voice and a willingness to create spaces in the classroom where all voices can be heard because all students are free to speak, knowing their presence will be recognized and valued. This does not mean that anything can be said, no matter how irrelevant to classroom subject matter, and receive attention—or that something meaningful takes place if everyone has equal time to voice an opinion. In the classes I teach, I have students write short paragraphs that they read aloud so that we all have a chance to hear unique perspectives and we are all given an opportunity to pause and listen to one another. Just the physical experience of hearing, of listening intently, to each particular voice strengthens our capacity to learn together. Even though a student may not speak again after this moment, that student's presence has been acknowledged.

Hearing each other's voices, individual thoughts, and sometimes associating these voices with personal experience makes us more acutely aware of each other. That moment of collective participation and dialogue means that students and professor respect—and here I invoke the root meaning of the word, "to look at"—each other, engage in acts of recognition with one another, and do not just talk to the professor. Sharing experiences and confessional narratives in the classroom helps establish communal commitment to learning. These narrative moments usually are the space where the assumption that we share a common class background and perspective is disrupted. While students may be open to the idea that they do not all come from a common class background, they may still expect that the values of materially privileged groups will be the class's norm.

Some students may feel threatened if awareness of class difference leads to changes in the classroom. Today's students all dress alike, wearing clothes from stores such as the Gap and Benetton; this acts to erase the markers of class difference that older generations of students experienced. Young students are more eager to deny the impact of class and class differences in our society. I have found that students from upper- and middle-class backgrounds are disturbed if heated exchange takes place in the classroom. Many of them equate loud talk or interruptions with rude and threatening behavior. Yet those of us from working-class backgrounds may feel that discussion is deeper and richer if it arouses intense responses. In class, students are often disturbed if anyone is interrupted while speaking, even though outside class most of them are not threatened. Few of us are taught to facilitate heated discussions that may include useful interruptions and digressions, but it is often the professor who is most invested in maintaining order in the classroom. Professors cannot empower students to embrace diversities of experience, standpoint, behavior, or style if our training has disempowered us, socialized us to cope effectively only with a single mode of interaction based on middle-class values.

Most progressive professors are more comfortable striving to challenge class biases through the material studied then they are with interrogating how class biases shape conduct in the classroom and transforming their pedagogical process. When I entered my first classroom as a college professor and a feminist, I was deeply afraid of using authority in a way that would perpetuate class elitism and other forms of domination. Fearful that I might abuse power, I falsely pretended that no power difference existed between students and myself. That was a mistake. Yet it was only as I began to interrogate my fear of "power"—the way that fear was related to my own class background where I had so often seen those with class power coerce, abuse, and dominate those without—that I began to understand that power was not itself negative. It depended on what one did with it. It was up to me to create ways within my professional power constructively, precisely because I was teaching in institutional structures that affirm it is fine to use power to reinforce and maintain coercive hierarchies.

Fear of losing control in the classroom often leads individual professors to fall into a conventional teaching pattern wherein power is used destructively. It is this fear that leads to collective professorial investment in bourgeois decorum as a means of maintaining a fixed notion of order, of ensuring that the teacher will have absolute authority. Unfortunately, this fear of losing control shapes and informs the professorial pedagogical process to the extent that it acts a barrier preventing any constructive grappling with issues of class.

Sometimes students who want professors to grapple with class differences often simply desire that individuals from less materially privileged backgrounds be given center stage so that an inversion of hierarchical structures takes place, not a disruption. One semester, a number of black female students from working-class backgrounds attended a course I taught on African American women writers. They arrived hoping I would use my professorial power to decenter the voices of privileged white students in nonconstructive ways so that those students would experience what it is like to be an outsider. Some of these black students rigidly resisted attempts to involve the others in an engaged pedagogy where space is created for everyone. Many of the black students feared that learning new terminology or new perspectives would alienate them from familiar social relations. Since these fears are rarely addressed as part of progressive pedagogical process, students caught in the grip of such anxiety often sit in classes feeling hostile, estranged, refusing to participate. I often face students who think that in my classes they will "naturally" not feel estranged and that part of this feeling of comfort, or being "at home," is that they will not have to work as hard as they do in other classes. These students are expecting to find alternative pedagogy in my classes but merely "rest" from the negative tensions they may feel in the majority of other courses. It is my job to address these tensions.

If we can trust the demographics, we must assume that the academy will be full of students from diverse classes, and that more of our students than ever before will be from poor and working-class backgrounds. This change will not be reflected in the class background of professors. In my own experience, I encounter fewer and fewer academics form working-class backgrounds. Our absence is no doubt related to the way class politics and class struggle shapes who will receive graduate degrees in our society. However, constructively confronting issues of class is not simply a task for those of us who came from working-class and poor backgrounds; it is a challenge for all professors. Critiquing the way academic settings are structured to reproduce class hierarchy, Jake Ryan and Charles Sackrey emphasize "that no matter what the politics or ideological stripe of the individual professor, of what the content of his or her teaching, Marxist, anarchist, or nihilist, he or she nonetheless participates in the reproduction of the cultural and class relations of capitalism." Despite this bleak assertion, they are willing to acknowledge that "nonconformist intellectuals can, through research and publication, chip away with some success at the conventional orthodoxies, nurture students with comparable ideas and intentions, or find ways to bring some fraction of the resources of the university to the service of the ... class interests of the workers and other below." Any professor who commits to engaged pedagogy recognizes the importance of constructively confronting issues of class. That means welcoming the opportunity to alter our classroom practices creatively so that the democratic ideal of education for everyone can be realized.

NOW THAT YOU'VE READ

1. How similar or dissimilar is your campus to the college campus that bell hooks describes?

2. How does social class affect the classroom, according to hooks?

3. She argues that social class differences are more important than racial or ethnic or gender differences. How do you respond?

4. hooks writes, "Students who enter the academy unwilling to accept without question the assumptions and values held by privileged classes tend to be silenced, deemed troublemakers." How do you respond?

READING

Selections from *Pro(se)letariets*

Preface; Introduction; **Pat Smart; Steve Oakley; Roxanne Bocyck**

BEFORE YOU READ answer the following questions:

1. What do you make of the title *Pro(se)letariets*, a blending of the words "proletariat" and "prose"?

2. Think about how literacy often depends on *access* (to materials, transportation, education, money). Jot down some examples in your own life where you have had access to literacy or moments where you have been denied access. What were some of conditions that shaped your access to literacy? For example, did your race, gender, class, etc. play a role in this?

3. Throughout these pieces, you may notice words or phrases that are unfamiliar to you. While you read, highlight or note these examples and be sure to research what they mean!

Sections to Read:
- "Preface." pp. 7-8
- "Introduction." pp. 9-10
- Smart, Pat. "Untitled (UK)." *Pro(se)letariets*. pp. 29-31.
- Oakley, Steve. "No Right to Write (UK)." *Pro(se)letariets*. pp. 77-78.
- Bocyck, Roxanne. "A Capitalist Fairy Tale (USA)." *Pro(se)letariets*. pp. 94-99.

NOW THAT YOU'VE READ

1. In the Preface to *Pro(se)letariets,* Steve Parks and Nick Pollard describe how this project emerged as a way to validate working-class voices. Does it succeed? What values do you think come from a working-class community publication?

2. Each of these writers discuss class, particularly working-class identity. Sometimes class comes through overt discussions of money, while other times it's more subtle, such as how some people have access to education, clothing, healthcare, publishing opportunities, etc. What examples of class, or class differences, do you notice in your reading? How do the writers describe being working-class or how does this show up in their writing (think of descriptions and language usage)?

3. Do these pieces, and the descriptions of working-class identity, make you think about your own class identity? What are some examples of class in your own life? Remember, class can intersect with experiences of race, gender, and sexuality, as well.

4. The writers in this book are part of a *transnational* project. That is, these experiences of literacy occur across national boundaries (here, England and the United States). And your reading of these texts continues the circulation of this writing across borders. What are other examples of writing or literacy practices that might be considered transnational? To begin, think about your own heritage or learning experiences. Describe how you see local instances of literacy in your own community, in your own lives, contributing to broader, transnational understandings of literacy.

WRITING ASSIGNMENT

REVISION

Using the feedback you received from your teacher and peers, please select the strongest part of your argument then complicate it with your reading of the second round of texts. Please note that we are looking for a re-vision—that is, a re-seeing of your project in light of new information and feedback. We are not interested in rewrites that contain sentences stuck into the first draft or minor edits in a digital project to "fix" the issues raised in your instructor's comments or to correct surface errors.

This will be largely a new project. Of course, you can borrow from and make use of meaty sections of your first draft. But it's important to remember that editing is not the same thing as revision.

Your revision should be the equivalent of at least one page longer. In addition, please highlight the sections of your revision that differ from the original, or explain the differences that emerge in your new piece if it is not an essay.

ASSIGNMENT

GROUP PRESENTATION

For your midterm, you and a couple of your colleagues will work together to produce a presentation synthesizing the work you've done so far this term and a product to circulate this information. This assignment has two parts: (a) a group presentation and (b) a short, individually authored essay in which you reflect upon the experience.

For Part I: Group Presentation

Please follow these steps:

- Read each other's papers and revisions.
- Note the definitions of literacy that emerge.
- Select the most compelling examples of literacy acquisition and/or practices from each.
- Collaborate on the best ways to represent this information visually.
- Produce a visual representation that clearly communicates your findings. This can take multiple forms, including but not limited to a poster, PowerPoint presentation, Prezi, iMovie, infographic, etc. Be creative!
- Prepare a brief (5 minutes maximum) presentation so that you can communicate orally to the class. You might use TED Talks as your inspiration for this part of the midterm.

Please note that listing the literacy definitions will not likely make for a riveting visual or oral presentation. In other words, please consider your audience.

For Part II: Reflective Project

Create a reflective project addressed to your instructor (1-2 pages), in which you address the following issues related to personal responsibility: Consider the concept of personal responsibility as it applies to the work you have completed for the course thus far. What has it meant to take "personal responsibility" when creating your individual writing assignments thus far? Define your understanding of plagiarism. What is it and why does it matter? What role does the issue of plagiarism play when one is taking personal responsibility for one's work? How can you avoid plagiarism, even cases of accidental plagiarism (which aren't at all uncommon, actually)? What did you learn about personal responsibility from the group project you just completed? How did it differ from taking personal responsibility when writing your essays on your own? If we see collaboration and plagiarism are on a spectrum, where do they become separate? Said another way, what is the distinction between the two? What was your role in the group presentation? How, specifically, did your group divide up responsibilities/duties? What were your specific duties? How well did you do? What about the rest of your group? What were they assigned to do? How well did the other group members do in meeting their obligations? How do you feel about the group presentation, now that it's over? Good? Bad? A little of both? Frustrated? Be as candid and as specific as you feel you need to be. This will only go to your instructor. It's entirely confidential.

CHAPTER 3

Dominant and Vernacular Literacies

In this chapter, we will discuss how literacy is often separated into dominant and vernacular forms. Throughout your life, you've been asked to participate in many forms of dominant literacies. For instance, throughout high school, you were probably asked to write a 5-paragraph essay. When you take state tests in K-12 for assessment purposes or to get into college (such as the SAT and ACT), these tests are written in standard English and are administered by states, companies, or institutions in order for students to show their proficiency in a particular subject. Because of these conditions, standardized tests or genres such as the 5-paragraph essay have become a dominant form of literacy in many ways.

However, these dominant forms of writing are by no means the best or only forms of writing. Each and every day people write using literacies learned outside of traditional learning spaces. We learn in kitchens and clubs, on sports teams and in digital communities. These vernacular spaces, filled with ordinary people, are constantly shaping how we understand and use literacy. One goal of this chapter is to dispel a hierarchy that places dominant literacies as better than or more powerful than vernacular literacies. Instead, we hope to show how people use these literacies in complex and exciting ways.

READING

● ● ● ● ● ● ●

Creating a Community: Literacy Events in African-American Churches

Beverly Moss

For her dissertation, Beverly Moss did an ethnographic analysis of her home church, which led her to examine other African-American churches and—eventually—developed into an important book on the subject (*A Community Text Arises: A Literate Text and a Literacy Tradition in African-American Churches*, 2002). The article that follows offers the early results of the extensive study on which *A Community Text Arises* was based.

BEFORE YOU READ answer the following questions:

1. What sorts of "literacy events" do you understand to be a regular part of a church community with which you have some familiarity? Remember, Beverly Moss is analyzing what literacy scholar Shirley Brice Heath calls "literacy events": "Any action sequence involving one or more persons in which the production and/or comprehension of print plays a role" (from *Ways with Words: Language, Life, and Work in Communities and Schools*, Cambridge UP, 1983). So what literacy events are involved with a church community you know? What kinds of texts can be found? How are they used? What "literacy events" surround their use?

Creating a Community: Literacy Events in African-American Churches

Beverly J. Moss

Introduction

Background

This chapter, like other chapters in this volume, examines literacy in a social institution or community other than the mainstream academy—the African-American church. In examining a literacy event to which most members in the African-American community have been exposed, I use Heath's (1982) definition of a literacy event: "Any action sequence, involving one or more persons, in which the production and/or comprehension of print plays a role" (p.92). The African-American sermon fits this definition, and it is the major literacy event that most African Americans have been exposed to in their communities, including those African Americans who do not attend church.

Over the past few years our discussions about literacy have taken a new direction, one long overdue—looking at literacy in nonacademic communities. A major tension in the discussion of literacy centers on the way literacy is defined or, more accurately, how people who are perceived to be literate and people who are perceived to be not literate are characterized. This issue relates to how we characterize and contrast with academic literacy? Before addressing these questions, it is necessary to provide some background information on the African-American church and preaching tradition and to introduce the three churches in which the highlighted literacy events take place.

The role of the church in the African-American community has been unsurpassed by any other institution (Hamilton, 1972; Smitherman, 1977). Smitherman (1977) states that "the traditional African-American church is the oldest and perhaps still the most powerful and influential black institution" (p.90). Theologian C. Eric Lincoln (1974), emphasizing the impact of the church on African-American people, states that "[their] church was [their] school, [their] forum, [their] political arena" (p.6). Lincoln (1974) also asserts that "whether one is a church member or not is beside the point in any assessment of the importance and meaning of the Black church" (p.115), and Mays and Nicholson (1933) assert that the "Negro church is one of the greatest perhaps the greatest channel through which the masses of the Negro race receive adult education....It becomes the center of religious, moral, and intellectual teaching" (p.58). This role of the African-American church is not a new one. Many reports focus on the role of the church and religion in helping African Americans survive slavery in American in the 18th and 19th centuries. Blassingame (1979) states that "slaves found [in religion] some hope of escape from the brutalities of daily life" (p.130). Frazier (1974) points to Christianity as the force that bonded slaves from many diverse backgrounds (p.16).

Features of African-American preaching. The characteristics which are the core of African-American preaching are the very features that make the sermon a literacy event worthy of study and that provide more insight into literacy acquisition and functions in African-American communities. These essential characteristics of African-American preaching can, I believe, lead us to think more complexly about literacy, literate behaviors, and literate texts.

Mitchell's *Black Preaching* (1970) is probably one of the most complete explorations of African-American preaching. Mitchell suggests that African-American preaching takes place only in dialogue, and he credits the congregation with "making the dialogue a normal part of the black preacher's sermon" (p.95). Mitchell (1970) characterized the dialogue as that which occurs when a member of the congregation responds "because he identifies with something the preacher has said...he is at home, he is interested in what the preacher is saying because he is involved, crucially involved in the issues as the preacher shapes them with scriptural reference and skillful allegory" (p.97). In other words, as the typical African-American sermon is being shaped by the preacher, he or she depends on the participation of the congregation in completing that sermon.

This dialogic quality contributes to another essential characteristic in African-American preaching: African-American preachers must create a sense of community between themselves and their congregations. Mitchell (1970) states that through the sermon "one has to establish a kind of intimate fellowship" (p.185). It is this task of creating a sense of community or "intimate fellowship" and its connection to the sermon that I concern myself with in my discussion of features of the sermon. That is, one of the major features of the sermons in the churches that I studied is that the texts are used to create and maintain a sense of community. This feature sets this literacy event apart from the essay—the major academic literacy event—because of the sermon's dependence on both participants, preacher and congregation to be considered a successful text in the community. African-American preachers, like other rhetoricians, can only be successful at setting up this dialogue if they know their audience and their needs.

Mitchell's (1970) characterizations of African-American preaching can be condensed to two major points:

1. Black preachers must preach in the language and culture of their people no matter how educated the preachers are.

2. The preacher must address the contemporary man and his needs. (p.29)

The first point is similar to one raised by St. Augustine (1958) who states that preaching is a rhetorical act and that the preacher/rhetor must, if necessary, speak the language of the people to reach them. One key difference between Augustine and Mitchell is that Mitchell sees this role as a necessity for being successful in the African-American church, whereas St. Augustine views it somewhat as a last resort. The second point stresses knowing enough about the congregation, being connected enough with them, to know what's important to them. This kind of knowledge and skill, prerequisites for building a community, makes African-American preachers quite effective in reaching their congregation. The dialogic quality of the text and the creation of a community through the text make the African-American sermon a distinctive text.

The Ministers and Their Churches

Each minister in the study held a bachelor's degree, had seminary training, and currently held the position of pastor in a mainstream African-American church. With the inclusion of the term *mainstream*, I excluded storefront churches where memberships are generally small, and there is less likelihood that the preachers have gone through formal training. Even though each church in the study belongs to a different denomination, even denomination falls within the reformed tradition in which the sermon is the key part of the service. Also, the Sunday services are similar in format and follow in the tradition of the African-American church, and even though each preacher is marked by fairly different individual styles, each is firmly within the tradition of African-American preaching discussed earlier in the chapter.

G. Davis (1983) argues that in spite of differences among denominations and preaching styles "the sermon structure identified...as African-American describes sermons preached from hundreds of Black pulpits across American without regard to denominational affiliation. That sermon structure is cultural" (p.30). The only noted exception to Davis's statement may be seen in African-American Catholic churches, where the structure of the service does not permit or invite the kind of sermons that are commonplace in most other African-American churches.

Meeting the Manuscript Minister

The most important distinction among the three preachers for the purposes of this study is the amount of writing they do in preparing their sermons. The minister who writes and uses a full manuscript from which he delivers his sermon is referred to hereafter as the *manuscript minister*, a term used by the manuscript minister himself. The manuscript minister pastors a church located on the South Side of Chicago, which in 1992 celebrated its 30th anniversary. This church has approximately 5,500 members and an annual budget of approximately $2,000,000. It is the largest church in the study, and to accommodate the large numbers of people who attend this church, the minister normally preaches at two services, one at 8 a.m. and one at 11 a.m. This congregation will be moving into a newly built worship center within a year.

Licensed to preach at 17 years old, and ordained eight years later, this minister has been a pastor since 1972. He has a B.A. in English, an M.A. in literature, an M.A. in the History of Religions, and a doctoral degree in Divinity. This minister's seminary training focused on academic scholarship rather than preparation to preach. He explains that this kind of training has an influence on what he preaches, specifically his understanding of the African-American religious tradition in the context of world religions. In addition, he serves as an adjunct professor with the Seminary Consortium for Urban Pastoral Education.

This manuscript minister's biographical sketch gives evidence of his deep commitment to education. Also, he is deeply committed to addressing political and social issues as well as religious issues. His sermons contain many illustrations that concern politics from the local level to the global level such as criticisms of Chicago politician Ed Vrdolyak, former U.S. President Ronald Reagan, and former South African President P.W. Botha. He does not shy away from relating Biblical politics to world politics nor does he shy away from criticizing politicians from the pulpit. Some of these references to politics are impromptu, but most of them are parts of the written sermons. This minister also educates his congregation about different cultures, telling them about the cultures of the people in the countries he visits, particularly the cultures of the peoples of color. He constantly introduces Hebrew and African concepts to the congregation in the context of a particular sermon's message. His focus on the bonds between peoples of color was evident to me after two months of observation. In short, he is a well-educated, charismatic man whose command of language and knowledge of the Bible and religions of the world are displayed in his sermons.

Meeting the Manuscript Minister's Congregation

Some churches reflect their denomination's teachings, some reflect the congregations' wishes, and other churches reflect their ministers' visions. This church falls into the latter category. Many of the programs that exist in this church are a result of the manuscript minister's philosophy and ideas brought to fruition. His effectiveness as a pastor can be measured by the growth of the congregation and the church's programs since his arrival over 20 years ago. The membership has grown from less than 100 to approximately 5,500 members. The church now has a federally approved credit union, a reading, writing, and math tutorial program, a day care center, a legal counseling service, a large pastoral counseling staff, an educational program that concentrates on educating the church membership about their religious and cultural roots as an African people, broadcast ministries, and much more.

The manuscript minister stresses to his congregation that they should be "unashamedly Black and unapologetically Christian." This statement is part of the oath that the congregation takes when accepting new members into the church. During the time that the data were collected, this church was always full, with standing room only. Worshippers arrived 50 minutes before the service starts so that they can get seats in the sanctuary.

The congregation of this church is viewed as middle-class by many members of Chicago's African-American community. However, the minister views his congregation as a mixed group. He takes pride in the diversity of the congregation. Yet, although the members of this church represent a range on the socioeconomic ladder, there are a large number of people who are professionals; judges, lawyers, doctors, educators, businessmen and women, entertainers, and so on. A TV documentary which aired nationally addressed the perceived "middle classness" of this church ("Keeping the faith," 1987). It is a church that stresses education, yet it does not make the less formally educated feel uncomfortable. Its apparent upward mobility makes this church appealing to those who identify with the upwardly mobile. In fact, many members of the congregation drive to Chicago's South Side from Chicago suburbs.

Despite its middle-class identification, this church is rooted in the tradition of the African-American church, and the minister is rooted in the tradition of African-American preachers. My interviews with this minister confirmed what I had observed previously: that this manuscript minister takes great pride in being identified as "in the tradition of black preachers." He believes in making connections between the traditional African-American church and the contemporary African-American church, and in using the language of the African-American community in his sermons. This use of the language is much more than just speaking; it is also establishing a sense of community, communicating ideas and attitudes about African-American people, and promoting certain community values.

Meeting the Nonmanuscript Minister

The second preacher in the study prepares no manuscript from which to preach and usually no written notes. He pastors a church, located in a North suburb of Chicago, that has approximately 800 members. Even though the church is in a Chicago suburb, it is located just across the northern border of Chicago and has very strong ties to the city. Many of its members live in Chicago. Like the manuscript minister, the nonmanuscript minister also preaches at two Sunday morning services, at 8:00 and at 11:00. This church, rich in history, celebrated its 122nd anniversary in 1992.

This preacher initially came to this area as a faculty member at a nearby well-known seminary. He was on the faculty at this seminary for 15 years. During the latter years of his faculty appointment, he also served as senior pastor of this church, probably one of the few professors who also pastured a church full time. In his church he is addressed by his academic title "Dr_ _ _ _ _" rather than "Reverend _ _ _ _ _." This minister brings to this church not only a traditional training of years of preaching experience mostly in smaller churches, but also a scholarly foundation. And although this scholarship includes the study of noted Western philosophers such as Heidegger and Kant, this minister has devoted much of his scholarship and his ministry to African-American theological issues.

Like the manuscript preacher, the nonmanuscript preacher has a basic philosophy that guides his ministry. That philosophy, which is printed on the church bulletins, is "faith and freedom for African-American people." He says that he is "unapologetically a race preacher." Committed to his people, this minister's philosophy and commitment affects his sermon preparation and consequently his sermons. Through my interviews with this minister I learned that his experiences as preacher at a southern church and at divinity school in the South played a major role in his training to be a pastor to African-American people. Born in a Midwestern, white-collar city, it was his experiences in the South that introduced him to the traditional African-American worship patterns that so many African-American preachers exemplify. He now describes the congregations of many urban churches as full of transplanted Southerners who are used to the Southern African-American tradition of worship, a sentiment echoed by Davis (1985) who notes the important influence of the Southern African-American church tradition on African-American churches in general.

When discussing methods of communicating with his congregation, the nonmanuscript minister focused on verbal and nonverbal language. He relies on gestures to communicate as well as words. The nonmanuscript preacher explains that in the African-American church he reaches some people with words; he states, for instance that, "celestial skies means heaven for some, but those words mean nothing to people ruled by emotions. A gesture, however, pointing upward and looking upward has the meaning of heaven for those people who attach less meaning to words." This raises the issue of how much value some people attach to words in this setting. It also raises the issue of how this minister and others identify and communicate with the multiple levels of audience that make up their congregations. This minister, as evidenced by his identification of the different kinds of language use to which people respond, has a special awareness of this multiple audience issue. More importantly, he seems to meet the needs of his congregation.

Finally, of great importance when discussing this nonmanuscript minister is his commitment to political and social issues. It is very obvious that he sees the pulpit as the perfect place to discuss politics. During the time that I attended services and collected data, I noted that the minister regularly discussed local, state, national, and international politics. Many times, issues of politics were used as illustrations in a sermon. Tied to political issues raised in the pulpit are social and economic issues. One sermon began with a discussion of the impact of AIDS on the African-American community. The politically centered discussions focus on their impact on African-American people, in keeping with this minister's identification of himself as a race preacher.

Meeting the Nonmanuscript Minister's Congregation

The oldest of the three churches in this study and located in a middle-class suburb, this church's location suggest that it serves a predominantly middle-class African-American population. Indeed, many of its members fit that label. Like the congregation in the manuscript minister's church, this church has a large number of African-American professionals. There are teachers, judges, lawyers, doctors, businesspersons, and corporate executives in this congregation. In addition, because this church is located very near a major university, there are a large number of African-American college students, both at the undergraduate and graduate level, who attend this church.

This church, unlike the other tow churches in the study, is not located in an African-American neighborhood; people drive from various distances to get to Sunday morning service. In spite of these facts, the minister indicated that he does not really see his church as middle class, although he recognizes that there are a large number of professionals and what he calls intellectuals in his congregation. His perception does assist him in not preaching above the heads of those who are limited in their vocabulary and educational levels or who do not respond as enthusiastically to verbal stimuli.

The church's organizations are concerned not only with the operation of the church but also with education and community fellowship. This church has an administrative staff consisting of the senior pastor, executive assistant pastor, and assistant pastors in charge of special ministries, educational ministries, and youth ministries. There are the traditional deacon, trustee, and usher boards. There is also a library committee and a group that runs a precollege seminar for church members who are going off to college. The focus on education reflects one of the priorities of the minister, who promotes the value of higher education in his sermons.

In addition, this church has numerous organizations that promote fellowship among the congregation such as the singles' ministry, the widows' and widowers' club, the bowling league, and the softball team. There is also a church-run marriage counseling program. These organizations and programs show how many diverse groups the church tries to serve. It also emphasizes the church as the center of not only religious and political activities but social activities as well.

Meeting the Partial Manuscript Minister

The third preacher in the study, hereafter referred to as the partial-manuscript minister, writes approximately 25% of his sermons. He brings into the pulpit with him a written text that physically resembles a sentence outline but that seems to include far more information than an outline usually does. The partial-manuscript preacher pastors a 78-year-old church on the far South Side of Chicago. This church, with approximately 550 members on roll (only half attend regularly), has one morning service at 11 a.m.

I learned of the partial-manuscript minister's church through an acquaintance who is a member of that church. This acquaintance described his minister as one who did not write his sermons. So it was the search for the nonmanuscript minister that brought me to this church. What I found, when I talked with the minister, was that he wrote too much to be considered a nonmanuscript minister (approximately one-fourth of his sermon was written), and he wrote too little to be considered a manuscript minister. However, this minister places himself more on the nonmanuscript end than the manuscript one. I refer to him as a partial-manuscript minister to distinguish him from the nonmanuscript minister.

This minister is the youngest of the three ministers in this study. After leaving the military he became pastor of his first church in 1974, and he has been a minister for 25 years and pasturing over 18 years. He has the least amount of education of the three ministers in that he was completing his graduate work (master's level) at the time of this study. However, he has studied in several seminary programs which, although they do not offer graduate degrees, prepare ministers to preach and pastor a church. He even stated in one of his sermons I collected that he goes to seminars and takes courses on preaching and the ministry to become a better communicator. What this congregation has is a model, the minister, who is constantly trying to improve himself as a preacher and pastor, mostly through education.

This minister's effectiveness is measured by his congregation's admiration of him, admiration which seems to cover the preacher and the man. When discussing his preaching, he said his sermons were arranged a certain way because he wasn't good at other kinds of arrangements, particularly topical arrangements. Yet, he also questioned the legitimacy of preaching topical sermons. He describes himself as being more of an exegetical preacher, which he views as the most legitimate type of preaching. Many works on preaching support him (H.G. Davis, 1958; W. Thompson, 1981). Exegesis involves close reading of the scripture as a basis for the sermon. It deemphasizes choosing a sermon from outside the Bible as the other two ministers often do. This minister's sermons closely resemble line-by-line literary explications of text. He is by far the more conservative in personality and philosophy of the three preachers.

He rarely included any political statement in his sermons during the time that I was in his church. The extent of his political statements was to urge people to vote in the upcoming election, a statement he made during the announcements, not during the sermon. His style is not to mix politics and religion in the pulpit, on one occasion he did use the pulpit to tell women not to wear pants to any function held at the church because some members had complained. This policy suggests the conservative nature of this church. The partial-manuscript minister basically sees the pulpit as the place to expound on the word of God. This is reflected in his sermons and interviews. This minister believes that sermons should be explanations of the Bible. His goal is to explain the Bible to his congregation as best he can.

Meeting the Partial-manuscript Minister's Congregation

The congregation, like their minister, can be described as low key. Holiness churches generally have the reputation, in the African-American church community, as being even more active and expressive than most African-American churches. Congregants also have the reputation of "staying in church all day." I even asked my acquaintance how long the service was when he first suggested that I visit his church. He said, "it's never more than two hours, unlike most holiness churches." This congregation and its service did not fit the image I had of how their service was supposed to be, an image which was shaped by my experiences with holiness churches in the rural South.

The low-key nature of the congregation is evident in many ways, most notably in how the congregation proceeds through the service. As in the other churches, the congregation is more active in some parts of the service than they are in others. Yet, their participation is not as intense or perhaps as verbal as in the other two churches. For example, when the senior choir sings, the congregation generally listens fairly quietly rather than standing or clapping to indicate that they are moved by the song. This could be because the choir sings anthems and spirituals more so than gospel music, and anthems and spirituals, which sometimes move people to tears, do not seem to invite the same kind of vocal responses from the congregation as do gospel songs.

The partial-manuscript minister's congregation is most vocal during the sermon and after the sermon. During the sermon, the congregation participates in the call-and-response patterns that are traditional in the African-American church, but the response seems limited to a few verbal statements. I noted that the congregation rarely showed their excitement by standing or clapping during the sermon, even during the climax. Yet, many members, especially men, answer the preacher during the sermon with "amen" and "umm hmm" or an affirmative nod of the head, and the congregation consistently answers [the minister] as a group "yes," "that's right," and "Lord." In addition, individual voices can be heard over the group responding "preach" along with other comments. As in the other churches, the more excited the minister becomes (when he raises his voice), the more vocal the congregation becomes. The more low key this minister is during the sermon, the quieter the congregation. Unlike the other two ministers, this minister seems to "wind down" during his climax, and his congregation "winds down" with him. The congregation's response reflects the minister's preaching style—straightforward and reserved, but not so low key that the service does not resemble a traditionally expressive African-American church service. However, I saw few people outwardly carried away by emotion in this church as I did in the other two churches.

Because this church is smaller than the other two churches, more members of the congregation know each other; consequently, they know when there are visitors, even when the visitors do not stand to identify themselves. I was recognized right away as new, and members of the congregation came up to me after the services each Sunday to greet and welcome me, treatment that other visitors and new members also received. Because few members knew about my research, they saw me as a potential member. I was constantly asked if or when I would join their church. I was surprised that more of the congregation's outgoing personality did not appear during the service.

Differences and Similarities

Although the three churches are similar in the format of their service, the manuscript minister's church and the nonmanuscript minister's church are more similar to each other than they are to the partial-manuscript minister's church. In a sense the partial-manuscript minister's church is a very traditional church. There are the normal organizations: deacon board, board of trustees, usher board, choirs, Sunday schools, youth groups, and so on. With the exception of the usher board and the choirs, most of these organizations are traditionally dominated by men, especially the leadership positions.

The usher board and choirs, traditionally female dominated, are organizations that have almost no role in the decision-making process of the church. In this particular church, men hold the leadership positions of almost all of the organizations. During my weeks of observation, I never saw a woman in the pulpit of this church. In contrast, the churches of the manuscript and nonmanuscript ministers have large ministerial staffs including women, who also have roles in other phases of the church. Both churches also have nontraditional organizations, such as singles groups. The manuscript preacher's church has African-American men's and women's organizations, and the nonmanuscript preacher's church has a widow(er)'s organization.

I note these differences in church organizations and the role of women because they reflect not only different philosophies of denomination but also of preachers and that affects how the preachers view their congregations. Consequently, their sermons are affected.

Although I have noted some differences, one major similarity which should be noted is the active youth groups and youth programs of each church. Each church has regular Youth Sundays when the youth run the entire worship service, including preaching. The youth also have organizations and other programs which are integral parts of the church. Because the youth at each church are so active, they are vitally involved in their churches, constantly exposed to and, indeed, deeply entrenched in the tradition of the African-American church and, therefore, its literacy traditions. This exposure to the sermon may have important consequences for how these youth and other members of the congregation view formal discourse, written and oral.

Literacy Events and Literacy Practices

This chapter focuses mostly on the sermon, but that is not the only literacy event that exists in the African-American church. Therefore, this chapter includes a brief discussion of other literacy events in these three churches which occur during Sunday worship services. It is these other literacy events that provide the context from which the sermon takes place.

Literacy Practices in the Manuscript Minister's Church

At first, one might think that the typical worship service at this church revolves around oral language use. And indeed, the sermon, which is the major activity of the service, is an orally performed event, as are the various prayers throughout the service, is an orally performed event, as are the various prayers throughout the service. However, before the congregation hears this sermon, they most likely have participated in several reading acts. Upon entering the sanctuary, worshippers are given bulletins by the ushers. These bulletins average 12 pates of written material.

The bulletin, used to present the order of worship and to make churchwide announcements, is the method that this church uses to proved non-sermon-related information to its congregation. Although many of the same announcements are read orally by one of the associate pastors each Sunday, it is this bulletin that lets the congregation know what activities are occurring in the church from week to week. Also included in this bulletin are a list of sick and shut-in members of the church, apartment advertisements, employment opportunities, and sometimes editorial essays from the desk of the pastor. This is by far the most effective method of disseminating information to the congregation. Usually before each service officially starts, most members of the congregation are using the time to read their bulletins. The information in these bulletins also becomes the basis of the talk by the pastor who highlights important information. In this case the congregation uses writing as a source of information.

The bulletin also contains the order or worship for each service. This is a church that rarely deviates from the printed order of worship in the bulletin. This order of worship appears almost ritualistic. Every Sunday the service opens with the choral introit, an opening choral number, and the Lord's Prayer. The next two acts are reading acts. The congregation sings an assigned hymn which can be found printed on an insert in the bulletin or in the hymnal. Then they participate in the responsive reading which is also printed in the bulletin and in the back of the hymnal. These two acts are performed every Sunday, and at the center of these acts is a written text. It is clear that the written Order of Worship provides structure to the service, serving the function for which it is named. Using writing as an ordering device then becomes one use of literacy in this church.

The elements in the worship service that change from Sunday to Sunday are the songs and the sermon. Because of the ritualistic nature of the service, the written Order of Worship may be more a tradition than a necessity, and if so, what kind of message is sent to the congregation about the value of writing in this situation? In African-American churches in which the Order of Worship is not consistently written, the services generally proceed in an orderly fashion but are far longer than in the churches in which the Order of Worship is written.

If one looks only at the Order of Worship, one may be puzzled by its seeming rigidity in what has been traditionally seen as the spontaneous nature of the African-American church. However, by attending the services of the manuscript minister's church, I found that within this structured service is opportunity for spontaneity by the preacher(s) and the congregation, particularly when the choir sings, during prayer time, or during the sermon. It is during these three times, when the congregation has no written text to guide them through these acts, that they seem most involved as measured through their verbal and physical responses. They are attentive through other parts of the service, but their responses are rather mechanical. Anytime the congregation reads a text, they become more passive participants as if they are listening to a lecture. However, during the times when there is not written text such as the choir's musical selections, the invocation, altar call prayer, and the sermon, the congregation becomes more active by responding vocally, clapping, standing, or some combination of the three. In short, the congregation becomes part of a dialogue.

In the sermon, the manuscript minister invites these responses. He believes that the sermon is a dialogue, not a lecture, and that the congregation should be actively involved. He sees this practice as marking a major difference between the African-American worship service and most white worship services. This practice, referred to as "call and response" (Holt, 1972) is a mainstay of the sermon event. Therefore, in this particular setting, reading is a passive act, but listening, which is normally viewed as a more passive act than reading, is far more active.

Listening to the sermon, the songs, and the prayers means answering the minister when he "hits home," or singing along or calling on Jesus to "help me," encouraging the preacher with "come on preacher" or "I know that's right," and saying "Amen" or countless other responses to let the preacher or the singer or the person praying know that you are participating in the act. Two of the more popular responses during the sermons are "preach" and "come on minister." Whether the speaker has a written text or not is not an issue for this congregation. So whatever the congregation may learn about language from a sermon or a prayer, they learn through the oral/aural mode. This is the norm (or interaction) in this church as well as in most other African-American churches I have attended over the past 25 years. And this norm is attached to an oral performance just as there are norms attached to the reading act. For the congregation these acts, prayers, and sermons are speech events that are detached from whatever written text from which they may have originated. Yet, this minister's sermons are based on written texts.

Just as the channels of language change throughout the order of service, that is, oral and written language are both used alternately throughout the service, the many acts within the Order of Worship (Lord's Prayer, invocation, ritual of friendship, altar call, sermon, hymn of invitation, etc.) result in different "keys" (Hymes, 1972). Hymes uses "key" to refer to the tone or manner of a particular act. The tone during the ritual of friendship is upbeat and lively, whereas the tone during the altar call is very serious and intense, and during the sermon the "key" may change many times. In this particular setting, there are many elements that may signal "key" from how loud the congregation is singing to how much feedback they give the preacher to how stationery the manuscript minister is during his sermon to the intonation patterns of this minister. During the services of this church, key is tied to the Order of Worship as well as to what is said and done. Because the congregation generally knows what should happen next in the service, they also know the appropriate tone and manner in which to perform an act. During my period of observation, neither the minister nor the congregation gave any indication of any inappropriate responses.

The manuscript minister best signals the key through his intonation patterns in his sermons and his physical gestures as he preaches. This minister's use of intonation and rhythm not only signals his feelings and emotions but also guides the congregation's responses to the sermon. For instance, in every sermon the manuscript minister establishes a pattern of repetition with words and intonation. As he moves toward the end of this pattern, his voice rises and along with it the congregation's responses become more vocal, louder; the clapping becomes more intense. In short, the response level rises with the minister's rise in intonation.

Literacy Practices in the Nonmanuscript Minister's Church

The nonmanuscript minister's church resembles the manuscript minister's in the way that written texts are used in the service. As in the manuscript minister's church, this church has a printed Sunday bulletin that includes the order of the service, announcements, names of the sick and shut-in, and sometimes forms to fill out (e.g., Vacation Bible school registration). The bulletin averages approximately 7 pages per Sunday. Although most of the announcements are in the bulletin, there are a few that are not and therefore must be read to the congregation. Every Sunday, someone, usually the same person, highlights many of the announcements in and out of the bulletin. This printed bulletin, combined with the oral reading of announcements, seems to be an effective means of disseminating information. And as stated earlier, it provides the order of the service.

This order of service includes two reading acts in addition to reading the bulletin—the responsive reading, which is a part of most church services, and the hymn of celebration, both of which are found in the hymnal. Not other reading acts are read by the congregation; instead, someone reads to the congregation. These reading acts tend to occur early in the service before the sermon. The scripture, however, is generally read by one of the assistant pastors. Many members read along (silently) in their own Bibles, as does the congregation in the manuscript minister's church. Most of the service proceeds according to the program. The congregation is generally low key during this part of the service, participating when they are supposed to.

The only time that feedback occurs before the sermon is when the choir sings a particularly moving arrangement of a song or when some announcements are read that invite feedback. For example, one Sunday, members of the singles ministry performed a brief commercial to advertise the church picnic which was to occur in the near future. It drew great responses from the audience. There are several occasions when the choir sings songs that have many members of the congregation singing along, standing and clapping, and a few times physically feeling the sprit and shouting, although shouting is rare in this church. For the congregation, everything in the service is an oral speech event except the two previously mentioned reading acts. Again, as in the manuscript minister's church, in this church, language is predominantly oral; therefore, one must deduce that most of what the people in this congregation learn about language use in this setting, they learn from and through the oral mode.

Literacy Practices in the Partial-Manuscript Minister's Church

The services in his church are similar to the services of the other two churches in that they also follow a written Order of Service printed in the Sunday bulletin. This bulletin averages four to five pages (front and back) per Sunday. Much smaller than the bulletins of the other two churches, this bulletin has on its cover a picture of the church and the biblical statement, "I was glad when they said unto me, Let us go into the house of the Lord." This cover statement illustrates the differences between this church and the other two churches, namely, that the first two churches explicitly combine their religious and social missions for the world to see. The partial-manuscript minister's church, in contrast, pushes social (and political) missions into the background and pushes its religious mission to the front. This is not to say that the other churches do not place their religious missions at the top of their priorities. Indeed, they do. However, they seem to consider their social mission as part of their religious mission.

Usually, the bulletin at the partial-manuscript minister's church includes one page devoted to the Order of Service, another devoted to a list of the sick and shut-in, a page or two that lists announcements, and finally a page which lists church officers and regular weekly church activities. Also, on the last page of each bulletin is a space called "sermon notes" where parishioners can take notes on the sermon. That is unique to this church. The other two churches provide no space in the bulletin to take notes on the sermon. This space is very small, but by virtue of its existence, one may assume that the idea of taking written notes is not an alien idea. My acquaintance in this church even told me that many people including himself take notes during the sermon. As I looked for this during my observation, I found that the people I noticed taking notes were the younger, more educated members who had been introduced to me by my acquaintance, then a doctoral candidate in biomedical engineering, and his wife, a medical doctor. Very few of the other members of the congregation take any kind of notes during the sermon.

This church's order of worship only deviates from what is printed in the bulletin when there is a guest speaker, and even the, the deviation is slight. The congregation moves through the order of worship in a very straightforward manner. The services open with the same hymn each week and a scripture which is printed in the bulletin. This call-to-worship scripture was the same three times out of the five weeks of services for which I have tapes. The congregation reads this call to worship aloud as a group, but there is no responsive reading as it is done in the other two churches. However, as in the other two churches, there are musical selections, announcements, scriptural readings, and as in the manuscript minister's church, an altar call in each service.

Also like the other churches, this church adds to the bulletin communion-related concerns on every first Sunday when they celebrate communion. In addition, during the time of my observation, a memory verse was assigned in the bulletin each week. The congregation was given the book, chapter, and verse of the passage which they were to look up and memorize. This verse changes each week, unlike in the manuscript minister's church, where a memory verse is assigned every month and is printed in the weekly bulletin. For both of these churches, assigning a memory verse encourages the congregation to learn the Bible. In African-American churches there is great value attached to being able to recite Bible verses from memory because it indicates that you know the Bible.

As in the other two churches, in the partial-manuscript minister's church, oral language dominates the service, particularly for the congregation. For them the most important part of the service, the sermon, is oral and aural, whereas for the minister, it is oral and written. Written texts are the basis for his sermons. The written texts that the congregation regularly uses during the service are the bulletins, the hymnal, and for a brief 60 seconds or so, the Bible.

The Sermon as a Literacy Event: The Ties That Bind

One of the more well-known facts about African-American sermons is that they are characterized by a call-and-response pattern, in which the congregation provides feedback to the minister throughout the sermon. This audience participation pattern is always prevalent in the minds of the three ministers in this study. It is this pattern that prompts each minister to characterize the sermon as a dialogue and because of this characterization to distinguish African-American sermons from most other American protestant sermons (there are some exceptions) which more closely resemble a monologue. This dialogic pattern is the rhetorical device that acts as the foundation for the other three devices I focus on in this section.

In the ministers' discussions of their sermon preparation, each seems acutely aware of the role of the congregation in the construction of a successful sermon. Even the manuscript minister who writes practically all of his sermons speaks of making room for the congregation to participate in the sermon. What these ministers do in their "texts" is to invite audience participation by using the sermon to create and maintain a community. In a sense, viewing the sermon as a dialogue between minister and congregation makes the sermon a community text that is written (or created) through a collaboration between minister and congregation. What I examine in the remainder of this chapter are the features used by the ministers in the sermons that contribute to this sense of community and create space for the dialogue.

Much of the success and/or effectiveness of the three ministers depends on their creating a bond between themselves and their congregations. Also, because part of people's identities are linked with the communities in which they hold memberships, when these preachers use sermons to construct communities, they are also constructing not only their identities, but also the identities of the members of the congregation.

Why is it important to create this sense of community? According to the ministers, placing themselves in the congregation and seeing themselves as part of the group, helps them keep their sermons relevant to the congregation, helps build trust between the minister and the congregation, and therefore, makes it easier for the congregation to hear and accept the message that the minister is preaching. Ultimately, these three ministers try to eliminate distance between them and the congregation through the sermon; yet, they must maintain the "proper" distance because of their leadership positions. Already we can see the multiple functions of this literacy event as well as its multidimensional nature.

The rhetorical strategies that the ministers use to construct and maintain community range from the seemingly simple reliance on first person plural pronouns to the more complex reliance on personal narratives and shared information. Various rhetorical devices are used by these ministers to construct community. It is also important to note that the theme of community also pervades the sermons as a mechanism for emphasis.

"We, The People"

One of the most obvious strategies that each minister consistently uses to help establish a sense of community is the employing of the collective pronouns *we, our,* and *us*. This strategy is a favorite of these ministers, and although it is not unique to African-American sermons (see Jellema, 1988), it is a feature that they use effectively. When the ministers use this strategy, they are tapping into the multiple levels of community represented in their churches as well as establishing their relationships with those communities. Consider the following examples from two different sermons in which the manuscript minister invokes at least three communities: his specific church community, the community of Christians, and society at large. As he taps into these three communities, his membership in these communities is also emphasized:

> Example 1: Some of the meanest most miserable ungodly people I know got more degrees behind they names and make more money than most of us will ever see in a lifetime.

> Example 2: We not at the pinnacle and we not in the pits. We just in between. Nothing to complain about and nothing to write home about either. We're not on a constant high no matter what kind of rhetoric we spout. And we not continuously in the dumps. Oh we have our moments like everybody else. But for the most part we find ourselves hanging around that gray area called in between.

In the first example, the pronoun *us* is so subtly used that we almost miss it. Based on its linguistic context, we can reasonably deduce that the community that the manuscript minister is tapping into is the specific church community. More interesting than the community that he taps into is that he includes himself in this community with the rest of the congregation. He is constructing his identity as a "regular guy" out there in the pew with little money just like everyone else in the church. Yet, he has a BA, two MAs, and was working toward a doctorate (which he has obtained since the study). He drives an expensive car, makes a most respectable if not enviable salary, and lives in an upper middle class Chicago neighborhood (in the church parsonage). But he constructs an identity that downplays his credentials and status.

It's important to this minister that he not separate himself from the congregation based on socioeconomic issues. That is seen even more clearly in the second example taken from the first few minutes of one the manuscript minister's sermons. In this example, *we* can have at least three referents—the church community, the Christian community, and the community of people in general. The primary audience seems to be the church community; yet, there are no cues that signal a specific community. Again, the minister establishes himself as a member of all of these communities, constructing his identity and contributing to the construction of their identities as a group. The congregation's apparent acceptance of their identities as shaped in this example (through nods of the head, amens, and other comments) marks their contribution to the dialogue that constructs their identities.

Another prominent community which the ministers, particularly the manuscript and nonmanuscript ministers, reference consistently is the African-American community. This is no surprise given the philosophies of those two ministers. They constantly emphasize their identities as African Americans and try to get their congregation to do so as well. Therefore, many times, the collective pronouns refer to the African-American community to which the ministers and their congregations belong. Consider the following example from the manuscript minister and a later example from the nonmanuscript minister:

Example: The God of Harriet Tubman is an *us* God—Community
The God of Martin Delaney is an *us* God—Community
The God of Ida B. Wells is an *us* God—Community

These names refer to famous African Americans from the past. One reading of this passage is that the God of these noteworthy African Americans who struggled yet accomplished much is a God of the people—a God who embraces African Americans. He is not a *them* God—a God for the rich and powerful only, or a God for whites only. African Americans are part of the community too. Here, the theme of community is intertwined with constructing the community. This passage is also one of those examples, which I address later, of using an assumed shared knowledge between minister and congregation to construct and maintain community.

An example of the nonmanuscript minister using collective pronouns to emphasize the African-American community occurs in statements such as the following:

Example: We can no longer stand in this world as second class in the economic world, but we got to think big.

Previous statements in the sermon signal that we refers to African Americans. The nonmanuscript minister implies that he, along with his other sisters and brothers, needs to think big. Of course, after being in this church for only a couple of weeks, it is clear that this minister thinks big consistently and that he is really trying to get African Americans in general, and his African-American congregation in particular, to think big. In this case, the minister is trying to change the perceived identity of the community. Yet, he has chosen not to place himself apart from the community he is addressing.

"I Can Witness"

This strategy of using collective pronouns to bind the ministers with their congregations seems obvious and simple, but its functions, as shown above, are subtle and complex. A less obvious strategy in creating and maintaining a community in the sermon is the use of personal narratives and testimonial-like statements. Again, this pattern is prevalent in both the manuscript and nonmanuscript ministers' sermons. These ministers' reference to themselves as individuals in the sermons most often take the form of personal stories, testimonies, and testimonial-like statements. In these churches there appears to be an implied distinction between testimonies and what I refer to as testimonial-like statements. A person who testifies, who gives a testimony, usually gives a detailed account of some tragedy or down time in his or her life. The account ends with how God brought him or her through this bad time. The testimony is usually quite specific. A testimonial-like statement is a more general version of "testifying;" for example, "God has lifted me up when I was down." Yet, we do not know what the down period was. My field notes contain several entries concerning how excited and vocal the congregations become in the midst of these ministers' stories or testimonies.

During interviews, each minister commented on how African-American churches value personal stories from the ministers. The partial-manuscript minister explains this value most succinctly: "In black churches, the people want to know what God has done for you [the minister]. What can you testify to?" The ministers gain more credibility and authority when they can show their congregations that they know what they are preaching about because they have been down and survived, they have been scared and conquered the fear, they have had experiences which have paralleled those of the people in the pew, and they have persevered and prospered. These personal stories provide the congregation with a more intimate view of the minister.

In sharing something personal, be it poignant or funny, these ministers forge even stronger bonds between themselves and the congregations; hence, they are strengthening community ties. The following example is a personal narrative that the nonmanuscript minister uses as an illustration in his sermon about Abraham:

> I was in the Marine Corps. I was training in Parris Island. I learned something at Parris Island. It was back in those days in 1954 when they was killing marines down there. Marines died on forced marches. I went down there right after six marines were drowned. When I got there the first thing I heard when I got off the bus, somebody said "move." Then he called me a name that just hurt me to my heart. When he called me he said move it you [blank] and I went to him and said sir, just a minute. I said I'm "—" Then he called me another name. I don't care who the [blank] you are. It took me a whole week. My heart just lay bare. I was hurt to the core. But every time in the morning they could get up early when you are tired they would come in and say "move it." We just got in bed. "Move it."

> My friend and I were put in swimming. I never swam in my life. I didn't know how to swim. They took us into the pool. One day there we were. I thought we were going in there to learn how to doggy paddle. Stand on the side, put your feed up and down,

learn how to swim the normal and intelligent way. There we all were there buck naked standing over the side of the pool. I remember all of us lined up. DIs standing on the side over there. There was a young brother named Logan standing next to me. I said, "Logan guess we're going to learn to swim in a minute. They going to teach us how to do this." Logan said, "Yes I've been waiting for this." Then they told us I want you to bend over just like that (demonstrates to congregation). All of us bent over then I heard this loud crack, "Move it!" I turned and looked back and said, "Do you mean?" "Yes, move it." I looked at Logan and said, "We're on this island out here. We're not going to get out of here. I better move." Logan said "Are you sure?" I said, "Yes." I jumped in. I took a risk. When I jumped in I went down. There I was swallowing the whole pool. I went up and down again. I started out the third time. They threw something out and pulled me out....Brothers and sisters God is often saying to us and you know something I moved at least four times, almost drowned at least four times. But the fifth time I got out there. I found a way of swimming like nobody has ever seen before. I got out that pool. I was not going to drown out there anymore. Brothers and sisters what I'm saying to you. God said it to Abraham, "Move it."

This lengthy example is actually two smaller stories within one longer one, and it highlights this preacher's skills as a storyteller. Storytelling, be it personal or biblical, is a dominant rhetorical device that this minister uses throughout his sermons. The story above is one of his most successful ones as measured by the large amount and loud volume of feedback he receives from the congregation. In this example, the minister shows himself as a naïve, sometimes frightened young man who overcomes these drawbacks by taking a risk, by moving forward. This characterization of him as naïve and frightened is in direct conflict with the person that he seemingly is now. He has a confident, self-assured presence. One might view him more as a drill instructor than a naïve marine private. Therefore, sharing this story about himself with the congregation shows the congregation a different, more vulnerable side of him.

This minister also uses the testimonial-like examples in his sermons to the same effect as he uses the narrative:

Example: A Jesus that I know lives. He is not a dead Jesus. This Jesus that I serve, this Jesus that I know is alive. The Jesus is at this table right now (inaudible) Jesus, he's alive. He lives. How do I know he lives? Because he walks with me and he talks with me. He tells me I am his own. Jesus is the life of the world. Jesus puts joy in my life. Jesus gives me peace when I'm sorrow...

Example: Well what do I get from it? You see these degrees that I've got? Well I see. They're not there just for me. But one is for my father, one is for my grandfather, one is for my great-grandfather, one is for those generations yet unborn. I've come a long way. And don't stop me now. I am what I am Thank God. I am so glad to be (inaudible). Thank you Jesus. I am what I am. Don't mess with me. Don't mess with me.

The latter example is fascinating because it relates to the earlier example from this minister of thinking big, and it contributes a new dimension to the issue of constructing an identity through the sermon. Although the manuscript minister emphasizes how he is just like everybody else, this minister emphasizes how he is just like everybody else, this minister emphasizes how he is not like everybody else. The latter example emphasizes his degrees. The earlier narrative emphasizes how he takes risks. He is constructing an identity of himself as a strong-willed, aggressive, upwardly mobile person. He wants his congregation to reach his heights and not accept being "just plain ole folks." He wants them, particularly his African-

American congregation, to construct an identity different from that which society has given the. And the implicit message is that he should be the role model for this reconstruction of identity.

Even though the nonmanuscript minister appears to distance himself from his congregation by emphasizing his successes, he, in fact, is trying to decrease the gap by appealing to them to rise to his heights and by showing them that his successes were for those who had come before him and for "generations yet unborn." He emphasizes his dedication to his people and, implicitly, his faith that his risks will pay off. The evidence of the value of his strategy is the positive response of the congregation; their level of feedback increases; they respond vocally, and they applaud with a great deal of energy. Through this focus on himself, this minister skillfully manages to maintain community ties, and he skillfully yet subtly establishes some standards for community behavior: taking risk, thinking big, and so on.

The final example below fits into two categories. It is another example of the testimonial-like statement, and it is an example that introduces the strategy of using shared information between minister and congregation to emphasize community ties.

> *Example*: I don't sing...because of thunderous ovations and grand audiences. I don't sing...because I've got a voice like James Cleveland, Dave Peaceton, or Teddy Pendergrass. I don't sing because I think I got a solo voice, and I might get discovered by some record company. I sing to praise him. I sing to my little light shine. I sing... because God has been good to me. I sing because I'm happy and I praise him and I say thank you Lord. I sing because I'm free. And I praise him. I sing because I know he watches over me.

As the manuscript minister delivers this part of his sermon, much of the congregation stands and applauds, waves their hands, and responds with encouragements such as "preach," "yes," "amen," "thank you Jesus," and other phrases. As they are responding to the minister's words about himself and his relationship with God, there also seems to be a kind of transformation which takes place. The congregation is moved by the witnessing of the minister, but they also identify with him. That is, the "I" in the example becomes a collective "I" that refers not only to the minister but also to the community of believers in that congregation. This minister is no longer speaking for himself but for the community as well. This takes the personal testimony to a new dimension in which the minister's story becomes the people's story.

The manuscript minister says that one of his goals when he prepares his sermons is to seek this collective voice. He views himself as part of the congregation and asks himself, "What do I need to hear today?" He is successful only if he is so much a part of the congregation that he sees himself in them, and they see themselves in him; hence, the "I" becomes representational. When the minister and congregation identify with each other so strongly, the community ties are more deeply embedded, the minister is more firmly entrenched as a role model, and his or her use of language and literacy is more influential.

"The Knowledge We Share"

The previous example provides a segue into the final feature of the literacy event on which this chapter focuses—relying on shared knowledge. These ministers relied on shared knowledge between themselves and their congregation to signal community identification. That is, the ministers assume that their congregation, by virtue of their membership in various communities, has a body of knowledge about certain topics, that that this knowledge is part of their culture. Therefore, these ministers assume that they do not need to explain certain references that come under the auspices of these topics. Many of the examples in the sermons point to an assumed shared knowledge of popular culture, of the Bible, and most often, of African-American culture and history. The previous example emphasizes a knowledge of African-American music, both secular and gospel. James Cleveland was a well-known African-American gospel singer. David Peaceton is most recently known as a rhythm and blues singer, and Teddy Pendergrass is noted for being a soul singer. All of these singers are popular in the African-American community and noted for their great voices. The manuscript minister assumes that this information is knowledge that the community shares, therefore, there is no need to explain.

In addition to the three references that rely on shared or given information, this example also taps into the community knowledge of music in a different way. Included in the minister's example are lyrics from the popular gospel song "His Eye Is On the Sparrow." This song is not unique to the African-American community, and it is a very popular song. "I sing because I'm happy/ I sing because I'm free/I know that he watches over me" are lyrics found in this song. Never in the sermon does the minister make mention of the song title. Again, he assumes that the congregation knows the song. Using song lyrics as examples, either gospel or secular, is a common device for the manuscript and nonmanuscript ministers. In interviews each minister emphasized how important music is in the African-American community, particularly in the African-American worship tradition. Music is so important that it becomes part of the text and, therefore, part of the literacy event. Neither of these ministers make clear distinctions between secular and sacred music.

As I mentioned earlier, the ministers also assume a shared knowledge of African-American history. Earlier in this chapter, I discussed an example from the manuscript minister that employed collective pronouns and focused thematically on community: "the God of Harriet Tubman is an *us* God....community/ the God of Martin Delaney is an *us* God...community/ the god of Ida B. Wells is an *us* God...community." The minister mentioned other famous African-American historical figures. Again, he offers no explanation of who these people were. His assumption is that people in the community know these people, and if they do not, they should know and better find out about their history and culture, or that those who do not know are not in the community. Being in the community and not having the shared knowledge becomes, for some, a motivation to learn—a subtle teaching device like many of the strategies discussed earlier.

Using examples from the culture of his congregation not only emphasizes the value of the culture but also signals that the minister knows the music, history, literature, and ways of the community. When we assume memberships in the same communities, then we feel comfortable assuming that other members of that community are familiar with much of the same information. Tapping into that familiarity, that common ground, through the text is a major function of the sermon. Tapping into that familiarity also allows the ministers to move their congregations from the familiar to the unfamiliar, by beginning with what people know—a sound pedagogical strategy.

Conclusion

I had three major goals in this chapter: (a) to describe the major literacy events and their functions in three African-American churches; (b) to describe and analyze the features and functions of the African-American sermon, the major literacy event in

African-American churches; and (c) to compare and contrast models of literacy in three African-American churches with models of literacy in the academy. The discussion of the first goal provides a context for discussing the second goal, a description and analysis of the African-American sermon, which in turn provides the basis for the third goal. All of the literacy events discussed meet Heath's (1982) definition of a literacy event: "Any action sequence, involving one or more persons, in which the production and / or comprehension of print plays a role" (p.92).

Even though each of the three churches represents a different denomination and has ministers with different styles, there was some consistency in the kinds of literacy events which took place in each church. The most obvious literacy event in each church beyond the sermon was represented in the church bulletin. The bulletin's major function was to disseminate information, but it also served as a structuring device by providing the Order of Worship for the service and as a mnemonic device, reminding the congregations of the verse they were to memorize weekly or monthly.

Other literacy events in both the manuscript and nonmanuscript minister's churches included responsive readings of the scriptures from either the bulletin or the hymnal. And one of the more interesting yet overlooked literacy events in each church was the songs assigned. At least one song in each church functioned as a reading act. That is, the song was either printed in the bulletin or in the hymnal. The literacy events mentioned above are typical kinds of literacy events recognized and/ or used in the academy because they involve reading print. They are, as this chapter demonstrates, part of the ritualistic services at most African-American churches and many protestant churches in general.

The atypical literacy event in this institution is the major one—the African-American sermon. The description of the features of the sermon has shown its uniqueness both as a literacy event—an ongoing process—and as a literate text. The textual features of the sermon which I have focused on are (a) use of collective pronouns in the sermon, (b) use of personal narratives and testimony, (c) reliance on shared cultural knowledge, and (d) the dialogic quality of African-American sermons. Because of its foundational role, the fourth feature—the dialogic quality—could not be treated separately; instead, it is shown to be an integral part of each textual feature. The ministers use these prominent sermonic features to create a community in their churches. The text—the sermon—becomes the major instrument by which to construct and maintain community ties and identities.

As the analysis has shown, the first three features are rhetorical devices that the ministers use in their sermons to draw them closer together with their congregation. The ministers use collective pronouns and personal narratives to shoe their congregations that they are no different than the people sitting in the pews, that they [the ministers] can identify with their congregation. The third device calls for the ministers to display their understanding of cultural knowledge, thus establishing community insider/ outsider status. These are all devices that encourage the congregation to involve themselves in the making of the text. Seeing themselves as part of the text, as being able to provide feedback and respond to the minister as part of the sermon, is a traditional characteristic of African-American sermons, and it is this process that is the essence of the fourth device—the dialogic quality.

The final goal—comparing and contrasting literacy in these African-American churches with literacy in the academy—is best understood by examining the implications of this study. First, this study suggests that because of the dialogic quality of African-American sermons and the focus on constructing community identities through the sermon, no fixed boundary between speaker and audience exists. Instead, participant roles constantly switch back and fort during the sermon. Even when a minister writes his sermon, as the manuscript minister does, he understands, allows, and, in fact, needs audience participation to complete the text. Audience participation in performance events, such as the sermon, is an Afrocentric concept characteristic of many African-American communities' performance-oriented events (R.F. Thompson, 1983).

The dialogic nature of the text also suggests, because of the lack of fixed boundaries, that the sermon can realistically be viewed as a community text. As he conceives of and shapes the sermon, the minister has no real ownership of the text. The ministers in this study argue that once a sermon is preached, it is no longer their sermon. There appears to be no concept such as ownership of text or intellectual property. Yet, academic literacy holds as one of its most sacred principles the ownership of words. These ministers also suggest that even if they preach the same sermon twice, it really is not the same sermon. Once the audience changes, the dialogue changes, and, therefore, the sermon changes. In other words, the sermon can never be decontextualized. Much of its meaning is determined by the participants.

As the boundaries are blurred between speaker and audience, so too are the boundaries between oral and written patterns in the sermons. Even through the sermon is an orally performed event, it also represents a literate text, one that uses varying degrees of writing and speech. This integration of speech and writing is part of the text of the sermon and once more points to the blurred boundaries and seamlessness that surround the sermons. This seamlessness can be found not only within the sermons. This seamlessness can be found not only within the sermons, but also within the service that surrounds the sermon (see Mountford, 1991). That is, neither the sermons nor the service can be easily segmented into discreet sections.

The blurred boundaries between speech and writing are most evident when one considers how many devices the manuscript and nonmanuscript ministers' texts have in common, even through one minister wrote everything down and preached verbatim from his written text, and the other wrote nothing. Because the sermon is an orally performed event, one is inclined to think of it as only an oral text, but the sermons are generally rooted in biblical scriptures—a written text. In addition, these ministers are highly literate men (as defined by the academy) whose lives are deeply influenced by written words. Yet, clearly, they do not view writing and speaking as an either/or dichotomy; in their communities, writing and speaking are intertwined and interdependent. The boundaries blur.

The nonfixed and blurred boundaries which characterize these ministers' sermons point toward a model of a literate text that is far different from the model that most quickly comes to mind when one thinks of the kind of literate text that dominates in school—the academic essay. The academic essay is generally characterized by its fixed boundaries between media and genres, its radical individualism and monologic quality, its decontextualized meaning, and its traditional definitions of intellectual property. These are features of the essayist tradition.

Although some argue that this is an ideal rather than a real model of the academic essay, it is still the model from which we operate in the academy and which we use to measure most other models and to measure students. Even though collaboratively written texts are acceptable texts in the academy, the text is still one that uses the monologic model. No matter how many writers a collaborative text may have, the writers strive for only one voice to be heard, as if there were only one writer and there were no audience involvement in the text.

Thus, the African-American sermon stands as a model of a literate text which in many ways is the antithesis of the academic essay and promotes a type of literacy which is the antithesis of the most popular academic notion of literacy. Like those who point to electronic and hypertextual forms of literacy, this study suggests that the academy must broaden its definition of literacy and, in addition, its conceptualization of the literate text and the "writer" or "owner" of that text. Privileging the essayist tradition of literacy leaves the academy unable and unwilling to recognize and validate types of literacies from other communities. One powerful consequence of this weakness is that we ignore the richness of literacies that our students from nonmainstream communities bring to the academy, literacies that could be used to help many of these students to more easily expand their knowledge base to include academic literacies. Most seriously, we also close ourselves off from opportunities to learn more about the diverse cultures and literacies represented in our classrooms. If multiculturalism and diversity are the future of the academy, then so is multiliteracy.

References

Blassingame, J. (1979). *The slave community: Plantation life in the antebellum south.* New York: Oxford University Press.

Davis, G. (1985). *I got the word in me, and I can sing it, you know.* Philadelphia: University of Pennsylvania Press.

Davis, H.G. (1958). *Design for preaching.* Philadelphia: Fortress Press.

Fishman, A. (1988). *Amish literacy: What and how it means.* Portsmouth, NH: Heinemann.

Frazier, E.F. (1974). *The Negro church in America.* New York: Shoeken Books.

Hamilton, C. (1972). *The black preacher in America.* New York: William Morrow.

Heath, S. (1982). Protean shapes in literacy events: evershifting oral and literate traditions. In D. Tannen (Ed.), *Spoken and written language: Exploring orality and literacy* (pp. 91-117). Norwood, NJ: Ablex.

Heath, S. (1983). *Ways with words.* Cambridge: Cambridge University Press.

Holt, G.S. (1972). Stylin' outa the black pulpit. In T. Kochman (Ed.), *Rappin' and stylin' out* (pp. 189-204). Chicago: University of Chicago Press.

Hymes, D. (1972). Models of the interaction of language and social life. In J.J. Gumperz & D. Hymes (Eds.), *Directions in sociolinguistics: The ethnography of communication* (pp. 35-71). New York: Holt, Rinehart and Winston, Inc.

Jellema, L. (1988). *Rhetoric and economics in television evangelism: What evangelists say and do to bring in money.* Unpublished doctoral dissertation, University of Illinois at Chicago.

Keeping the Faith. (1987, February). *Frontline* [television program]. Chicago: PBS, WTTW.

Lincoln, C.E. (1974). *The black experience in religion.* Garden City, NY: Doubleday.

Mays, B., & Nicholson, J. (1933). *The negro's church.* New York: Negro Universities Press.

Mitchell, H. (1970). *Black preaching.* Philadelphia: Lippincott.

Moss, B. (1988). *The black sermon as a literacy event.* Unpublished doctoral dissertation, University of Illinois at Chicago.

Mountford, R. (1991). *The feminization of the Ars Praedicandi.* Unpublished doctoral dissertation, The Ohio State University, Columbus, OH.

Philips, S. (1972). Participant structures and communicative competence: Warm Springs children in community and classroom. In C. Cazden, V. John, & D. Hymes (Eds.), *Functions of language in the classroom* (pp. 370-392).

St. Augustine. (1958). *On Christian doctrine* (D.W. Robertson, Trans.). New York: Bobbs-Merrill Company.

Scollon, R., & Scollon, S. (1981). *Narrative, literacy and face in interethnic communication.* Norwood, NJ: Ablex.

Scribner, S., & Cole, M. (1981). *The psychology of literacy.* Cambridge, MA: Harvard University Press.

Smitherman, G. (1977). *Talkin' and testifying'.* Boston: Houghton-Mifflin.

Spradley, J.P. (1979). *The ethnographic interview.* New York: Holt, Rinehart and Winston.

Spradley, J.P. (1980). *Participant Observation.* New York: Holt, Rinehart and Winston.

Street, B.V. (1984). *Literacy in theory and practice.* Cambridge: Cambridge University Press.

Szwed, J.F. (1981). The ethnography of literacy. In M. Farr (Ed.), *Writing: The nature, development, and teaching of written communication* (pp. 13-23). Hillsdale, NJ: Erlbaum.

Taylor, D., & Dorsey-Gaines, C. (1988). *Growing up literate.* Portsmouth, NH: Heinemann.

Thompson, R.F. (1983). *Flash of the spirit.* New York: Random House.

Thompson, W. (1981). *Preaching Biblically.* Nashville: Abingdon.

Weinstein-Shr, G. (1986). *From mountaintops to city streets: An ethnographic investigation of literacy and social process, among the Hmong of Philadelphia.* Unpublished doctoral dissertation, University of Pennsylvania, Philadelphia.

NOW THAT YOU'VE READ

1. What have been your experiences with what Moss calls here the "African-American sermon"? If you have no direct experiences with this, what experiences have you had with a church community you know well? Are your experiences similar to those Moss articulates? Different? In what ways? What are we to make of these similarities? These differences? If you haven't had many direct experiences with a particular church, work with what you do know about the literacies associated with church. (How you know what you know about churches.)

2. What are the "features of African-American preaching" as Moss describes them? List them and then reflect upon what conclusions we can draw from that list.

3. What are the literacy practices Moss observes? Name at least three. What else can we learn from these lists and the patterns that emerge from them?

4. If your experiences are with religious institutions quite unlike the ones Moss describes, reflect on those experiences and unpack them for us. What texts are involved at these church services? What do members of the congregation typically say before, after, and during the service? What "norms" are "attached to the oral performance" of the texts involved (perhaps the sermon) and which are "attached to the reading act" (Moss 102)?

READING

Learning to Serve: The Language and Literacy of Food Service Workers

Tony Mirabelli

Tony Mirabelli is a Tutorial Coordinator at University of California-Berkeley, where—in 2001, he earned his PhD in Education in Language, Literacy and Culture. His article, "Learning to Serve: The Language and Literacy of Food Service Workers," examines the literacy practices involved in restaurant work in many of the same ways Moss looked at the African-American church. Like Moss, Mirabelli had extensive personal experience with these literacy events and practices as they manifest themselves in the contexts he investigates. The following article examines an Italian-American restaurant where he worked as a waiter for two years.

BEFORE YOU READ answer the following questions:

1. What sorts of literacy events and practices do you understand to be a regular part of food service work? Have you ever worked in a restaurant? If not, the time you've spent in one or more restaurants will help you answer these questions. Make use of that knowledge. Might the literacy practices required of workers in what Mirabelli calls "diner restaurants" differ from those required of fast-food service workers? How? What literacy practices and events are involved with a restaurant you know particularly well? What kinds of texts can be found? How are they used? What "literacy events" surround their use?

2. According to the following essay, "how language is spoken, read, or written in a restaurant may be vastly different from how it is used in a classroom.... How the waitress or waiter understands and uses texts such as the menu and how she or he 'reads' and verbally interacts with the customer reflect carefully constructed uses of language and literacy" (145). What does he mean by this? Do you agree? Why or why not?

Learning to Serve: The Language and Literacy of Food Service Workers

Tony Mirabelli

Bitterwaitress.com is one of the newest among a burgeoning number of worker-produced websites associated with the service industry.[1] The menu on the first page of this website offers links to gossip about celebrity behavior in restaurants, gossip about chefs and restaurant owners, accounts from famous people who were once waitresses,[2] and customer-related horror stories. There is also a forum that includes a "hate mail" page that posts email criticisms of the website itself, as well as general criticisms of waitressing, but the criticisms are followed by rebuttals usually from past or present waitresses. Predictably, most of the criticisms either implicitly or explicitly portray waitresses as ignorant and stupid. One email respondent didn't like what he read on the customer horror story page and sent in this response:

> If you find your job [as a waitress] so despicable, then go get an education and get a REAL job. You are whining about something that you can fix. Stop being such a weakling, go out and learn something, anything, and go make a real contribution to society .... Wait, let me guess: you do not have any marketable skills or useful knowledge, so you do what any bumbling fool can do, wait on tables. This is your own fault.

This response inspired a number of rebuttals of which the following two best summarize the overall sentiment expressed in response to the rant above. The first is from the webmaster of *bitterwaitress.com*:

> Is it possible that I have an education, maybe I went to, oh say, Duke, and I just waitressed for some free time? Or that there are very many people in the industry who do this so that they CAN get an education? Not all of us were born with a trust fund.—There is, I might add, considerably more or less to a job than a "clear cut" salary. If you ... live in New York, ... you'll know that empty stores and un-crowded subways are half the reason to work at night. By the way, what are the three Leovilles? What are the two kinds of tripe? Who was Cesar Ritz' partner? What is the JavaScript for a rollover? I guess I would have to ask a bumbling fool those questions. So, tell me then.

The second is from a mother of four:

> I might not have a college education, but I would love to see those so called intelligent people get a big tip out of a bad meal, or from a person who is rude and cocky just because that's the way they are—that takes talent and its not a talent you can learn at any university. So, think about it before you say, "poor girl—to dumb to get a real job ...."

Assumptions that waitresses (and waiters) are ignorant and stupid and that waiting on tables contributes little to society are not new. The rebuttals to commonplace, pejorative understandings of the food service industry suggest, however, that there is complexity and skill that may go unrecognized by the general public or institutions such as universities. Indeed institutions, particularly government and corporate entities in the United States, like the Bureau of Labor Statistics or the National Skills Labor Board, define waiting on tables as a low skilled profession. By defining this kind of work as low skilled, there is a concomitant implication that the more than one-third of America's work force who do it are low skilled.

Service occupations, otherwise known as "in-person" services (Reich, 1992) or "interactive services" (Leidner, 1993; MacDonald and Sirianni, 1996), include any kind of work which fundamentally involves face-to-face or voice-to-voice interactions and conscious manipulation of self-presentation. As distinguished from white-collar service work, this category of "emotional proletariat" (Macdonald and Sirianni, 1996) is comprised primarily of retail sales workers, hotel workers, cashiers, house cleaners, flight attendants, taxi drivers, package delivery drivers, and waiters, among others. According to the U.S. Bureau of Labor Statistics (1996), one-fifth of the jobs in eating, drinking, and grocery store establishments are held by youth workers between the ages of 16 and 24. While this kind of work is traditionally assumed to be primarily a stop-gap for young workers who will later move up and on to other careers, it also involves youths who will later end up in both middle- and working-class careers. It should not be forgotten that more than two thirds of the workers involved in food service are mature adults—many or most who began their careers in the same or similar industries. Interactive service work is a significant part of the economy in the U.S. today, and the Bureau of Labor Statistics predicts that jobs will be "abundant" in this category through 2006.

Economists such as Peter Drucker (1993) suggest that interactive service workers lack the necessary education to be "knowledge" workers. These economists support general conceptions that service work is "mindless," involving routine and repetitive tasks that require little education. This orientation further suggests that these supposedly low skilled workers lack the problem identifying, problem solving, and other high level abilities needed to work in other occupations. However, relatively little specific attention and analysis have been given to the literacy skills and language abilities needed to do this work. My research investigates these issues with a focus on waiters and waitresses who work in diners. Diner restaurants are somewhat distinct from fast food or fine-dining restaurants, and they also epitomize many of the assumptions held about low skilled workplaces that require interactive services. The National Skills Standards Board, for instance, has determined that a ninth-grade level of spoken and written language use is needed to be a waiter or a waitress. Yet, how language is spoken, read, or written in a restaurant may be vastly different from how it is used in a classroom. A seemingly simple event such as taking a customer's food order can become significantly more complex, for example, when a customer has a special request. How the waitress or waiter understands and uses texts such as the menu and how she or he "reads" and verbally interacts with the customer reflect carefully constructed uses of language and literacy.

This chapter explores these constructed ways of "reading" texts (and customers) along with the verbal "performances" and other manipulations of self-presentation that characterize interactive service work. In line with Macdonald and Sirianni (1996), I hope this work will contribute to the development of understandings and policies that build more respect and recognition for service work to help ensure it does not become equated with servitude.

Literacy and Contemporary Theory

In contrast to institutional assessments such as the National Skills Standards Board (1995), current thinking in key areas of education, sociology, anthropology and linguistics views language, literacy, and learning as embedded in social practice rather than entirely in the minds of individuals (Street, 1984; Gee, 1991; Lave and Wenger, 1991; Kress, 1993, 1995; Mahiri and Sablo, 1996; New London Group, 1996; Gee, Hull, and Lankshear 1996). As earlier chapters in this book have noted, Gee (1991: 6)—a key proponent of this conception of literacy—explains that to be literate means to have control of "a socially accepted association among ways of using language, of thinking, and of acting that can be used to identify oneself as a member of a socially meaningful group or 'social network.'" In a similar fashion, research work located explicitly within workplace studies proposes that literacy is "a range of practices specific to groups and individuals of different cultures, races, classes and genders" (Hull et al., 1996: 5).

In most societal institutions, however, literacy, continues to be defined by considerations of achievement and by abstract, standardized tests of individual students. Also, there is a decided focus on printed texts over other mediums of communication like visual and audio. Such a focus limits our understanding of literacy in terms of its use in specific situations in multiple modes of communication. The New Literacy Studies orientation that shapes the work reported in this book argues that literacy extends beyond individual experiences of reading and writing to include the various modes of communication and situations of any socially meaningful group or network where language is used in multiple ways. The New London Group (1996), for example, claims that due to changes in the social and economic environment, schools too must begin to consider language and literacy education in terms of "multiliteracies." The concept of multiliteracies supplements traditional literacy pedagogy by addressing the multiplicity of communications channels and the increasing saliency of cultural and linguistic diversity in the world today. Central to this study is the understanding that literate acts are embedded in specific situations and that they also extend beyond the printed text involving other modes of communication including both verbal and nonverbal. In this chapter, I illustrate something of the character of literacies specific to the "social network" of waiting on tables and show how they are distinct from the conceptions of literacy commonly associated with formal education. This is not simply to suggest that there is a jargon specific to the work, which of course there is, but that there is something unique and complex about the ways waiters and waitresses in diners use language and literacy in doing their work.

Methodology

Taken together, extant New Literacies Studies research makes a formidable argument for the need to re-evaluate how we understand literacy in the workplace—particularly from the perspective of interactive service workers. The research reported here is modeled after Hull and her colleagues' groundbreaking ethnographic study of skill requirements in the factories of two different Silicon Valley computer manufacturing plants (1996). Instead of studying manufacturing plants, the larger research study I conducted and that underpins the study reported here involves two diner restaurants—one that is corporately owned and one that is privately owned. In this chapter, however, I focus only on the one that is privately owned to begin addressing the specific ways that language use and literacy practices function in this kind of workplace.

To analyze the data, I relied on some of the methodological tools from the work of Hull and her colleagues (1996). In short, I looked at patterns of thought and behavior in the setting; I identified key events taking place; I did conversational analysis of verbal interactions; and, I conducted sociocultural analyses of key work events.

The data used in this chapter came from direct participation, observation, field notes, documents, interviews, tape recordings, and transcriptions, as well as from historical and bibliographic literature. I myself have been a waiter (both part-time and full-time over a ten-year period), and I was actually employed at the privately owned restaurant during my data collection period. In addition to providing important insights into worker skills, attitudes, and behaviors, my experience and positioning in this setting also enabled access to unique aspects of the work that might have otherwise gone unnoticed. The primary data considered in this chapter were collected during eight-hour periods of participant observation on Friday and/or Saturday nights in the restaurant. I chose weekend nights because they were usually the busiest times in the diner and were therefore the most challenging for the workers. Weekend shifts are also the most lucrative for the restaurant and the workers.

Lou's Restaurant

Lou's Restaurant[3] is a modest, privately owned diner restaurant patterned in a style that is popular in the local region. It has an open kitchen layout with a counter where individual customers can come and sit directly in front of the cooks' line and watch the "drama" of food service unfold while enjoying their meals. The food served at Lou's is Italian-American and it includes pastas, seafood, and a variety of sautéed or broiled poultry, beef, and veal. As is often the case with diner restaurants, Lou's has over ninety main course items, including several kinds of appetizers and salads, as well as a number of side dishes. The primary participants focused on in this chapter are three waiters at Lou's: John, Harvey, and myself.

After finishing my master's degree in English literature and deciding to move out of the state where I taught English as a Second Language at a community college, I ended up working as a waiter for two years at Lou's. This work allowed me to survive financially while further advancing my academic career. At the time I began my study at this site, the only waiter to have worked longer than two years at Lou's was John. Like myself, John began working in the restaurant business to earn extra money while in school after he had been discharged from the Marines, where he had been trained as a radio operator, telephone wireman, and Arabic translator. Two days after his honorable discharge, he started working in the restaurant that four years later would become Lou's. He subsequently has worked there for ten years. John also is the most experienced waiter at Lou's, and although the restaurant does not have an official "head" waiter, John is considered by his peers to be the expert. In an interview, he noted that it took almost ten years before he felt that he had really begun to master his craft.

Harvey might also be considered a master waiter, having been in the profession for over thirty years. However, at the beginning of the study he had been with Lou's for only two weeks. He was initially reticent to participate in the study because he said he lacked experience at this restaurant, and "didn't know the menu." Having left home when he was 14 years old to come "out West," over the years he had done a stint in the Air Force, held a position as a postal clerk, worked as a bellhop and bartender, and even had the opportunity to manage a local cafe. He decided that he did not like managerial work because he missed the freedom, autonomy, and customer interaction he had as a waiter and took a position at Lou's.

The Menu

Harvey's concern over not knowing the menu was not surprising. The menu is the most important printed text used by waiters and waitresses, and not knowing it can dramatically affect how they are able to do their work. The menu is the key text used for most interactions with the customer, and, of course, the contents of menus vary greatly from restaurant to restaurant. But, what is a menu and what does it mean to have a literate understanding of one?

The restaurant menu is a genre unto itself. There is regularity and predictability in the conventions used such as the listing, categorizing, and pricing of individual, ready-made food items. The menu at Lou's contains ninety main course items, as well as a variety of soups, salads, appetizers, and side dishes. In addition, there are numerous selections where, for example, many main course items offer customers a choice of their own starch item from a selection of four: spaghetti, ravioli, french fries, or a baked potato. Some of the main course items, such as sandwiches, however, only come with french fries—but if the customer prefers something such as spaghetti, or vegetables instead of fries, they can substitute another item for a small charge, although this service is not listed in the menu. In addition to the food menu, there is also a wine menu and a full service bar meaning that hard liquor is sold in this restaurant. There are twenty different kinds of wine sold by the glass and a selection of thirty-eight different kinds of wine sold by the bottle, and customers can order most other kinds of alcoholic beverages.

In one context, waitresses and waiters' knowing the meaning of the words in the menus means knowing the process of food production in the restaurant. But this meaning is generally only used when a customer has a question or special request. In such situations the meaning of the words on the page are defined more by the questions and the waiters or waitresses' understanding of specific food preparation than by any standard cookbook or dictionary. For example, the *Better Homes and Gardens New Cook Book* (1996) presents a recipe for marinara sauce calling for a thick sauce consisting of tomatoes, tomato puree, peppers, carrots, celery, and garlic all sautéed and simmered for over thirty minutes. At Lou's, a marinara sauce is cooked in less than ten minutes and is a light tomato sauce consisting of fresh tomatoes, garlic, and parsley sautéed in olive oil. At a similar restaurant nearby—Joe's Italian Diner—marinara sauce is a seafood sauce, albeit tomato based. Someone who is familiar with Italian cooking will know that marinara sauce will have ingredients like tomatoes, olive oil, and garlic, but, in a restaurant, to have a more complete understanding of a word like *marinara* requires knowing how the kitchen prepares the dish. Clearly, the meanings of the language used in menus are socially and culturally embedded in the context of the specific situation or restaurant. To be literate here requires something other than a ninth-grade level of literacy. More than just a factual, or literal interpretation of the words on the page, it requires knowledge of specific practices—such as methods of food preparation—that take place in a particular restaurant.

On one occasion Harvey, the new but experienced waiter, asked me what "pesto" sauce was. He said that he had never come across the term before, and explained that he had never worked in an Italian restaurant and had rarely eaten at one. Pesto is one of the standard sauces on the menu, and like marinara, is commonly found on the menus of many Italian-American restaurants. I explained that it comprised primarily olive oil and basil, as well as garlic, pine nuts, Parmesan cheese, and a little cream. Harvey then told me that a customer had asked him about the sauce, and since he could not explain what it was, the customer did not order it.

On another occasion a mother asked Harvey if her child could have only carrots instead of the mixed vegetables as it said in the menu. Although he initially told her this was not possible, explaining that the vegetables were premixed and that the cooks would have to pick the carrots out one by one, the mother persisted. After a few trips from the table to the cooks' line, Harvey managed to get the carrots, but the customer then declined them because everyone had finished eating. Later, I explained to Harvey that it would have been possible to go to the back of the restaurant where he could find the vegetables in various stages of preparation. While the cooks only have supplies of pre-mixed vegetables on the line, Harvey could have gone to the walk-in refrigerator and picked up an order of carrots himself to give to the cooks.

Harvey's interactions with his customers highlight how much of what he needs to know to be a good waiter is learned within the specific situations and social networks in which that knowledge is used. The instantiation of the meaning of words like *pesto* and *marinara* often occurs in the interaction between co-workers as well as with customers. Conversation becomes a necessary element in achieving an appropriately literate understanding of the menu.

Harvey's understanding and use of the menu and special requests also involves more than his knowledge of food preparation. It involves the manipulation of power and control. Sociocultural theories of literacy consider the role of power and authority in the construction of meaning (Kress, 1 993). From his perspective, the order of carrots was not simply an order of carrots, but a way of positioning one's self in the interaction. The customer saw her desire for the carrots as greater than what was advertised in the menu and thus exercised authority as a customer by requesting them despite Harvey's attempt to not make the carrots an option. While such a request might seem fairly innocuous in isolation, when considered in the specific situation of Lou's at that time—that is, peak dinner hour—it becomes more complex.

Special requests and questions can extend the meaning of the menu beyond the printed page and into the conversation and interaction between the waiter or waitress and the customer. Furthermore, special requests and questions can be as varied as the individual customers themselves. The general public shares a diner restaurant menu, but it is used by each individual patron to satisfy a private appetite. How to describe something to an individual customer and satisfy their private appetite requires not only the ability to *read* the menu, but also the ability to *read* the customer. This is achieved during the process of the dinner interaction, and it includes linguistic events such as greeting the customer or taking food orders and involves both verbal and non-verbal communication. In such events the meaning of the menu is continually reconstructed in the interaction between the waitress or waiter and the individual customer, and as a text functions as a "boundary object" that coordinates the perspectives of various constituencies for a similar purpose (Star and Griesmer, 1989); in this case the satisfaction of the individual patron's appetite. The degree to which private appetite is truly satisfied is open to debate, however. Virtually everyone who has eaten at a restaurant has his or her favorite horror story about the food and/or the service, and more often than not these stories in some way involve the menu and an unfulfilled private appetite.

In addition to being a text that is shared by the general public and used by the individual patron to satisfy a private appetite, the menu is also a text whose production of meaning results in ready-made consumable goods sold for a profit. The authors of a printed menu, usually the chefs and owners of the restaurant, have their own intentions when producing the hard copy. For example, it is common practice to write long extensively itemized menus in diner restaurants like Lou's. As was pointed out earlier, Lou's menu has over ninety selections from which to choose, and many of these can be combined with a range of additional possible choices. Printing a large selection of food items gives the appearance that the customer will be able to make a personal—and *personalized*—selection from the extensive menu. In fact, it is not uncommon for patrons at Lou's to request extra time to read the menu, or ask for recommendations before making a choice. The authors of the printed menu at Lou's constructed a text that appears to be able to satisfy private appetites, but they ultimately have little control over how the patron will interpret and use the menu.

The waiters and waitresses, however, do have some control. While customers certainly have their own intentions when asking questions, waitresses and waiters have their own intentions when responding. When customers ask questions about the menu, in addition to exercising their own authority, they also introduce the opportunity for waiters and waitresses to gain control of the interaction. A good example of how this control could be manipulated by a waiter or waitress comes from Chris Fehlinger, the web-master of *bitterwaitress.com*, in an interview with *New Yorker* magazine:

"A lot of times when people asked about the menu, I would make it sound so elaborate that they would just leave it up to me, " he said, "I'd describe, like, three dishes in excruciating detail, and they would just stutter, 'I, I, I can't decide, you decide for me.' So in that case, if the kitchen wants to sell fish, you're gonna have fish." He also employed what might be called a "magic words" strategy: "All you have to do is throw out certain terms, like *guanciale*, and then you throw in something like *saba*, a reduction of the unfermented must of the Trebbiano grape. If you mention things like that, people are just, like, 'O.K.! '" (Teicholz, 1999)

The use of linguistic devices like obfuscating descriptions and "magic words" is not unusual—particularly for waiters in fine dining restaurants. In *The World of Waiters* (1983), Mars and Nicod examined how English waiters use such devices to "get the jump" and gain control of selecting items from the menu. Their position of authority is further substantiated in fine dining restaurants by the common practice of printing menus in foreign languages, such as French, because it shifts the responsibility of food ordering from the customer, who often will not understand the language, to the waiter.

While diner restaurants generally do not print their menus in incomprehensible terms, they do, as at Lou's, tend to produce unusually long ones that can have a similar effect. But, diner menus like Lou's which offer Italian-American cuisine do use some language that is potentially unfamiliar to the clientele (e.g., *pesto*). The combination of menu length and potentially confusing language creates frequent opportunities for waiters and waitresses to get a jump on the customer. Customers at Lou's tend to ask questions about the meaning of almost every word and phrase in the menu. Not being able to provide at least a basic description of a menu item, as shown by Harvey's unfamiliarity with pesto, usually results in that item not being ordered.

Knowing what a customer wants often goes beyond simply being able to describe the food. It also involves knowing which descriptions will more likely sell and requires being able to apply the menu to the specific situation. For instance, in the following transcription I approach a table to take a food order while one customer is still reading the menu (Customer 3b). She asks me to explain the difference between veal scaloppini and veal scaloppini sec.

Tony:	(to Customer 3 a and Customer 3b) hi
Customer 3b:	what's the difference between scaloppini and scaloppini sec?
Tony:	veal scaloppini is a tomato-based sauce with green onions and mushrooms / veal scaloppini sec is with marsala wine green onions and mushrooms
Customer 3b:	I'll have the veal scaloppini sec
Tony:	ok / would you like it with spaghetti / ravioli / french fries
Customer 3b:	ravioli
Customer 3a:	and / I'll get the tomato one / the veal scaloppini with mushrooms
Tony:	with spaghetti / ravioli / french fries
Customer 3a:	can I get steamed vegetables
Tony:	you want vegetables and no starch? / it already comes with vegetables / (.) (Customer 3a nods yes) ok / great / thank you
Customer 3a:	thanks

The word *sec* functions not unlike one of Fehlinger's "magic" words. Customers who are interested in ordering veal frequently ask questions about the distinction between the two kinds of scaloppini. I discovered over time that my description of the veal scaloppini sec almost always resulted in the customer ordering the dish. It seemed that mentioning marsala wine piqued customer interest more than tomato sauce did. One customer once quipped that marsala was a sweet wine and wanted to know why the word *sec*—meaning *dry*—was used. I replied that since no fat was used in the cooking process, it was considered "dry" cooking. In situations like this the menu is situated more in a conversational mode than a printed one. The transition from print to spoken word occurs due to the customer's inability to understand the menu, and/or satisfy his or her private appetite which results in a request for assistance. As a result the waiter or waitress can become the authority in relation to not only the printed text, but within the interaction as well. Eventually, I began to recommend this dish when customers asked for one, and the customers more often than not purchased it.

This particular food-ordering event also is interesting with regard to the customer's request for steamed vegetables. When I asked what kind of pasta she would like with her meal, she asked for steamed vegetables. The menu clearly states that vegetables are included with the meal along with the customer's choice of spaghetti, ravioli, or french fries. When she requested steamed vegetables, I simply could have arranged for her to have them and persisted in asking her which pasta she would like, but instead I anticipated that she might not want any pasta at all. I knew that, while it was not printed in the menu, the kitchen could serve her a double portion of steamed vegetables with no pasta. Most importantly, this customer's ability to order food that would satisfy her private appetite depended almost entirely upon my suggestions and understanding of the menu. Mars and Nicod (1984: 82), discussing a situation in a similar restaurant noted a waiter who would say, "You don't really need a menu . . . I'm a 'walking menu' and I'm much better than the ordinary kind . . . I can tell you things you won't find on the menu." Examples like this illustrate not only how waitresses and waiters gain control of their interactions with customers, but also how other modes of communication—such as conversations—are used to construct complex forms of meaning around printed texts like menus. Thus, the meaning of words in a menu are embedded in the situation, its participants, and the balance of power and authority, and this meaning manifests itself in more than one mode of communication.

Reading menus and reading customers also involves a myriad of cultural distinctions. Although there is not the space to discuss them here, age, gender, race, and class are all relevant to interactions between customers and waiter or waitress. The argument can be made that diner restaurants like Lou's promote a friendly, family-like atmosphere. Historically diners in the U.S. have been recognized as being places where customers can find a familial environment. Popular media today support this characteristic particularly via television—where restaurant chains explicitly advertise that their customers are treated like family, and a number of television situation comedies have long used restaurants, diners, bars, and cafes as settings where customers and employees interact in very personal and intimate ways. This cultural atmosphere can have a tremendous impact on interactions with the customers. There is sometimes miscommunication or resistance where a customer may or may not want to be treated like family, or the waitress or waiter may or may not want to treat a customer like family. At Lou's, in addition to having an intimate understanding of food production and being able to describe it to a customer in an appealing fashion, reading a menu and taking a customer's food order also requires the ability to perform these tasks in a friendly, familial manner.

The following example reveals the complexity of meanings involved in taking a customer's food order and the expression of "family." Al is a regular customer who almost always comes in by himself and sits at the counter in front of the cooks' line. He also always has the same thing to eat, a side order of spaghetti Marinara, and never looks at the menu. Perhaps more important to Al than the food he eats are the people he interacts with at Lou's. He will sit at the counter and enjoy the badinage he shares with the other customers who sit down next to him at the counter, the waitresses and waiters as they pass by his seat, and the cooks working just across the counter. On this particular evening, however, he was joined by his son, daughter-in-law, and young adult granddaughter, and rather than sitting at the counter, he sat in a large booth. Although I immediately recognized Al, I had never waited on him and his family before, I was not sure how informal he would like the interaction to be. So I began with a fairly formal greeting saying "hello" instead of "hi" and avoided opportunities to make small talk with Al and his family:

Tony:	hello::=
Customer 2d:	=hello
Al:	hey (.) what they put in the water? / I don't know / is it the ice or what is it?
Customer 2s:	(chuckles from Customer 2d, Customer 2s and Customer 2c)
Tony:	does the water taste strange?
Customer 2s:	no
Tony:	do you want me to get you another water?
Al:	no / I don't want any water
Tony:	ok
Al:	I had a couple of drinks before I came
Customer 2s:	(chuckles)=
Tony:	(in reference to the water tasting strange) =it could be / it could be / I don't know
Customer 2d:	(to Customer 2s) are you having anything to drink?
Customer 2s:	I'll have a beer / American beer / you have miller draft?
Tony:	(while writing down the order) miller genuine
Customer 2d:	and I'll have a tequila sunrise
Al:	(to Customer 2d) what are you having?
Customer 2d:	tequila sunrise
Al:	oh / you should fly / you should fly
Tony:	(to Customer 2a) al / you want anything
Customer 2s:	(to Customer 2a) a beer? / or anything?
Al:	no / I've had too much already
Customer 2s:	are you sure
Customer 2d:	we'll get you a coffee later
Tony:	(nod of affirmation to daughter-in-law)
Al:	I've been home alone drinking
Tony:	ugh ogh:: / (chuckles along with Customer 2s)

Al's comments about the water tasting funny and his drinking at home alone both provided opportunities for me to interact more intimately with Al and his family, but instead I concerned myself solely with taking their drink orders. Al's desire for me to interact in a more familial manner became more apparent when I returned to take their food order.

Customer 2d:	(as the drinks are delivered) ah / great / thank you
Tony:	(placing drinks in front of customers) there you go / you're welcome

Al:	(to Customer 2s) so we're flying to vegas (mumbles)
Tony:	all right / you need a few minutes here?
Customer 2s:	no / (to Customer 2a) are you ready or do you want to wait?
Customer 2d:	you made up your mind yet?
Al:	(mumble) made up my mind yet
Customer 2d:	oh / ok
Tony:	al / what can I get for you?
Al:	I said I haven't made up my mind yet
Tony:	oh / ok (everyone at the table chuckles except Al)
Al:	I always have pasta you know / I would walk out there (points to the counter) the guy says / I know what you want
Tony:	ok / I'll be back in a few minutes
Customer 2d:	come back in a few minutes / thanks

While I misunderstood Al when I asked if he was ready to order, for him the greater transgression was simply asking if he was ready to order. Al expected me to know what he was going to eat because he's a regular; he's like family. He wanted a side order of spaghetti marinara and didn't want to have to speak regarding his food order. To be successful in fulfilling Al's private appetite required more than the ability to describe food according to individual customer preferences. A side order of spaghetti marinara represents not merely a food item on a menu, nor a satisfying mix of pasta and tomatoes, but also, depending on the way it is ordered and served, a gesture of friendliness: "I always have pasta you know / I would walk out there (points to the counter) the guy says / I know what you want." To be literate with a menu also means knowing when and how to express emotion (or not express emotion) to a customer through its use.

Being able to take a customer's order without him or her reading the menu or being able to fulfill a special request not printed in the menu are important ways of expressing friendliness and family at Lou's. John, the most experienced waiter on staff, often can be found running to get an order of homemade gnocchi from the back freezer and delivering them to the cooks when they are too busy to get back there themselves. Or, he might step in behind the bar to make his own cappuccino when the bartender is busy serving other customers. On one occasion, like many others, John had a customer request a special order called *prawns romano*, a pasta dish consisting of fettuccine with prawns in a white sauce with green onions, tomatoes, and garlic. This is not listed on any menu in the restaurant, but it is something that the cooks occasionally offer as an evening special. John politely asked whether or not the cooks could accommodate his customer's request, and they complied. One can frequently hear John greeting many of his customers with some variation of, "Can I get you the usual?" Alternatively, in the case of special requests, some variant of, "That's no problem" is an often used phrase. Just like a friend for whom it would be no problem, John attempts to satisfy his customer's special requests in a similar fashion.

Yet, friendliness is often a feigned performance. Being friendly is an experiential phenomenon that is learned through participation. To be a good waitress or waiter generally requires being able to perform friendliness under any number of circumstances. To be successful at the practice of being friendly requires performing certain techniques over and over until they can be performed on an unconscious level: Referred to as *emotional labor* (Hochschild, 1983: 6-7) this kind of work "requires one to induce or suppress feeling in order to sustain the outward countenance that produces the proper state of mind in others." Emotional labor also is an integral part to how a waitress constructs meaning in a menu. While emotional labor may not yield the same monetary results in restaurants like Lou's, it is still essential to the work. For example, John is masterful in the way he utilizes emotional labor. On one particularly busy evening John was trapped in a line at the bar waiting to place his drink order. He was clearly anxious, and was looking at his food order tickets to see what he needed to do next. The crowd of customers waiting to be seated spilled out of the foyer and into the aisle near where the waitresses and waiters where waiting to place their drink orders. One customer, who recognized John, caught his attention:

John:	hi=
Customer:	=hi can I get a glass of wine
John:	sure (.) what do you want
Customer:	are you busy
John:	NO (.) I got it (.) what do you want

John's friendly "hi" and over emphatic "no" were intended to suggest to the customer that he was not busy, when he clearly was. As he later explained, he knew that the customer knew he was really busy, but he also knew that if he was friendly and accommodating, the customer probably would give him a nice tip for his trouble, which the customer did. His feigned amiability in agreeing to get the customer a drink was more or less a monetary performance. John had learned to use language for financial gain. One should not be fooled by the apparent simplicity in the preceding interaction. While it may be brief, being able to be friendly and accommodating under extreme circumstances like the "dinner rush" requires years of practice in a real work setting learning to be able to say, "hi—sure—NO, I got it."

Although interactions with customers have been presented individually, the reality of how these events occur is quite different. Unlike fine-dining restaurants where the dinner experience can extend over a few hours, diners operate on high volume serving to a great number of patrons in a short amount of time. George Orwell, reflecting on the difficulty involved in this work, wrote, "I calculated that [a waiter] had to walk and run about 15 miles during the day and yet the strain of the work was more mental than physical. . . . One has to leap to and fro between a multitude of jobs—it is like sorting a pack of cards against the clock" (Orwell, 193 3). Because one person may be serving as many as ten tables or more at one time, the process of serving each individual table will overlap with the others. Food orders are taken numerous times in a half-hour period during busy dinner hours at Lou's. The preceding transcriptions were taken from tape-recorded data collected on Friday evenings around 7 o'clock. My own interactions were recorded during a period when I had what is referred to as a *full station*, meaning that all of the tables under my supervision were filled with customers. By this point in the evening I had two customers at the counter, a party of four and six parties of two, for a total of eighteen customers—all of whom were in the process of ordering their meals within the same half-hour to forty-five minute period.

Literacy practices in this environment are nothing like those found in traditional classrooms, but they might be more comparable to those found in the emergency ward of a hospital or an air-traffic controller's tower. Interaction with texts and participants takes place in a rapid succession of small chunks. During the dinner hours, there are no long, drawn out monologues. Time is of the essence during the busiest dinner hours for all participants involved: from the waiters and waitresses to the cooks, bartenders, and busboys. In two hundred lines of transcribed dialogue during a busy dinner period, for example, I never paused longer than thirty-nine seconds, and no participant spoke more than forty-one words in one turn. Even these pauses were usually the result of other work being completed, such as preparing a salad or waiting to order a drink. During this period, virtually all the conversation, reading, and writing were related to the immediate situational context. As this research has shown, language use was far more complex than one might assume in situations and events that involve taking a customer's food order. In addition to knowing how food is prepared, what will appeal to specific customers, and how to present this in formation in a friendly manner, the waiter or waitress must also remain conscious of the number of other tables waiting to have their orders taken and the amount of time that will take. Reading menus and reading customers requires the ability to think and react quickly to a multitude of almost simultaneously occurring literate events.

Conclusion

Menus at Lou's are texts that are catalysts for interaction between staff and customers, and their meaning is firmly embedded in this interaction. Meaning is constructed from the menu through more than one mode of communication and between a variety of participants. This process involves knowledge of food preparation, use specific linguistic devices like magic words and other ways of describing food, the ability to read individual customers' tastes and preferences, the general expectation to perform in a friendly manner, and all during numerous virtually simultaneous and similar events. Yet, there is much left unconsidered in this chapter, particularly regarding the nature of power and control. While waitresses and waiters are frequently able to manipulate control over customer decisions while taking a food order, this control is often tenuous and insignificant beyond the immediate interaction.

Little also has been said in this chapter about the role of management. Extensive research has already been done in the area of management control, literacy, and worker skills (Braverman, 1974; Hochschild, 1983; Kress, 1993; Leidner, 1993; Hall, 1993; Hull et al., 1996; Macdonald and Sirianni, 1996; Gee, Hull, and Lankshear, 1996). These researchers consider how literacy practices are manipulated by management to maintain control over the worker. Whether it be scientific management where workers are deskilled and routinized, or Fast Capitalism where forms of control are more insidious and shrouded in the guise of "empowering" the worker, there is little research on interactive service work beyond the fast food industry that explores how this rhetoric plays itself out in a real world situation. This leaves open to debate questions regarding the effectiveness of Fast Capitalism as a form of control over the worker. While my research has shown that waiters and waitresses can exercise some level of authority, skill and wit through their use of language with customers, they must also interact with management and other staff where authority and control plays out in different ways.

In the end, however, the customer has ultimate authority over the waiter or waitress. Diner waitressing has a long history of prejudice dating back to the beginning of the industrial revolution and involves issues of gender regarding our general perceptions and ways of interacting (Cobble, 1991; Hall, 1993). Waitressing is integrally tied to domesticated housework and likewise has historically been treated as requiring little skill or ability. In fact, the stigma of servitude that plagues waitressing and other similar kinds of work are not only the result of less than respectable treatment from management, but from customers as well. In her sociological study of diner waitresses in New Jersey, Greta Paules sums it up best:

> That customers embrace the service-as-servitude metaphor is evidenced by the way they speak to and about service workers. Virtually every rule of etiquette is violated by customers in their interactions with the waitress: the waitress can be interrupted; she can be addressed with the mouth full; she can be ignored and stared at; and she can be subjected to unrestrained anger. Lacking status as a person she like the servant, is refused the most basic considerations of polite interaction. She is, in addition, the subject of chronic criticism. Just as in the nineteenth century servants were perceived as ignorant, slow, lazy, indifferent, and immoral (Sutherland 1981), so in the twentieth century service workers are condemned for their stupidity, apathy, slowness, competence, and questionable moral character. (1991: 138 -139)

The low status of waitressing and waitering belies the complex nature of this kind of work and the innovative and creative ways in which such workers use language.

Notes

[1]Some of the more than 20 websites I have found so far like waitersrevenge.com are award winning. They include sites for taxi drivers, hotel workers, and the like.

[2]How to appropriately refer to waitresses and waiters is not a simple decision. Terms like *server* and *food server* are alternatives, but all are problematic. I personally do not like *server* or *food server* because they are too closely related to the word servitude. The waiter/waitress distinction is problematic not simply because it differentiates genders, but also because it is associated with a kind/class of service. Often in fine-dining restaurants today both men and women are referred to as waiters, but it is more commonly the practice in the "diner" style restaurant to maintain the distinctive terms. This is historically connected to the diner waitressing being regarded as inferior to fine-dining waitering because it was merely an extension of the domesticated duties of the household.

[3]Pseudonyms have been used throughout this chapter.

Works Cited

Better homes and gardens new cook book. (1996). New York: Better Homes and Gardens.

Braverman, H. (197 4). *Labor and monopoly capital: The degradation of work in the twentieth century.* New York: Monthly Review Press.

Bureau of Labor Statistics. (1996). Washington, D.C.: U.S. Department of Labor.

Drucker, P. (1993). *Innovation and entrepreneurship: Practice and principles.* New York: Harperbusiness.

Cobble, S. (1991). *Dishing it out: Waitresses and their unions in the 20th century.* Urbana: University of Illinois Press.

Gee, J. (1991). *Sociolinguistics and literacies: Ideology in discourses.* New York. Falmer.

—-, Hull, G., and Lankshear, C. (1996). *The new work order: Behind the language of the new capitalism.* Sydney: Allen & Unwin.

Gowen, S. (1992). *The politics of workplace literacy.* New York: Teachers College Press.

Hall, E. (1993). Smiling, deferring, and good service. *Work and occupations,* 20 (4), 452-471.

Hochschild, A. (1983). *The managed heart.* Berkeley: University of California Press.

Hull, G. (Ed.). (1997). *Changing work, changing workers: Critical perspectives on language, literacy, and skills.* New York: State University of New York Press.

—- et al. (1996). *Changing work, changing literacy? A study of skills requirements and development in a traditional and restructured workplace. Final Report.* Unpublished manuscript. University of California at Berkeley.

Kress, G. (1993). Genre as social process. In B. Cope and M. Kalantzis (Eds.), *The powers of literacy: A genre approach to teaching writing* (pp. 22-37). London: Falmer.

—-. (1995). *Writing the future: English and the making of a cultural innovation*. London: NATE.

Lave, J. and Wenger, E. (1991). *Situated learning: Legitimate peripheral participation*. New York: Cambridge University Press.

Leidner, R. (1993). *Fast food, fast talk: Service work and the routinization of everyday life*. Berkeley: University of California Press.

Macdonald, C. and Sirianni, C. (Eds.). (1996). *Working in the service society*. Philadelphia, PA: Temple University Press.

Mahiri, J. and Sabio, S. (1996). Writing for their lives: The non-school literacy of California's urban African American youth. *Journal of Negro Education*, 65 (2), 164-180.

Mars, G. and Nicod, M. (1984). *The world of waiters*. London: Unwin Hyman.

New London Group. (1996). A pedagogy of multiliteracies: Designing social futures. *Harvard Educational Review*, 66 (1), 60-92.

NSSB (National Skills Standards Board). (1995). *Server skill standards: National performance criteria in the food service industry*. Washington, DC: U.S. Council on Hotel, Restaurant and Institutional Education.

Orwell, G. (1933). *Down and out in Paris and London*. New York. Harcourt Brace.

Paules, G. (1991). *Dishing it out: Power and resistance among waitresses in a New Jersey Restaurant*. Philadelphia, PA: Temple University Press.

Reich, R. (1992). *The work of nations*. New York: Vintage.

Star, L. and Griesmer, J. (1989). Institutional ecology, translations and boundary objects: Amateurs and professional in Berkeley's Museum of Vertebrate Zoology, 1907-1939. *Social Studies of Science*, 19.

Street, B. (1984 April 5). *Literacy in theory and practice*. London: Cambridge University Press.

NOW THAT YOU'VE READ

1. What's Lou's restaurant like? What was Mirabelli's role there? Who's Harvey? Who is John? What were their roles there?

2. Mirabelli describes "the restaurant menu [as] a genre unto itself" (149). What does he mean by this? How does he describe the variety of ways this genre is put to use? What literacy events surround the use of the menu at Lou's, at least as they are articulated in this essay? How do these compare with the literacy events you've witnessed at other restaurants?

3. Not only must the menu be "read" and acted upon, but the food service worker must also "read" the customer. What does it mean to "read" the customer? How do literacy practices further complicate the work of a server?

4. The essay suggests that "literacy practices in this environment are nothing like those found in traditional classrooms." A better comparison, according to Mirabelli, might be "the emergency ward of a hospital or an air-traffic controller's tower" (158). What does he mean by this comparison? What other comparisons can you make that might serve as a good analogy for the way literacy functions in the various restaurants with which you are most familiar?

READING

The Coming Apocalypse

Richard Miller

BEFORE YOU READ

1. What do you make of the title?

2. Given the title, what do you expect the essay to be about?

3. What are your expectations of how methods of communication will be changing in the coming years?

4. Should students be able to use their phones or other connected devices in class? Why? Why not?

The Coming Apocalypse

Richard Miller

Nice title, eh?

We are fortunate to be living through the greatest change in human communication in human history. This change is bigger and more momentous than our distant ancestors' slow crawl from the muck to dry land where, over great swaths of time, they came to grunt at one another meaningfully. It is more significant than the invention of the alphabet. It is more important than anything that was set in motion by the grinding gears of the Guttenberg printing press. It is more transformative than the telephone, the television set, the satellite have been or will ever be. Obviously, the Internet could never have come into being without these earlier creations. But its communicative powers surpass all the preceding technologies for enabling and enhancing human understanding combined. Right now, anyone equipped with the least bit of intelligence and the slightest modicum of ambition can make his or her thoughts available via the Internet to a global audience instantaneously and at virtually no cost. While Luddites and historians of science wring their hands over this development and call for caution in assessing the impact of the digital revolution, the World Wide Web proliferates with abandon, leaving in its wake the wreckage of institutions once thought eternal: the newspaper industry, the textbook industry, the US postal service. Indeed, it is fair to say that the Internet provided the infrastructure that has enabled instant global, economic collapse. No other means of human communication has ever had the capability to travel so far so quickly to such devastating effect. Like the Internet, the most pressing problems of our time are all global in scope: in addition to the global economic collapse, there is global climate change, the global "war on terror," the global energy crisis, and the ticking global population bomb. How do we prepare students to think on such a scale? In such a context, it seems almost ludicrous to ask if writing has a meaningful role to play in the hot, flat, and crowded world that looms in the global populations near future. We are living through the greatest change in human communication in human history, but you would never know this from visiting language arts classrooms across the country. Far from evolving in relation to the globalization of experience, our teachers, our curricula, and our expectations of education remain frozen in time, preserved like some prehistoric insect in a golden drop of amber.

Last weekend, I helped my eighth-grade daughter with her latest English assignment. She's been working her way through a curriculum that is virtually unchanged since I was in eighth grade more than thirty years ago. *Catcher in the Rye. To Kill a Mockingbird. A Midsummer Night's Dream. 1984. The Diary of Anne Frank.* Watergate. The Fall of the Berlin Wall. Desert Storm. Sarajevo. The L.A. Riots. 9/11. What used to be known as The Second Gulf War, but is now known as the wars in Iraq and Afghanistan. Choose your own life-changing historic events; whatever you choose will pass through the sieve of the middle school curriculum without a trace on its way to oblivion. Why study such things, when one can read about the angst of a boy in private school in the late forties; race relations in the fifties; a vision of 1984, also written in the late forties; an account of the Holocaust from World War II? The message of the middle school language arts curriculum is quite clear: literature is a refuge for those who don't want to or are incapable of contending with the present. And so, following Anne Frank and Elie Wiesel, my daughter's class watched *Hotel Rwanda*, after which they were assigned the task of composing a letter to the editor about the coverage of genocide. (Yes, they are brought up to the present in one giant step via film not print.) A letter to the editor. About genocide. Did your class visit Google Earth, where there is an ongoing effort to map the Rwandan genocide? Did you learn about the Genocide Prevention Mapping Initiative that seeks to document all genocides, past and present? The Holocaust Mapping Initiative? Let me back up. Did you look at anything that wasn't print or video? All right then, Letter to the Editor it is. When the ink dries, we'll climb back into our horse and buggy, sealed envelope in hand, and head to the post office, satisfied that we've done our best to voice our disapproval of—what was Clinton's famous phrase, the one that allowed the atrocities in Rwanda to unfold in our own time? Oh yeah—"acts of genocide."

What is writing for? Let's begin with the following definition and see how far we can take it: writing is a technology for advancing thought. In this formulation, "advancing" means both "to make visible" and "to move forward." Writing enables us to take the thoughts in our heads and make them visible to ourselves and to others; and, once our thoughts are visible, writing also provides the means for moving our thoughts forward—through clarification, expansion, qualification, revision, retraction. Who is writing for? The problem that has bedeviled writing instruction since its inception has been the status of the audience. Teachers say over and over to their students, "Think of your audience." And the students say under their breath, in unison, "We are. It's you." There is, by definition, no real audience for student writing. The abiding fiction of the writing classroom is that students can be fashioned into a proxy audience for the writing produced in that class. Assignments create a writing situation: a letter to the editor; an argument; an act of persuasion; a description. The student work is circulated; discussion of its rhetorical effectiveness occurs—and by this we mean its ability to generate discussion among people for whom writing has, by and large, no rhetorical power. The semester ends and all that writing goes to the dump. And why not? The very obviousness of this solution should give one pause. Why don't universities preserve the writing solicited from students? Why isn't there a national archive of student writing, from the turn of the century to the present? Would there be an audience for these materials? Would anyone roam the stacks which, surely, would circle the globe? It is only with the advent of the Web that such an archive has begun to be assembled. But its purpose is not to provide material either for assessing the effects of writing instruction over time, say, or for tracking shifting conceptions on the function of writing's value in the academy. Rather, the database that is continually being amassed by TurnItIn.com exists to address the only audience outside the classroom with a lasting interest in student writing: teachers hoping to catch a thief. And, in this instance, one would be hard pressed to say that either the members of this audience or those on staff at TurnItIn are actually interested in reading student work. The queries to the database generate the "reading," such as it is: the audience waits for the "read out," which reveals whether or not Paper A is, in fact, a version of some other paper already sitting on TurnItIn's servers. In this arena, student writing is not a technology for advancing thought; it is evidence of an irresistible temptation to deceive.

It's not just student writing that is in search of an audience. Over the past two decades, self-sponsored reading has fallen in every age group, according to the trembling prose of the NEA's much discussed report, Reading at Risk. Novels? Down. Poetry? Down. Drama? Down. (The report predates the explosion in reading in the micro-genres of: text messages; wall posts to Facebook; tweets; RSS feeds; scrolling instant messages.) The only growth area? Self-sponsored acts of creative writing. Poems, diary entries, blogs, fan fiction, screenplays. Picture the graph: self-sponsored acts of reading declining across the board; self-sponsored acts of writing on the rise. We are becoming a nation of writers in search of an audience. And, to put this another way, a nation for whom writing is nothing more than a tool for self-expression, the means for tracing the topography of the prison house of identity.

Now, if you take the departmental point of view, it is reasonable to see all this as evidence that the forces of destruction are massing on the horizon. And more. Print newspapers moving online or closing altogether. University presses considering anything to stay in business: weighing marketability as an important criterion during the review process; printing only on demand; getting out of paper altogether and offering only e-books. The paradox of a public that seems to be reading all the time, but largely in 140 character blasts on palm-sized screens. An economic collapse that has, in a few short months, wiped away tens of billions of dollars in endowment accounts across the country, leaving colleges and universities scrambling for revenue streams that can support basic operations. So the perfect storm: more students, who are even more underprepared to work with print, paying more to be in bigger classes with teachers who trained for a kind of expertise that is no longer valued and, perhaps, not even necessary. So framed, what remains but feelings of betrayal, sadness, rage, impotence? Since the advent of post-secondary writing instruction, teachers have bemoaned the sorry state of student composing skills. But what differs about the current cries de coeur and those that have defined hallway chatter about the trials of grading student themes from times past is that the anguish now is produced by the a real decline in the power of print. David Wiley's recent declaration that universities will be "irrelevant" by 2020 and Mark C. Taylor's New York Times Op-Ed, "End the University as We Know It," are only the two most recent examples of the delight some faculty take in telling others about the failure of the academy to change with the times. And in the commentary that followed each of these set pieces, one side weighed in to extol the virtues of research for research's sake and the other side lambasted the willfully obscure, everyone getting a boot in, paying tribute to the alluring fiction that the fate of higher education might be determined through arguments carried out in the Web. Institutions, though, like economic systems, are remarkably durable.

It is true enough that higher education is struggling with the paradigm shift from a universe that had at its center the highly credentialed content expert who generates individually-authored print documents fully protected by copyright to a universe that has at its center collaborative networks of mentors and learners who work with information freely available on web. But it's worth remembering that the paradigmatic paradigm shift—from geocentrism to heliocentrism—didn't happen in a day. Indeed, it was in 1633 that the Vatican tried Galileo for heresy because of his insistence that earth revolved around the sun and it was nearly 400 years later, in 1992, when Pope John Paul stated publicly that the Catholic Church had erred in its treatment of Galileo. So, how long can it take an established institution to acknowledge a paradigm shift? One measure starts the stopwatch with the publication of the Dialogue Concerning the Two Chief World Systems in 1632 and stops it with the declaration of plans to install a statue of Galileo in the Vatican in 2008. And then restarts it, with the January 2009 announcement that plans for the statue have been abandoned and the funds diverted to an educational institution in Nigeria, where they will be used to foster a better understanding of the "relationship between science and religion," according to a church official. How long? In practical terms, maybe forever.

While officials at the Catholic Church try to decide if Galileo belongs in the Vatican or out in the gardens or scattered to the earth's four corners, NASA celebrated the 400th anniversary of Galileo's use of the telescope with a final repair visit to Hubble. In nineteen years orbiting far above the earth's distorting atmosphere, the Hubble Space Telescope has collected data that is transforming cosmology. An expanding universe? A multiverse? How does one think these thoughts?

I have a confession to make. I'm more interested in creative thought than in critical thinking. I think work in the humanities has been both stimulated and paralyzed by the race to expose the flaws in the conceptual foundations of this or that hermeneutic system. And I might as well admit that I also have difficulty with the larger claim that the primary aim of work in the humanities is to generate knowledge. If one is dealing with work that is either nonfalsifiable or inconsequentially falsifiable, then one isn't involved in the generation of knowledge. Rather, one is moving between the realms of belief and subjective experience, tracing the inner landscape that defines our humanity. Finding the limits of what we know is an abiding activity of higher education and an essential part of clearing space and time for future endeavors to better understand the human condition. But equally important are the efforts to get to work in that newly cleared space. My interest in pedagogy is an expression of my desire to find ways into the spaces that have been laid waste by critique, analysis, argumentation. How, for example, to build a model for education once the university has been declared a ruin, branded irrelevant, yoked to the dead carcass of the automotive industry and sent careening off a cliff? How to create a classroom where students are asked to sit with real world problems, to engage with multiple variables simultaneously, to plunge into the bottomless sea of information that has been unleashed by the World Wide Web? For those who believe, as I do, that one of the university's primary responsibilities is to promote the acquisition of knowledge in depth, there has never been a more exciting time to be involved in higher education. What the World Wide Web provides is the opportunity to work with the most powerful media of our time on the project of making thought visible. And, of course, the great challenge posed by our technologically-saturated time is that our movement from moment to moment is punctuated by distractions that know no bounds: text messages, phone calls, the ringing signal of the inbox. And, too, we work in an environment where the ready availability of information serves to degrade the value of all information, promotes superficiality, and cedes the official version of any given event to the top link on Google. Teaching thinking as the process of making and testing connections has always been a wayward, messy, reckless business. (This has been clear since the Platonic dialogues, though the description of Socrates' engagement with his interlocutors as a "method" has served to occlude this fact.) This is why universities are necessary and will continue to be necessary. The paradigm shift in the nature of human communication hasn't altered the nature of thought; it has, however, transformed what it means to teach in ways that have yet to be generally recognized or understood. What will it mean to teach when Internet access is truly ubiquitous? When everyone is equipped with a handheld convergence device that provides immediate access to everything stored on the web? When the open course movement succeeds in putting together free, online curricula for all areas of the undergraduate curriculum, taught by the best teachers of our time? When Google finishes scanning every book ever printed and the results are available to the curious the world over 24/7? I don't know how these questions will be answered by administrators, teachers, students, and parents in the years ahead. But for anyone interested in literacy, the making of meaning, the movement across time of our hardwired drive to narrate, this is anything but an apocalyptic moment. It's a time that invites invention, creativity, improvisation, experimentation. At Rutgers, we've put together an immersive learning environment where students are working collaboratively on exploring what a multimedia visual essay might be. We've chosen the non-existent genre of the visual essay because, while multimedia composition has been used for decades to sell stuff, to tell stories, and to report the news, it hasn't been used to fulfill the other primary responsibility of the university—namely to promote the generation of new ideas. Here again, as with its written counterpart, the visual essay is a means to forestall argumentation in order to pursue the kinds of insights that emerge via deliberation, speculation, and meditation. By design, the space we've created for this work—the Plangere Culture Lab— doesn't function like any classroom the students or the teachers have been in before. Though the Lab is kitted out with a bunch of high tech equipment to facilitate composing with still images, video, and sound, the emphasis in the Lab is not on the glitzy gizmos and their magical powers. Instead, we emphasize the eventual ordinariness of the work we're doing. We tell the students we can foresee a time—not necessarily in the distant future—when entry-level composition will involve working with a video editor rather than a word processor, a time when the final document will not be a paper submitted to the teacher, but rather a piece published to a site like YouTube and shared with the class as a whole. We tell the students that the video editor is a technology for extending thought, just like writing, and that the work of the Lab is to explore and exploit its potential. In the Plangere Culture Lab, the emphasis is on producing examples of what it might mean to make the process of thinking visible. My collaborators and I know what we don't want to be doing. We're determined to move beyond the advertisement, the public service announcement, the music video, the documentary, the feature length movie—the genres established before multimedia composition was brought within the reach of anyone who had a laptop. But we also want to move beyond the early versions of multimedia academic content that now populate the web: talking head videos, unedited vodcasts and podcasts of lectures, material that isn't shaped through post-production. What we're doing now is to figure out how to live and work and think in the space. And so, we've brought in lab mentors, interns, and undergraduates in to think creatively with us about what it would mean to generate idea-driven visual content that has a place in the university. (The results of our ongoing efforts to produce what we are currently terming "an idea portfolio" may be seen at http://www.youtube.com/user/newhumanities.)

No, it's not really an apocalypse. It's an opportunity to redefine the pedagogical function as promoting a tolerance for ambiguity, as cultivating informed curiosity, as encouraging connective thinking about multi-variant real world problems, as preparing students to think and communicate in and with the most powerful medium of our time. Who wouldn't want to be involved with that?

NOW THAT YOU'VE READ

1. What is Miller arguing in this essay?

2. How is he making use of the word "apocalypse"?

3. What kinds of ways might you be encouraged to make use of technology in your classes? In other words, what are the opportunities that your teachers are missing?

4. What is your response to the "idea portfolio" in the YouTube video? What might you add to it?

WRITING ASSIGNMENT

TENSIONS IN LITERACY

In "The Coming Apocalypse," Richard Miller asks, "What is writing for?" At this point in the term, we are asking you to expand your notions of literacy practices. Using Miller's question and discussion as your starting point, bring your own experience as a writer in different settings into conversation with the other readings for this assignment. What are some of the arenas in which you are highly literate—arenas you may not have previously thought of as involving any sort of literacy? What are some of the tensions among your literacy arenas? Please analyze those tensions, making use of your experience and of your reading. Please be specific. This essay should be 4-5 pages (or an equivalent*) and should begin with a meaningful title.

*NOTE: When thinking of the areas you are highly literate or not, you might also think of different genres of writing. For instance, a waiter (as in Mirabelli's case) might be literate in various restaurant practices (creating menus, perhaps speaking and writing in Italian and English) and taking orders (often requiring a shorthand). That is, try to think expansively about literacy examples.

READING

● ● ● ● ● ● ●

Literate at Home But Not at School: A Cambodian Girl's Journey from Playwright to Struggling Writer

Ellen Skilton-Sylvester

BEFORE YOU READ

1. What do you make of the complete title of this essay ("Literate at Home But Not at School: A Cambodian Girl's Journey from Playwright to Struggling Writer")?

2. Given the title, what do you imagine this essay will examine?

Literate at Home but Not at School: A Cambodian Girl's Journey from Playwright to Struggling Writer

Ellen Skilton-Sylvester

Through my writing I found myself again after a long time of being lost. I learned who I was in the past, who I was then, and who I wanted to be in the future. There I finally found freedom in writing. I flew in the sky with my pencil and notebook. (Ngo, 1994)

In more than 3 years of participant observation in home and school contexts with seven young Cambodian girls in Philadelphia, it became quite clear that there was a big separation between school literacy and home literacy in the lives of these girls.[1] At home, it was possible to imagine many of them "flying in the sky with their pencils and notebooks," but at school, this image was much more difficult to visualize. Fro the girls in my study, across home and school contexts, there were differences in written genres, differences in the social and academic prestige of writing, differences in the functions of writing, and incredible differences in volume and quality of written text. Their experiences with writing took place within a social, academic, and cultural context in which writing often had negative connotations.

At the school these girls attended, being good at literacy had quite negative peer-group consequences. In describing why she had a hard time relating to the academically oriented members of her class, one middle school student described them disdainfully in terms of their literacy practices. She explained, "They're always reading books. All the time. If I see them and try to talk to them, they can't even talk because they're reading some book" (fieldnotes, 4/4/94). This student devoured magazines and romances outside of school but made a point not to become a "school-oriented reader." Another Cambodian teenager explained what makes someone popular in this way: "Smart people are not popular." When I asked who is popular, she said, "class officers...people who get in trouble. Bad people" (interview, 5/23/94).

The peer culture at this school was complemented by an academic culture in which true engagement in the work of school was rare. Much of the work students were asked to do was quite disconnected from their interests and lived experiences. In many situations, I saw students focused on filling in blanks on worksheets, copying already written texts that they could not comprehend, getting better grades for copying the summaries of books from the back cover than for writing their own, and being evaluated based on whether or not they had finished an assignment but not on how they had finished it or what they had written on the page (Skilton-Sylvester, 1997). In those cases where literacy activities at school overlapped with the interests and experiences of students (e.g., journals, pictures, autobiographies), they were often seen as peripheral to the "real work of school."

Because the families of the girls in my study are refugees, we also need to consider the role that literacy has typically played in rural Cambodia and how this influences family literacy practices in the United States. Aside from monks, many Cambodians, women especially, have had little formal schooling and have little knowledge of the Khmer or the English script. Several of the Cambodian women I know in Philadelphia find it both physically and cognitively challenging to write on a page. Ina study of women in Cambodia, Ledgerwood (1990) highlights the emphasis on oral performance throughout Cambodia's history, even when there were written texts available. Ledgerwood also discusses the suspicion many had of those who were highly literate. This historical stance toward those who are literate was reinforced by the genocide of Pol Pot's regime in which being literate was a reason for being killed.

In spite of the social, academic, and cultural reasons for a young Cambodian woman to turn her back on reading and writing if given a choice, several of the girls I worked with most closely enjoyed an active writing life at home that was nearly invisible at school. Once girl in particular, Nan, who was in third, fourth, and fifth grade during the 3-year fieldwork period, had been held back once and struggled with academic literacy throughout the time I knew her. However, she was a prolific writer outside of school and had explored several genres: plays, fictional and nonfictional stories, captioned pictures, letters.

In order to understand Nan's experiences with writing, one must be careful not to construct artificial dualisms about her ethnolinguistic background or her writing. First, it is not accurate or helpful to conceive of Cambodians in the United States as bicultural. Ledgerwood, Ebihara, and Mortland (1994) explain why the refugee experience of Cambodians in the United States makes understanding culture much more complex than simple notions of biculturalism:

> One needs to abandon a view of Khmer refugees as biculturals...and exchange it for a perspective that sees war, flight, camp life and resettlement as a series of distinctive cultural experiences that have far-reaching impact on refugees....Americans trying to understand Khmer refugees in the United States explain behavior they do not understand by saying "That is Cambodian." It may be, but it has been influenced by the intervening experiences and by the particularities of the experience of being newcomers in a strange environment (pp. 18-19, 20).

All the parents of the Cambodian girls I knew had spent a few years in refugee camps, as had the oldest children. Nan, the focal child in this chapter, was born in the United States, but her parents' experiences of refugee camp life deeply colored her sense of what it means to be Cambodian.

While it is tempting to see Nan's struggles primarily as a mismatch between her home and school practices, it is also true that her own very particular subjectivities—her ways of being in the social worlds of home and school—played a powerful role in framing her literacy practices in both contexts. Heller (1999) has recently shown how students with similar cultural and linguistic backgrounds can respond variously to the linguistic, academic, and social demands of schooling; they meet the overt expectations of the school while at the same time finding ways to meet their own needs as well. In reviewing the ethnographic literature on how student subjectivity is related to school experiences, Levinson (1998) highlights the ways in which it is limiting to think of students' selves as being imported into the school context:

> *Student subjectivity, while formed in important ways outside the school, also comes to be (re) formed within the space of the school itself.* Contingencies of school and student culture play a significant role in this outcome, and the eventual form that subjectivity takes depends on processes of cultural production and affiliation not entirely predictable from the patterns of enculturation outside the school. (Levinson, 1998, p. 267; emphasis added).

In fact, this debate is quite similar to that sketched earlier on how limiting it is to think of Cambodians in America as merely living out their intact Cambodianness—brought with them across miles and miles of ocean—in a new context. In much the same way, Nan did not arrive in school with a predetermined set of practices that she imported into the school context. Instead, she came to school with a set of resources that continued to expand and be reshaped as she negotiated with particular teachers and particular peers to, in Dyson's (1993) words, use writing to do "social work." Learning to write in school is a complicated process that involves negotiating with the expectations and evaluations of multiple "imaginative universes," which do not always make their values explicit (Dyson, 1993, p. 17).

Nan was able to do significant "social work" through her writing outside of school, I want to argue, but had a hard time accomplishing the social work of school through her writing. Other researchers have discussed the distinction between the school and non-school writing done by students both in and out of school (Camitta, 1993; Dyson, 1993; Finders, 1996). In her study of junior high school girls, Finders (1996) describes the two literate systems at work in these girls' lives. On the one hand, students engaged in "sanctioned literacies" that teachers were aware of and supported. And on the other, students also engaged in a "literate underlife" that allowed them to break with the official conventions of the sanctioned literacies and to express more controversial opinions. I believe that understanding Nan's literate underlife is valuable in part because it allows us as educators to imagine how the knowledge of writing she does in fact have could serve as a bridge to engaging in other more sanctioned literacies.

What can we learn from out-of-school literacy practices that could help us reshape what happens in schools around literacy? Is it possible that the kind of investment Nan demonstrated in her out-of-school writing could be fostered in her in-school writing as well? If students believe that the best return on their investment comes from their peers, and if their peers see literacy as an unpopular activity, how can we convince them that reading and writing in school are worth their energy and attention?

Context, Participants, Methods

Nan's school and home were located just blocks from a major university. Although predominantly African American, the neighborhood included a concentration of Cambodian families not far from the elementary school Nan attended. Nan, her two younger sisters, her older brother, and her parents lived in a one-bedroom apartment not far from the elementary school. Her parents had come from rural Cambodia and struggled to find economic stability in the urban landscape in Philadelphia. Nan's family was on public assistance, and her parents also did seasonal work picking berries at different times of the year. Unlike her cousins' parents (who lived in the same building), neither of Nan's parents spoke English and both had had very little schooling in Cambodia. Nan's apartment was always a welcoming, warm, and comfortable place for me to be, but it was clear that her family was struggling to make ends meet, with few of the resources needed to succeed economically in urban Philadelphia.

The data presented in this chapter are part of a larger ethnographic study (Skilton-Sylvester, 1997) documenting the identities, literacies, and educational policies that are part of the lives of several Cambodian women and girls in Philadelphia. The fieldwork on which this chapter is based consisted of weekly tutoring sessions over a 3-year period with Nan and her cousins in either of their apartments (located in the same building on different floors). These sessions focused primarily on homework structured around the particular needs of individual girls in any given week. But as we built relationships, they extended to weekend trips to the museum, to my apartment, or to local parks. The girls often gave me drawings, paintings, and writings as parting gifts, especially Nan. And at the end of our tutoring sessions, they also often performed skits, dances, ice-skating competitions, and lip-synching in the living room. As themes emerged from the data, I interviewed the girls about their points of view concerning particular findings or issues.

Fieldwork also included regular visits to the neighborhood elementary school. I had visited the English for Speakers of Other Languages (ESOL) classrooms in this school regularly for a year before I met these particular girls as part of another research project. These regular visits to the school continued during the early phases of my work with Nan, her sisters, and her cousins. During the second year of tutoring the girls, I spent several months visiting each of their ESOL classrooms and each of their grade-level classrooms. In addition, I interviewed each girl's ESOL and grade-level teachers.

I focus on Nan in this chapter because there are such dramatic differences between her in-school and out-of-school writing identities and products. Although the girls were from similar cultural, linguistic, and socioeconomic backgrounds, their school trajectories were not so similar. Nan's younger sister and her cousin both now attend an academic program at a local high school. Nan, however, is on the nonacademic track and still struggles to get to class and to not give up on school all together (personal communication, 2/2/00). Nan interests me greatly both because the resources she brought to school were often invisible or devalued and because I can imagine other possibilities when I see her out-of-school writing. In the right classroom, her enthusiasm for making meaning through print, pictures, and performance could have been a resource to build on in learning to use writing as a tool to do the social work of school.

Taller than her sisters, brother, and cousins, with shoulder-length dark hair, Nan spent a lot of time imagining that being white and American would be better than being Asian and Cambodian American. She also spent a lot of time imagining a glamorous future for herself, possibly in Hollywood. Perhaps more than any of the other girls, she devoted much energy to managing her relationships with her peers.

Nan viewed her academic limitations as linked to her "Cambodianness," as demonstrated by the choices she made in finding an American name. Although other girls had likewise chosen American names, Nan seemed to tie her ability to choose the right American name to her success at school. In fifth grade,[2] she began writing "Mandy" before her Cambodian name on all her homework sheets. Just before she did this, I noticed what a difficult time Nan was having copying down her homework. When I later realized that she had copied all her homework very, very neatly for several days, I asked her what had changed. She replied, "I changed my name to Mandy. Now I can copy my homework." Later I noticed that Nan had adopted still another name, Stacey, a choice she again connected to her academic identity: "When I was Mandy, I was too lazy, so I changed it to Stacey" (fieldnotes, 2/1/95). I would argue that at some level, Nan sensed that she did not have the resources she needed to succeed in school but that if she could somehow be someone else, she might be able to flourish.

Nan's Out-of-School Writing

The prolific nature of Nan's out-of-school writing always amazed me, as did the way she alternately used such writing to tackle tough subjects and create fantasies. The variety in her writing and the joy with which she produced it were also startling—in part because her school experiences were so challenging. Her ESOL teacher remarked, "I don't' think Nan will ever test out of ESOL" and went on to talk about the difficulty Nan faced because she "writes in circles" (fieldnotes, 5/10/94). Her fourth-grade teacher expressed similar doubts: "She's lacking in a lot of the basics in reading and writing skills....She's going to go into fifth grade. My concern is a lot of them are going to go into fifth grade and they're not really ready....Nan wouldn't be able to do the fifth-grade math" (taped interview, 6/2/94).

Meanwhile, outside of school Nan appeared unable to stop writing. I collected more examples of out-of-school writing from Nan than from the other six focal girls in the larger study combined. During our tutoring sessions at her family's apartment, Nan regularly wrote something to give to me when she had finished her homework. In fact, many times I had to encourage her not to rush through her schoolwork in order to finish it quickly and be able then to write a story. During the fieldwork period, she gave me 25 pieces of writing. This out-of-school writing spans several genres: pictures without words (2), pictures with captions (5), multipage fictional stories with pictures (4), stories/reports about real events with pictures (6), letters to me (6), a questionnaire (1), a play (1), and one picture that combines several genres: a picture with a memo to me including a few sentences about the weather (this format was characteristic of much of the daily writing done at her school).

Nan's Strengths

When I compared Nan's in-school and out-of-school literacy practices, one of the first things I noticed was how her oral, visual, and creative focus was often at odds with what mattered most in the school writing she encountered. Whereas at home her strengths as a speaker, an artist, and a storyteller were assets, at school such strengths did not help her master the powerful discourse in which the written word is more valued than speech, words are more important than pictures, and accuracy often matters more than meaning.

Orality and Performance

When Nan wrote at home, it was first and foremost an enjoyable experience. She was totally engaged with the process and could not wait to "perform" what she had written for an audience. To her, writing was meant to be read orally for an audience. There were often many mistakes in her writing, and she usually had some trouble reading what she had written. It was when her written work was performed orally that it really came to life, as she paraphrased the words on the page. She consistently strayed from the text of the story, even though she held the story in front of her. And she often crafted a much more complicated story as she "read" during the performance. This practice of reading texts orally fits with a tradition in Cambodia, whereby performance is an essential aspect of reading (Ledgerwood, 1990, p. 72).

For the women and girls in my study, orality and literacy were connected. Even in English, a Cambodian practice of viewing performance as part of reading crossed generations, socioeconomic classes, and levels of English (see Thierry, 1978). An emphasis on oral performance could certainly be found by looking at the reading goals of adult Cambodians in Philadelphia. Many discussed their desire to learn better pronunciation as they discussed their reading skills, and most read out loud even if they were reading alone. The tendency to see speech and performance as part and parcel of literacy fits well within what has been written about Khmer literacy practices in Cambodia (Ledgerwood, 1990; Thierry, 1978). Interestingly, although most Cambodian children in Philadelphia are not learning to read and write in Khmer, they continue a tradition of performance and oral reading in the context of their English literacy.

An emphasis on orality, while not present in the grade-level classrooms of the Cambodian girls in my study, complements a historical and current emphasis on spoken language in ESOL classrooms in the United States. The well-known audiolingual method does not foreground reading and writing, especially at the lower levels. Observational and interview data that I collected from elementary and middle schools similarly revealed an emphasis on oral language in ESOL. This focus was a common source of tension between grade-level teachers and their ESOL colleagues, since reading and writing are key components of academic work outside the ESOL classroom (Skilton-Sylvester, 1997).

In fact, reading and writing were key concerns in the development of a "New Instructional Model" for Asian ESOL students; this mandated curriculum resulted from a class action suit filed against the school district: *Y.S. v. School District of Philadelphia*.[3] As the new program was developed, there was consensus that ESOL needed to focus on more than just oral English if the program was going to prepare students to succeed in their grade-level classes. It is particularly important that there be an emphasis on reading and writing in ESOL when bilingual students, such as the Cambodian girls in this study, are often fluent *speakers* of English by the time they reached second grade.

My findings show the congruence between an oral/performance orientation of Cambodian students at home and the emphasis on oral language in the ESOL classroom. Such a continuity can make for a good match between home and school practices in relation to ESOL. This was particularly noticeable for Nan, who attended and ESOL class that regularly required students to read aloud from their journals (Skilton-Sylvester, 1997). In this setting, Nan was able to use her oral strengths in ways that were connected to her out-of-school writing practices. This congruence often makes it possible for Cambodian students such as Nan to be more engaged in their work in their ESOL classrooms than in their "regular" classrooms. However, for children and young adults, success in the grade-level classroom (especially in the upper grades) depends more and more on so-called decontextualized literacy skills that do not include an oral component. What is missing, then, is a bridge between the "comfort zone" represented by oral language use and the different demands outside of home and ESOL contexts.

Visual Images

In looking at Nan's writing, it is clear that visual images overshadow the words on the page in most of her texts. Quite a talented young artist, she took great pride in her drawing abilities. When asked what she wanted to do when she grew up, she explained why she wanted to be an artist: "Because I like to draw and I draw good. When I come and paint at your house, I'll make something pretty." After her cousin's comment that she wanted to be a lawyer because she could make a lot of money, Nan added to her earlier response, saying: "I want to be a cartoonist and work at Disney World and make a lot of money at Disney World and Hawaii and everywhere" (fieldnotes, 5/14/94).

In *Before Writing*, Kress (1997) explores the semiotic systems that children have at their disposal before they become writers. One key system of signs is pictures, and Kress makes a compelling point that, in this regard, children are in step with the world at large. As he suggests, words are literally being pushed off the page in current newspapers and textbooks where visual images are prominent. According to Kress, while we discuss with panic the ways in which children are oriented to television and video, we ignore the fact that modes of communication are increasingly visual. In teaching children about writing, we tend to see pictures as superfluous; they are there to complement the writing but are often not "counted" in school contexts as a part of making meaning. Kress believes that we think of pictures as expressions of children's feelings but not as ways that they communicate their interest. Of the 25 pieces of Nan's writing that I analyzed for this chapter, just 4 have no pictures/graphic image accompanying the text: 3 letters and 1 play. In all the others, pictures are a key, if not the main part, of what Nan created. (See, for example, Figure 3.1, a picture she drew of my husband and me.) Kress discusses how difficult it is for children to go from a semiotic system in which form and function are closely matched to a writing system in which symbols themselves are quite distant from what is meant. As he explains, "For children who learn alphabetic writing, the path is from drawing images to the drawing of sound, a path which takes them across a chasm which not all manage to negotiate, a shift from spatial display to sequences in time" (Kress, 1997, p. 137).

Nan's orientation to visual images is common among children her age, but her orientation to drawings and pictures also coincides with Cambodian practices in the United States that value visual images over written texts in the transmission of culture. Many scholars have discussed the importance of television and video for Cambodian families in the United States (Hardman, 1994; Hornberger, 1996; Smith, 1994). Television has become a way of remaining connected to the home culture through Chinese videos dubbed in Khmer. In Cambodian homes, it is videos, photographs of family members, and posters of scenes from Cambodia—not books or magazines—that allow Cambodians in Philadelphia to remain connected to their homeland.

Creating a Message

Watching Nan compose something for school was quite a different experience from watching her compose something for her own purposes. Her difficulties with spelling and grammar in English never seemed to get in her way when she was writing a story or a letter for her own purposes. Her focus on creating a message and her ability to use oral language and pictures to supplement her meaning made it possible for her to write without being particularly focused on whether the form of her message fit the spelling and grammatical conventions expected at school. There were times when this orientation didn't' work for the reader, but it worked for Nan as an out-of-school writer. For example, one of her earliest stories, entitled "The Store is Come Tonight," is quite difficult to follow, even with pictures:

> One day the man owner a stor he said to the stor! stor! stor! give me a moeny. So his pocker is a picture of a stor so the man is a number of a stor. So his mother say are you are Right day! his mother say, you must put it in your pocker. So the man mother Leater go to the New big store and owner of the store Right Now. The End.

Even given the benefit of knowing Nan personally and being able to examine the accompanying pictures, it was hard for me to decipher this story. It has something to do with a man getting some money and buying a big new store, but many of the details are lost. As in much of her writing, in this piece Nan did a better job putting her personal thoughts and ideas on paper than communicating them to a reader. One of the interesting aspects of this story is the way that Nan gets the spelling of *store* right in some cases but not in others. This isn't, then, an instance of not knowing how to spell the word, but one in which getting the form right is not what matters most.

In her out-of-school writing, Nan was able to compose much clearer stories as time went on when she controlled the topic and the genre. One of her most polished writings (and also one of the last I collected) is a play entitled "Daytime":

Lindsey:	Oh, it seem sad that my sister's had forgot about my birthday, Oh, will. (Lindsey walks out of the room).
Lemming:	I didn't not want Lindsey to think we're not thinking about her birthday party
Karen:	Oh, it's OK Lemming don't worry she will know soon (put her hand on Lemming shoulder).
Banky:	Ha, want me to tell her (sitting on Manny's lap)
Lemming, Karen:	big mouth
Manny:	Ha don't say that to he she is just an tiny little sweet girl.
Karen, Lemming:	but
Manny:	no but (Linda—stuck her tongue at them)
Manny:	go to sleep
Banky:	did you buy everything
Manny:	Oh no, we can because we have no money
Banky:	Ha we have no moeny But we could make a card for her

One of the things that is most interesting about her mastery of this genre is that it is a written version of oral speech. In merging her oral strengths with writing, Nan produced a piece of writing that contains the most standardized language of any of her texts. The play is also the only piece of writing besides three letters that does not have a picture to accompany it. In writing down speech, it seems that Nan did not need visual "data" to represent her ideas; rather, the genre itself helped her to compensate for some of her difficulties with capitalization and punctuation because it is clear who is speaking each line. Although she replaces *will* for *well* in the first line, the only other spelling error is *moeny* for *money* in the last line.

Kress (1997) distinguishes between the representation of a message—what an author wants to say or mean—and the communication of a message—how an author gets that meaning across—as two central aspects of school writing suggests that she emphasized representing the message using both words and pictures. She was often so absorbed in creating her text that its representation took precedence over communication. In addition, her ability to communicate to the reader/listener outside of school was not based primarily on the form of the words she used in her text. She relied on pictures and oral explanation to supplement the written word. Outside of school, she often performed her texts; this "performance" also occurred in her ESOL classroom, where she regularly read from her journal, but rarely in other school contexts. Dyson (1993) suggests that privileging communication over performance is common in academic writing in which "the composer is never a performer, only a communicator" (p. 16). In her academic writing, where form mattered more and where she often could not supplement her words with pictures or embellish the text with oral performances, Nan struggled more with both representing and communicating her message.

It is also important to note that power relationships at home were quite different from those Nan experienced at school. At home she had significant prestige as the most fluent writer of English and the kind of power that comes when immigrant and refugee speak more English than their parents (Auerbach, 1989; McKay & Weinstein-Shr, 1993). At school, as a nonnative (and struggling) writer of English and an elementary student, she had vastly less power. These shifts in prestige and power relations influenced Nan's ease with composing. As Kress (1997) explains, "Participants who have greater power are able to force other participants into greater efforts of interpretation. They have a different notion of 'transparency' than other participants who have less power and have to make every effort to produce messages which truly require minimal efforts of interpretation" (p. 14).

Transparency of message was something Nan actively struggled with in her school writing, as demonstrated when she was asked to write a report about a black explorer named Matthew Henson. As she wrote, Nan referred to photocopies of several encyclopedia pages about him (of which a few portions were missing) and struggled to make sense of what she had read. She also wrestled with what to write if she weren't going to copy directly from the published text. When Nan wrote stories for her own purposes, she rarely worried about spelling and easily constructed new texts. In contrast, as she worked on this assignment, spelling and accuracy became very important as she realized that this writing would be judged by how well it followed spelling rules and how much it was connected to the actual facts of Matthew Henson's life (fieldnotes, 12/14/94). The first draft of her report reads as follows:

> Mattrew was born in 1837. he was an exporter he was black he was lucky because ~~it help him~~ every people thought he was their family. he explorer Greenland North pol. Mattrew helped Aruther parory He was ~~Story~~ that people would Story ~~and~~ gave up and he dies in 1855.

After talking about her text for a while, we worked on revising it together. The final version of her story ended up like this:

> Matthew was born in 1837. He was an explorer. Matthew helped Admiral Peary. Admiral Peary was a very famous explorer who discovered the North Pole. Matthew was black. He was lucky because the Eskimo people thought he was their family. He explored Greenland and the North Pole. He was strong. Other people would give up, but he didn't. He died in 1855.

In this genre, Nan's strengths were not readily available as resources. There was no link to oral speech or to visual images that would help her construct her message. As in much academic writing, she had only words to use as tools for conveying her message. Especially because of her positioning as a student and as a nonnative speaker of English, she needed to make her message as transparent and accurate as possible for the reader. All the meaning needed to be contained in the words she wrote. As a result, this assignment was a real challenge for her because she simultaneously had to focus on accuracy, representation, and communication without the oral and visual tools that assisted her in out-of-school writing.

Nan's Written Meaning-Making

In analyzing Nan's out-of-school writing, three questions are important in understanding the texts themselves: What is she writing? To whom is she writing? And why is she writing? Sociolinguistic studies of written language have tended to focus on the form of the writing, its context, the functions it serves, and the roles and statuses of the writer(s) audience. (For a review of this literature, see McKay, 1996.) Only recently have sociolinguists concerned themselves with the content of writing (Hornberger & Skilton-Sylvester, 2000). Here I examine not only the form of Nan's writing but the topics that she chose to write about as well.

Understanding the audiences Nan wrote for its especially important, since so much of school writing is done solely for the teacher to read. Notions of audience are quite connected to issues of purpose and function. In Camitta's (1993) study of out-of-school writing at a Philadelphia high school, she found that audience and purpose intersected in significant ways for adolescents:

> Personal and creative writing is motion toward intimacy, and...its exchange weaves the strands of friendship and understanding....For adolescents, writing is personal and social, an act of invention in which everyday actions are shaped and influenced by the content and by the symbolic value of written texts (p. 243).

As I show in the analysis that follows, the genre/content, purpose/function, and audience of Nan's out-of-school writing were quite different from those of her school writing. In part, this analysis can explain why she was such an engaged writer at home and such a disengaged writer at school.

Genre

Although Nan's out-of-school writing included several different genres, she was most comfortable with narrative stories and letters to people she knew. Even the accounts that she wrote about real events had a storylike quality to them. Most of her fictional and nonfictional writing began with "One day..." For example, two nonfiction stories about me started: "One day is a girl name Miss Ellen." Here's the shorter version of this story:

> One day is a Girl name Msr. ELLEN
> Who like to teach a student
> her name is <u>ELLEN</u>
>
> She like to teach a lettle student

Another nonfictional story that started this way recounted how Nan's friend had thrown away the disposable camera she had taken to school. This story begins "One day I give my camera to my freind." All of her fictional stories (except the play) also began in this same way; for example: "One day it was a cloud and it was so cold." Nan's fictional and nonfictional stories as well as her single-page and multipage stories shared this storytelling mode. Her multipage stories were different in that each concluded with "The End." In all of the other fictional and nonfictional writing, the only other story that ended this way was the one about the camera. These beginnings and endings show, I think, that she had mastered aspects of the story genre and preferred it over other kinds of writing. More than half of her writing used these "story-oriented" conventions. The emphasis on narrative in her out-of-school writing illustrates the somewhat narrow set of conventions that she was comfortable working within. Clearly, as a student she needed to master other genres. What is unfortunate is that her rhetorical knowledge of storytelling was not made visible in ways that would allow her to make comparisons to alternate ways of making meaning in the classroom.

The other genre that Nan used most often was the letter. She wrote six letters to me during the fieldwork period, several around the time of my wedding. For example:

Dear Mrs, Mr, Ellen and Paul

Have a very good time I wish
you and Paul have a baby so we
can see what he or her looks like

We wish	Fr, Bnom* Rem
he or her	Family
well be	To you and and
pretty and	Mr. Paul
cute	

In this letter, Nan showed that she knew some of the conventions for writing a letter, such as starting with "Dear" and ending with some kind of closing. She didn't use a typical convention for letters, but rather the kind of headings often found in memos or on gifts. She ended with a section that shows whom the note is from and whom it is to. Although she still struggled with punctuation (there is non in this writing sample), she did capitalize appropriately, making it easier to distinguish the boundaries between ideas.

About a year later, Nan sent me a letter in the mail which shows that she had figured out several other letter-writing conventions:

Dear Mrs. Ellen

How are you! Thanks for the letters you sent to us. Did you know I have got a crush on a boy name Tommy he's cute and he's in 7th grade he's my typ but he have a girlfriend I got a crush on him since's he frist came to this school went he didn't have a girlFriend yet. please write back what should I do.

Love. Tiff
ask know ask ←— — — — AKA
Nan

P.S. wish you a nice time
my friend knew I like him thy say they'll hook
me up with him
wish you like my letter

In this later letter, Nan demonstrated that she had learned about closing personal letters and that she could also append a "P.S." for additional thoughts. She used more punctuation, and she had also learned a common preteenage convention of putting "AKA" after her name to include both a nickname and her more formal name. Although she used this convention correctly, she incorrectly indicated that it stands for "ask know ask" rather than "also known as." In this case, Nan had learned the form but did not completely understand the meaning.

Certain features of the school genres she regularly produced can be found in the writing she did outside of class. I first noticed this practice in the writing of Nan's younger sister, Chamran. After a huge struggle with reading and writing in first and second grade, one day Chamran asked me if she could write a story. This was a monumental event because she had never asked to write something for fun. When I gave Chamran a piece of paper, she wrote her name in the top right corner of the page and then put "Spelling" as a title centered at the top of the page and numbered from one to ten down the left-hand side. In her first piece of out-of-school writing, she had decided to compose a spelling test. This was the genre that she felt most comfortable with and the only kind of "story" she knew how to write. In contrast, Nan always embraced story writing. The one exception was a picture at the top of which she had written "Today is Monday, January 18, 1993. It is a cold and sunny." This type of note consisting of the date and a short sentence about the weather was typically written on the chalkboard in the ESOL classes at her school.

Content

Before looking at particular themes in Nan's out-of-school writing, I would like to draw attention to one general feature of its content—the fact that in most of the texts I analyzed, women and girls are the main characters. The only exceptions in the writing she gave me are the "store opening" story, which had a man as its main character and the drawing of me with my husband (see Figure 3.1). At one point during the fieldwork period, Nan told me that she had added a boy character to a story she was writing about a girl who encountered some bees. When she rewrote the story to include the boy, she changed the title to reflect this change. Interestingly, although the female character had a name, she did not name this boy. When I asked her why she had made the decision to add a boy to her story, Nan explained: "My friend told me it is better if there's a boy, too."

This example shows that Nan talked about her writing with her friends and sometimes took their advice about the content of what she was composing. It also shows that when writing for her own purposes, the content of her writing was typically connected to her own interests and experiences as a girl. Although the topic of her writing was not always herself, it was the starting point for much if not all of what she wrote. This is yet another way in which the school writing Nan did differed from the writing she did on her own, for she was often not able to include herself or her experiences in her school writing (Skilton-Sylvester, 1997).

In Nan's out-of-school writing, there was a dual emphasis on fantasy and reality. Her thematic focus ranged from (1) seemingly mundane topics (such a story about her mother cooking, as story about seeing a bird in a tree, and a letter telling me that she had drawn a lot of pictures); to (2) fantasy topics (such as one about dressing in glamorous dresses and dancing, several about participating in my wedding, and a few that take place in nonurban settings quite unlike her neighborhood—settings with trees, birds, flowers, and single-family homes with chimneys); to (3) topics about difficult realities (including one about a fictional family living in poverty and another about a girl who cannot go to school because she is pregnant).

An example of the first set of topics about seemingly mundane realities is a text about her mother cooking. It included a picture of an overhead light and a table set with plates, forks, knives, and spoons. The text reads, "My mom is making a fried. But it is good to eat." Even in this apparently straightforward story, one can see the ways that Nan situated herself, not just as a reporter of what she saw, but a creator of written realities. She wrote this text as if she were writing a description of something that she had witnessed, but she also transformed the message in ways that vary from reality. Nan's' family did not own a table; they typically ate sitting on the floor. They also ate using chopsticks, not forks, knives, and spoons. Even in this seemingly straightforward story, Nan created a reality with her message; she didn't merely transcribe it. The insertion of a table, chairs, and silverware fit with Nan's interest in the lives of the families she saw on TV and of other Americans. She regularly interviewed me about my family's practice and asked if we ate the way that people do on television. Her choice also fit with her ambivalence about being Cambodian.

Nan: I don't' want to be Asian American. I want to be just American.
Me: Why?
Nan: Cause it's better.
Me: Why is it better?
Nan: It just is. (fieldnotes, 2/5/95)

In her pictures and stories, she sometimes had the power to "Americanize" her family in ways that did not fit her lived reality.

Nan's ability to create new realities was even more present in the writings that clearly included fantasy content. In these stories, she created the content completely, rather than basing it partially on her own lived experience. The same is true of her later drawings (see Figure 3.2). In these stories and pictures, the figures were typically who are dressed in long, elaborate gowns. Another example can be seen in the story called "The Pretter Girls" ("The Pretty Girls"): "One day it was six pretter girls and They all dances Pretter like a pretter women that has a picture for me. Some of the pretter girls were asleep now." This particular story and drawing had six girls, all in full-length gowns with one lying down and sleeping at the bottom of the page; in many others Nan created similar situations in which women are described as pretty and are dressed quite formally and extravagantly. Her interest in stories about formal occasions became more intense before my own wedding; Nan spent a long time talking about what I would wear and how pretty I would look.[4]

The final set of themes have to do with fictional stories written about difficult realities; they are not about Nan but instead address issues that are relevant to her life. In addition to challenges similar to those facing other girls in school, the Cambodian girls in my study often had significant family responsibilities that outweighed those of their brothers or their non-Cambodian classmates, strict rules about interacting with the opposite sex, and uncertainty about their language abilities or limited experience with participation patterns found in the classroom (Skilton-Sylvester, 1997).

In addition, the girls often worried about getting pregnant early, a fear closely linked to concerns about not finishing school and a potential version of their futures. When I visited college campuses with Nan's older cousin Ty, her mother kept lecturing her about how important it was not to get pregnant if she were allowed to live on campus (Skilton-Sylvester, 1997). On a similar topic, in fourth grade Nan wrote the following story entitled "The girl that can not got out of School":

One day she went home with not to tell the teacher. The teacher cannot found her. The girl went up the sky and down the dry and then she got home early. But she forgot to go to school. The teacher was very happy that she did not go to school. The girl said "Oh no." In the next morning, she did not go home. Her mother was very sad because she did not go home. The girl's mom give her a wedding. The girl cry today. The girl is a mommy and the girl's mother is a grandmother and she have a baby. The girl cannot go to school because she had a baby. The End.

While the title seems to suggest that the girl cannot get out of going to school (i.e., she has to go to school), the story ends by stating that she can't go to school. This might be just an inadvertent mix-up, but I think it may also point to ambivalence about school, which is supposed to be a place where people want to be but often is not. It is also interesting (and disturbing) that the teacher in the story is happy when the girl doesn't come to school. Although this story line may not have been directly applicable to Nan's experience with school, there were certainly times for all the girls in this study when they did not feel good about going to school, often because of peer relationships and negative connotations associated with being in ESOL. For example, Nan's youngest sister Chamran once asked me when I would come to her class to visit again "because sometimes I don't have any friends." She went on to explain that her friend "took" her other friend by saying that Chamran wasn't good at ESOL (fieldnotes, 6/2/94). At other times, discomfort with school had more to do with academic struggles. Nan's older cousin Saporn talked about her difficulty in school this way: "I'm doing so bad in school. I've never been this scared. I study and study and I fail, but my other friends, they didn't even study and they know how to do it. It just doesn't make any difference. I study and it does nothing" (fieldnotes, 2/22/95).

Most of the pictures that Nan drew for "The girl that can not got out of School" illustrate directly what was happening in each segment of the plot, except in the first section when the girl left school early, and there are a few rhyming words that don't makes sense: "the girl went up the sky and down to the dry." The picture in Figure 3.3 shows a car near the school with what looks like a young man in it; in this context these words seem to allude to what she is doing with him. Since most Cambodian girls Nan's age don't' seem to know too much about pregnancy, it makes some sense that whatever she is doing with this boy is in almost indecipherable terms. (One of her cousins who is the same age was surprised that I didn't have a baby when I got home from my week-long honeymoon.)

It is also noteworthy that the girl in the story sees the boy under the guise of school. This fits with my understanding of the uses of an "education" label in increasing freedom and mobility for young women. If an event is seen as a school event (i.e., going to the library, meeting a tutor), girls and young women can often do things they wouldn't ordinarily be able to do (dancing with a boy, wearing a sleeveless dress). As Kulig (1994) states, "There are many opportunities for freedom here for these young women because they attend school where they can meet and spend time with young men without parental supervision" (p. 139).

This story says a lot, I think, about the fear girls have about not living up to their parents' goals for their future. The fears expressed by Nan about getting pregnant as a teenager are an example of this. However, it is important not to see their fears simply in terms of the disruption of having a baby as a teenager. Nan's story also seems to express well both the ambivalence these girls often have about school and a sense that they do not always feel wanted when they are there. In a more general way, this story illustrates the fact that going or not going to school is often a gendered process; that is, that processes that influence girls (i.e., pregnancy, needing to take care of siblings, rules about interactions with the opposite sex, marriage) can be in conflict with being a student.

Clearly, in the content of her writing, Nan did not focus primarily on the specifics of her own everyday reality. Instead, she transformed those realities, dreamed of other realities, and worked out fears about current and/or future realities. Although her own life was typically the starting point, she often created her stories at the intersection of fact and fiction. My analysis of the reading and writing that these students did in school indicates that outside of the ESOL classroom, there were few opportunities to write with their own lives (or the lives of other Asian Americans) as a starting point. The writing that these girls did in school focused much more on fact than on fiction, making Nan's stories sometimes seem like false representations of the facts, rather than her own "trying on" of different possibilities.

Audience/Function

Unlike much of Nan's school writing, for which the teacher was the only audience and the purpose of writing was often "to finish the assignment for a grade," Nan's out-of-school writing had multiple audiences and served multiple functions. I was surprised to see how much copying students were required to do in their school writing, especially in the early grades. I was also somewhat surprised to hear Saporn, Nan's cousin, say that students got higher grades when they copied something from the book than when they wrote something themselves (fieldnotes, 5/30/94). Saporn's copying during middle school could be framed as plagiarism, but it could also be seen as a product of many years of school training in which copying was the main genre of school-based writing. In fact, in first grade, almost all Chamran's homework had to do with copying. From this perspective, Saporn used the training that she received in elementary school, despite the fact that the rules for writing had changed. She had developed few skills for meeting the writing expectations of middle school and high school.

The notion that it matters more to put something on the page than to write something good or original was echoed many times in the comments of these school-aged girls. As Saporn explained, "Sometimes when I copy what I write, I don't even know what it means anymore" (fieldnotes, 2/25/94). Not knowing what things mean seemed to hamper other aspects of writing for some of the girls. Ty, for example, thought that not knowing the meaning made it hard for her to spell words. She questioned, "They asked me about the spelling of the words, but I don't know what they mean, how can I know how to spell them?" (fieldnotes, 6/2/95).

In contrast to the school writing Nan had to do, her out-of-school writing had multiple audiences and multiple functions. For example, letter/note-writing was something that Nan (and the other girls) did a lot and not just with me. They regularly used letters to repair and maintain relationships, write to members of the opposite sex, and keep in touch with friends (Skilton-Sylvester, 1997). In fact, when Nan sent me the letter about her crush on a boy, she also included a copy of the note that had been passed back and forth between her and her friend about this boy. In the note, parts were crossed out as new messages were exchanged:

Whatever you name Tommy
Why you ask me if I like him
Because I'm gonna hook you up with him
No I got a boy already
Who?
My friend brother in Maine name Timmy

This strategy of maintaining relationships through writing was particularly appealing to these girls in part because it was difficult for many of their parents to read what they had written. Neither of Nan's parents could read in English, so a note was a safe way for her to communicate even about things that her parents might not want her to talk about (i.e., a crush on a boy). So, in addition to there begin a real audience, the value of communicating in this way also connected to a "nonaudience"— knowing, that is, that one's parents could not read what was written.

Although Nan often focused more on creating and representing her message than on being sure it was communicated as she intended, it is clear that her out-of-school writing was always done to be shared with someone. In some cases, it was performed; in others, it was passed along to show her interest in a topic or to show that she cared about the receiver. In our tutoring sessions, she gave me pieces of her writing as gifts when I left, as something of value that she had created. Another example of this practice can be seen from the story line of her play "Daytime," when disappointed girls cannot buy a birthday present for their sister: "We have no money but we can make a card for her." Here is the foundation of the audiences and purposes Nan imagines as she writes. Although she struggled in school and did not have much money, Nan was able through her pencil and paper to give those around her a creation that was part of herself. In this way, writing was a limitless resource for connecting with others outside of school.

Investment

Understanding Nan's experiences with writing requires thinking about her investment (Norton Peirce, 1995) in using and learning about writing. This notion acknowledges that power relationships and other particulars of the context can shape identities and language practices at any given point in time. Norton Peirce's (1995) term *investment* is connected to the idea that those who are learning a new language need to believe that they have the "right to speak," that what they say will be heard and responded to with interest, respect, and action. Drawing on Bourdieu's (1977) work, she suggests that we cannot assume that listeners always grant those who are speaking (or writing) English as a second language the "right to speak."

I believe that Nan's experiences with writing in home and school contexts can be understood in terms of investment, identity, and the right to speak. In thinking about Nan's experiences with school writing, it would be easy to conclude that she was just no motivated, that she simply had little interest in print. What her out-of-school writing shows is that she could be incredibly invested in using and learning about the written word when she was granted the right to write and knew that there were those who really wanted to listen to her thoughts, experiences, and ideas. At school, when she was framed as a "struggling writer" and where the purposes of writing were not primarily to "do social work," she was often unable to reveal her literacy strengths. In her ESOL classroom, however, where she was given the opportunity to "perform" parts of her journal for her classmates, she was able to demonstrate some of her literacy strengths within the school context. At home, where she was framed as storyteller and playwright, she wrote with great enthusiasm and creativity. We have often failed in schools because we tell students we want them to speak/compose their thoughts on paper, yet we constrain their "right to speak" by making our responses primarily evaluative. As teachers, we are often not a real audience, and so it is difficult for students to invest in the work we are asking them to do. Nan's engagement in the writing of her ESOL classroom shows, however, that when purpose and audience are meaningfully constructed, she was able to claim the right to write within the classroom context.

Implications for Teachers and Schools

Both Norton Peirce (1995) and Cummins (1997) point to the important role that teachers can play in shaping the identities students have at school. In discussing what makes it possible for language-minority students to succeed, one of the key elements Cummins (1997) stresses is "the identity options that are being opened up or closed off for students" (p. 425) in the school context. Similarly, Norton Peirce (1995) discusses this changing subjectivity of students in different contexts and concludes that because identities can be shaped by those who listen to students and read their texts, educational intervention can really have an impact. Norton Peirce (1995) suggests:

> Motivation is not a fixed personality trait but must be understood with reference to social relations of power that create the possibilities for language learners to speak.... It is their investment in the target language that will lead [learners] to speak....The lived experiences and social identities of language learners need to be incorporated into the formal second language curriculum (p.26).

My study has shown, however, that if students' lives only enter the school walls through writing that is on the periphery of how students are ultimately evaluated, we have not created the bridge needed to make the out-of-school strengths of a student such as Nan visible when she is tackling academic literacy. It is also important, as Zamel (1993) has pointed out, that we not merely prepare students for the academic world that already exists, but that we work to make that academic world take the realities of writing in a second language into consideration in evaluation.

Nan's writing also highlights the importance of visual and oral discourse in the ways she augmented the meaning-making she dos with letters and words. Bridges need to be built between these mulitsensory messages and the ways that school writing is often judged and interpreted based on the messages that the words themselves convey. Kress (1997) suggests, "As texts draw more and more overtly on visual means of communication, the skills and knowledge of visual design and display will need to be fostered as a central part of any literacy curriculum" (p. 58).

If schools are to compete with peer groups for the investment of students, it needs to be clear to students that they have something to gain by learning school writing conventions. This "return on investment" needs to be more than a good grade. We need to show the doors that open up if one can write "transparent" messages as part of academic discourse. Even more, we need to show that there is an immediate return on students' investment in school writing, that this writing is being written for real audiences and real purposes beyond evaluation.

In Nan's writing, there was just one time that a school writing genre visibly appeared in her out-of-school writing (that is, when she place a date at the top of a page and described the weather). Her genres of choice—fictional stories and pictures and letters—were not typical genres she was asked to write in school. The genres that she liked best had an emphasis on creative storytelling and personal connections, two features often not present in school writing. The one place where school and out-of-school genres intersected was in the journal that she kept in ESOL class that she was often able to read aloud to her classmates. The journal captured both the creativity and the emphasis on relationships that are central characteristics of the genres that she most often picked, and it included a performance element that also highlighted her strengths. Unfortunately, journal-writing was not a type of genre that had much importance at school, so this link was not a powerful bridge between her home and school writing practices. Also, in other classes I observed, journals were not linked to performance but were primarily used as communication tools to discuss ideas and thoughts with an audience that included the teacher, but no necessarily other students.

During Nan's fourth-grade year, I spent a significant period of time her grade-level classroom. Her teacher, Mrs. Jackson, explained that she was at a second-grade reading level and that the school had recently adopted a textbook series that meant that all students in a particular grade read the same text at the same time. This was quite difficult for Nan, who got the most out of the lesson when the stories were read out loud or listened to on tape. It appears that her comfort in speaking in the classroom could also have been used as a bridge. Mrs. Jackson explained, "Well, the Cambodian girls are very quiet, very timid....Nan on the other hand is very vocal. I mean, whether she has the right or wrong answer or has any idea what you were talking about, she'll offer an answer to a question" (taped interview, 6/2/94). Even so, much of the "language work" that went on in her fourth-grade classroom was "over her head." On one of the days that I observed the class, while much of the class read a story, Nan worked in a small group of students focusing on phonics exercises from a workbook not associated with the main text (fieldnotes, 5/22/94).

When Mrs. Jackson spoke about writing instruction in her classroom, she first mentioned the lesson that she thought was most successful that year. It was an exercise the children did after reading a story that contained a lot of similes; most of the students then successfully created similes of their own. As Mrs. Jackson goes on to discuss what her goals were for writing instruction, one can sense how much she wanted writing to be fun for her students:

> One thing I work on from the very beginning is just building sentences....I work on creative writing and my feeling is writing is just something the kids should do. We do through all the writing process. I go through all the steps—brainstorming, the rough copy, the editing, the final copy. It takes maybe a whole week to do one story. An my goal is not so much to get a finished piece of work that is grammatically correct, punctuation and all. My goal is to get a story that shows some imagination and shows that the child was able to go through those steps, was able to...get their ideas down....I will grade them, but I don't put the marks all over the paper. *So my goal is that by the end of the year, they've had an enjoyable experience writing....* We read autobiographies in the book and then from that we just took of and wrote an autobiography. (taped interview, 6/2/9, emphasis added)

The writing Nan most often did in her fourth-grade classroom clustered around three types: (1) writing based on readings done in class, (2) creative writing in which students showed their ability to go through the writing process, and (3) workbook exercises that included individual words or the construction of sentences.

There are several ways in which Nan's strengths from her out-of-school writing could have been evident here—the emphasis on meaning-making in creative writing (rather than on correctness) and the writing of autobiographies were both potential pathways for Nan to participate in school writing. However, the emphasis in the creative writing process was on communication for the teacher who would be grading the writing and not on performance or relationship-building through the writing. Also, pictures were not a part of the meaning-making she did for these creative writing activities. In addition, because the readings were often inaccessible to Nan, the writing of autobiographies or the writing of similes might have been difficult to even begin to understand.

It is not difficult to imagine that the classroom context could be one in which oral and visual meaning-making exists alongside written communication, where both teachers and students are an authentic audience for the written work of others in the classroom, and where the purposes for writing are connected to multiple real reasons why class members would want to communicate with each other. And in fact, in some of the many classrooms I visited, this very kind of writing instruction did occur. If Nan had been in such an environment, her abilities as a playwright might have been a springboard for doing the social work of school through writing.

Aside from the ways that writing instruction occurred in the classroom, two other factors might have made Nan's writing trajectory quite different. First, if she had learned to read and write in her native Khmer, there is reason to believe (Garcia, 1999, in press; Snow, Burns, & Griffin, 1998) that she might not have fallen so far behind her native-English-speaking peers in her ability to understand and create texts in English. Like Nan, all her sisters and cousins struggled with the technical skills of reading and writing in the early grades, and this continued to make them fall farther and farther behind their peers. Much of Nan's writing, although expressive, creative, and interesting, did not meet the expectations of school personnel for what children of her age should be able to accomplish with print.

Nan's in-school writing was also influenced by her perception of herself within the school context. As I mentioned above, student subjectivities are "(re)formed within the space of the school itself" (Levinson, 1998, p. 267). Nan was a part of a peer culture in which being literate was not the pathway to popularity. Part of why Nan's out-of-school writing was more visible than her in-school writing may have had to do with the fact that mastering "sanctioned literacies" was seen as the key to unpopularity. Her desire to win popularity, however, was also connected to the fact that she saw herself losing at the academic game. As we saw earlier, Nan believed that adopting an American name was a good way to achieve better academic results. At some level, when she was not in her ESOL classroom, she had given up on herself as someone who could do "sanctioned literacy" and so it is not surprising that her "literate underlife" was so much more vibrant that what she did at school.

Nan did find some success in her ESOL classroom, where she was able to use her multimodal resources to perform literate acts in the classroom, where many of the students had similar reading and writing difficulties, and where her linguistic and cultural differences were "normal." However, the reading and writing she did in ESOL was not the kind of reading and writing she was expected to do outside it. The engagement she experienced with writing out-of-school shows that she saw the potential power of the written medium to convey meaning and build relationships—to "do social work" with writing. Nan's out-of-school literacy resources—and those of many nonmainstream students in U.S. schools—can be a foundation for school literacy if we are able to read the words and the worlds that children bring with them to school and help them to engage in new and related words and worlds as they use writing to do the social work of school. There are many things to learn by looking at Nan's out-of-school writing in relation to her in-school writing. It is abundantly clear that we, as teachers, have as much to learn from Nan as she from us.

Notes

[1] The research reported in this chapter was made possible in part by a grant from the Spencer Foundation. The data presented, the statements made, and the views expressed are solely the responsibility of the author.

[2] Most of the girls did not choose American names until high school.

[3] *Y.S. v. School District of Philadelphia* was a class-action suit filed in 1985 on behalf of Asian students in Philadelphia. The resulting court mandate included restructuring curriculum, placement, and staffing in schools with a significant number of Asian students.

[4] She was, in fact, somewhat disappointed by how informal my wedding was, which did not fit with how (fueled by television) she imagined such an event. At one point she told me, "You have to have a pink cake like they did on *Full House*" (one of her favorite television shows).

References

Auerbach, E.R. (1989). Toward a socio-contextual approach to family literacy. *Harvard Educational Review, 59*(2), 165-181.

Bourdieu, P. (1977). The economics of linguistic exchanges. *Social Science Information, 16,* 645-668.

Camitta, M. (1993). Vernacular writing: Varieties of literacy among Philadelphia high school students. In B. Street (Ed.), *Cross-cultural approaches to literacy* (pp. 228-246). Cambridge, UK: Cambridge University Press.

Cummins, J. (1997). Minority status and schooling in Canada. *Anthropology & Education Quarterly, 28*(3), 411-430.

Dyson, A.H. (1993). *Social worlds of children learning to write in an urban primary school.* New York: Teachers College Press.

Finders, M.J. (1996). "Just girls": Literacy and allegiance in junior high school. *Written Communication, 13*(1), 93-129.

Garcia, G.E. (1999). Bilingual children's reading: An overview of recent research. *ERIC/CLL Newsbulletin.* ERIC Clearinghouse on Language and Linguistics, Center for Applied Linguistics.

Garcia, G.E. (in press). Bilingual children's reading. In M. Kamil, P. Mosenthal, P.D. Pearson, & R. Barr (Eds.), *Handbook of reading research* (Vol. 3). New York: Longman

Hardman, J. (1994). *Language and literacy development in a Cambodian community in Philadelphia.* Unpublished doctoral dissertation, University of Pennsylvania, Graduate School of Education, Philadelphia.

Heller, M. (1994). *Linguistic minorities and modernity: A sociolinguistic ethnography.* New York: Longman.

Hornberger, N.H. (1996). Mother-tongue literacy in the Cambodian community of Philadelphia. *International Journal of the Sociology of Language, 119,* 69-86.

Hornberger, N.H. & Skilton-Sylvester, E. (2000). Revisiting the continua of biliteracy: International and critical perspectives. *Language and Education: An International Journal, 14*(2), 96-122.

Kress, G. (1997). *Before writing: Rethinking the paths to literacy.* New York: Routledge.

NOW THAT YOU'VE READ

1. In what out-of-school writing activities was Nan involved? How did Nan use out-of-school writing? How do these uses compare with the ways in which she made use of writing in school?

2. Nan was clearly much more interested/invested in her out-of-school writing. Why might that be, according to Skilton-Sylvester? Do you agree with Skilton-Sylvester's conclusions? Why or why not?

3. In the opening pages of Skilton-Sylvester's essay, she asks "What can we learn from out-of-school literacy practices that could help us reshape what happens in schools around literacy? Is it possible that the kind of investment Nan demonstrated in her out-of-school writing could be fostered in her in-school writing as well? If students believe that the best return on their investment comes from their peers, and if their peers see literacy as an unpopular activity, how can we convince them that reading and writing in school are worth their energy and attention?" (64). What do you think? How would you respond to Skilton-Sylvester's question?

READING

Ban Fascism

Roger Mills

BEFORE YOU READ

1. What does "fascism" mean?

2. In recent months, "fascism" has been used often by many groups across the globe. Can you describe any current discussions surrounding fascism? How is this term being used? Toward whom? In what contexts is it being used?

3. What do you see as the value of political writing?

Section to read:

Mills, Roger. "Ban Fascism (UK)." *Pro(se)letariets*. pp. 112–117.

NOW THAT YOU'VE READ

1. Mills writes about the first time he saw a sign which read "BAN FASCISM." In this short piece, he argues that writing and art are meaningful whether or not they appear in a prestigious location or by a prominent author/artist: "The work of those graffiti artists is as deep and honourable as anything hanging in the National Gallery." This reading is also about identity: Which people can create meaningful art/writing? Do they have to be famous, rich, from a certain background? This is a version of

PRO(SE)LETARIETS

The Writing of the Trans-Atlantic
Worker Writer Federation

Edited by Audrey Burns, Alicia Landsberg,
Evan Smith, Jesse Uruchima

the tensions between dominant/vernacular literacies as well. Describe your view of this debate and other examples that come to mind.

2. "BAN FASCISM" is about a literacy event (seeing the words "BAN FASCISM" for the first time), and then learning about various connotations or contexts of this phrase. It also intersects with identity on a political level by implicitly asking *who or what has authority to write or participate in shaping the world around us?* Think about a time when a piece of art (a symbol, an image, an advertisement) stood out to you and why. "Read" the image as if you are reading a piece of writing. What stands out to you? Can we understand your example as a form of literacy?

3. How might we see Mills' piece as being political?

WRITING ASSIGNMENT

REVISION

Using the feedback you received from your teacher and peers, please select the strongest part of your argument then complicate it with your reading of the second round of texts.

Please note that we are looking for a re-vision—that is, a re-seeing of your project in light of new information and feedback. We are not interested in rewrites that contain sentences stuck into the first draft to "fix" the issues raised in your instructor's comments or to correct surface errors. This will be largely a new paper. Of course, you can borrow from and make use of meaty sections of your first draft. But it's important to remember that editing is not the same thing as revision.

Your revision should be at least one page longer or an equivalent for digital or multimodal projects. In addition, please highlight the sections of your revision that differ from the original or describe these changes for your instructor.

CHAPTER 4

(Re)defining Literacy in Our Lives

In the chapters leading up to this one, you have been reading about literacy experiences in everyday life, exploring your own and those of others, expanding your understanding of what literacy means, and exploring the tensions between dominant and vernacular literacies. Let's bring these conversations together. What does this mean for readers and writers in a variety of contexts?

In this chapter, we will think about the material conditions in which texts are created, produced, and circulated. As you read this chapter, think about the various forms of writing you do (in class, at home, for organizations, work, fun, etc.): What types of writing do you produce? What genres (essays, lab reports, memos, fanfiction, blogging)? What types of language do you use? Where does your writing circulate? (Who reads it? How do they access this writing? Does it cost anything?) These questions show us that writing doesn't just happen. Instead, our writing is shaped by our experiences, the tools we use to write, and the conditions around us, including financial, social, and sometimes even political factors.

To think about these points, we will read parts of *Dreams and Nightmares* written by Liliana Velásquez. This provides another example of how literacy extends beyond local spaces to have transnational implications. That is, literacy happens not only in our local communities but also across national boundaries. Often, in the United States, we might think about literacy within the context of English and from what we know of as an American-based view of literacy. But, of course, literacy happens every day beyond these narrow examples— across linguistic and national borders. As you'll see in your book, *Dreams and Nightmares* is written in both English and Spanish. Velásquez details her journey from Guatemala and the literacy practices she used in order to survive political, social, and economic hardship as she immigrated to America. Ultimately, this book was produced in America and is now read and accessed by anyone who can purchase the book online. In order for this book to be produced though, multiple people came together to raise money at universities, through CrowdRise, and pulled together resources. In this way, we see how the book you're reading was impacted by factors beyond the writing itself.

READING

● ● ● ● ● ● ●

Selections from *Dreams and Nightmares*

Liliana Velásquez

BEFORE YOU READ

Please note: In previous chapters, you have read short pieces, poems, and articles. In this chapter, we will read an entire book. However, your focus and reading strategies for this will probably be different. We would like you to focus on pages 9–117 and 191–207. (Each page of text is in Spanish followed by a translation in English). This book will be longer than your other readings for this class, but the goal for this reading is more about what the book represents than looking closely at each and every line of text. While you read, think about the journey of the narrative and the factors that shaped this book. Think too about the questions of access, materiality, movement, violence, and sponsorship that have shaped the fact we are even able to read a book detailing a 14-year-old immigrant's journey in a first-year writing class.

1. As you read, think about the conditions that inspired this book, and the implications of this book even existing! For instance, what does it mean for a 14-year-old girl to flee her country and then be able to tell her story? How does Liliana's narrative relate to the views of literacy and language that we've discussed? What does this story add to our discussions?

2. Look at the book *Dreams and Nightmares*. Flip through the pages, paying attention to images, language, the people involved in its production, where it was produced, and even the book's materiality (how it feels, how it's put together, how it looks). What do you notice about this book?

3. We see from the book cover that *Dreams and Nightmares* is a story of immigration, or writing about the literal movement of people across geographic borders. Can you think of a story of immigration or movement across borders in your own life or family's history? Did your language or literacy practices change with this movement?

DREAMS AND NIGHTMARES

I fled alone to the United States when I was fourteen

SUEÑOS Y PESADILLAS

Huí sola a los Estados Unidos cuando tenía catorce años

LILIANA VELÁSQUEZ

edited and translated by
editado y traducido por MARK LYONS

NOW THAT YOU'VE READ

1. Liliana Velásquez travels through and describes multiple settings (her home in Guatemala, in the desert, on trains, in villages, a detention center, Philadelphia, etc.). Focus on one of these settings and note how she describes it. What descriptions does she use? Does literacy play a role in this setting? How so? Think about the work we've done on literacy sponsors, discourse communities, the role of access, and the material conditions that shape our narratives.

2. Think about each of the chapter titles in Part II of our textbook (Narrating Literacies; Expanding Notions of Literacy Practices; Dominant and Vernacular Literacies; (Re)defining Literacy in Our Lives). How does *Dreams and Nightmares* embody each of these themes? Does Velásquez complicate, change, or reinforce your ideas of literacy?

WRITING ASSIGNMENT

FINAL PROJECT

For this final assignment, we ask that you reflect on the reading and writing you've done this semester—specifically, the ways your understandings of what it means to be literate have changed. To begin, you may want to think about and address the following questions:

- In what settings are you most aware of language? Why?
- What does it mean to be part of a community? What does membership require?
- More specifically, what does it mean to be outside that community? And how do you navigate being part of, perhaps, multiple communities simultaneously?
- What happens to your ways of using language in the process of becoming an "insider" within a community?
- What readings have you found the most engaging and useful? Why? Do these readings match up with your view of literacy? Why or why not?

As with all assignments from this course, we would like you to think broadly and creatively about how you might best represent your ideas. Of course, this will involve a written product, but it can also take a variety of forms and genres. This project consists of two (2) products:

1. A **final project** that addresses the above questions and explores how your understanding of being literate has changed. (For instance, you could produce a narrative story that reflects on key artifacts—images, movies, songs, photographs, menus, locations, etc.—from your literacy communities while you describe shifts that you've noticed in these literacies.)

2. A **reflective piece** that supplements this project. The reflection is a dialogue between you and your instructor, where you "talk through" ideas you have come to, articulate questions you might still have, and provide context for your ideas. This can take multiple forms. For instance, you can write a reflective essay. You could produce an audio reflection. You could also annotate your project with "comments" in a Word document or Google Drive.

Please quote from *your own writing* to mark changes in your thinking and from several of the readings you've found most engaging or useful. Your final project should be at least 6 pages (or a suitable equivalent if you are using a different form) and should begin with a meaningful title.

What We'll Be Looking For:

- Is your project engaging? Is it creative? Does it show nuanced thinking of literacy that has developed throughout the course?
- Does your project show specific instances of how and where your thinking has developed about literacy?
- Does your project show thoughtful engagement with the readings, conversations, and activities from the course?

- Does your project address how literacy and communities are intertwined?
- Does your reflective piece add context for your thinking about literacy? Does it show specific moments of thinking and explicitly address ideas, questions, and your process of working on this project?

PART III

Literacies in Context

If among the o
f its pervading
whic significan
idden from all
depts the preg

Introduction

Shannon Carter

---

lit·er·a·cy (lit′er-e-sē) n.

1. The condition or quality of being literate, especially the ability to read and write.

2. The condition or quality of being knowledgeable in a particular subject or field: cultural literacy; biblical literacy.

con·text (kän′t ekst′) n.

1. The part of a text or statement that surrounds a particular word or passage and determines its meaning.

2. The circumstances in which an event occurs; a setting.

The title of Part III is "Literacies in Context." Of course, you already know this. We draw your attention to the title not because we think you are unaware of its exsistence but because we rarely make much use of titles, at least not beyond locating the text it labels and turning past the cover on which the words are printed.

BEFORE YOU READ any further, take another look at the keywords that make up the title of this section. Given these keywords (as defined in the box above), what do you expect this section will be about? Tie this information to what you already know about the course itself. What do you imagine you will be expected to read? To write? To do with these reading and writing projects?

Not surprisingly, the subject of "Literacies in Context" is, like the rest of this textbook, literacy. That means we will be concerned with your development as a writer, reader, and researcher, as well as the ways in which these activities (literacy) function in the world beyond ourselves (and in our own lives beyond the walls of our classrooms).

In doing so, we work from two, complementary assumptions: first, that writing (and reading) is, as Jacqueline Jones Royster puts it, a "people-oriented enterprise" (27), and second, that texts do not exist except as "texts in use." Before you picked up this textbook, for example, its meaning lay dormant, pressed silent between the pages on which these words are written. As reading theorist M.J. Tonjes puts it, "a text is gobbledygook unless the reader can breathe meaning into it" (10). The writer must do the same, infusing the voices involved on his or her end of the conversation with enough power to sustain the conversation until the reader arrives.

Literacy (reading and writing) exists only when it is active, alive, and in "conversation" with real people posing real problems—people with real lives and histories who are asking these questions and having these conversations some place rather than in some abstract, cognitive no-place where mysterious writers write for "general" audiences.

Why Is Literacy a Good Subject for a First-Year Writing Course?

> [O]ur cornerstone course must resist conventional but inaccurate models of writing. A re-envisioned FYC [First Year Composition] shifts the central goal from teaching "academic writing" to teaching realistic and useful conceptions of writing—perhaps the most significant of which would be that writing is neither basic nor universal but content- and context-contingent and irreducibly complex.
> —Doug Downs and Elizabeth Wardle

Though it probably seems counterintuitive to say so, the greatest obstacles to learning to write "college-level essays" in any course rest not in what you don't yet know about writing but rather in *what you've already learned* about it; in other words, most unsuccessful student writers struggle to apply writing "rules" that are, in fact, inappropriate for the vast majority of "real" writing situations (see especially Street, Gee, Hull, Schultz, Brodkey, Barton and Hamilton, Cope and Kalantzis, Harrington, Adler-Kassner, and Carter among others).

It's not that you didn't learn the rules the first time around. You did. No doubt you've had plenty of successful writing experiences in previous courses. When pressed, many writers can parrot the very same writing "rules" we know to be circulating among even the most effective writers (never use "I" in formal writing; be clear and concise; the thesis statement should appear at the end of the first full paragraph). No, it's not that struggling writers didn't get it. It's just that while these rules may have been entirely appropriate guidelines for the context in which they originally learned them, these rules are unlikely to be equally applicable to every single writing context in which writers may later find themselves (History, Biology, American Literature), despite what they've been taught about the autonomy and portability of these rules. Still, as Brian V. Street explains, "individuals, *often against their own experience*, come to conceptualize literacy as a separate, reified set of 'neutral' competencies, autonomous of social context" (114, emphasis mine).

According to key research in literacy studies—much of which is included among the readings in this textbook—many teachers' attempts to simplify and universalize writing (through rules, through "general writing instruction") actually block access to any meaningful sort of literacy development. Writing is not neutral; it is, as Jacqueline Jones Royster explains, a "people-centered enterprise." In other words, "all language use . . . is an invention of a particular social milieu, not a natural phenomenon" (21). In fact, "discourses operate at the hands and the will of a *people,* rather than instruments or forces of nature" (25, emphasis in original). For this very reason, general writing instruction with neutral goals like producing in students "clarity of prose" and "stronger research skills" is problematic; people exist in communities, and communities— even academic ones—are never entirely autonomous but always already "people-oriented" and therefore reproduce "[a particular] discourse [that] is a configuration of knowledge and its habitual forms of expression, which represents a particular set of interests" (Cope and Kalinowitz 21)—interests that are neither "universal" nor "generalizable" but rather time-based, people-based, place-based, and situation-specific.

To a great extent the key theoretical framework for this textbook's approach relies on two overlapping theoretical traditions: the New Literacy Studies (NLS) and activity theory.

1. "NLS approaches," according to Brian V. Street, "focus on the everyday meanings and uses of literacy in specific cultural contexts and link directly to how we understand the work of literacy in educational contexts" (417). In other words, NLS is primarily concerned with the way literacy manifests itself in various out-of-school contexts and, through these findings, exposing the artificiality and irrelevance of formal literacy education as it exists in most *in*-school contexts.

2. Activity theory has its roots in Vygotskian psychology and is largely concerned with human practice as an

   "activity system": goal-directed, historically situated, cooperative human interactions, such as . . . a job interview, a "date," a social club, a classroom, a discipline, a profession, an institution, a political movement, and so on. The activity system is the basic unit of analysis for both cultures' and individuals' psychological and social processes. . . . Activity systems are historically developed, mediated by tools, dialectically structured, analyzed as the relationship of participants and tools, and changed through *zones of proximal development.* (Russell 54-55, emphasis in original)

   A zone of proximal development, according to Lev Vygotsky, is

   "the distance between the actual developmental level as determined by independent problem solving and the level of potential development as determined through problem solving under adult guidance, or in collaboration with more capable peers" (86).

Whereas NLS focuses mostly on the *social* nature of literacy, activity theory emphasizes the goal-oriented behaviors that make up the activity system we call "literacy." When literacy is understood as a social practice, however, activity theory requires us to examine the social contexts in which these activities are mediated and reproduced. Thus, we will be inviting you to examine the ways in which literacy is a social practice (activity system) and, therefore, deeply situated and context dependent.

Before we leave our discussion about *why* we have chosen to shape the assignments and readings in the ways we have, it may be useful to take a look at a rather compelling argument David Russell has made to demonstrate the futility of teaching students "to write" or "to improve their writing" in any general way (see "Activity Theory and Writing Instruction"). To this end, Russell "draw[s] an analogy between games that require a particular kind of tool—a ball—and activity systems (disciplines, professions, businesses, etc.) that require a particular kind of tool—the marks we call writing" (57). In this sense, teaching players to use a ball or "to improve their use of a ball" in any general way is no less absurd than teaching writers to improve their "writing" in any general way. As he explains:

> Some people are very adept at some games and therefore at using some kinds of balls, whereas they may be completely lost using a ball in another game because they have never participated in it. (I play ping-pong pretty well, but my 9-year-old daughter laughs at my fumbling attempts to play another game with a ball of a similar size—jacks.) However, ways of using a ball (ball handling, if you will) are "generalizable" to the extent that in two or more games the tool (ball) is used in similar ways and for similar object(ive)s. A good croquet player might easily learn to putt, or a good tennis player might learn squash. However, *there is no autonomous, generalizable skill called ball using or ball handling that can be learned and then applied to all ball games.* (Russell 57, emphasis mine)

The activity "ball handling" exists as a recognizable practice only within the particular communities of practice using the ball—the game for which the ball is intended. The tool (ball) varies from game to game ("large, small, hard, soft, leather, round, oblong") in response to the objective of the game itself, the history of the game as it relates to the overall objective and key strategies players typically use to reach that objective, and so on. A ping-pong ball makes little sense as a tool in a football game. In football, the objective (to reach the opponent's goal) and the material conditions of the playing field (very large) demand that the ball chosen be able to travel vast distances. An oblong shape is, therefore, most appropriate, and uses of this oblong-shaped ball within a given activity system (football) must achieve the objective of reaching the opponent's goal in ways that do not violate the rules and values established and maintained within the communities of practice of which football is a part.

Literacy cannot be reduced to an autonomous skill set, but neither can it be reduced to particular *content*. The content thus becomes shared knowledge among members of a given community of practice, and these members both produce and maintain the "content" most appropriate for them and their key objectives. The knowledge football players/viewers/coaches/fans share is multifaceted, dynamic, and historically situated. Football and its rules are historically situated, and they are not even consistent throughout the relevant communities of practice, as college football differs in some ways from high school football, which differs still further from professional football. The rules, tools, and objectives for fans within this community of practice also differ from the objectives of the players, which differ again from the coaches and those officiating this sport.

Thus literacy, and, therefore, literacy education, must be treated as entirely dependent upon context, which is what we will do here. In other words, the current English 1102 curriculum is designed to resist the pervasive myth that literacy is an autonomous and completely portable skill set by guiding students through key scholarship and then their own ethnographic research into the ways literacy functions in specific contexts and for specific purposes.

Over the past several years, my own teaching, administrative, and scholarly work has become increasingly shaped by my growing appreciation for vernacular literacies—video game literacies, Star Trek literacies, and Anime literacies, among others—as represented not only by our students but also in, among other things, Deborah Brandt's *Literacy in American Lives* (2001), Cynthia Selfe and Gail Hawisher's *Literate Lives in the Information Age: Narratives of Literacy From the United States* (2004), Steven Johnson's *Everything Bad Is Good for You: How Today's Popular Culture Is Actually Making Us Smarter* (2005), and, especially, work in the New Literacy Studies (like James Paul Gee's *What Video Games Have to Teach Us About Learning and Literacy* [2003] and *Situated Language and Learning: A Critique of Traditional Schooling* [2004]). The readings included in this textbook further illustrate the complexity, intellectual rigor, and challenges presented by literacy practices required of us in out-of-school contexts.

In response to the persuasive conclusions these and similar studies in multiple literacies illustrate, even the most conservative readings of literacy have to accept that literacy itself has changed and, as the world moves from a print-based culture to a digital one, it will only continue to change. All this makes teaching writing much more complicated than ever before, but knowing this better enables writing teachers to help students make more deliberate use of the literacies they already possess in order to further develop the variety of literacies required of them at the college level. Thus, our textbook is designed to help you develop what I have called elsewhere "rhetorical dexterity"—the ability to effectively read, understand, manipulate, and negotiate the cultural and linguistic codes of a new community of practice based on a relatively accurate assessment of another, more familiar one" (14). In the pages that follow, you'll learn much more about how one develops rhetorical dexterity, including "What Is a Community of Practice?" (pages 314–318) and why knowing this matters.

As I continue to take vernacular literacies seriously, I have been amazed to find the intellectual rigor and rhetorical sophistication embedded in rhetorical spaces that extend beyond the academy, especially those spaces rarely understood to have anything to do with the kinds of writing students are expected to do at school. As you look at out-of-school literacies in these new ways, I believe you will be similarly impressed. Perhaps you already are.

Assignments

Ethnography

Ethnography is a method of studying and learning about a person or group of people. Typically, ethnography involves the study of a small group of subjects in their own environment. Rather than looking at a small set of variables and a large number of subjects ("the big picture"), the ethnographer attempts to get a detailed understanding of the circumstances of the few subjects being studied. Ethnographic accounts, then, are both descriptive and interpretive; descriptive, because detail is so crucial, and interpretive, because the ethnographer must determine the significance of what she observes without gathering broad, statistical information. ("What is Culture?" Learning Commons)

The subject of this textbook is *literacy* as it exists when put to use by real people for specific purposes and in specific places. The reading and writing assignments that follow are designed to (1) introduce you to the general conversation in literacy studies through key scholarship that offers arguments and evidence in support of the theoretical framework I described above while (2) generating the space you need (and deserve) to test/resist/expand those arguments as presented. All the readings, assignments, and activities included in this section are sequenced to guide the successful development of your own, original, *literacy ethnography*—a study of literacy as it functions in the lives of a person or group of people. "Ethnography"—both as a research method and a means of sharing the findings of this research—is "the study of people in cultures; also the text that is written based on that study" (*FieldWorking*, 500).

The roots of the word are *ethno-,* meaning "peoples," and *-graphy,* meaning "writing." It's "the study of lived experience" (Brodkey). In other words, an ethnography is "the telling of a people's story, . . . a piece of written (down) culture, a book, an article or essay that examines certain elements, ideas, or behaviors in a particular research site" (*Translating Culture,* 312; 15). In our ethnographies, the subject will be literacy as experienced in everyday lives. As Barbara Gleason has said of teaching ethnographic inquiry, "[a] primary reason for the suitability of ethnography to a writing course is the opportunity it affords for studying language form, language practices, and communication in actual contexts of usage" (46).

No doubt this sounds intimidating right now. Please don't worry. Your instructor and the assignments, activities, and readings that follow will guide you through this process step by step. In a few weeks, you will be more than ready to begin to make meaningful contributions to the field regarding the ways in which literate practices manifest themselves within a particular context, among a particular community, or across the lives of people, perhaps from different places and across multiple generations.

As you will learn in the pages that follow, ethnographic research is not uncommon in first-year writing. In many cases, first-year writing programs training students to conduct ethnographic research ask them to investigate a particular community and somehow "represent" that community through fieldwriting. As Sunstein and Chiseri-Strater explain in the popular textbook *FieldWorking,*

> Fieldwriting is a skill that requires close observation, careful documentation, and rendering of data into thick descriptions of informants within their cultural spaces. To be an accurate and sensitive fieldwriter, you'll need to manipulate your multiple data sources, call on your informants' voices, examine your reflective writing, and craft a text so that it will give your reader a sense of participating in the fieldwork you've experienced. (305)

We want you to develop the skills required to be "accurate and sensitive fieldwriters," but we also want you to shape this fieldwriting in ways that will, first of all, develop in you the metacognitive awareness necessary to negotiate a variety of different writing tasks in a variety of different rhetorical contexts. In other words, by asking *you* to investigate and share the way literacy functions in everyday life, we help you understand literacy in reality-based and people-oriented ways—ways that require you to examine each new rhetorical context, the project at hand, and your own goals as writers before making any decisions about which rules or strategies to apply.

By focusing on literacy as both an object of scholarly inquiry and the product reproduced through said scholarly activities, we treat first-year composition as "a course about how to understand and think about writing in school and society" (Wardle and Downs 9). By focusing on literacies as they exist *in context*, and asking students to contribute to this scholarly conversation, we help these beginning college writers develop a better understanding of "the ways writing works in the world and how the 'tool' of writing is used to mediate various activities" (9). More importantly, we make that writing really matter—not as an empty exercise but as a chance to create *real* knowledge.

To this end, "Part III: Literacies in Context" begins an exploration of the ways in which literacy may be understood as a social practice (Barton and Hamilton) and different metaphors people typically use when they talk about literacy (Barton). Next, you'll be asked to develop your own working definition of literacy and associated concepts like literacy events and literacy practices. In doing so, you'll be encouraged to investigate your own lived experiences with and memories of reading and writing, including the ways in which literacy exists among people in your own life. That is, you'll read with and against the ways in which these scholars define literacy and test these definitions against your observations of literacy in everyday life. What does it mean to approach literacy as context dependent, social, and "people-oriented" (Jones Royster)? The first major writing assignment invites you to answer that question based, in no small part, on your own observations of literacy as it manifests itself in everyday life. Sounds familiar, doesn't it? This is, indeed, a key goal of your final ethnographic project. This assignment, like all the others in this section, is designed to get you started on that project right away.

Next, you'll learn more about communities of practice and the ways in which they limit and shape what counts as "literacy," including the rules, terminology, and behaviors accepted. Like your first assignment, this second major writing assignment serves as another step toward your final project. Throughout, please keep in mind the ultimate goal of "Part III: Literacies in Context"—to develop rhetorical dexterity, "the ability to effectively read, understand, manipulate, and negotiate the cultural and linguistic codes of a new community of practice based on a relatively accurate assessment of another, more familiar one" (*The Way Literacy Lives*, 22). You will also read and reflect upon what it means to be an ethical researcher when studying the lived experiences of everyday literacy. The formal writing assignment at the end of this chapter will ask you to identify a particular community of practice (CofP) with which you are familiar, articulate the ways in which it functions as a CofP, and develop a "Code of Ethics" you would want a researcher to follow if he or she were to study your CofP. You'll apply these same codes to your own original research, leading to your final project—an ethnographic inquiry into literacy in everyday life.

In the following chapter, you'll analyze literacy ethnographies that should (a) inform your understanding of how writing and reading work in a variety of contexts and (b) serve as models for the final research project you'll be expected to undertake. You'll read about a variety of places in which literacy is put to use and how these places and the needs of the people inhabiting them largely determine the shape and function of literate behavior (in church, in a restaurant, at home, in classrooms). Many of the readings included in this chapter also examine the ways in which out-of-school literacy practices are often and largely usurped by in-school ones, despite the inaccuracies of these school-based models in representing the way literacy actually functions in the real lives of people in and out of school. The major assignment will invite you to represent not only the findings published in a selected literacy ethnography but the ways in which the researcher set up the study that led to these findings. This close analysis of a study's research design will help prepare you to develop your own research plan, which is the subject of the next assignment—the research proposal. At this point, you will know what you plan to research and how you plan to go about studying this aspect of ordinary, everyday literacy.

The chapters that follow are designed to help you conduct your research in productive ways—from the collection of relevant data to analysis of that data to the final write-up of that interpretation. Remember, ethnography is both the process of conducting field research and the essay that results from that research.

You're the Expert!

In her study of the various ways writing instruction is often used by student writers and their teachers, Cheryl Geisler argues that writing cannot be successfully used by learners to create knowledge except among those marked as "experts." We agree. That's why we have designed this textbook with the assumption that you *are* (and can become) the expert. Your research in this course does not merely reproduce existing knowledge. Instead, you are being asked to create *new* knowledge. We agree with Geisler who insists that "learning already extant knowledge and making new knowledge are quite distinct activities. . . " (101). Too often, Geisler argues, students are assumed to "learn extant knowledge," leaving the creation of "new knowledge" to "academic professionals." In other words, instructors often expect students to "use writing primarily for the 'lay' purpose of learning extant knowledge made by others more 'expert' than they." She continues:

> These two groups, even though they inhabit the same institutions and organize their activities around interactions with texts, are generally worlds apart with respect to knowledge, separated across what I have called the Great Divide between expert and layperson (Geisler, 1994)

We do not believe in that Great Divide that treats the student as "layperson" and the instructor as "expert." Of course, your instructor has a great deal of expertise in the subject of writing—how writing works and how to best guide students in developing increasingly sophisticated writing practices. However, we also believe that when provided with support such as what we provide in this book guided by your savvy instructor, students can create "new knowledge" as well. That is exactly our goal here: shifting the lens as a student writer from that of a "layperson" (non-expert) to an expert (contributing, through their own, original research, new knowledge rather than simply regurgitating knowledge produced by others assumed to be an "expert." Our goal in this textbook is absolutely this—to *create new knowledge* not merely transmit existing knowledge.

We approach writing instruction with a critical theoretical framework that insists that educators liberate learners by refusing to participate in what Paulo Freire calls the "banking model" of education, insisting instead that we make use of "problem-posing" education. In the former, "education . . . becomes an act of depositing, in which the students are the depositories and the teacher is the depositor [and] . . . the scope of action . . . [for the student] extends only as far as receiving, filing, storing the deposits" (*Pedagogy of the Oppressed*, 72). In the latter, however, "people develop their power to perceive critically *the way they exist* in the world *with which* and *in which* they find themselves; they come to see the world not as a static reality, but as a reality in process, in transformation" (83). In doing so, they come to "name" that world, which is, according to Freire and other critical theorists, crucial for any real meaningful learning to take place. As Freire explains, "to exist, humanly, is to *name* the world, to change it. Once named, the world in its turn reappears to the namers as a problem and requires of them a new *naming*. . . . Dialogue is the encounter between men [sic], mediated by the world, in order to name the world" (88). Geisler accepts the importance of this "problem-posing" education, but argues that writing is "at odds with learning—when learning is characterized as the acceptance of a web of cultural knowledge" (116), when "students" are treated as "depositories" of knowledge rather than creators of it (Freire 72). "We write," Geisler argues, "both to contribute to and to counter the current trajectory of our culture" (116).

Thus "writing to learn" "extant knowledge" may be ineffective, but writing to create new knowledge is, in fact, what "motivates us to pick up the pen (or turn on the computer) in the first place" (Geisler 116). Teaching students to write (or to use a ball) in any general way is problematic from the standpoint of application as neither writing "skills" nor knowledge of writing as content separable from the context in which it is used enable writers to create knowledge. However, it is also problematic from the standpoint of motivation, as general skills instruction or lessons in "general" knowledge ("what every American needs to know") ask writers to accept without critique the "cultural facts and values" perpetuated in the academy. Teaching what Joseph Petraglia calls "General Writing Skills Instruction" (or "GWSI") is, therefore, oppressive because it necessarily and consistently validates the "content" shared by scholars in our various disciplines and invalidates the content shared among members of communities of practice not directly associated with the academy. As Geisler explains, "the move to professionalize can, in fact, be defined as a move to remove knowledge from the public sphere" (116). We should instead make use of what Antonio Gramsci calls "organic intellectuals." As Gramsci argues, "there is no human activity from which every form of intellectual participation can be excluded" and everyone carries on some form of intellectual activity. . . , participates in a particular conception of the world, has a conscious line of moral conduct, and therefore contributes to sustain a conception of the world or to modify it, that is, to bring into being new modes of thought." Thus, "organic intellectuals" can be agents of change in ways "traditional intellectuals" cannot.

We believe you are more than capable of making meaningful contributions to the field of writing studies and beyond. In doing so, you will become "agents of change" and "writing to learn" will, therefore, become a much more transferable skill for you—and for us. When we treat your ethnographic projects as existing within a very real and much larger scholarly conversation in which they function as the "organic intellectuals" who are capable of making knowledge that is, in fact and in many ways, much more meaningful than that being generated by "traditional intellectuals," we've developed in your first-year writing classroom an activity that extends far beyond the walls of that classroom (see, especially, Robillard).

You are ready. Let's dive in.

Works Cited

"About the New London Group and the International Multiliteracies Project." *Education Australia Online*, 10 Aug. 2005.

Barton, David, and Mary Hamilton. *Local Literacies: Reading and Writing in One Community*. Routledge, 1998.

Brodkey, Linda. "Writing Ethnographic Narratives." *Written Communication*, vol. 4, no.1, Jan. 1987, pp. 25-50.

Carter, Shannon. *The Way Literacy Lives: Rhetorical Dexterity and the "Basic" Writer*. State U of New York P, 2008.

Cope, Bill, and Mary Kalantzis, editors. *Multiliteracies: Literacy Learning and the Design of Social Futures*. Routledge, 1999.

Downs, Doug, and Elizabeth Wardle. "Teaching About Writing, Righting Misconceptions: (Re) Envisioning 'First-Year Composition' as 'Introduction to Writing Studies.'" *CCC*, vol. 54, no. 8, June 2007.

Freire, Paulo. *Pedagogy of the Oppressed*. Bloomsbury Academic, 2000.

Geisler, Cheryl. *Academic Literacy and the Nature of Expertise: Reading, Writing, and Knowing in Academic Philosophy*. Lawrence Erlbaum, 1994.

---. "Writing and Learning at Cross Purposes in the Academy." *Reconceiving Writing, Rethinking Writing Instruction*, edited by Joseph Petraglia, Lawrence Erlbaum, 1995, pp. 101-120.

Gleason, Barbara. "Connected Literacies of Adult Writers: Work Ethnography in College Composition." *Multiple Literacies for the 21st Century*, edited by Brian Huot, Beth Stroble, and Charles Bazerman, Hampton Press, 2004.

Gramsci, Antonio. *Selections from the Prison Notebooks*. Edited and translated by Hoare and G. Smith, International Publishers, 1971.

Petraglia, Joseph. "Introduction." *Reconceiving Writing, Rethinking Writing Instruction*, edited by Joseph Petraglia, Lawrence Erlbaum, 1995, pp. xi-xvii.

Robillard, Amy. "Young Scholars Affecting Composition: A Challenge to Disciplinary Citation Practices." *College English*, vol. 68, no. 3, 2006, pp. 253-70.

Russell, David R. "Activity Theory and Process Approaches: Writing (Power) in School and Society." *Post-Process Theory: Beyond the Writing-Process Paradigm*, edited by Thomas Kent, Southern Illinois U P, 1999.

---. "Activity Theory and Writing Instruction." *Reconceiving Writing, Rethinking Writing Instruction*, edited by Joseph Petraglia, Lawrence Erlbaum, 1995, pp. 51-77.

Schultz, Katherine, and Glenda Hull. "Locating Literacy Theory in Out-of-School Contexts." *School's Out!: Bridging Out-of-School Literacies with Classroom Practice,* edited by Glenda Hull and Katherine Schultz, Teacher's College P, 2002, pp. 11-31.

Street, Brian V. "Autonomous and Ideological Models of Literacy: Approaches from New Literacy Studies." *Media Anthropology Network,* Jan. 2006, pp. 17-24, http://www.philbu.net/media-anthropology/street_newliteracy.pdf.

---. Street, Brian V. "Recent Applications of New Literacy Studies in Educational Contexts." *Research in the Teaching of English*, vol. 39, no. 4, May 2005, pp. 417-423.

---. *Social Literacies: Critical Approaches to Literacy in Development, Ethnography and Education.* Longman, 1995.

Vygotsky, L. S. *Mind in Society: The Development of Higher Psychological Processes.* Harvard U P, 1978.

CHAPTER 1

What Is Literacy?

In this chapter, we begin our exploration of literacies in context by examining the ways in which literacy functions in a variety of places for a variety of purposes. Our starting place is with a deceptively simple term—*literacy*. What does it mean? What does it *really* mean?

Options for Navigating "Chapter 1: What is Literacy?"

The goal of this first chapter is to get you thinking about reading, writing, and texts in new ways. To that end, we have provided essays that approach literacy in different, albeit complementary ways—as "cultural ecologies" (Selfe and Hawisher; Barton), for example, and a "social practice" (Barton and Hamilton). We have also included a set of interview questions that invite you to explore digital literacies in your own lives and direct connections to a related, digital book that considers digital literacies experienced by people across the globe (*Transnational Literate Lives in Digital Times*), the latter of which includes videos of interviews with these same people.

The culminating assignment for this chapter asks you to develop your own working definition of literacy, literacy practices, and related terms—building, in part, upon the way these terms are taken up by the readings we have included here. With that end in mind, your instructor may ask you to read all of these important texts to inform your developing definitions. Or, if time is short, your instructor may assign only a portion of these readings, inviting you to skim the others quickly in search of information, keywords, or evidence that grabs you. Your instructor may ask you to interview a classmate or maybe even yourself based on the Interview Protocol we have provided, which Hawisher and Selfe used to develop the article that follows "Becoming Literate in the Information Age." However, your instructor may not require you to read the article itself but, rather, skim it quickly for information you may find useful in composing your first major writing assignment. Your instructor may ask you to read the article by Hawisher and Selfe instead of conducting the interview. Or your instructor may assign both the interview and the article. Perhaps your instructor will assign only the interview and invite you to select interviews from the authors' digital book *Transnational Literate Lives in Digital Times* (Berry, Selfe, and Hawisher). They may even invite you to select your own readings from those provided. This textbook is designed to guide you in deep collaboration with your instructor.

In other words, all of the materials included in this chapter—like everything else we've selected for this textbook—are part of a sequenced approach to writing, whereby each reading and writing activity prepares you for the next and so on. In this chapter, you are developing a working definition of literacy and related terms. To do so, you will need to engage with a variety of texts that take up this same task from a variety of angles. We leave it up to your instructor to determine the best path through Chapter One to lead you to this first major writing assignment. In subsequent chapters, each of which build upon the previous one, the path we've provided will include fewer readings. We just need to provide a range of opportunities for you to enter this complex, ongoing scholarly conversation, which will provide the context for the research and writing you will be doing this term.

BEFORE YOU READ, spend some time with the interview protocol Cynthia Selfe and Gail Hawisher used to collect the data that would eventually become the article that follows: "Becoming Literate in the Information Age: Cultural Ecologies and the Literacies of Technology." You'll then be asked to take into account your own experiences with literacy as you read about metaphors people typically use when talking about literacy (Barton) and arguments for a "social theory of literacy" (Barton and Hamilton).

Remember the final project in this course is a literacy ethnography. For that project, you may decide to conduct interviews with family members using the interview protocol that follows. Something to think about. For now, please use this interview protocol to collect information about your own literacy experiences and those of a classmate. Take excellent notes. You'll use this information in your first major assignment, which you can find on page 309 in this chapter.

For this activity: Use this interview protocol to interview a classmate about their literacy experiences. Your instructor may not require you to address every question. Before you begin, review the questions below and decide a plan of action. What are you most interested in learning about your own reading and writing experiences or those of a classmate? Hone in on that section of questions. If it is not as fruitful as you hoped, you can always move to a different line of questioning. The goal here is to stimulate memories of reading and writing— specific, detailed, and compelling. After interviewing your classmate, you may be asked to make use of this information to introduce him or her to the rest of the class.

Interview Protocol

From Cynthia Selfe and Gail Hawisher's *Literate Lives in the Information Age* (Mahwah, New Jersey: Lawrence Erlbaum Associates, 2004, 237-42).

[NOTE: The brackets mark portions of text the authors of *Writing Inquiry* have added in order to update and/or clarify the questions asked by Selfe and Hawisher in their original interviews more than a decade ago.]

We're doing research to find out primarily how people came to computers and what their experiences using computers have been. We're interested in what experiences different generations of people living in the United States have had with computers.

Demographic Information
Name:
Current Occupation:
Previous Occupations:
[. . . .]

Let me get down a few facts about your family as you were growing up.

Immediate family members and ages:

How would you describe your family circumstances?

Income Level:
  Growing up:
  Now:
Parents' [or Guardian's] Literacy Histories (e.g., literacy values, education, reading/writing/computing activities):
Did your parents value literacy? How? Any literacy stories?
Parents' [or Guardian's] Education and Professions:

Can you tell us a bit about yourself? Where were you born? Where did you grow up? What was your family like? What are you like?

Place and date of birth:

Where did you live?
  Growing up:
  Now:

Schooling History:
  Elementary   College
  High School Other

Early Exposure to Literacy/Computers
Can you tell us how/when/why you learned to read and write?

Can you tell us the story about when, where, and how you first came in contact with computers? [Do you remember a time without computers?]

Do you remember what the prevailing images/representations of computers [and related technologies like smartphones and social media] were when you were growing up (e.g., movies, television, magazines, books)?

At home

If your family had a computer at home when you were growing up, can you tell us the story of buying the computer? Who bought it? When? Why? [If you can't remember a time when you didn't have a computer in your home, what's your earliest memory of bringing a new computer into the home?]

Can you tell us how much the computer cost? Can you talk about how significant/serious that investment was in terms of your family's regular budget?

For what purposes did you use the computer [growing up]?

Can you tell how a typical session might have gone in your home computing environment? [Where was it in the home, for example?]

How often did you use the computer [growing up]? What contributed to your use of it or not? Are there any stories/incidents that you can remember about this?

Can you remember any books/texts about computers that you had at home? Any that you read? Any computer games?

Can you identify any images that you remember about computer use?

What did you and your [family members] use the computer for at this time?

At school

[What are your earliest memories of using computers at school? Where were they? Did every classroom have one? More than one? Did you regularly visit a separate computer lab?] What was your motivation? Age? Who helped? How did they help? What kind of support did you have? In what classes did you learn to use the computer? [Were you taught how to use the computer directly or did you just learn how by using the computer to complete an assigned project? If the latter, describe the project and how completing this assignment helped you learn how to use the computer more effectively.] How much access did you have to a computer per day/week/month?

[Based on your earliest memories of computer use in the schools,] describe your use of the computer. Who was there? What times of day? What were the surroundings like?

For what purposes did you use this computer [again, based on your earliest memories of computer use in the schools]?

For what purposes did other kids use computers at the school when you were first learning to use technology? As you continued to learn?

Can you tell how a typical session might have gone in this environment?

What determined how frequently you used the computer? Are there any stories/incidents that you can remember about this?

Can you remember any books/texts about computers [or related technology] that you had access to at school? Any that you read? Any computer games played or otherwise available at school?

Can you identify any images that you remember about computer use that you encountered at school? Educational images?

What did your family think about computers [and your use of them in school]? Your parents [or guardians]? Siblings? Uncles and aunts? Cousins? Grandparents? What values did they place on this activity? On your participation in [computer-based] activities? On their role? Do you have any stories you can tell us that would illustrate the value your family placed on computers or computer literacy [as learned at school]?

Did you read about computers [or related technology]? If so, where? When? [Why?]

Can you remember any pictures of computers or computer use [or related technology] that struck you as memorable? Where did you see these? [What did you see? What made them memorable to you?]

Current Exposure

Do you (or your family) own a computer *now*? More than one? If so, please describe it [/them].

If "yes"

Can you tell us the story of buying your current computer? Who bought it? When? Why?

Can you tell us how much the computer cost? Can you talk about how significant/ serious that investment was in terms of (your, your guardian's, your family's, [or whomever purchased it]) regular budget?

[If a desktop], describe for us where you keep your computer at home? [What room?] What are the things you have around your computer? What items of furniture do you associate with the computer?

[If a laptop or other portable device, where do you keep it? How do you transport it, where, and how often?]

For what purposes do you use this computer (e.g., what kinds of work, what applications)?

For what purposes do [the people in your life] use computers? Who taught them? Who provides support?

[How often do you find yourself online? What motivates you to get online?] What do you use it for?

Tell the story of how you learned to use the computer [in the ways you do today]. What was your motivation? Who helped? What kind of support [did you] have?

What are the rules associated with using your computer, [whether they be self-imposed or imposed by another person]? Why make up these rules? How do they affect you?

Can you identify books/texts [online or physical] that you have easy access to? Any that you read? [Access regularly? To what end?]

Also

Do you currently have access to a computer [that you do not own yourself]? Where (work, school, [public library, someone else's house, a paid-use place like FedEx Kinko's, elsewhere])? When? For how long? How do you get there? How much does it cost to use this computer [if anything]? [If you pay to use the computer,] how do you get that money to pay for access?

Describe the surroundings in which you use this computer: Who is there? What times of day? What are the surroundings like?

For what purposes do you use this computer?

For what purposes do other students/co-workers/[others] use the computer?

Can you tell how a typical session might go in this environment?

Tell the story of how you learned to use the computer in this environment, [or perhaps how you found yourself using this computer]. What was your motivation? Who helped? What kind of support did you have? Do you continue to have?

What are the rules associated with using a computer in this environment? Who made up these rules? How do they affect you?

[. . .]

Can you describe your current level of skill with computers? Novice, competent, expert? Any stories about your expertise?

What do you think about computers now? Why? [Do you find yourself thinking about computers at all? Try hard to come up with an answer to this question, even though computers are as ubiquitous as televisions and toasters today so you probably rarely think of them at all.]

What do your family members think about computers now? Your parents [or guardians, children, siblings, aunts or uncles, grandparents, friends]? What values do they place on computer use? On your [use of computers]? On [the role of computers in everyday life]? Do you have stories you can tell us that would illustrate the value your family and friends now place on computers or computer literacy?

What values does the educational system currently place on computer use? Do you have any stories you can tell us that would illustrate the value your schools now place on computers or computer literacy?

How/when/where/why do you see yourself using computers in the future?

Do you read about computers [and/or related technology]? If so, where? When? What do you read [about computers and related technology]?

Can you identify any images of computer use that have struck you recently? [Like what?] Where have you seen these images?

Do you use a particular brand of computer? If so, why? Which one? Names of [most used] programs [or applications?]

Anything else you'd like to say about your relationship with computers [or related technologies]?

Further Discussion

The questions for Hawisher and Selfe's Interview Protocol were written in 2004. In terms of digital technology, that is a *very* long time ago. Throughout (in brackets) we tried to update this Interview Protocol as much as possible. Update this Interview Protocol for today. What questions should an interviewer ask about the development of digital literacies that aren't included in this current Interview Protocol? For example, social media wasn't a thing in 2004, at least not in any significant way. Do we need questions referencing Facebook, Twitter, Tumblr? What else? How would you phrase these questions? What might you learn by asking these new questions that isn't invited by the questions included in the above Interview Protocol?

NOTE: If you think digital literacy will be of concern for you in your own ethnographic project, you may decide to use these new questions alongside or in addition to the ones Selfe and Hawisher used for their study more than a decade ago. As we will remind you throughout, everything you develop in response to the readings, assignments, activities in this book can be useful fodder for your final ethnographic project. Hold onto it! Your future self will thank you!

Activity

Take a look at *Transnational Literate Lives in Digital Times* by Patrick W. Berry, Gail E. Hawisher, and Cynthia L. Selfe, published in 2012—nearly a decade after the book for which they developed the original interview protocol. You can find this digital project at our companion website for this textbook (www.fountainheadpress.com/writinginquiry).

Read the Introduction section, particularly the "Notes on Method." As you do so (a) think about the constantly evolving nature of digital technology in your own life and in the spaces around you; (b) listen to some interviews; (c) consider how their digital literacy experiences compare with your own; (d) think about what all this may mean for your own (developing) literacy ethnography.

Hold onto your responses. You may find these useful in upcoming writing assignments.

Discussion Questions

1. What do you notice that differs from your own experiences and those represented in Berry, Hawisher, and Selfe's book?

2. How do you understand the meaning of "transnational" from what you've read? Give examples.

3. Do you see transnational literacy functioning in the spaces around you? What are the ways in which you notice this coming up, being discussed, being navigated by others or yourself?

4. Take note of the different modalities represented (images, videos, transcripts, etc.). What are the varieties you notice? How are they used? How might you incorporate them into your own work?

READING

Becoming Literate in the Information Age: Cultural Ecologies and the Literacies of Technology

Gail E. Hawisher and Cynthia L. Selfe

Hawisher and Selfe argue that the field of literacy studies often sets its sights solely on school-based alphabetic "traditional" literacies at the exclusion of technologically based literacies. In the early part of the century, literacy scholars began to pay more attention to the fact that writers—especially our students— were often engaging in digital or technological literacies more often than alphabetical print-based literacies. Hawisher and Selfe were pioneers in this research, and what followed were studies on students' online gaming, tweeting, filmmaking, activism, and more.

BEFORE YOU READ consider the following questions:

1. What do you think the phrase "literacies of technology" means? Why might we use the plural *literacies* in this context?

2. What contexts informed your own technology literacies? Hawisher and Selfe point to cultural, material, educational, and familiar contexts that influence and are influenced by literacies of technology. How did these contexts influence your technological literacy practices?

Becoming Literate in the Information Age: Cultural Ecologies and the Literacies of Technology

Gail E. Hawisher and Cynthia L. Selfe
with Brittney Moraski and Melissa Pearson

The increasing presence of personal computers in homes, workplaces, communities, and schools over the past twenty-five years has brought about dramatic changes in the ways people create and respond to information. In the United States, for example, the ability to read, compose, and communicate in computer environments—called variously technological, digital, or electronic literacy[1]—has acquired increased importance not only as a basic job skill[2] but also, every bit as significant, as an essential component of literate activity.[3] Today, if students cannot write to the screen—if they cannot design, author, analyze, and interpret material on the Web and in other digital environments—they may be incapable of functioning effectively as literate citizens in a growing number of social spheres. The ability to write well—and to write well *with* computers and within digital environments—we believe will continue to play an increasingly important role in determining if students will be able to participate and succeed in school, work, and community.

Despite the growing importance of these new literacies, however, and despite statistical reports[4] that document patterns of computer diffusion and use in U.S. homes, schools, and the culture at large, we have only begun to understand how people, both in and outside our classrooms, acquire and develop—or fail to acquire and develop—the literacies of technology. Over the years, we have learned from early studies with word processing that writers might compose differently with computers but probably not better (Hawisher, "Research"); we have learned that online venues can assist in encouraging intellectual engagement (Cooper and Selfe) but that these online spaces are probably no more egalitarian than their face-to-face, classroom counterparts (Romano). Today, we hear anecdotes of students who demonstrate extraordinary abilities with the new technologies and those of students who know from first-hand experience of the difficulties family members face when it comes to developing electronic literacies. But while outstanding scholars from the U.S. and abroad, such as Deborah Brandt; Gunther Kress; Bertram Bruce; Robert Yagelski; Carmen Luke; James Paul Gee; Juliet Merrifield, Mary Beth Bingham, David Hemphill, and Kathleen P. Bennett deMarrais, have started to trace the historical, cultural, economic, political, and ideological factors affecting—or being affected by—people's acquisition and development of literacy, in general, and digital literacies, more specifically, we still know less than we might about the relationship between digital and nondigital literacies.[5]

In this article, we discuss the literacy narratives of two participants, Melissa Pearson, an African American woman born on 25 August 1964 in Fort Jackson, South Carolina, into a middle-class Baptist family in the military, and Brittney Moraski, a white woman born on 28 August 1986 into a middle-class Catholic family in the rural Upper Peninsula of Michigan. These two stories are culled from a larger investigation of literate lives in the information age.[6] Our hope is that these case studies will help readers appreciate the importance of situating literacies of technology—and literacies more generally—within specific cultural, material, educational, and familial contexts that influence, and are influenced by, their acquisition and development.

In foregrounding the significance of multiple contexts for electronic literacy efforts, we hint at the many related factors that shape, and are shaped by, people's adoption of computers as literacy tools and environments: social contexts; educational practices, values, and expectations; cultural and ideological formations like race, class, and gender; political and economic trends and events; family practices and experiences; and historical and material conditions—among many, many other factors. We refer to these contexts as the *cultural ecology* of literacy and, with this term, we attempt to signal the complex web within which both humans and computer technologies coexist, and all communication takes place.

We believe five key themes emerge from a reading of these cases as set within their respective cultural ecologies, and we explicate each theme in later sections of this article:

- Literacies have *life spans*. These lifespans differ within particular patches[7] of a cultural ecology.
- *People can exert their own powerful agency in, around, and through digital literacies.* In particular cultural ecologies, some individuals may even confound society's expectations regarding race, class, age, and gender.
- *Schools are not the sole—and, often, not even the primary—gateways through which people gain access to and practice digital literacies.* English composition teachers often have little connection to, and a limited understanding of, the range of literacy practices that happen in digital environments reached through other gateways.
- *The specific conditions of access have a substantial effect on people's acquisition and development of digital literacy.* Thus, access to computers— and to the literacies of technology—cannot be accurately represented as an isolated or monodimensional formation. Rather, access is best understood as part of a larger cultural ecology. Physical access to computers is necessary but insufficient for the acquisition and development of digital literacies.
- *Families transmit literacy values and practices in multiple directions.* Information about, and support of, literacy can flow both upstream (from younger people to older people), and downstream (from older people to younger people), and across media (print to electronic environments or from electronic to print environments).

Some notes on method

In 1998, inspired by an outstanding talk Brandt gave at the University of Louisville's Thomas R. Watson Conference on her oral-history literacy project, we began a relatively large-scale study to identify how and why people in the U.S. acquired and developed (or, for various reasons, failed to acquire and develop) the literacies of technology between the years of 1978 and 2003. During that period, personal computers—as relatively cheap and durable, mass-produced and mass-marketed machines—became commercially available for the first time to many families, entered composition classrooms across the nation in large numbers, and were broadly accepted by many school-aged children as the composing tool of choice. Since that time, these machines have become so ubiquitous that their many effects are becoming increasingly invisible.[8] Before our cultural memory of this important time faded entirely, we wanted to document the period during which these machines first found their way into—and altered—the fabric of our culture.

The larger project from which these case studies come consists of more than 350 literacy narratives from people who participated in life history interviews or completed online a technological literacy questionnaire. (See Appendix.) We recruited participants primarily through school settings, calling first on colleagues and students we knew from around the U.S. We also identified participants through the recommendations of these initial volunteers. As a result, the brothers, sisters, other relatives, and friends of the people we contacted also became part of our informant pool—secretaries, former domestic workers, graphic artists, technical communicators, factory workers, program directors, nurses, and managers, among just a few of their current and former occupations. At the time of their interviews people ranged in age from thirteen to sixty-nine and hailed from more than twenty-five different states from every section of the U.S. We have also invited participants whose stories we feature in our book (Selfe and Hawisher *Literate Lives*) to become coauthors of the published work that grows out of the investigation.[9]

We have chosen to focus on the stories of Melissa and Brittney because we think they provide an interesting pair of cultural tracings—albeit fragmentary and incomplete—of how personal computers found their way into the lives, homes, schools, and workplaces of some people within the U.S. during the period we are studying. For these two women, the introduction of personal computers, a relatively cheap and durable example of technology, was associated with periods of major social, educational, and technological change, times during which peoples' lives, and literacies, were altered in fundamental ways.[10]

Because these two women grew up under markedly different circumstances, we believe their cases will also help readers further appreciate the importance of situating technological literacy in specific cultural, material, educational, historical, and familial contexts—in particular, contexts characterized by varied levels of support (social, economic, educational, technological) for electronic-literacy efforts. As the work of Brian Street, James Gee, Harvey Graff, and Deborah Brandt reminds us, we can understand literacy as a set of practices and values *only* when we properly situate our studies within the context of a particular historical period, a particular cultural milieu, and a specific cluster of material conditions.

Finally, we feature these women and their stories because they resonate with parts of our own stories as women working in composition: the ways in which these women's lives are situated historically and culturally; their backgrounds and gender; the ways in which they have learned to use and cope with technology; the schools they have attended or in which they teach; their experiences as students; the teaching they have experienced; their relationships with family and friends; and the literacies they share with us.

Throughout this article, we also corroborate these two primary cases with references to the stories of other participants in our project: among them, Paula Boyd, born in Chicago, Illinois, in 1969; Nichole Brown, born in Greenville, South Carolina, in 1971; Damon Davis, born in Detroit, Michigan, in 1978; Josh Gardiner, born in Escanaba, Michigan, in 1987; Charles Jackson, born in Salt Lake City, Utah, in 1985; Karen Lunsford, born in Minot, North Dakota, in 1968; Mary Sheridan-Rabideau, born in Oak Lawn, Illinois, in 1967; and Dean Woodbeck, born in Vicksburg, Michigan, in 1956.[11]

The cultural ecology of digital literacy in the 1960s and 1970s: the story of Melissa Pearson

When Melissa Pearson was growing in South Carolina during the 1960s, her African American family valued literacy both as a route to prosperity and as an intellectual practice. Her father's career in the U.S. Army, which began after he dropped out of high school and enlisted, influenced much of Melissa's childhood and, indeed, shaped much of her life. While in the armed services, her father completed high school and college, a trajectory that, as Melissa sees it, propelled the family into the Black middle class in the South:

> When he finished college in the army, he was offered a chance to go to the officer's candidate board and took that. So, he moved from...one class...to another....and this all took place when I was born or very, very early in my life.

Melissa's mother finished high school and then began studying nursing at Bennett College for Women, a historically black college. Her career, however, assumed second place to her husband's. As Melissa notes:

> Um, my mother graduated from high school. I think it was the class of 1961. I remember this because the whole family has to celebrate her class reunion around Christmas time. I mean it's a whole community thing because it was the last all black high school in her town....she is one of twelve children. Most of her siblings except for maybe herself and another sister all went to Bennett College which is a historically black college in South Carolina. And they either went into nursing school at Bennett or... teacher's training...So, um, I have a family full of educators.

> But my mother dropped out of college in her sophomore year when she met my father and, um, became a military wife and so she worked as, she was going to school to be a nurse and she worked as a, um, CNA, a certified nurse's assistant, for a long time.

The military context of the family's life—as shaped by national and world events—influenced Melissa's literacy values and practices both directly and indirectly. In the decade leading up to her birth, Fidel Castro had become well ensconced in Cuba; the Soviet Union had launched Sputnik in 1957, established the administration of Nikita Khrushchev in 1958, and had shot down Gary Powers's U2 spy plane in 1960. In the U.S., during the years preceding Melissa's birth, citizens had elected John F. Kennedy to the office of President in 1960; Miami-based Cuban refugees had invaded the Bay of Pigs in 1961; and the Cuban missile crisis had unfolded in 1962. During the early years of the Cold War, people had begun building fallout shelters in their backyards and holding atomic bomb drills in public schools, and the nation's military was on high alert.

During this same tumultuous period, computers were in the process of becoming a major social force. Growing out of an alliance between the U.S. military effort and scientists after World War II, these machines changed rapidly after the first mainframe—dubbed ENIAC—was completed in 1945. That machine included 17,468 vacuum tubes, weighed 30 tons, took up approximately 1,000 feet of floor space, ran on 130-140 kW of electricity, and worked at a speed of 100 kHz. By 1951, UNIVAC I, the first commercially successful, general purpose computer, had been purchased by the United States Bureau of Census (White), and by 1958 (just five years before Melissa was born) the U.S. had established the Advanced Research Projects Agency in the Department of Defense (DARPA) to support the development of computer-based research (Kurzweil). This research remained primarily dependent on mainframe computers, which were large and expensive, but spin-off applications, which required an increasingly computer-savvy workforce, had begun to affect the curricula and literacy practices of universities and schools across the country (Castells, *The Information Age* series).

Most project participants who pursued higher education and who were over thirty years of age first encountered computers in college. By the 1970s, many research institutions had begun to teach computer programming as part of the effort to educate an increasingly savvy workforce. But the access that people had to computers was often far from ideal, and, frequently, the conditions of this access limited their enthusiasm for literacy practices in digital environments. As another study participant, Dean Woodbeck, eight years Melissa's senior, pointed out,

> I had to take...Fortran....[W]e had punch cards, and you would have to do a stack, and they had this, you know, there was this machine that had a keyboard that you typed on and it coded the punch card [with] whatever you were typing in....

> You could have 80 cards in your stack [and you] ran the stack through this reader, and then you went away for awhile because it didn't generate a printout right away. So you'd maybe go in the morning...and run your program, [and] um, go to class, you know, [and] come back a couple hours later. Sometimes you came back the next day to see if the program ran or not and, there it was...sitting in your mailbox. The program...may have said "Error;'...and you'd have to do it over again....So then you would have to go back to your punch cards and say, "OK, did I make a typo here?"

> Or, you know, if you dropped them [the cards] and put them back together in the wrong order—everything had to be in a certain order—it [the computer] would just spit [the cards] back at you....Oh, I hated it...

As computers became smaller, faster, and more flexible during the 1960s, innovations associated with computer technology had leaked into the realm of popular culture, where they affected Melissa's life. By 1965, for instance, ComSat's Early Bird, the first television satellite, was put into orbit, and one of the first broadcasts to use this technology covered a 1966 protest march against the war in Vietnam (*The 1900s*). The Vietnam Conflict, of course, was a war in which Melissa's father fought on behalf of the U.S. Even in this context, however, Melissa's own personal understanding of computers, remained limited. As she explained,

> [I remember]...my father saying something about how, um, war systems and things are managed on a computer, you know, and having some cognition about what that was although I couldn't picture what kind of computer....I imagined someone sitting there with a cape [and a] keyboard...I guess.

The Cold War was far from the only threat facing the nation or the only macrolevel factor that affected Melissa's early literacy practices and values. In 1963, one year before she was born and the same year in which President John Kennedy was assassinated, a bomb killed four children at a Black church in Birmingham, Alabama, and 250,000 people listened to Reverend Martin Luther King, Jr., deliver his "I Have a Dream" speech in Washington, DC. Civil unrest followed—in Harlem, Philadelphia, Chicago, and Jacksonville. In summer 1964, the year of Melissa's birth, Reverend King won the Nobel Peace Prize, and President Lyndon B. Johnson signed the Civil Rights Act. By 1966, when Melissa was two years old, Malcolm X had been assassinated, and Reverend King had led a five-day march in Selma, Alabama.

These events, too, had their direct and indirect effects on Melissa's literacy values and practices, and those of her family. Influenced by the national context of unrest and hoping to avoid the mayhem that marked early school desegregation efforts, Melissa's mother enrolled her in an all-Black Montessori school in 1967 and an all-Black Catholic primary school in 1968. By this time, computers were assuming an increasing presence in the public sphere, in part because of their influence on mass media. As Melissa entered and progressed through elementary school, for instance, computer technology had made it possible for families to view the broadcast of the first Super Bowl in 1967; the coverage of Reverend King's assassination in 1968; and Neil Armstrong's walk on the moon in 1969 (*The 1900s*). The time into which Melissa had been born and within which she would grow up would continue to be characterized, to a great extent, by technological events like these, even though her personal access to computers, for various reasons, would take another twenty or so years.

During Melissa's childhood, the high value her family placed on literacy continued to affect her life and approach to education:

> Well, um, my father...[was] always...reading all the time. You know, if I look back over the times in our lives, I can always see him stretched out with the paper or some kind of manual or some kind of book or something. I always remember him as a reader....

> Um, but my father's punishment...for me...when I was younger, I had to copy the dictionary....If I got in trouble and was being irresponsible, I had to write a paper about responsibility...and privilege.

> Um, my mother, my mother was like a romance novel reader right before she went to bed. That was her little thing. She would read these little Danielle Steele's or some kind of Harlequin [novel]....

In 1976, just one year before the first fully assembled microcomputers rolled off the production line and began trickling into U.S. schools, Melissa's father began a tour of overseas duty in Italy and Germany. Moving with her family, Melissa attended military-supported institutions during much of her junior high and high school years wherever her father was stationed. When asked about moving so much, both in the United States and in Europe, she says that she accepted her many moves throughout school "with a grain of salt-and that the transitions weren't so bad:" Her main memory has to do with coming back from Germany to stateside schools in the South:

> I just don't remember having too much stress [from moving]. The only thing I can remember is when I was in Germany, there was so much enrichment that went on outside the classroom that made you a lot smarter than you realized you were becoming. You know, you just got really savvy about some things and then when I came back to the States and I was confined to the classroom again, because I went to a civilian school for junior and senior year, I found it, I just got really edgy, you know, I got really bored—I really wanted the go-see kind of education again.

Melissa's family returned to the U.S. in 1980 where her father, now as a lieutenant colonel, was stationed in Fort Stewart, Georgia, and Melissa graduated from high school in 1983. She went on to attend the University of South Carolina and Georgia Southern University through her sophomore year in college and then joined the army herself in 1986.

Although Melissa had benefited a great deal from her education outside the United States, neither the U.S. military schools of Europe nor the high schools and universities she attended at home provided her with access to the new microcomputers that were coming to populate U.S. schools. According to both government and private-sector reports published during this period,[12] as well as the narratives of many other participants in this project, the dispersion of the new technology was—and continues to be—unevenly aligned along the related axes of race and class in U.S. public schools. This inequity was to prove embarrassingly persistent, even into the 1990s (e.g., United States, *Falling*). Nichole Brown (another African American in this project) who came from a working class family and was educated in the South seven years after Melissa, describes her own perception of this situation succinctly, "I thought...[computers were] something that rich people and spoiled kids had. I knew that I would never have one. Not even a question."

Despite these inequities, the country had begun to realize that computer expertise, however defined and however unevenly distributed, was an important key to success in an increasingly technological culture. Melissa noted:

My first memory of a computer? A computer for me was something to be used by skilled people. And it was so far out of my grasp. It probably was not until I was well out of high school—I'm even thinking that it was after the army—yeah, it was when I worked in a bank. All I knew was how to flip it on, put my little password in, and do my own work.

Although Melissa's first experiences with computers occurred in the army as she came in contact with mainframe technology, she discounted them. These data entry efforts, as she explained, were limited by her understanding of the system with which she was interacting:

...it was something really quick. I punched [the data] in. I didn't cognitively think of the system, you know, the computer was like this whole other entity and you just put it [data] in there. If it was to like crash, I had no idea....I probably didn't even know how to turn it on, you know, when I came into work it was on, you know.

But once Melissa started working with computers, she seemed to have no fear of plunging right in:

It wasn't until I wanted this temporary job and it required that I have data processing skills on a certain kind of computer. I lied. I lied. I made my résumé sound like I knew every computer program out there and hadn't even learned on it. I was writing stuff like Lotus, you know, and didn't even know what it meant. Excel, didn't even know what it meant. I'm like, yeah, I do it, I do it, you know. And so when I got the job—I did get the job, because, you know, I've got the gift I guess. I got the job and I remember that on the first orientation day I took the manual home to the computer and I read and I studied that thing all night and the next day I knew how to turn it on, I knew how to get into the program, I knew how to input information just from like familiarizing myself with that manual. And I had those people convinced. I had them convinced that I knew what I was doing on the computer. So that catapulted me into other jobs that required computer skill and I just, that's what I remember doing, getting the book. It all came with the book.

In the same way that Melissa, as a child, remembered her father learning from the army manuals that she watched him read, Melissa took on computers. She read the instruction manuals, educated herself through self-application packets, and "learned Excel, learned Lotus, learned Word, learned e-mail." Finally in the 1990s, Melissa bought a Packard Bell personal computer.

Computers—for Melissa and many other participants in our project—denoted privilege; they were for important people, for government professionals, or for bank officials who handled money and important documents. From her father, Melissa also learned that computers required a particular kind of expertise and that they gave those who worked with them a certain kind of power over their own lives and those of others. Melissa's determination and middle-class status, reinforced daily by her life in the military, played a significant role in helping her enact agency in and around digital environments.

In 1989, Melissa married her husband, whom she met in the army, left nursing as a profession, and resigned her own post in the armed services. She maintained her connection with military life, however, as she moved from place to place with her husband who remained in the military until 1999. Outside the military, she found life, "a little crazy":

> [Out of the army] I worked as a member services representative in the credit union for a while. That was okay except it really got on my nerves to work with civilians because there was no structure. You basically would do whatever you wanted to do. Whatever you wanted to do; nobody cares about your title or anything. And that drove me nuts a little while. Because I was [so] much a part of the military structure with my husband being in, my father being in, and it was just so engrained [in me] that I found the whole civilian working structure a little crazy. I moved back to the States and worked odd jobs, part-time things, until I became a paraprofessional in a middle school.

Her work in the middle school was sufficiently rewarding that it gave her the motivation to go back to school and finish her degrees, even though she had also become a mother and had borne two children during this time.

In 1996, Melissa first attended a community college (in the town where her husband's military career finally deposited them) and then went on to a four-year university in the same town, receiving her bachelor's and master's degrees in English from the University of Illinois, Urbana-Champaign. Funding for her master's degree was provided through a special Scholar's Fellowship from Parkland College that enabled Melissa to return to Parkland as a full-time faculty member in 2000. Since then she has gone on to accept a tenure-line faculty position with Midlands Technological College, an outstanding two-year college in Columbia, South Carolina.

By the time of her interview in 2000, when Melissa was thirty-six, she had already become a Web author through her coursework at the University of Illinois (see Figure 1) and was teaching students in her college-level English classes the intricacies of word processing, page-layout software, online conferencing, and Web site development. She had, in addition, bought her first car online, purchased CD-ROM books for her children, and admitted to having little respect for businesses that lacked a serious Web presence. She also reported teaching her oldest child, Justin, to read on the computer:

> During the time that he [Justin] was...almost two years old, I spent a lot of time on the computer that we had just gotten. And, you know, of course he's curious about what I'm doing, and he would come in and, um, I would just sit there and say, "This a 'j'"—you know, we were talking about his name, JUSTIN. And eventually when he would see the letters go up on the screen he began to associate and...pick them out and I'd say, "Point to 'j:'" He would point to a "j" and it would go up on the screen. And, um, you know, being two I didn't think that he...could associate the actual keyboarding and the monitor. But, um, that was where he would go and pick out his letters: "Is

It's All About Me!!!

Introduction

My Online Portfolio

this a 'c' right here?"—you know, that kind of thing....Later on, I didn't quite do that with his brother...They are 19 months apart, but, um, he had exposure through, uh, a daycare program where they had like a computer camp for little toddlers and stuff. So he had exposure that way and so they are constantly doing computer stuff at school...They are just surrounded by computers...

Most recently, with her brother, Melissa has made business cards on her computer. She has also used her Web access to visit chat rooms, vote in Harris and Gallup polls, and cruise the Internet to learn more about issues like immigration, when the Elian Gonzalez case was in the news in 2000, and police violence, when Amadou Diallo was shot by police in New York in 1999. As she noted,

> I have an opportunity to gaze into the political arena or the social arena on the World Wide Web and actually read it and internalize it. Not that I believe everything that's coming across it. But if I don't, if I get to one site, and I read it, and I go onto another site, I can at least contrast what the inconsistencies are.

Melissa also noted that she wanted to help her mother start an e-business selling gift baskets over the Web and had plans to purchase her own domain name and create a Web site for this purpose. Her most recent decision, however, is to earn a doctorate with a focus on service learning, a specialty she has worked hard to develop in her master's degree research and community college teaching. With her growing confidence in online venues, she plans to earn this degree through a distance-learning program.

The cultural ecology of digital literacy in the 1980s and 1990s: the story of Brittney Moraski

Between 1964, when Melissa was born, and 1986, when Brittney was born, the first large-scale computer network, ARPANET, had been created; John Vittal had invented the first fully functional e-mail system; and Queen Elizabeth II had sent her first e-mail message. Also within this period of time, BITNET, a successor to ARPANET, had come into being, matured, and been linked to other computer networks that were emerging around the world. The network of networks that resulted from these connections—known as the Internet—had also started to expand at an exponential pace. By Brittney's first birthday, it connected more than 10,000 host computers; by her second birthday, more than 60,000 hosts; and by her third birthday, more than l0,000 hosts. By the time Brittney was five years old, the computer code for the World Wide Web had been released, making it possible to create digital texts out of words, images, and sounds and to publish them on the Internet. By the time she was seven, the first graphical browser Mosaic, released at the University of Illinois, had begun to pique the public's interest in the Web.[13] This rapid pace of technology change was about to accelerate rather than slow over the subsequent decade, generating effects that would change the lives of Brittney's white, middle-class Catholic family in Michigan's rural Upper Peninsula. Although Brittney would attend both elementary and secondary school in the same small town where she was born, she knew at an early age that the digital world she would inherit placed a premium on computer-based literacies.

As with Melissa's parents, Brittney's mother and father were her first literacy teachers, and they held literacy practices in high esteem. Her mother, who had attended a year and a half of college, "always enjoyed reading," and her father, a sixth grade teacher who holds a master's degree in education, "constantly reads magazines on ultralight and powered parachute flying," in addition to daily newspapers. As Brittney notes, her parents

> ...never stressed the importance of education—it...[was] unnecessary....Even in childhood, my brothers, sisters, and I...instinctively understood the importance of education.

Unusually poised for a fifteen-year-old at the time of our initial interview, Brittney reported that she always had her "nose in a book" and—like Melissa and many of the other respondents in our study—attributed her love of reading and learning to her family's literacy practices and values:

> [They were]...fantastic about reading to me. I was read to constantly, especially during car rides. Such diligence and attention from my family members has no doubt played a major role in the development of my intellectual facilities....

> [Now] I enjoy history, and I found *Robert Kennedy: His Life* by Evan Thomas to be a fantastic book. I've read many books on the Holocaust, including *Night* by Elie Wiesel and *The Diary of Anne Frank*. I'm beginning to become interested in classical literature (I loathed it before) and recently read *The Pearl* by John Steinbeck. I read the news articles on Yahoo! to stay current in world and national affairs and subscribe to *Time* magazine. I enjoy writing essays and research papers and love creating web sites.

Unlike Melissa, whose Web authoring began later in life and was the culmination of several years of computing, Brittney began to author Web sites as a child. Twenty years after Melissa's early school experiences, Web sites, research papers, and essays exist side by side for Brittney as natural companions. As thirteen-year-old Josh Gardiner, a contemporary of Brittney's, and another study participant, explained when we asked him to describe how centrally computers figured in his life and his ability to communicate with other people, "They rank right up there with air" (Interview, 11 June 2003).

The first computer that Brittney remembers in the house was her brother's, and it was on this machine that Brittney began her digital literacy practices when she was five:

> My brother Garrett got a computer when I was young, and I remember that I had a dinosaur (my passion at the time) program in which I made a printout that read:

> brittney ligh moraski is 5years old. her sisters and brothers names are courtney and leslye and brittney garrett brett brandon dad [bob] mom [beth] mitzi is are best friend in the world.

Brittney also used a computer when she visited the home of a family friend, Mitzi Barra. As a result, by the time Brittney got to school, she had already associated computers with literacy, self-expression, and fun:

The increasingly close relationship between literacy and computer technology that helped shape Brittney's early reading and writing experiences at home (at a microlevel) reflected a similar linkage at school (at a medial level) and within the larger cultural ecology (at the macrolevel). By 1990, when Brittney was four years of age, the State of Michigan supported educational computing in K-12 school sites. During the same time period, the Michigan State Board of Education published a report, *Education: Where the Next Century Begins,* that called for the development of a five-year state technology plan that would help ensure citizens of "the necessary technological skills for employment" (Michigan).

As a result of these factors and others, when Brittney began second grade, in 1994, 68.4% of fourth-grade students, 82.3% of eighth-grade students, and 86.9% of eleventh-grade students nationwide were writing stories or papers on computers (United States, *Condition*), and 43% of fourth-grade teachers and 17% of eighth-grade teachers nationwide reported using computers to teach reading (Coley et al.). This rapid expansion of computer-based literacy efforts took place within a global context in which the World Bank and the United Nations had already established their own Web sites; Bulgaria, Turkey, Kazakhstan, Ghana, and Kenya had been connected to NSFNET; and the World Wide Web was growing exponentially (Zakon). It is little wonder that as Brittney grew up and progressed through the grade levels in school, she was keenly aware of the increasingly important role that computer-based exchanges were playing in the world and increasingly adept at communicating within digital environments.

At the microlevel of personal literacy practices and values, Brittney remembers developing her own digital literacy through a process of working and learning collaboratively in Mitzi's company.

> I just dove into computers as a young child, and I used it, especially in word processing, often before many of my peers. I used Microsoft Works in fourth grade to create my graphs and papers for my science fair project. A huge amount of credit goes to the Barra's (Mitzi and her father) for my technological progression—they taught me everything. I would go over to Mitzi's house and together we would try (and try) to

create the things necessary for my homework. It took us hours to learn how to create a graph in Works.

I didn't have a computer of my own until I was a sixth grader, so the only time I used the computer was when I was at her house. Needless to say, I spent an extraordinary (and worthwhile) amount of time there throughout my childhood. Her (and her family's) help and support has been tremendous.

At home, Brittney rapidly became the technology expert. And—like Melissa and many people who came of age in a technological world—she passed her growing expertise upstream to her parents, teaching them how to send e-mail, connect to the Internet, and use Microsoft Money, a finance management program. By the time Brittney had completed sixth grade in 1998 and had her own computer, she had begun to use the Internet daily, joining 57 million other U.S. citizens (Treese) and 147 million people globally (Paquet) who also had access to the Internet.[14]

Computers became a major part of Brittney's social life as well. As a sophisticated fifteen-year-old, she observed that computer-based literacy had become a means of extending the personal relationships of her friends:

My friends embrace technology because it allows them to communicate with their friends, makes homework assignments easier, and allows them to create cards and posters....When my friends have crushes with certain guys...the computer becomes an important flirting tool. Getting that guy on your instant-messenger list can result in conversations that may lead to "going out."

By the time that Brittney arrived at high school in 2001, she was thoroughly aware that she was a citizen of a nation dependent on computers and a world moving rapidly, if unevenly, toward technological connection. But not all of her contemporaries or near contemporaries shared the same level of access to computer technology that Brittney enjoyed. Other study participants and near contemporaries of Brittney, for instance—especially those raised in poverty, educated in schools with high populations of students of color, and lacking the material resources needed to purchase access to computers—had very different experiences. As Damon Davis, for example, an African American who was twenty-one when we first interviewed him in 2000, noted about his own childhood, "...[F]rom where I'm from, computers were not the big thing... No computer at home, uh, actually nobody I knew in the neighborhood had one."

Despite inequities both within and outside of the United States (Castells), however, a snapshot of computer use taken at this point in history would show that computer use was growing rapidly in many parts of the world. More than 93 million Internet host systems had been registered, and the World Wide Web had reached a size well over a billion indexable pages (Zakon). Brittney was part of a generation that recognized that those nations with the healthiest economies, and the largest share of world markets, were also those with the highest investment in computer technologies. Within this historical context, Brittney was to become one of the estimated 605.6 million people worldwide who today have moved their communication activities online ("How Many Online?").

Before Brittney was sixteen, she was reading books on Web design, HTML coding, using programs like Photoshop, and enrolling in online distance education classes to supplement her education in a small, rural town. In junior high, as she noted, a great deal of her day was spent in online literacy activities, although she believed her outdated computer had cramped her style to some extent:

I have a moderately slow, nondescript PC computer. It has been jazzed up recently, however—one of Mitzi's brothers helped me to install a CD burner, more memory, and an additional hard drive.

...I spend a tremendous amount of time using a computer!....I have the Internet at home, and I use it for a multitude of functions. I access my Spanish course online, send and receive emails, use Yahoo! Messenger to check news headlines and see how my stocks are doing, purchase stocks though ShareBuilder, buy books and CDs at Half.com or Amazon.com, use M-W.com to look up the definitions of words, chat with friends on ICQ, update the school's website, look up topics that interest me, download songs, search for scholarships or contests, learn more about the college admissions process and visit the sites of my preferred universities, look for upcoming camps or workshops, research for homework, and more, and more, and more! One recent example of how I use my computer: We were asked at [my church group] to choose a patron saint and report on it the next week. Well, I used Yahoo! and Google to find sites that list patron saints, and pretty soon I was at catholic-forum.com, trying to find my "personal" saint. I eventually settled on St. Catherine of Alexandria, the patroness of wisdom, philosophers, scholars, and students, but I was tempted to choose St. Vitus, who guards against oversleeping!

Although Brittney used computers in school, her *preferred* gateway for such literacy activities was her own home or that of Mitzi. In these places, Brittney could shape the conditions of her access to meet her specific needs and interests. In part this was true because Brittney's computer skills had quickly outstripped those of many of her teachers—particularly those who taught English. And, while Brittney was appreciative of those instructors who took the trouble to enter her digital world and tolerant of their initial efforts, she was also realistic about the time it would take for adults to catch on to the dynamic technologies that were already a part of her life. She was brutally frank about the instruction she felt her school could offer students like her:

I appreciate [it] when my teachers embrace technology—I understand that it can be a scary thing. However, very few teachers use technology in the classroom. While my algebra teacher has a website that he uses to post homework, the art teacher at school gives PowerPoint presentations, and my health teacher had us take a computerized test to see if we were right or left brained, there is little use of dynamic technology in school, but I'm certain that this will change as the years progress.

I think my personal initiative in understanding and utilizing computers will serve me better than what my school has taught me. But that's really life in a nutshell. We do best at things we have a genuine interest in, not those that are spoon-fed to us.

Brittney's assessment of the educational system she inhabited was both accurate and incisive. Although her teachers were supportive of her computer-based learning activities and had even chosen her to attend a summer institute on computer-based communication, many of Brittney's online literacy practices remained invisible to the instructors with whom she worked daily. This was true, at least in part, because many of these online literacy activities fell outside the relatively narrow bandwidth of the conventional practices her teachers recognized as literate behavior.

None of Brittney's teachers, for instance, realized that her extensive exchanges in chat rooms helped to define her attitude toward face-to-face conversations and her sophisticated ear for nuance in verbal exchanges. Similarly, Brittney's developing understanding of visual literacy was generally invisible to her high school teachers, as were her digital composing efforts that combined both alphabetic and visual elements. As a result, only Brittney herself knew how much her online activities—for instance, her growing understanding of visual design—had begun to contribute to the success of her conventional alphabetic assignments. She explained:

> Lately....I've realized that the aesthetic quality and layout of a website greatly determines its credibility and effectiveness...I think cleanliness, readable fonts, and professional-looking graphics are very important....It is important to "read" graphics and understand the relationship between text and how it is displayed. (i.e. bold text = main idea, small text = footnote)....

> When I write conventional texts, I...use visual layouts to contribute to the true message of my writing.

Given her situation, by the time she entered high school, Brittney had become quite adept at leading a double life in terms of her literacy practices and values. To please her teachers for most of her academic classes, she composed what she called "conventional" texts like the following book report entitled "Schindler's List" (see Figure 2). But to challenge herself and to engage in the literacy practices she knows will matter most to her when she graduates, she contributes to her school's Web site and designs visual PowerPoint texts like "Honduras 2001," about a social action project she undertook with members of her community (see Figure 3). Importantly, Brittney's experiences in this regard mirror those of a number of other young people in our project. Charles Jackson, for instance, an avid computer gamer when we interviewed him at the age of sixteen, also had what he considered to be limited computer-based instruction and access to computers in school. Charles considered home to be his primary gateway to the literacies that he would need to succeed in college and to prosper as a gaming entrepreneur. Although his school did acquire a computer lab when he was in the second grade, Charles had only minimal access to these machines and limited help from teachers in learning to use them. As he explains, when his instructors did integrate computers into their classroom work, they focused on conventional, alphabetic literacy:

> I had about an hour a week [on the computers]. [And] if I was lucky I could [also] use them for 10 minutes before recess....

> The teachers helped me learn about computers, but I don't think they really knew what they were doing. They were new to computers like we were. They helped us out by encouraging us to use them and to help us learn to read and write with them.... They taught us to use word processors and encyclopedias on computers....

> I do a lot of computer coding. Mostly C++ stuff. I do a lot of writing for my games. I try to come up with ideas. I just sit down and try to come up with ideas. Often I will write down a plot or [try] different methods of coding to get a camera angle to work or a certain character to move, stuff like that.

Thus Charles engages a great deal in the kinds of analytical thinking often prized in schools, but most of this thinking and writing is done out of school, extracurricularly, in his role as a gamer.

Figure 2: Brittney's print essay.

Brittney Moraski
February 13, 2002
English, Book Report

Schindler's List

Schindler's List, a novel by Thomas Keneally, prevails in its account of the Holocaust and Oskar Schindler's uncanny heroism. The novel fails, however, to convey the very human and personal suffering of European Jewry at the hands of the Nazis. Schindler's List presents a cut-anddry recitation of the tragedies of the Holocaust and does not leave the reader with a strong sense of personal loss at its conclusion. The author's use of complex and, at times, incorrect sentences detracts from the story and makes it difficult to read. The faults of the novel, however, disappear in Steven Spielberg's film adaptation of Schindler's List. The movie presents the horrors of the Holocaust visually, and most importantly, poignantly. While Spielberg's film captures an essence of the Holocaust that Keneally's words do not express, it is only when the movie and novel are used in concert that the history of the Holocaust is   appropriately depicted.

While Schindler's List has considerable faults, it does present an amazing story. Keneally's cantankerous sentences may discredit the flow of the novel, but the lives of Oskar Schindler and the Schindlerjuden are so intriguing that the story itself remains captivating. Schindler, a Nazi Party member, used his clout and authority within the Reich to protect over a thousand Jews during the Holocaust. An important industrialist, Schindler contracted Jews, otherwise imprisoned in labor and death camps, to work in his factories under the guise that they were essential workers and that their efforts were necessary to keep up the production of German Army supplies. In his concentration camps, prisoners were cared for and fed. Schindler forbade SS guard beatings and executions of prisoners. While life in Schindler's camps was not easy, the Schindlerjuden (Schindler's Jews) considered them a paradise. People on Schindler's list had hope, and better yet, a guarantee of a future beyond the war.

While Keneally does an impressive job telling the Schindlerjuden's story, his book lacks the emotional impact that most Holocaust literature possesses. Keneally's style of writing fails in describing the enormous tragedies of the Holocaust. Since a majority of the characters in Schindler's List survive the Nazi's Final Solution, their stories lack a certain amount of tragedy and devastation. Readers of the novel are not adequately exposed to the brutality and atrocities present throughout the Holocaust, and, consequently, are not left with a sense of personal grief or loss at the novel's end.

The film version of Schindler's List, directed by Steven Spielberg, debuted in 1993. The threehour video was a winner of seven Academy Awards, including Best Picture and Best Director, and was considered by many to be one of the greatest films of all time. Spielberg's video succeeds in its portrayal of the Holocaust because it uses imagery to make its impact. Spielberg's Schindler's List brings the chilling anti-Semitic jeers of village children and the brutality and sheer iniquity of SS guards to the screen. The palpable horror and grief in Jewish families becomes heart-wrenchingly real in the video, and history, however distant, supercedes time and exposes the physical agony of those affected by the Holocaust.

The whole of Schindler's List is more than the sum of a moving novel or a cinematic piece of art. Together, the novel and video complement each other, preserving a wide breadth of the Holocaust for future generations to learn and grow from. With the gravity of its subject matter, Schindler's List, as a novel and a movie, stands as a testimony, a written and visual witness, to what cannot be forgotten.

What these narratives suggest to us

The narratives presented here comprise only a small portion of the story of how people and their families adapted their literacy values and practices to computer-supported environments from 1978 to 2003 in the United States. Although we cannot generalize from these personal narratives to larger populations, these life history interviews have helped us generate key themes that may provide rich direction for further study and exploration. Here we present some thoughts on those emerging themes, discussing them in relation to the narratives presented above and to those of other participants in our study.

The cultural ecology and lifespans of literacies

Almost without exception, the narratives suggest to us that literacies may accumulate more rapidly in the lives of some people when a culture is undergoing a particularly dramatic or radical transition, much as Brandt (*Literacy*) and Miles Myers have indicated. During such periods of macro-order change, people like Melissa and Brittney and many of the other participants learn to value and practice both past and present forms of literacy, often simultaneously. In our contemporary culture, for example, which is undergoing a complicated and messy transition from a modern world of superpower nations and manufacturing might to a postmodern world of global commerce and the rhizomatically organized exchange of digital information, change is both dramatic and rapid. Hence, it is no surprise that literacy scholars have noted multiple literacies emerging, accumulating, combining, and competing: among them, print and digital literacies (Deibert), conventional alphabetic literacies (Brandt, *Literacy*), visual literacies (Kress; George), and intertextual forms of media literacies (George and Shoos).

However the narratives we've presented here also indicate that new forms of literacy may not simply *accumulate* in specific cultural ecologies.[15] Rather, in the lives of individuals, groups, and communities in different patches of an ecosystem and in ecosystems as a whole, literacies have *lifespans*. Specific literacies emerge; they overlap and compete with pre-existing forms; they accumulate, especially, perhaps, in periods of transition; they also eventually fade away. And, depending on the ecological conditions, some may fade faster than others.

Examples of emerging, competing, and fading literacies are not difficult to find. All the participants we have mentioned in this particular article, for example, have adopted e-mail as their primary form of communication at a distance, and so, for them, the literacy involved in writing letters by hand is fading. The specific literacy practices associated with letters handwritten on paper fit well in a culture characterized by an educational system that provided constant practice in cursive writing, a corporate sector based primarily in the United States, and a relatively cheap and reliable postal service that hadn't been compromised by deliveries of anthrax in envelopes. E-mail, similarly, as a literacy practice fits remarkably well with the growth of electronic networks, global markets, and international financial systems.

Fit and the lifespans of particular literacies, of course, will vary among individuals, and communities, within regions and ecological patches. For Brittney, Charles, Damon, and Josh, for instance, literacies that are primarily alphabetic are fading; they have, as Kress notes, taken a "turn to the visual" ("English") and to the multimodal (Cope and Kalantzis). On the microlevel, these young people recognize the excellent fit between emerging digital literacies and the current cultural ecology. However, this same situation does not hold for other people of their age who occupy different ecological patches. Scholars such as Manuel Castells and Pippa Norris have pointed out that while some people (like Josh and Charles) have the opportunity to rely primarily on instant-messaging systems, e-mail, and chat rooms as they communicate with similarly equipped friends in Germany, Italy, or the Netherlands, a teen living in poverty in some parts of Nigeria or China, or on an under-resourced Native American reservation in the United States may not have the same opportunities to pursue such practices or may not be interested in doing so.[16]

Importantly, the overdetermined ecological relationships among literacies, social formations, and technological systems also emerge from the stories we have told. On the macro- and medial levels, the new literacies of Brittney, Charles, Damon, and Josh could not have flourished, indeed would not have been necessary, without the invention of the World Wide Web, fast Web browsers, and efficient Web search engines. Nor could they have existed without new kinds of hardware and software that supported both word and visual processing, multimodal design, and global communication. Similarly, these new literacies would not have experienced such widespread growth without the accompanying explosion of online communities that used chat rooms, experimented with digital photography, played games online, and designed Web sites—communities made up of people who shared the interests of some of the participants in this study. In addition, their interests were supported—at one level or another—by parents and friends who were also convinced of the increasing value of digital literacies, the growing enthusiasm of educators who understood the communicative potential of technology, the technologizing of U.S. workplaces, the establishment of federal and state programs for technological literacy, the increasing investment in information services, the influence and growth of globalization and transnational finances, and many more factors at micro-, macro-, and medial levels. All of these factors—and others—have contributed to a cultural ecology in which technological literacy practices have been, and continue to be, valued.

Figure 3: A visual composition that Brittney creates for a self-sponsored literacy task

Literacy, technology, and agency

The literacy narratives we have discussed here also indicate that people manage to exert their own very real and potent agency in, around, and through digital literacies, thus shaping the environment for their own literacy practices through actions that have effects at micro-, macro-, and medial levels of social operations.

This understanding corroborates the work of Anthony Giddens who notes that people both shape and are shaped by the social systems within which they live in a complex duality of structuration—that "every competent member of every society" not only "knows a great deal about the institutions of that society" but also draws on this understanding of "structure, rules and resources" to make changes in the surrounding environment (71). Andrew Feenberg, too, contends that people can productively shape and influence technological systems in both their design and their use, even as these systems themselves shape and influence people's lives.

For us, it is comforting to see how people like Melissa, Brittney, and other participants in the study have succeeded to some extent in shaping the social and historical circumstances within which they live. Their actions—their decision to learn to compose, create, and communicate in computer environments; the ways they have shaped their own appropriate conditions of access to these environments; the steps they have taken to advance their knowledge and expertise within these environments; the significant literacy exchanges they have undertaken with people outside their own culture, country, and age group, although often occurring in micro-level social environments (i.e., in families, in peer groups, in everyday contexts of living)—also extend beyond these environments to the medial level (e.g., workplaces, schools, organizations) and macrolevel (e.g., regional, national, multinational) contexts. These people's sense of their own communicative agency in digital environments remains strong and persists, despite the discouraging computer experiences they have had and the poor reception their literacy efforts have sometimes received from teachers and parents.

We do not want to indicate with this discussion, however, that people can *always* accomplish anything they want within the social structures they inhabit or that their actions are always effective in the ways they intend. Clearly, people are constrained by any number of influential factors: age, class, race, gender, handicap, experience, opportunity, and belief systems are among only a few such factors. A number of our participants, for example, most especially women, felt that their gender was not an asset to them as far as technological literacy was concerned, and several texts suggest the difficulties some women and girls face in electronic environments (e.g., Blair and Takayoshi; Cassell and Jenkins; Hawisher and Sullivan; Hawisher and Selfe "Teaching"), There continues to be strong support for the perception that boys are more likely to use computers extensively than girls and to excel in their use of them. Justine Cassell and Henry Jenkins note in *From Barbie to Mortal Combat*, for example, that "among secondary school-aged children (eleven to eighteen years), boys are at least three times more likely to use a computer at home, participate in computer-related clubs or activities at school, or attend a computer camp" (12). The literacy narratives generated from our study tend to substantiate Cassell and Jenkins's contentions.

Our study also suggests, however, that while some girls may participate less in computer activities, many *do* participate. When Paula Boyd, now 34, for example, was in junior high, she was a regular at the local mall and its video game arcade, despite the fact that her girlfriends preferred to hang out in the mall proper rather than in the arcade. Brought up in a working class family, Paula has always felt comfortable around computers and serves as a role model today for many younger (and older) women in her work directing a learning center at Parkland Community College. Sixteen-year-old Brittney, similarly, seldom feels that being a girl hampers her in her pursuit of digital literacy. As long as she has the encouraging support of family, friends, teachers, and community, she is able to engage in the computer-based literacy practices she prizes. At the same time, however, she recognizes the complicated nature of gender differences and acknowledges that sometimes, because she is a girl, she feels "slightly, though not wholly, out-of-place" (personal communication, 2 February 2003). As an example, she notes the following:

> Just recently I toured my area's intermediate school district vocational training program as part of a school trip, and I visited the PC tech dept. as part of the tour. From touring the class I could see that the students in the class were predominately male, and in some sense that was slightly intimidating. Still, the teacher who led the tour treated me (the only female in the group) equally and respectfully, and while I don't think my treatment in that class would be any different than the male students, I imagine that it would take me time to adjust to such a learning environment.

She goes on to tell us about the computer camps in which she participated, admitting that in all-male settings she's less likely to "show off" her computer expertise or admit that she doesn't understand something. She concludes, however—and everything we know about Brittney supports her conclusion—that "[her] gender may play some role in [her] experiences with technology, but it is not (nor never will be) influential enough to stop [her] from enrolling in a C++ course or, most importantly, venturing out of [her] comfort level to learn something new" (personal communication, 2 February 2003). We are confident that her high aspirations for excellence and her acts of literacy themselves will continue to thrive throughout her college years. But, at the same time, we do worry that other young women less confident about their capabilities in digital environments may have less success, and we are disheartened that the gender ratio in many computer settings remains so imbalanced. If the first decade of the twenty-first century is anything like the preceding decades, we must acknowledge that a chilly climate for women often extends to computer-based literacy environments today (Takayoshi; Kramarae; Hawisher and Selfe, "Teaching").

In addition, the actions people *do* undertake—because they take place within a complex cultural ecology—always have what Giddens calls "unintended consequences" (56) that overflow the bounds of peoples' intentions. Melissa, for instance, went back to earn a college degree ostensibly to become qualified to teach in a middle school. During her undergraduate and graduate years, however, when she was already thirty years old and a wife and mother, her easy access to, and particular facility with, the new technologies convinced her that she should follow a different route. As she put it in an email message, the results of her efforts have been gratifying:

> My interest now in computer literacy affords me access both socially and professionally. I'm INCLUDED in communities, rather than being on the margins doing what an African American woman might stereotypically do, which is often nothing related to technology if she is in Education or Liberal Arts. Reflecting on my earlier experiences, I'm certain that had I not lied, and then obtained the manual, and had I not been self-motivated in acquiring a computer of my own, my employability and mobility would have been drastically different.... (personal communication, 29 January 2003)

Certainly Melissa's persistence contributed to her success, but other factors in the cultural ecology contributed as well. She attended a community college that, at the time, was sponsoring an excellence program aimed at recruiting minority faculty members, and Melissa's qualifications made her a superb prospect. Without this opportunity, Melissa may never have become a college teacher, one who now regards her work with the new information technologies as a definite asset. Her welcoming relationship with computers also seems to fly in the face of society's common construction of how middle-class, adult women respond to the new information technologies. As noted, being a woman is customarily cast as an obstacle to acquiring the literacies of technology (e.g., Cassell and Jenkins; Jessup). But we hypothesize (based in part on our larger study) that the military culture, in which technology is just a part of everyday life for women as well as men (Katzenstein and Reppy), may work in women's favor as far as information technologies are concerned. Karen Lunsford, a white woman in our study four years younger than Melissa, has this to say about her early memories of computers as an air force dependent when she was 10 years old:

> One of the earliest real computers that I remember was in, um, we were in Alabama, we were there for one year from 1978 to 1979.... And [my father] was taking courses of some sort, and he had a simulation computer that he brought home and it had a daisy wheel printer in it. It didn't have a screen. And I remember he brought it home, he linked it to the telephone and we were playing *Star Trek* on it.

For Karen and her sister, computer games rapidly became a family activity, and, often, with their emphasis on war and military maneuvers, the games themselves were merely an extension of Karen's immersion in a military culture already saturated with technology. While Melissa may not have taken to mainframe computer technology as a member of the military, she nevertheless as a military dependent understood computers as integral to what her father and the military were all about.

In addition to the military, however, Melissa's immersion in the African American culture, in which young women are encouraged to take charge (hooks), may well have shaped her future work with computers. Hortense Spillers, a black feminist at Cornell University, argues that early on, given the experience of their lives, black women were exempt from some racially dominant expectations of white feminine behavior, behavior that excluded, for instance, expertise with machines. This cultural exemption may well have helped some African American women, in this case Melissa (and perhaps Nichole), claim a subject position that allows black women to take pride in their own technological expertise.

Gateways to the literacies of technology

This project has reminded us that people often acquire and develop the literacies they need in places other than the classroom where, often, instructors tend to limit literacy activities to the narrow bandwidth of conventional written English (Selfe et al. "Stasis"). Nonetheless, schools, along with workplaces, communities, and homes, represent the major gateways through which people in the United States have gained access to computer technology over the last twenty-five years. In general, our interviews indicate that the more gateways people have open to them, the more likely they are, over their lifetimes, to acquire and develop effective sets of digital literacy skills and to value these literacies of technology. The relative importance of these gateways in people's lives varies according to the needs and motivations of those who use them, the timing of these needs within individual lives, the historical contexts in which such gateways exist, and the sets of social circumstances which shape them—all factors that influence the cultural ecology in which people acquire electronic literacies.

Of particular note in the cases that we have collected from young people who have come to value and practice various digital literacies is the fact that schools are not currently uniform in their predispositions to digital literacy, in general, and to visually rich—and multimodal[17]—digital literacies, more specifically. Although the various educational institutions these people have attended as students, for instance, value computer-based literacies at some level, in English composition classes and in most official assessments of communication ability, the focus is primarily on conventional, alphabetic, and print literacy.

To a large extent, this valuing of official forms of alphabetic and print literacy is generational. Such literacies have, after all, been the major shaping forces in the educational experiences of faculty members teaching at these schools and, thus, in the ongoing formulation of their official grading and evaluation standards. The primacy of alphabetic and print literacies has also affected the hiring decisions of these educational institutions—and the values of employers who recruit their graduates and expect these people to be able to meet minimal standards. The culture of print and alphabetic literacy exerts, too, a powerful force on the expectations of parents who enroll children at these educational institutions and the historically defined literacy ideals of the larger society in which the educational institutions exist and are expected to thrive.

This contested situation—in which print-based and alphabetic literacies continue to compete at many levels with some students' computer-based literacies that often exceed the alphabetic—may help explain why most English composition teachers who have worked regularly with Brittney, Charles, Damon, and Josh have not addressed their new media literacies on a systematic basis. Raised and educated in a culture that valued, and continues to value, alphabetic and print literacies, many of these teachers remain unsure of how to value new media literacies, unsure how to practice these new literacies themselves, and unprepared to integrate them at curricular and intellectual levels appropriate for these particular young people. In this context, teachers cannot take full advantage of the literacy strengths computer-savvy kids bring to the classroom and may miss some important opportunities to link their own instructional goals to the developing literacy strengths of these talented young people.

Workplace settings have provided a second major gateway for electronic literacy—as Melissa's and other participants' narratives suggest. Since the 1980s, businesses and corporations have become increasingly dependent on computer-based communications.[18] Driving this dependence have been the forces of globalization, the rapid growth in computer manufacturing[19] and in the information technology sector, government policies designed to increase the export of U.S. computer goods and services, and the rapid innovation and decreasing costs characterizing the computer industry. As a result of these related trends, workplaces have provided many employees with both access to technology and the pragmatic motivations for taking advantage of this access. This historical tracing does not suggest, however, that access to computer technology in the workplace has been equitable. Computer use in the workplace, as in schools, also continues to be differentially distributed along the axes of race and income as we have already noted.

Communities also serve as critical technological literacy gateways by providing access to social groups in which people form friendships that frequently support technological literacies, such as those Brittney has encountered, but also by providing public access facilities, such as community centers, community networks, and libraries for people's online literacy practices. The 2002 U.S. government report, *A Nation Online*, revealed that many in the U.S. who lack access to computers and the Internet at home turn to libraries for access, and this was certainly true for several of the participants in our study. Time and again, they mentioned libraries as important gateways for literacy activities. Older participants spoke of the Carnegie libraries and the weekly trips each made to the library to borrow books, and the younger participants, like Damon, not only borrowed books but also talked about writing school papers with word processing and doing research on the Web at local libraries. Significantly, *A Nation Online* reports that "a far higher percentage of Hispanic (39 percent) and Black (45 percent) children rely solely on public access facilities to use computers than White children (15 percent)" (United States, Nation 9). Thus these public access facilities also help address the inequitable computing conditions that remain constant and seemingly insurmountable as problems in the U.S.

And, finally, families and homes provide the fourth major gateway through which people come to the literacies of technology. Within the environment of their homes, parents again and again provided a rich environment in which the participants learned and practiced print and digital literacies. Parents bought computers that they could sometimes ill afford in order to give their children and themselves greater educational and economic opportunities. When the participants became parents, such as Melissa, they too made sure that their own children had a wide assortment of electronic resources at their fingertips. In fact, compared to the latest U.S. Census Bureau's statistics on the percentage of households in the U.S. owning a computer, the participants in our study are probably more likely to own computers than the average U.S. resident. Fifty-four million households in the U.S., or 51%, had at least one computer in August 2000 (Newburger). As many of the participants seemed to know intuitively, household ownership of computers along with Internet access—and thus ready access to online reading, writing, and communicating at home—has been a major factor contributing to people's high degrees of proficiency with digital literacies.

Access and its complications

Importantly, access is a much more complexly rendered social formation than we have heretofore recognized. While physical access to computers is necessary, it is not sufficient for developing digital literacies (Hawisher, "Accessing"; *Spanning*; DeVoss et al.). Rather, the specific *conditions* of access (and the timing of these conditions) seem to be important in determining when and how people acquire and develop effective sets of technological literacy skills—or, indeed, if they choose to do so.

Although it is difficult to indicate the scope and complexity of the ecological relationships that affect the conditions of people's access, we can illustrate these principles a bit more specifically by tracing how they play out at various levels in the lives of the two women we have featured in this article. At a *macro*level, for example, Melissa's and Brittney's access to technological literacy was affected by large-scale historical, political, and economic factors such as, but not limited to, the development of microcomputers in the late 1970s, the resulting expansion of the U.S. computer industry in the 1980s (Freeman; McConnell; Moris; Warnke), the Clinton administration's decision to invest in technology as the economic engine that would drive the country's economic expansion in the 1990s (Selfe), and the ongoing partnership between universities and the military industrial complex (Castells, *The Rise*). All of these converging factors exerted a great tendential force in our culture, feeding the rapid development of microcomputers, contributing to the falling costs of these devices, and affecting the availability of computers in schools, workplaces, communities, and homes.

The condition of Melissa's and Brittney's access to technology was also affected at *medial* levels by the different institutions, organizations, and professions that exerted shaping influences—often, but not exclusively, bureaucratic and institutional in nature. For example, Melissa, as a bank employee, was required to make use of a limited number of applications on which the banking industry had begun to depend and which were becoming standard for managing accounts. Similarly, Brittney's school had a computer-use policy that dictated a much more limited range of use at school where her movements online were constrained by firewalls and filters designed to prevent her from accessing material educators considered inappropriate for her age group.

*Micro*level factors similarly affected the conditions of these women's access to technology. Melissa's marriage and birth of her children led to her work in a middle school, which propelled her back into higher education at a time when computers were more readily available for her literacy efforts. Her courses and work with other graduate students and faculty spurred her interest in Web authoring that was made all the easier by her now owning a computer. In Brittney's case, her brothers supported her early attempts to use computers at home, and her family supported her efforts with financial resources. Brittney also had a close friend in her community who used computers, educational opportunities that exposed her to computers, and a home life that could accommodate personal computers with a minimum of space reallocation.

The transmission of digital literacy values and practices

Perhaps most fascinating, the cases we have collected form a complex mapping of the routes by which literacy values and practices are passed along within individual families. Under the right conditions, literacy practices and values—both print and electronic—can flow upstream as well as downstream in a family. An NPR/Kaiser/Kennedy School poll conducted in 1999, for example, found that 33% of adults reported asking their children for help with computer problems, and 55% of the children reported asking their parents for such help (adult's survey question 32, children's survey question 14) ("Survey Shows"). Thus, it is not surprising to find that Brittney's older brother influenced his younger sister's values regarding computer-based literacy practices, nor is it unusual that Brittney had, in turn, taught her parents how to send e-mail and connect to the Internet. And Melissa, similarly, introduced her brother and mother to ways in which the literacies of technology could support their emerging business projects. Three years Melissa's junior, Mary Sheridan-Rabideau, another participant in our study who initially valued computers less than some of her contemporaries and whose well-educated parents valued them not at all, eventually went to the trouble to outfit a computer she purchased for her parents with coded keys to facilitate their learning. Today, although her parents still struggle with the technology, they remain connected. Paula, similarly, made sure her extended family in Chicago was connected through e-mail so that, for her own convenience, she'd have family members to whom she could send email regularly. Other interviews we have completed for this project—including Dean's and Charles's—also indicate that these intrafamily patterns affect peoples' access to computers, with computers being passed from children to parents, from parents to children, from aunts to nieces, from mothers-in-law to daughters-in-law, and from grandchildren to grandparents.

As we continue...

The stories we have told here are not complete histories. Chosen from more than 350 interviews, excerpted, and reduced, they comprise only a very small portion of some larger national narratives: how individuals and families have adapted their literacy values and practices to computer-supported environments; how people's access to computers has varied, in part, along the axes of race and class; how and why technological literacy has thrived within the cultural ecology existing within the United States from 1978 to the present; how people have struggled to acquire computer-based literacies in an attempt to improve their own prospects or those of their children; how children have shared computer-based literacies with adults and how adults have shared with children.

We recognize (and hope readers do as well) that no one story we have told here and, certainly, not this collection of stories can be considered indicative or representative of any larger population. There are far too many stories that remain uncollected, unheard, unappreciated for such larger narratives to be completely or even accurately rendered. We also recognize that drawing conclusions from a limited set of data is always dangerous business, so we approach the task with caution and hope readers will do so as well.

This recognition, however, does not serve to diminish the value of the first-hand accounts like those we have told here. On the contrary, to us, these literacy histories have proven to be richly sown with insights that have immediate face validity. And we hope that other faculty members, parents, policy makers, and program directors will react to them in the same way.

For us, some of the more surprising discoveries to come from the autobiographies we have collected focus on how little teachers of English, composition, and communication know about the many literacies students bring to the classroom. Our professional radar is tuned so narrowly to the bandwidth of print and the alphabetic—to school-based and workplace writing—that we miss a great deal of the more interesting and engaging self-sponsored reading and composing students do on their own time. These activities, these values remain generally invisible to us. And because we often miss such activities, our instructional practices and values, our interests, and the texts we read and compose may be moving further and further away from those that students consider important.

Under these conditions and with the best of intentions, writing instructors—ourselves among them—face the danger of teaching in ways that ignore the considerable strengths in technological literacies that some students bring to our classes. As a result, we fail to build on the literacies that students already have—and we fail to learn about these literacies or why they seem so important to so many students. We also fail, as we deny the value of these new literacies, to recognize *ourselves as illiterate* in some spheres. And in this intellectual arrogance, we neglect to open ourselves to learning new literacies that could teach us more about human discursive practices.

With regard to computer technology more specifically, these stories also suggest to us how important it is to remember, as teachers, that all students are not the same (Faigley). They inhabit different patches of a larger cultural ecology. They come from different backgrounds and have had access to different technology gateways. They have differing proclivities and support for technological agency; they have differing family traditions and friends. Thus, we must show caution in designing computer-supported lessons that assume too much or too little or misjudge students' motivations. And we need to be increasingly wary about assuming that school is the primary gateway for learning about and using technology.

But changing people's attitudes toward literacy is not a simple or easy task. Many composition instructors have been raised and educated in a world that focuses on alphabetic, print literacy. Many faculty lack training in digital literacies, and many lack access to the technology and professional support systems that could help them feel more confident in these realms. This may be especially true, as we have pointed out elsewhere, in institutions that have high populations of students of color and poor students. And it may be especially true in schools hard hit by recent budgetary cutbacks in which the U.S. has sacrificed school funding to military spending and international warfare.

However, faculty members can start to change their attitudes about literacy—to broaden their understanding of, and appreciation for, students' literacies—by attending as closely to students' online reading and composing practices as they do to their own more traditional writing practices; by listening closely, and with open minds, to what students are saying about the role of new-media compositions in the world they inhabit; and by expanding their definitions of "texts" and "composing" practices to include a range of other behaviors: among them, reading and composing images and animations; creating multimedia assemblages; combining visual elements, sounds, and language symbols into alternatively organized and presented forms of communication in digital environments.

More than anything, instructors can discipline themselves to become increasingly open to a flexible understanding of composing and composition instruction, not more constrained. We can remind ourselves of our professional responsibilities as scholars of language to recognize, study, and address a full range, rather than a narrow bandwidth, of semiotic practices and channels: those that may use images, animations, sounds, and multiple media; those that represent newly emerging literacies *as well as* established literacies *and* competing literacies *and* fading literacies. Composition teachers can also remind themselves and students about how specific historical periods and cultural ecologies shape, and are shaped by, literacy standards, values, and practices (emerging, established, competing, *and* fading). And in doing this work, they can help students negotiate and reconcile the contested values and practices associated with the various kinds of reading and composing work they currently do for different classes in school; in family, peer-group, and community settings; and in the workplace. This kind of work will also pay dividends as students change their reading and composing habits and encounter differing habits from differing cultural ecologies, over the course of their lifetimes.

Finally, the literacy narratives on which we have focused in this article suggest that closing the gaps associated with information technologies in the lives of some people will depend not on providing them with access to computers through one technology gateway but on providing them with access through several such gateways—school, workplace, community, and home. The specific *conditions* of access—and how these are aligned in our country with interrelated formations of race, class, and gender—must be addressed in order to assure productive environments within which the beginning steps of physical access can make a real difference. One necessary element of these conditions must be a broad understanding and valuing of multiple literacies—emerging, competing, and fading—in home, school, community, and workplace environments. And it is in schools and universities—in our roles as teachers—that we are uniquely positioned to make a difference in the literate activities of students.

None of these changes in literacy, of course, can be addressed in isolation from the larger cultural ecology within which computers—and the acquisition and development of the literacies of technology—exist. But all of them can make a difference in peoples' literate lives during this information age.

Appendix: Interview Protocol

We're doing research to find out primarily how people came to computers and what their experiences using computers have been. We're interested in what experiences different generations of people living in the United States have had with computers.

Demographic Information

Name:
Current Occupation:
Previous Occupations:
Nationality:
Race:
Orientation (only if volunteered by subject):
Let me get down a few facts about your family as you were growing up. Immediate family members and ages:

How would you describe your family circumstances?

Income Level
    Growing up?
    Now?

Parents' Literacy Histories (e.g., literacy values, education, reading/writing/computing activities):

Did your parents value literacy? How? Any literacy stories?

Parents' Education and Professions:

Can you tell us a bit about yourself? Where were you born? Where did you grow up? What is your family like? What are you like?

Place and date of birth:

Where did you live?
    Growing up:
    Now:

Schooling History:
    Elementary
    College
    Secondary
    Other

Early Exposure to Literacy/Computers

Can you tell us how/when/why you learned to read and write?

Can you tell us the story about when, where, how you first came in contact with computers?

Can you tell us the story about when, where, how you *first learned* to use computers?

Do you remember what the prevailing images/representations of computers were when you were growing up? (e.g., movies, television, magazines, books?)

At Home

If your family had a computer at home when you were growing up, can you tell us the story of buying the computer? Who bought it? When? Why?

Can you tell us how much the computer cost? Can you talk about how significant/serious that investment was in terms of your family's regular budget?

For what purposes did you use the computer when you first started? As you continued to learn?

Can you tell how a typical session might have gone in your home computing environment?

How often did you use the computer? What contributed to your use of it or not? Are there any stories/incidents that you can remember about this?

Can you remember any books/texts about computers that you had at home? Any that you read? Any computer games?

Can you identify any images that you remember about computer use?

What did you and your siblings and parents use the computer for at this time? As you continued to use it?

At School

Tell the story of how you first learned to use the computer at school: What was your motivation? Age? Who helped? How did they help? What kind of support did you have? In what classes did you learn to use the computer? How much access did you have to a computer per day/week/month?

Describe your use of this computer: Who was there? What times of day? What were the surroundings like?

For what purposes did you use this computer?

For what purposes did other kids use the computer at school when you were all first learning to use technology? As you continued to learn?

Can you tell how a typical session might have gone in this environment?

What determined how frequently you used the computer? Are there any stories/incidents that you can remember about this?

Can you remember any books/texts about computers that you had access to at school? Any that you read? Any computer games?

Can you identify any images that you remember about computer use that you encountered at school? Educational images?

What did your family think about computers? Your learning computers? Your parents? Sisters and brothers? Uncles and Aunts? Cousins? Grandparents? What values did they place on this activity? On your participation? On their role? Do you have any stories you can tell us that would illustrate the value your family placed on computers or computer literacy?

What did your friends think about computers: What values did they place on this activity? On your participation? On their role? Do you have any stories you can tell us that would illustrate the value your friends placed on computers or computer literacy?

What did your teachers/the school you went to think about computers: What values did they place on this activity? On your participation? On their role? Do you have any stories you can tell us that would illustrate the value the educational system placed on computers or computer literacy?

Did you used to read about computers? If so, where? When?

Can you remember any pictures of computers or computer use that struck you as memorable? Where did you see these?

Current Exposure

Do you (or your family) own a computer *now*? If so, please describe it. If "yes"

Can you tell us the story of buying the computer? Who bought it? When? Why?

Can you tell us how much the computer cost? Can you talk about how significant/serious that investment was in terms of (your, your parents, your family's) regular budget?

Describe for us where you keep the computer in your house/apartment/dorm room. What are the things you have around the computer? What items of furniture do you associate with the computer?

For what purposes do you use this computer? (e.g., what kinds of work? what applications?)

For what purposes do your siblings/parents/children use the computer? Who taught them? Who provides support? (e-mail?)

Do you access the Web? What do you use it for?

Tell the story of how you learned to use the computer in this environment. What was your motivation? Who helped? What kind of support did you have? Do you continue to have?

What are the rules associated with using a computer in your home/apartment/dorm? Who made these rules up? How do they affect you?

Can you identify books/texts about computers that you have access to at your home/apartment/dorm? Any that you read?

Also

Do you currently have access to a computer someplace other than at home? Where (workplace? school?) When? For how long? How do you get there? How much does it cost to use this computer? How do you get that money to pay for access?

Describe the surroundings in which you use this computer: Who is there? What times of day? What are the surroundings like?

For what purposes do you use this computer?

For what purposes do other students/co-workers use the computer? Can you tell how a typical session might go in this environment?

Tell the story of how you learned to use the computer in this environment: What was your motivation? Who helped? What kind of support did you have? Do you continue to have?

What are the rules associated with using a computer in this environment? Who made these rules up? How do they affect you?

Can you identify books/texts about computers that you have access to at your school/ workplace/ other? Any that you read?

Can you describe your current level of skill with computers? Novice, competent, expert? Any stories about your expertise?

What do you think about computers now? Why?

What do your family think about computers now: Your parents? Sisters and brothers? Uncles and Aunts? Cousins? Grandparents? Your friends? What values do they place on computer use? On your participation? On their role? Do you have any stories you can tell us that would illustrate the value your family and friends now place on computers or computer literacy?

What values does the educational system currently place on computer use? Do you have any stories you can tell us that would illustrate the value your schools now place on computers or computer literacy?

How/when/where/why do you see yourself using computers in the future?

Do you read about computers? If so, where? When? What do you read on computers?

Can you identify any images of computer use that have struck you recently? Where have you seen these images?

Do you use a particular brand of computer? If so, why? Which one? Names of programs?

Anything more you'd like to say about your relationship with computers?

Notes

[1] By *technological literacy* or *literacies* we mean the practices involved in reading, writing, and exchanging information in online environments, as well as the values associated with such practices— cultural, social, political, and educational. For us, the term differs from *computer literacy* in that it focuses primarily on the word *literacy* and, thus, on communication skills and values rather than on the skills required to use a computer. To distinguish technological literacy from computer literacy, literacy scholars have also used the related terms *electronic literacy* (Sullivan and Dautermann; Selfe and Hawisher, "Historical Look"), *digital literacy* (Tyner), and the *literacies of technology* (Hawisher and Selfe). We use the last term, literacies of technology, as an all-encompassing phrase to connect social practices, people, technology, values, and literate activity, which, in turn, are embedded in a larger cultural ecology. All these terms are synonymous with our use of technological literacy, and we use them in this article interchangeably. In all cases, they focus on literacy practices and values in online environments rather than on the skills required to use computers themselves.

[2] Evidence of the increasing importance placed on computing as a prerequisite for many available jobs is not difficult to come by. For various takes on this pattern, consult the Hudson Institute's *Workforce 2020* (Judy and D'Amico), the *Digital Workforce* report issued by the Office on Technology Policy (Meares and Sargent), and *Futurework* issued by the U.S. Department of Labor.

[3] See Paul Prior's *Writing/Disciplinarity* for a particularly apt discussion of literate activity, technological or otherwise. He writes, in part, that "writers and readers are inescapably situated in particular places and in the moment-to-moment flow of lived time...Literate activity...is not located

in acts of reading and writing, but *as* cultural forms of life saturated with textuality, that is strongly motivated and mediated by texts" (138, emphasis in original).

[4] Compare, for example, the *Falling through the Net* series (United States) issued by the National Telecommunications and Information Administration during the Clinton presidency from 1995 to 1999 and during the Bush administration in 2000, along with the more recent 2002 *A Nation Online* (United States).

[5] We couple the concept of "literacy" with technology while recognizing the unease with which some scholars view the proliferation of terms like "digital literacy," "visual literacy," "media literacy," and so forth. Anne Wysocki and Johndan JohnsonEilola, for example, have argued that "when we speak...of [alphabetic] 'literacy' as though it were a basic, neutral, contextless set of skills, the word keeps us hoping...that there could be an easy cure for economic and social and political pain, that only a lack of literacy keeps people poor or oppressed" (355). And, increasingly, of course, this same kind of thinking is applied to online literacy practices. Gunther Kress (*Literacy*) also suggests that *literacy* is an inappropriate word to link with terms not specifically aimed at "[making] messages using letters as the means for recording that message (23)." For Kress, not only is the move imperialistic (many cultures don't use the concept of literacy, and still others don't even use letters or an alphabet), but also it's also confusing. According to Kress, the move allows us to conflate too simply the individual competencies required to make meaning in multimodal contexts. Nevertheless, we endorse linking *literacy* with words, such as *technological, digital, electronic* as well as the all-encompassing "literacies of technology." We believe that by naming these abilities "literacies," we signal the enormous importance they hold for living in today's literate world. James Gee (*What Video*) would seem to agree. By emphasizing "the idea of different sorts of multimodal literacy" (14) and by asserting that "both modes and multimodality go far beyond images and words to include sounds, music, movement, bodily sensations, and smells" (14), he too extends the reach of "literacy." For Gee, "in the modern world, print literacy is not enough. People need to be literate in a great variety of different semiotic domains" (*What Video* 19). We agree.

[6] An extended account of this project and the life-history narratives it generated appears in Cynthia L. Selfe and Gail E. Hawisher's *Literate Lives in the Information Age: Narratives of Literacy from the United States*. This project has been funded, in part, by generous support from the National Council of Teachers of English, the Society for Technical Communication, Michigan Technological University, and the University of Illinois, Urbana-Champaign.

[7] In using the term *patch*, we are indebted to the work of Jay L. Lemke. In *Textual Politics*, he writes:

> ...activities in human communities are interrelated both in terms of exchanges of matter and energy and in terms of relationships of meaning. The fundamental unit of analysis will turn out to be a "patch," a mini-ecosystem containing human organisms in interaction with their social and material environments according to both cultural and ecological-physical principles. The patch is part of a mosaic of other patches each with its own unique history, all interacting and forming a larger scale patch in a larger scale eco-social system....underlying them are the interconnected doings, the ecological and social processes that link organism to organism, organism to environments, and which at smaller scales operate to constitute organisms, artifacts, landscapes, dialects, communities, cultures, and social individuals as self-organizing systems. (94)

When we use the term *patch*, we refer to the smaller eco-units of families, peer groups, institutions, professions, etc.

[8] See Bertram C. Bruce and Maureen Hogan's chapter for a fascinating discussion on "The Disappearance of Technology." They argue that

> [a]s technologies embed themselves in everyday discourse and activity, a curious thing happens. The more we look, the more they slip into the background. De spite our attention, we lose sight of the way they give shape to our daily lives. This disappearance effect is evident when we consider whether a technology empowers people to do things that would be difficult, or even impossible otherwise. (270)

[9] Importantly, we have asked the participants on whom we focused to coauthor their own case studies with us. We were influenced in this decision by Caroline Brettell's *When They Read What*

We Write, a collection that presents a series of perspectives on studies like ours—anthropological projects, ethnographies, and life histories—and talks about the ways in which modernist approaches to such writing have often suffered from the limited perspectives of academics and professional scholars who, as Donald Schoen notes, still cling to an understanding of "the superior academic value of 'pure knowledge' inherited from the 'model of technical rationality' that has been influential in all American social sciences" (27). As Alexandra Jaffe points out in the Brettell collection, this kind of approach to research claims a "distance between observer and observed" that is, to a great extent, an "ethnographic fiction;' one that scholars have employed to assure "control over [their] 'subjects'" (51). As a corrective to this modernist approach, Brettell and others in her collection suggest an alternative method of having subjects talk back, comment on, modify, change, correct scholars' interpretations of what they said. Talking back, as Jaffe goes on to say, helps to undermine professional ethnographers' "ability to construct an unproblematic Other, and hence, an unproblematic self" (52). In our experience, the reflexivity established by this dialogue is not only a positive and productive characteristic of postmodern anthropology but also, as Jaffe points out, a realistic and "essential condition of interaction with the people we study" (51). See Gail E. Hawisher and Cynthia L. Selfe's "Collaborative Configurations" for further discussion.

[10] For an extensive explanation of the role that networked computers have played in bringing about change and ensuring certain political phenomena an extended global impact—among them, international terrorism, religious fundamentalism, the Green movement, and feminism—see Manuel Castells's three-volume series, collectively entitled *The Information Age: Economy, Society, and Culture*. In addition, the New London Group, in their recently published book, *Multiliteracies: Literacy Learning and the Design of Social Futures*, explores the role that computer networks and technological communications systems have played in multiplying and transforming individuals' "lifeworlds" (see Cope and Kalantzis).

[11] The extended life-history narratives of these participants can be found in the chapters they have coauthored within *Literate Lives in the Information Age* (Selfe and Hawisher) or in other work we have published.

[12] See the Clinton administration's *Falling through the Net* series (1995, 1998, 1999, 2000), issued by the National Telecommunications and Information Administration (United States), and the 1997 Educational Testing Service report by Richard Coley, J. Crandler, and P. Engle, *Computers and Classrooms: The Status of Technology in U.S. Schools*.

[13] These markers of Internet development and many others can be found in *Hobbes' Internet Timeline*, v5.6, compiled by Robert H. Zakon. Zakon's timeline chronicles the growth of the Internet, focusing primarily on the development of hardware, software, and networking systems. This timeline, and others, can be accessed from the Web site of the Internet Society at <http://info.isoc.org/internet/history/> or at <http://www.zakon.org/robert/internet/timeline/>.

[14] We do not mean to suggest by this statistic that access to the Internet has been or has become evenly distributed around the world or within the U.S. The distribution of technology has been uneven and aligned along existing axes of race and socioeconomic status—globally (cf., Castells; Norris) and nationally (cf., United States, *Falling*; "Digital Divide"; Castells; United Nations, *Human Development*; Selfe). In addition, at various times and depending on the current cultural ecology, technology has also been differentially distributed along the axes of age (cf., Pastore; Pew Internet Project, "Gray Gap" and "Wired Seniors"), gender (cf., Cassell and Jenkins; United Nations, *Human Development*; Jessup; Pew Internet Project, "Tracking"), and geographic location (cf. Castells; United Nations, *Human Development*; Norris), both nationally and globally.

[15] In 1995 in her groundbreaking article, "Accumulating Literacies," Deborah Brandt noted that literacies—with the invention of computer-based communication technologies—were proliferating in the years marking the end of the 20th century. Computer-based literacies imparted a "complex flavor even to elementary acts of reading and writing...creating new and hybrid forms of literacy where once there might have been fewer and more circumscribed forms" (651).This "rapid proliferation and diversification of literacy" (651), Brandt continued, places increasing pressure on those in the U.S. whose ultimate success may be "best measured as a person's capacity to amalgamate new reading and writing practices in response to rapid social change" ("Accumulating" 651).

[16] For further information on the diffusion of technologies among Native Americans in the U.S., see James Casey, Randy Ross, and Marcia Warren.

[17] See Bill Cope and Mary Kalantzis, and Gunther Kress and Theo Van Leeuwen.

[18] For explorations of this claim, compare William Johnston and Arnold Packer; Richard Judy and Carol D'Amico; Carol Meares and John Sargent; and the U.S. Department of Labor's *Futurework*.

[19] Published in 1996, volume 119, number 8 of the *Monthly Labor Review* provides an excellent historical snapshot of how computers were shaping the U.S. economy at that time. Among the articles in this issue, we recommend those authored by Laura Freeman, William Goodman, Sheila McConnell, Francisco Moris, and Jacqueline Warnke.

Works Cited

Blair, Kristine, and Pamela Takayoshi, eds. *Feminist Cyberscapes: Mapping Gendered Academic Spaces.* Stamford: Ablex, 1999.

Brandt, Deborah. "Accumulating Literacy: Writing and Learning to Write in the Twentieth Century." *College English* 57.6 (1995): 649-68.

_____. *Literacy in American Lives.* New York: Cambridge UP, 2001.

_____. "Literacy Learning and Economic Change." *Harvard Educational Review* 69.4 (1999): 373-94.

_____. "Sponsors of Literacy." *College Composition and Communication* 49.2 (1998): 165-85.

Brettell, Caroline, ed. *When They Read What We Write: The Politics of Ethnography.* Westport: Bergin and Garvey, 1996.

Bruce, Bertram C., ed. *Literacy in the Information Age: Inquiries into Meaning Making with New Technologies.* Newark, DE: International Reading Association, 2003.

Bruce, Bertram, and Maureen P. Hogan. "The Disappearance of Technology: Toward an Ecological Model of Literacy." *Handbook of Literacy and Technology: Transformations in a Post-Typographic World.* Ed. David Reinking, Michael C. McKenna, Linda D. Labbo, Ronald D. Kieffer. Mahwah, NJ: Lawrence Erlbaum, 1998. 269-81.

Casey, James, Randy Ross, and Marcia Warren. *Native Networking: Telecommunications and Information Technology in Indian Country.* April 1999. Benton Foundation, Washington, DC. 1 Aug. 2003 <http://www.benton.org/ publibrary/native/indexnew.htmi>.

Cassell, Justine, and Henry Jenkins, eds. *From Barbie to Mortal Combat.* Cambridge: MIT P, 1998.

Castells, Manuel. *End of the Millennium.* Malden: Blackwell, 1998. Vol. 3 of *The Information Age: Economy, Society, and Culture.* 3 vols. 1996-1998.

_____. *The Power of Identity.* Malden: Blackwell, 1997. Vol. 2 of *The Information Age: Economy, Society, and Culture.* 3 vols.1996-1998.

_____. *The Rise of the Network Society.* Malden: Blackwell, 1996. Vol. 1 of *The Information Age: Economy, Society, and Culture.* 3 vols. 1996-1998.

Coley, Richard J., J. Crandler, and P. Engle. *Computers and Classrooms: The Status of Technology in U.S. Schools.* Princeton, NJ: Educational Testing Service, 1997.

Cooper, Marilyn M., and Cynthia L. Selfe. "Computer Conferences and Learning: Authority, Resistance, and Internally Persuasive Discourse." *College English* 52.8 (1990): 847-69.

Cope, Bill, and Mary Kalantzis, eds. *Multiliteracies: Literacy Learning and the Design of Social Futures.* New York: Routledge, 2000.

Deibert, Ronald J. *Parchment, Printing, and Hypermedia: Communication in World Order Transformation.* New York: Columbia UP, 1997.

DeVoss, Danielle Nicole, Joseph Johansen, Cynthia L. Selfe, John C. Williams, Jr. "Under the Radar of Composition Programs: Glimpsing the Future through Case Studies of Electronic Literacy." Ed. Lynn Z. Bloom, Donald A. Daiker, and Edward M. White. *Composition*

Studies in the New Millennium: Rereading the Past, Rewriting the Future. Carbondale: SIU P, 2003.

"Digital Divide Basics Fact Sheet" 2003. *Digital Divide Network*. Benton Foundation, Washington, DC. 1 Aug. 2003. <http://www.digitaldividenetwork.org/content/stories/index.cfm?key=168>.

Faigley, Lester. *Fragments of Rationality: Postmodernity and the Subject of Composition*. Pittsburgh: U of Pittsburgh P, 1992.

Feenberg, Andrew. *Questioning Technology*. New York: Routledge, 1999.

Freeman, Laura. "Job Creation and the Emerging Home Computer Market." *Monthly Labor Review* 119.8 (1996): 46-56.

Gee, James Paul. *Social Linguistics and Literacies: Ideology in Discourses*. London: Falmer Press, 1990.

_____. *What Video Games Have to Teach Us about Learning and Literacy*. New York: Palgrave Macmillan, 2003.

George, Diana. "From Analysis to Design: Visual Communication in the Teaching of Writing." *College Composition and Communication* 54.1 (2002): 11-39.

George, Diana, and Diane Shoos. "Dropping Bread Crumbs in the Intertextual Forest: Critical Literacy in a Postmodern Age." *Passions, Pedagogies and Twenty-First Century Technologies*. Ed. Gail E. Hawisher and Cynthia L. Selfe. Logan: Utah State UP, 1999. 115-26.

Giddens, Anthony. *Central Problems in Social Theory: Action, Structure, and Contradiction in Social Analysis*. Berkeley: U of California P, 1979.

Goodman, William. "The Role of Computers in Reshaping the Work Force." *Monthly Labor Review* 119.8 (1996): 37-45.

Graff, Harvey J. *The Legacies of Literacy: Continuities and Contradictions in Western Culture and Society*. Bloomington: Indiana UP, 1987.

Hawisher, Gail E. "Accessing the Virtual Worlds of Cyberspace." *Journal of Electronic Publishing* 6 (2000). 22 July 2003 <http:/ /www.press.umich.edu/jep/ 06-01/hawisher. html>.

_____. "Research and Recommendations for Computers and Composition." Ed. Gail E. Hawisher and Cynthia L. Selfe. *Critical Perspectives on Computers and Composition Instruction*. New York: Teachers College P, 1989. 44-69.

Hawisher, Gail E., and Cynthia L. Selfe. "Collaborative Configurations: Researching the Literacies of Technology." *Kairos* 7 (2002). 22July 2003 <http://english.ttu.edu/kairos/7.3/binder2.html?cover web/hawisher/index.htm>.

_____. "Teaching Writing at a Distance: What's Gender Got To Do With It?" *Teaching Writing with Computers: An Introduction*. Ed. Pamela Takayoshi and Brian Huot. New York: Houghton Mifflin, 2003. 128-49.

Hawisher, Gail E., and Patricia Sullivan. "Women on the Networks: Searching for E-Spaces of Their Own." Ed. Susan Jarratt and Lynn Worsham. *Feminism and Composition Studies: In Other Words*. New York: MLA, 1998. 172-97.

_____. "How Many Online?" September 2002. *NUA*. 31 July 2003 <http://www.nua.ie/surveys/how_many_online/>.

Hooks, bell. *Talking Back: Thinking Feminist, Thinking Black*. Boston: South End P, 1989.

Jaffe, Alexandra. "Involvement, Detachment, and Representation on Corsica." *When They Read What We Write: The Politics of Ethnography*. Ed. Caroline Brettell. Westport: Bergin and Garvey, 1996. 51-66.

Jessup, Emily. "Feminism and Computers in Composition Instruction." *Evolving Perspectives on Computers and Composition Studies: Questions for the 1990s*. Ed. Gail E. Hawisher and Cynthia L. Selfe. Urbana: NCTE, 1991. 336-55.

Johnston, William B., and Arnold H. Packer. *Workforce 2000: Work and Workers for the Twenty-First Century*. Indianapolis, IN: Hudson Institute, 1987.

Judy, Richard W., and Carol D'Amico. *Workforce 2020: Work and Workers in the Twenty-First Century*. Indianapolis, IN: Hudson Institute, 1997.

Katzenstein, Mary Fainsod, and Judith Reppy, eds. *Beyond Zero Tolerance: Discrimination in Military Culture*. New York: Rowman and Littlefield, 1999.

Kramarae, Cheris. *The Third Shift: Women Learning Online*. Washington, DC: AAUW Educational Foundation, 2001.

Kress, Gunther. "'English' at the Crossroads: Rethinking Curricula of Communication in the Context of the Turn to the Visual." *Passions, Pedagogies, and Twenty-First Century Technologies*. Ed. Gail E Hawisher and Cynthia L. Selfe. Logan: Utah State UP, 1999. 66-88.

_____. *Literacy in the New Media Age*. London: Routledge, 2003.

Kress, Gunther, and Theo Van Leeuwen. *Multimodal Discourse: The Modes and Media of Contemporary Communication*. London: Edward Arnold Ltd., 2001.

Kurzweil, Raymond. *The Age of Intelligent Machines*. Cambridge: MIT P, 1990.

Lemke, Jay L. *Textual Politics: Discourse and Social Dynamics*. London: Taylor and Francis, 1995.

Luke, Carmen. "Cyber-Schooling and Technological Change: Multiliteracies for New Times." *Multiliteracies: Literacy Learning and the Design of Social Futures*. Ed. Bill Cope and Mary Kalantzis. New York: Routledge, 2000. 69-91.

McConnell, Sheila. "The Role of Computers in Reshaping the Work Force." *Monthly Labor Review* 119.8 (1996): 3-10.

Meares, Carol Ann, and John F. Sargent. *The Digital Workforce: Building Infotech Skills at the Speed of Innovation*. Washington, DC: U.S. Department of Commerce and the Office of Technology Policy, 1999.

Merrifield, Juliet, Mary Beth Bingham, David Hemphill, and Kathleen P. deMarrais Bennett, eds. *Life at the Margins: Literacy, Language, and Technology in Everyday Life*. New York: Teachers College P, 1997.

Michigan. Department of Education. *Michigan's State Technology Plan, 1992-1997*. Lansing: Office of Educational Technology, 1992.

Moris, Francisco A. "Semiconductors: The Building Blocks of the Information Revolution." *Monthly Labor Review* 119.8 (1996): 6-17.

Myers, Miles. *Changing Our Minds: Negotiating English and Literacy*. Urbana: NCTE, 1996.

Newburger, Eric. "9-in-10 School-Age Children Have Computer Access." 6 Sept. 2001. *U.S. Department of Commerce News*, Economics and Statistics Administration, Bureau of the Census, Washington, DC. 28 July 2003. <http://www.census.gov/Press-Release/www/2001/cbol-147.html>.

The 1900s: American News and Lifestyle Headlines from 1900-1999...plus a Century of Sound (1999-2000). Archer Audio Archives. 27 July 2003 <http:// archer2000.tripod.com/index.html>.

Norris, Pippa. *Digital Divide: Civic Engagement, Information Poverty, and the Internet Worldwide*. New York: Cambridge UP, 2001.

Paquet, Cheri. "Report Counts 147 Million Global Net Users." 12 February 1999. CNN.com. 31 July 2003 <http://www.cnn.com/TECH/computing/9902/12/globalnet.idg/>.

Pastore, Michael. "Older Americans Lack Confidence in Computing Skills." The Big Picture: Demographics. 3 April 2000. *Cyberatlas*. l Aug. 2003. <http://cyberatlas.internet.com/big_picture/demographics/article/0,,5901_333251,00.html>.

Pew Internet Project. "The Gray Gap." 21 Sept. 2000. *Who's Not Online*. Pew Internet and American Life Project, Washington, DC. 1 Aug. 2003 <http://www.pewinternet.org/reports/reports.asp?Report=21&Section=ReportLevel l&Field=Level1ID&ID=56>.

_____. *Tracking Online Life: How Women Use the Internet to Cultivate Relationships with Family and Friends.* 10 May 2000. Pew Internet and American Life Project, Washington, DC. 1 Aug. 2003 <http://www.pewinternet.org/reports/toc.asp?Report=ll>.

_____. *Wired Seniors: A Fervent Few Inspired by Family Ties.* 9 September 2001. Pew Internet and American Life Project, Washington, DC. 1 Aug. 2003 <http://www.pewinternet.org/reports/toc.asp?Report=40>.

Prior, Paul A. *Writing/Disciplinarity: A Sociohistoric Account of Literate Activity in the Academy.* Mahwah, NJ: Lawrence Erlbaum, 1998.

Romano, Susan. The Egalitarianism Narrative: Whose Story? Which Yardstick? *Computers and Composition* 10.3 (1993): 5-28.

Schoen, Donald. *The Reflexive Practitioner.* New York: Basic Books, 1983.

Selfe, Cynthia. *Technology and Literacy in the Twenty-First Century: The Importance of Paying Attention.* Carbondale: SIU P, 1999.

Selfe, Cynthia L., and Gail E. Hawisher. "A Historical Look at Electronic Literacy." *Journal of Business and Technical Communication* 16.3 (2002): 231-77.

_____. *Literate Lives in the Information Age: Narratives of Literacy from the United States.* Mahwah, NJ: Lawrence Erlbaum, 2004.

Selfe, Cynthia, Gail E. Hawisher, Patricia Ericsson. "Stasis and Change: The Role of Independent Composition Programs and the Dynamic Nature of Literacy." *A Field of Dreams: Independent Writing Programs and the Future of Composition Studies.* Ed. Peggy O'Neill, Angelo Crow, Larry Burton. Logan: Utah State UP, 2002. 268-77.

Spanning the Digital Divide: Understanding and Tackling the Issues. 2001. Bridges.org, South Africa. 29 July 2003. <http://www.bridges.org/spanning>.

Spillers, Hortense J. "Who Cuts the Border: Some Readings on 'America.'" Ed. Hortense Spillers. *Comparative American Identities: Race, Sex, and Nationality in the Modern Text.* New York: Routledge, 1991.1-25.

Street, Brian V. *Social Literacies: Critical Approaches to Literacy in Development, Ethnography, and Education.* New York: Longman, 1995.

Sullivan, Patricia, and Jennie Dautermann, eds. *Electronic Literacies in the Workplace: Technologies of Writing.* Urbana, IL: NCTE, 1996.

"Survey Shows Widespread Enthusiasm for High Technology." February 2000. *NPR Online.* 2 Feb. 2003 <http://www.npr.org/programs/specials/poll/technology/>.

Takayoshi, Pamela. "Building New Networks from the Old: Women's Experiences with Electronic Communications." *Computers and Composition* 11.1 (1994): 21-35.

Treese, Win. *The Internet Index* (no. 22). 22 May 1998. 31 July 2003 <http://www.treese.org/intindex/>.

Tyner, Kathleen. *Literacy in a Digital World: Teaching and Learning in the Age of Information.* Mahwah, NJ: Lawrence Erlbaum, 1998.

United Nations. Human Development Research Organization. *Human Development Report 2001: Making New Technologies Work for Human Development.* 2001. United Nations Development Program, New York: Oxford

UP. 1 Aug. 2003 <http://hdr.undp.org/reports/global/2001/en/>.

United States. Department of Commerce. *Falling through the Net: Defining the Digital Divide.* July 1999. National Telecommunication and Information Administration, Washington, DC. 27 July 2003 <http://www.ntia.doc.gov/ntiahome/digitaldivide/>.

_____. _____. *Falling through the Net: A Survey of the "Have Nots" in Rural and Urban America.* July 1995. National Telecommunications and Information Administration, Washington, DC. 27 July 2003 <http://www.ntia.doc.gov/ntiahome/digitaldivide/>.

_____. _____. *Falling through the Net: Toward Digital Inclusion: A Report on Americans' Access to Technology Tools.* October 2000. Economic and Statistics Administration, and

National Telecommunication and Information Administration, Washington, DC. 27 July 2003 <http://www.ntia.doc.gov/ntiahome/digitaldivide/>.

_____. _____. *Falling through the Net II: New Data on the Digital Divide.* July 1998. National Telecommunication and Information Administration, Washington, DC. 1 Aug. 2003 <http://www.ntia.doc.gov/ntiahome/net2/>.

_____. _____. *A Nation Online: How Americans Are Expanding Their Use of the Internet.* Feb. 2002. National Telecommunications and Information Administration and Economics and Statistics Administration, Washington, DC. 27 July 2003 <http://www.ntia.doc.gov/ntiahome/dn/index.html>.

_____. Department of Education. *The Condition of Education 1997.* 1997. National Center for Educational Statistics 97-388, Washington, DC. 1 Aug. 2003 <http://nces.ed.gov/pubsearch/pubsinfo.asp?pubid=97388>.

_____. Department of Labor. *Futurework: Trends and Challenges for Work in the 21st Century.* Washington, DC: Dept. of Labor, 1999.

Warnke, Jacqueline. "Computer Manufacturing: Change and Competition." *Monthly Labor Review* 119.8 (1996): 18-29.

White, Stephen. *A Brief History of Computing: Complete Timeline.* 1996-2004. 27 July 2003 <http://www.ox.compsoc.net/swhite/timeline.html>.

Wysocki, Anne Frances, and Johndan Johnson-Eilola. "Blinded by the Letter: Why Are We Using Literacy as a Metaphor for Everything Else?" *Passions, Pedagogies, and Twenty-First Century Technologies.* Ed. Gail E. Hawisher and Cynthia L. Selfe. Logan: Utah State UP, 1999. 349-68.

Yagelski, Robert. *Literacy Matters: Writing and Reading the Social Self.* New York: Teachers College P, 2000.

Zakon, Robert H. *Hobbes' Internet Timeline, v7.0.* 1 April 2002. Zakon Group LLC. 27 July 2003 <http://www.zakon.org/robert/internet/timeline/>.

NOW THAT YOU'VE READ

1. Hawisher and Selfe use a method of study called a case study. What is your understanding of a case study, and what might a case study help you learn about literacy? Imagine a case study you might design to better understand how literacy functions within a context.

2. Hawisher and Selfe identify five key themes that emerge from their case studies:
   - literacies have life spans
   - people can exert their own powerful agency in, around, and through digital literacies
   - schools are not the sole—and often, not even the primary—gateways through which people gain access to and practice digital literacies
   - the specific conditions of access have a substantial effect on people's acquisition and development of digital literacy
   - families transmit literacy values and practices in multiple directions

   Did any of these findings surprise you? Have you noticed any of these findings in your own thinking about literacy and sponsorship?

3. Hawisher and Selfe claim: "We do not want to indicate with this discussion, however, that people can *always* accomplish anything they want within

the social structures they inhabit or that their actions are always effective in the ways they intend. Clearly, people are constrained by any number of influential factors: age, class, race, gender, handicap, experience, opportunity, and belief systems are among only a few such factors." What evidence of this claim do you see in the article? In other articles you've read this semester? In your own experience or knowledge of others' experiences?

4. Near the end of the article, Hawisher and Selfe discuss issues of access and its complications. What is access, and how is this concept relevant to our studies of literacy and literacy sponsorship?

5. Hawisher and Selfe conclude their article with this warning to writing scholars: "Our professional radar is tuned so narrowly to the bandwidth of print and the alphabetic—to school-based and workplace writing—that we miss a great deal of the more interesting and engaging self-sponsored reading and composing students do on their own time." Have you noticed this exclusion in other texts you have read this semester? As you study literacy, how can you be sure to be inclusive of these more "interesting and engaging" literacy practices?

READING

Talking About Literacy

David Barton

By now you are aware that "literacy" can be a slippery term. You and your classmates may be wondering: What does it mean? When do we use it? Can it be overused? Is *everything* a literacy? David Barton is a scholar who takes on this question. This article shows why this debate is complicated and why the language we use to describe a concept matters.

BEFORE YOU READ answer the following questions:

1. What is a metaphor? How do metaphors help us understand concepts? What metaphor have you heard that helped you understand a concept?

2. Given what you have already learned about literacy, what kinds of metaphors might you imagine would be useful for learning about literacy as a concept?

Talking about Literacy

David Barton

Metaphors for literacy

Like a germ that learns to enjoy penicillin, illiteracy consumes all the armies sent to fight it. No matter what we do about it—and we do a good deal, contrary to complaints from the literacy lobby—the condition persists. Depending on how you count them, adult illiterates make up anywhere from a tenth to a fifth of the Canadian population. We have no reason to think their number is shrinking, and some reason to fear that it is growing...social evil...illiteracy is caused...The remedy...

The metaphors are clear in this leader from the *Financial Times* of Canada on 4 July 1988. Ideas of disease and warfare come over in every word. The author of this emotive writing, Robert Fulford, then went on to make some interesting points about the *illiteracy* of the ghostwriting of speeches for politicians, thus stretching the term in a different direction.

Such metaphors are common in the media and in public discussion. In an interview on television the then Archbishop of Canterbury argued that the inner-city riots in Britain in 1991 were due to 'a matrix of illiteracy and delinquency and other wrongdoing'. Around the same time a leading British politician referred to a situation where there was 'not a high level of literacy so people were excitable and likely to be led astray'. Again the metaphors are clear, and especially revealing if you observe how literacy is juxtaposed with other negative terms suggesting weakness and crime.

The disease metaphor particularly is very pervasive. It can be used to damn the illiterate, as in the examples above, or it can be used to praise the literate. An example of the latter is to be found in Bruce Chatwin's novel *Utz*; referring to Prague in the mid-twentieth century, the narrator comments: 'The Soviet education system, I felt, had worked all too well: having created on a colossal scale, a generation of highly intelligent, highly literate young people who were more or less immune to the totalitarian message' (1988, p. 118). There is a great deal on literacy to draw out of this quote and I will return to it later on. For the moment, the idea that literacy is an inoculation, making one *immune* to brain-washing, is a further example of the disease metaphor.

Talking about a disease which has to be eradicated is also a common way in which literacy is discussed as a social issue. Powerful images can be built up with this metaphor, as in a recent newspaper headline: '12-year-olds caught in epidemic of illiteracy'. Further links are suggested by a cursory glance at other newspaper headlines: across the world illiteracy is often linked with criminality, with not being able to get a job, and with being a drain on the economy.

To move to another metaphor, a view of literacy which is at the root of much educational practice is that of treating it as a skill or set of skills. This has been very powerful in the design of literacy programmes at all levels of education. The acts of reading and writing are broken down into a set of skills and subskills. These skills are ordered into a set of levels starting with pre-reading skills and they are then taught in a particular order, each skill building upon the previous. Literacy is seen as a psychological variable which can be measured and assessed. Skills are treated as things which people own or possess; some are **transferable skills**, some are not. Learning to read and write becomes a technical problem and the successful reader and writer is a **skilled** reader and writer. As an educational definition of literacy, this view is very powerful, and it is one which spills over into the rest of society. It is often drawn on in government strategies for literacy.

It is important to realize that this idea of skills is a particular way of thinking about literacy; it is no less a metaphor than the disease metaphor. Everywhere there are metaphors for talking about reading and writing, some very graphic, others less so. Paulo Freire, for example, presented the idea of traditional literacy education as being **banking**, where knowledge is deposited in a person. It is a *thing*, almost an object which is given and received; shifting the metaphor slightly, empty people are filled up with literacy. He contrasts this deficit view with a view of literacy as a form of empowerment, as a right, as something which people do, a process rather than a thing.

Everyone has a view of literacy, and opinions on the subject are often held tenaciously. These views are expressed through metaphors. However, different metaphors have different implications for how we view illiteracy, what action might be taken to change it and how we characterize the people involved. For example, if illiteracy is a disease, then the people involved are sick, it should be eradicated, and experts need to be called in to do the job. If it is a psychological problem, then therapy or counselling are needed. Other metaphors call for training, empowerment, special education or social support. The participants might be construed as students, customers, clients or recipients. The blame, if it is blameworthy, might be attributed to fate, the individual, the school, the family, or the social structure. Note that some metaphors are within the education sphere, while others branch out into counselling, therapy and elsewhere. In all of them literacy has been socially constructed. Kenneth Levine discusses this (1985, p. 172) and has a tentative chart of different social ways of talking about illiteracy. Table 2.1 is an updated version of this.

Table 2.1 Some ways of talking about literacy

	Condition	Response	Means	Goal	Application
1	Sickness	Treatment	Clinical intervention	Remittance	
	Handicap	Rehabilitation	Compensatory aids	Alleviation	Dyslexia
2	Ignorance	Training	Instruction	Mastery	Orthodox literacy tuition
3	Incapacity	Therapy	Counselling	Adjustment Assimilation Autonomy	
4	Oppression	Empowerment	Political organization / legislation	Rights	Conscientization
5	Deprivation	Welfare	Reallocation of material resources	Benefit	Positive discrimination
6	Deviance	Control	Isolation Containment Physical coercion	Correction Conformity	Negative discrimination

Another approach is to view literacy in terms of access to knowledge and information. To be literate is to have access to the world of books and other written material. When viewed this way, the word literacy itself has become a metaphor which has been applied to other areas. This has happened with terms like **cultural literacy**, **computer literacy**, **information literacy**, **visual literacy** and **political literacy**. Here we see literacy loosely as understanding an area of knowledge.

The trouble with metaphors for literacy such as that of a disease or a set of skills is that they are limited in scope and do not capture the breadth of what is involved in reading and writing. I want to explore this, but first it is necessary to say some general words on metaphors and theories, in order to make clear the approach being taken in this book.

Theories and metaphors

In arguing for a different way of thinking about literacy, it is important to be very conscious and reflective about this activity. We need to be very clear about the language we are using. Throughout, I will be scrutinizing and deconstructing many of the concepts which structure and scaffold the ideas of literacy. This will include notions of **reading**, **writing**, **skill**, **illiterate**. The discussion will also embrace many ideas and concepts which do not appear at first to be directly related to literacy, such as when we examine what is meant by terms such as **learning**, **evolution**, **mainstream culture**. In addition, in slipping from discipline to discipline it will be obvious that terms are used in different ways. What I am trying to do is to find a way of talking about literacy which can bring together insights from these different areas. What is needed is not exactly a definition of literacy; rather we need a metaphor, a model, a way of talking about literacy. What sort of activity is literacy?

Before addressing this set of questions, it is necessary to say a few words about metaphors in general, how they work and what their role is. The notion of metaphors used here is broader than the everyday use of the term. I will describe what I mean by metaphor, then I will look at some definitions of literacy and describe some of the ways of talking about the subject which are developing in the field of literacy studies. When this has been done I will move on to another metaphor for literacy.

As part of living we all make sense of our lives; we can talk about what do; we explain and justify our actions, our feelings and our intentions. We construct theories to make sense of the world. Our theories affect our action, just as our emotions and our intentions affect our actions. We adjust and change our theories in the light of experience. This applies to literacy as much as to any other part of life. Everyone has a view of literacy; everyone in some way makes sense of it. Everyone who uses terms like **reading** has a theory of the nature of literacy underlying their use of the word. I am going to call these views of literacy people's **everyday theories** of literacy. They are sometimes called **folk theories**. I prefer everyday theories, as folk already has the idea in it that they are not really true and is therefore pejorative in some sense.

These points about everyday theories apply equally to the theories of the specialist, the professional, the researcher. These people have theories which they (we?) are often more conscious of. However, these theories, which I will call **professional theories**, are developed and changed in a similar manner to everyday theories. The main differences between everyday and professional theories are that the latter are often more articulated and explicit; often they aim to be more general; they can be checked in more systematic ways; they are formalized into a seemingly impersonal body of knowledge and they are often passed on in an explicit way by teaching. These bodies of expert knowledge often have higher status and more authority, partly by getting into print. Particular theories can be backed by government policies and then promoted and supported by extensive funding. These official theories become dominant. They can be legally enforced and become the orthodox authoritative way of seeing an issue. Nevertheless, professional theories can be wrong, misleading and harmful and they are not necessarily superior to everyday theories. It is important not to give special privilege to professional theories as being inevitable right, or perfect, or as replacing everyday theories.

I distinguish everyday theories and professional theories but they are similar in kind. In people's actual lives they overlap. Social science and other theories *leak* into life, to use another metaphor. They provide the terminology and framework for talking about an area. For example, some of the concepts of Freud's theories about the mind and the subconscious have passed into everyday language. Another example would be views on child care, where the theories of psychologists and others influence everyday practices, including ways of talking about children. It is important to realize that professional theories can influence everyday discourse but in many areas, as far apart as nuclear energy, medical knowledge and general public understanding of science, there are questions raised about the role of professionals and the status of expert knowledge.

When talking about theories of literacy so far, one of the main professional theories underlying media, politicians' and parents' talk is that of literacy as a set of skills. It is a professional theory, embodied in textbooks and teaching materials, taught in institutions, supported by a legal infrastructure and guiding much literacy instruction in schools and colleges. It also leaks into life and forms part of people's everyday theories of literacy. The idea of skills and levels becomes the way parents talk about their children's progress; this approach may suggest, for example, that as a set of skills reading is best taught by a teacher, that learning to read should be isolated from other learning, and that the parents have no independent role in a child's learning to read.

The leak between everyday and professional theories works in both directions. As well as professional theories influencing everyday discussion, there is an influence in the opposite direction. Professional theories are articulated mainly in words from everyday life; words like 'intelligence' or 'evolution' are given more technical meanings, as researchers try to talk in a more precise manner. Nevertheless, professional theories are incomplete and are expressed partly in ordinary language. Inevitably, everyday usage fills the gaps left in these theories. The teacher of literacy at any level is partly guided by professional theories put over in training courses, but teaching is guided equally by everyday knowledge which fills out and completes the partial professional theories. This is inevitable and is part of the nature of theories; it is not some failure of professional theories. Another result of this mixing of different sorts of theories is that it is not clear whether common academic theories, such as 'the great divide' between oral and literate or the superiority of the alphabet over other writing systems, are mainly everyday theories or professional theories. This argument about the role of everyday theories in professional theories is relevant throughout the book and should be borne in mind in several of the discussions.

Another aspect of theories which is important for the discussion on literacy is that they are developed from experience in particular areas; they are then stretched to cover larger areas. The example of literacy as a set of skills will be given later as an illustration of this. Our knowledge is always partial and we need to generalize our experience to make sense of more of life. As a consequence, the backing for our theories is always partial. Mistakenly, we often look for one answer to cover everything, so that theories which are half true get extended too far to cover inappropriate areas.

Theories also differ in what they emphasize. This has its roots in the fact that theories differ in what they set out to do. Take, for example, the idea of individual differences in how quickly children learn to read. If you need to classify children in school and later in college, then grading and sorting become very important. Individual differences in how children learn to read, however small and impermanent, become highly salient. In another theory such differences might be completely irrelevant. Or to give another example related to literacy, issues of access and power are important in critical approaches to literacy, while in other theories they could hardly even be plausible concepts.

Metaphors and thinking

In the approach being taken here I am also making certain assumptions about the mind and thinking: crucially, there is an internal world, there is an external world, and there is some relation between the two. I will be taking a **constructivist** view of this, where people construct a mental model of the external world, with language at the centre of the construction. As a starting point, our theories are articulated in language, and in everyday language. One way of doing this is with metaphors, through the words we use, the labels we give things and the names we give to activities. This is a normal use of language and, in fact, there is no alternative to it. We use language to imagine what the world is like and what it might be like.

Most of language relies on metaphors, most words and relations between words are metaphors. One reason for this is that we need metaphors for talking about things which are not concrete. A common starting point is the physical world. We use physical distance to talk about time, for instance, as in 'the week ahead' or 'from Monday to Friday'. Crucially, metaphors for the mind are often structured from the physical world too; this relates to literacy with such ideas as that of putting thoughts into writing. The skills metaphor, which posits a set of abilities which we either have or do not have, represents another very physical metaphor. We internalize the physical as metaphors for representing the abstract. I will not pursue this in any detail here. (And it is not essential for you to believe this in order to continue reading. I will just keep to the parts which are necessary for a discussion about literacy.)

Another shift between different areas is the way we use 'say' for 'read', 'see' for 'understand', 'talk' for 'write'. This is interesting in that since listening is aural and reading visual, they get mixed around: 'I don't see what this book is saying', or in this book where I write 'what I am talking about is...', or a letter I received which asked me to '...say in writing the things we discussed on the phone'. This is common everywhere, including the teacher talking to the young child in the beginning reading classroom, and we are usually oblivious of the fact that we mix these modalities. One researcher even reports the anecdote of the child who thought herself deaf because she could not hear the letters whispering to her—she could not hear what the letters said.

Something further to say about metaphors is that they themselves are part of larger systems; they fit together and form discourses, which are coherent ways of representing the world (Gee, 1996; Fairclough, 1992). Words are situated within the structures of other words. Metaphors are part of whole theories. They are like the tips of icebergs, in that the words we use bring whole theories with them. Using one aspect of the visual metaphor for understanding can imply others. Looking more broadly, concepts like **intelligence**, **evolution**, **society** and **the individual** are also used within the frameworks of broader discourses, although these might be more difficult to ascertain. These terms are important as **organizing ideas**. They organize a domain and stretch beyond a domain. Intelligence and evolution are two organizing ideas used in everyday thought. They are theories, they are metaphors of everyday thought. Simultaneously, they do two opposing things for the areas they are applied to—such as when talking about literacy. On the one hand, they enrich our everyday thinking; at the same time they constrain it. These other words inevitably have to become part of the discussion of literacy. Even seemingly innocent everyday terms when discussing literacy such as **mainstream**, **western**, or the insidious use of 'our' when discussing literacy practices assume that the reader and writer share cultural practices. (I am also guilty of this.) These terms need to be unpacked.

We need these organizing principles to help us make sense of the complex world we live in. A good theory or metaphor illuminates. It takes you further, it provides new insights and makes new connections. Concepts link with other concepts and we need to group them together. This view of metaphor will recur; it is an essential aspect of the constructivist view of language of chapter 5. It has implications for how people make sense of the world, how children develop, and what language is.

Definitions of literacy

Looking for a precise definition of literacy may be an impossible task; the idea that complex concepts are susceptible to dictionary-like definitions is probably a myth. Nevertheless, dictionaries codify some view of usage, and dictionary definitions can be a useful starting point on the way to a broader view of literacy, a theory of literacy. We need a way of talking about literacy which can encompass these definitions. In this section I will explore what can be learnt from dictionaries and the information they provide. It is a useful place to start as long as we do not confuse the meaning of a word with its etymology and we are not searching for some basic real or literal meaning. Although there is obviously a link, dictionary definitions also need to be distinguished from people's actual usages of words in their everyday speech.

The words **reading**, **writing** and **literacy** have many meanings. **Reading** can go from the mechanical uttering of the newsreader to the innumerable levels of interpreting any text. In the sense of understanding meanings, reading has always been applied to a wide range of phenomena, including the reading of barometers, tea-leaves and facial expressions. The word has now been extended to include the different interpretations people—readers—might have of a poem, a novel or a film. Reading is deconstructing.

The English word **writing** has a systematic ambiguity so that a good writer is on some occasions a neat scribe and accurate speller, while on other occasions the term means a creative author, whether the texts are academic essays, novels or advertising copy. Which of these two meanings of writing should be dominant is a constant conflict in education, whether in the primary school or in the adult education class. We will return to these terms in the chapters on children's learning and on educational metaphors.

Literacy is a fairly recent English word and its meaning is being extended. I am using the term to cover new broader views of reading and writing, and that is how it is being used in several disciplines and in terms like emergent literacy, used in education. As already pointed out, it is extended in another way to mean competent and knowledgeable in specialized areas, with terms like computer literacy, economic literacy and political literacy. People talk of different 'literacies', so that different media can be discussed, and film literacy, for example, can then be contrasted with print literacy.

Tracing the historical changes in how dictionaries deal with such words is instructive. With literacy there are actually four words to consider: literate, illiterate, literacy and illiteracy and there can be both nouns, an illiterate, and adjectives, literate behaviour. Going back to Samuel Johnson's first dictionary of English in 1755, only one of the terms we are interested in, illiterate, is to be found. I have examined 20 dictionaries published in the nineteenth century and early in the twentieth century. *Barclay's Dictionary* of 1820 also only has illiterate. Illiteracy is found in *Walker's Critical Pronouncing Dictionary* of 1839 with the caveat that it is an uncommon word. Literate, but only in the sense of educated or learned, sometimes appears too. There will be examples later of how in contemporary life the term is sometimes used to mean educated and how sometimes it is contrasted with education.

Literacy is not found in a dictionary dated 1913 but appears in dictionaries from 1924 on. There is also a change in the meaning of literate. A new meaning 'being able to read and write' is added. This meaning gradually grows in importance, so that in contemporary dictionaries, such as the *COBUILD English Language Dictionary* or the *Concise Oxford*, it is the first meaning, with 'educated' given as a subsidiary meaning.

The full-length *Oxford English Dictionary* has literate in the sense of educated right back in 1432, with a second meaning of one in holy orders coming later. I assume from the evidence of the other dictionaries that it was not a very common word. Illiterate dates from 1556 and is the only one of these four terms which Shakespeare uses; illiteracy dates from 1660. It is more than 200 years before literacy appears, in 1883 in a sentence from the *New England Journal of Education* about Massachusetts being 'the first State in the Union in literacy' (although the *Random House Dictionary* places 'literacy test' more than a decade earlier). Its origin is given as being from the word 'illiteracy'. Literate in the sense of being able to read and write, the opposite of illiterate, does not appear until 1894. Some of the quotes in the dictionary give a flavour of the historical connotations of the term. A quote from 1859 talks of putting 'the literate and the ignorant' on one level. A quote from 1628 refers to 'a weakling or illiterate'. The claim from 1894 could still be debated today, that 'literates contribute a larger percentage of their class to the criminal ranks than do illiterates'. In addition, illiterates are not cast totally in a negative light: there was a concern in 1865 that as a result of 'intellectual tests the army will exclude from it the dashing illiterates whose stout hearts and strong thews and sinews made it what it was under the Duke'.

Application of the term literacy to other areas such as economic literacy and computer literacy is much more recent. The *Oxford English Dictionary* has a quotation from 1943 referring to economic literacy. The idea of literacy in a communications medium is represented by a quote from the *BBC Handbook of 1962* which refers to television and 'our skills in understanding the medium and our own literacy in it'. Other dictionary examples of the terms include musical literacy, sexual illiteracy and a house being described as having an illiterate design.

Linguists talk of unmarked and marked terms, where with pairs of opposites the natural, normal, default and common word is the unmarked, such as 'honest', and the other derived word is marked, as in 'dishonest'. One might expect literacy to be the unmarked term and illiteracy the marked version which is derived from it. But in terms of history and frequency of usage illiteracy, a fairly pejorative term, is the natural or unmarked term and literacy comes from it. Illiteracy belongs to a class of words—disability is another example—where the longer word with an additional morpheme is the unmarked. Literacy and illiteracy do not have to be paired together, of course. Literacy is sometimes contrasted with **orality**, or with another neologism **oracy**. **Nonliterate** can be used as a less pejorative sounding alternative to illiterate; or the two can be used with different meanings, illiterate meaning not being able to read within a culture which is literate, while nonliterate covers people in a culture which has never had literacy. Even talk of a literate culture is an extension of the word beyond the idea of literacy being a property of individual people.

Literate is also contrasted with **numerate**, a word going back only to 1959 in the dictionary, where it was deliberately coined in a British report by the Central Advisory Council for Education, along with **numeracy** and **innumeracy**. The authors of the report are quite conscious of coining the words, unlike most new words, which slip into the language unannounced. In the report the words are contrasted with literate, literacy and illiteracy. A different and much older meaning of numerate as counted or numerated goes back at least to 1432, a similar age to literate in the *Oxford English Dictionary*.

Translation of these terms brings its headaches, puzzles and contradictions. Literacy does not easily translate into French, while there is no easy English equivalent of the French sense of *ecriture* as 'writings', and *illetrisme* as 'unlettered' is not common in English. Jean-Paul Hautecoeur (1990) points out that in the world of adult education *illetrisme* is used in France, whereas *analphabetisme* is more common in other French-speaking places such as Quebec. A word like 'unalphabetized' exists in other languages including Spanish, Italian, Greek and Danish. Note that it is a partisan word: in its make-up there is the idea that an alphabetic writing system is necessary in order to be literate. In several languages there is a verbal equivalent, like *alfabetizar* in Spanish, meaning to make literate. In English alphabetize is something you might do to a list or even to a writing system, but not normally to a person. English lacks any such verb for the act of making people literate.

I will give two examples where I have encountered problems with translation. These demonstrate the confusions which can result. Firstly in Angers, France a group of us from different countries planning an adult education conference argued amicably about the contents of the conference, about whether it should be generally on literacy or specifically on problems with writing. We then argued confusedly about the title. The English-speaking side felt the French wanted a general conference on literacy but then inexplicably wanted the title to be restricted to 'Writing'. After a morning of cross-cultural miscommunication, it was the patient translators who first realized that the problem was one of translating the term literacy.

A second problem arose in a seminar when a group of us were discussing a paper which compares print literacy and film literacy. Firstly with Japanese, and then also with Greek and Danish, we discovered the difficulty (or impossibility) of translating a term like film literacy into other languages. Take Japanese, for example: it has a word for illiteracy equivalent to sentence-blindness and made up of the two characters *mon mou*, and the word for literacy means the recognition of letters. However, the word could not be used to mean film literacy or computer literacy. A general word for competence or knowledge could be used but it would not make the link with literacy. In Japanese one would say the equivalent of 'the ability to appreciate films', or 'the ability to manipulate computers'. Where computer literacy has been used the term has been directly transliterated into Japanese.

Literacy studies

The meaning of the word literacy is to be found not just by examining dictionary entries. It has become a unifying term across a range of disciplines for changing views of reading and writing; there has been such a growth of study in the area that it is now referred to as **Literacy Studies** or the **New Literacy Studies**.

The history of the term, and the field, can partly be seen in the way titles of key books have staked claims to the area. Prior to 1980 hardly any books mentioned literacy in the title. In the early 1980s there were one or two a year. This increased during the decade and 15 books published in 1991 had 'literacy' in the title. The titles reveal a great deal. One of the first key books in the field was *Language and literacy: the sociolinguistics of reading and writing* (Stubbs, 1980). There is clearly a definition of literacy in that title. This was followed in 1981 by *The psychology of literacy* (Scribner and Cole, 1981) which at the time seemed a challenging title, claiming so much more than books entitled *The psychology of reading*. Already we knew that it relates to the 'social order' (Cressy, 1980) and that there is a 'literacy myth' (Graff, 1979). Although a short article rather than a book, a whole methodological approach was suggested with 'The ethnography of literacy' (Szwed, 1981). Others then asserted that literacy has a 'social context' (Levine, 1985) and is 'socially constructed' (Cook-Gumperz, 1986). It has theory underlying it as well as practice (Street, 1984). It relates to 'popular culture' (Vincent, 1989) and it is 'emergent' in children (Teale and Sulzby, 1986). Other words in titles make links with literacy, including orality, empowerment, involvement, culture and politics, right up to interest in 'ideology in discourses' (Gee, 1996), or it simply goes under the heading *The new literacy* (Willinsky, 1990).'Ecology' is one more link, one which can bring together many of these strands.

More recently, a wide range of studies of literacy practices in different settings have been published. Literacy practices in a variety of different 'worlds' are presented in Hamilton et al. (1994) and in a range of different 'situated' settings in Barton et al. (2000). Community literacies have been studied in Australia (Breen et al., 1994) and South Africa (Prinsloo and Breier, 1996). The personal letter-writing practices of Pacific islanders are examined in Besnier (1993). Wagner studied Arabic speakers in Morocco (1993). American studies have often been of the literacies of minority communities, such as Moss (1994), Reder (1987, 1994) and Perez (2004). Moll's work relates the school and community practices of Hispanics in the southern United States (1994,see also Gonzalez et al., 2005). Merrifield et al. (1996) studied two distinct communities, urban Appalachians and Californian immigrant Americans, exploring their literacies and learning in different contexts. Minority bilingual communities have also been studied in Britain (Saxena, 1994; Bhatt et al., 1996; Baynham, 1993; Gregory, 1996; Martin-Jones and Jones, 2000a). Some researchers have focused on particular social institutions, such as literacy in religious groups (Fishman, 1988, 1991;Kapitzke, 1995) or in the workplace (Gowen, 1992; Gee et al., 1996; Belfiore et al., 2004). A similar ethnographic approach has been taken by researchers investigating children's literacies at home and at school (Schieffelin and Gilmore, 1986; Mahiri, 2004, also in the case studies in Moje and O'Brien, 2000, and to some extent in Serpell et al., 2004), and children's nonformal literacies (Carnitta, 1993; Maybin, 2006). Denny Taylor has produced a series of studies of literacy within families (Taylor, 1983, 1996, 1997; Taylor and Dorsey-Gaines, 1988). Fingerer and Drennon (1997) studied the impact of participation in literacy programmes on adults' practices outside the class. In chapter 4 I describe some of these studies of literacy practices in more detail.

In this book, I restrict myself mainly to print literacy. This means saying little about orality on the one hand, and on the other hand, different media. This is deliberate, and discussion throughout will make it clear how this is in many ways a practical decision to do with restricting the topic to a manageable one. I have taken print literacy as a starting point for understanding a much broader field; for me, there is something to say about written language in a fairly precise way which would not be possible in a broader, more diffuse and less focused discussion. Having said this, I also emphasize throughout the book that the borders of what counts as print literacy are becoming increasingly fuzzy and that one cannot isolate print literacy from other forms of meaning-making when trying to understand the complexity of people's lives or the demands of education and other spheres. Gunther Kress in particular talks of **multimodality** and how print literacy is intertwined with other modes, especially the visual mode, and how reading changes as society shifts from a reliance on the page to reading the screen. (See Kress and van Leeuwen, 2001; Kress, 2003; Snyder, 2002.)

A key to new views of literacy is situating reading and writing in its social context. In the books named above many people in different disciplines have been moving in the same direction. I will draw attention to just a few of them here, describing more in later chapters and drawing upon their ideas throughout. I will begin with three important academic studies, the work of Sylvia Scribner and Michael Cole, Brian Street, and Shirley Brice Heath. Their studies are well-known and have been extremely influential. In their different ways they provide three threads to weave together to represent the beginnings of literacy studies and they have become classics in the field.

They are part of different research traditions but they actually have a great deal in common. All three academic studies looked at particular societies in detail, examining separate groups within a society and how they use literacy. They start from everyday life and what people read and write. They observe closely and they are willing to make use of a wide range of evidence. Each study makes comparisons between groups in a society, teasing out differences, but they avoid making grand generalizations. Rather, they make points about the particular situations they have studied. They provide ideas for other people looking at specific situations. Equally importantly, they raise more general questions about what is meant by literacy. Part of what comes with these studies is a recognition of the complexity of the idea of literacy and the fact that much of our understanding of it is not obvious. This leads to new definitions of literacy.

Briefly, Scribner and Cole, working within traditions of cross-cultural psychology, carried out a fascinating study of the uses of literacy among the Vai of north-west Liberia. Their study was very detailed, covering the writing systems, how people learned to read and write, the uses of literacy. Their methods included interviews, observations and a whole battery of psychological tests. They provide detailed descriptions of different forms of literacy, including those which are learned informally and which exist outside the educational system.

Their book (1981) is a very readable account of their work. In it we can see how they shift their ideas from the notion of literacy as a set of skills with identifiable consequences. They are edging towards their alternative notion of a **practice account** of literacy, arguing that literacy can only be understood in the context of the social practices in which it is acquired and used. They conclude their study:

> Instead of focusing exclusively on the technology of a writing system and its reputed consequences...we approach literacy as a set of socially organized practices which make use of a symbol system and a technology for producing and disseminating it. Literacy is not simply knowing how to read and write a particular script but applying this knowledge for specific purposes in specific contexts of use. The nature of these

practices, including, of course, their technological aspects, will determine the kinds of skills ('consequences') associated with literacy. (Scribnerand Cole, 1981, p. 236)

There is a great deal to do with definitions in this quote and I will return to it. For the moment, we can see in their work that the move to attending to social aspects of literacy inevitably involves a shift in the ways of studying and researching the topic. It is a shift from a psychological paradigm to a social paradigm. In reading their book you can trace the development of their thinking as their research unfolds. They move away from traditional psychological thinking with the notion of discrete individual variables which can be added together towards other approaches. They begin to talk in terms of literacy practices, a term which will be central to the discussion of the next chapter. Their work has also been influential more generally in new work bringing together psychology with other disciplines concerned with locating individuals in their cultural contexts. These are loosely described as socio-cultural approaches.

Heath and Street have a different starting point. They begin from more descriptive social and anthropological methodologies. Street studied Islamic villagers in Iran; he lived there as an anthropologist and carried out ethnographic fieldwork. Part of this included examining people's reading and writing. He describes his approach as an **ideological** approach to literacy, one that accepts that what is meant by literacy varies from situation to situation and is dependent on ideology. He contrasts his approach with **autonomous** approaches which claim that literacy can be defined separately from the social context. He describes how: 'the meaning of literacy depends on the social institutions in which it is embedded...[and]...the particular practices of reading and writing that are taught in any context depend upon such aspects of social structure as stratification...and the role of educational institutions' (Street, 1984,p. 8). Like Scribner & Cole he talks in terms of practices. His distinction between ideological and autonomous has proved to be a powerful one and has been taken up by people studying many areas, including potentially difficult topics for a social account such as assessment (see for example, Hill and Parry, 1994).

The third study is Heath's work in the south-eastern United States. Her book, *Ways with words* (1983) is another book which is very enjoyable to read. She developed close ties with three Appalachian communities in the United States over seven years and used ethnographic and sociolinguistic methods to provide detailed descriptions of people's uses of reading and writing in the home and in the community. Having a clear idea of the reading and writing done in the home and the community, she then turned to school, examining the relation between home literacies and school literacies. When defining literacy Heath comments: '...the concept of literacy covers a multiplicity of meanings, and definitions of literacy carry implicit but generally unrecognized views of its functions (what literacy can do for individuals) and its uses (what individuals can do with literacy skills)' (Heath, 1980, p. 123). This contrast between what literacy does for people and what people do with literacy has been taken up by several researchers. Heath's work has been important in getting people to focus on actual instances where people use reading and writing in their day-to-day lives, **literacy events**. It has been influential throughout education; it has made educators examine in detail the literacy in classroom activities, and it has made them think about what reading and writing goes on in the home and the community.

Here I have concentrated on what these three studies have to say about definitions of literacy. To round this out as a mini-history of literacy studies, two general collections of papers were published in 1985 (Olson et al., 1985; De Castell et al., 1986) and a reader not long after (Kintgen et al., 1988). Then the subject was on its way, with books and articles almost too numerous to keep up with. This has been a brief overview. Work by other people and references to a range of studies will be woven into the text in the next few chapters.

So far I have dealt with academic researchers. Another person who has contributed to social approaches to literacy, but from a very different direction, is the Brazilian educator Paulo Freire. His is a distinct approach to literacy going back more than 40 years. He has been very influential throughout the world in the area of adult literacy and I have already referred to one of his metaphors, that of education as banking; his work will come up again in several places, in relation to metaphors, in terms of literacy and thought, and when discussing adult literacy programmes. There is continuing interest in his approach, notably in work in the United States with adults learning English and in literacy programmes in developing countries. Some examples in the US are Auerbach and Wallerstein (2004), Shor (1987); and in Britain, Kirkwood and Kirkwood (1989). In developing countries, there has been a continuing interest in the REFLECT programme, developed on the basis of Freire's work (see Archer and Cottingham 1996, and see ch.13).

In many ways Freire is starting from a different place from the other people mentioned so far; he has different aims, he is asking different questions and, crucially, underlying his approach is a different view of literacy. He makes explicit the fact that in practical terms literacy teaching takes place within a social context. Adults in the world today who cannot read and write tend to be the poorest, the least powerful, the oppressed. It is the inequalities in the world which foster illiteracy. Accepting this and examining it is the starting point of his approach. Literacy teaching begins with a critical examination of society and of the participants' relationship to it. Literacy education inevitably involves change and the first step is analysing and understanding one's own position in society. Inevitably, questions concerning the inequalities of power in the teaching relationship and more broadly in society have a central role. Like others, Freire is very aware that literacy can be used for different purposes, that it can have *domesticating* effects and that it can have *empowering* or *liberating* effects. It gets defined in very different ways. The link between his work and the academic studies is that he demonstrates from a different direction that there is not a monolithic 'thing' called literacy.

One way in which literacy studies is linked to more general shifts in thought is the way in which the topic is described as **critical**. Freire's is an explicitly critical view of literacy. Critical can mean several things. There is a sense in which all education is critical, to the extent that it involves teaching people to reason, evaluate and think clearly. This is basic and important, but it loses some force when all educators claim to be critical and empowering. Another sense of critical is what I am doing here, subjecting the term literacy to examination, analysis and deconstruction, and coming up with a critical discourse on the topic. Such deconstruction can result in a critical examination of public usage, of media images, and of current educational provision—hopefully in a constructive way.

In addition, there is a further sense: critical literacy links up with critical theory, an umbrella term for much more general approaches to the nature of knowledge which emphasize how social structure affects individuals, and describe the inequalities in access and power which constrain what people can do in their lives (Giroux, 1983; Livingstone, 1987; Gee, 1996; Luke and Walton, 1994). In this sense links can also be made with critical approaches to the study of language such as Clark et al. (1990, 1991).

Literacy studies has the potential to have an influence at all three of these levels, relating to theories of inequality and searching for practical ways of empowering people, giving them a right to the possibilities of literacy. While social approaches to literacy are not inevitably critical, many people, such as Luke (2005), see a critical approach as an essential part of a social approach. As Mary Talbot puts it, 'Looking at language critically is a way of *denaturalising* it—questioning and making strange conventions which usually seem perfectly natural to people who use them. It can help *empower* them in the sense of giving them greater conscious control over aspects of their lives especially how language shapes them' (Talbot, 1992, p. 174).

Looking for a metaphor

Literacy studies covers a wide area, and I will deal with many different topics. It is hard to jump from children in schools, to adults at work, or to many different cultures and different historical periods, as well as describing in brief what language is and what learning consists of. I want to bring these diverse topics together, to integrate and expand upon them. We need a way of talking about literacy which can encompass all this. To keep it all in mind a metaphor would be useful.

So far I have called this a social approach to literacy. However, it is more than just adding the social as an extra dimension, a variable to be taken account of. Literacy has a social meaning; people make sense of literacy as a social phenomenon and their social construction of literacy lies at the root of their attitudes, their actions, and their learning. Nevertheless, in starting from the social, it is important to make clear that, as they exist at present, social approaches are not in themselves adequate. Adding the prefix 'socio-' to a word is not a magic way of conveying the meaning of good, or easy, or politically acceptable. One problem with social approaches is that they usually treat important psychological concepts like thinking, learning and memory as basic unquestionable and unanalysable concepts. In Jean Lave's terms (1988, p. 18), it regards them as 'unexamined primitive elements'. In addition, social approaches do not necessarily have a historical perspective and they may not be dynamic in the sense of viewing people as active decision makers.

It is important not to reject psychological approaches out of hand. There are certain psychological traditions which have been the basis of work on reading and writing. Alone they are inadequate. However, there are other traditions which are becoming more prominent, such as that drawing on the work of the Russian psychologist Lev Vygotsky, which aim to bridge the gap between social and psychological. Vygotsky was concerned with the social origins of thought. In particular he traced how children's 'internal' thinking develops out of their 'external' social interactions with other people. Researchers moving in the same direction use various terms to describe their approach including constructivist or constructionist, socio-historical, socio-cognitive, socio-cultural and activity theory. One metaphor which can be useful in drawing together the social and the psychological is the metaphor of ecology.

The ecological metaphor

Originating in biology, ecology is the study of the interrelationship of an organism and its environment. When applied to humans, it is the interrelationship of an area of human activity and its environment. It is concerned with how the activity—literacy in this case—is part of the environment and at the same time influences and is influenced by the environment. An ecological approach takes as its starting point this interaction between individuals and their environments.

In the social sciences the idea of ecology goes back at least to Gregory Bateson, who linked up biological notions of ecology with anthropological and psychological concerns about the nature of human thought, referring to his collected works as *Steps to an ecology of mind* (1972). Two other early uses of the term are Bronfenbrenner's (1979) work on the ecology of human development and Gibson's work on the ecology of perception (1979). Some of these early uses may now seem simplistic, such as Bronfenbrenner's Russian dolls one inside the other, used as a way of visualizing how activities are situated in different layers of context: this is too static a model, making different contexts and environments seem very fixed. When applied to human activity more recently the idea of ecology has often been used to situate psychological activity, placing it in a more complete social context and a dynamic social context where different aspects interact.

An example of this development is Neisser's work on the ecology of memory (1982) showing the importance of studying how people use memory in natural contexts in their everyday lives. He is highly critical of the achievements of a hundred years of laboratory-based experimental studies of memory, and he argues for a more ecologically based approach, that is, a more naturalistic approach. His book begins with an article arguing point-by-point the importance of studying natural memory and criticizing the methods of experimental psychology; it is instructive to reread the article replacing the word 'memory' with the word 'reading'. Many of his criticisms of studies of memory apply equally well to studies of reading. Another use of the term ecology associated with psychological studies has been the idea of **ecological validity**. Researchers use the term to question whether experimental studies of psychological activity are valid reflections of natural everyday contexts. Other examples include work on the ecological basis of child development.

Within the sociology of language and sociolinguistics there is a separate tradition of using the term ecology. This dates back to Einar Haugen's (1972) work in the United States tracing the extent to which immigrants kept their own languages or changed to using the majority language, English. Another example is the work of Michael Clyne (1982) in Australia who uses ecology to mean the study of the environment which favours maintaining the community language. A more recent use has been Peter Mulhausler's (1992), who points out the need to focus on factors related to the ecology of a dominated language, rather than on the language itself if one is interested in its preservation.

I want to use the ecological metaphor to summarize and integrate what is known about literacy today. One advantage is that it has been used in both psychological and social traditions. In addition, a biological or organic metaphor of some sort has been used by several people when discussing reading and writing. Freire refers to domestication; many people talk of the roots of literacy. Yetta Goodman (1984) refers to the soil in which growth of literacy takes place. I want to develop these fragments, using the whole metaphor, making it more explicit.

The ecological metaphor actually produces a whole set of terms which can provide a framework for discussions of literacy. Terms like **ecological niches**, **ecosystem**, **ecological balance**, **diversity** and **sustainability** can all be applied to the human activity of using reading and writing. Some of the ideas in books on biological ecology are worth exploring to see how far the metaphor can be taken: for example, that communities themselves are not self-perpetuating or reproductive, individuals are; that the structure and patterns in a community are the product of processes at the level of the individual. And that change occurs at the individual level: the consequences but not the mechanisms occur at the community level.

In recent years, some researchers have come to write about societies and ecologies as both having the properties associated with **complex systems**. Complex systems are made up of many elements which interact with each other repeatedly. Over time, these processes of interaction lead to what is called the **emergence** of new patterns, features and structures, which are generated from the constitutive elements of the system but cannot be reduced to them. In the natural sciences, ideas of emergence have been used explain how complicated and intricate structures, such as wasps' nests, ant colonies or slime moulds, can arise from the ongoing interaction of very simple processes (Johnson, 2001). In the social sciences, the emergence of a range of social structures including languages and literacies (see Sealey and Carter, 2004) has been explained in terms of similar processes. There are several ways in which literacy is also an ecological issue in the current popular sense of a political issue to do with the environment. First, languages are vanishing at a remarkable rate; they are disappearing at such a rate that most of the languages of the world are likely to disappear within the lifetime of today's schoolchildren. Literacy may be aiding this, but it can also have a role in changing it. For ecological reasons there is a need to protect these languages and the cultures they often embody. I will return to the issue of endangered languages and the role of literacy in sustaining them in chapter 13.

Secondly, dominating languages like English need to maintain their diversity and variety. There are several English languages, not one English. The dangers of a push to a monocultural view of any language are great. The edges are its vitality, and variety ensures its future. There is much diversity in language: there are different genres of language, different languages and different scripts. An ecological approach emphasizes diversity, and in the original biological senses of ecology, sees it a virtue. Diversity is a source of strength, the roots of the possibilities of the future. This is just as true when applied to the diversity of languages and literacies. Again literacy has a role in maintaining diversity; it can be seen as the main force of standardization of languages, or it can have an important role in maintaining the range of variation in language.

Thirdly, there are communication technologies which can change the balance of languages and cultures, often in ways which have not been thought out. In the natural world there is technology available which means that whole forests can be destroyed and the earth transformed at remarkable rates, irrevocably and with unthought-of-ecological effects. The same is true of language and literacy. Large-scale communication, such as the internet, means that sudden and irreversible changes are taking place. Technology beyond a human scale is speeding up ecological change.

Ecology seems to be a useful and appropriate way of talking about literacy at the moment, and of bringing together its different strands. Using the term changes the whole endeavour of trying to understand the nature of reading and writing. Rather than isolating literacy activities from everything else in order to understand them, an ecological approach aims to understand how literacy is embedded in other human activity, its embeddedness in social life and in thought, and its position in history, in language and in learning. **Ecological** will be used in these several senses. If at this point a succinct statement of what is meant by an ecological approach is needed, I would say that it is one which examines the social and mental embeddedness of human activities in a way which allows change. Instead of studying the separate skills which underlie reading and writing, it involves a shift to studying literacy, a set of social practices associated with particular symbol systems and their related technologies. To be literate is to be active; it is to be confident within these practices. The rest of the book will be devoted to amplifying this.

NOW THAT YOU'VE READ

1. Consider the metaphors for literacy outlined in the article. Do any of them correlate with ideas you have ever had about literacy and its purposes? Do you now see these metaphors as problematic now that you have read more about literacy?

2. Barton scrutinizes the following terms in this article:
   - reading
   - writing
   - skill
   - illiterate
   - learning
   - evolution
   - mainstream culture

   Consider the scrutiny he applies to these concepts. Does his analysis help you to better understand the problematic nature of metaphors often associated with literacy? How might you create better metaphors using his terminology analysis?

3. We tend to think of literacy as something that is positive and a goal for all, but this article shows how discussions of literacy have, at times, been used to categorize people in an oppressive manner. Beyond the examples here, can you think of additional examples of when literacy can be used against someone or as a way to categorize or separate people?

4. Barton concludes his article by claiming "Ecology seems to be a useful and appropriate way of talking about literacy at the moment, and of bringing together its different strands. Using the term changes the whole endeavor of trying to understand the nature of reading and writing. Rather than isolating literacy activities from everything else in order to understand them, an ecological approach aims to understand how literacy is embedded in other human activity, its embeddedness in social life and in thought, and its position in history, in language and in learning." Break down this quote and explain what Barton means. How does the term ecology, as Barton explains it, better serve a literacy scholar?

READING

Literacy Practices

David Barton and Mary Hamilton

In the following excerpt from *Local Literacies* (1998), David Barton and Mary Hamilton articulate what they call a "social theory of literacy." Rather than treating literacy as a skill that, once acquired, is equally applicable to a variety of contexts, Barton and Hamilton define literacy in terms of "practices" ("what people do with literacy") and events ("activities where literacy has a role"). For your major writing assignment, you will be asked to develop your own working definition of literacy. As you read the following essay, keep in mind the metaphors people use when talking about literacy (Barton's "Talking About Literacy") and the ways in which our lived experiences with the technologies of literacy limit and shape our approaches to reading and writing.

BEFORE YOU READ answer the following questions:

1. In the excerpt that follows, Barton and Hamilton put forth a "social theory of literacy" and describe the ways in which it differs from the much more common assumption that literacy is a set of skills one carries with them and applies to a text in order to make sense of it. As they explain in the introduction to their book-length study of which the following essay is a part,

   > *Literacy is primarily something people do; it is an activity, located in the space between thought and text. Literacy does not just reside in people's heads as a set of skills to be learned, and it does not just reside on paper, captured as texts to be analyzed. Like all human activity, literacy is essentially social, and it is located in the interaction between people.* (3)

   Respond to this quote. Is this how you have seen described literacy in other contexts? Where do you see literacy "located?" Where have you been taught to "locate" literacy? In the heads of readers and writers? In the texts themselves? What does it mean to locate literacy "in the interaction between people"?

2. Without doing any research at all, think about the ways in which you have heard and/or seen the word literacy used and write all those ways down. Do you find a pattern among them? What is this pattern?

3. Barton and Hamilton discuss literacy in terms of "events" and "practices" rather than "skills." How do you see a literacy event or literacy practice differing from what we often describe as a literacy "skill"? Why might it be productive to think of literacy in these new ways?

Literary Practices

David Barton and Mary Hamilton

A Social Theory of Literacy: Practices and Events

In this chapter we provide a framework in terms of a theory of literacy. It is a brief overview of a social theory of literacy. This can be seen as the starting-point or orienting theory, which the detailed studies in this book then expand upon, react to and develop. We define what is meant by literacy practices and literacy events and explain some of the tenets of a social theory of literacy. This is pursued in Barton and Hamilton (1998), where a further example of situation literacies not covered in this book can be found.

Figure 1 Literacy as a Social Practice

> - Literacy is best understood as a set of social practices; these can be inferred from events which are mediated by written texts.
> - There are different literacies associated with different domains of life.
> - Literacy practices are patterned by social institutions and power relationships, and some literacies are more dominant, visible and influential than others.
> - Literacy practices are purposeful and embedded in broader social goals and cultural practices.
> - Literacy is historically situated.
> - Literacy practices change and new ones are frequently acquired through processes of informal learning and sense making.

We present here the theory of literacy as social practice in the form of a set of six propositions about the nature of literacy, as in Figure 1. The starting-point of this approach is the assertion that *literacy is a social practice*, and the propositions are an elaboration of this. The discussion is a development on that in Barton (1994, pp. 34-52), where contemporary approaches to literacy are discussed within the framework of the metaphor of ecology. The notion of *literacy practices* offers a powerful way of conceptualizing the link between the activities of reading and writing and the social structures in which they are embedded and which they help shape. When we talk about practices, then, this is not just the superficial choice of a word but the possibilities that this perspective offers for new theoretical understandings about literacy.

Our interest is in social practices in which literacy has a role; hence the basic unit of a social theory of literacy is that of *literary practices*. Literacy practices are the general cultural ways of utilizing written language which people draw upon in their lives. In the simplest sense literacy practices are what people do with literacy. However, practices are not observable units of behaviour since they also involve values, attitudes, feelings, and social relationships (see Street 1993, p. 12). This includes people's awareness of literacy, constructions of literacy and discourses of literacy, how people talk about and make sense of literacy. These are processes internal to the individual; at the same time, practices are the social processes which connect people with one another, and they include shared cognitions represented in ideologies and social identities. Practices are shaped by social rules which regulate the use and distribution of texts, prescribing who may produce and have access to them. They straddle the distinction between individual and social worlds, and literacy practices are more usefully understood as existing in the relations between people, within groups and communities, rather than as a set of properties residing in individuals.

To avoid confusion, it is worth emphasizing that this usage is different from situations where the word *practice* is used to mean learning to do something by repetition. It is also different from the way the term is used in recent international surveys of literacy, to refer to 'common or typical activities or tasks' (OECD/Statistics Canada 1996). The notion of practices as we have defined it above—cultural ways of utlising literacy—is a more abstract one that cannot wholly be contained in observable activities and tasks.)

Turning to another basic concept, *literacy events* are activities where literacy has a role. Usually there is a written text, or texts, central to the activity and there may be talk around the text. Events are observable episodes which arise from practices and are shaped by them. The notion of events stresses the situated nature of literacy, that it always exists in a social context. It is parallel to ideas developed in sociolinguistics and also, as Jay Lemke has pointed out, to Bahtkin's assertion that the starting point for the analysis of spoken language should be 'the social event of verbal interaction,' rather than the formal linguistic properties of texts in isolation (Lemke 1995).

Many literacy events in life are regular, repeated activities, and these can often be a useful starting-point for research into literacy. Some events are linked into routine sequences and these may be part of the formal procedures and expectations of social institutions like work-places, schools, and welfare agencies. Some events are structured by the more informal expectations and pressures of the home or peer group. Texts are a crucial part of literacy events and the study of literacy is partly the study of texts and how they are produced and used. These three components, practices, events, and texts, provide the first proposition of a social theory of literacy, that: *literacy is best understood as a set of social practices; these are observable in events which are mediated by written texts.* The local literacies study was concerned with identifying the events and texts of everyday life and describing people's associated practices. Our prime interest there was to analyse events in order to learn about practices. As with the definition of practices, we take a straightforward view of events at this point, as being activities which involve written texts; discussion throughout this book returns to the definitions of these terms. An example of an everyday literacy event, taken from the local literacies study, is that of cooking a pudding; it is described in Figure 2.

Figure 2 Cooking Literacy

When baking a lemon pie in her kitchen, Rita follows a recipe. She uses it to check the amounts of the ingredients. She estimates the approximate amounts, using teacups and spoons chosen specially for this purpose. The recipe is hand written on a piece of note-paper; it was written out from a book by a friend more than ten years ago. The first time she read the recipe carefully at each stage, but now she only looks at it once or twice. The piece of paper is marked and greasy by having been near the cooking surface on many occasions. It is kept in an envelope with other hand-written recipes and ones cut out of magazines and newspapers. The envelope and some cookery books are on a shelf in the kitchen. The books range in age and condition and include some by Robert Carrier. Sometimes she sits and reads them for pleasure.

Rita does not always go through the same set of activities in making the pie. Sometimes she makes double the amount described in the recipe if more people will be eating it. Sometimes she cooks the pie with her daughter Hayley helping her where necessary. Sometimes she enjoys cooking it, at other times it is more of a chore, when times is limited or she has other things she would rather do. Rita has passed the recipe on to several friends who have enjoyed the pie.

Rita does not always follow recipes exactly, but will add herbs and spices to taste; sometimes she makes up recipes; at one point she describes making a vegetable and pasta dish similar to one she had had as a takeaway meal. She exchanges recipes with other people, although she does not lend her books.

Once one begins to think in terms of literacy events there are certain things about the nature of reading and writing which become apparent. For instance, in many literacy events there is a mixture of written and spoken language. Many studies of literacy practices have print literacy and written texts as their starting point but it is clear that in literacy events people use written language in an integrated way as part of a range of semiotic systems; these semiotic systems include mathematical systems, musical notation, maps, and other non-text based images. The cookery text has numeracy mixed with print literacy and the recipes come from books, magazines, television, and orally from friends and relatives. By identifying literacy as one of a range of communicative resources available to members of a community, we can examine some of the ways in which it is located in relation to other mass media and new technologies. This is especially pertinent at a time of rapidly changing technologies.

Looking at different literacy events it is clear that literacy is not the same in all contexts; rather, there are different *literacies*. The notion of different literacies has several senses: for example, practices which involve different media or symbolic systems, such as a film or computer, can be regarded as different literacies, as in *film literacy* and *computer literacy*. Another sense is that practices in different cultures and languages can be regarded as different literacies. While accepting these sense of the term, the main way in which we use the notion here is to say that literacies are coherent configurations of literacy practices; often these sets of practices are identifiable and named, as in *academic literacy* or *work-place literacy* and they are associated with particular aspects of cultural life.

This means that, within a given culture, *there are different literacies associated with different domains of life*. Contemporary life can be analysed in a simple way into domains of activity, such as home, school, work-place. It is a useful starting point to examine the distinct practices in these domains, and then to compare, for example, home and school, or school and work-place. We begin with the home domain and everyday life. The home is often identified as a primary domain in people's literacy lives, for example by James Gee (1990), and central to people's developing sense of social identity. Work is another identifiable domain, where relationships and resources are often structured quite differently from in the home. We might expect the practices associated with cooking, for example, to be quite different in the home and in the work-place—supported, learned, and carried out in different ways. The division of labour is different in institutional kitchens, the scale of the operations, the clothing people wear when cooking, the health and safely precautions they are required to take, and so on. Such practices contribute to the idea that people participate in distinct *discourse communities*, in different domains of life. These communities are groups of people held together by their characteristic ways of talking, acting, valuing, interpreting, and using written language. (See discussion in Swales 1990, pp. 23-27.)

Domains, and the discourse communities associated with them, are not clear-cut, however: there are questions of the permeability of boundaries, of leakages and movement between boundaries, and of overlap between domains. Home and community, for instance, are often treated as being the same domain; nevertheless, they are distinct in many ways, including the dimension of public and private behaviour. An important part of the local literacies study was to clarify the domain being studied and to tease apart notions of home, household, neighbourhood, and community. Another aspect is the extent to which This domain is a distinct one with its own practices, and the extent to which the practices that exist in the home originate there, or home practices are exported to other domains. In particular, the private home context appears to be infiltrated by practices from many different public domains.

Domains are structured, patterned contexts within which literacy is used and learned. Activities within these domains are not accidental or randomly varying: there are particular configurations of literacy practices and there are regular ways in which people act in many literacy events in particular domains of life. These include family, religion, and education, which are all social institutions. Some of these institutions are more formally structured than others, with explicit rules for procedures, documentation and legal penalties for infringement, whilst others are regulated by the pressure of social conventions and attitudes. Particular literacies have been created by and are structured and sustained by these institutions. Part of the study aims to highlight the ways in which institutions support particular literacy practices.

Socially powerful institutions, such as education, tend to support dominant literacy practices. These dominant practices can be seen as part of whole discourse formations, institutionalized configurations of power and knowledge which are embodied in social relationships. Other vernacular literacies which exist in people's everyday lives are less visible and less supported. This means that *literacy practices are patterned by social institutions and power relationships, and some literacies are more dominant, visible, and influential than other.* One can contrast dominant literacies and vernacular literacies which exist, and with exploring their relationship to more dominant literacies.

People are active in what they do and *literacy practices are purposeful and embedded in broader social goals and cultural practices.* Whilst some reading and writing is carried out as an end in itself, typically literacy is a means to some other end. Any study of literacy practices must therefore situate reading and writing activities in these broader contexts and motivations for use. In the cooking example, for instance, the aim is to bake a lemon pie, and the reading of a recipe is incidental to this aim. The recipe is incorporated into a broader set of domestic social practices associated with providing food and caring for children, and it reflects boarder social relationships and gendered divisions of labour.

A first step in reconceptualising literacy is to accept the multiple function literacy may serve in a given activity, where it can replace spoken language, enable communication, solve a practical problem, or act as a memory aid—in some cases, all at the same time. It is also possible to explore the further work which literacy can do in an activity, and the social meanings it takes on. For instance, there are ways in which literacy acts as *evidence*, as *display*, as *threat*, and as *ritual*. Texts can have multiple roles in an activity and literacy an act in different ways for the different participants in a literacy event; people can be incorporated into the literacy practices of others without reading or writing a single word. The acts of reading and writing are not the only ways in which texts are assigned meaning (as in Barton and Hamilton 1998, Chapter 14).

It is important to shift from a conception of literacy located in individuals to examine ways in which people in groups utilise literacy. In this way literacy becomes a community resource, realised in social relationships rather than a property of individuals. This is true at various levels; at the detailed micro level it can refer to the fact that in particular literacy events there are often several participants taking on different roles and creating something more than their individual practices. At a broader macro level it can mean the ways in which whole communities use literacy. There are social rules about who can produce and use particular literacies and we wish to examine this social regulation of texts. Shifting away from literacy as an individual attribute is one of the most important implications of a practice account of literacy, and one of the ways in which it differs most from more traditional accounts. The ways in which literacy acts as a resource for different sorts of groups are a central theme of Barton and Hamilton (1998), which describes some of the ways in which families, local communities, and organisations regulate and are regulated by literacy practices.

A person's practices can also be located in their own history of literacy. In order to understand this, we need to take a life history approach, observing the history within a person's life. There are several dimensions to this: people use literacy to make changes in their lives; literacy changes people and people find themselves in the contemporary world of changing literacy practices. The literacy practices an individual engages with change across their lifetime, as a result of changing demands, available resources, as well as the possibilities and their interests.

Related to the constructed nature of literacy, any new theory of literacy implies a theory of learning. *Literacy practices change and new ones are frequently acquired through processes of informal learning and sense making* as well as formal education and training. This learning takes place in particular social contexts and part of this learning is the internalisation of social processes. It is therefore important to understand the nature of informal and vernacular learning strategies and the nature of situated cognition, linking with the work of researchers influenced by Lev Vygotsky, such as Sylvia Scribner, Jean Lave, and colleagues (Scribner 1984; Lave and Wenger, 1991). For this it is necessary to draw upon people's insights into how they learn, their theories about literacy and education, the vernacular strategies they use to learn new literacies. We start out from the position that people's understanding of literacy is an important aspect of their learning, and that people's theories guide their actions. It is here that a study of literacy practices has its most immediate links with education.

NOTE

This chapter is adapted from pages 6-13 of D. Barton and M. Hamilton, *Local Literacies: Reading and Writing in One Community,* Routledge, 1998, with permission of the publishers.

REFERENCES

Barton, D. (1994) *Literacy: An Introduction to the Ecology of Written Language*, Oxford: Blackwell.

Barton, D. and Hamilton, M. (1998) *Local Literacies: Reading and Writing in One Community*, London: Routledge

Clark, R. and Ivanic, R. (1997) *The Politics of Writing*, London: Routledge

Gee, J.P. (1990) *Social Linguistics and Literacies: Ideology in Discourses*, London: Palmer Press.

Heath, S. (1983) *Ways with Words: Language, Life and Work in Communities and Classrooms*, Cambridge: Cambridge University Press.

Hoggart, R. (1957) *The Uses of Literacy: Aspects of Working-Class Life*, London: Chatto.

Lave, J. and Wenger, E. (1991) *Situated Learning: Legitimate Peripheral Participation*, Cambridge: Cambridge University Press.

Lemke, J. (1995) *Textual Politics: Discourse and Social Dynamics*, London: Taylor and Francis.

OECD/Statistics Canada (1996) *Literacy, Economy and Society*, Ontario: OECD.

Scribner, S. (1984) 'Studying working intelligence,' in B. Rogoff and J. Lave (eds) *Everyday Cognition: Its Development in Social Context*, Cambridge, MA: Harvard University Press.

Street, B. (ed.) (1993) *Cross-cultural Approaches to Literacy*, Cambridge: Cambridge University Press.

Swales, J. (1990) *Genre Analysis: English in Academic Research Settings*, Cambridge: Cambridge University Press.

Taylor, D. and Dorsey-Gaines, C. (1988) *Growing Up Literate: Learning from Inner-city Families*, London: Heinemann.

NOW THAT YOU'VE READ

1. According to Barton and Hamilton, "literacy practices are patterned by social institutions and power relations and some literacies are more dominant and visible than others" (64). What do they mean by this? Unpack this quote as it relates to your own literacy experiences.

2. To illustrate their definition of literacies, Barton and Hamilton provide an example of Rita's cooking literacy as she makes a lemon pie. Create a representation—a chart, a list, a map, a diagram, or something else—that

shows all of the elements involved in this illustration. Be sure to include connections to other people (like the friend who gave Rita the recipe) in your representation.

3. Reflecting on your representation of Rita's cooking literacy, think about the literacies in which you participate, and where you participate in them (Barton and Hamilton refer to these different places as "domains"). Schooling is an obvious one since you are a student and there are likely others as well (a religious affiliation or a club or fraternal organization membership, for example). How do you show you have developed literacies in each of these domains? What skills, behaviors, and other factors are involved?

WRITING ASSIGNMENT

DEFINING LITERACY

This first writing assignment calls upon you to define key terms that will frame the research project you will undertake this term. To do so, you'll need to (a) address common misconceptions about these seemingly simple terms, (b) offer reasons such definitions are inaccurate at best, and (c) articulate new, more appropriate definitions of relevant terms. You need to develop working definitions of literacy, text, literacy practices, and literacy events, then consider what it means to approach literacy as a social practice. In preparation for this essay, you should reflect upon your initial understanding of these concepts and the specific, extensive ways the assigned readings in Chapter 1 disrupted previous expectations. Your overarching task in Writing Assignment 1 (WA1) is to "redefine literacy" as informed by the conversations represented in this chapter and in your in-class discussions on the same. However, doing so will require you to define additional, deeply related terms like "reading," "writing," "text," "literacy practices," and "literacy event."

Successful WA1s will address the above prompt, in part, by making extensive, meaningful use of Hawisher and Selfe's "Becoming Literate in the Information Age," Barton's "Talking About Literacy," Barton and Hamilton's "A Social Theory of Literacy Practices and Events," and (if your instructor assigns it) Hamilton's "Expanding New Literacy Studies: Using Photographs to Explore Literacy as a Social Practice." In this essay, you should not only redefine literacy but explain why it is necessary to redefine literacy and related terms.

WA1 includes two parts. The first part is a traditional, academic essay; the second part (no more than one page) is a glossary of 4-5 terms (no more than two sentences per definition). The terms included in your glossary should be addressed in the essay portion as part of your overall attempt to redefine literacy. WA1 should be approximately 3-4 pages in length, including the glossary, and adhere to regular essay requirements: 12 pt. Times New Roman Font, standard heading, and double spaced with 1" margins.

CHAPTER 2

Research Ethics and Communities of Practice

In the previous chapter, we talked about what literacy is and how we might *redefine* it to be relevant to us. Literacy is happening, not some static thing that sits in our textbook. Part of the reason that literacy constantly changes is because *we* (people and communities) change it! Here, we will discuss (1) how we might understand a "community" or various communities, (2) how our research can be ethical within these communities, and (3) what ethical research means and why ethical research matters.

To go back to the idea that literacy is constantly evolving based on communities, take, for instance, the moment when the animated, fictional character Homer Simpson's famous exclamation "Doh" became part of the *Oxford English Dictionary*. Or how J.K. Rowling's creation of a school called Hogwarts affected whether some children or adults wore scarlet and gold to support Gryffindor, or green and silver to support Slytherin, and made sports such as Quidditch become a well-known term (and a new sport across college campuses!). Or, how the use of the phrase "Winter is Coming" on *Game of Thrones* is now often referenced on memes, t-shirts, and in response to people who are fans of the show. These are three examples of how people (through popular culture) and their followers (their community of fans) have participated in the creation of words, phrases, behaviors, and dress styles of various communities (in this case, fans of *The Simpsons, Harry Potter,* and *Game of Thrones*). However, it's likely that even if you don't consider yourself a "fan" or an "insider" of these communities that you are somewhat aware of their influence. Or, for perhaps more familiar examples, think about how you might identify someone as part of a sports team, a military branch, or a particular profession. Here, what might distinguish people as part of a community is how they are dressed (the uniform they wear), the materials they use (for a football player: cleats, helmet, jersey, long socks, and pads to begin), how they act (saluting officers, for instance), and the language they use (such as a football quarterback yelling "Blue 42, blue 42" as their new play). Of course, these are just quick examples, but what they begin to show us is how communities of practice are all around us. We will delve into what makes a community of practice (see Carter in this chapter).

In this chapter, we will also explore how ethnographic research—a kind of research that originated in sociology which allows a researcher to study a group of people—necessitates *ethical* interaction with people, places, and ideas.

Through this research, we must consider the ethics involved in researching communities that we are both part of and, perhaps, entirely apart from. In 1979, the Office of the Secretary for the Department of Health, Education, and Welfare released "The Belmont Report" which describes "Ethical Principles and Guidelines for the Protection of Human Subjects of Research." This report describes historical moments that show the mistreatment of human subjects, particularly those who have been marginalized by their socioeconomic, racial, ethnic, or dis/ability backgrounds:

> For example, during the 19th and early 20th centuries the burdens of serving as research subjects fell largely upon poor ward patients, while the benefits of improved medical care flowed primarily to private patients. Subsequently, the exploitation of unwilling prisoners as research subjects in Nazi concentration camps was condemned as a particularly flagrant injustice. In this country, in the 1940's, the Tuskegee syphilis study used disadvantaged, rural black men to study the untreated course of a disease that is by no means confined to that population. These subjects were deprived of demonstrably effective treatment in order not to interrupt the project, long after such treatment became generally available. ("The Belmont Report")

In order to counter these atrocious misuses of power and research, "The Belmont Report" establishes three basic principles for the ethical treatment of human subjects. These include:

1. **"Respect for Persons"** which is described as "first, that individuals should be treated as autonomous agents, and second, that persons with diminished autonomy are entitled to protection. The principle of respect for persons thus divides into two separate moral requirements: the requirement to acknowledge autonomy and the requirement to protect those with diminished autonomy."

2. **"Beneficence"** which is articulated so that "persons are treated in an ethical manner not only by respecting their decisions and protecting them from harm, but also by making efforts to secure their well-being. Such treatment falls under the principle of beneficence. The term 'beneficence' is often understood to cover acts of kindness or charity that go beyond strict obligation. In this document, beneficence is understood in a stronger sense, as an obligation. Two general rules have been formulated as complementary expressions of beneficent actions in this sense: **(1)** do not harm and **(2)** maximize possible benefits and minimize possible harms."

3. **"Justice"** is described as such: "Who ought to receive the benefits of research and bear its burdens? This is a question of justice, in the sense of 'fairness in distribution' or 'what is deserved.' An injustice occurs when some benefit to which a person is entitled is denied without good reason or when some burden is imposed unduly. Another way of conceiving the principle of justice is that equals ought to be treated equally. However, this statement requires explication. Who is equal and who is unequal? What considerations justify departure from equal distribution? Almost all commentators allow that distinctions based on experience, age, deprivation, competence, merit and position do sometimes constitute criteria justifying

differential treatment for certain purposes. It is necessary, then, to explain in what respects people should be treated equally. There are several widely accepted formulations of just ways to distribute burdens and benefits. Each formulation mentions some relevant property on the basis of which burdens and benefits should be distributed. These formulations are **(1)** to each person an equal share, **(2)** to each person according to individual need, **(3)** to each person according to individual effort, **(4)** to each person according to societal contribution, and **(5)** to each person according to merit."

To follow these basic principles, researchers must adhere to the following applications for their research: "informed consent, risk/benefit assessment, and the selection of subjects of research" ("The Belmont Report"). Broadly speaking, these procedures require researchers to inform participants of their procedures, obtain consent from volunteers, reflect on their methods for gathering and analyzing data, and adhere to "moral requirements that there be fair procedures and outcomes in the selection of research subjects" ("The Belmont Report"). The ways these procedures are taken up in research differ based on the context of the project, but these principles are set in place to deeply encourage the ethical treatment of humans in research projects.

For this course, you obviously won't be doing medical experiments that could cause direct harm to a person. However, because we will be interacting with people (which includes their emotional, physical, mental, and social well being), we must still be ethical in our research. Therefore, we will read examples about ethical ethnographic research by Seth Kahn and Tabetha Adkins. We will also read the "CCCC Guidelines for the Ethical Conduct of Research in Composition Studies." CCCC, or the Conference on College Composition and Communication, is one of the governing bodies of the field of Writing Studies. The information you read here has been recently revised by scholars doing research similar to the ethnographic research we are asking of you! This document also provides a current look at how the field of Writing Studies is taking up questions of human interaction within research—something that is constantly evolving to account for changes in research, technology, and communities!

Based on these insights, we will discuss what it means to be ethical researchers in a variety of contexts. As we've suggested throughout this textbook, literacy is constantly shifting based on the contexts in which it is used. Research ethics are similarly contextual because we navigate them in relation to the communities, institutions, places (digital and geographical), and ideas in our research. As researchers, we must be malleable with our ethical practices—or able to be shaped and *responsive to* the communities at hand. Some questions we will discuss include: How do we show respect to various communities? What types of actions or behaviors are (in)appropriate in certain contexts? Why are these actions or behaviors (in)appropriate? For instance, does the community you're thinking about have a particular dress code, way of speaking, language pattern, set of rules, code of conduct, etc.? In other words, in this chapter we will talk about what makes a community *a community* and how people are insiders, outsiders, or inhabit a space in between these distinctions and, finally, how we should approach research involving "human subjects" (people) based on such information.

READING

What Is a Community of Practice?
Shannon Carter

BEFORE YOU READ:

1. Speculate for a moment. Have you ever heard the term "community of practice" before? If so, in what context? If not, what do you think a community of practice might be?

2. What does the term "community" mean to you? What communities do you belong to? How do you know? How do others know?

3. What might the concept "communities of practice" have to do with literacy in and/or beyond school?

What Is a Community of Practice?

Shannon Carter

Learning to read and write for college is not really about memorizing rules. Instead, it's about understanding and being able to emulate the rules that constitute literate behavior within a particular group—often called a "discourse community." What is a discourse community? In her collection of previously published essays *Academic Discourse and Critical Consciousness* (1992), Patricia Bizzell defines a "discourse community as a group of people who share certain language using practices." She continues: "These practices can be seen as conventionalized in two ways. Stylistic conventions regulate social interactions both within the group and in its dealings with outsiders. . . . Also, canonical knowledge regulates worldviews of group members and how they interpret experience" (222). Discourse communities then regulate not only *how* one should interact within the associated social spaces (stylistic conventions) but *what* the subject of such interactions can profitably be (canonical knowledge). For our purposes, however, "communities of practice" seem more appropriate than "discourse communities" because the former stresses literacy as an *activity* rather than a state of being (via membership or ability to meet universal standards).

"Communities of practice" are relations of people who have in common a "shared competence and mutual interest in a given practice" (Choi 143), be that repairing Xerox machines (see Orr 1996 and Brown and Duguid 1991), recovering from alcoholism (see Lave and Wenger, 1990), writing as a college student in a history class, or countless other activities in which a person may be involved. The concept first emerged in the Lave and Wenger study of the ways in which various communities of practice teach newcomers the practices valued and reproduced in those communities (midwives, meat cutters, tailors, and recovering alcoholics in Alcoholics Anonymous). According to Lave and Wenger, a "community of practice is a set of relations among persons, activity, and world over time and in relation with other tangential and overlapping communities of practice." The term "impl[ies] participation in an activity system about which participants share understandings concerning what they are doing and what that means in their lives and for their communities" (98).

My brother is a musician, a systems engineer and a video game enthusiast; thus, his literate practices cover multiple communities of practice, such as (1) an *electronic music community,* which includes the user-guide for his keyboard and other music equipment, the software designer's explanation about the functions of the programs he purchased to compose and produce his music, the ad copy for this merchandize, the forums he frequents to discuss current electronic music and share clips, and so on; (2) *a video game community* which includes the others involved in his experiences with multi-player games like *Fallout* and *Skyrim,* the various documents users produce to assist other players ("Frequently Asked Questions," "Walkthroughs," "Cheats"), and so on. The list is almost infinite.

Another way to think of a "community of practice" is in terms of what James Paul Gee calls "affinity groups":

> People in an affinity group can recognize others as more or less "insiders" to the group. They may not see many people in the group face-to-face, but when they interact with someone on the Internet or read something about the domain, they can recognize certain ways of thinking, writing, valuing, and believing as well as the typical sorts of social practices associated with a given semiotic domain. This is to view the domain externally. (*What Video Games Have to Teach Us About Learning and Literacy*, 27)

In other words, according to Gee, literate members of a particular affinity group (read "community of practice") can identify one another in ways non-members cannot. Only other highly literate connoisseurs of wine, for example, know the difference between a person who understands wine and a person who is merely faking it. Unless the difference is very obvious (perhaps the "faker" is trying to pass off *Strawberry Hill* or *Blue Nun* as "fine" wine), I can't tell because I am not a member of that affinity group. Only those who are can identify those who are not.

What those literate members are "reading" in order to distinguish other literate members from those attempting to behave as members is what Gee refers to as the "external design grammar." That is, "the principles and patterns in terms of what one can recognize as what is and is not acceptable or typical *social practice and identity* in response to the affinity group associated with a semiotic domain." According to Gee, "you know, consciously or unconsciously, the external design grammar of [a particular] semiotic domain" if you answer "yes" to questions like these:

> Do you know what counts as thinking, acting, interacting, and valuing like someone who is into "modernist architecture" [or wine or first-person-shooter games or web design or neuroscience]? Can you recognize the sorts of identities people take on when they are in their domain? Can you recognize what counts as valued social practices to the members of the affinity group associated with the semiotic domain of modernist architecture [or wine or first-person shooter games or web design or surfing or neuroscience] and what counts as behaving appropriately in these social practices? (30)

I am reminded of a high school classmate of mine in a coastal town in Texas (Corpus Christi, a coastal town in South Texas) in the 1980s who successfully adopted three very different identities in as many years—a new one for each year he was in high school: as a sophomore he was "punk" (with quite an impressive Mohawk, sometimes green, sometimes blue); as a junior he became a surfer; his senior year he transformed into what we called back then a "kicker," a cowboy of sorts. Each year he'd "hang out" with the appropriate friends (affinity group/community of practice), wear the appropriate clothing, and even change his body language to fit the group. Even the way he spoke changed: from "hardcore" as a punk (as in, "That's f***king hardcore, man!") to "bra" as a surfer (for "brother," perhaps, as in "What's up, bra'? Heard the surf report this morning! Let's cut") to "fixin'" as a kicker ("I'm fixin' ta' git outta here"). Each identity shift was seamless—at least it appeared to be. In other words, Mike had developed high levels of rhetorical dexterity. He wasn't an outsider in any group he chose to join, at least not that I could see. However while his move into a new group each fall looked seamless, it couldn't have been entirely so because these groups certainly did not bear much crossover (conflicting literacies at the core value systems shaping each subgroup).

Still, Mike was able to read and embody not only the "external design grammar" of each group, but also what Gee calls the "internal design grammar." "Internal design grammar" refers to the "principles and patterns in terms of what one can recognize what is and is not acceptable or typical *content* in a semiotic domain" (or "community of practice"). Knowledge of the "internal design grammar" of a particular community of practice can be confirmed when one can answer "yes" to these questions: "Do you know what counts as a modernist piece of architecture" (or fine wine or a "choice" ocean wave, etc.)? "What sorts of buildings count as typical or atypical of modernist architecture?" What sorts of music counts as typical or atypical punk? What sorts of wines (from which regions) are wine connoisseurs likely to find most valuable (or least) and for what reasons? "Do you understand what counts and what doesn't count as a possible piece of content in theoretical linguistics?" in composition studies? In neuroscience?

The "internal design grammar" involved in Mike's various identity shifts is a bit harder for me to determine, especially given my own lack of literacy in these semiotic domains. However, we may assume that as a surfer he not only had to know how to surf, but how to dress, walk, talk, and perform like a surfer (the external design grammar); he also had to know and appreciate the music that surfers typically listen to (and why), the films they were likely to see, the equipment (and brand names) they were likely to find most valuable for their various surfing activities, and so on (the internal design grammar—the content). As a punk, he would also need to know what sorts of music was typically considered most valuable to members of this affinity group (and why), the films most typical of this semiotic domain (community of practice), the short history of punk rock music and the key players, the philosophical principles (of anarchy, etc.) underlying the punk rock movement, and other similar content.

At least from a distance, it seemed that Mike had developed a productive knowledge of the internal and external design grammars making up these various cliques—so much so that he was able to move from punk to surf to cowboy rather swiftly and without incident. He seemed to know, instinctively, how to recognize *the points of contact* and *dissonance* among these different groups; music (punk, country), clothing (combat boots, cowboy boots), hair style, and language drew these groups together and kept these groups apart. Mike knew how to tell the difference and embody the similarities.

However, I can only imagine that his rapid identity shifts were less simplistic than they seemed. The boundaries between various high school cliques are rather sharp and pronounced; the borders guarded rather openly; outsiders (fakes, "posers") identified quickly and conspicuously. Because the boundaries were so clearly drawn,

Mike knew when he had changed groups, and so he was able to pick up the appropriate lens (the philosophical principles and value sets by which the affinity group functions) necessary for him to view those groups outside the boundaries of his own as other members would.

Such identity shifts are much more problematic when we are dealing with moves from home to school to church to work rather than from one high school clique to another, especially when those moves are complicated by race, class, and all the sociohistorical and material circumstances that surround these identity shifts. Literacy is profoundly tied up with identity. According to James Paul Gee, "semiotic domains encourage people new to them to take on and play with new *identities* (51, emphasis mine). "By a semiotic domain," Gee means, "any set of practices that recruits one or more modalities (e.g., oral or written language, images, equations, symbols, sounds, gestures, graphs, artifacts, etc.) to communicate distinctive types of meanings." Examples of semiotic domains include cellular biology, postmodern literary criticism, first-person-shooter video games, high-fashion advertisements, Roman Catholic theology, modernist painting, mid-wifery, rap music, wine connoisseurship, through a nearly endless, motley, and ever changing list. (18)

In keeping with the social function of language, then, Gee urges us to "think first in terms of what I call semiotic domains and only then get to literacy in the more traditional terms of print literacy (17). Thus, he continues,

> If we think first in terms of semiotic domains and not in terms of reading and writing as traditionally conceived, we can say that people are (or are not) literate (partially or fully) in a domain if they can recognize (the equivalent of "reading") and/or produce (the equivalent of "writing") meanings in the domain. (19)

Those literate in "cellular biology . . . first-person-shooter video games, high-fashion advertisements, Roman Catholic theology, modernist painting," and "wine connoisseurship," for example, make up several different communities of practice—communities that include other cellular biologists or players of first-person-shooter games or connoisseurs of wine. Because I wish to emphasize the social function of literacy, I hope you will continue to think of the *people* involved in these various communities of practice rather than just the literate strategies they employ; thus, developing new literacies in new communities of practice means, as Gee explains, "*taking on and playing with new identities*. . . . All learning in all semiotic domains requires identity work. It requires taking on a new identity and forming bridges from one's old identities to the new one (51, emphasis in original).

The wine connoisseur, then, who wishes to develop new literacies as a cellular biologist must take on the identity of a cellular biologist. The person highly literate as a designer and consumer of high-fashion advertisements who wishes to learn how to play first-person-shooter games must take on the identity of the gaming shooter. In order to be taken seriously as a surfer by the other surfers around him, Mike had to leave his punk persona behind and take on the identity of the surfer. At times the new identity differs so little from the old one that learning these new literacies is no more complicated than learning new strategies based on the old ones. Other times the difference between the old identity and the new one is so profound that one must discard the previous identity entirely in order to adopt the new one and/or decide against learning the new literacy altogether. In no small way, the communities of practice with which you most identify determine the way you approach any literate act, and without developing rhetorical dexterity—a meta-awareness of the points of contact and points of dissonance between these two developing literacies—such associations make learning new literacies improbable or at least so jarring that it is difficult to pull through. That's why we are asking you to dig into what you already know very well, making use of these familiar literacies to learn new ones.

Works Cited

Bizzell, Patricia. *Academic Discourse and Critical Consciousness.* U of Pittsburgh P, 1992.

Choi, Mina. "Communities of Practice: An Alternative Learning Model for Knowledge Creation." *British Journal of Educational Technology.* 37.1 (2006): 143-146.

Gee, James Paul. *What Video Games Have to Teach Us About Learning and Literacy.* Palgrave, 2003.

Lave, Jean and Etienne Wenger. *Situated Learning: Legitimate Peripheral Participation.* Cambridge UP, 1991.

NOW THAT YOU'VE READ

1. How can a high school clique be a community of practice? What are the rules for discourse within a high school clique? How do they vary from clique to clique? Who writes the rules? Who enforces them?

2. How can videogames be a community of practice? What are the rules for discourse within a video game (and about video games)? Who writes these rules? Who enforces them?

3. Choose one more community of practice from this essay and think about it in terms of "rules": What are the rules within this community of practice? Who writes these rules? Who enforces them?

4. Come up with two communities of practice not mentioned in this essay.

5. What might all this have to do with writing and reading—in college or beyond?

READING

Putting Ethnographic Writing in Context
Seth Kahn

BEFORE YOU READ answer the following questions:

1. Think about a community of practice that you consider yourself a part of: Is it a sports team? A club? An academic discipline? Is it a religious institution? A political party? Your family? A particular cultural background? Brainstorm how you might describe this community of practice. What words, feelings, or ideas come to mind?

2. Once you've thought of your community of practice, notice what helps you know you're part of this community. For example, are there particular values or ideas you share? What are they? Are there particular ways your community distinguishes itself with clothing, language, the work people do? Take notes of all the things that you can think of to describe this community.

3. What types of literacy practices do you use within this community of practice? Do you write or read? Are you speaking? What languages, dialects, or jargon do you use? What are you speaking about? Who are you speaking to? What genres of writing does your community use?

Putting Ethnographic Writing in Context
Seth Kahn

If you're like most students, you may wonder why your writing instructor is asking you to do *ethnographic writing*.¹ You may have a vague idea of what ethnography is—what anthropologists do when they live in faraway places for long stretches of time, trying to understand what makes a culture unique or interesting. You may wonder what studying cultures in detail, conducting fieldwork and interviews, has to do with writing papers for your college classes.

Anthropologists James Spradley and David McCurdy answer the question concisely when they say, "A good writer must be a good ethnographer" (4). Ethnographic writing challenges you to consider everything that's interesting and difficult about writing; it pushes you to *generate, collect, analyze,* and *synthesize* more material than you've probably had to work with in one paper before. Moreover, because ethnographies are about actual people, the assignment makes you think about *ethics* (how you're presenting information, how that information might affect people if made public, being as accurate as you can) and *knowledge* (what it is you really know at the end of the project and how you present that knowledge without sounding more confident than you should). And finally, because these projects generally take a long time and you write constantly while doing them, you'll have plenty of time to reflect on and understand how you're learning and changing as writers along the way.

Along with the benefits to your writing, ethnography really highlights and emphasizes human relationships: between participants and researchers; between writers and readers of ethnographic narratives/ reports; between students and teachers in classrooms. If all goes well, you'll find that your writing helps you navigate those relationships. That is, ethnographic writing can, when it works well, do more than produce interesting papers: it can improve your understanding of people and their ways of thinking/talking; it can improve the lives of the people you write about; it can help you reflect on your own positions within cultures.

One big lesson you should learn is that ethnographic writing, when it works well, does not—in fact cannot—follow a conventional formula for essays. It requires you to experiment with style, voice, structure, and purpose in ways you probably haven't before. To help you see what I mean by that, I'll at times evoke my own experiences as an ethnographer and teacher of ethnographic writing; the mixture of narrative and analysis should give you an idea—not necessarily a model—of the ways that traditional and non-traditional academic writing conventions work for this kind of project.

Some Nuts and Bolts: What Ethnographers Do

The term most synonymous with *ethnography* is *participant-observation research.* Ethnographers study *cultures,* i.e., the relationships, rituals, values, and habits that make people understand themselves as members of a group (or society, or what have you). We do so by spending lots of time in the cultures we study, interacting with members, watching and learning from how they act and talk, participating in their activities, and talking with them about how they understand their groups and their lives. That is, we adopt a stance that's both distanced (observing) and interactive (participatory), and good ethnographic writing emerges from the juxtaposition of those stances. Good ethnographic writing also acknowledges the effects we have on the cultures we study—which, I'll contend below, is both inevitable and desirable—and the effects those cultures have on us.

Put simply then, ethnographers: observe, participate, interact, analyze, reflect, write, rethink, and describe cultures, their members, and our own involvements with them. What pins together all these ways of thinking and seeing is that they all either happen in—or directly lead to—*writing.* I can't even pretend to generate an exhaustive list of all the writing you'll do for your project, but here's some of it:

1. Pre-writing: reflections on what you know about the culture you'll study, what you think you know, your biases and predispositions towards its members, the questions you're interested in trying to answer, and more.

2. Introductions/consent forms: letters/emails to group members explaining your project and asking for permission to do it; consent forms for participants to sign, indicating that they understand your project and agree to be involved in it.

3. Fieldnotes/interview notes/transcripts: notes on your visits to the group/ research site; notes taken during interviews with participants; transcripts of interviews with participants; descriptions of physical locations, settings, physical artifacts, and so on.

4. Journal: a running internal monologue, so to speak, of your thinking throughout the project—what you're seeing, what you think is important, what you need to pursue further, what you're confused about, who you need

to make sure you interview, and/or anything else that helps you keep track of your ideas; some instructors might require occasional "progress reports," which are slightly more elaborated, formal versions of journal entries.

5. Drafts and revisions of ethnographies: your write-up of the project will require multiple drafts and major overhauls in organization/structure, voice, and content, all of which should help you understand your own points as much as they help your readers. Your instructor might even require that you share drafts of your paper with participants in your study.

If you're still wondering what this assignment can teach you about writing, then understand also that this list is not only incomplete, but also not in any necessary order. You'll probably find that your process is *recursive,* e.g., that a journal entry near the end of the project might call on you to re-interview a participant, or that something you'd forgotten about in your fieldnotes makes you rethink your analysis in a third draft of the paper. And, just as importantly, you may find that sharing your notes, transcripts, and drafts with participants in your project heightens your awareness of what some of us call the *ethics of representation,* i.e., the responsibility to our participants to ensure that what we say about them is fair, reasonable, and accurate.

Learning from Experience

One of the driving forces behind assigning ethnographic writing is that people learn more from direct experience than from second-hand experience (e.g., reading, lectures). When we ask you to go out into the field to do your participant-observation research, we're expecting you to learn a lot more about the culture you study than you could by reading about it, or listening to somebody else talk about it. We're also expecting that all the writing you do about it will help you come to terms with what you know, both by making you make sense for yourselves about what you're experiencing, and by making you make sense of it for readers.

If you've written personal reflective essays (like many college admission essays, as well as assignments you might have done for courses), then you've done some of what I'm describing; you've written a narrative in order to help you reflect on an experience, to help you learn or understand something about yourself, and to make that as clear as you can to somebody else. Ethnography also requires you to do this kind of *inductive reasoning,* which means that you collect and consider evidence and experience without a hypothesis or conclusion in mind; your analysis and descriptions explain what you've learned, rather than confirming or disconfirming what somebody else already claimed or knew. But ethnography is different from personal reflective writing in at least these two ways. First, rather than writing about experiences you've *already had,* most of the writing you'll do is about experiences *you're having.* That is, your writing can actually change your situation in ways that reflecting on the past can't. Second, while you're certainly part of the story you're experiencing and writing, you're also writing about *other people,* which comes with a set of responsibilities that can become very complex very quickly.

Learning from Somebody Else's Experience

You can, of course, learn from other people's experiences, too. I want to tell you the story of my first ethnographic project. The project, a study of a graduate-level literature course, should help you see in concrete terms what I've been describing:

the kinds of writing involved, and some of the ethical issues that arise from talking about real people and real events, with real implications.

Fall 1996 semester: for a research methods course (most graduate students are required to take at least one methods course, in which we learn to do the professional scholarship we'll have to do as faculty), our major assignment, which would span about eight weeks, was to pick a course in our department, negotiate access to the course with the professor, and do participant-observation research for about five weeks, leaving the last three weeks to write an ethnographic description of fifteen to twenty pages.

The first half of the research methods course had gone smoothly. We studied ethnographic techniques: negotiating access (convincing participants to let us study their cultures), interview strategies, ways of taking fieldnotes, and types of data analysis. We read two full-length ethnographic studies—Elizabeth Chiseri-Strater's *Academic Literacies* and Bonnie Sunstein's *Composing a Culture*—as well as two books that theorize the importance of *writing* to ethnographic research: anthropologist Clifford Geertz's *Works and Lives: The Anthropologist as Author* and sociologist John Van Maanen's *Tales of the Field: On Writing Ethnography*. I'll return to the Geertz text later; for now, suffice it to say that our entire class believed we'd been well trained to do participant-observation research, and to write interesting and ethically responsible accounts of our experiences.

I decided to approach a professor I had taken a course from before; the course I wanted to study examined relationships between jazz music and literature in the 1950s. I had really enjoyed working with him, and he had some teaching habits I wanted to examine while I wasn't a student in his course. He was intrigued by the idea, and because we'd developed a solid working relationship, he quickly granted access. His only request, one you shouldn't be surprised to encounter, was that I share the final paper with him.

The fieldwork went fine. Over five weeks, I attended class three times each week for fifty minutes; took fieldnotes on the nine students and the professor (an average of five handwritten pages per day); interviewed everybody, some more than once (a total of fifteen interviews, averaging about twenty minutes). The professor gave me copies of his syllabus and all the assignments, as well as examples of work students had done earlier in the semester so I could see the kinds of topics they were interested in researching. In all, I had hundreds of pages of notes, course documents, students' work, and my own journals.

By the time I was done with the fieldwork, I knew how I would focus my description and analysis—which, in retrospect, was part of the problem. What I found, in brief, from my research was what I thought I'd find—a professor who knew his material inside-out, who worked hard to involve students in conversations, who cared as much as anybody I've ever known about his students, but who at times responded to students' comments in ways that seemed dismissive or sarcastic. As a result, the students were sometimes confused about how to respond to the professor's questions and discussion prompts, which frustrated the professor into sometimes sounding even more sarcastic, hoping to lighten the mood but often doing just the opposite.

I had plenty of evidence to write a good paper demonstrating what I'd learned.

We spent two weeks drafting and revising the papers, and receiving extensive feedback from classmates and the professor of the research methods course. All the feedback emphasized readers' needs for more direct evidence: anecdotes from class meetings; sections of interview transcripts; relevant pieces of the syllabus and course materials. By the time I submitted the final draft, I believed I had represented the central issue of the class in a readable, interesting, and believable way. My professor, Wendy, (mostly) agreed. She gave me an Aon the paper, an A in the course, and I thought I'd had a positive learning experience.

I had, but not the one I anticipated. Here's what Wendy wrote about my study in a textbook that incorporates a lot of the work and experiences of graduate students in her courses:

> I have had a classroom mini-ethnography cause consternation to a colleague who had allowed one of my students to study him. Consent forms were signed. Classroom reports were drafted and commented on and shared: novice work, much learning. The teacher who was portrayed in the classroom study was—with some reason— much dismayed to read his portrait. I was able to assure him that the student had no intention of publishing that work. (He didn't, particularly after talking to the teacher, whose work he actually admired no matter how his report played out, and he had even less intention of doing so when he realized his informant was upset.) (Bishop 122)

Wendy's description is much more careful and rational than mine was; I wrote in my journal, after the professor reacted to what I'd written:

> I can't believe this guy! I can't believe he called me, at home, after midnight last night to yell at me about my paper. We were on the phone for an hour while he disputed everything I said, except the actual facts! Was I wrong when I said [. . .], or when I described his way of [. . .], or [. . .]? [I'm leaving out specific details to protect his identity]. Everything I said was right! It's not my fault if he's offended by his own behaviors.

Once I calmed down (a few days later!), I began to understand the professor's reaction: not so much that I'd included specific unflattering details, but that I'd made him look unprofessional (while I thought he looked quirky and interesting). He was an award-winning faculty member, understandably concerned that a published version of my paper could harm his reputation—an example of what I meant before when I talked about some of the ethical problems that arise from ethnographic writing. In retrospect, I wish I had shown him a draft of the paper while I was working on it so that he'd had a chance to respond, and perhaps clarify, what he believed were misrepresentations and misunderstandings on my part. I also learned a hard lesson about seeing situations from the perspectives of *all* participants; while my paper represented the students' frustrations at length, it didn't account for the professor's nearly well enough.

Risks and Benefits for Participants

Because you're writing about real people in real life in your ethnography, your words have potentially profound consequences for the people you write about. I was devastated by the professor's response to my paper. Somebody I respected was very upset about what I'd written, and beyond his hurt feelings, he was concerned that my piece might affect his professional life. And I would soon teach my first research-writing course, having just experienced first-hand what happens when an ethnographic writer upsets a participant. The professor whose course I'd studied made it quite clear that we were no longer friends, and only once since then have we had any contact at all. He felt *betrayed,* a term I borrow from composition researcher Thomas Newkirk's essay, "Seduction and Betrayal in Qualitative Research." Newkirk contends that because qualitative research is inductive (we don't know what we'll see until it happens), there's no sure way to ensure that participants won't be unhappy about what researchers find; moreover, informed consent not only can't stop this from happening, but also may lull participants into a false sense of security during the project.

Because I wrote the paper for a class with no intention of ever publishing it, the professional consequences for the professor were minimal; that's not to say, of course, that his feelings weren't hurt by the experience. However, even your fieldnotes can have consequences, and you need to be very careful to protect the identities of your participants, even if you don't expect anybody else to see what you write. One former student of mine left his notebook on a table at his site one afternoon, and when he returned five minutes later, two of his participants were reading it. One of them discovered that her boyfriend was cheating on her with another group member; within two days the group had disbanded, and one participant wound up in the hospital with injuries from the ensuing fight.

Situations this dramatic are rare; I've read about 700 ethnographies and count fewer than ten with the potential to endanger any of the participants. The point is that they can be, and you should take steps to minimize the danger: never use anybody's real name or anything that easily identifies them; ask participants to check your notes about them for accuracy, and respect requests not to reveal certain details; make sure participants have signed consent forms. None of these is fail-safe, but they should all be habitual.

Your ethnographic research and writing can, of course, be beneficial for you and your participants, too. Several of my students have discovered, during their projects, significant ways to help their groups. One student, who studied a dance troupe at the university where I did my doctorate, found that the biggest problem they faced was the absence of a regular practice space; she used the evidence she developed in her research—specifically the time members spent worrying about and looking for practice space instead of practicing, and the number of prospective members they lost because they looked disorganized— to argue for a dedicated room, and the group still uses the room to this day. Another studied a university office that provided escorts to students crossing campus late at night. His thesis in the first draft of his paper was that the service was under-utilized, largely because it was understaffed and underfunded. When he showed the draft to the office's director, however, he learned the office had been well-funded and well-advertised for many years, but had slipped off the university's radar. His study, particularly evidence that the staff didn't take its public relations responsibilities very seriously because they didn't have enough people to serve more students, helped the office's director develop a convincing argument to resume funding and public relations work so that the service got the resources it needed.

These projects helped their writers to see the significance of their own writing in very direct terms. One reason their papers worked so well is the *authority* (a somewhat different kind of authority than conventional academic writing demonstrates, a distinction that will be clearer shortly) with which they represented the cultures and the issues. Earlier, I mentioned anthropologist Clifford Geertz and sociologist John Van Maanen, both of whom have been extremely influential among ethnographers in helping us understand what ethnographic writing is good for. Geertz especially, in a book called *Works and Lives: The Anthropologist as Author,* develops two concepts that have become crucial to my understanding of ethnographic writing. First is *ethnographic authority.* In simple terms, the problem is that for decades, anthropologists and sociologists had treated ethnography as if it were a science, i.e., as if it could/should result in objective descriptions of cultures. By the 1960s, ethnographers had begun to realize that objectivity isn't possible in this kind of research; when I said in the second paragraph that ethnography makes you think about the kind of knowledge you make from doing it, this is what I was introducing. To be taken seriously as research, the writing has to demonstrate a level of rigor that many academic disciplines believe is best represented by scientific reportage (like chemistry lab reports—very thoroughly detailed, step-by-step descriptions of processes; careful analysis of results; style that excludes any mention of the researcher; etc.). But with the realization that ethnography doesn't work like a science, ethnographic writers had to think about other ways to establish authority for their work.

Geertz presents the second major concept from *Works and Lives* in the deceptively simple phrase, "being there":

> The ability of anthropologists to get us to take what they say seriously has less to do with either a factual look or an air of conceptual elegance than it has with their capacity to convince us that what they say is a result of their having actually penetrated (or, if you prefer, been penetrated by) another form of life, of having, one way or another, truly 'been there.' (4–5)

As he unpacks this phrase throughout the book, it becomes possible to paraphrase it in another deceptively simple way, i.e., ethnographic authority results from being able to present details and insights that only the writer would know, because the writer was there and readers weren't.

The logic here is circular (authority comes from sounding like an authority)—mostly. Geertz's goal is a little more complicated than I've put it. We haven't explored yet his assertion (or recognition) that issues of writers' *voices* and *styles* are as relevant to ethnographic authority as the writers' *content*. Let me be clear here: nobody would argue that strong voice and style can override bad content; the data/findings/ results have to be strong (in the sense that they're specific, concrete, and analyzed carefully) before presentation matters. But, whereas traditional scientific discourse assumes that personal voice and style are distractions from content, Geertz posits that content, by itself, doesn't really accomplish anything; the knowledge that ethnography produces emerges from the relationships formed among writers and readers. The students in my classes whose projects directly benefited their cultures were all able to construct relationships of trust with their readers—exactly what I failed to do in my project I described earlier—helping the data make the case that something needed to change on behalf of their groups. It's hard to imagine that happening if they hadn't "been there." Another way that ethnographers can benefit participants in our research is by establishing a relationship of *reciprocity*. The principle, in the abstract, is simple—in return for inviting us into their worlds and letting us take information from them, we agree to return the favor by performing services of various kinds for community members. Literacy researcher Ellen Cushman, in her book *The Struggle and the Tools,* describes this exchange between members of a black Muslim mosque and herself as an example:

> [A]rea residents invited me to attend the mosque with them (this group of Muslims happened to be particularly private and only allowed Whites to attend if invited by a member). With their invitation, I was granted entry into a religious arena that I would have been hard pressed to enter otherwise [. . .]. In like fashion, I invited residents [participants in her study] to use the computer facilities of the private university I

attended. Because this institute was private, residents would have been hard pressed to use the computers without my invitation. (23)

Much of her work with the residents of an inner city neighborhood also involved helping them deal with government agencies, advising high school students on college prospects, and similar activities.

Further, the principle of reciprocity signifies a commitment ethnographers make to developing personal relationships with research participants. Not only does reciprocity establish a relationship that goes beyond *taking;* it also allows ethnographers and participants to collaborate in the process of learning about each other, and learning about themselves. As ethnographers, we aren't watching lab rats run through mazes or observing processes in laboratories. We are real people, involving ourselves in the lives of other real people, with real consequences for all of us.

The takeaway value of these concepts (consent, reciprocity) is that you need to respect your participants and make sure you're not exploiting them and their goodwill just for the sake of your grades. Along with heightened attention to writerly authority (the discussion of Geertz earlier), concern for participants as a primary feature of ethnography is the most important shift following from the realization that ethnography isn't a science.

Putting Ethnographic Writing in Historical Context

If ethnography isn't science, then what is it? Why do we talk about it as *research?* If its primary goal—as least as I've been putting it—is to benefit the cultures and participants in studies, then why do ethnographers pay so much attention to procedures, kinds of data, style, voice, authority—all the academic-sounding concerns I'm raising in this essay? The answer, at least my answer, to that question is complicated. To understand it well, it's helpful to know some history of where ethnography and ethnographic writing came from.

Most scholars in Anthropology (ethnography's "home" discipline) agree on two predecessors of ethnography: missionary work and travel writing, beginning as early as the seventeenth and eighteenth centuries. Anthropologist Dell Hymes traces the tradition back to ancient Greece, marked by the beginnings of sea-faring international commerce (21), contending that trade couldn't happen successfully unless traders understood the cultures they were trading with. Other anthropologists (Clifford Geertz; James Clifford; George Marcus; many more) likewise describe the peak of European/Christian missionary work, claiming that missionaries had to study and document the cultures in which they worked, and that the texts they produced were often extremely detailed descriptions of cultures—structures, membership, hierarchies, value systems, rituals, customs. Missionaries' purposes weren't *academic,* i.e., their task wasn't primarily scholarly, but they established the habit of *writing up* their findings.

Their writing, however, didn't need to appeal to an especially wide audience, or an audience that needed to be convinced that the "findings" were rigorous. Their audience was themselves, their churches, and other missionaries who would follow them into similar regions. As people began traveling more in the nineteenth century, many of whom were traveling in lands that missionaries had explored and written about, a new kind of cultural document emerged: travel writing. Nineteenth-century travel writing borrowed from missionary writing the habit of presenting detailed accounts of places, people, customs, rituals, and so on, but more with an eye towards representing the exotic, exciting elements of those cultures. The purpose was to highlight the *otherness* of foreign cultures in order to encourage people to visit them, or to feel like they'd shared the experience of visiting them, without recognizing (or caring about) the risk of stereotyping or marginalizing those cultures.

These forms of pre-ethnographic writing were crucial to developing the discipline of Anthropology, establishing the habits of writing detailed and (ideally) interesting texts about cultures other than the writers.' But missionary and travel writing also laid the seeds for two major ethical problems plaguing ethnographers since: the *imperial* and *colonial* critiques. The *imperial* critique contends that ethnographers bring cultural assumptions and agendas with us when we enter new cultures, and (almost) inevitably try to impose those agendas and values on those cultures—which is, by definition, what missionaries do. I'm not accusing missionaries of anything insidious; I'm making the point that their understandings of other cultures are instrumental (they serve specific purposes) rather than intellectual. As an ethnographer, you'll discover, if you haven't already, that it's very hard not to do this. You can't help but see cultures in terms you're comfortable with. For now, as long as you're not trying to convince members of the cultures you're studying to *think like you do,* to share your beliefs instead of your trying to understand theirs, you're on the right track.

The *colonial* critique emerges more directly from the habits of travel writing, positing that simply taking data from a culture without giving anything back exploits the members of those cultures for personal gain (for academics, that usually means publications and conference presentations; for you, it means course credit and a good grade), leaving the cultures in the same conditions we found them. For many decades, anthropologists studied cultures that were isolated, pre-industrial, and very often on the brink of disappearing or being controlled by powerful nations. My earlier discussions of risks and benefits, especially the notions of respect and reciprocity, developed in direct response to these critiques.

With the shift away from seeing ethnography as science, possibilities for its usefulness have expanded significantly. No longer is ethnography a direct descendent of missionary work, an effort to romanticize the voyeurism of wealthy travelers, or a scientific effort to document different cultures—although it still wrestles with all of those influences. Instead, ethnography is a means of engaging and understanding cultures and cultural differences with respect and care for the members of those cultures.

Learning from a Better Experience

Most of what I've discussed in the last two sections (Risks and Benefits; Historical Context) I learned after I'd struggled with the research project I described earlier. Although I couldn't know then what I know now, at least you can know some of it. In the same spirit but on a happier note, I'll finish this essay by describing a—not to put too fine a point on it—better ethnographic project, one that embodies what I learned. The goal is for you to see what these concepts look like in practice. Although this project was much bigger and more complex than what you're doing, you should be able to see what it looks like to design and conduct a study that incorporates the kinds of care and respect for participants I'm calling for, and to see how various forms of writing contribute to making that happen.

My PhD dissertation, called *Grassroots Democracy in Process: Ethnographic Writing as Democratic Action,* merged my interests in *doing* and *teaching* ethnographic writing. I had taught ethnographic writing in my courses for years, studied what other ethnographic writing teachers do, and studied ethnographic theory and practice in other disciplines. What would happen if I did ethnography in a course where I was teaching ethnography? How would what I'd learned about research ethics, collaborative knowledge-making, and authority play out as I tried both to enact and teach them? I was also interested, as a teacher whose scholarly work speaks primarily to other teachers, in exploring the difficulties of being both the instructor and the researcher in the same setting.

In order to do what I'd learned—and, because I'd already started publishing articles about research ethics, to practice what I preached— a key goal of the project was making sure that the students' needs never became subordinate to mine. I needed to collect data: fieldnotes from every class and conference, transcripts of interviews, the students' writing, course materials, and so on. I also needed not to to push their projects in ways that fit my expectations. Most importantly, I needed to make sure that the students' learning was always the focus of our activities.

For the most part, we could say that I was trying to build the kind of *reciprocal* relationship that Ellen Cushman calls for. Anthropologist Robert Jay probably describes what I was after a little more precisely: a relationship of collaboration and trust. The goal, that is, wasn't simply to return favors to participants, but to establish a relationship in which we all worked together on a common project that benefitted all of us equally as a result. As early as 1969, anthropologists were beginning (and I can't overemphasize that word—even forty years later many anthropologists don't fully subscribe to this position) to privilege the well-being of their research participants above even their own research agendas. Jay declares:

> In future field work I shall place first a mutual responsibility to my whole self and to those I go to learn from, in agreement with my desire to relate to them as full equals, personal and intellectual. I shall try to use my relationships with them to find out what topics are relevant to each of us, to be investigated through what questions and what modes of questioning, and for what kinds of knowledge. I should wish to make the first report for them, in fact with them; indeed it may be that written reports would seem to us redundant. (379)

Jay might sound preachy (he does to me), but his point is important. Ethnographers always have to remember that our work can have serious implications for our participants. As such, we share the responsibility to make those implications: (1) as positive as possible; and (2) collaboratively determined with our participants. By engaging our participants as collaborators, we make sure their needs are just as important as ours; our studies serve their aims as much as ours; and they benefit from participating in them as much as we do.

In my project, students collaborated as fellow researchers primarily by reading, responding to, and discussing every word of my fieldnotes during the semester. Every two weeks, I'd distribute all my notes. They'd read them for homework, and then we'd discuss them. They corrected any mistakes or misattributions in the notes. The discussions would focus on issues they saw recurring or emerging, what they found interesting or anomalous, and questions they had either about the method or the data. Thinking through all this information with the students was stimulating; they had ideas and noticed patterns I wouldn't have, which I carefully credited them with in the dissertation. More important than the direct benefit to me was the sense of collaboration this practice generated among them. Because the group really understood the project as a collaboration rather than an imposition, they spoke candidly about contentious issues, and were willing to trust that when I asked them to do seemingly strange activities, I wasn't just experimenting on them.

I also designed the course so that everything students did for my study helped them with their ethnographies; everything we did served two purposes at once. When they read and commented on fieldnotes, for example, they were collaborating and helping me understand our class, but they were also learning valuable lessons about fieldnote-taking and data presentation. About halfway through the semester, I asked them to interview each other about our class; the transcripts provided me with insights into their thoughts about the semester, while at the same time allowing them to practice interviewing techniques. An exercise late in the semester, in which they reflected on what they thought somebody would need to know in order to do well in the course, helped them learn to synthesize and make claims about vast amounts of data, while showing me what struck them as important, annoying, useful, and distracting about the way we conducted ourselves in class.

By the end of the semester, I had a pretty good idea what my ethnography would say. Its central claim, that involving my students in my project helped them do theirs better, seemed clear and supportable. However, I also knew from my last experience that the obvious claim certainly wasn't all there was to it, and I needed to write and think a lot more about what I'd learned. I was lucky I had lots of time—more than a year—to write slowly and revise extensively; also, I was lucky to have two readers who worked very hard to provide feedback. The upshot of that long process was a project that made a much better claim than the one I'd started with. Yes, the ethnographies from that semester were better than ones I'd read before, but there was more to it than simply that they'd participated in somebody else's study while doing their own. I realized, after months of writing and rewriting, that all the writing we'd done (fieldnotes, comments on fieldnotes, interviews, in-class exercises) had been the catalyst for the students' improved work. That is, the fact that we wrote with, for, and about each other all semester long had helped the students understand what they were engaged in much more richly than they would have otherwise.

You shouldn't be taking my project as a model for yours. But you will, I hope, see one way of working with and through the major concepts I've laid out in the essay (the lessons to be learned about writing: the significant ethical issues that arise from representing other people; and the possible benefits of ethnographic research and writing). Rather than seeing this part of the text as instructions, I'd rather you feel inspired, or provoked—either way, prepared—to think your way through your own projects. The best feature of ethnographic writing is that whatever happens, it's important and interesting as long as you make it so by writing well about it. That's the hardest thing about it, too; nobody can provide you with a precise formula for the writing. You have to work that out by drafting, working with feedback, and revising.

Conclusions and (In)Conclusions

I hope you've learned enough about ethnography's problems and possibilities to understand *why* we ask you to do it. It's connecting events with how you understand them; with how your understanding connects to your participants' understandings; how all of those understandings interrelate, conflict with, and affirm each other; how you expect your readers to make sense of all that in a way that's meaningful for them; and how all that contributes to the lives of your participants and yourself.

Those are lofty goals. You may have noticed that I said little about writing any of my own ethnographic texts; that's partially because this collection limits texts to a certain length, but more importantly because you can only sort through these problems of representation and authority, and of collaboration and mutual respect, by writing your own way through them. Your writing, the feedback you get, and your revision processes will all make you see these problems as connected and complicated; keep writing, and you'll find your way.

Discussion

1. Perhaps the most complex problem facing ethnographic writers is the problem of representing your research participants ethically. How have the theoretical and anecdotal evidence in this chapter helped you think about how to do that?

2. As I was drafting and revising this essay, I asked several classes to read it. There was strong disagreement among my students over which sections they found most convincing: the more traditionally academic, or the more narrative/anecdotal. How would you answer that question, and why?

3. Based on any fieldwork you've already done (if you've begun), or you can imagine doing, what specific strategies can you suggest for avoiding imperial and/or colonial critiques of your own research?

4. What lessons that you're learning about ethnographic research can you imagine applying to other kinds of research and writing that you do as college students, or beyond?

Works Cited

Bishop, Wendy. *Ethnographic Writing Research: Writing It Down, Writing It Up, and Reading It.* Portsmouth, NH: Boynton-Cook/Heinemann, 1999. Print.

Chiseri-Strater, Elizabeth. *Academic Literacies: The Public and Private Discourse of University Students.* Portsmouth, NH: Boynton-Cook/Heinemann, 1991. Print.

Clifford, James. "Introduction: Partial Truths." *Writing Culture: The Poetics and Politics of Ethnography.* Ed. James Clifford and George E. Marcus. Berkeley, CA: U of California P, 1986. 1–26. Print.

Cushman, Ellen. *The Struggle and the Tools: Oral and Literate Strategies in an Inner City Community.* Albany, NY: State U of New York P, 1998. Print. Geertz, Clifford. *Works and Lives: The Anthropologist as Author.* Stanford, CA: Stanford UP, 1988. Print.

Hymes, Dell, ed. *Reinventing Anthropology.* New York: Pantheon, 1972. Print.

Marcus, George. *Ethnography through Thick and Thin.* Princeton, NJ: Princeton UP, 1998. Print.

Newkirk, Thomas. "Seduction and Betrayal in Qualitative Research." *Ethics and Representation in Qualitative Studies of Literacy.* Ed. Peter Mortensen and Gesa E. Kirsch. Urbana, IL: National Council of Teachers of English, 1996. 3–16. Print.

Spradley, James, and David A. McCurdy. *The Cultural Experience: Ethnography in Complex Society.* Chicago: Science Research Associates, 1972. Print.

Sunstein, Bonnie. *Composing a Culture: Inside a Summer Writing Program with High School Teachers.* Portsmouth, NH: Boynton-Cook/Heinemann, 1994. Print.

Van Maanen, John. *Tales of the Field: On Writing Ethnography.* Chicago: U of Chicago P, 1988. Print.

NOW THAT YOU'VE READ

1. Kahn describes types of writing that can be incorporated into ethnographic research. What are they? And what can you add to this list? Can you think of other styles of writing or presenting information that might be useful to use?

2. Read the following passage, and reflect on it:

"Ethnographic writing challenges you to consider everything that's interesting and difficult about writing; it pushes you to generate, collect, analyze, and synthesize more material than you've probably had to work with in one paper before. Moreover, because ethnographies are about actual people, the assignment makes you think about ethics (how you're presenting information, how that information might affect people if made public, being as accurate as you can) and knowledge (what it is you really know at the end of the project and how you present that knowledge without sounding more confident than you should). And finally, because these projects generally take a long time and you write constantly while doing them, you'll have plenty of time to reflect on and understand how you're learning and changing as writers along the way" (175).

Think about what "public" means here and how that might affect what you write and to whom.

3. What points can you take away from Kahn's piece about doing *ethical* research? What concepts should you keep in mind, as you continue your own fieldwork? Note key passages and ideas that you can refer to throughout your project.

READING

Ethnographic Research Ethics and Amish Values
Tabetha Adkins

BEFORE YOU READ answer the following question:

1. Can you imagine any situations or contexts in which the ethical plans you make for your research might actually be inappropriate or unethical?

Ethnographic Research Ethics and Amish Values

Tabetha Adkins

This article is based on my experiences interviewing 25 members of an Amish community in southeast Ohio for my dissertation on the community's literacy practices. I see this text as a response to calls from scholars like Sharon McKenzie Stevens who says in her *Ethnography Unbound* chapter "Debating Ecology: Ethnographic Writing that 'Makes a Difference,'" scholars can no longer simply engage in discussions of whether to write self-reflexivity but must also address "what form of reflexivity to adopt and to what purpose" In this article, I show how the theories of ethical ethnography—theories to which I am very committed—led to some interesting problems in my study of the Amish. I also address which traditional ethnographic methods did not work, which approaches were successful, and what I would like to see come from these kinds of discussions.

The Amish, as many mainstream Americans know, are a religious group whose ancestors immigrated to the United States in the early eighteenth century to seek religious freedom. The Amish are known for "living simply"—that is, they do not use modern conveniences like electricity, cars, or computers as a sacrifice to God. While there are many different denominations or, in the native Pennsylvania Dutch word *Orndung,* the basic tenant of Amish belief comes from *The Bible,* I Peter 2:11, which tells Christians to live "in the world but not of it." As a result, the Amish are typically seen as a characteristically private group of people. I was able to interact with a group of Amish individuals living in southeast Ohio because many of the members of this community are friends and neighbors of my husband's (fiancé at the time of the study) family. It is important to note that my husband's family is not Amish; they are simply farmers who spend a good deal of time with their Amish neighbors.

My primary concern in designing this project was to engage the community in a way that was responsible, ethical, and reflexive. I knew that Amish participants could potentially and understandably resist my attempts to learn about their reading and writing practices, especially since I, as a university professor, represent state-sanctioned education and institutions. Historically, the Amish have fought for the rights to educate their children in the manner dictated by their traditions and faith, and this fight was especially brutal in Ohio where, as Hostetler and Gertrude Enders Huntington show in *Amish Education: Education in the Family, School, and*

Community, Amish fathers were imprisoned for refusing to send their children to state-supported schools (39). The 1972 Supreme Court decision *Wisconsin v. Yoder* gave Amish families the legal right to educate their children as determined by their faith and traditions, but many of the participants in this study attended school before *Wisconsin v. Yoder* and knew of the struggles their fellow-Amish suffered at the hands of local governments and school boards. It was important to me, then, for participants to understand that my goal was not to make a value judgment on their education model, literacy practices, or lifestyles but to learn about their literacy practices. With these goals in mind, I tried to create a research design that was as transparent and reflexive as possible.

I obtained approval from my university's Institutional Review Board (IRB) before beginning the 25 interviews. Upon gaining this approval, I first approached Matthew, a bishop for the community, and asked his permission to interview him. I wanted Matthew to understand the nature of my presence in the community, so that as a leader of the community, he could give guidance to others who had questions about my intentions. Among ethnographers, there is a precedent for interviewing community leaders before engaging with the community as a whole. Sylvia Scribner and Michael Cole state that in their study, "in each town we began our interviewing with the chief and the elder statesmen, as a courtesy and because they usually requested that we begin in this way" (45). My experience with the Amish community leads me to believe that this was the right decision, because if Matthew had heard second-hand that an outsider was asking questions about the community's reading and writing, his reaction could have had a negative effect not only on my study but also on my relationship with the Amish community members.

During this first interview, I could see almost immediately that there were problems with my IRB approved informed consent forms. Matthew had many questions about the form. He could not understand why categories like "Privacy," "Risk," and "Compensation" were present if all I wanted to do was talk about reading and writing. I allowed him to read the questions I wanted to ask, and seeing these questions put him at ease. I explained that the consent form uses academic conventions that are required by the university. However, it was clear to me that in composing this form, I had considered the wrong audience; I was writing for the IRB, not for the Amish. Although the form was relatively free from "academic jargon," phrases like "the data will be stored on a password-protected computer" and the inclusion of telephone numbers should have been revised. I learned quickly that in a community where computers are absent, there is no perceived difference between a computer and the Internet, so some community members thought I was placing their personal data on the Internet. And in hindsight, what phones did I think the Amish would use to call me or the IRB at my university? Perhaps I should have began my study by asking Matthew to help me with my informed consent form, because he provided very useful feedback that informed the rest of my study; he suggested that I allow all interview participants to see the questions in advance, so I did. In the interest of transparent research, I have included those questions at the end of this article.

A second complication of the data-gathering process was one I anticipated and for which I was prepared. Ethnographers generally agree that a tape recorder is an essential tool of good ethnography. The problem this method created for my research is that the Amish, who believe they are made in God's image and, in accordance with Exodus 20: 4 which warns Christians against "mak[ing] for yourself a carved image—any likeness of anything that is in heaven above," do not allow themselves to be photographed or audio recorded since an audio recording is, in a sense, a photograph of one's voice. Andrea Fishman addresses this conundrum in her own study of the Amish, stating that she was given permission to use a tape recorder but found that "the big black box" (tape recorder) was too much of a distraction to her participants who were not used to having such technology present (11-12). I therefore prepared to write with pen and paper participants' responses to my questions. I developed an elaborate note-taking code that allowed me to use symbols and abbreviations for commonly used terms like Amish, English, church, school, family, et cetera. At the end of every interview, I read my notes back to the participant to ensure I had not misunderstood any of their responses. After leaving an interview, I sat down immediately to write "reflective remarks" and to interpret my symbols and abbreviated notes into a longer narrative as is suggested by methodologists Matthew Miles and A. Michael Huberman (66).

When I imagined how the interviews would take place, I pictured myself sitting with participants at their kitchen tables, talking without interruption for half an hour. But as many ethnographers report, this ideal scenario is rare whenever research occurs outside of the academy. Scribner and Cole explain thusly:

> Individual sessions were not always private sessions. Every effort was made to secure quiet and privacy for the respondent by interviewing inside our rented houses; during especially hot spells, interviewers set up tables and chairs under trees remote from public walk-and-lounge ways. Even with these precautions, the novelty of the proceedings, especially for the first few days after our arrival in a town, tended to attract a fringe of interested observers. Onlookers offered comments from time to time on the interview conversations. These intrusions represented little threat to the integrity of the information secured on personal history, but we had to take into account in our data analysis their potential contaminating influence on responses to attitude questions and experimental tasks. (46)

Indeed, I shared similar intentions of privacy when I planned my research. These plans did not take into account, however, several factors that affected my research experience. First of all, I underestimated the hectic schedule of the average Amish man, woman, and child. Instead of finding a quiet place to sit and talk, participants found time for our chats between planting rows of corn, while completing tasks for the upcoming school auction, while hand-stitching quilts, and during the clean-up from a sibling's wedding. During the first day of interviews, I quickly realized that I would not always have the convenience of a kitchen table to spread out my interview materials, nor would I always be able to have the undivided attention of an interview participant. Instead, I found myself balancing my notebook on my hip while standing in a blacksmith's forge or making funny faces at a crying baby. Like Scribner and Cole, I did not feel that these interview conditions affected the integrity, honesty, or quality of the answers participants provided. Instead, I felt that this gave me a better understanding of the participants' lives and created a more organic research atmosphere.

Secondly, while I anticipated that the fact that I am unfamiliar, not Amish, and curious would make some participants uneasy, I was surprised by how much the presence of my primary informant, Jeanie, my (non-Amish) mother-in-law, put many participants at ease. When she volunteered to take me to different Amish homes and businesses, I imagined her as a silent observer who introduced me to potential interview participants and then waited in the car. Instead, Jeanie stayed to watch the interviews—she was present at 22 of the 25 interviews—and at times, she engaged in conversation with the participants. For example, on one occasion, an interview with Joseph was not going as well as I had hoped. Joseph had been interviewed by someone he identified as a college student at Ohio State University several years earlier when his son was a patient the University's hospital. This student had asked Joseph many questions he described as "embarrassing" and had conducted the interview in a private room; the entire experience made Joseph uneasy and angry. This occurrence made him distrustful of people asking for interviews, and especially of people from universities. I assured him that I had the utmost respect for the people of this community and mentioned specifically the kind treatment I had received from the Amish members of the community when a member of my (then) fiancé's (now husband's) family died the previous summer. Seeing that Joseph could relate to this, Jeanie added that she had more Amish friends than non-Amish friends and that she really enjoyed getting to know the Amish people in the neighborhood. This statement seemed to comfort him, and Joseph then allowed me to continue the interview. He even seemed to enjoy our conversation.

When I reflected on this later and asked Jeanie about her comments, she said that she felt she could help. And while many scholars of research methods and ethics might argue that Jeanie's influence on the interviews may have negatively affected the outcome, I argue that the social conditions present in this community create a unique research situation for which any research methods class or text could not prepare me. The value placed upon privacy and preserving a way of life force the Amish to be careful about whom they interact with; as a result, it is important to know who people are. Knowing this, Jeanie always introduced me as her "future daughter-in-law" and specified to which of her sons I engaged.

Getting to "know" people—a value important to my Amish participants—was the greatest surprise of the study. Again, the study would not have been possible if I had not created these kinds of relationships. To borrow Bruce Horner's words, these relationships were critical to the *demands,* not the dilemmas of the study (14).

Since my data-collection period ended, many participants have asked my in-laws about me, my research, and the progress of my scholarship. Some participants have even sent me presents: Ezekiel sent me a mug with the name of his business printed on it; Caleb sent me an article from a newspaper about a business pretending to use Amish artists to craft "Amish stoves"; Jacob sent me an Amish man's Sunday hat to display in my office with my Amish made quilt. Experiences like these—connecting with people, developing relationships—are what drew me to ethnography as a research method in the first place. While some methodologists like Michael Quinn Patton warn ethnographers of growing too close to participants for fear of "going native," I would argue that in this case, my bond with the community only led to better results since familiarity and friendship, not college degrees and institutional support, are what create credibility and trust in the Amish community (568).

Another methodological choice I made concerned compensation. Because I was a graduate student living on teaching assistant wages at the time of this study, I decided to not offer compensation to interview participants. In hindsight, it is clear to me that even if I could have provided financial compensation, I made the right decision because participants would have been confused by the concept for which they were being paid. In this community, families make their money with labor, not with conversation or ideas. Academics, of course, are used to being paid for their ideas, but in the Amish community, this concept is a foreign one. This notion, like the language on the IRB form, serves as another example of the conflict between academic and Amish values. Instead of compensating individual participants for their time and responses, I decided to follow the advice provided by Katrina Powell and Pamela Takayoshi in their article, "Accepting Roles Created for Us: The Ethics of Reciprocity." Like Powell and Takayoshi, I wanted to find a research model that removed the power dynamic inherent in research. Most importantly, I wanted the Amish to benefit somehow from this experience. I decided that I could help the larger community by buying a quilt from their annual auction for which community members donate quilts, furniture, farm animals, and baked goods that are sold to support the private parochial Amish schools for the entire school year. While this transaction was certainly to my advantage—I acquired a beautiful piece of art created by people I admire and respect—I came to see this arrangement as one the Amish would appreciate; the generosity of a few members of the community—those who decided to participate in the study—benefited the entire community, as my purchase helped support the community-sustained schools.

While I believe that ethics and the research traditions of IRB, informed consent, and ethnographic "distance" for the subject are essential for creating solid research and protecting subjects, my experience has prompted me to rethink some of these traditions. Certainly, researchers concede that every research situation is different, but it is unethical to suggest that the approach for every context should be the same. In this article, I have addressed the research methodologies presented most often to students of ethnography and how these methods either worked or did not for my study of an extra academic group, the Amish. My goal was to show how these methodologies, while good guides toward ethical practices, do not always work when we leave the safe confines of the academy to conduct literacy research. Since writing scholars are turning to communities outside of the academy more and more, it is most important that when we teach these methodologies, we also equip student ethnographers with tools to critically think through the interesting scenarios they may be faced with in the field.

Works Cited

Fishman, Andrea. *Amish Literacy: What and How it Means*. Portsmouth, NH: Heinemann, 1988. Print.

Horner, Bruce. "Critical Ethnography, Ethics, and Work: Rearticulating Labor." *Ethnography Unbound: From Theory Shock to Critical Praxis*. Eds. Stephen Gilbert Brown Sidney I. Dobrin. Albany, NJ: State U of New York P, 2004. 1334. Print.

Miles, Matthew B. and A. Michael Huberman. *Qualitative Data Analysis*. 2nd ed. Thousand Oaks, CA: Sage, 1994. Print.

New King James Bible. Nashville: Thomas Nelson, 1997. Print.

Patton, Michael Quinn. *Qualitative Research and Evaluation Methods*. 3rd ed. Thousand Oaks, CA: Sage, 2002. Print.

Powell, Katrina and Pamela Takayoshi. "Accepting Roles Created for Us: The Ethics of Reciprocity." *College Composition and Communication* 54.3 (2003): 394-422. Print.

Scribner, Sylvia and Michael Cole. *The Psychology of Literacy*. 1981. Cambridge, MA: Harvard, 1999. Print.

Stevens, Sharon McKenzie. "Debating Ecology: Ethnographic Writing that 'Makes a Difference.'" *Ethnography Unbound: From Theory Shock to Critical Praxis*. Eds. Stephen Gilbert Brown and Sidney I. Dobrin. Albany, NJ: State U of New York P, 2004. 157-180. Print.

Wisconsin v. Yoder, 406 U.S. 205 (1972), Supreme Court of the United States. In Depth Write up of the Supreme Court Case. Web. 10 June 2008.

1. In what kinds of circumstances would you change your research plans? Is it more important to conduct the research project as you imagined it or adjust to the needs, values, and ideas of your participants?

2. What are the ways in which Adkins adjusted her research to be more ethical? Give examples. What struggles did she face?

READING

CCCC Guidelines for the Ethical Conduct of Research in Composition Studies

BEFORE YOU READ, answer the following questions:

1. Based on the readings you've done already for this chapter, what questions do you have about ethical research?

2. As you think about your own communities and ethnographic projects more broadly, what possible tensions or issues might arise in response to ethics and ethical treatment?

CCCC Guidelines for the Ethical Conduct of Research in Composition Studies

Preamble

The CCCC represents teachers and researchers of composition and communication in all possible genres, media, contexts, and exigencies; for the purpose of these guidelines, "writers" and "writing" will be all-encompassing, and the term "researcher" will refer to anyone who undertakes a study. We embrace numerous subfields, many of which have also issued their own ethical statements and have published commentary about conducting research that should be consulted. As members of the CCCC, we share a commitment to protecting the rights, privacy, dignity, and well-being of the persons who are involved in our studies, whether as participants or co-researchers. These guidelines are intended to assist researchers in fulfilling this commitment.

The following guidelines have been informed by U.S. Federal policies, regulations, and laws on the ethical conduct of research;[1] however, they do not replace or supersede them. Researchers who conduct studies outside of their home countries should also refer to the policies, regulations, and laws that govern the locales where the research takes place. The U.S. Office of Human Research Protections maintains a listing of international standards that may be consulted.[2]

The following guidelines apply to all efforts by scholars, teachers, administrators, students, and others that are directed toward publication of a book or journal article, presentation at a conference, preparation of a thesis or dissertation, display on a website, or other general dissemination of the results of research and scholarship. The guidelines apply to formally planned investigations. They likewise apply to emergent studies that discuss the writers and unpublished writing that researchers encounter in other ways, such as when teaching classes, holding student conferences, directing academic programs, conducting research in nonacademic settings, or going about their professional, civic, and personal lives.

U.S. Federal policy allows an exception for studies that researchers conduct solely for the purpose of improving their own practice, or solely for discussion within their own institution. To confirm that a study falls under the exception, researchers should follow local review processes. Moreover, even in studies confirmed as exceptions (granted an exemption), CCCC members carefully protect the rights, privacy, dignity, and well-being of their participants and co-researchers. These guidelines suggest ways to accomplish this goal.

Compliance

As researchers, we learn about and comply with all policies, regulations, and laws that apply to our studies. Many institutions have an Institutional Review Board (IRB)[3] or alternative review process to which we submit our plans for advance review and approval. We then conduct our studies in accordance with the approved research plans. We also confirm with the IRB or alternative review committee if we believe a proposed study should be allowed an exception (granted an exemption). If we work at or are students at an institution without an IRB or alternative review process, then we contact colleagues at other institutions so we can learn about and follow procedures that IRBs require.[4]

Although we comply with the final decision of our IRBs or alternative review processes, we recognize that members of the review committee may need to be educated about the particular methods and methodologies of writing research. As researchers, we negotiate with committees about IRB requirements or restrictions that hamper research unnecessarily and without benefit to participants. Moreover, we engage in ongoing conversations with regulatory agents to advise them in developing policies, regulations, and laws that take into account the methods and methodologies of writing research.

We acknowledge that mere compliance with policies, regulations, and laws does not necessarily guarantee the ethical conduct of research (see Maintaining Competence).

Maintaining Competence

As researchers, we strive to refine our competence and to keep apprised of ongoing ethical discussions for several reasons:

1. Understandings of and definitions of ethical research practices are constantly negotiated among members of a discipline or subfield;

2. New experiences among researchers and participants may raise new ethical issues; and

3. Formal policies, regulations, and laws continually evolve (See the "Selected Bibliography" section).

We assure that we are appropriately trained and prepared to conduct the studies we undertake, and we likewise assure that our co-researchers and assistants are appropriately trained and prepared. Training and preparation may include activities such as enrollment in classes, review of relevant published research and methodological discussions, and consultation or collaboration with other experienced researchers.

Researchers who are supervisors of and/or collaborators with novice researchers (such as undergraduates, graduate students, postdoctoral scholars, colleagues new to a discipline/subfield, and participant-researchers) should maintain frequent and open discussion of research procedures with those in their charge as the studies are conducted and disseminated.

Recruiting

Some studies may include populations who may be considered vulnerable and protected, including but not limited to children and adolescent minors, students, prisoners, pregnant women, military veterans, disenfranchised groups, persons with disabilities, and adults with legal guardians. In these cases, as researchers, we consult carefully with the IRB/reviewing agencies, colleagues, and (when allowed) with prospective participants to develop a protocol that protects their rights, privacy, well-being, and especially, dignity.

When conducting studies with individuals who are perceived to have less institutional power or others whose well-being depends on the researcher's opinions, decisions, or actions, we take special care to protect prospective participants from adverse consequences of declining or withdrawing from participation.[5]

To avoid situations in which students feel that their decision to participate (or not) in a study might affect their instructor's treatment of them, we recruit participants from other classes or other sources. If the topic of the research or other special circumstances require that the study involve our own students, then we use measures to avoid coercion or perceived coercion, such as confirming students' voluntary participation after grades are submitted or asking colleagues to conduct the actual data collection.

Obtaining Informed Consent

When asking people to volunteer to participate in (or in the case of co-researchers or novice researchers, collaborate in the design and execution of) a study, we provide participants a copy of the consent document and explain the study in a way that enables the participants to understand the following points:

1. The purpose of the research and its possible benefits.

2. Why the participant was recruited.

3. What the participant will be asked to do and how long it will take.

4. What we plan to do with the information or data obtained from participants.

5. Any potential discomforts, harms, or risks one might incur as a result of participating and how we plan on minimizing any potential discomforts, harms, or risks.

6. Any potential benefits (separate from compensation, if any) participants may experience from the study.

7. Whether or not we intend to include data in research reports that would render participants identifiable. (We always honor participants' requests that disseminated reports contain no personally identifiable information, including data that would make them identifiable to persons familiar with the research site. We acknowledge that sometimes a conflict may emerge when some participants want to remain anonymous and others want to be recognized, and we resolve the issue before presenting, publishing, or reporting on the study.)

8. How confidential data will be stored and who will have access to confidential data and materials, particularly in the case of research teams/co-researchers. If data and materials are to be included in an archive, we receive explicit consent (see "Conducting Studies Involving Archival Work").

In addition, we emphasize the following points:

1. Participation is completely voluntary.

2. Participants can decline to answer any questions instead of withdrawing from the study.

3. Participation is an ongoing and constantly negotiated process between the participants and the researcher or research team.

4. If anonymity for participants is not possible, then we are explicit about this constraint.

5. Participants may withdraw at any time without penalty or loss of benefits to which they are otherwise entitled.

For studies involving vulnerable populations who have parents or legal guardians, we obtain written permission from the parents or legal guardians in addition to the assent of the prospective participant or we seek permission from IRBs for a waiver of consent. If required, we also gain the permission of sponsoring institutions, such as public schools or private workplaces. We are careful to determine that whatever terms of access we agree to are consistent with the stipulations of applicable IRB regulations and the provisions of these guidelines.

We always provide those invited to participate in a study an opportunity to ask questions. When asked questions by participants during or after a study, we reply in a timely manner.

In the case of classes in which undergraduate and graduate students are collaborators in research projects, we guide their work toward best practices and acknowledge their collaboration in any presentation, publication, or report.

These guidelines concerning informed consent are intended to complement (not replace) any additional requirements of applicable policies, regulations, and laws.

Conducting Studies Involving Classes

When conducting studies involving classes, we give primary consideration to the goals of the course and fair treatment of all students. Toward that end, we take the following measures, whether the students are members of our own classes or are from classes taught by colleagues:

1. We design our studies so that participation is completely voluntary.

2. We assure that volunteering, declining to volunteer, or deciding to withdraw after volunteering will not affect a student's grade.

3. We assure that pursuit of our research goals will not hinder achievement of the course's educational goals.

4. We assure that all students will receive the same attention, instruction, support, and encouragement in the course. For example, studies may be conducted so that instructors do not know who participated or not until the class is over.

5. We assure that reports on the research do not include information about students who did not volunteer.

6. If there is a possibility that one or more of the volunteering students have changed their minds since the study began, we obtain confirming consent at the end of the course.

7. In the case of classes in which undergraduate and graduate students are collaborators in research projects, we guide our work toward best practices and acknowledge their collaboration in any publication.

Conducting Studies Outside the Classroom

When conducting studies in sites outside the classroom, we give primary consideration to the contexts of our research and to the fair treatment of all participants. Toward that end, we take the following measures:

1. We design our studies so that participation is completely voluntary.

2. We assure that volunteering, declining to volunteer, or deciding to withdraw after volunteering will not affect participants or a participant's standing at the research site.

3. We assure that pursuit of our research goals will not hinder achievement or operation at our research site.

4. We coordinate and discuss our research plan with site leaders/administrators before proceeding with research.

5. We assure that reports on the research do not include information about participants who did not volunteer.

6. In the case of research projects in which participants, undergraduate, and/or graduate students are collaborators, we guide our work toward best practices and acknowledge their collaboration in any publication.

7. When conducting research with protected/vulnerable populations, we follow federal guidelines to ensure our research is ethical and legal.

Conducting Studies Involving Digital/Online Media

When conducting studies involving digital/online media, we are particularly aware that researchers' and participants' expectations regarding the public/private, published versus unpublished documents, informed consent, sensitivity of the data, vulnerability of the participants, identifiability of the data, and other aspects of the research study must be negotiated.[6] We recognize that these expectations are often contingent and may shift in response to revised trajectories in disciplinary research practices; newly introduced, innovative technologies; and the multifaceted histories that specific digital/online communities have experienced. As a result, we should explicitly justify our research choices and our positioning as researchers when we plan, conduct, and publish our studies.

We do not assume, for example, that all digital/online communications are available for research studies simply because they can be accessed. Nor do we assume that we must always receive express permission from authors before citing their digital/online materials. A balance must be struck between these extremes, a balance that is informed by institutional regulation, consultation with published research and other researchers, discussion with members of the online communities themselves, and sensitivity to and understanding of the expectations that authors (including student authors) may have had in posting their materials.

We are also aware that promising anonymity to participants may be impossible when conducting certain digital/online studies. Communication technologies may not be secure enough for discussing sensitive topics. Likewise, search engines have become increasingly powerful in their capacity to locate text strings. Materials that are protected behind a firewall or password today may become readily available tomorrow as passwords are compromised, the mode of access changes, a database is archived, or other modifications in technology occur that are beyond the researcher's control. Instead, we may need to integrate practices that take into account these possibilities, such as finding alternate means of communicating with participants; turning off the collection of IP addresses in online survey services; asking participants' permission to use real names; allowing participants to review interview data before employing them; and so on.

Researchers interested in digital/online media are encouraged to consult the more extensive ethical guidelines published by researchers in these subfields, including those by the Association of Internet Researchers. In addition, they are encouraged to consult the many and lengthy discussions found in the provided Bibliography.

Conducting Studies Involving Archival Work

As researchers, we often consult library resources, museums, and other archival materials. These already collected materials are not governed by IRB review. However, we are aware that some archival materials may have been assembled without ethical consideration for all cultural stakeholders involved, and that understandings of ethical standards may shift over time. As researchers, we are alert to these concerns and debates, and when we choose to use these archival materials, we strive to represent them and their multilayered, multivoiced contexts accurately and fairly.

The following guidelines speak to studies that involve living participants, plus the intent to generate, construct, and curate an archive. Such a study typically requires an IRB's/review committee's approval. For example, as researchers, we may collect and analyze a large sample of student or professional documents, and then make the documents available for use by other researchers. When we plan to build a new archive as a component of a study, we need to negotiate several considerations:

1. As researchers, we are sensitive to our participants as cultural stakeholders in a long-term archive of materials. We explicitly ask for permission to include a participant's materials in an archive. In some cases, stakeholders may actively collaborate on building the archive. Negotiations over what materials to include and exclude should be explicit, and they may need to consider

the archival materials' impact on the descendants of those whose work is included.

2. Libraries and other institutional repositories may not be able to accept materials from studies involving human participants unless their own versions of permission forms are collected in addition to informed consent letters. (These additional permissions often address intellectual property and access issues.) As researchers, we consult early in the process with the intended host to determine what conditions may apply and what procedures to follow.

3. We must balance accessibility to the archive with both the participants' and the future researchers' rights to privacy. When we create archives, we organize the artifacts and the information about their provenance so that the organization is clear and consistent. If we create or adopt data-mining tools for digital archives, we facilitate access to the artifacts without violating the researchers' privacy. When we compile culturally sensitive records, we are careful to follow procedures to maintain participants' anonymity when permission to use real names is not granted (for example, by removing identifying information and/or by embargoing materials until an agreed-upon date).

4. We acknowledge the impact that different cataloging, data-mining, coding, and other software may have in shaping our access to and interpretation of archival information. When building an archive, and when reporting on materials in an archive, we explicitly name and justify the relevant software used.

5. We strive to ensure the proper long-term storage and preservation of artifacts, whether they are physical or digital materials.

Conducting Studies Involving Assessment Data

Studies involving assessment data may include outcomes data, portfolio evidence, survey data, directed self-placement scores, interviews, and so on. According to U.S. Federal policy, if such studies are conducted solely for the purpose of internal assessment (e.g., placement testing, improving a program), they are typically considered exceptions. As researchers, we confirm the exception (request an exemption) as well as any local requirements (e.g., anonymity of data) with our IRB/review committee.

If we plan to present, publish, or report on assessment data beyond the local institution, then we submit a protocol for advance review and approval by the IRB/review committee.

Using Unpublished Writing Collected Outside of an IRB-Approved Study

When studying unpublished writing samples that have been collected outside of a study approved by an IRB or other process, we, (and, when applicable, our undergraduate/graduate researchers, collaborators, and colleagues), determine whether our planned use of these samples is consistent with the policies governing research at our institutions and, if different, the institution at which the samples were collected.

When using unpublished writing samples for reasons outside of research purposes (e.g., textbook samples, writing samples collected for writing consultant or teacher training), we determine whether our use of these samples is consistent with the policies governing student privacy at our institutions, and, if different, the institution at which samples were collected.

We continue to apply to these materials the same ethical guidelines we employ when analyzing and reporting on data collected under the auspices of an IRB-approved study. We are also mindful that copyright regulations may apply to these materials.

Quoting, Paraphrasing, and Reporting Statements

In our publications, presentations, and other research reports, we quote, paraphrase, or otherwise report unpublished written statements only with the author's permission. That permission may be indicated by written consent, or (in digital/online research) through click-through approval on a form, and/or through another procedure approved by an IRB or alternative review process. We likewise seek permission to quote, paraphrase, or otherwise report a spoken statement that a participant has made with the expectation that it will remain private. U.S. Federal policy allows an exception to be made for spoken statements made while participants are speaking in or attending a public forum (the definition of which may be contingent upon institutional regulation, previously published research, and the expectations of the participants involved).

When quoting, paraphrasing, or reporting unpublished writing and when reporting (with permission) oral statements made in private, we respect the writer's or speaker's wishes about whether or not to include the writer's or speaker's name or identifying information. When the writer or speaker is a member of a vulnerable/protected population with a parent or legal guardian, we obtain permission from a parent or legal guardian in addition to the assent of the prospective participant. When we use an informed consent process approved by an IRB or similar committee, we have obtained the necessary permission.

We do our best to represent language/meaning accurately, understanding that meaning-making is often negotiated, shifting, multivoiced, and changeable over time. We report written and spoken statements in ways consistent with the collected data, and avoid deliberately misrepresenting participants' words. We provide contextual information that will enable others to understand the statements the way the writer or speaker intended. When in doubt, we check the accuracy of the reports and interpretations with the writer or speaker. We are especially sensitive to the need to check interpretations when the writer or speaker is from a cultural, ethnic, or other group different from our own.

When discussing the statements that we quote, paraphrase, or otherwise report, we do so in ways that are fair and serious, and that avoid harm.

Describing Individuals and Groups

We describe individuals and groups fairly and accurately, in ways that are accountable to the data, observation, or other evidence on which the descriptions are based. We describe people in ways that are fair and serious, avoid harm, and protect privacy.

Using Video, Audio, Photographs, and Other Identifiable Representations of Participants

Because video, audio, photographs, and other representations (e.g., cartoons) of participants in the studies that we conduct allow individuals to be identified, we include them in conference presentations, publications, or other public displays only with written consent (or other approved procedure for receiving consent) from all persons whose voices and/or images were recorded or shown. When the person recorded is a member of a vulnerable/protected population with a parent or legal guardian, then we obtain permission from the parent or legal guardian in addition to the assent of the prospective participant. When we use an informed consent process approved by an IRB or similar committee, we have obtained the necessary permission.

One exception allowed by U.S. Federal policy are instances when the recording was made while participants were speaking in or attending a public forum (the definition of which may be contingent upon institutional regulation, previously published research, and the expectations of the participants involved).

Working with Co-Researchers and Co-Authors

Research studies often rely upon the assistance of many people, not only the participants, but also those who organize and perform data collection, those who assist with coding, those who analyze information, and so on. We are generous in acknowledging these contributions, whether by name or general category (e.g., reviewers of the manuscript).

In some cases, participants in and/or other contributors to a study should be considered co-researchers and/or co-authors. Determining who should be a co-researcher and/or co-author depends on disciplinary convention, institutional regulation, and local expectations. Ideally, participants who become co-researchers and/or co-authors benefit, learn, and gain insight/knowledge through the collaborative process. We strive for reciprocal relations. Participants who become co-authors should be made aware that a designated "author" on a publication has legal privileges (e.g., copyright) and ethical obligations for the acceptable conduct, representation, and/or dissemination of the study.

Co-researcher status and/or co-authorship may be determined at the beginning of the study, or they may emerge during the course of the study. In either case, expectations about who can use what data, and under what circumstances, should be negotiated and made explicit. Many institutions have a representative, committee or office (such as the IRB office or Ombuds Office) that can assist in negotiating these expectations to avoid conflicts.

Working with Editors/Publishers

When accepting manuscripts for publication or other public display, editors and publishers should assist in maintaining ethical standards without unduly burdening the researcher. For example, editors/publishers should doublecheck for occasions where identifying information has been incorporated accidentally into a manuscript, or for representations of participants that may be misunderstood.

Publishers also recognize the difference between informed consent letters (as approved by an IRB or other reviewing committee) and copyright release permissions. If anonymity has been promised to participants, it is inappropriate to demand copies of the signed informed consent letters.

Indicating Possible Financial Conflicts of Interest

In accordance with U.S. Federal guidelines, for any presentation, publication, or report on a study, the researcher(s) shall make full disclosure of all possible financial conflicts of interest with an entity connected to the research topics. (Research conducted under the auspices of other nations should accommodate those nations' regulations regarding conflicts of interest as well.) The following exceptions are allowed:

1. Amounts less than $5,000 per calendar year per entity and associated entities
2. Book royalties
3. Instances when an author's or speaker's stated affiliation is with the entity or associated entities.

This policy applies to all researchers associated with the study. Presenters at a conference will also disclose if an interested entity has paid some or all of the expenses related to performing the study and/or attending the conference.

Full disclosure can consist of statements in the methods section, acknowledgements, footnotes/endnotes, or, in the case of a presentation, a statement on a slide or handout. The exact amount of financial remuneration need not be disclosed, but, except for the cases indicated above, the fact that remuneration was received must be stated.

Selected Bibliography

CCCC has compiled a selected bibliography of sources on the ethical conduct of research involving human participants. It is available at http://www.ncte.org/cccc/resources/positions/ethicalconductbiblio.

Notes

[1] Information about these policies, regulations, and laws can be found at the U.S. Department of Health & Human Services, Office of Human Research Protections, http://www.hhs.gov/ohrp/

[2] The International Compilation of Human Research Standards, http://www.hhs.gov/ohrp/international/index.html

[3] An institutional review board is a committee established under the federal regulation for the protection of research participants (45 CFR 46). Each IRB is legally responsible for assuring that all research involving human participants that is conducted under the aegis of its institution complies with this regulation. For more information, visit the website of the federal Office for Human Research Protections: http://www.hhs.gov/ohrp/

[4] In several cases, institutions without IRBs have made arrangements with a local institution with an IRB to conduct the reviews.

[5] This sentence is adapted from the American Psychological Association Ethics Code, 3.08. http://www.apa.org/ethics/code/

[6] This section has been informed by work by Heidi McKee & James E. Porter. "The Ethics of Digital Writing Research: A Rhetorical Approach." College Composition and Communication 59.4 (2008): 711–749, and by the Association of Internet Researchers' 2002 and 2012 reports, Ethical decision-making and Internet research: Recommendations from the AoIR ethics working committee, located at http://aoir.org/ethics/Researchers may also be interested in the Statement of Principles and Best Practices by the Oral History Association, located at http://www.oralhistory.org/about/principles-and-practices/

NOW THAT YOU'VE READ

1. Refer to the "Obtaining Informed Consent" section and discuss answers and think through to the following points, using Tabetha Adkins' example of research. Adkins might not say these phrases, but what information can you

glean from her piece in response to these points? You will use these points later on to create your own Informed Consent Form for your ethnography.

The CCCC Guidelines for the Ethical Conduct of Research in Composition Studies states:

"When asking people to volunteer to participate in (or in the case of co-researchers or novice researchers, collaborate in the design and execution of) a study, we provide participants a copy of the consent document and explain the study in a way that enables the participants to understand the following points:

1. The purpose of the research and its possible benefits.

2. Why the participant was recruited.

3. What the participant will be asked to do and how long it will take.

4. What we plan to do with the information or data obtained from participants.

5. Any potential discomforts, harms, or risks one might incur as a result of participating and how we plan on minimizing any potential discomforts, harms, or risks.

6. Any potential benefits (separate from compensation, if any) participants may experience from the study.

7. Whether or not we intend to include data in research reports that would render participants identifiable. (We always honor participants' requests that disseminated reports contain no personally identifiable information, including data that would make them identifiable to persons familiar with the research site. We acknowledge that sometimes a conflict may emerge when some participants want to remain anonymous and others want to be recognized, and we resolve the issue before presenting, publishing, or reporting on the study.)

8. How confidential data will be stored and who will have access to confidential data and materials, particularly in the case of research teams/co-researchers. If data and materials are to be included in an archive, we receive explicit consent (see "Conducting Studies Involving Archival Work").

In addition, we emphasize the following points:

1. Participation is completely voluntary.

2. Participants can decline to answer any questions instead of withdrawing from the study.

3. Participation is an ongoing and constantly negotiated process between the participants and the researcher or research team.

4. If anonymity for participants is not possible, then we are explicit about this constraint.

5. Participants may withdraw at any time without penalty or loss of benefits to which they are otherwise entitled" (CCCC Guidelines for the Ethical Conduct of Research in Composition Studies).

EXAMPLE
CODE OF ETHICS

Preamble

As a researcher, my goal is to obtain information about a certain subject. When researching, there are certain rules necessary to solicit information from people involved in any study to ensure my research is conducted as ethically as possible. Therefore, my research will be guided by the following Code of Ethics.

Of course, every situation will be different, and the researcher will have to judge how to proceed based on her or his own judgment. Regardless, every interaction with the individuals involved in my study—from data collection to analysis to writing up the results—will be guided by these principles.

Responsibility to People

1. Researchers have a primary obligation to ensure the safety of the people they study, minimizing any risks they may encounter.

2. Risks involved in research like this include the potential discomfort participants may suffer when responding to questions and the time commitment required of them. It is vital that researchers take every precaution to protect the people involved in their study.

3. The researcher will respect the wishes of each individual he or she studies.

4. The researcher will protect the persons studied from harm.

5. The researcher will treat each person according to individual need.

6. The researcher will not disclose the identity of the persons studied unless explicitly given permission by the research participant in writing via an Informed Consent Form.

7. The researcher will ask for the consent of the persons studied (see #6 above).

8. The researcher will not take advantage of the persons studied in any way.

Other Responsibilities

1. The researcher will not make up false accounts.

2. The researcher will handle conflicts in a dignified manner according to the principles outlined in this Code of Conduct.

3. The researcher will be truthful.

Conclusion

The researcher will apply this to any type of research conducted. The guidelines above shall be honored and noted in times of conflict. However, some guidelines may overlap with other obligations made with the researcher. The guidelines set are general and are made to give a precedent of behavior when conducting research.

EXAMPLE

INFORMED CONSENT FORM

NOTE: You will need to submit Informed Consent Forms from every individual with whom you interact for your study, whether that is through interviews, surveys, or other means. The following example is for an interview. If you are using another research tool such as a survey or focus group, you may adapt the following form accordingly.

Name of Researcher

Contact Information for Researcher

I understand that I am being interviewed and recorded for an ethnographic research project conducted by _____ (name of student researcher) for _____ (class) at _____ (school) taught by _____ (name of teacher). I agree to let him/her use the interview to write a paper for the class. It will not be used for any other purpose. I have been informed that if I become uncomfortable at any time during the interview, I do not have to answer questions or I can ask to have the tape or video recorder (if used) turned off. I am aware that I can request that a pseudonym be used. I understand that by signing this form, I give permission for the interview to be used for the purposes stated above.

Do you agree to participate in the interview	YES	NO
Can the interview be recorded?	YES	NO
Should a pseudonym be used instead of your real name?	YES	NO

If you wish for me to use a pseudonym, do you have a preferred name you would like to be used?

Signed: _____

Date: _____

WRITING ASSIGNMENT
RESEARCH ETHICS IN COMMUNITIES OF PRACTICE

For WA2, you will be exploring the concept of literacy practices as you demonstrate your understanding of the ethical responsibilities of any research involving "human subjects" or, as we prefer to call them, "research participants." Now that you have read "What is a Community of Practice?," "Putting Ethnographic Writing in Context," the CCCC's "Guidelines for the Ethical Conduct of Research in Composition Studies," and "Ethnographic Ethics and Amish Values," reflect on a community of practice to which you belong. Consider the following: if someone were to research your community, how would you want to be treated? How would you want your community members to be treated? What would you want the researcher to know or understand prior to entering the community? What would you expect of them? Require of them? What practices could the researcher follow to show respect to your community? What issues should be treated with sensitivity?

Once you have reflected on how you would want your community to be treated, we will move toward creating your WA2 product. WA2 is made up of **three (3) short parts**.

Part 1 (no more than one page) is a "Code of Ethics" that you will give to the people you will study for your own ethnographic research project. You are welcome to use the example as a template for your own Code of Ethics. You can use this directly or adapt as needed.

Part 2 (no more than one page) is an Informed Consent Form that each person you interact with in your ethnography will fill out and sign. Again, use the Informed Consent example provided to create your own. You can use this directly or adapt as needed.

Part 3 (2-3 pages) is the bulk of this assignment—a reflective essay in which you reflect on your decisions for creating the Code of Ethics and Informed Consent Form. Consider again that community of practice of which you are a part that we've asked you to reflect upon in conversation with the Code of Ethics and Informed Consent Form. How are you defining "community of practice" (see Carter)? Were a researcher to come into your community of practice, what would you need him or her to consider with respect to what you've learned thus far about research ethics (see Adkins, the "CCCC Statement," and Kahn)? How do the Code of Ethics (CE) and Informed Consent (IC) forms you developed address the concerns you've raised with respect to your own community of practice? What were you thinking about when you crafted the CE and IC? What challenges did you face? What questions do you have moving forward? Here, you should think about and explain what values and practices you see as important in your ethnographic research and use the chapter's readings as well to articulate key points, questions, ideas, or struggles about ethical research as you move forward.

CHAPTER 3

Analyzing Literacy Ethnographies

> Not all research is conducted in the library. In fact, the library may be just a
> starting point, providing you with an overview of your topic and the background
> information you need in order to undertake field research. Field research
> includes making observations, conducting interviews, and using questionnaires.
> In fact, researchers often combine two or more of these methods in a research
> project.
>
> (John Trimbur, The Call to Write, 509)

For several weeks, you have been preparing for this culminating project—an
ethnographic inquiry about writing as it is experienced by ordinary people in
everyday life. In fact, any one of the formal writing assignments you've written
thus far can serve as fodder for your more formal—and more extensive—
ethnographic project. As Bruce Ballenger explains in his popular textbook, *The
Curious Writer*, "The real value of trying ethnography isn't that you'll be writing
lots of ethnographies in other classes—you probably won't. Instead, writing an
ethnographic essay will test your research skills by bringing them out of the
academic and into the field" (390). "Field Research" is what ethnography is all
about, as you've read in previous chapters (see, especially, Carter's introduction
to Part III and Kahn's essay "Putting Ethnographic Writing in Context"). Before
we do, however, let's spend some time thinking about how ethnographies are
generally constructed.

According to anthropologist Clifford Geertz,

> Doing ethnography is like trying to read (in the sense of "construct a reading
> of") a manuscript—foreign, faded, full of ellipses, incoherencies, suspicious
> emendations, and the tendentious commentaries, but written not in
> conventionalized graphs of sound but in transient examples of shaped behaviors.
> (10)

In preparation for their article "Becoming Literate in the Information Age" (see
Chapter One), for example, researchers Gail Hawisher and Cynthia Selfe "read"
the literacy technologies experienced of several people of different generations
in the United States as they describe them. In preparation for their book *Local
Literacies,* the introduction of which you read in Chapter One (see "Literacy
as a Social Practice"), David Barton and Mary Hamilton follow four people in
a small community in Lancaster, England, interviewing them and observing
them to understand how they use literacy in their day-to-day lives—local media,
participation in public life, family activities, and leisure pursuits.

Indeed, all of the articles included in "Part III: Literacies in Context" required the author(s) to undertake field research of some kind—field observations, interviews, surveys, or some combination thereof. In most cases, the studies published here involve what sociologists and anthropologists call "thick descriptions" of individual experiences as they make up a larger group rather than attempts to make generalizations across a particular culture (or cultures). Even in these cases, however, the researcher will draw some conclusions about a larger group based on the "thick descriptions" they present and every research project certainly begins with some assumptions about how the subjects might be "read." In other words, as Geertz explains it,

> Although one starts any effort at thick description, beyond the obvious and superficial, from a state of general bewilderment as to what the devil is going on—trying to find one's feet—one does not start (or ought not) intellectually empty handed. Theoretical ideas are not created wholly anew in each study; as I have said, they are adopted from other, related studies, and, refined in the process, applied to new interpretive problems. If they cease being useful with respect to such problems, they tend to stop being used and are more or less abandoned. If they continue being useful, throwing up new understandings, they are further elaborated and go on being used. (27)

Thus your deep and extensive readings of key research in literary studies in previous chapters were a necessary prerequisite to conducting your own ethnographic study of literacy practices. However, while the previous studies may have offered you a good overview of the kinds of work being done in the field of literacy studies (and what has been discovered about literacy by investigating these out-of-school contexts), the field research process itself has thus far remained relatively abstract. In this chapter, we will help you understand the specific, concrete steps involved in designing field research like this and how you develop your own, original literary ethnography.

What we see in the ethnographies presented thus far are the researcher's findings and conclusions presented in such a way as to support their key arguments about the subject at hand. What we don't see much of, however, are the steps they took to choose the subject, locate an appropriate "group" to investigate, develop an effective procedure for collecting the requisite data, interpret them, draw appropriate (supportable) conclusions, and then present them to readers in ways that support the researcher's key arguments.

For primarily this reason, it seems appropriate to go back to these essays and analyze them from the ethnographer's point of view. Let's do that now.

Reverse Engineering

To "reverse engineer" is to study or analyze an existing object (a video game console, for example, or the motherboard of a computer) in order to understand the design, construction, and operation of that object—perhaps to produce a copy or an improved version. To better understand how literacy ethnographies "work," we are going to "reverse engineer" a published literacy ethnography to see (1) the way the author designed the original study and (2) the scholarly conversation to which the essay is contributing.

To that end, the first object of our analysis is the following essay, "Literacy Sponsors and Learning: An Ethnography of Punk Literacy in Mid-1980s Waco." Eric Pleasant wrote this essay as a first-year student in the writing program at Texas A&M University–Commerce, building upon much of the scholarship you have read thus far. For these and many other reasons, it is an excellent object for our reverse engineering session.

READING

Literacy Sponsors and Learning: An Ethnography of Punk Literacy in Mid-1980s Waco

Eric Pleasant

Eric Pleasant wrote the original version of this essay as part of the first-year writing program at Texas A&M–Commerce, the very first semester we began asking students to conduct original ethnographic research in literacy studies. To do so, he worked through readings and assignments very much like the ones you've taken on this semester. He then submitted his final project to the national journal *Young Scholars in Writing: Undergraduate Research in Writing and Rhetoric*. They invited him to revise it for publication in this competitive venue, so Eric worked closely with his professor on his campus (Shannon Carter) and another at the University of Montana (Doug Downs) to develop the version of the essay you see here, which was published in the 2008 issue of this journal. Two lessons we hope you'll learn from Eric's experience:

1. The work you are doing in this course has a potential audience that extends far beyond your classroom. Eric's essay has been read by scholars, teachers, and students around the world. It has even been re-published in other books about undergraduate research as an "exemplar" model. Yours can, too. If you are interested in submitting your final project to *Young Scholars in Writing,* as well, talk to your instructor and/or Google the journal title and look for "submission" information.

2. The writing, research, and inquiry-based work represented in your work thus far leads researchers in a wide range of often unexpected directions. As you can see from the student examples on the companion website for this textbook, the topics for these literacy ethnographies is limited by little more than access and your imagination.

Literacy Sponsors and Learning: An Ethnography of Punk Literacy in Mid-1980s Waco

Eric Pleasant

> Literacy is primarily something people do; it is an activity, located in the space between thought and text. Literacy does not just reside in people's heads as a set of skills to be learned, and it does not just reside on paper, captured as texts to be analyzed. Like all human activity, literacy is essentially social, and it is located in the interaction between people.
>
> —David Barton and Mary Hamilton

As you walk in, you instantly notice your surroundings. You are entering a dark room with an almost oppressive atmosphere. Animal bones hang from the ceiling. The walls are painted black. Flyers promoting upcoming shows have been pasted one on top of the other throughout the room. Artwork on the flyers consists of skeletons, monsters, and an array of unflattering caricatures of people such as Ronald Reagan, Hitler, and the pope. Band names upon the flyers are as brash as the images: Dead Kennedys, Millions of Dead Cops, Agent Orange, Marching Plague, and the Offenders. Phrases such as "There is no justice, just us" and "We're just a minor threat" are graffitied across the walls, promoting a sense of unity outside the bounds of traditional societal values. At the opposite end of the room is a stage. Groups of kids are standing together looking at you with seeming tribal defiance. Most of these people have leather jackets adorned with spikes and band names or logos similar to the ones on the walls. Some have hair that has been spiked, shaved, or colored with Day-Glo hues that scream, "I am not a normal member of society!" You have just entered the netherworld of the Cave Club, Austin, Texas. The year is 1985 and you have come to see the psychedelic punk rock band the Butthole Surfers.

I am one of the people walking into the club. I look at my four best friends. We are five white adolescents aged fifteen to eighteen from Waco, Texas. How did we get here? How do we fit into this extremely closed group of people we see around us in the club? These other youths have a reputation of hating outsiders to the point of showing extreme aggression. All of a sudden, one of the people in the club sees and recognizes us. He nods and walks up. The band takes the stage and opens its set with crazy, insane-sounding rants that lead into straight-ahead, hard-driving drums and guitar—this is stripped-down, in-your-face music. The punk walking up grabs one of my friends. No words are spoken. He puts his arm around my friend's shoulders and pulls him into a swirling pit of kids. The music picks up. The rest of us look at each other, grin, and run to join the human maelstrom. We do fit in here!

Punk as Literacy

Fitting in, in this case, means that we had acquired the requisite punk literacy necessary to survive or thrive in this environment. Acquiring the literacy of such a nontraditional, new, and relatively nonstudied or reported subculture necessitated nontraditional modes of learning. Traditional definitions of literacy are generally limited to the study of written text; such a definition limits this project to our reading of the verbal snapshot detailed above. But there is so much more going on here. As David Barton and Mary Hamilton's definition shows us, "Like all human activity, literacy is essentially social, and it is located in the interaction between people" (42).

Within the context of traditional literacy, the words on the flyers, jackets, or walls are relatively meaningless. Within the bounds of the second and more relevant definition, my opening scene becomes a plethora of literacy. Every aspect of the room is a source of learning: the color of the walls, the art on the flyers, the bones on the ceiling, the interaction of the people. These things alone may not have meaning, but in this instance, the question becomes what kind of subculture would choose this setting for interaction.

In "Literacy, Discourse, and Linguistics," James Paul Gee defines what he means by "literacy studies" and pushes us beyond more traditional definitions of literacy.

> At any moment we are using language we must say or write the right thing in the right way while playing the right social role and (appearing) to hold the right values, believes, and attitudes. Thus, what is important is not language, and surely not grammar, but saying (writing)-doing-being-valuing-believing combinations. These combinations I call "Discourses" with a capital "D." [. . .] Discourses are ways of being in the world; they are forms of life which integrate words, acts, values, believes, attitudes, and social identities as well as gestures, glances, body positions, and clothes. (6–7)

In regard to my project, Gee's concept of literacy provides a frame to consider the opening scene in this paper. What are the ideas, unifying concepts, and sources of self-identity among the people in the room? Every detail becomes something from which one can learn in order to blend within this unique subculture of attitudes, ideas, beliefs, and appearances. The words and art on the walls, flyers, and jackets begin to represent not just words, but the ideas and values of the culture creating them. The appearance of these groups of people in the room, from their clothing and hair to the way that they are standing, becomes a source of literacy in its own right. For those experienced in this scene, it is fairly simple to tell who is new, who is experienced, and eventually, who belongs within this group. After some time within the culture, appearance begins to assume less importance than mannerisms, slang, and ability to successfully interact.

Cultural Sponsors of Literacy

Like Lauren B. Resnik, I am examining "literacy as a set of cultural practices that people engage in" (117). This study explores literacy practices associated with punk culture, paying particular attention to the ways in which we, in Gee's words, "acquired the Discourses" of punk culture. How did these five middle-class teenagers from suburban, Baptist Waco manage to get to this point? What drew us together and what were the different forms of sponsorship from which we assimilated different aspects of punk literacy? Therefore, this project looks at a sub-subculture of punks in mid-1980s Waco, Texas, for the ways in which my friends and I, in the words of Deborah Brandt, "pursue[d] literacy" and how punk "literacy pursue[d]" us (33).

As Brandt discusses in "Sponsors of Literacy," every aspect of our lives affects our literacy. Sponsors range from family, friends, and teachers to setting, family background, socioeconomic standing, and exposure to ideas. All forms of sponsorship direct us and influence our literacy development. Literacy itself influences the direction of further development. Sponsorship and literacy become the proverbial "snowball" within which we develop; its shape over time is dictated by the layers of learning, background, and exposure inside.

In order to study this sub-subculture, the Waco group of punks, I first detail the backgrounds of a group of five people within it: Eric (me), Matt, Harry, Judson, and Fred. Each received a survey that assessed their backgrounds, similarities, and differences—information that is invaluable in understanding the eventual development of the group. This group of friends is the direct result of the various forms of literacy sponsorship within our lives: people, setting, and backgrounds.

Family Backgrounds

Given the socioeconomic status of our families, we each consider ourselves to come from middle- or working-class backgrounds. Four of us have parents with college and postgraduate educations, and all our parents completed high school. We each view our parents as people who worked their way up to more economic stability and better social standing through their own efforts—pulled themselves up by their bootstraps, so to speak—and attained more comfortable lives by hard work and/or education. Our aspirations to attend a university were instilled in all of us by our parents. In essence, we grew up believing that hard work and education were the only ways to achieve and maintain a stable, fulfilling life. We were a fairly social group that was exposed and privy to the benefits of a decent education. Some of us attended public schools while others attended private schools, and all were active in student government, social, and academic groups in high school.

As complex and different as our family histories were, instability in our home and family life is something to which we were all exposed. Three of us came from families that were comprised of divorced and remarried parents. Matt and I were raised much of our lives by single mothers. Many of us were drawn to each other in an attempt to create our own family of friends.

Community Culture

One extremely influential force in our lives did not come from our schools, religions, or families, but from our geographical area: Waco, Texas. The significance of this location cannot be stressed enough. Waco is part of the "Southern Bible Belt"; it is very much a Southern Baptist town, dominated by Baylor University. Although only one of us was specifically raised Southern Baptist, for five adolescents beginning to develop their own identities and life philosophies, this community influence played a huge role. We were all dealing with the typical adolescent crises. The constant struggle to find our own voices often meant coming face-to-face with opposing beliefs that were generally much more conservative in nature than the beliefs we were developing on our own. As Barton and Hamilton explain, "literacy practices are purposeful and embedded in broader social goals and cultural practices" (44). Our family situations may have led us to one another, but it was the conservative climate of our hometown—a climate we found alienating—that provided the glue that held our group together and led us to punk.

Our personalities all reacted to this conservative setting with a sense of defiance and sometimes outright anger. When questioned about what attracted them to punk culture, survey respondents listed angst as a main factor. Punk was both a form of music and a collective that allowed and encouraged its members to speak openly. Freedom of expression was, in 1980s punk, a defining element of the culture. We found this liberating and highly enticing. Anger and desire to change the world around us were easily expressed through the medium of punk music and were often reflected in dress and attitude, which placed importance on shock value.

Class Conflict

This leads to another prevalent answer to the question of what attracted us to the punk culture: class conflict with our peers. Many of us grew up exposed to a class structure in which we did not necessarily fit. All of our parents had achieved a certain level of success, but we still found ourselves in conflict with some of our peers. We all came from working, middle-class families that struggled to attain their class standing. While we may have reached some small level of privilege by our high school years, we were still painfully aware at times of the socioeconomic background from which we had come. The public schools some of us attended were in the more affluent parts of town. When I attended a college prep school, I was receiving financial aid for tuition from a scholarship. Essentially, we came from fairly financially comfortable families by this time, but we were still surrounded by peers from much more affluent families than ours. This basic conflict of social standing resulted in us feeling not quite part of the same society as our classmates. We chose a culture in which class was not an issue.

One reply to the question of what drew us into this culture differed from the others: "I do not know if anything necessarily 'drew' me to any scene; rather, it is simply where my life took me. I don't think that I sought the scene; instead, the scene was secondary to the friendships. [. . .] Simply put, it was the friendships that brought me to the scene—the scene itself was merely a collateral aspect of the friendships." I have since asked all those surveyed and each agrees with this answer. In short, our subculture was not necessarily defined by punk. Rather, it was defined by our group of friends—who happened to be punks.

Pop Culture

Our musical tastes prior to punk were similar: each of us listened to heavy metal and classic rock, and some listed classic country music as well. Most of us had been influenced by older siblings and parents. (Most of us had siblings who had come of age in the late '70s.)

Other media that influenced our development included television and film. We were the quintessential "Pop Culture" generation. Everyone cited horror and science fiction as an influence: growing up with the electric babysitter (TV), we were inundated with campy horror and science fiction films of the '50s, '60s, and '70s. Movies such as *Planet of the Apes*, *Forbidden Planet*, and *Plan 9 from Outer Space* were among our favorites; we were all seeing the *Star Wars* movies and watching *Star Trek* reruns after school. Collecting toys merchandised by these movies was also a common bond. "Disposable" entertainment such as plastic toys and low-budget B-movies were often the forms of media that we were drawn to and cherished.

We grew up reading the Bible and comic books, and as we grew older, we all became intrigued by authors such as Joseph Heller, Kurt Vonnegut, C. S. Lewis, Tolkien, and John Irving. It is evident that our early and middle childhood imaginations revolved around science fiction, camp, and horror. We were all relatively intelligent youths and had all made As and Bs in school to this point. Reading was a pastime that had fueled our imaginations and begun to shape our personalities.

These developments occurred independent of each other; none of us met until high school. This taste for comic books, science fiction, horror, and ultimately our early outlook on life had developed of its own accord, free from each other's influence. Obviously, like people are drawn to like people. In our case, some of our likes and dislikes were so similar that it seems, in retrospect, inevitable that we would become close friends. Even in a town the size of Waco, it was only a matter of time until our paths crossed and we realized we were kindred spirits.

The pop culture we grew up with was as much an influence on us as the community and "place" in which we were raised, and it was also a significant influence on the subculture to which we later belonged. Our collective tastes and similar backgrounds encouraged a mutual respect for each other, which fueled a sense of belonging and family. The common thread that was stressed by each member of the group is that we were all seeking a family of our own making. We wanted to belong with people whom we had chosen and who had chosen us. We created our own stable environment that allowed us to exchange ideas, share perspectives, and nurture our individual personalities. We had grown up in a community that didn't understand us, in homes that were sometimes unstable and volatile. Within our group, we exchanged ideas and were receptive to new concepts. We frequently shared new books, new movies, and new thinking. Thus, our various early literacy sponsors were not merely people; they were the culture of our surroundings as well as the actual place we were raised. By the time we met and formed strong bonds of friendship, we were just waiting for something new and exciting or explosive to come into our lives. That something was punk.

Developing Punk Literacy

> Sponsors are a tangible reminder that literacy learning throughout history has always required permission, sanction, assistance, coercion, or, at minimum, contact with existing trade routes. Sponsors are delivery systems for the economies of literacy, the means by which these forces present themselves to—and through—individual learners. They also represent the causes into which people's literacy usually gets recruited.
> —Deborah Brandt

When studying a subculture (or, as Gee would call it, a Discourse), it is interesting to look at the origins of different behaviors, beliefs, terminology, and ultimately all of the different elements that define it. Where do people learn to behave in an acceptable manner among their peers? Various subcultures have their own social practices, which eventually become forms of literacy. Written texts, even the simplest ones, are translated into action and applied within the group, and one group's texts and practices may seem completely foreign to another. As noted at the beginning of this essay, I am attempting here to understand "the social conditions under which people actually engage in literate activities" (Resnick 117). Inasmuch as punk culture and music were hard for us to come by, it is important to understand literate activities involved in the perpetual cycle of discovery and introduction that sponsored and advanced our increasing punk literacies. That's just what I will do here. While our punk literacy was culturally sponsored, as I have analyzed, I want to look in particular at how my group of friends used different forms of sponsors and literacy in order to educate ourselves about the punk subculture and, eventually, how we became accepted into that tight-knit social environment.

We had each experienced limited exposure to punk music. One of my earliest sponsors was a friend from California who had introduced me to bands such as Black Flag, X, and Fear. Judson's early sponsorship came in the form of a radio show called *The Rock and Roll Alternative*. Matt was already involved with new wave music. Harry and Fred were both exposed to punk by friends or family. Thus, we did not necessarily introduce each other to punk, but had some interest in the music prior to meeting.

However, once we met, we became involved in a perpetual cycle of discovery and introduction. We shared every aspect of the music or culture that we learned about with each other. This perpetuated sharing of facets of the culture that we discovered produced a geometric learning curve. In a way, we became sponsors to ourselves.

One of our primary sources of information about punk culture and music came from its actual records. We would listen to *Rock and Roll Alternative* and hear a band we liked. Then we would special-order the band's records from the local music store. Most included sleeves with lyrics and occasionally pictures of the band. Listening to the band, we would read the lyrics, learning the songs and what the band was talking about. The pictures showed how the band dressed. As we eagerly exchanged records among ourselves, our own group literacy began to develop. We were learning the slang, the dress, and the fashion of another culture prior to direct, personal exposure. This gave us an advantage when we began going to see bands in Austin or Dallas, where there were established punk cultures. Because we went to see only bands we liked, we were already familiar with their music and knew most of the lyrics before we saw them perform. We were "punk literate," albeit without much real-life, direct exposure to the punk scene. We adapted our dress and style from the pictures on the records and learned a new language from the music. Thus, the records were extremely influential sponsors.

Television was another sponsor for us. Although there was very little true exposure to punk culture on TV, we did manage to find a few programs, movies, documentaries, and late-night videos that gave us a glimpse into the world of punk rock. A late-night show called *Night Flight* played some of the more controversial, less commercial music videos. These were aired after midnight on Friday and Saturday. Some of these early music videos influenced the way we dressed and exposed us to some of the more obscure bands, whose records we could then order. The same program also offered documentaries that showed us what was going on in the larger cities on the West and East coasts. Interviews on the programs taught us about other bands and different music scenes. It was almost a continuous cycle of information from media and records leading back to more information from the same sources, all leading to more learned behavior that we put into practice within our sub-subculture and, eventually, within the larger subcultures at the music venues.

One incredibly important factor in our development was exposure to other groups at shows. The records, lyric sheets, and media had provided us with the basic tools we needed to go to the show and not stick out. However, fully assimilating into the larger scenes of Austin and Dallas took a little longer. Anyone who attends live music venues knows that there are always different groups of people standing around talking. Attending the punk shows provided us with a good way to observe different mannerisms and types of dress, and to pick up some of the different slang terms. The more events we attended, the more people began to recognize us. Eventually, we began to feel that being the "Waco guys" was something we didn't need to hide. We began to make friends within the Austin and Dallas punk community. We were no longer singled out in a bad way. Simply stated, we established our credibility and earned respect. We had progressed to the point that we were comfortable and regarded as extended members of the community. The more we were exposed to the other music scenes, the more we were accepted by the punk community.

Punk Literacy in Practice (and in the Making)

Now that I have outlined our individual histories and different modes of learning and assimilation, I will review some of the characteristics of our Waco punk "sub-subculture." During the mid1980s, we were a relatively small group, initially very isolated from the active, direct persuasion of the larger punk culture in other cities. Accordingly, we developed some distinct unifying aspects.

Philosophically, we always tried to maintain an open-minded approach to other individuals and cultures. We felt that different ideas and culture should be treated with respect. The general rule in our early days was that we wanted to be introduced to and learn concepts that originally seemed foreign to us. Our reading material was often inclined to be political or subversive in nature. We traded books by authors such as Camus, Nietzsche, and Solzhenitsyn. *The Anarchist Cookbook* provided quite a bit of enjoyment and inspiration. We freely exchanged ideas and philosophies that melded with our pop culture past. The result was that our group was drawn together on a more cerebral level than some of the larger punk subcultures to which we were eventually exposed.

As punk culture developed within some of the larger cities, I at times witnessed a somewhat "testosterone"-driven form of punk. During the later 1980s, many of the people drawn to this culture were not attracted to it for the same reasons we were. As punk music and fashion became more popular, some of the people we encountered at larger music venues were like the ones who had, four years earlier, relished chasing us out of fast food establishments and trying to pick fights with us. Some had the stereotypical "jock" mentality and thought that a punk show was a great place to thrash around and beat up people. The mentality in the larger punk scene was not always similar to our much smaller and more isolated scene. Unfortunately, this mentality began to appear in scenes throughout the States. George Hurchalla observed the same thing, writing in his book *Going Underground*: "The core of people making the music and putting on the shows was tight. We all were kinda dorky kids into punk rock. We weren't into all the violence and tough guy posturing [. . .] in other scenes" (279).

It pains me that this later form of punk is so often its main image. In contrast, we had been shaped by early sponsors into a group of young people drawn to this culture by intellectual and developmental desires. We wanted to feel our own voice and learn about others, in an open-minded and unrestricted manner. Nor was this motivation indigenous to Waco; these ideas were blossoming throughout the country. According to Mark Anderson of the Positive Force record label in 1985,

> Punk is not [. . .] the latest cool trend or even a particular form of style or music, really—it is an idea that guides and motivates your life. The Punk community that exists, exists to support and realize that idea through music art, fanzines and other expressions of personal creativity. And what is this idea? Think for yourself, be yourself, don't just take what society gives you, create your own rules, live your own life. (qtd. in O'Hara 36)

In the early days of our Waco subculture, we discovered the "do-it-yourself" attitude of punk. This part of the early punk culture encouraged us to make our own fashion, and, as our punk literacies increased, the relative inaccessibility of punk fashion further "sponsored" our do-it-yourself choices. At that time, it was nearly impossible to go into a store and purchase prefabricated punk-look fashion, so every aspect of our fashion was do-it-yourself. We discovered ways to buy regular, plain T-shirts and transform them into more suitable and desirable attire. We quickly learned that stencils could be made out of any material, such as paper or cardboard, and with spray paint, we were able to make shirts that said anything we wanted. Leather jackets originally came in the form of motorcycle jackets, which we would decorate with ink pens and paint. We styled our hair in the backyard with pet-grooming clippers. While bright-colored hair dye wasn't readily accessible to us in Waco, we figured out that our hair could be bleached white and then colored with Kool-Aid drink powder in concentrated form. The spikes in our hair were made to stand up with Knox gelatin.

We also learned to go to new places. In the formative years of our subculture, we learned from some of the bigger scenes that mainstream clubs and bars were not receptive to punk rock shows. Instead, venues often came in the form of alternative "gay" bars. An early alliance was formed between much of the gay culture and the punks; because punk culture originally embraced open-mindedness, the gay culture of the time seemed a natural ally, as both were often viewed as outcasts and nonconformists. Thus, we were able to persuade proprietors of gay bars to allow "our" bands to play. Eventually, we persuaded a predominantly African American club to let us bring records in once a week to play our music. Our group's determination thus caused us to form somewhat unconventional associations with others with whom we might otherwise never have connected. In retrospect, these alliances and friendships seem logical; but at the time, we were merely doing what we felt we had to do to nurture our fledgling music scene. None of us knew or suspected that these actions would introduce us to cultures that would enrich our lives and lead us to a higher state of social consciousness as we became adults.

During these years, we were introduced to soul, jazz, dance, and hip-hop music. Our view of punk was that we should listen to anything we found enjoyable. At least for my group of friends, the punk culture was not defined by punk music. Classical, new wave, new age, jazz, metal, hardcore, hip-hop, etc. are all forms of music that have remained in our lives.

Another characteristic of the group from this period was the reemergence of the skateboard scene. Skateboarding had begun its resurgence in the late 1970s. Its new popularity had started on the West Coast at the same time as punk emerged there, and skate culture became interconnected with punk culture. One of our favorite pastimes was to skate drainage ditches. Eventually, we were able to acquire enough wood to build our own ramp, affording us an inexpensive way to entertain ourselves. The skate culture had great impact on our clothing fashion and slang.

Lasting Effects of Sponsored Literacy

The "do-it-yourself," or DIY, attitude of punk permeated every aspect of our sub-subculture. Will and determination were the means by which we had our fashion, our music, and our entertainment. This drive is still visible in each of our lives today: the entire group has gone on to realize educational and/or business success. The drive that was the catalyst to form our friendships and create our sub-subculture is the same drive that has allowed us to attain some of our goals.

Every aspect of our lives, friendships, and subculture has been a direct result of our early sponsors. The forces that drew us together—background, family, education, culture—were all aspects of sponsorship that had shaped us to that point. The tools we used to assimilate and educate ourselves on punk were further sponsors in our development. Variations of these same tools are still used today in our educational or professional endeavors. Our subculture—or, more importantly, every aspect of our lives—has been the culmination of every sponsor (positive or negative) and every action that has brought us to our current state. Such analysis makes clear why Barton and Hamilton conclude: "Like all human activity, literacy is essentially social, and it is located in the interaction between people" (42). Our group's developing punk literacy was a clear case in point.

Works Cited

Barton, David, and Mary Hamilton. "A Social Theory of Literacy Practices and Events." *Local Literacies: Reading and Writing in One Community*. New York: Routledge, 1998. 6–13. Rpt. in Carter 42–53.

Brandt, Deborah. "Sponsors of Literacy." *College Composition and Communication* 49.2 (1998): 165–85. Rpt. in Carter 12–38.

Carter, Shannon, ed. *Literacies in Context*. Southlake, TX: Fountainhead, 2007.

Gee, James Paul. "Literacy, Discourse, and Linguistics: An Introduction." *Journal of Education* 171.1 (November 1989): 5–17.

Hurchalla, George. *Going Underground*. Stuart, FL: Zuo, 2005.

O'Hara, Craig. *The Philosophy of Punk: More Than Noise*. San Francisco: AK, 1999.

Resnick, Lauren B. "Literacy in School and Out." *Literacy: An Overview by 14 Experts*. Ed. Stephen R. Graubard. New York: Noonday, 1991. Rpt. in Carter 116–33.

NOW THAT YOU'VE READ

Analyze the Field Research Design

Based on your reading of Pleasant's essay, how did he design his study? Your instructor may decide to make this an in-class activity or one you do on your own. Either way, analyzing Pleasant's field research design will prepare you to design your own ethnographic research project, which is your next step.

To figure this out, answer the following questions (questions inspired by the "components of culture" as described by James Spradley). Not all will be relevant, but most will. If you run across a question that seems entirely irrelevant to the study you are analyzing, skip it.

1. (Space): What is (are) the location(s) in which this analysis took place?

2. (Actors): Who are the members of this group/subgroup as represented in this article? Describe them.

3. (Texts/Objects): What texts are involved in this study? As you consider this question, remember your own working definition of literacy and the ways in which Pleasant defines literacy in his article. What are some of the objects of literacy used as a regular part of the activities in which the members of this group engage?

4. (Literacy Events): In what literacy events do the members of this group or subgroup engage? How do we know? What does this mean?

5. (Literacy Practices): Describe one or more of the literacy practices within a selected literacy event (as described in response to the previous question).

6. (Goals): What do the members of this group or the group as a whole want to achieve and/or accomplish? What role(s) does literacy play in this?

7. (Feelings): How do members of the group feel about the literacy events, practices, or related activities (as described in response to some of the previous questions)?

FIELD RESEARCH METHODS

1. Why/how did the researcher choose the population he or she sampled?

2. Did the researcher choose to observe the subjects? Survey them? Interview them? A combination of observation, survey(s), and/or interview(s)?

3. Why did the researcher make the choices he or she made (regarding field research method—observation, survey, and/or interview)?

4. How does the focus of the researcher's inquiry shape his or her research plan?

5. What conclusions does the researcher draw from his or her investigation? Given the data as presented in this article, do these conclusions seem appropriate? Why or why not? If not, what might be some alternative ways to interpret that data?

It is important that your study make good use of the many options of field research, but it is also important that your project be clearly situated in the ongoing conversation regarding the subject at hand. That's where the articles you've read in previous chapters come in (i.e., Barton, Barton and Hamilton, Kahn, etc.). What has already been said about the subject under investigation? What is missing in the conversation, as you are reading it? How is your project going to fill the research gap you say now exists in the scholarly conversation surrounding your topic? It may be useful to think of the research project you choose to undertake as part of an "ongoing conversation," something that many argue may be best understood in terms of the "Burkean Parlor"[1]:

> Imagine that you enter a parlor. You come late. When you arrive, others have long preceded you, and they are engaged in a heated discussion, a discussion too heated for them to pause and tell you exactly what it is about. In fact, the discussion had already begun long before any of them got there, so that no one present is qualified to retrace for you all the steps that had gone before. You listen for a while, until you decide that you have caught the tenor of the argument; then you put in your oar. Someone answers; you answer him; another comes to your defense; another aligns himself against you, to either the embarrassment or gratification of your opponent, depending upon the quality of your ally's assistance. However, the discussion is interminable. The hour grows late, you must depart. And you do depart, with the discussion still vigorously in progress. (Burke, 110-111)

In other words, the scholarly conversation regarding literacy and the various forms it takes in a variety of contexts has been going on for a long time—long

---

1 Burke, Kenneth. *The Philosophy of Literary Form: Studies in Symbolic Action.* Berkeley: University of California P, 1941.

before you began reading, discussing, and writing in response to the essays included in the previous chapters—and it will continue long after you turn in your final project and move on to other courses and your life beyond college.

However, after "listening" to parts of the ongoing conversation (as represented by essays in the previous chapters), you are in a much better position to join the conversation in more formal ways. Think of how you defined literacy in your first writing assignment, for example. In your final project, you should make extensive use of both the articles published in this textbook and your own writing assignments, including the key arguments they present, but you should also add to them though your own field research.

ASSIGNMENT: GROUP PRESENTATION
ANALYSIS OF LITERACY ETHNOGRAPHIES

For this assignment, you will work with at least two other students to read, discuss, summarize, synthesize, analyze, and present one of the literacy ethnographies available in Chapter 3, all of which are examples of the kind of research you will undertake in this course. This assignment is made up of two parts:

- Part I: Poster Presentation—As a group, you will develop a Poster Presentation that includes the following information: (a) title of study, (b) main argument, (c) research question(s), (d) glossary of key terms (2-3), (e) community of practice (research participants), (f) research methods, (g) research ethics, (h) findings, and (i) implications for your own research project. (See the following page for details and additional guidance for each category and a template you can use to develop your poster.) On the day of our Poster Presentation, you'll post these around our classroom and we'll wander around to hear about your work, much as you will when you present your own, original research at your school's display of student learning, such as a Celebration of Student Writing.

- Part II: Reflections—Individually, you will write a one- to two-page reflective memo that describes your experiences reading, discussing, synthesizing, summarizing, and rhetorically analyzing this study. This will be shared only with your instructor and in confidence. You might take some time to answer one or more prompts provided to guide the development of your group poster, especially if you do not feel you were able to adequately address it/them in the Poster Presentation. When and how often did you meet? What happened when you met? How did you go about dividing up the workload? How did that go? How did you decide to develop the Poster Presentation itself? What were your contributions (and why)? What contributions did others make? What else can you tell me about the process. I recognize collaboration can be difficult and often unpredictable. For this and other reasons, this reflective memo will be shared only with your instructor.

BEFORE YOU BEGIN THIS GROUP ASSIGNMENT:

Through your close reading of Eric Pleasant's literacy ethnography, you have begun using "reverse engineering" to understand his field research design and the scholarly conversation to which he was contributing. As we discussed, Pleasant did not necessarily answer these questions explicitly himself. However, you should be able to determine the answers by reverse engineering the essay ("product") he developed based on his original research.

For your Group Assignment as described above, we ask you to dig a little deeper into the research design of a different literacy ethnography. In preparation for that, we'd like to go through the same process required of you for this group assignment by analyzing Pleasant's essay together.

Author First Name, Last Name. "Title of Study"

Group Members:

ARGUMENT/"SO WHAT?"

Main argument of study: Provide two to three sentences here that pins down what the author argues his/her study proves and why that matters. Every study needs to address the "So What?" question.

RESEARCH QUESTION(S)

List the major question(s) the research project is attempting to answer. Every study has them. Yours will, as well.

GLOSSARY OF KEY TERMS

Every study defines key terms carefully. Since these are studies of literacy, expect to find terms like those you defined in your own WA1 defined in this one. How is this study using these terms? You can quote directly from the study or summarize the relevant terms.

RESEARCH PARTICIPANTS

Who is involved in this study? Define the targeted "community of practice." Every study defines not only the people involved but *why these particular research participants* and not others. In other words, what is the relationship between the targeted research participants and the study's goals?

RESEARCH METHODS

How did the researcher approach this study? What did he/she *do*? Interviews? Surveys? Field observations? Some combination thereof? As you analyze the research methods involved in this study, think about what they may have to teach you about your own research project.

RESEARCH ETHICS

Think again about your own WA2 and the "Code of Ethics" you created to guide your own research. What steps did the researcher take to ensure she/he approached research participants ethically and responsibly? How do you know? Were those steps appropriate? Adequate?

FINDINGS

Here, help us understand what the researcher discovered through his/her research. How did he/she answer his/her research questions? How did the research methods undertaken lead the researcher to these conclusions?

IMPLICATIONS

What did you learn about ethnography by analyzing this study? About setting up a major argument and dealing with the "so what?" question? About developing relevant research questions? About identifying appropriate research participants and approaching them ethically? About possible research methods? How does study of literacy compare/contrast with others you have read? What implications might your analysis of this study have for your own research? (collectively or individually or both)?

The questions driving your analysis of Pleasant's essay are exactly the same ones you will answer to (a) develop your Group Presentation, as articulated on page 365 and (b) design the research proposal for your own literacy ethnography (see page 388 for assignment details for the Research Proposal, Chapter 4). The better you understand how other researchers have gone about designing their own studies, the better position you will be in to jump in yourself. If you already know the sort of study you'd like to undertake at this point, even better. Keep that in mind throughout this process and your research proposal will almost write itself!

Your own literacy ethnography, like the research you have read and analyzed thus far, should include the following information: (1) a main argument, (2) at least one research question, (3) definition(s) of key term(s), (4) research participant(s), (5) research methods, (6) research ethics, (7) findings, and (8) implications.

The Central Claim

Every study makes an argument—a central claim. In academic writing, this is rarely an adversarial stance. Perhaps you have written essays like that before: for or against gun control, for example. That's not how academic writing usually works. Instead, you are making a contribution to an ongoing conversation. Remember the Burkean Parlor defined in the previous section. The conversation started before you arrived, and it will likely continue long after you leave. So while you are in that "Burkean Parlor," what will be your contribution? What's your central claim?

Pleasant's central claim is that his acquisition of "punk literacy" is both an example of what David Barton and Mary Hamilton call "literacy as a social practice" and, by extension, a direct challenge to traditional definitions of literacy that limit reading and writing to autonomous skill sets. In your own research, for example, you may identify other ways in which literacy functions as a social practice. From this, you would develop your central claim. As Pleasant describes it in his own project, "This study explores literacy practices associated with punk culture, paying particular attention to the ways in which we, in [James Paul] Gee's words, 'acquired the Discourses' of punk culture" (138).

However, research like this rarely begins with the central claim. You should begin with at least a vague idea about what you'd like to contribute to the conversation about literacy as represented in this book and your own original research project. However, you are unlikely to be able to state that claim in informed and convincing ways until you have conducted your research, entered the field, interviewed and/or surveyed your participants, etc.

This may sound counterintuitive, given your previous experiences with writing in school. Have you been taught to decide the position you are going to take on an issue (for or against gun control, for example) *before* beginning your research project? If so, you are not alone. That likely meant you then went to the library or, more likely, began searching library databases or even Googling to locate articles that supported your position. That meant your research taught you very little. You knew your position going in. The research you conducted was meant only to confirm what you already believed.

However, we believe research is about *inquiry* not *confirming what we already know.* By this, we mean the research process should teach you things you could not know before beginning that process. The process itself should take you (and your reader!) in surprising directions, leading you to conclusions that not only challenge your own expectations but those of others. That's where your central claim comes in. What is your original contribution to the ongoing conversation? That's the answer to the "so what?" question, as well. Why does your research matter? Well, your central claim—if original—is why your research matters. We did not know this before. Now that you've conducted your research, we know something new. From there, others can build on the research you've conducted. You've become part of the larger scholarly conversation.

Research Question(s)

Every study begins with a research question, which will relate closely to the central claim that emerges from your study. Literacy ethnographies are not terribly formulaic, so every study may not identify that research question as, specifically, a research question. However, you can infer that information based on a close reading of the published study. Though he doesn't articulate his research question outright, Pleasant's research question can be determined a few different ways:

- Look at his title. It begins with "Literacy Sponsors and Learning." "Learning" is a relatively generic term so you may not be able to glean much information there—at least not yet. "Literacy sponsors," however, is a unique term. Scan the article, and you will find this term was coined by literacy scholar Deborah Brandt, whose article "Sponsors of Literacy" is included in Part II of this textbook (see Table of Contents). So, based on this information, you can guess that he will be concerned with the ways in which his punk literacy was "sponsored."

- Read the first few paragraphs of his study. From the above discussion regarding his central claim, you know how he is answering his research question. Work backward, as contestants on *Jeopardy!* might. Remember how that quiz show works: Alex Trebek gives them an answer (answer: "a hired killer") in a particular category (category: "3 + 3"), and the contestant has to come up with the question (question: "What is a hit man?").

- Similarly, you can look at Pleasant's answer (his "central claim"): Pleasant's central claim is that his acquisition of "punk literacy" is both an example of what David Barton and Mary Hamilton call "literacy as a social practice" and, by extension, a direct challenge to traditional definitions of literacy that limit reading and writing to autonomous skill sets.

Given that answer, what's his research question? What about this: "How does punk literacy function as a social practice?" Combine this with what you gleaned from his title, and what might be another related research question? Perhaps,

"How might punk literacy be learned as a social practice? In other words, how and by whom is punk literacy 'sponsored'" (Brandt)?

Research Participant(s)

Who is involved in this study? Define the targeted "community of practice." A study should define not only the people involved but why these particular research participants and not others. In other words, what is the relationship between the targeted research participants and the study's goals (research questions)?

The participants ("community of practice") in Pleasant's study include himself and his four best friends when he was a teenager in Waco, Texas, in the 1980s. As he puts it in his study, after setting the scene in the punk club where he participated in this community of practice, "I am one of the people walking into the club. I look at my four best friends. We are five white adolescents aged fifteen to eighteen from Waco, Texas." (357).

Research Methods

What research methods did the researcher use to answer his or her research question(s)? How did the researcher approach this study? What did he or she do? Conduct interviews? Surveys? Field observations? Some combination thereof? As you analyze the research methods involved in this study, think about what they may have to teach you about your own research project.

Pleasant describes his research methods plainly and directly:

> In order to study this sub-subculture, the Waco group of punks, I first detail the backgrounds of a group of five people within it: Eric (me), Matt, Harry, Judson, and Fred. Each received a survey that assessed their backgrounds, similarities, and differences—information that is invaluable in understanding the eventual development of the group. This group of friends is the direct result of the various forms of literacy sponsorship within our lives: people, setting, and backgrounds. (358)

Research Ethics

What steps did the researcher take to ensure he or she approached research participants ethically and responsibly? How do you know? Were those steps appropriate? Adequate? What concerns do you have about the research ethics guiding this study?

Findings

Here, help us understand what the researcher discovered through his/her research. How did she/he answer his/her research question(s)? How did the research methods undertaken lead the researcher to these conclusions?

Implications

What did you learn about literacy ethnographies by analyzing the research undertaken by others? About setting up a major argument? About developing relevant research questions? About identifying appropriate research participants and approaching them ethically? About possible research methods? How does the study of literacy compare/contrast with others you have read? What implications might your analysis of this study have for both your own studies (collectively or individually or both)?

Begin Your Group Project:

1. You need a group. Your instructor may choose your groups or provide a mechanism through which you can identify potential group members. However, your instructor may also invite you to select your own group members.

2. Once you have a group, work with them to select a literacy ethnography from those presented at the companion website for *Writing Inquiry* at http://www.fountainheadpress.com/writinginquiry (again, your instructor may assign these). Your options include:
   - Alvarez, Steven. "Brokering the Immigrant Bargain"
   - Bowen, Lauren Marshall. "Resisting Age Bias in Digital Literacy"
   - Cushman, Ellen. "Elias Boudinot and the *Cherokee Phoenix*: The Sponsors of
   - Literacy They Were and Were Not"
   - Fishman, Andrea R. "Becoming Literate"
   - Hogg, Charlotte. "The Space Between Public and Private: Rural Nebraska Women's Literacy"
   - Jacobs, Dale. "Marveling at 'The Man Called Nova'"
   - Kynard, Carmen. "'New Life in This Dormant Creature': Notes on Social Consciousness, Language, and Learning in a College Classroom"
   - Mahiri, Jabari. "Reading Rites and Sports: Motivation for Adaptive Literacy of Young African-American Males"
   - Mirabelli, Tony. "Learning to Serve: The Language and Literacy of Food Service Workers"
   - Nordquist, Brice. "Mobile Collaborations"
   - Simon, Kaia. "Daughters Learning from Fathers: Migrant Literacies that Mediate Borders"

3. Meet as soon as possible to divvy up the workload. You may decide to assign each group member two or three categories as represented in the assignment description and template provided on pages 367–371. Everyone in the group should answer the final category— "Implications"—because the implications the article analysis may have on your own individual studies will likely differ.

4. Get to know the categories for which you are responsible very well. Review the questions associated with those categories carefully. Take notes as necessary to ensure you understand them well.

5. With your categories and associated questions in mind, read the selected article carefully, pen in hand and paper or Word document on computer in front of you for notes. Mark the places in the article that appear to address the categories for which you are responsible. Write down (or type) the answers to the questions. Summarize your response to each selected category as clearly and briefly as possible to ensure it (a) clearly communicates your findings and (b) fits the template provided on page 368 (a one-page poster).

6. Meet again to share your answers, decide how to divvy up workload between designing the poster (based on contributions to each category from the group) and presenting this information to the class.

7. Develop your "Poster Presentation," which should follow the template you used to answer the questions offered on page 368. You can download a PowerPoint version of that template for your presentation at our companion website (www.fountainheadpress.com/writinginquiry). When you meet, you should also each share your responses to the "Implications" category. One person should be responsible for developing a summary of everyone's responses to the "Implications" category to be inserted into the poster template.

8. Present this information to the class, using your poster as a visual aid. We recommend limiting these presentations to ten minutes. Consider the following format:
   – Introduce yourselves.
   – Provide the title and author, and explain (briefly) why you selected this article over the other options.
   – Present information for each category in the order suggested by the template for the Poster Presentation. Each person should contribute information on the category for which they contributed their written summary.

9. Thank the class and, if there's time, invite questions.

10. Do not forget to submit your anonymous, individual reflections regarding your experiences with this group project (see assignment sheet on page 367). Collaborating can be incredibly rewarding. It can also be very difficult. Sometimes it seems like everyone is contributing equally, giving it their all and taking the project very seriously. Sometimes, it may seem like you are the only one doing the work and keeping up with internal deadlines set to meet this assignment's requirements. Your instructor will provide you with guidance, of course. Unfortunately, there is no real way to know how well a group is going to work together until they begin working together. As you can see, this textbook is a collaborative effort. We work well together.

For us collaborating on this particular project, working together has been very rewarding. We are much smarter together than we are alone, and we all feel we can trust one another to pull her own weight, meet deadlines, and contribute strong, smart, relevant work. However, we all have had previous opportunities to work together on other projects, both large and small (articles, other books). That puts us at an advantage you are unlikely to have. We already knew we worked well together. Yet we have also learned the hard way that collaboration can be very unpleasant indeed. We've each collaborated with one or more people on other projects where the collaborator failed to do what they promised to do (on time or, more than once, *at all)*, contributed subpar or, at times, largely irrelevant work, or were simply difficult personalities who, we learned, simply did not play well with others. That's a key reason why we want you to share this information with your instructor—anonymously. We want to know what worked well for you, what didn't, how you divided up your workload, who contributed what (and/or didn't), and all the other experiences with collaborating on a group project that are not visible from the Poster Presentation itself.

Goal: Completing this deep analysis of a published literacy ethnography and hearing about others puts you in an excellent position to develop your own literacy ethnography—especially your next major assignment, the Research Proposal, which is the subject of the next chapter.

CHAPTER 4

Designing Your Research Plan

Now that you have a good working definition of the object of study (literacy), explored potential research topics (through your writing assignments), read, discussed, and analyzed existing studies (through your various assignments, including your group presentation), you are more than ready to set up your own literacy ethnography. It may seem like an intimidating prospect, but you are ready. We promise! In this chapter, we will explore how.

Ethnographic research is *qualitative* research, as opposed to *quantitative* research.

> **Definition: *Qualitative Research*,** including <u>ethnography</u>, is primarily *exploratory* research. It is used to gain an understanding of underlying reasons, opinions, and motivations. It provides insights into the problem or helps to develop ideas or hypotheses for potential quantitative research. It requires close, careful, and extensive observations and interviews with a smaller data set than is required of ***Quantitative Research***, which is characterized by much, much bigger data sets. Where Qualitative Research can provide what an ethnographer calls a "thick description" of targeted populations and problems, Qualitative Research uses very large data sets and statistics to provide a "bird's-eye" view of the targeted issues. Quantitative Research is a formal, objective, systematic process in which numerical data are used to obtain information about the world.

Your research project is a literacy ethnography—*qualitative* research not quantitative. Here are a few examples of literacy ethnographies undertaken by former students:

> **Stephen Williams, "The (Il)literate Linemen":** "This literacy ethnography explores the lives of two men who have been labeled 'illiterate' according to the traditional definition, all of whom have experienced a great deal of success as employees at a local company that installs telephone lines (a supervisor and a co-worker). This project challenges common definitions of 'literacy' as they apply to the success of people who—despite evidence that these men cannot read or write in traditional ways—have developed very successful, albeit unique approaches to the extensive literacy practices required of their jobs. By focusing on how these men successfully negotiated the extensive paperwork required of their jobs, my study illustrates their particular practices in overcoming traditional literacy in non-traditional ways."

371

Stacie Gonzales, "Broken, Yet I Smile": "a study of what I call 'literacies of empowerment' within a home for women who have suffered from abuse. Part literacy autoethnography, part ethnography, I explore the role played by writing (and drawing) in working through the inevitable pain, vulnerability, and loss experienced—by these battered women and, through them, by myself."

Hunter Joyce, "Past Panels: The Influence of Our Literacy History": "a study of the ways in which previous experiences with texts affect present reading and writing practices. My project focuses on the reading of comic books as described by readers and creators of comics."

Jeremy Borden, "Like Father, Unlike Son: An Authoethnography of Literacy Between Father and Son": "an autoethnography on the different literacy practices between father and son, and the resulting influences on the social relationship between the two."

In the previous chapter, you analyzed a published literacy ethnography to understand the project's research design, findings, and contributions to the ongoing scholarly conversation. Each study taught us something different about the way reading and writing work in a variety of contexts and within the lived experiences of people. Yours will, too.

Your research, like any qualitative research, will occur in six distinct though deeply related phases. Your Research Proposal, the culminating project for this chapter, will articulate the way your research design will help you successfully navigate each of these phases.

Phase 1: Prepare for the Field and Design Your Research Question

Read. Write. Discuss. Read some more. Reflect. Read. Reflect. All of the assigned readings thus far, all of your assignments—indeed everything leading up to this point—has been preparation for the field. To prepare for the field, Stephen, Stacie, Hunter, and Jeremy all read many of the same articles you have read. Scholars like David Barton and Mary Hamilton inform their definitions of literacy.

Near the end of this phase, which will take place in the current chapter and your next major writing assignment (Research Proposal), you will define a research question and topic worthy of exploration (and accessible). Reflect, discuss, and read some more. Through their essays and other assignments, these students began to identify research questions and topics worthy of exploration. You will, too. In fact, you likely have already begun to do so. For Stephen, Stacie, Hunter, and Jeremy, these topics had deep personal connections. The topics emerged from their everyday, lived experiences in conversation with the scholarship they were reading in their classes.

Stephen worked for the telephone company. Early in the semester, he learned his direct supervisor could not read or write in traditional ways. He had been working with this man for years, yet Stephen never noticed he was illiterate. They had extensive paperwork to attend to at the beginning of their day, in the field, and at the end of each workday. Because he was reading about and discussing literacy so much in his first-year writing class, he started paying more attention to the way texts functioned in his daily life. He began to notice that his boss often drove, so Stephen found himself identifying all the relevant information from the documents guiding that day's work without any meaningful input from his boss. Finally, he asked him directly. From that delicate, difficult conversation, Stephen learned that his boss was, according to traditional definitions, "illiterate." From there, his research question began to take shape: *"How can people who might be identified as functionally illiterate successfully navigate the literacy practices required of their jobs?"* Interested in the answer? Stay tuned. We'll return to Stephen's study as it helps illustrate the other phases. The lesson here: pay attention to the way people interact with texts in your daily life. Many students have found excellent research questions right under their noses.

Stacie knew immediately what she wanted to be the focus of her study: a home for abused women and their children, where she had spent some time as a child and where she currently volunteered. She knew they used writing quite a bit as part of group and individual therapy. Her initial research question became, *"How do women and their children use reading and writing to work through the pain they experienced by their abuser(s)?"* This is a fine question. However, working with children is challenging. As you learned in Chapter 2, researching children, incarcerated people, and pregnant women is strongly discouraged by all governing bodies overseeing "research involving human subjects" (Institutional Review Board, the Federal Policy for the Protection of Human Subjects [45 CFR 46]). For this and other reasons, Stacie changed her research question to include only adult women. Given the sensitive nature of this study, she limited her focus still further to include only two women from this particular shelter. Importantly, she had a close personal relationship with these women based on her own, personal connections to this shelter as a former resident and current volunteer, *and* these women expressed an eagerness to participate in her study, as long as she did not refer to them directly by their own names (see Chapter 2 on research ethics). The lesson here: effective, ethical research often depends upon your existing relationships. Stacie would not have been able to undertake this research project had she not had this close personal relationship with the women involved and this particular research site. You cannot undertake research involving vulnerable populations like victims of domestic violence unless you (a) have a deep, long-lived, personal connection and (b) the potential participants agree to participate without coercion. Remember your Informed Consent Form, Code of Ethics, and everything you learned about research ethics from Chapter Two? That information is vital. Never, ever put your research participants at risk. Never cause them any undue harm. Respect their wishes. Respect them.

Hunter loved comic books. He had been a fan of them throughout his entire life. Early in the semester, he interviewed and was interviewed by a classmate based on Deborah Brandt's "Interview Protocol" from Part II, Chapter One (see pages 28–30), an activity not unlike the one based on Hawisher and Selfe's "Interview Protocol" provided in Chapter One, which you likely used to conduct an interview with a classmate at the beginning of the term. Whereas Hawisher and Selfe's Interview Protocol concerns digital literacies, Brant's concerns print-based ones. Based on his interviews, he was surprised to learn how much his own past experiences shaped his approach to and love of comics. Other than the comic strips printed in the newspaper, the person he interviewed had never read a single comic book. He became increasingly interested in that disconnect. His research question: *"How do past literacy experiences help shape approaches to reading comic books?"* The lesson: multiple lessons can be learned from this and our other examples, but we'd like to call your attention to one in particular—the rest of this textbook includes research tools and related information you might find useful as you develop your own literacy ethnography. Thumb through the rest of this textbook, and see what you find.

Jeremy immediately began to consider the significant differences between the ways in which his father approaches digital literacy and the way he experienced digital literacy in his own life. Like Hunter, this line of questioning began with an Interview Protocol—in Jeremy's case, the one Hawisher and Selfe used to develop their project on the ways in which people experience digital literacies. For his project, Jeremy generated what is called an "autoethnography":

> Autoethnography is an approach to research and writing that seeks to describe and systematically analyze (*graphy*) personal experience (*auto*) in order to understand cultural experience (*ethno*) (Ellis, 2004; Holman Jones, 2005). This approach challenges canonical ways of doing research and representing others (Spry, 2001) and treats research as a political, socially-just and socially-conscious act (Adams and Holman Jones, 2008). A researcher uses tenets of autobiography and ethnography to do and write autoethnography. Thus, as a method, autoethnography is both process and product. (Ellis, Adams, and Bochner)

The "cultural experience" Jeremy was working to understand is digital literacy as it manifests itself across generations in a single family living in the same town and attending the same schools in different historical periods. His research question: *"How might two men from different generations experience digital literacy in the same place (home, town, and school)?"* Jeremy was raised in the same town as his father, and he attended the same schools. The lesson: the researcher can be a research participant in his or her own literacy ethnography. Hunter was a research participant in his study of comic book literacies, though the majority of his study was based on data collected from interviews and site observations of other people so his study is properly defined as an ethnography. Jeremy, however, was a key research participant in his study, which centered on literacy in his family and their relationships as developed through reading and writing. Whereas Hunter's study included himself as one of many research participants, Jeremy's centered almost entirely on his own life and family relationships. That makes Jeremy's project an autoethnography rather than an ethnography.

An autoethnography is a perfectly legitimate genre of research. It is difficult, however, for a wide variety of reasons. For one, an autoethnography is not simply a personal story. It is research that involves extensive data collection and analysis. The research and analysis for an autoethnography is no less rigorous than that required for an ethnography. Even more difficult in an autoethnography is the getting the critical distance required to make meaningful observations and draw reliable conclusions. It is *your* life, of course. To compose a successful autoethnography, Jeremy had to work twice as hard to obtain the critical distance necessary to conduct accurate field observations and interpret the data he collected. In the end, it was worth it. However, it was not easy.

Phase 2: Select Research Tool(s)

What research tool(s) is most appropriate for your project? How can you tell?

For your research tool, you have several options: (a) interviews, (b) field observations, and/or (c) close reading of literacy artifacts. Most researchers use some combination of these tools. In what follows, I will define each of these tools and discuss the ways in which these student researchers used them in their own literacy ethnographies.

- *Interviews:* This research tool should be pretty self-explanatory. An interview is a face-to-face, online, or telephone meeting during which information is obtained.

Jeremy wanted to understand literacy experiences across generations—specifically his father's and his own. His primary focus was *digital* literacies, so he based his interviews on the interview protocol provided by Hawisher and Selfe (see Chapter 1, pages 242–247). This interview protocol, as you know, guided their own research for their article "Becoming Literate in the Information Age" and related book *Literate Lives in the Information Age* (2004). To this end, he "interviewed" himself and his father.

Initially, Hunter was interested in how comic book readers' literacy history shapes their approach to superhero comic books—specifically, Batman comics. In an attempt to answer his research question (see above), he chose to interview two people. Both were first-year students who lived in his dorm: one who self-identified as an avid reader of comic books and one who had never read a comic book. [Tip: Select research participants to whom you have access.] Hunter was more interested in their literacy experiences with print-based texts than digital ones, however, so he decided not to use the interview protocol Jeremy utilized (from Hawisher and Selfe). To guide this interview, Hunter utilized the interview protocol developed by Deborah Brandt for her book *Literacy in American Lives,* which you can find in "Part II: Experiencing Literacy," Chapter One of this book (pgs. 28–30). Brandt studied ordinary, everyday literacy experiences with print-based texts across generations. Selfe and Hawisher built directly upon Brandt's study, focusing instead on ordinary, everyday literacy experiences with digital texts across generations.

Stephen's study of his functionally "illiterate" colleagues required extensive use of two different kinds of interviews. First, he interviewed his supervisor and co-worker based on the same Interview Protocol Hunter used (from Deborah Brandt), which helped him understand the ways in which these men experienced literacy across their life spans. He went in with the understanding that even though these men could not read and write in the traditional sense, they were still very intelligent, successful people. As Mike Rose explains in *The Mind at Work: Valuing the Intelligence of the American Worker* (2005),

... when we dismiss the intelligence necessary to install a new toilet in an older home, color hair without drying it out, or effectively serve a restaurant full of hungry customers, we "develop limited educational programs and fail to make fresh and meaningful instructional connections among disparate kinds of skill and knowledge." (216)

After interviewing his two research participants guided by Brandt's Interview Protocol, Stephen interviewed them again based on a second set of questions very specific to his own study. For this phase, he had only one planned question: "How do you deal with all the paperwork required of this job?" His follow-up questions emerged during the interviews themselves. From these interviews, he learned that both men relied heavily on co-workers during the workday (recall Stephen's supervisor drove while Stephen read from the forms guiding the day's work on telephone lines around town) and family (both had wives and children who helped them complete the requisite paperwork that summed up each day's work, which they submitted the following morning).

EXERCISE

Thinking About Research Tools

Think about these interview protocol in terms of the studies discussed thus far. Jeremy chose to use Hawisher and Selfe's interview protocol to study literacy experiences in his family. Hunter chose to use Brandt's interview protocol to understand how previous literacy experiences might shape a person's approach to reading a comic book.

1. What makes Hunter's choice appropriate given his research question?

2. How might Hunter's study change were he to utilize Hawisher and Selfe's interview protocol on digital literacies instead of Brandt's interview protocol on print-based literacy? Would he need to rethink his research question? If so, how? What might a new, more relevant research question be, based on data guided by Hawisher and Selfe's Interview Protocol?

3. How might Jeremy's study change were he to utilize Brandt's interview protocol on print-based literacies instead of Hawisher and Selfe's interview protocol on digital ones? Would he need to rethink his research question? If so, how? What might a new, more relevant research question be based on using data guided by Brandt's Interview Protocol?

- *Field Observations:* Field observations are methods a researcher uses to observe people in "real" locations and situations. Since our focus is literacy, the field observations help researchers focus on how real people put texts to use in real situations and to what ends.

Stacie's study was built almost entirely around field observations (and close readings of cultural artifacts, as we will explain in a moment). For her study, she gained permission from her two friends at the shelter (see above) to observe four writing sessions—two with a facilitator from the shelter and two without.

During all of these sessions, the women were working on a series of brief, autobiographical sketches. The former were two sessions during which these women were working together, sharing portions of their essays with one another and asking for feedback. The other two sessions were similar activities with a facilitator present.

In addition to the interviews we've already mentioned above, Hunter's study included two focus groups that met two times (each). One group included only regular comic book readers. The other included only those who never read comic books. He wanted to know how these two groups would approach the reading of comic books, so he placed about ten of his own comic books in the middle of the floor and invited them to "have at it." He recorded what he observed during these literacy events.

- *Close reading of literacy artifact:* In his classic essay, "Artifact Study: A Proposed Model" (1974), E. McClung Fleming argues, [e]very culture, however primitive or advanced, is absolutely dependent upon its artifacts for its survival and self-realization." This is certainly true of reading and writing in our world.

In addition to interviews, Stephen's study included a close reading of our literacy artifacts: (a) the "Job Board" posted in the staff workroom at his telephone company, where key information about the day's objectives are posted by management each day; (b) a completed "Daily Workflow Report," which workers are required to pick up at the beginning of each workday, outlining the location of each job and required tasks involved; and (c) two completed "Daily Job Reports"—one from each of his research participants—which workers were required to fill out at the end of each work day outlining the activities of that day. The "Daily Job Reports" were the forms these men completed with the help of their families each night, so they provided important information about the ways in which these individuals negotiated the texts required of them without the benefit of traditional literacy skills.

In addition to field observations of her research participants working on their autobiographical sketches, Stacie closely observed and analyzed excerpts from their writing and drawing activities selected by the authors themselves. Both Stephen and Stacie also used these literacy artifacts in the interviews themselves, inviting the research participants to comment on their direct experiences with these texts as readers, writers, artists, and workers.

EXERCISE

Thinking About Research Tools

Consider a research question you might undertake for your literacy ethnography. What tool(s) do you believe would be most appropriate and why?

1. Interviews: If you were to interview someone for your own literacy ethnography, whom might that be? How might this person inform your research question? What sorts of access do you have to this person? Do you believe this person would be interested in and available to participate? How

do you know? What interview questions would you ask and why, given your research question?

2. Field observations: If you were to conduct field observations, what would you observe? How might these observations inform your research question? What sorts of access do you have to this site? What would you be looking for? Remember our focus is literacy. Where are the texts? Literacy practices? Literacy events?

3. Analysis of Literacy Artifact: If you were to analyze a cultural artifact of literacy ("object" of literacy), what would you choose? Why? How might a close analysis of this artifact inform your research question? What sorts of access do you have to this artifact? What would you be looking for? Again, remember our focus is literacy.

- *Analysis of Photographs:* Yet another research tool is to analyze photographs representing literacy events, as Mary Hamilton explains in her extremely informative essay "Expanding New Literacy Studies: Using Photographs to Explore Literacy as a Social Practice." You'll find this essay on our companion website at www.fountainheadpress.com/writinginquiry.

Phase 3: Design Your Research Plan

This is the focus of the current chapter. For your Research Proposal, you will need a research question, relevant research tool(s), discussion of how you will work to protect the participants involved in your research (see "research ethics" in Chapter 2), a copy of your interview questions, if relevant, and "Code of Ethics" and "Informed Consent" (see Chapter 2). We'll offer much more information about how to approach your research design below.

Phase 4: Enter the Field and Begin Data Collection

Fieldnotes (FNs) play a key role in ethnographic research like this, whether this is an interview, field observations of a research site and/or activity, or close analysis of a cultural artifact. You'll find a guide for collecting fieldnotes in Chapter 5, when we begin the actual research process. We'll discuss that process in much greater detail in the next chapter, including providing examples from a recent ethnography. For now, just know that FNs are notes you take "in the field"—during a site visit, an interview, or a close reading of a given cultural artifact. Use your senses—what do you see, hear, smell, and, potentially even feel or taste.

Phase 5: Analyze Your Data

At a certain point, you have to stop collecting data and begin to analyze the data. In the following chapter, you'll receive extensive guidance on how to effectively move from data collection (see "fieldnotes" above) to data analysis. We will cover this in the next chapter.

Phase 6: Write It All Up

You'll use your fieldnotes and data analysis exercises to generate your final ethnographic essay.

You should be able to draw directly from your previous writing assignments, as well, including the research proposal you will be developing as your next major assignment. Everything you do in each phase of the research process is designed to help you compose an effective final ethnographic essay. Chapter 5 will give you exactly what you need to write up your literacy ethnography.

ACTIVITY

IDENTIFYING YOUR RESEARCH QUESTION AND DEVELOPING YOUR RESEARCH PLAN

You have already completed Phases 1: Prepare for the Field and Define Your Research Question. It is now time for Phases 2-3: **Select Your Research Tool(s) and Design Your Research Plan.** That means that before you do anything else, you will need to pin down the specific, concrete plans that will guide your entry into the field—i.e., the research site and/or your interviewee's location (Phase 4).

The following exercise should help get you started on this important process.

Directions: In this activity, you should begin by considering what data you will need to begin answering the major question or issue that drives your project. Your goal in this activity is to pin down the community of practice and/or literacy artifacts you will need to observe and/or interview to begin answering that important research question.

Goal: Focus your research plan so you will know where you need to go and what you need to do when you "enter the field" and begin collecting your data.

Step I: What is your research question? This doesn't need to be set in stone. Can't think of one? Review your previous essays. Consider research questions driving the articles you have read, analyzed, and discussed in previous chapters. Brainstorm. Talk it over with classmates. It will come to you. Not there yet? Put a pin in it for now and move onto Step II.

Step II: Freewrite for about five minutes in response to the people you might interview, the sites you may observe, and/or the artifacts/materials you might collect and analyze to help you answer the key research question and issue you would like to investigate through your final research project.

Step III: Share and discuss results with your partner, in preparation for sharing it with your class.

Step IV: Are you ready to enter the field now? To be sure, answer the following questions as completely as you can. Remember you used these in the previous chapter to analyze at least one essay from a previous chapter. Take them on again, this time for your own study.

These questions will require you to speculate—or hypothesize—based on your currently limited information on the subject. You haven't yet collected or analyzed your data yet, so you won't be able to answer any of these questions definitely yet. That's not the point. The point is to imagine the form your study should take *before* you undertake it. A hypothesis is, essentially, an informed "guess" scientists or other researchers make to guide the study they intend to undertake. A hypothesis is made on the basis of limited evidence as a starting point for further investigation. That's what the research proposal is designed to be—your starting point.

1. (Space): What is (are) the location(s) in which this analysis might take place? (Note: your study need not take place in any particular location. Consider the research projects we've discussed thus far. Neither Hunter's project on comic book literacies nor Jeremy's project on digital literacies were dependent upon a single location. In Stephen's study, one location played a minor role—the staff workroom at his telephone company. Stacie's study was based at a shelter for victims of domestic violence, but the bulk of her data was collected through interviews and close analyses of literacy artifacts.
   - Will your study be dependent upon a particular space? If so, which one? Why?
   - Do you have access to this location? How?
   - How will field observations of this space help you answer your research question?

2. (Actors): Who are the members of this group/subgroup in your proposed study? Describe them.
   - Why these actors and not others?
   - Do you have access to these "actors"? How?
   - How will information gleaned from these people help you answer your research question?

   Hunter's "actors" were readers and non-readers of comic books; the "actors" in Jeremy's study were himself and his father.

3. (Texts/Objects): What texts are likely to be involved in this study? As you consider this question, remember your own working definition of literacy (Writing Assignment 1).
   - What objects of literacy do you think may be used as a regular part of the activities in which the members of this group engage? How can you find out?
   - Why these texts and not others?
   - Do you have access to these texts? How?
   - How will this information help you answer your research question?

   Again, you will not know the answer to these questions in any definitive way yet. That's a purpose of your study, which will follow the development of your Research Proposal. However, you can guess at this point. Because he worked at the telephone company, for example, Stephen knew the kinds of paperwork he'd likely need to consider in his study of the literacy practices his functionally illiterate co-workers would have to navigate. Those were, necessarily, the texts he decided he would need to analyze.

4. (Literacy Events): In what literacy events do you believe members of this group or subgroup are likely to engage? How will you find out?
   - Why these literacy events in particular?
   - How will this information help you answer your research question?

The literacy events in Stephen's study included the following: (a) reading and discussing the "Daily Workflow Report" in the work truck throughout the workday, as it guided them from job to job; (b) filling out the daily "Job Report" at the end of each day, where the workers summarize the activities they completed during that workday.

5. (Literacy Practices): What literacy practices will you be looking for?
   - Why these literacy practices in particular?
   - How will this information help you answer your research question?

   The difference between a "literacy event" and a "literacy practice" may be difficult to discern, but drop the word "literacy" and you'll get it quite easily. What is an "event"? How does an "event" differ from "practice"? An event is a concert, for example. A practice is the moves a pianist makes within that event (concert)—fingers moving up and down the keyboard, eyes moving across the page, left to right, to interpret, line-by-line, the notes and translate those into moves upon the keyboard to generate the desired sound. We could, in fact, consider a concert a "literacy event," in this sense. To enact this literacy event, the pianist sits down at her piano and begins to interact with the text (musical score) in particular ways. The ways in which the pianist interacts with this text during this literacy event are the literacy *practices.*

6. (Goals): What do you imagine the members of this group or the group as a whole want to achieve and/or accomplish?
   - What role(s) does literacy play in this?
   - How will you find out?
   - How will this information help you answer your research question?

   The goals for the literacy events in Stephen's study were to (a) successfully navigate a workday, getting to the right job locations at the right time and performing the assigned jobs successfully and (b) accurately and promptly summarizing the jobs performed throughout the day so their supervisors are happy, enabling them to keep their jobs or perhaps even earn raises and promotions.

7. (Research Tool): What research tool will best enable you to answer your research question? Interviews? Field observations? Close analysis of literacy artifacts? Some combination thereof? How? What makes this/these research tool(s) the best ones for the job, given your research question and goals?

8. (Summary): Summarize your responses to the above questions as completely as possible. Share them with a classmate. This information will form the basis of your Research Proposal, your next major writing assignment.

WRITING ASSIGNMENT
RESEARCH PROPOSAL

Your research proposal is your plan for data collection. It is necessarily flexible, and things may not always go according to plan (that's okay!). Even so, it is crucial that you have a plan. The research proposal asks you to question what you know, what you don't know, and what you hope to know. Also crucial are the ways in which you are going to treat the community you are investigating and the data you are collecting to represent them (all with great respect, of course!).

Your Research Proposal must include:

1. your working definition of literacy (see Writing Assignment 1, Chapter One);

2. a discussion of what you hope to accomplish;

3. an explanation of why the research is important to you and how you have framed the central questions or lines of inquiry for your research (your research question);

4. a discussion of the spaces (locations), actors (people), texts, literacy events, and/or literacy practices you plan to study and their relevance to your research question (see responses to exercises on previous pages);

5. a description of the access you have to the locations, people, texts, literacy events, and/or practices you listed in response to the previous questions (What is your connection? How will you obtain the access you need to conduct this study?);

6. a statement describing the ways in which you will approach your data collection, analysis, and write-up that will ensure the participants in your study will be treated with the utmost respect and that the process will follow the ethical principles set by university researchers and the Institutional Review Boards that oversee such work (see Chapter 2). Who will you approach for permission, for example, and why this particular person(s)/group and not another?;

7. a discussion of how you will obtain signatures on the requisite forms and a draft of the permission forms you intend to use;

8. a detailing of your research plan (When and where will you research, and how?);

9. a description of the methodology for your research (How will you collect the data and why this method as opposed to another?); and

10. a discussion of how your research connects to the wider scholarly community discussing such subjects (Where's the literacy? How will this project contribute to the larger scholarly conversation in literacy studies, especially as represented in our course readings?).

As you write, keep in mind that your responses to the guiding questions listed above should be integrated into a coherent essay. Your paragraphs should not stand as separate, isolated responses to the questions but should be held together as a cohesive proposal by the exploration of what you want to research, why you want to research this in particular, what makes it important, and the connection you can make between your research in this local context and the larger scholarly conversation in literacy studies.

Your Research Proposal must include the following:

- a three- to four-page essay that responds to the items listed above;
- a copy of your Code of Ethics (see Writing Assignment 2 in Chapter Two); and
- a copy of your Informed Consent Form (see Writing Assignment 2 in Chapter Two).

CHAPTER 5

Entering the Field

In this chapter, we take up the next two phases: data collection (Phase 4) and analysis (Phase 5).

X	Phase 1: Prepare for the Field and Design Your Research Question
X	Phase 2: Select Your Research Tool (Interviews? Field observations? Close analysis of literacy artifact? Some combination thereof?)
X	Phase 3: Develop Your Research Proposal
	Phase 4: Enter the Field and Begin Data Collection
	Phase 5: Analyze Your Data
	Phase 6: Write It All Up! (see Chapter 6)

Now that you have a good grounding in literacy studies, working definitions of important terms like literacy, literacy events, texts, reading, writing, a better understanding of what others have said about how literacy is put to use by real people in real locations and over time, a research question that hasn't yet been answered in the work you've read thus far, and a research plan (see "Research Proposal" in previous chapter), *you are ready to "enter the field."* This means you'll be collecting your data (Phase 4) and then analyzing that data (Phase 5). In this chapter, we will by providing a range of useful tools to help you do just this. As with every writing and reading assignment thus far, anything you generate in response to these activities may end up in your final project. It doesn't have to, of course, but these activities and readings are designed to help you generate as much material as possible that might be directly relevant to your final ethnographic project. That means you should be able to draw prose directly from your responses to these readings, activities, presentations, and assignments.

Before we move too far into the nuts and bolts of data collection and analysis, let's return to a literacy ethnography we analyzed together in Chapter 3: Eric Pleasant's "Literacy Sponsors and Learning: An Ethnography of Punk Literacy in Mid-1980s Waco." His introductory paragraphs set the stage for his study, as they should. At first glance, they also may seem to represent what it means to "enter the field" in research. As readers, we are, essentially, entering the field with him: a punk club in Austin, Texas, where the popular Dallas-based band the Butthole Surfers were about to play. However, that club is not actually the "field" in the sense meant by researchers—at least not directly. Through extensive data collection (interviews, analysis of literacy artifacts) and analysis, Pleasant was able to construct this "verbal portrait" with which he began his final ethnographic essay. You'll be asked to do the same.

The culminating assignment for this chapter is a Verbal Portrait, for which Pleasant's introductory paragraphs serve as a model (see pages 356–357). As Pleasant did in his own project, a version of your own Verbal Portrait can serve as the introductory paragraphs for your final ethnographic essay. Like Pleasant, however, you cannot compose your Verbal Portrait without first collecting and analyzing data based according to the plan outlined in your Research Proposal (see previous chapter). You need not wait until you have collected and analyzed *all* your data before composing your Verbal Portrait (see the student example provided on page 408, which is based largely on a single extended interview). However, you will have to collect and analyze *some* of the data—an interview or two, two site visits, close analysis of two literacy artifacts, or a combination thereof—to compose your Verbal Portrait. After this assignment, you will need to collect and analyze your remaining data and—guided by your instructor and information provided in Chapter 6—develop your final ethnographic essay. The goal of the current chapter is to provide methods for and examples of data collection and analysis.

EXERCISE

Review (again) the opening paragraphs of Eric Pleasant's "Literacy Sponsors and Learning: An Ethnography of Punk Literacy in Mid-1980s Waco." As you do so, think about the data he needed to gather and analyze in order to compose this Verbal Portrait.

- Did he visit the club and take notes? That seems unlikely doesn't it, given that his description illustrates the club as it would have appeared to him and his friends in the 1980s, twenty years before he began researching this essay? Perhaps he visited it during the time of his research? We'd have to assume it still existed, right? And if it did, would it have been a better choice to develop a Verbal Portrait of how it looks today? Why or why not?

- If he did not visit the club—at least not the 1980s version of the club, given his lack of a time machine—how did he gather the data he needed to compose this Verbal Portrait? What research tools did he use?

- As you read, be thinking about your own research project. What might you learn from analyzing Pleasant's work about effective ways to collect and analyze data to present via your own Verbal Portrait?

As you walk in, you instantly notice your surroundings. You are entering a dark room with an almost oppressive atmosphere. Animal bones hang from the ceiling. The walls are painted black. Flyers promoting upcoming shows have been pasted one on top of the other throughout the room. Artwork on the flyers consists of skeletons, monsters, and an array of unflattering caricatures of people such as Ronald Reagan, Hitler, and the pope. Band names upon the flyers are as brash as the images: Dead Kennedys, Millions of Dead Cops, Agent Orange, Marching Plague, and the Offenders. Phrases such as "There is no justice, just us" and "We're just a minor threat" are graffitied across the walls, promoting a sense of unity outside the bounds of traditional societal values. At the opposite end of the room is a stage. Groups of kids are standing together looking at you with seeming tribal defiance. Most of these people have leather jackets adorned with spikes and band names or logos similar to the ones on the walls. Some have hair that has been spiked, shaved, or colored with Day-Glo hues that scream, "I am not a normal member of society!" You have just entered the netherworld of the Cave Club, Austin, Texas. The year is 1985 and you have come to see the psychedelic punk rock band the Butthole Surfers.

I am one of the people walking into the club. I look at my four best friends. We are five white adolescents aged fifteen to eighteen from Waco, Texas. How did we get here? How do we fit into this extremely closed group of people we see around us in the club? These other youths have a reputation of hating outsiders to the point of showing extreme aggression. All of a sudden, one of the people in the club sees and recognizes us. He nods and walks up. The band takes the stage and opens its set with crazy, insane-sounding rants that lead into straight-ahead, hard-driving drums and guitar—this is stripped-down, in-your-face music. The punk walking up grabs one of my friends. No words are spoken. He puts his arm around my friend's shoulders and pulls him into a swirling pit of kids. The music picks up. The rest of us look at each other, grin, and run to join the human maelstrom. We do fit in here!

Entering the Field: Data Collection

To enter the field does not, necessarily, mean entering a physical space. As you can see from Pleasant's Verbal Portrait, sometimes entering a physical space is not even possible. He had no time machine, so he relied extensively on memories of the experiences collected through his interviews with that group of friends twenty years after that concert in 1985. This particular concert and location were not the primary focus of this project. Instead, the Verbal Portrait serves as a representative example designed to introduce readers to the general topic that is the focus of the study—in this case, the way he and his friends developed "punk literacy" in a relatively isolated town in Texas with no "punk scene" and long before the Internet existed. His essay, again based on interviews with other members of his subgroup and explorations of his own memories about this time, revealed strategies like purchasing records through the mail, subscribing to "zines" (again through the mail) that likewise articulated the fashions, music, philosophy, and terminology associated with punk culture. No less important were the concerts he and his friends would attend, including this concert at a club in Austin, a couple hour's drive from his home in Waco. To learn more about the specific data collection process Pleasant went through, return to his complete essay.

"The field," in Pleasant's case, was one built from memories collected via interviews. In Hunter's case, "the field" he entered was his own creation—"field observations" of the focus groups that were an important part of Hunter's study on comic book literacies discussed in the previous chapter. The "field," in his case, was the living room in his dorm, where he placed his precious collection of *Batman* comics in the middle of the floor and invited his research participants to "have at it." To collect his data, Hunter, like Pleasant and all the other researchers we've discussed thus far, relied on two deeply interrelated research tools: (1) the Research Portfolio and (2) Fieldnotes.

Research Portfolio

The **Research Portfolio** is a place where you collect every scrap of paper, photograph, literacy artifacts like flyers or writing samples, notes (including Fieldnotes, described below), interview transcripts, signed Informed Consent Forms, and everything else you generate and collect throughout your research process. Artifacts collected in your Research Portfolio might also include photographs, brochures, pamphlets, letters written from one community member to another, menus, timesheets, employee reports, church bulletins, newsletters, sketches, songs, and advertisements. The only requirement for an item to be considered appropriate for your Research Portfolio is that it's relevant to the subject of your study.

"At first," as Sunstein and Chiseri-Strater explain,

> . . . you may find it strange to collect wrinkled scraps of paper, lists on napkins, or snippets of conversation you've overheard, but by gathering them in your portfolio, you'll see how they might fit into your larger project. . . . [O]ver time, you will see that it is a focused, not random, collection of artifacts and writing that lend shape to your fieldwork. Unlike a scrapbook, where pieces are fastened down, in this portfolio, you can move, remove, and replace your data to see potential patterns and structures. (57)

Because this flexibility is so important in the early stages of your research/ writing process, you may find it useful to begin with an accordion-style folder in which you collect these items. Soon enough, however, it will become necessary to begin organizing them in a three-ring binder—a process that will again require great flexibility and quite a bit of reflection and analysis (see the following chapter).

In the Research Portfolio for his ethnographic study of how his functionally "illiterate" coworkers and supervisor at the telephone company navigated the texts required of their jobs, Stephen collected, among other things, copies of the various forms employees had to read and fill out at the beginning and end of each shift, the work schedule, minutes from monthly meetings, photographs of signage posted around the workroom and of the inside of the work truck, where much of the negotiation of relevant texts took place as they guided them to the location of each "job" and the duties they were required to perform at each job site, notes from his interviews with these research participants, and the Informed Consent Forms these employees signed to give their permission to be interviewed (see Chapter 2), as well as the Code of Ethics he wrote to guide his research. Not everything collected in his working Research Portfolio made it into the final project. However, he collected all of these materials regardless, since there is no real way to know what you really need until you sharpen your focus through additional data collection and—most importantly—*analysis*.

Fieldnotes

> *Fieldnotes: "The observations written by a researcher at a research site, during an interview, and throughout the data collection process"* (*Fieldwork*, 501)

Basically, fieldnotes (FNs) are notes you take "in the field"—during a site visit, an interview, or a close reading of a given artifact. Use your senses—what do you see, hear, smell, and potentially even feel or taste? Writing FNs is more than a process of remembering and getting it down on paper. Rather, writing FNs promotes learning and deepens understanding about what has been seen and heard in the field, during interviews, close readings of literacy artifacts, and/or photographs of literacy practices.

Fieldnotes are the heart and soul of this kind of research. Again "field" here is not, necessarily (though sometimes) a literal, physical space. As we've already discussed, interviews can also be considered field observations and rely on the same research tool: fieldnotes. Stephen relied on fieldnotes to collect data during interviews with his seemingly "illiterate" co-workers at the telephone company that was the focus of his study. He received permission to record his interviews, which he found useful. He also relied on fieldnotes to collect data from his close analysis of selected literacy artifacts like the "Job Reports" that his research participants filled out at home after each work day with the help of their families to summarize the work they undertook in the field that day.

Strategies for Taking Fieldnotes

Fieldnotes take many forms, but the key ingredients are these.

1. Close, objective, unbiased observations through the senses;

2. Your own reflections, questions, potential interpretations, and ideas about what you are observing, objectively, through your senses; and

3. Keeping #1 and #2 separate, so your notes reflect the data you collect in as objective a way as possible.

You'll take these FNs in two separate steps:

- (Step I): *Jottings*, which are the notes you take in real time, in the process of the field observations. Jottings are devices intended to encourage the recall of scenes, events, relevant quotes, or other details in the construction of some broader, fuller FN account. What is "key" won't be clear right away or always, and what seems "key" at one point may not necessarily appear as key later in the research process. For primarily these reasons, it is important to write down as much as you can as quickly as you can.

- (Step II): *Expanded FNs*, an expanded, more formal set of notes you write up based on the "jottings" collected in the field. To be as useful as possible, you should spend some time "expanding" your FNs as soon as you complete your field observations. For example, as soon as you shake hands with your interviewee at the end of your interview, head straight for your desk and write up your expanded FNs while the event is still fresh in your mind.

  For Expanded FNs, you will be turning your recollections and jottings (see Step I) into detailed written accounts that will preserve as much as possible about what you noticed and now feel is significant. Expanded FNs require a complex process of remembering, filling in, elaborating, and commenting upon FNs in order to provide a full, written account of witnessed scenes and events and other relevant details (including findings emerging from close readings of literacy artifacts and/or photographs). *Tip: write to yourself as a future researcher first.* As a future reader of your own FNs, you anticipate a detailed reading in order to code (we'll discuss the coding process later) and analyze the notes for a paper or an article. Attempt to keep it open-minded, though, allowing for new insight and information as your research process unfolds.

Exercise

Taking Fieldnotes

Directions: Take some fieldnotes in your classroom. Your classroom is unlikely to be the subject of your own research project, but this is a good way to experiment with the process before you begin collecting data for your own research.

Step I: *Jottings.*

- Set up the page for your "jottings." At the top of the page, place your name, the date, time, and location of your fieldwork. Right now, this may seem silly. However, as you begin collecting your own FNs, these identifying markers will be vital. Otherwise, it will be almost impossible to keep track.
- Divide your sheet into two columns. This version of FNs are called "Double-Entry Notes," for obvious reasons. "Making such distinctions" between your objective observations and your personal reflections regarding those observations "allows the fieldworker to become aware of the differences between verifiable, tangible facts about the chosen fieldsite and his or her thoughts and feelings about those facts" (FW, 500).

Name? Date? Time? Location?

Observations	Reflections
On the left side, record only your observations. Do not analyze them.	On the right side, record only your personal reflections about the subject of your field observations (in this case, your classroom).
Use your senses! Write down as much as possible and be as specific as possible. When you begin your own research, this will be particularly important because you never know what might become important later.	Prompts to consider:
Prompts to consider:	<ul><li>What surprises you about what you are observing?</li><li>What confuses you?</li><li>What questions arise as you conduct these observations?</li><li>What key terms or new vocabulary words are emerging through these observations?</li><li>What strikes you as odd? Puzzling? Anything? What can you make of this at this point? What's to be learned?</li><li>What are you noticing now in this seemingly very familiar space that you never notice before? What are you to make of that disconnect? How has this exercise made the familiar strange, and what meaning can you derive from that information?</li></ul>
<ul><li>*Look*—What do you see? What are people wearing? How is the classroom decorated? Because your focus for this project will be literacies in context, identify texts around the classroom, technologies of literacy (on the walls, doors, in the hands of and near classmates, etc.).</li><li>*Listen*—What do you hear? Shuffling of papers? Feet on the floor? Scribbling of pens? What else? Listen carefully. Can you hear the sound of the air conditioner humming along? Muffled conversations from a class down the hall? What about outside the building? A dog barking in the distance? Listen closely, considering not only what is in the room with you but what may be beyond. As noted earlier, you never know what may become important later.</li></ul>	

Observations	Reflections
• *Smell*—What odors do you notice? What do you recognize? What seems unrecognizable? Write it all down. • *Taste*—Okay, this may seem like a very strange sense to document in this context. And it is. No one is asking you to lick the desk or anything else in the room for that matter. Perhaps you merely taste spearmint from the gum you popped into your mouth after lunch and before class. If there is nothing to document regarding "taste" here, skip this sense. • *Touch*—Consider the feel of the pen in your hand or keyboard under your fingertips. The floor under your feet. Your feet in your shoes. The desk. The seat. The temperature in the room. Again, anything you can take in via this sense may be worth documenting. Of course, it may not. You may feel particularly silly writing down sense impressions like these. Don't give in. Trust the exercise. You can adapt it later to your own research, needs, context, and goals. The main objective with these jottings is to get down as much information as you can as observed through your senses. Leave all the judgments, insights, questions, and other reflections for the other side of the page. This side is for objective, observable facts only!	• What insights can you draw from these observations? About texts and the way people use them? About writing instruments? About writing technologies? About reading? About writing? About literacy? About anything else? Any ideas for further research emerging from these observations? What might you like to know more about? • From your observations thus far, what really stands out? What seems most important? Why?

Step II: *Expanded Fieldnotes*.

- Translate your "jottings" (above) into prose. Again, write the date, time, and location at the top of the page. Title it "Expanded Fieldnotes," just to keep track of everything. Address it to your future self, as a researcher. This may seem particularly silly now, especially since you are unlikely to make your classroom the subject of your ethnographic project. However, this practice will be particularly useful later, as you tell your future self to consider particular lines of inquiry, test new hypotheses, and look at patterns or outliers you have begun to identify in this particular set of field observations. Your future self will thank you for it. So go ahead and address it, "Dear _____. Come on. No one is looking. This is for you.
- Summarize your general observations, focusing on what stands out as puzzling, intriguing, surprising, in need of further study.
- What surprised you?
- What intrigued you?
- What seemed odd or out of place or otherwise puzzling?
- What questions emerged from this set of field observations?
- From these observations, what seems worth pursuing further?

- From these observations, what conclusions are you beginning to draw about the meaning of literacy, texts, writing, writers, reading, readers, literacy practices, literacy events, and the like? Anything?
- What implications might all this and this exercise in particular have for your own research project?

Use these questions and this method to collect field observations for your own study. Whether you are conducting field observations of a specific place, as you did in this exercise, or during an interview, an analysis of a literacy artifact, or other data, the method is much the same.

For each field observation—whether that be in a physical space like your classroom, an interview conducted face-to-face, by phone, online, or other means, a literacy artifact, or a photograph depicting literacy events and practices (a method described by Mary Hamilton in her essay found at our companion website)—you will always begin with "jottings" that separate your sense impressions (left side) from your reflections (right side), followed as quickly as possible with the Expanded Fieldnotes that summarize your observations and reflections and give you a map for where to take your project next.

Stephen received permission from his research participants to record the interviews he conducted with his co-workers at the telephone company. Even though Stephen listened to the recordings he collected, he found the "jottings" he took during the initial interview to be even more useful materials in his analysis. Before he began the interview, he folded a sheet of paper in half (vertically). As he spoke with his interviewee, he'd write down phrases he found particularly interesting, puzzling, or otherwise worthy of further consideration (observations, on the left side of the page in the Double-Entry Fieldnotes described above). He also wrote down questions he had, or insights, or possible connections to other data collected or analyzed previously (reflections, on the right side of the page in the same Double-Entry Fieldnotes). Many of the questions he found himself asking through reflections were those listed in the exercise above that invited you to collect fieldnotes in your classroom.

Immediately after each interview, he would go directly to a quiet corner of the workroom at the telephone and develop his Expanded Fieldnotes. At the top of the page, he'd write the date and time of the interview (when it began and ended) and the location (most often, in the work truck at the end of a shift). Again, he used the questions listed in the exercise above regarding field observations in your classroom. A few times—with a headset plugged into his phone, where he had recorded the interview—he found himself returning to the recording to flesh out phrases he wanted to quote directly but couldn't quite capture completely in the moment of the interview itself. There, in his Expanded Fieldnotes, he began making connections, developing potential answers to his research question, identifying areas for further inquiry, and potential questions he'd like to answer in a follow-up interview or based on other data collected, perhaps through a close analysis of literacy artifacts like job reports (also based on "jottings," then "Expanded Fieldnotes").

Eric began his study with brief interviews conducted largely via email with the group of friends with whom he had developed his punk literacy decades earlier. They had remained relatively close in the years since, so he had ready access to their contact information. First, he called each of them to tell them what he was doing, ask them if they would be willing to participate, and walk them through the information provided on his Informed Consent Form. Next, he emailed a set of five questions and the Informed Consent Form to each participant with a requested deadline of one week. He worked hard to ensure the questions asked did not require extensive answers, as he did not want to burden them with a time-consuming task and he planned to follow up with a phone interview where additional information seemed necessary after initial data collection and analysis. As soon as he received the first response and Informed Consent Forms, he sat down at his computer, opened a Word document, and created a table with two columns—again, like Stephen and the other researchers, he used the left side for observations and the right side for reflections, guided by the same questions and additional support provided by the classroom field observation exercise above. The "jottings" require a date, time, and location. Since the exchange took place online, he typed the date and time upon which he emailed the interview questions *and* the date upon which the interviewee sent his responses. For the location, he wrote "email."

When dealing with an online exchange, observations through the senses may seem particularly silly. However, you might find later that you would like to develop a Verbal Portrait of yourself taking in this data for the first time, especially given the memories a project like Eric's might evoke in yourself— sitting on a recliner in your den, laptop atop a pillow on your lap, a printout of the emailed interview on the table next to you alongside your iPhone and earbuds, textbook open to page X, and a half-full cup of tea. You can hear the soft breathing of your sleeping dog on the floor next to you and children playing kickball on the cul-de-sac outside your front door. You write down these sense impressions just in case they prove useful later, then settle in to focus your "field observations" on the interview itself. You notice the interview was returned to you about two hours after you sent it. You write, "fast response time—two hours" in the left column. In the right, you jot down "Wow, that was fast; I wonder what that means. Is he as eager to remember those times as I am? Of all my friends, I thought he'd take the longest. As teenagers, we were always waiting on him. Anything worth further exploration there in my future research? Will be interesting to find out how quickly the others respond." You continue to summarize and reflect upon his responses. In his answer to the third question about materials they remembered collecting to learn about punk music and culture, he mentions a zine you hadn't thought about in many, many years. He writes down the name of the zine in the left column (observations) and, in the right, he writes, "I LOVED that thing! What might I learn by applying this 'field observation' technique to that zine? It's a literacy artifact, without a doubt. I know I still have a copy in that box in the upstairs closet. I'll grab that next." From the zine, his interviewee says he learned about "new bands" and "concerts" (you'd have written this information about what the interviewee learned in the left column, since that's an "observation" without analysis). "I learned that and much more. Definitely a lot there to explore."

After completing the "jottings" on this interview, perhaps he prints out the document, makes a new cup of tea, and opens a new document titled "Expanded Fieldnotes." The date, time, and location are the same as the jottings. Here, again, he uses the questions guiding the field observations of the classroom above, including what surprises him, intrigues him, or puzzles him. He'd certainly write something about the zine his friend referenced. He might write something about the quick response time for the interview. After writing observations of the scene in which he wrote his initial jottings, he may decide that could be a neat way to begin his Verbal Portrait—recalling the scene in which he began walking down memory lane based on this research project for an English class. Of course, he goes with a Verbal Portrait of a music venue in 1985, but he may not know that this early in the research process. He provides himself with information about future research paths (the zine, the response time for other interviews, etc.). Then he prints out the Expanded Fieldnotes and adds those with the initial jottings, the print-out of the email, and the Informed Consent Form to his Research Portfolio before heading upstairs to unearth that zine for another set of field observations (jottings and then Expanded Fieldnotes).

ADDITIONAL EXERCISES

Extensive guidance and practice for field observations of Interviews, Photographs, and Literacy Artifacts can be found at our companion website.

Data Analysis

Throughout the data collection process, you will be continually analyzing that data. Part of that process begins on the right side of your "Double-Entry Fieldnotes" ("jottings")—the place where you include your reflections, questions, and things that stand out, confuse, intrigue, or attract your attention for other reasons. You are beginning to analyze again when you turn those "jottings" into the Expanded Fieldnotes that are your goal immediately following any individual field observation that yields the *jottings* referenced above. That's where you'll summarize your observations, identify any problems or setbacks, begin to formulate potential avenues for further research, rich areas for additional inquiry, initial interpretations based on observations, and thoughts on what you found surprising, intriguing, or confounding. It is, in fact, not enough to merely *describe* what you learn in the field, through your interviews, and/or your close analysis of a selected literary artifact or photograph. You have to *analyze* those observations as well, and then report your findings.

Thus, your data analysis will include at least the following tools:

- **From Jottings to Expanded Fieldnotes:** As we've already discussed, each field observation (physical site, community of practice, interview, literacy artifact, and/or photograph) should be captured in real-time (as you are reading, listening, and/or observing), followed as immediately as possible by your expansion of these notes—summarizing what you observed, what that might mean, and what you need to consider/do next. These are, of course, your starting point.

- **The Code Book:** After you have collected at least two sets of fieldnotes, it is time to begin developing "codes" that will help you further analyze the data you are collecting.

According to anthropologist Andrew Asher,

> Analysis of ethnographic data begins with a process of coding. This is the generating of words and short phrases, called codes, and assigning them to sections of . . . [collected data] in order to summarize and/or interpret the meaning of the [collected data]. We describe a process that begins with open coding, to uncover patterns that arise in the data, and moves to a process of closed coding, to elaborate on those initial patterns and solidify understanding of the relationships between themes. ("A Practical Guide to Ethnographic Research")

The codes you develop are up to you. To generate your Code Book, consider (a) your research question and (b) recurring themes you see emerging from your research.

Example

Code Book

What follows is the Code Book from Hunter's study of comic book literacies. Remember his research question: *"How do past literacy experiences help shape approaches to reading comic books?"*

He knew he wanted to understand how past experiences influenced current approaches to comic books. To develop his Code Book, he began by looking at his research question and his first two sets of Expanded Fieldnotes. He noticed in his two sets of Expanded Fieldnotes based on two different interviews that one person was motivated to pick up a comic book based on a movie about a superhero. The other person, interestingly, found himself even less interested in reading comics about superheroes after watching that same movie. From there, he developed both the code for "influenced by movie" ("I2") and "negative influence" ("NI"). On both interviews he placed "I2" next to the section where they discussed movies. On the second interview next to that same section, he added the second code: "NI" ("negative influence"). These codes would become increasingly important to him as he continued collecting and analyzing data.

It is important to note that the Code Book is rarely developed in one sitting. Most often, the researcher begins the Code Book after compiling the first two sets of Expanded Fieldnotes in conversation with their research question. However, the Code Book is revised and extended after the researcher learns more about his or her subject based on further data collection, analysis, and refinement in response to the research question.

- I1 = Influenced by book
- I2 = Influenced by movie

- I3 = Influenced by person
- I4 = Influenced by environment
- I5 = Influenced by other
- I6 = Influenced by a character/story
- I7 = Influenced by text/script/words (in general)
- I8 = Influenced by comic strips
- I9 = Influenced by work/job
- PI = Positive Influence
- NI = Negative Influence
- E1 = Effect on teaching methods
- E2 = Effect on learning methods
- E3 = Effect on social skills
- E4 = Effect on morals/beliefs/ethics
- E5 = Effect on emotions
- E6 = Effect on scheduling/planning
- CH = Comic history fact
- CH2 = Major turning point in comic history
- CH3 = Comic book stat

- **The Conceptual Memo** is a product of concentrated effort to identify and develop analytic themes while still actively involved in the field and writing fieldnotes. In other words, this is your attempt to explore what FNs taken over a specific period of time might *mean* and anticipate next steps. While a single set of FNs captures a single observation taken at a particular time, the Conceptual Memo calls upon you to look at a set of FNs and begin analysis. The Conceptual Memo is *sustained, analytic writing.*

A "memo" is, according to the *Cambridge Dictionary,* "a written report prepared especially for a person or group of people and containing information about a particular matter." The "information about a particular matter" that is the subject of your Conceptual Memo is—like your Expanded FNs and the Interpretive Memo, which we will discuss next—your *data collection and analysis.* The "person or group of people" for whom this memo is prepared is, in fact, your future self as a researcher. What do you need to know? For each observation, your Expanded FNs offer your future self an overview or summary of that observation, a discussion of any problems or setbacks you encountered, and an exploration of any patterns, insights, or potential breakthroughs you see emerging.

A "concept" is, of course, a general idea or notion. That is, what might the data you have been collecting thus far *mean*? What general ideas or notions have you begun to develop based on the data collected that might help you begin answering the research question that is driving your study? Consider the Conceptual Memo as a portrait of your research thus far. What are the important items or recurring themes emerging from your study thus far? How do these fit together? How do these themes and relationships fit into the larger structure of your study?

In other words, what might this study actually mean? You probably won't know enough to answer the last question, but begin projecting. What *might* it mean? Also use this short analysis to think through what else you might need to do/ know. What does this analysis suggest you need to do next? To find out next? To observe next? Another interview or so? With whom and why? What will be the focus? Another set of field observations or so? Where/how/why? Outside reading that might complement your study and help you make sense of it? Additional literacy artifacts? Of course you won't need all of this, but think through what's next by reviewing your study thus far.

The Conceptual Memo differs from the Expanded Fieldnotes primarily with respect to the number of observations it covers. Your Expanded FNs cover only one observation. Your Conceptual Memo must address at least two observations as represented in your expanded FNs.

To generate a Conceptual Memo, begin by:

1. selecting two sets of expanded fieldnotes;

2. offer an overview or summary of the FNs together as a group;

3. considering both sets of FNs together, identify any problems or setbacks you have encountered thus far and/or solutions you've begun to implement to address problems identified in at least one set of FNs; and

4. begin identifying patterns you see emerging across these two sets of FNs.

The Conceptual Memo is a key place to begin applying your Code Book. You may also find it necessary at this point to revise your codes to better represent the direction your study is beginning to take you. Before you can really begin making your Conceptual Memo meaningful, you need to further develop relevant codes for analyzing (coding) your materials. Your "codes," as we've noted, are the terms and themes you use to sort your data—likely codes emerge from your conceptual framework and research questions. Most likely at this point, you continue developing and refining your Code Book at the same time you compose your Conceptual Memos, one feeding into the other and vice versa.

Across these two sets of FNs, apply relevant codes, which will help you begin tracing relevant patterns more clearly. You should also underline, tag, or highlight five to 10 details that stand out for you. After you have finished coding your FNs, include in your Conceptual Memo a summary of the patterns you see merging as identified through your coding process. Anything you write for your Conceptual Memo, like anything else you generate throughout the data collection and analysis process, can serve as potential text for your final ethnographic paper.

Feeling Overwhelmed?

We understand, but we really hope you'll take this minute to breathe, close your eyes, and believe us when we say: "You can do this!" Truly. Although it may seem like a lot to take in, you are taking this larger, complex project in small, bite-sized pieces. The Conceptual Memos, like your Expanded Fieldnotes, are *informal* writing assignments, designed specifically to help you collect and make sense of the data you are bringing together in an attempt to answer your research question. Typically, instructors check to see that you have composed these documents; however, these research-in-process documents are not graded like your major writing assignments. These are working, informal documents for *you,* designed to help guide and organize your research throughout the process. In other words, the Expanded FNs and Conceptual Memos should make the research process *less* intimidating and overwhelming, not more. Often the only time your instructor will see these documents will be in the Research Portfolio you submit as part of your Final Project.

After you have had a chance to compose Conceptual Memos based on all the FNs you've collected, you are ready to move onto the final step before writing up your final ethnographic essay: the Interpretive Memo. We will talk about the Interpretive Memo in the next chapter, as a first step to moving the data you've collected and analyzed throughout your research process into your Final Project.

A Verbal Snapshot: Insider Perspective

As noted throughout, your FNs (including the Expanded FNs and the Conceptual Memo) play a central role in your ethnographic project. The major writing assignment that follows invites you to translate the data collection and analysis you've been doing thus far into a narrative form you can use directly as part of your final ethnographic essay. Consider the following example, which—like Eric Pleasant's essay on developing "punk literacy"—the researcher chose to use as a way to open her final ethnographic essay.

EXAMPLE

From Carmen Kynard's "'New Life in This Dormant Creature': Notes on Social Consciousness, Language, and Learning in a College Classroom" (see Chapter 3— one with the group project, "Analyzing Literacy Ethnographies")

> It was my first day at my urban, four-year college in Bronx, New York. I was waiting for the previous class to leave so that I could go in, set up chairs in a circle, and write an agenda on the board. As all the students filed out of their classrooms, an explosion of sound, seemingly antithetical to the voices of bellowing professors ten minutes before, range through the hallways: the rapid swirls of Spanish that sometimes, and sometimes not, moved through fusions of Spanglish; urban, African American English twisted around the words from my radio when tuned into HOT 97's Blazin Hip Hop and R&B; the swift, yet sometimes punctuated nuances that West African languages seem to dance through; varied versions of Patois which seem to meld together these urban Ebonics and nuances of West African language systems yet add on something else; and then Frenchified sounds spun onto African cadences from Haitian and

Francophone African students. On that first day, however, these were mostly the sounds of the hallway and not the sounds of the classrooms.

Before my classes start, I like to take a look around and see how students present themselves to the world--like the big baggy pants that the boys especially like to wear. While the looseness may seem lax, I know from watching the flop-over process of the leg bottoms that it takes quite a bit of tinkering to achieve that perfect number of layers on both pant legs. The young women mostly wear bell bottomed pants also with a carefully manipulated, new foldover at the bottom. There are thick-soled boots in black or the latest blond and red leathers that make their walking more like thumping across the ground. Sneakers and casual boots ironically have these thick heels also, but these are made according to Michael Jordanian concepts of flight with colorful air pockets laid into the sides. The fellas' well-tapered sides take on adult significance when replacing their baseball caps (which have bris folded just right in the middle to form a perfect arc over their round faces), or their wool caps topped off in the shape of a banana, or the doo-rags that snuggle the roundness of their heads. The young women have their hair pulled back very tightly to showcase an explosion of curls at the nape of their neck or long cornrows lining the contours of their heads. Most seem to experiment with dark-lipsticked lips outlined with an even darker, outer edge.

My description of these images is not meant to serve as a mere backdrop for an academicized, ethnographic story. These images represent a specific lens through which I look to construct the contours of the landscape of my classroom. The episodes I recreate here marked a semester begun with a mandatory brunch-type affair for freshman instructors where an administrator, one of the few people of color in the room who was not a peer tutor, offered an ominous warning. He explained that these students required a different kind of education. These students, he argued, wear doo-rags to class and traverse the classroom and hallways wearing walkmen. As such, they are unlike his own Latino son, who had gone to the best private schools and was currently attending an ivy league school. His son was ready for intellectual work (based solely on his not having a walkman and doo-rag) in a way that "our students" simply were not. The administrator's utterance was greeted with attentive nods by the petit bourgeois in the room disguised as educated/educators. I would argue that this administrator's system of logic comprises the everyday discursive and ideological apparatuses that operate underneath curriculum and instructor for working-class students of color, which also includes: "these students" belong in remedial courses only, cannot write and speak except in "street language," do not know how to think, have no work ethic (i.e. do not come to class, turn in work late, etc.).

Discussion Questions:

1. Based on this opening, what do you expect this ethnographic essay to be about? To support your answer, point to specific passages in this example.

2. What role does the description of this setting lay in establishing the framework for this essay?

3. Without reading the entire essay, which is available at the companion website for this textbook, what do you believe the research question to be based on these opening paragraphs?

4. Think about the author's research process: If this were your project, what research tools do you believe would be most useful in collecting the requisite data? Interviews? Site visits? Analysis of literacy artifacts? Some combination thereof? Why these research tools and not others?

5. Think about the author's research process: To conduct this study, the author conducted field observations and analyzed data collected through tools like Expanded FNs, a Code Book, and Conceptual Memos. Based on the research question to which you believe this essay is responding (see answer your #3) and the possible research tools (see answer to #4 above), identify five codes this researcher might use to effectively analyze her data to answer her research question. Defend your choices and explain how she might make use of these codes in her research process.

WRITING ASSIGNMENT

INSIDER PERSPECTIVE/VERBAL PORTRAIT

This essay calls upon you to make extensive use of the ethnographer's research tools (interviews, observations, fieldnotes) to offer an insider's perspective of the people, places, and/or communities of practice that have been the focus of your study. For this assignment, your focus should be on one or more of the following:

- an interview with a key participant (at least one hour);
- field observations of a community of practice (at least two visits on two different days); and
- cultural artifacts (at least two different artifacts).

To generate this essay, you should rely on your Expanded Fieldnotes and Conceptual Memos, as described earlier in this chapter. Ideally, this essay can serve as an introduction to your final ethnographic essay, just as it has in the examples from Eric Pleasant's and Carmen Kynard's essays provided in this chapter.

Writing from an "Insider's Perspective" requires selective perception, which should involve choices based on the overall sense you hope to communicate: What insights have you gained from your field observations, Expanded FNs, and Conceptual Memos? How might this description of place, people, communities of practice, literacy events, and/or literacy artifacts help set the stage for an essay in which you reveal these insights—ideally in response to the research question driving your ethnography?

Consider, for example, Carmen Kynard's description of a classroom at a college in the Bronx. How did she describe her students? Her administrators? How did Eric Pleasant go about describing the club in Austin, Texas, in the 1980s, where he developed aspects of what he calls his "punk literacy"? How did these descriptions contribute to each researcher's key arguments? Insights derived from their field observations?

Your description involves more than making an inventory or listing details. It also involves making deliberate choices:

- focusing on some elements of the landscape or people and ignoring others;
- narrowing your gaze to a specific place, cultural artifact, or personal detail and rejecting others as you do so; and
- utilizing particular metaphors and descriptions and abandoning others as inappropriate.

Throughout, your descriptions should be based on evidence found in your fieldnotes. Even so, your "Insider's Perspective" can be an amalgamation of different field observations, rather than a single one alone. Pleasant's description, for example, was based on memories of a club he visited with friends on a few different occasions, all of which occurred more than twenty years before he wrote his ethnography. Details emerged from his own reflections of this time combined with interviews he conducted with the friends with whom he conducted this "punk literacy" so long ago, evidence of which he found not in one single set of fieldnotes but across multiple field observations, reflections, and Conceptual Memos.

STUDENT EXAMPLE
LITERACY IN A SMALL TOWN

Tamika Jones

Rain pattered against my car as I stare at the dilapidated house. Panes, long ago rotten, hang from a single nail near the windows of the house. Spots of mint green paint peel back to reveal the board frame. What once was a flower bed now is a forest for overgrown shrubbery and an endless vine. The neighbors sat smoking on the front porch. Their stares were focused on me, or possibly my car. I found myself thinking that if I was smart I would back out of the driveway and forget this entire interview. I had not visited in so long; the possibility that he would remember me was slim.

Just as I decided that the best idea was to complete my project without disturbing him, the front door of 1214 South 5th Street. Standing, hunched from age, stood the oldest man I had ever had the privilege of meeting. Over the rain, I listened to him wheeze out, "Well, honey, are you coming in or are you just going to sit there?"

Slowly I got out of the car, making sure to lock my doors and stare down the neighbors. Rain drops fell on me and my spiral notebook. I was about to conduct my first ever interview, with one of my dearest friends. Robert Spearman, a 98-year-old war veteran, sat hunched in the only chair not occupied by cats. His afternoon lunch sat cold by his chair and was beginning to attract the attention of several brave kittens. He pulled a threadbare blanket over his legs and thicker one that I had made for him across his shoulders. As I waited for him to settle, his head slowly slumped to one side, the only position of late that made him feel better. "Well, honey, it's been awhile."

Sighing, I know I should visit more often. College seems to get in the way. I'm glad for the project, because it lets me combine the people I want to see with the things I have to do. "Mr. Spearman, I was wondering if I could talk to you about your youth." He nods and I fear he didn't hear me. "I want to use our talk in a project I'm doing, but I need your permission to use it." I read him the form so he doesn't have to search for his glasses. He nods then leans over for a pen. I hand him the paper. Looking at me, he asks, "My signature or my X?"

Thus begins our lengthy talk about his youth. Most of the time I spent I won't be able to use for my project. I did learn several things about him and his opinions. More to the point of my project though, I learned about a century ago. I asked him questions about what he thought the definition of literacy was. His reply was colorful. "It is," he said, "what the government says it is. It's can you read."

"Read what?" I pushed him.

"Words."

Szwed, the first reading we read in my English 1302 class, believed that words were on "[...] handbills, signs, graffiti, sheet music, junk mail, cereal boxes, captions on television, gambling slips and racing tips sheets, juke-box labels, and pornography" (Szwed 8). According to Mr. Spearman being able to read those things is what made one literate. He never said anything about being able to understand what the words meant. As long as one could read the words, one was literate.

I expected a response like that, especially, after his comment on his signature. His father, I learned, was an illiterate man. When he signed for something, he was forced to put his X. Instead of schooling, work on the farm took precedents. His father slaved over crops and never once was taught to read a single word. More important he could not sign his own name. He was forced to make his mark, an X, on all official documents.

"That didn't mean he wasn't smart," Mr. Spearman defended, "He was. He would catch me doing naughty things. He was a smart man. He just wasn't educated."

Mr. Spearman, who after his father's death, moved to the city and attended all twelve grades of public school. He could read and calculate. Most importantly to him, he could sign his name. He learned all of the basics and then some. "I was educated. That doesn't mean I was smart. But I could read," he boasted.

His pride in his ability struck me as odd. Reading the words, is no longer the main focus. Instead, today we decipher the meaning behind each word and assign a separate unstated meaning to it. Everyone can read. Street signs, magazine headlines, store billboards and cereal boxes are a staple in society's reading material. Some people read these things multiple times a day. To Mr. Spearman it was still a feat. He was able to read. Curious, I asked about his pride.

"Well, honey, I was the youngest. My brothers had to get jobs. The family was poor and Mom couldn't work enough to keep us all fed. So my brothers worked. I got to go to school. I got to learn."

It was privilege. He wanted to learn. He wanted to read. The idea struck me as reminiscent of what students are told about the old days. A time when people were more appreciative of the opportunities they were given. Mr. Spearman got to read while his brothers didn't. He got to sign his name. For many years, he was the only fully literate sibling. When the family was home after work, he would read to them from whatever was nearby: an old newspaper or the bible.

As I tried to remember to keep on topic, I asked him about what he thought technology is. His response was, "That thing I don't understand, like that box in your hand, or one of them mobile phone deals. Half the time I don't understand the TV."

Then he got up from his chair. His bones creaked as he stood. I grabbed his arm to help balance him out as he led me to his back room. An old record player sat on a side table next to a chair identical to the one he just left. Bookshelves full of records, books and old teapots, lined the room. He pulled a record out and began the process of getting it to play. I watched as efficiently started the music. Collapsing into his chair, he closed his eyes. His head bobbed back and forth the melody of old jazz. "This is the only technology I need," he stated.

Quietly I listened to the crackle of the recording and bittersweet sound of the saxophone. Things began to fall in perspective in that little room. "…literacy is best understood as a set of social practices." (Barton and Hamilton, 24). Mr. Spearman didn't need anything more than the ability to read and write. This is comparable to his use limited use technology; he only needs to be able to operate an old record player. If one can consider him to be his own community then one can consider him literate. "Appeals to individuals to enhance their functional skills might founder on the different subjective utilities communities and groups attach to reading and writing activities." (Scribner 40). He does not have to have any skills other than the ones' he possess to be able to function in society.

He is a literate individual, even by today's harsh standards. He can read, interpret and comprehend. Though, his skills may not be as advanced as others, he still possesses the ability. According to most of our reading this makes him literate.

CHAPTER 6

Writing It Up

In this chapter, we continue our exploration of literacies as experienced by ordinary people in our everyday lives. We'll begin by considering how to move from the data you've collected into interpreting this data and writing it up into an ethnographic project. Throughout this chapter, you'll be creating an interpretive memo, drafting and revising your Final Project (an ethnographic portfolio that will emerge from your research portfolio), and developing a poster presentation for an event where you will present your ethnographic findings.

We are committed to including field research in our teaching because it gives you an opportunity to teach yourself and others something real, immediate, and special about your subject—something you probably wouldn't find in a book or journal. Ideally, it gets you involved in your subject in ways that library research alone just can't match. As teachers, we find the prospect of our students having this kind of experience and this kind of involvement genuinely exciting.

Each term our students learn things about their lives and experiences as members of a community of practice and teach those things to us, and learning from them has transformed our own experiences as teachers.

Performing field research helps you grow intellectually and helps you claim true ownership of your writing. We want you to break free of formulaic approaches and to engage actively and curiously with ideas. The heart of this book is more about thinking than it is about writing, which plays a significant role in thinking but without critical thinking you'd have nothing meaningful to write about. It's about growing intellectually and cultivating a richer academic experience. Because of the personal involvement it entails, field research is a vital contributor to these processes.

We look forward to seeing how you approach your final project and what you have to teach us.

So far, we've gone from Fieldnotes to Conceptual Memo. Now, we will move to Interpretive Memos and into the Final Ethnographic Portfolio. So, let's begin.

Interpretive Memo

We will start with an **Interpretive Memo**. The Interpretive Memo is your opportunity to begin drawing forward firm interpretations of data collected, elaborating on concepts developed through your Interpretive Memos and other means, and linking codes and bits of data together into meaningful phrases you might use directly in your final ethnographic essay. As with the Conceptual Memo, the Interpretive Memo requires you to combine close reading with analytic coding.

In writing the Interpretive Memo, you should seek to explore relationships among your coded FNs and Conceptual Memos and provide a more sustained examination of a theme or issue by linking discrete observations together. This is your final step before you begin writing up your final ethnographic essay.

By this point, you will have composed Conceptual Memos in response to all of the FNs collected. For the Interpretive Memo, place all your Conceptual Memos in front of you. You should have composed at least two Conceptual Memos.

1. With pen in hand and Code Book in front of you, code the Conceptual Memos, looking for recurring themes, patterns, and relevant evidence. Underline or highlight sentences or ideas you think would work well in your final ethnographic essay. Concepts that seem important. Phrasing that you really like and would like to reuse.

2. Provide an overview or summary of all the research you've conducted, including any setbacks you encountered throughout the process, solutions you may have implemented to address setbacks experienced, and insights you've developed based on your own original research about how writing works, how ordinary people put texts to use in everyday contexts, or other arguments that might contribute to the ongoing scholarly conversation in literacy studies, the discipline represented in the essays you've read thus far. This can be the starting place for the actual prose you develop for your ethnographic essay. In fact, this is where you should find your central argument.

ASSIGNMENT

FINAL PROJECT: Ethnographic Portfolio

For your final project, you will compile an ethnographic portfolio, beginning with choosing 5-8 pieces of your work throughout this course: different genres, informal jottings, and fieldnotes. You will curate these pieces into a portfolio, along with your final ethnographic project and a reflection of your work. This reflection can occur through the inclusion of an introduction and conclusion to your ethnographic project; the reflection might also be a separate piece of work at the end of your portfolio; or, your reflective statements could also be included in a digital file (such as a Word document or Google doc) using the "new comment" feature. You may also decide that your ethnography work might best be presented in a form that is not entirely a textual essay. For example, some students may find that comics, videos, blogs, photographic essays, podcasts, etc. could represent their literacy ethnography better than alphabetic text. Therefore, we encourage you to brainstorm ways to make your project unique (and representative of the communities you're researching) with your instructor. **Said another way, be innovative with how you present your findings! The details below are a starting point, but we encourage you to adapt these to your findings.**

*Note: if you are not writing a 10-15 page essay, you should think about the rigor (brainstorming, drafting, editing, revising, etc.) involved in this work and use these same views to guide your work regardless of its form or genre.

In other words, for your Ethnographic Portfolio, you might turn in a digital file consisting of:

- 5-8 pieces of your ethnographic work-in-progress (informal notes, responses, interview scripts, fieldnotes, Conceptual Memos, Informed Consent Forms, Code of Ethics, images you reflect on, surveys, etc.)
- An ethnographic project (10-15 pages, or an equivalent using multimedia)
- A reflection (which can be through an introduction and conclusion or by other means that you see fit for your own project).

For this ethnographic portfolio, you will be analyzing, synthesizing, and writing up the research you've been doing all semester. The beauty of all the levels and layers of work you've done is that it is unique to you and your experience and interests. No one else will have done the assignments in the same ways or talked to the same people or made the same observations. Therefore, you are now positioned to speak as an expert.

For instance, much of the work for this final portfolio has been generated in the writing assignments. You might think about using the Verbal Portrait, definitions from WA1, your research proposal and questions, your research methods, Code of Ethics, Informed Consent Forms, Conceptual Memos, fieldnotes, etc. to begin your rough draft of this final project. In other words, you are not starting from scratch!

ACTIVITY

Beginning The Ethnographic Portfolio

Now that you have your interpretive memo, as well as your Research Portfolio, we will talk about how to move these items into your final project, an Ethnographic Portfolio. This Ethnographic Portfolio is a combination of the research and writing you've done all semester, as well as your final ethnographic product.

Once you get together your research portfolio and other documents from the semester, go through the following steps:

1. Read through all your notes, artifacts, extended fieldnotes, reflections, responses to discussion questions and, especially, your major writing assignments, Conceptual Memos, and Interpretive Memo (etc.)—with a highlighter in hand—and mark those moments and prose that seem most important to you, most interesting, most useful.

2. Share your Portfolio with a partner. Your partner should—with a different colored highlighter in hand—mark those moments and prose that seem most interesting/important/useful.

3. Read over all these highlighted bits and begin to make a list of these most important moments/ideas as you work through them. At this point it may be useful for you to indicate the sections of your portfolio (by number) that correspond with your separate list of important moments/ideas.

4. Search for patterns in your list and make a new list of those patterns. NOTE: It may be useful at this point to make a photocopy of the first list of important points—from #3 above—and then cut it up into units that you can then manipulate (kinesthetically) to identify these patterns. We find that method very useful in our own research. That way we don't end up bound to the original list, which may be chronological or organized some other way that is totally logical when collecting and analyzing the research but not terribly useful in the final analysis and write-up. Or if you're a visual learner, is there a way to represent your important points through images, charts, etc.? Use this work to suit your learning style and process as a writer.

5. "From your list of patterns and connections, select ONE larger idea/pattern that interests you most; a larger pattern to which other ideas can then be connected." (from *Translating Culture*, "Ethnographer's Toolkit: Reviewing Fieldnote Analysis," Chapter 8).

6. "Create a focus statement/controlling idea/thesis statement from your observations" (also from *Translating Culture*, same as above):

Now you've got a focal point around which you can begin to organize your essay. Your starting point for that focus was the Interpretive Memo (see above), of course. Through this activity, you also have some terrific prose and ideas you can use to unpack that focus in the essay itself.

ACTIVITY
Creating a "Zero Draft"

THE NEXT STEP is to start developing prose, which you may begin to incorporate into your final write up. In each step, the best way to make it happen quickly is to allow yourself to develop what Anne Lamott has called "Shitty First Drafts" (see *Bird by Bird*), the same thing composition scholar Bruce Ballenger means when he teaches his students "The Importance of Writing Badly" (in *Genre By Example: Writing What We Teach,* Boynton/Cook, 2001) and journalist Jon Spayde celebrates in "The Miracle of Mediocrity" by providing a forum in which he, his wife (an artist), and their friends can make—deliberately and competitively—*bad* art (*Utne Reader,* March/April 2001 issue). As Spayde explains, "Nothing lifts the spirits like the making of bad art." For the purposes of this project, we'll call it a Zero Draft, a draft that has zero expectations. It is merely a space for you to brainstorm, write, think, and develop ideas free from judgment and assessment.

Remember, to create this Zero Draft, you can pull directly from anything you have written thus far, including the prose you and your partner highlighted in the previous activity. You can photocopy those pages with highlighted sections, for example, cut out the highlighted sections, spread them out on a large table or a floor, rearrange them as needed to make sense, and then paste them to sheets of paper in the order in which you'd like to see them.

For example, you might begin with large portions of your Verbal Portrait, then your central argument as it relates to your Verbal Portrait, then your definitions of literacy and related terms (from Writing Assignment 1, perhaps), then a description of your research methods (consider borrowing from your Research Proposal) and research ethics (consider pulling from your Writing Assignment 2), and findings (as you've discovered them through your Extended Fieldnotes, Conceptual Memos, Interpretive Memo, and in activities like those in the current chapter).

Thus, the Zero Draft doesn't come out of nowhere. You've been working toward it the entire semester.

Once you have developed a Zero Draft—a deliberately rough ("shitty"/bad) draft—you are ready to sharpen it up, fill in the gaps, and iron it out. That may require reorganizing. It may require starting over. It may require little more than cutting, extending, or merely cleaning it up. Whatever the case, wait until you have a draft to begin that revision process.

*** Once you complete the Zero Draft, you can move to the next stage. But don't rush! Writing is different for everyone, so this activity can take a class period or longer for even the Zero Draft. The next part will take longer, as you sit with ideas and revise them through multiple sessions of working.***

THEN, revise, peer review, "thicken your draft," revise some more, review your Research Portfolio again, revise some more, get feedback from your instructor, revise some more.

ACTIVITY

Putting Together an Ethnographic Portfolio-in-Progress

This activity moves you through the three parts of your overall final Ethnographic Portfolio that will be due.

REMEMBER, your final project will consist of the following:

ARTIFACTS: 5-8 pieces or artifacts of your ethnographic work-in-progress (informal notes, responses, interview scripts, fieldnotes, Conceptual Memos, Informed Consent Forms, Code of Ethics, images you reflect on, surveys, etc.)

ETHNOGRAPHIC PROJECT: An ethnographic project (10-15 pages, or an equivalent using multimedia)

REFLECTION: A reflection (which can be through an introduction and conclusion or by other means that you see fit for your own project).

ARTIFACTS:

1. Using the documents you have from your Research Portfolio and the semester, choose 5-8 artifacts that stand out to you in some way as meaningful.

   Write up short paragraph explanations about why these stand out. Do you think you did good work? Did you find some new information in this research? Did you learn something about your community participants? Were you confused by something? In other words, reflect on and describe your reasons for including these artifacts. It's important to remember that a good portfolio doesn't mean you're showing off polished material; sometimes, the best learning moments are when we see something that doesn't fit and work through it. So, make sure you provide a variety of artifacts in your draft portfolio.

ETHNOGRAPHIC PROJECT:

2. Think about your final ethnographic product, and develop answers or ideas for the following, as you consider what it will look like: Is this an essay? Is it a video? A blog? How are you going to curate your pieces into something interesting and innovative? What is the point of your ethnographic project? What do you want to get across to your audience about your community? Be sure to think about this "so what?" question throughout your drafting and revision.

3. Choose your starting point. What's a moment, description, answer, action, artifact, history, etc. that stands out to you? How are you going to bring your

reader into your writing to make him or her interested in your narrative? Work on developing this starting point. If you need additional guidance, try out the exercise below (from *Translating Culture*, "Ethnographer's Toolkit: 'Evoking Response,'" Chapter 7):

> While it may not be THE most important element of ethnographic writing, I want to encourage/emphasize the need for you all to evoke a response from the readers, to write in such a way that your writing will resonate with them on a visceral level. In order to help you facilitate this process, here are two specific writing exercises, each of which might be used as an intro for a final piece.
>
> 1. Begin with a personal narrative that focuses on your relationship with the topic. Tell a short story about the subject/culture/activity/person/ etc., trying the whole while to get the reader to *feel* your connection, not just understand it. In this 3-4 full-paragraph intro, you'll want to establish the connection, make clear how you feel/felt about it. How is it part of you? Don't make any conscious reference to the research yet. Just stick to what YOU know and feel about it from experience.
>
> 2. Choose a specific scene, instance, description of action, or the space of your research site (the Verbal Portrait will be most helpful here). Work to describe it, to bring it to the reader in such a way that he or she can "be there." You may refer heavily to some of the more recent response papers (reflections), working to improve your initial writing. Again, the best bits of writing will focus on ONE story or space.
>
> Regardless of whether you use this piece as your intro in the final draft, writing it now may help you think about how to engage the reader with your work, even as you work to make sure that there is a point to your research.

REFLECTION:

4. Consider the Reflection Overview and the Course Goals included here. Develop a list of the goals you think you accomplished this semester. Use these ideas as focal points for your reflection.

Overview

The purpose of the reflection is to consider the work you have done for the course in terms of the major course goals, with the overall goal of demonstrating what you have learned over the fifteen weeks of the semester.

Course Goals

As noted in the syllabus, the course goals include learning how to analyze, evaluate, or solve problems while communicating rhetorically for a particular audience and/or occasion. Using literacy ethnography, we have explored concepts of academic honesty and ethics, literacy usage, and developing ideas together with communities and collaborators.

See course syllabus for the specific ways these objectives are framed.

5. Develop a reflection considering the purpose of this class, our goals, and the work you've done throughout the semester: in class, at sites, on your own time, in conferences, etc. Consider the following questions:

> Has this course enabled you to see literacy anew? Has it challenged your definitions or understandings of literacy? What types of literacy have you analyzed or evaluated? What have you learned about communities of practice, research ethics, and developing ethnographic writing? Did your writing change when aimed for a particular audience?

What skills or methods have you used this semester? In what ways can you see these ideas, skills, or practices assisting, complicating, or transferring into other areas of your learning?

These questions are meant to help you develop a reflection about the semester, but this does not mean you should present a progress narrative. In other words, we do not need you to say, "I learned so much" just to appease us. Rather, grapple with these ideas and think through them. What did you learn? How did you learn it? What did you struggle with and why? What might you take away from, improve on, or continue thinking about beyond this course?

Be specific! Give examples, quote from and reference your own work, the readings, and discussions from the semester.

Wrapping Up

After completing your Interpretive Memo, the activities provided, and meeting with your instructors, peers, and writing tutors, you should have a rough draft of part of your final project. As you keep developing this work, remember that you are adding to work you've already begun.

Suggestion 1: Go back to previous exercises that you've completed. Go back to your Research Portfolio, comments from your instructor, classmates, or yourself. Trace the patterns again as they relate to your focal point/focus statement/controlling idea/thesis statement. If you've cut these units out, you may begin tracing these patterns by piling like items together. From there, you can begin to decide which moments/ideas will be most relevant and which you may consider leaving out. From these piles, develop an outline that might guide your draft. As you develop this outline, ask yourself, *"In what order should I present the key patterns/evidence/ideas emerging from my data?"*

Suggestion 2: Add evidence to each of your ideas. For example, if you talk about a key pattern you see, *show* your reader with examples. Do you have quotes, statistics, images, fieldnotes, interviews, etc. that allow you to fill in these gaps?

In other words, your ethnographic project should be rich with examples and specific details.

Suggestion 3: Just keep working! You have multiple resources, readers, and ideas around you. Be sure that you use the resources you have (teachers, peers, tutors, friends, yourself). **Also, remember you are ideally writing something that is interesting to you and your readers! So, make it interesting! What do you think it needs?**

ACTIVITY

Peer Review for Your Final Ethnographic Project

1. Fieldsite: What is the fieldsite here? It might be an actual place or some organization made up of people or it might just be the life histories of the people themselves. Whatever the fieldsite, it should be described in enough detail for you to know it well and be ready to enter it with the researcher. That means the researcher should have described it well enough in her ethnography. Do you feel she/he has?

2. Statement of Problem: What is the research question here?

   Is it sufficiently grounded in the relevant research in literacy studies? If not, what suggestions can you offer from our readings that might help bring the scholarly nature of the research question forward?

   Is the research question clearly stated? What might help clarify the question for you?

3. Methods: The researcher should make the research tools as clear as possible and tie those methods to the overall research question. What methods did the researcher use? Interviews? Surveys? Field observations? Some combination of the above? Something else? How did she/he work to treat the participants with the care and respect they deserve? How many participants were involved and how? How much time did the researcher spend in the field? What's the relationship between these methods and the research question?

4. Interpreting the Fieldwork: What recurring themes emerged from the research? Does the researcher effectively foreground those themes in terms of her/his research and connect them to the research question? Do you need to see more here?

5. What contribution does this study make to the larger scholarly conversation in literacy studies? Who does the researcher cite from our course readings and how does it work in terms of this study? Comb our course readings for relevant quotes and arguments. Offer at least two suggested quotes that might work well in terms of bringing the researcher's current study into conversation with the larger scholarly conversation.

6. Is it interesting? Star the most interesting part and explain what makes it so interesting.

7. Are there areas of the study you'd like to hear more about? Mark those areas and explain what you'd like to hear more about and why.

8. How about the current organizational structure? Any recommendations there?

9. The title? Any recommendations?

10. Anything else?

Acknowledgements